ArtScroll Tanach Series®

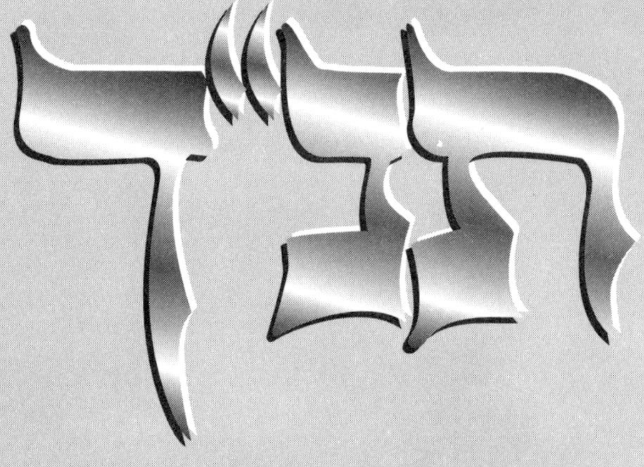

A traditional commentary on the Books of the Bible

Rabbi Nosson Scherman / Rabbi Meir Zlotowitz

General Editors

A PROJECT OF THE

Mesorah Heritage Foundation

TREI ASAR

Hosea / Hoshea
Joel / Yoel
Amos
Obadiah / Ovadiah

הושע
יואל
עמוס
עובדיה

Translation and Commentary by
Rabbi Matis Roberts

Overview:
The Later Prophets: Unity and Mission
by
Rabbi Joseph Elias

hosea / hoshe
joel / yoe
amos
obadiah / ovadiah

trei asar

THE TWELVE PROPHETS Vol. I: / A NEW TRANSLATION WITH A COMMENTARY ANTHOLOGIZED FROM TALMUDIC, MIDRASHIC, AND RABBINIC SOURCES.

Published by
Mesorah Publications, ltd

FIRST EDITION
First Impression . . . October 1995

Published and Distributed by
MESORAH PUBLICATIONS, Ltd.
4401 Second Avenue
Brooklyn, New York 11232

Distributed in Europe by
J. LEHMANN HEBREW BOOKSELLERS
20 Cambridge Terrace
Gateshead, Tyne and Wear
England NE8 1RP

Distributed in Israel by
SIFRIATI / A. GITLER – BOOKS
4 Bilu Street
P.O.B. 14075
Tel Aviv 61140

Distributed in Australia & New Zealand by
GOLDS BOOK & GIFT CO.
36 William Street
Balaclava 3183, Vic., Australia

Distributed in South Africa by
KOLLEL BOOKSHOP
22 Muller Street
Yeoville 2198, Johannesburg, South Africa

THE ARTSCROLL TANACH SERIES
TREI ASAR / THE TWELVE PROPHETS VOL. I

ISBN
0-89906-017-X (hard cover)
0-89906-018-8 (paperback)

Typography by CompuScribe at ArtScroll Studios, Ltd.
4401 Second Avenue / Brooklyn, N.Y. 11232 / (718) 921-9000

Printed in the United States of America by Moriah Offset
Bound by Sefercraft Quality Bookbinders, Ltd., Brooklyn, NY

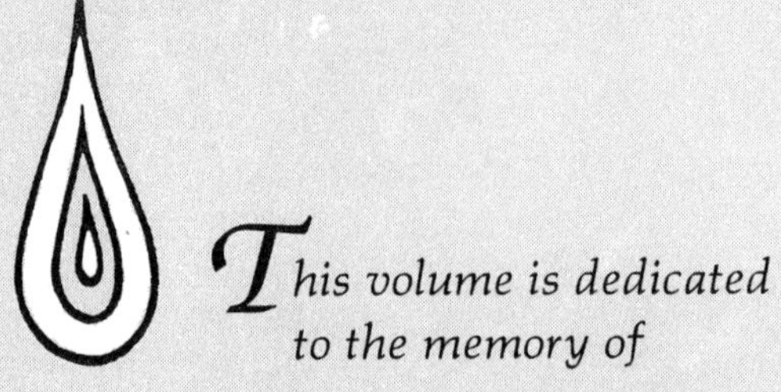

This volume is dedicated to the memory of

Rabbi Sholom Edelman

הרב שלום בן הרב אליעזר ז״ל

נפ׳ כ״ו תמוז תשנ״ה

He was one of those who kept the menorah of the Mirrer yeshiva burning brightly during its heroic exile to Shanghai.

Then, when the inferno was extinguished, he brought the Torah scholarship and idealism of Eastern Europe to Cong. Shaarei Tefillah of Perth Amboy, N.J. As halachic authority, teacher, mohel, and shochet, he gave the children of the New World a glimpse of the greatness of the Old.

His great loves were Torah study, Eretz Yisrael, and Klal Yisrael.

It is fitting that Trei Asar, which begins with omens of destruction and ends with prophecies of rebirth, should bear the name of a distinguished talmid chacham, who lived through the former and helped bring about the latter in our century.

Mrs. Ida Edelman
Eliezer and Linda Edelman,
Esther and Paul Stark,
and Shmuel Gamliel
and families

☙ Publisher's Preface

We are privileged to present this first volume of *Trei Asar/The Twelve Prophets.* In it we read how its great protagonists carried God's message to their contemporaries, and — if we read it well and contemplate it seriously — we hear them speaking to us, as well. Of the countless prophecies conveyed to Israel during the First Temple era, the ones preserved in Scripture were only those that were relevant to future generations. Thus, the soaring words and searing experience of Hosea, for example, were meant for us, as well as his contemporaries. But the words that are so beautiful and laden with meaning are extremely hard to understand; hence the need for this new translation and commentary.

The author of this volume is RABBI MATIS ROBERTS, whose previous work on several volumes of the ArtScroll Mishnah Series earned the respect of scholars and laymen alike. As *mashgiach* of Yeshivah Shaar HaTorah of Forest Hills, he has demonstrated a profound understanding of the sacred texts and of human nature, and the ability to make complex ideas comprehensible. The book was edited by YAAKOV ASTOR. The finished product is eloquent testimony to the skills of both of them.

We are grateful to the family of Rabbi Sholom Edelman ז״ל, which dedicated this volume. He helped bring the legacy of the Mirrer Yeshiva to America. By supporting the publication of this work in his memory, his wife and children perpetuate his ideals.

We are grateful to our dear friend Rabbi Raphael Butler, Executive Vice President of the Orthodox Union, for his constant interest and assistance in our joint cause of bringing Torah knowledge to our people.

We are honored that RABBI JOSEPH ELIAS consented to write the Overview. He is a thinker and scholar of unusual breadth and depth,

and we are proud to present his profound and enlightening essay to the public.

Many members of the ArtScroll staff were involved in the exacting task of typing and correcting the manuscript. We are grateful to MRS. BASSIE GUTTMAN, MRS. DVORY BICK, MRS. ZISSI LANDAU, MRS. FRIMI DANZIGER, MRS. BAS-SIYON DREBIN, MRS. ESTHER FEIERSTEIN, MRS. MIRYAM STAVSKY, and MISS UDI HERSHKOWITZ. MISS CHAYA G. ZAIDMAN had the responsibility of completing the work and paginating the entire volume, under the supervision of the acknowledged master of the craft, our esteemed colleague, REB SHEAH BRANDER. We are also grateful to MRS. FAYGIE WEINBAUM for her customarily meticulous proofreading.

In its two decades, the ArtScroll Tanach Series has enriched the lives and understanding of many. We hope, with God's help, to continue to do so, as more and more volumes of our Torah heritage are brought to our people.

Rabbi Meir Zlotowitz / Rabbi Nosson Scherman

☙ *Table of Contents*

◆§ *An Overview / The Later Prophets: Unity in Mission*

An Overview / The Later Prophets: Unity in Mission

I. Prophecy

קֶשֶׁר נְבוּאִי בֵּין הַיּוֹצֵר וִיצוּרָיו אֶחָד מִן הַיְסוֹדוֹת שֶׁל בְּרִיאַת הָעוֹלָם.

The link between the Creator and His creatures, by means of prophecy, is one of the foundations of the creation of the world.
(*Chazon Ish*, *Emunah U'Bitachon*, ch. 6)

Medium to the Nation

Ever since God communicated His will to Adam, mankind has been guided by Divine pronouncements addressed to such outstanding personalities as Noah, the Patriarchs, and Moses. Indeed, as Jewish philosophers (*Ikkarim* 3:12) have pointed out, it would have been inconceivable for God to have created the universe without providing the guidelines for man's mission on earth.

For the only time in history, He spoke not only to great individuals, but to the entire nation that He had chosen as His people and His messenger, and that would from that time onward be held to a higher standard of Divine service.

The apex of prophetic communication was the revelation at Mount Sinai, when God communicated His message to mankind. For the only time in history, He spoke not only to great individuals, but to the entire nation that He had chosen as His people and His messenger, and that would from that time onward be held to a higher standard of Divine service. Had Israel been equal to the great challenge of direct

communication from God, He would have continued to speak to the nation as a whole, but the Jews declared themselves unable to continue listening to the direct voice of God. They appealed to Moses:

> ... *If we continue to hear the voice of* HASHEM*, our God, any longer, we will die! For is there any human that has heard the voice of the Living God speaking from the fire, as we have, and lived? You should approach and hear whatever* HASHEM*, our God, will say, and you should speak to us whatever* HASHEM*, our God, will speak to you — then we shall hear and we shall do.*
>
> (*Deuteronomy* 5:22-24)

The people did not spurn God's message; they were afraid that the masses were not equal to the awesome holiness of prophecy.

Moses was upset with the people. Why should anyone forgo the opportunity to communicate directly with God? (*Rashi* ibid.). God, however, ratified their request, "... *they did well in all that they spoke* (ibid. 5:25). The people did not spurn God's message; they were afraid that the masses were not equal to the awesome holiness of prophecy. What they wanted was a level of communication that they in their human frailty could bear, while at the same time not remaining ignorant of God's will.

God acceded to both aspects of their request. He approved of their wish not to hear His voice directly. And He provided for them a different vehicle from which to hear His word. "From that time on, the Jewish people merited that God would send them prophets" (*Mechilta* to *Exodus* 20:16). Through their prophets, they would hear the word of God and be able to maintain a lofty level of devotion to Him.

Of these millions of Jews who achieved the height of human spirituality, the prophecies of only forty-eight men and seven women have been recorded in the Scriptures.

Indeed, our Sages teach that through the course of history, twice as many prophets arose among the Jews as there were Israelites who left Egypt (*Megillah* 14a). Yet, of these millions of Jews who achieved the height of human spirituality, the prophecies of only forty-eight men and seven women have been recorded in the Scriptures. (Their names are listed by *Rashi*, loc. cit.).

Moreover, even among these fifty-five, in many cases very few of their prophecies are recorded, as little as a sentence or two in some cases.

What does this say about their role? Should we measure the significance of a prophet by the number of lines allotted to him in Scripture? Is it fair to say that the fifty-five whose prophecies are recorded were greater people than those who are unnoted? Can we assume that the "Twelve Prophets" whose book we are about to begin were less important than Isaiah, for example, whose Book comprises more chapters than those of all Twelve Prophets combined?

Function of the Prophets

וּמִמַּה שֶׁיַּגִּיעַ לַנְּבִיאִים הוּא הֱיוֹתָם מִשְׁתַּלְּחִים בִּשְׁלִיחוּת מִמֶּנּוּ יִתְבָּרַךְ, וְהַיְנוּ כִּי לֹא זֶה הוּא עֶצֶם הַנְּבוּאָה וְאֵינוֹ מֻכְרָח כְּלָל בְּנָבִיא שֶׁיִּשְׁתַּלַּח לַאֲחֵרִים; אֲבָל עֶצֶם הַנְּבוּאָה . . . שֶׁהוּא הִתְדַּבֵּק בּוֹ יִתְבָּרַךְ וְהִגָּלוֹתוֹ יִתְבָּרַךְ אֵלָיו.

Part of a prophet's function may include being sent on a mission by God, may He be blessed, meaning that this in itself is not the essence of prophecy, nor is it at all necessary that a prophet be sent on a mission to others ... [Rather] the essence of prophecy is that one be attached to God, may He be blessed, and that one experience His revelation. (*Rabbi Moshe Chaim Luzzatto, Derech Hashem* 3:4:6)

A prophet is an individual who has purified his mind and nature to the point where he is able to receive the outpouring of God's spirit upon himself.

The sheer number of prophets of whom we know nothing indicates that a prophet is not necessarily sent on a specific mission or to deliver a message for eternity, or even to his own generation. Essentially, a prophet is an individual who has purified his mind and nature to the point where he is able to receive the outpouring of God's spirit upon himself (see *Rambam, Hilchos Yesodei HaTorah* 7:7; *Chasam Sofer, Even HaEzer* §40). Thus the earlier prophets were called רֹאִים, *seers* (*I Samuel* 9:9), because they were Divinely granted deeper insight, which enabled them to provide

spiritual and practical guidance to people, but they were not sent to be the leaders of the people. In contrast, the term נָבִיא [*Navi*], which essentially means a *preacher* (*Rashi, Exodus* 7:1), was commonly used for persons who exhorted others to go in the right way and prayed for them in their time of need (*Emes L'Yaakov, Genesis* 20:7). Obviously they had to be wise and righteous, but not necessarily Divinely inspired individuals.

Only in later years, when there was a need to send prophets to admonish the Jewish people and provide national leadership, did *navi* become the general appellation of a prophet. In commenting on *I Samuel* 9:9, Rabbi Yaakov Kamenetsky explained that this development marked a turning point in Jewish history, with the creation of the monarchy in Israel. The advent of a hereditary kingship meant that the heads of the state would not necessarily be righteous, as had been the case previously when God had chosen the leaders of the people, and none of those were succeeded by their children. Indeed, there was no shortage of kings who sullied the image of the Chosen People. Henceforth, the nation stood in great need of prophets with the mission of conveying נִיב ה׳, *the word of God*, to the people.

Not a Measure of Greatness

It is important, however, to note that prophets without such a mission were by no means unimportant to the community. On the contrary, they made a crucial contribution to the people, simply by their presence as personalities so closely in communion with God, and by providing guidance to their contemporaries. It was from them that people gained advice and direction, an understanding of the challenges and obligations they faced, and a true interpretation of the happenings of their time. Thus they inspired their contemporaries to go in God's way. Therefore, the fact that only a few or in some cases no prophecies whatever are passed on to us is no measure of these prophets' significance (see *Nevi'ei Emes*, pp. 110ff).

In a sense, the prophets whose teachings and even names are not recorded may be likened to great Torah leaders who never published their writings.

In a sense, the prophets whose teachings and even names are not recorded may be likened to great Torah leaders who never published their writings. It is natural that we are aware of the great contributions of the foremost scholars whose works are still studied avidly, but this does not mean that in its long history the Jewish people had no leaders who were of equal stature and whose guidance was critical to the survival of their contemporaries. Similarly, there were *tannaim* and *amoraim* who were mentioned in the Talmud as little as one time, but it would surely be inaccurate to say that the stature of the respective luminaries can be determined according to how many times they are listed. So, too, the prophets cannot be judged on the basis of whether and how extensively they are quoted in Scripture.

The *Vilna Gaon* indeed stated that these *seers* represented a higher level of prophecy than the *neviim*, the prophets who were the preachers and remonstrators of later generations. He understands the term *seer* to imply that they saw their revelation clearly, and did not require that God provide them with the words of prophecy (*Aderes Eliyahu, Balak*, and *Isaiah* 1:1; see *Oros HaGra*, pp. 194,196).

Apparently, the decline in the spiritual level of the people that marked the later period and required the presence of מוֹכִיחִים, or *providers of admonition*, also meant that the level of prophecy was diminished. Thus the fact that little or nothing is recorded about the activities of so many *seers* is no indication of their stature. The same is true of the later prophets. Even when they were sent with a specific message, it was not necessarily included in Scripture. As will be noted below, a prophet's personal stature was not the criterion that determined whether or not his prophecy would be included in Scripture

Nothing Minor

It is understandable that when we think of the paramount prophets — apart, of course, from Moses, whose prophecy was unequaled — we think of Isaiah,

As for the twelve prophets found in Trei Asar, the common wisdom considers them to be of lesser standing. But this is a non-Jewish appellation that is more than degrading.

Jeremiah, and Ezekiel, all of whose prophetic books total well over forty chapters. As for the twelve prophets found in *Trei Asar*, the common wisdom considers them to be of lesser standing; indeed, the Book of *Trei Asar* is often called the "Minor Prophets." But this is a non-Jewish appellation that is more than degrading. It reveals a profound misunderstanding of the nature of *Trei Asar* and the greatness of its protagonists *(Rabbi Shimon Schwab)*.

There was nothing minor about the *prophets* whose soaring words are gathered in *Trei Asar*; it was just that the prophecies included in *Trei Asar* are comparatively brief, and were therefore gathered in a single book so that they would not be lost (*Bava Basra* 14b).

Chaggai, Zechariah and Malachi "saw that the Divine Spirit was departing and that they would be the last prophets; they therefore wrote down their own prophecies and to them added the small prophecies."

Rashi explains (loc. cit.) that Chaggai, Zechariah and Malachi, who lived at the beginning of the Second Temple Era, "saw that the Divine Spirit was departing and that they would be the last prophets; they therefore wrote down their own prophecies and to them added the small prophecies."

By compiling this final volume of prophecies, these three prophets made sure that all the remaining prophecies needed by future generations would be preserved (see also *Yoma* 9b). As our Sages explain: נְבוּאָה שֶׁהוּצְרְכָה לְדוֹרוֹת נִכְתְּבָה, *Only such prophecy that was needed for later generations was written down.* In the case of some prophets only a few or even none of their utterances fell into this category. We should realize, however, that this did not reflect upon their function and importance.

II. The First of the Twelve

תְּחִלַּת דִּבֶּר־ה׳ בְּהוֹשֵׁעַ. וְכִי עִם הוֹשֵׁעַ דִּבֵּר תְּחִלָּה
וַהֲלֹא מִמֹּשֶׁה עַד הוֹשֵׁעַ כַּמָּה נְבִיאִים הָיוּ? אָמַר ר׳
יוֹחָנָן: שֶׁהָיָה תְּחִלָּה לְאַרְבָּעָה נְבִיאִים שֶׁנִּתְנַבְּאוּ
בְּאוֹתוֹ פֶּרֶק.

"The beginning of God's word came to Hosea" — did God then speak first to Hosea? Were there not many prophets from Moses to Hosea? Said Rabbi Yochanan: "He was the first of the four prophets [Hosea, Isaiah, Amos and Micah] who prophesied in this period." *(Bava Basra 14b)*

Hosea — A New Era

With Hosea begins not only Trei Asar, the Book of Twelve Prophets, but a new period in Jewish history.

With Hosea begins not only *Trei Asar*, the *Book of Twelve Prophets*, but a new period in Jewish history — and with it, a new role for the prophets of that time. In addition to the twelve of this Book, those prophets include Isaiah, Ezekiel and Jeremiah. Collectively, they are known as the נְבִיאִים אַחֲרוֹנִים, *Later Prophets*, even though almost all of them lived during the era described in the *Book of Kings*, which is included in the so-called נְבִיאִים רִאשׁוֹנִים, *Early Prophets*. (The Sages, in fact, refer only to Chaggai, Zechariah and Malachi as the "Later Prophets" (*Yoma* 9b), since they lived at the beginning of the Second Temple Era, centuries after the time of Hosea and his contemporaries.

Different Content

Clearly, the differentiation between the "early" and "later" prophets is not chronological, but a reflection of their different roles and the nature of their message. We do, indeed, find that the prophetic missions of those known as the later prophets were quite different from those of their predecessors. In the first place, the prophetic messages of the Early Prophets are integrated into the overall historical account of the happenings of the period, in contrast to the books

comprising the Later Prophets, which are composed primarily of distinct and explicit exhortative epistles (*Daas Sofrim*).

This difference of form is related to a fundamental difference of content. Faced with the transgressions of the Jewish people, the prophets preceding Hosea warned it of punishments that would befall it before long in *Eretz Yisrael* itself. These punishments consisted of the incursions and conquests of foreign enemies, such as the Canaanites who dominated the Land until the prophetess Deborah drove them out, and the Philistines, who were conquered under the leadership of Samuel and the kings he anointed; but these prophets did not refer to exile from the Land.

The Later Prophets spoke of long-term punishments. These later prophecies were a direct response to the decline of the Jewish people.

In contrast, the Later Prophets spoke of long-term punishments. These later prophecies were a direct response to the decline of the Jewish people, as suggested above (see p. xxi). They pleaded with the people to repent, and warned them that vain stubbornness would bring the destruction of the Temple, the fall of the state, and the exile of the people. The latter theme is mentioned only once, and then only in a very general way, in the earlier prophetic books (*Joshua* 23:15). With Hosea began a new period in the life of the Jewish people, and consequently a new focus in the nature of the prophecies addressed to it. Thus, according to the *Vilna Gaon*, the reason why the term *Neviim Achronim* was adopted for the prophets from Hosea on was not because of chronology, but because their prophecy had a unity of its own.

With Hosea began a new period in the life of the Jewish people, and consequently a new focus in the nature of the prophecies addressed to it.

III. Prophets of the Churban

מֵאֵמָתַי תַּמָּה זְכוּת אָבוֹת? אָמַר רַב מִימוֹת הוֹשֵׁעַ בֶּן בְּאֵרִי.

From which period in time did the merit of the Patriarchs lapse? Said Rav: "From the days of Hosea ben Be'eri" (*Shabbos 55a*)

Lost Protection

The detailed statement about the time of Hosea's prophecies, given in the first verse of the Book, highlights the fact that he spoke at a crucial moment in Jewish history.

A*barbanel* points out that whenever it is essential to the understanding of a prophecy, Scripture specifies the time period during which that prophet functioned (see also *Moreh Nevuchim* III:7). The detailed statement about the time of Hosea's prophecies, given in the first verse of the Book, therefore highlights the fact that he spoke at a crucial moment in Jewish history, during the reigns of four kings of Judah and one king of the Ten Tribes. It was during his long tenure as a prophet, Rav explains, that the Jews lost the protection of the merits of the Patriarchs, which had shielded them for many centuries until then.

But why should the good deeds of our forefathers ever have compensated for our own iniquities? Does not the Torah say that everyone is judged only according to his own good deeds and iniquities?

The Patriarchs attained such a lofty level of Divine service, marked by extraordinary dedication to kindness, truth and fear of God, that these qualities became natural attributes of their descendants.

Michtav MeEliyahu (I pp. 8ff, quoting Rabbi Chaim of Volozhin) explains that, in truth, only a person's own merits can protect him from Divine judgment. However, the Patriarchs attained such a lofty level of Divine service, marked by extraordinary dedication to kindness, truth and fear of God, that these qualities became natural attributes of their descendants. This enabled future generations to rise in spiritual stature and prevented them from falling to the lowest depths of depravity — that is, until the precious heritage of the Patriarchs had been exhausted and "they had used it up" (*Rashi*). At that point their spiritual level began to plunge and they could no longer count on God's special providential mercy. According to Rav, this precipitous decline happened in Hosea's time.

There are also other opinions as to the exact time when the Jewish people lost the merit of the Patriarchs (see *Shabbos 55a* and *Vayikra Rabbah* 36:5). Moreover, there is disagreement on what exactly this lapse signified (see *Tosafos* and *Michtav MeEliyahu* III pp. 74, 80). However, it is quite clear that there was a major change in the situation of the Jewish people in Hosea's time.

It is quite clear that there was a major change in the situation of the Jewish people in Hosea's time.

Earthquakes

The period was marked by the great earthquake that took place on the day King Uziah of Judah entered the Temple to offer קְטֹרֶת, *incense* (*Zechariah* 14:5; *Rashi,* following *Seder Olam,* explains *Isaiah* 6:4 as a reference to this earthquake, which is also mentioned in *Amos* 1:1 and was predicted by him, 3:15; see *Radak* and *Malbim*). Not being a Kohen, and therefore forbidden to perform the incense service, Uziah was struck with *tzaraas.* This desecration of the Sanctuary marked a turning point in the destinies of the Jewish people; indeed, the prophecy of Isaiah (ch. 6) indicates that it represented the beginning of the withdrawal of the *Shechinah*, the Divine Presence, from the Temple, step by step. This was the process that eventually led to the Temple's destruction (*R' S.R. Hirsch, Collected Writings* IV pp. 6-7).

Nevi'ei Emes points out that three great earthquakes are mentioned in *Tanach.* The first was at Mount Sinai (see *Ramban, Exodus* 2:15) when the *Shechinah* descended to dwell in *Klal Yisrael;* the next was in the time of Uziah, when the *Shechinah* began to depart; and the third, foretold by Zechariah, will mark the *Shechinah's* return in the days of Mashiach.

The tone of the prophecies from Hosea on, up to the return of the Jewish people from Babylonia, is set by Isaiah's words in reference to the second earthquake, as explained by *Rashi* (6:11): *They will not return until punishment has befallen them; they will go into exile and the cities will be desolate, without dwellers.*

Tentative Message

The warnings about the Destruction have a tentative note about them, as if that dreaded event could not be predicted with certainty (see *Daas Sofrim* to *Isaiah*

Only the merit of the forefathers had lapsed, but God's covenant with the Patriarchs remained binding.

6:11). In the first place *Rabbeinu Tam (Shabbos* 55a) stresses that only the *merit* of the forefathers had lapsed, but that God's *covenant* with the Patriarchs remained binding. This is shown every day by the fact that we continue to pray that He remember His *bris* [covenant] with them for our benefit. *Michtav MeEliyahu* (III p. 80) explains *Rabbeinu Tam's* view to mean that only individuals cannot count on the protection of זְכוּת אָבוֹת, *the merit of the Patriarchs*, but the nation as a whole can still invoke their covenant with God. Moreover, as *Maharal* stresses, through sincere penitence it is always possible to reverse harsh Divine punishment.

Consequently, we may see the strong admonitions of the Prophets as an effort to bestir the Jewish people to repentance in the face of threatening disaster. Understanding that they could no longer readily count on the merits of the Patriarchs, the people had to perceive the destruction of the Temple and exile from the Holy Land as a terrible possibility. They were urged, therefore, *Look up to your father Avraham, and to Sarah who bore you* (*Isaiah* 51:2), and seek to regain what they had taught you. *Hate evil, love good, and establish justice in court, so that perhaps HASHEM, the God of the multitudes, will grant favor to the remnant of Joseph* (*Amos* 5:15).

Thus the prophets had to shock Israel out of its complacency. Israel looked up to the Temple Mount and felt secure. The Temple would protect them and the merit of their forefathers made them impregnable — but the prophets had to show them they were wrong.

Thus the prophets had to shock Israel out of its complacency. Israel looked up to the Temple Mount and felt secure. The Temple would protect them and the merit of their forefathers made them impregnable — but the prophets had to show them they were wrong, that their own misdeeds had undermined the Temple's sanctity, and caused the *Shechinah* to begin its slow, painful withdrawal, until, by the time of the Babylonian conquest, the Temple had been reduced to an architectural shell without spiritual content. The prophets avoided outright predictions of destruction, however, because the Patriarchal covenant was still binding, and, as noted above, even the Patriarchal *merit* could be restored if there was national repentance.

IV. Message of the Twelve

אַף עַל פִּי שֶׁמֹּשֶׁה רַבֵּנוּ כְּבָר הִזְהִיר עַל קִיּוּם הַמִּצְוֹת הָיָה מֵרַחֲמֵי הָאֵ־ל יִתְבָּרַךְ לַחֲזוֹר וּלְהַתְרוֹת בָּעָם עַל יְדֵי נְבִיאָיו בְּעֵת הַצּוֹרֶךְ . . .אֲבָל לֹא הָיָה צוֹרֶךְ לְדוֹרוֹת בְּכָל דִּבְרֵיהֶם, רַק עִנְיָנִים שֶׁצְּרִיכִין בֵּירוּר יוֹתֵר . . .

Even though our teacher Moshe had already warned about observance of the commandments, Hashem, may He be blessed, in His mercy reiterated the warning to His people through His prophets, whenever it was necessary ... However, later generations had no need of all their teachings, only matters that needed more clarification [and these were committed to writing].

(*Beis Elokim* ch. 19)

Flowing from Sinai

Our Sages stress that if the Jewish people had not sinned, they would have received only the *Chumash* and the Book of Joshua, because it contains the boundaries of *Eretz Yisrael* (*Nedarim* 22b). In explanation, *Emes L'Yaakov* quotes *Rashi (Taanis* 9a) that "the *Chumash* is the foundation of *Neviim* and *Kesuvim,* which are all alluded to in the Torah." This implies that the essence of the Books of the Prophets would not have been lost to the nation, for it is contained in the Torah. Hence, we find in *Berachos* 5a that not the Torah alone, but also *Neviim* and *Kesuvim* were given at Sinai. No prophet is permitted to innovate; his task is to reiterate, explicate and elaborate on what the Torah teaches: "Said Rabbi Yitzchok: Whatever the prophecy in any generation, the prophets had received it from Sinai" (*Shemos Rabbah* 28:4). R' Yitzchok found in the Torah the soaring spirituality of Isaiah, but ordinary people did not. Thus they came to sin — and they needed the prophets to show them what they did not learn from the Torah.

No prophet is permitted to innovate; his task is to reiterate, explicate and elaborate on what the Torah teaches.

Rabbi Yitzchok Hutner has pointed out that the first prophetic book, *Joshua*, begins with a reference to the Torah (1:7), and the last prophetic book, *Malachi*, ends likewise (3:22). Thus, the beginning and end of the Prophets illustrate R' Yitzchok's teaching that the words of the prophets are actually an amplification of the Torah itself.

There was no need, therefore, to record all prophetic statements: "Only such prophecy that was needed for later generations was written down" (*Megillah* 14a). *Rashi* explains that the recorded prophecies were all meant "to call Jews to repentance or to provide guidance." These, too, of course, originate in the Torah, but the subsequent prophecies had to be recorded because the respective prophets spoke to future generations, as well as their own.

Rashi explains that the recorded prophecies were all meant "to call Jews to repentance or to provide guidance."

Each prophet, however, had his own particular style of speech and expression. It was reflected in his teachings and — if needed — preserved for posterity. Men of great stature, each of them expressed his own individuality (see *Chazon Ish*, quoted in *Nevi'ei Emes* p. 96, and *Emes L'Yaakov, Numbers* 30:82). Additionally, each of them responded to the particular needs of his time and emphasized what it required. Let us explore how Hosea's prophecy related to his own era.

Hosea's Symbolism

Hosea's book starts with God's command to marry a loose woman. It symbolizes the deteriorating relationship between God and Israel over the years from Sinai to the time of the prophet. The original closeness between them is described allegorically in *Shir HaShirim*, the *Song of Songs*. Lyrically, it describes the ecstatic relationship of a loving bride and groom, and our Sages compare the Revelation at Sinai to a marriage ceremony. But many years of sin had changed that. God's command that Hosea marry a faithless woman and have children by her symbolized the degradation of a union that had become worthless by Hosea's time. Yet, in spite of this, God refused to reject his people totally, and told Hosea to pray for them (*Pesachim* 87b).

Even the most repulsive object or person can attain value by serving as a means of achieving God's purpose.

Michtav MeEliyahu (II p. 285) points out a further lesson conveyed by this episode: Even the most repulsive object or person — in this case a woman of ill repute — can attain value by serving as a means of achieving God's purpose.

Message for the Future

During the period of the Later Prophets, the moral decline of the rulers and the harsh lot of the righteous was obviously a matter of transcending and perplexing concern to the people.

Beis Elokim draws attention to another lesson to be derived from *Trei Asar*. The prophet Habakkuk deals with the question of why evildoers often succeed while the righteous may suffer. This was clearly a timely subject, because, during the period of the Later Prophets, the moral decline of the rulers and the harsh lot of the righteous was obviously a matter of transcending and perplexing concern to the people. This also accounts for Habakkuk's emphasis on faith in God as the very foundation of our life as Jews (2:4). Can there be a prophecy more necessary for all future generations, especially those that would be mired in exile among cultures abhorrent to the values of the Torah, and subjugated by smug and prosperous oppressors?

Generally, the prophecies concerning the *Churban* had a profound and lasting impact. They taught the Jewish people that the fate it would suffer at the hand of its enemies was not a matter of accident or chance, but of Divine Providence. This was reinforced by the prediction of a redemption to come, which gave further meaning to the exile that was to precede it (*Nevi'ei Emes*). Then, all the suffering of the exile due to the sins of the Jewish people would finally culminate in the glorious era of Messiah and the fulfillment of God's purpose in creating the world.

Why could these teachings not be passed on to later generations by oral transmission?

Only written transmission made these ideas part of the eternal covenant between God and Israel, which is essentially in writing.

Nevi'ei Emes suggests that only written transmission made these ideas part of the eternal covenant between God and Israel, which is essentially in writing (see *Deuteronomy* 29:20). Furthermore, the written *Tanach* is a revelation of God's ways in the world (see *Exodus* 4:3) and the recorded prophecies are further

instances of this revelation. Indeed, the *Chazon Ish* (quoted in *Nevi'ei Emes*) described the writing of the *Tanach* as a continuation of Moshe's writing of the *Torah*. In a similar vein Rabbi Tzaddok HaKohen (*Tzidkas Hatzadik*, 72) describes the work of the prophets as the opening of new wellsprings of Divine spiritual influence in the world.

The Last Prophets

אַף עַל פִּי שֶׁלֹּא שָׁרְתָה שְׁכִינָה בְּבַיִת שֵׁנִי, מִכָּל מָקוֹם עִיקַּר הַתּוֹרָה וְזִיוָהּ וְהַדָרָהּ לֹא הָיוּ אֶלָּא בְבַיִת שֵׁנִי.

Even though the Shechinah did not dwell in the Second Temple, the essence of the Torah, its radiance and splendor, were only found in the Second Temple.

(*Pirkei Heicholos* ch. 27)

The last prophets represent the end of the prophetic era. They knew that there would be no further prophecies until Elijah would appear to herald the Messianic age.

Chaggai, Zechariah and Malachi, the last prophets, represent the end of the prophetic era. They knew that there would be no further prophecies until Elijah would appear to herald the Messianic age; hence, together with the other אַנְשֵׁי כְּנֶסֶת הַגְּדוֹלָה, *Men of the Great Assembly*, they closed the canon of the Sacred Scriptures, selecting which books of the prophets would become part of the eternal Written Torah. Indeed, with their death, רוּחַ הַקּוֹדֶשׁ, *the spirit of holiness* — in the narrow sense of prophecy — disappeared from the Jewish people (*Yoma* 9b). The special role these three prophets shared is highlighted by the fact that they all used the same Divine Name ה' צבא־ות, *HASHEM, Master of Legions*.

Each Divine Name represents a particular manifestation of God. It is well known, for example, that the Name *HASHEM* represents Divine mercy, and the Name *Elokim* represents Divine judgment. Thus the particular Divine name used by a prophet is an indication of his own mission, and of the specific aspect of Divine providence that he was appointed to convey (see *Ramban, Exodus* 3:13, and *Rashbam* 23:17). It has been suggested that the specific name ה' צבא־ות alludes

to the multitudes over whom God exercises His sway (see *Berachos* 31b). Concerning the building of the Second Temple, Chaggai (2:6) indeed declares that *the honor of the last house will exceed that of the first*, in that the other nations will view it with greater awe and reverence (*Yaaros D'vash*).

The destruction of the First Temple, the departure of the *Shechinah*, and the loss of prophecy, represented a terrible punishment. Yet perhaps it should not be seen in a purely negative light.

The Sages

There is a controversy among the commentators as to whether the return from Babylonia and the building of the Second Temple were meant to be a full redemption from exile or merely a preparatory stage for the long galus to come.

In the first place, the Sages assumed the role of the prophets. There is a controversy among the commentators as to whether the return from Babylonia and the building of the Second Temple were meant to be a full redemption from exile or merely a preparatory stage for the long *galus* to come. In any case, the circumstances surrounding the return made it clear that it would not be a full redemption (*Sotah* 36a; see *Emes L'Yaakov, Exodus* 12:2). The last prophets clearly conveyed to the Jewish people that the leadership in this new stage of Jewish history would lie in the hands of the Sages. Malachi, poignantly, ended his Book with the exhortation: זִכְרוּ תּוֹרַת מֹשֶׁה עַבְדִּי אֲשֶׁר צִוִּיתִי אוֹתוֹ בְחֹרֵב עַל־כָּל יִשְׂרָאֵל חֻקִּים וּמִשְׁפָּטִים, *Remember the words of Moses, My servant, that I commanded him at Horeb, decrees and ordinances upon all Israel* (*Malachi* 3:24).

The Sages explain (*Megillah* 15a) that Malachi is identical with Ezra, whose teacher was Baruch ben Neriah, the scribe of Jeremiah. Ezra became the leader of the Jewish people, and, with the Men of the Great Assembly, laid the foundation for the coming Rabbinic leadership of the nation. Here we see the transition from the prophets, represented by the prophetic tradition of Baruch ben Neriah, to the Sages, represented by the Great Assembly, which included the prophets Ezra, Chaggai, Zechariah, and Mordechai.

The *Netziv* explains that this shift was necessary because, with the change to an exile existence, it was no longer sufficient to pass on the Torah verbatim from generation to generation; there had to be a special emphasis on study in depth and clarification of the law, whenever and wherever questions arose (*Harchev Davar, Deuteronomy* 1:3).

With the change to an exile existence, it was no longer sufficient to pass on the Torah verbatim from generation to generation; there had to be a special emphasis on study in depth and clarification of the law, whenever and wherever questions arose.

It is true, as far as actual prophets were concerned, prophecy came to an end; but "it remained with the Sages" (*Bava Basra* 12a), who became the nation's new leaders. *Ramban* explains that prophecy through vision was lost, but not that which was attained "through the wisdom of the Sages and the truth perceived through the רוּחַ הַקֹּדֶשׁ, *the spirit of holiness*, that was within them." This spirit did not give them prophetic insights, but it aided them in their understanding of the Torah; thus they brought about an extraordinary flowering of Torah.

End of Miracles

A second development at that time is described in *Yoma* (29a): Rabbi Assi said: "Why is Esther compared to the dawn? (*Tehillim* 22:1). It is to tell us that, just as the dawn marks the end of the night — so did Esther mark the end of miracles."

It would appear that the end of open miracles, like the end of darkness, is to be welcomed. *Anaf Yosef* explains that the miracle of Purim so clearly established the truth of God's rule over the world and that He is the King of Kings that "many of the people converted to Judaism" (*Esther* 8:17). Henceforth, even though there could still be scoffers and unbelievers, the world, generally, acknowledged the existence of God. In a similar vein, *Malbim (Nitzavim)* points out that the foundation for mankind's recognition of God was laid by the prophetic prediction that destruction and exile would be followed by redemption. This brought recognition of God's power and providence. Thus, it would follow that neither miracles nor prophecy would be necessary any longer. Similarly, Rabbi

Even though there could still be scoffers and unbelievers, the world, generally, acknowledged the existence of God.

It would follow that neither miracles nor prophecy would be necessary any longer.

Tzaddok HaKohen relates the changes here described — the disappearance of prophecy and miracles — to the elimination of the *Yetzer Hara* of idol worship. As the forces of impurity and temptation were weakened by the termination of idol worship, there was less need for open Divine intervention.

The future would center around the concentration on Torah — as Malachi said in the last words of the Books of the Prophets:

Remember the words of Moses, My servant.

Rabbi Joseph Elias

Tishrei, 5756 / September 1995

hoshea

א דְּבַר־יְהוָה ׀ אֲשֶׁר הָיָה אֶל־הוֹשֵׁעַ בֶּן־בְּאֵרִי בִּימֵי
עֻזִּיָּה יוֹתָם אָחָז יְחִזְקִיָּה מַלְכֵי יְהוּדָה וּבִימֵי
ב יָרָבְעָם בֶּן־יוֹאָשׁ מֶלֶךְ יִשְׂרָאֵל׃ תְּחִלַּת דִּבֶּר־

⸎ Introduction

Hosea is counted as the first volume in the Book of *Twelve "Minor" Prophets* (תרי עשר). Of course, Hosea was by no means a "minor" prophet, nor were the others. However, since his book and those of the other eleven "minor" prophets are relatively small books in comparison to other books of Scripture, they were combined into one. In actuality, the nomenclature "minor" prophets is of non-Jewish origin (*Rav Shimon Schwab*). They were all the greatest of human beings as well as exceptional prophets.

Over the centuries, Israel produced millions of prophets. Nevertheless, only the words of those prophets which contained a message for the future generations were written down (*Megillah* 14a). Therefore, when we read about the sins of the Jewish people, and even the sins of the ten northern tribes, like worshiping idols of the Baal and Molech, it is important to realize that the prophet's messages are meant to have a bearing on us.

I

1. דְּבַר־ה׳ אֲשֶׁר הָיָה אֶל־הוֹשֵׁעַ בֶּן־בְּאֵרִי — *The word of* HASHEM[1] *that came to Hosea the son of Beeri.* This book contains [primarily] the words of rebuke and admonition that Hosea son of Beeri said to the people of Israel and Judah for the evil they pursued in the days of the kings listed (*Radak*).

Hosea's father Beeri was the same person as Beerah, a prince of the tribe of Reuven,[2] who was exiled to Assyria by Tilgath-Pilnesser (see *I Chronicles* 5:6).

1. Although the *Midrash (Bereishis Rabbah* 4:7) enumerates ten expressions of prophecy found in Scripture, *Abarbanel* reduces this list to three general categories with seven subgroupings:

(1) When the source of the prophecy (i.e., God) is emphasized, the term דְּבַר־ה׳, *the word of* HASHEM, or one of its derivative forms is used.

(2) If the verse stresses the role of the recipient of the prophecy (i.e., the prophet), then the expression חֲזוֹן, *the vision of*, or one of its subgroups, is employed [e.g., *Isaiah* 1:1].

(3) Should the subject of the prophecy (i.e., the individual or nation to whom the prophecy pertains) be of foremost importance, one of the forms of מַשָּׂא, *the burden of*, is utilized [e.g., *Nahum* 1:1].

Our verse begins with דְּבַר־ה׳, *the word of* HASHEM, accentuating that these are God's words. Perhaps it is the sensitive subject matter of this first prophecy which necessitates the emphasis of its Divine source. Certainly a person of Hosea's caliber would not degrade himself to marry a harlot, had the order not issued directly from God — the source of all prophecy (*Abarbanel, Introduction* to *HaChakirah HaShlishis*).

2. [Ascribing such greatness to Hosea's father is in line with a Talmudic dictum. If a prophet's father's name is recorded along with his own, then he is surely a second-generation prophet. If, however, the father's name is omitted, then the father was not a prophet (*Megillah* 15a).]

Abarbanel cites the dictum above and adds three other reasons for the inclusion or omission of a prophet's name:

(1) If the father is famous, well known for his righteousness and benevolence, then appending his name to his son's lends honor to the son. In effect this shows that the latter is worthy of his illustrious heritage [e.g., Hosea is deemed worthy of succeeding his father as prince of the tribe of Reuven (*I Chronicles* 5:6)].

1 The word of HASHEM that came to Hosea the son of Beeri in the days of Uziah, Jotham, Ahaz, [and] Hezekiah — the kings of Judah — and in the days of Jeroboam son of Joash, king of Israel. 2 The initial [words

He was called Beerah because he was a flowing source of Torah wisdom [from the word *be'er*, well] (*Yalkut Shimoni* from *Pesikta d'Rav Kahana*).

... בִּימֵי — *In the days of ...* When knowledge of the time period during which a particular prophet functioned is essential to the understanding of his words, then that period is delineated. But when the prophecy relates to some indefinite future date, then such details are omitted (*Abarbanel*).

בִּימֵי עֻזִּיָּה יוֹתָם אָחָז יְחִזְקִיָּה מַלְכֵי יְהוּדָה — *In the days of Uziah, Jotham, Ahaz, [and] Hezekiah — the kings of Judah.* [Hosea prophesied during the reigns of these four kings of Judah: Uziah — 3115 (645 B.C.E.) — 3167 (593); Jotham — 3167-3183 (577); Ahaz — 3183-3199 (561); Hezekiah — 3199-3228 (532).]

For ninety years Hosea prophesied the downfall of the kingdom of Israel — Uziah reigned 52 years (*II Kings* 15:2); Jotham, 16 (ibid. v.33); Ahaz, 16 (ibid. 16:2); and during the sixth year of Hezekiah's kingship (ibid. 18:10) the ten tribes were exiled (*Pesikta* 34:9).

וּבִימֵי יָרָבְעָם בֶּן־יוֹאָשׁ מֶלֶךְ יִשְׂרָאֵל — *And in the days of Jeroboam son of Joash, king of Israel.* Jeroboam was a descendant of Jehu, whose reign over the kingdom of Israel coincided with those of Uziah and Jotham over Judah (*Rashi*).[1] Due to their wickedness, the various kings of Israel who ruled during this period are not accorded the honor of being mentioned here. Nevertheless, Jeroboam — who was also guilty of idolatry — is cited. This is due to his refusal to accept the slander of Amaziah — a priest of idolatry — against the prophet Amos, when the former accused the latter of inciting rebellion against Jeroboam's throne (*Rashi* from *Pesachim* 87b; see *Amos* 7:10; comm. ibid.). In reward for this, he also succeeded in reconquering for Israel portions of their land which had been captured by gentile nations (*Mahari Kara*; see *II Kings* 14:25).

Malbim notes that the kingdom of Judah was under the dominion of the kingdom of Israel from the time that Joash conquered Amaziah king of Judah until twenty-four years into the reign of Uziah, who overthrew the yoke of Israel from upon Judah. Thus, during the first twenty-seven years of Jeroboam's rule, he held power over Judah as well as Israel. Thus for part of the time in which Hosea prophesied, Jeroboam's rule encompassed Judah as well. Therefore, although the verse cites only the kings of Judah under whose reign Hosea prophesied, it nevertheless mentions the monarchy of Jeroboam.

2. In the following verses, the prophet depicts a strange sequence of events, in which he weds a known prostitute at the Almighty's behest and has three children with her. The correct interpretation of these verses is the subject of great dispute. *Targum Yonasan* interprets the entire chapter metaphorically. None of these events occurred, nor did

(2) The literal meaning of the father's name may indicate greatness [e.g., Beeri means well of Torah knowledge (see *Yalkut* cited above)].

(3) Confusion with a contemporary of the same name is avoided when the father's name is also given [e.g., Hosea son of Beeri and not Hosea son of Elah].

1. [*Rashi*'s statement is perplexing as Jeroboam apparently ruled from 3112 (648 B.C.E.) — 3153, which coincided with the reign of Uziah but not with that of Jotham.]

א/ב יְהוָה בְּהוֹשֵׁעַ וַיֹּאמֶר יְהוָה אֶל־הוֹשֵׁעַ לֵךְ קַח־לְךָ אֵשֶׁת זְנוּנִים וְיַלְדֵי זְנוּנִים כִּי־זָנֹה תִזְנֶה הָאָרֶץ

they appear to have occurred in a prophetic dream. They are merely the medium used to depict the prophetic message that Hosea was commanded to import to the nation. *Ibn Ezra* follows a less radical approach: The events described did not actually transpire; they merely appeared in a prophetic dream to Hosea in order to convey the message that they symbolize. He categorically rejects the possibility that the Almighty would command His servant to perform so degrading an act as to marry a prostitute and have children from her. *Rambam (Moreh Nevuchim* 46:2) and *Radak* share this view.

The Sages of the Talmud (*Pesachim* 87a), however, interpret these events literally.[1] Hosea actually wed the harlot Gomer and she actually bore to him two sons and a daughter. This view is followed by *Rashi*, *Abarbanel*, and *Malbim* in their commentaries. [However, they too agree that the primary point of these actions was to convey a message of prophecy to the nation, and the events depicted thus symbolize the particulars of that message.]

תְּחִלַּת דִּבֶּר־ה׳ בְּהוֹשֵׁעַ — *The initial [words that] HASHEM spoke to Hosea.* The following are the first words of prophecy spoken to Hosea by the Almighty (*Rashi*). The Sages interpret: The first of Hashem's words were to Hosea. Did then Hashem speak first to Hosea? Were there not from Moses until Hosea many prophets? Said R' Yochanan: The first of the four prophets who prophesied at that time. And these are they: Hosea, Isaiah, Amos, and Michah (*Pesachim* 87a).

If Hosea predated Isaiah as a prophet, then why does the Book of *Isaiah* precede the Book of *Hosea* in Scriptural order? *Hosea*, because of its diminutive size, was made a part of the Book of Twelve Prophets. Since this book includes the Books of *Haggai*, *Zechariah*, and *Malachi*, with whom the era of prophecy ended, it is placed last in the order of *Prophets*. Had *Hosea* been assigned a place as a separate volume, it would probably have been first (*Bava Basra* 14b).

Others interpret this phrase as a preface to the remainder of the verse, based on a dialogue between Hashem and

1. *Abarbanel* defends the view of the Sages by explaining that the prophets were servants of the Almighty whose entire being was given over to the needs of the Jewish nation. Thus, they did not hesitate to perform acts which were personally demeaning or even harmful, in order to promote the general welfare of Hashem's nation, nor did the Almighty refrain from commanding them to do so. [It is axiomatic that any harm or shame caused to them by these actions are viewed as מְסִירוּת נֶפֶשׁ, *extreme self-sacrifice*, in service of the Almighty, and were rewarded generously in this world and/or the next.] *Malbim* notes as well that there is no actual prohibition against one who is not a *Kohen* taking a prostitute for a wife. Furthermore, we find clear examples of cases in which prophets were commanded to perform deeds which are otherwise prohibited. This is a הוֹרָאַת שָׁעָה, *a ruling for the moment* [permissible only by prophetic decree (see *Rambam Hil. Yesodei HaTorah* 9:2)]. Such a case was the erection of an altar by Elijah on Mt. Carmel, despite the prohibition against building altars other than the one in the *Beis HaMikdash*.

Abarbanel also strongly disputes *Ibn Ezra's* contention that the words of Scripture may be extracted from their literal meaning to such an extent. In those instances in which a prophetic vision is described as taking place, it is acceptable to interpret subsequent events as being part of that vision. Similarly, if the verse relates how the Almighty commanded a prophet to perform a specific symbolic act but does not describe him as actually doing so, it is possible that the command is merely symbolic. However, in a case such as ours, in which no previous prophetic vision is recorded, and Scripture explicitly describes the marriage of Hosea and Gomer as well as the birth of their children, there can be no question that the literal meaning is correct.

that] HASHEM spoke to Hosea; and HASHEM said to Hosea: Go take for yourself a wife of harlotry and children of harlotry, for the land strays from after

Hosea (*Pesachim* 87a): The Almighty said to Hosea, "Your children have sinned!" The appropriate response would have been, "They are Your sons, Your cherished sons, the sons of Abraham, Isaac, and Jacob. Extend to them Your mercy." However, not only did he not plead in this manner, he actually replied,"Master of the World, the entire world is Yours. Exchange them for another nation." Said the Holy One, Blessed is He, "What shall I do with this sage? I will say to him, 'Go and take for yourself a wife of harlotry and have her bear for you children of harlotry.' I will then say to him, 'Send her away from before you.' If he will be able to send [her] I too will send away Israel." Thus the Divine command to take a wife of harlotry was the "initial" response of the Almighty to Hosea's recommendation that He exchange the Jewish people for another nation (*Mahari Kara;* cf. *Alshich; Malbim*). [The latter, concluding response by Hashem to Hosea's recommendation is recounted in the Talmud (*Pesachim* 87b) as follows: "After she bore to him two sons and one daughter, Hashem said to Hosea, 'Should you not have learned from Moses your master, who separated from his wife when I spoke to him? You, too, separate yourself from her.' He replied, 'Master of the World, I have children from her and I am unable to divorce her.' Said the Almighty, 'If you — whose wife is a harlot and whose children are of harlotry, and you do not even know if they are yours or of others — [react in] this [manner], certainly Israel, who are the children of My tested ones — the children of Abraham, Isaac, and Jacob — one of the four acquisitions that I have in the world ... and you say that I should exchange them for another nation?' Once [Hosea] realized he had sinned, he rose to beg for mercy for himself. Said to him the Almighty, 'Before you request mercy for yourself seek mercy for Israel, for I have decreed upon them three decrees because of you.' He rose and begged for mercy and the decree was annulled. He then began to bless them, as it is stated (2:1): *And the number of the Children of Israel shall be etc.*"] Out of deference to the honor of Hosea, Scripture does not record the actual dialogue but merely alludes to it with the phrase, *The initial [words that] HASHEM spoke to Hosea* (*Alshich*).

לֵךְ קַח־לְךָ אֵשֶׁת זְנוּנִים וְיַלְדֵי זְנוּנִים — *Go take for yourself a wife of harlotry and children of harlotry.* Since you do not desire to reprove the Jewish people and arouse them to repentance (*Malbim*), [go place yourself into circumstances which will enable you to appreciate Mine]. Marry a prostitute and have from her children of harlotry — i.e., children about whom it will be impossible to ascertain whether they are actually yours or illegitimate children from another father (*Rashi* from *Pesachim* loc. cit.).

Alternatively: Go take a woman who is a known prostitute, as evidenced by the fact that although unwed she has already borne children (*Abarbanel*).

כִּי־זָנֹה תִזְנֶה הָאָרֶץ מֵאַחֲרֵי ה׳ — *For the land strays from after HASHEM.* Your taking of such a wife will serve as a symbol of Israel's situation. For they have been designated as My nation and sanctified to serve Me and cleave to Me. Nevertheless, they have strayed from My ways like a wayward wife, and performed iniquitous deeds which can be likened to children born of harlotry (*Abarbanel*).

Targum interprets the verse metaphorically: Go prophesy a prophecy upon the inhabitants of the cities of idolatry. According to this approach, the word קַח denotes teaching — teach them to repent (*Rashi*).

ג מֵאַחֲרֵי יהוה: וַיֵּלֶךְ וַיִּקַּח אֶת־גֹּמֶר בַּת־
ד דִּבְלָיִם וַתַּהַר וַתֵּלֶד־לוֹ בֵּן: וַיֹּאמֶר יהוה
אֵלָיו קְרָא שְׁמוֹ יִזְרְעֶאל כִּי־עוֹד מְעַט
וּפָקַדְתִּי אֶת־דְּמֵי יִזְרְעֶאל עַל־בֵּית יֵהוּא

3. In the year 2964 (766 B.C.E.) Jeroboam son of Nebot (*Jeroboam* I) rebelled against the rule of Rehabim son of Solomon (son of King David) and formed an independent Jewish kingdom in the north of *Eretz Yisrael.* Thus, by the time of Hosea (over 120 years later) two Jewish states existed — the smaller kingdom of Judah, comprised primarily of the tribes of Benjamin and Judah; and the kingdom of Israel in the north, comprised of the remaining ten tribes. The kingdom of Israel was eventually destroyed by Assyria; its populace was exiled and lost among the nations of Biblical times. Although the Talmud mentions that the "lost tribes" will eventually return to the body of the Jewish people (*Sanhedrin* 110b), their whereabouts, and the process by which they will be restored, is not known.

The prophet now goes on to describe the birth of a son, a daughter, and another son and the names they were given. According to *Ibn Ezra* and *Radak*, all of these occurrences symbolize events which occurred to the kingdom of the ten tribes of Israel. *Abarbanel* and *Malbim* understand them as encompassing both of the Jewish kingdoms, with *Abarbanel* interpreting them to extend even to the second commonwealth of Judah in the times of the second *Beis HaMikdash.* According to *Abarbanel*, each of the three children represents an event of destruction and tragedy in the history of the Jewish nation. *Malbim* understands them to represent different eras in the monarchies of Israel. *Targum* continues with his approach that all of the events are allegorical depictions of prophetic messages.

The following chronological chart should facilitate a clearer understanding of the different approaches to the prophecies which follow.

3112	Jeroboam son of Joash assumes throne of Israel
3115	Uziah assumes throne of Judah
3153	Zechariah son of Jeroboam succeeds his father for six months
3153	Shallum son of Yavesh ascends to throne of Israel for one month
This marks the end of the dynasty of Jehu	
3154	Menachem son of Gadi ascends throne of Israel
3164	Pekachiah succeeds his father Menachem
3166	Pekach son of Remaliahu ascends throne of Israel
3167	Jotham assumes throne of Judah
3183	Ahaz succeeds Jotham
3187	First stage of exile of kingdom of Israel; tribe of Naphtali exiled by Tiglath-Pilnesser of Assyria
3187	Hosea son of Elah assumes throne of Israel
3195	Second phase of exile of ten tribes — Shalmanesser exiles tribes east of Jordan River
3199	Hezekiah ascends throne of Judah
3205	Final exile of the tribes of Israel
3338	Final exile of kingdom of Judah and destruction of first Temple

וַיֵּלֶךְ וַיִּקַּח אֶת־גֹּמֶר בַּת־דִּבְלָיִם — *And he went and took Gomer the daughter of Diblaim.* Hosea went and took for a wife a well-known prostitute by the name of Gomer (*Radak*). The Sages understand her name to symbolize her station in life: Gomer — שֶׁהַכֹּל גּוֹמְרִין בָּהּ, *all finish with her* [i.e., they finish their act of intercourse and satiate their desire (*Rashi* to Gemara ad loc.)]. בַּת דִּבְלָיִם שֶׁדָּשִׁין בָּהּ כִּדְבֵלָה — *they tread upon her like a pressed fig* [denoting her constant availability for

HASHEM. 3 And he went and took Gomer the daughter of
Diblaim and she conceived and bore him a son. 4 And
HASHEM said to him: Call his name Jezreel for I will
shortly visit the blood of Jezreel upon the house of Jehu

sexual relations] (*Rashi* from *Pesachim* 87; cf. ibid.).

Abarbanel interprets her name as representing the eventual destruction of the Jewish nation that Hosea's marriage with her was meant to symbolize: גֹּמֶר — that the kingdom of Israel would be finished and destroyed; בַּת דִּבְלָיִם — that they would be withered and emaciated in their exile like a dried-out fig.

וַתַּהַר וַתֵּלֶד־לוֹ בֵּן — *And she conceived and bore him a son.* She bore a child לוֹ, *to him* — one who was clearly identified as the son of Hosea, as Gomer was still faithful to him at that time (*Malbim*).

This child represents the monarchies of Jehu and his descendants, under whose reign the nation of Israel was still clearly linked to the Almighty. Although they were already guilty of idolatry, they pursued this merely as a means to getting closer to the Almighty Himself[1] or as deities in addition to Him (*Malbim*).

Ibn Ezra interprets this son as representing only the generation which was to follow that of Jeroboam the son of Joash, in whose time the events depicted in the following verses took place. According to *Abarbanel*, the son is symbolic of those catastrophes themselves.

Targum renders: And go and prophesy upon them that if they will repent they will be left in peace and if not they will be like unripe figs falling from the tree. And they continued to perform evil deeds.

4. קְרָא שְׁמוֹ יִזְרְעֶאל — *Call his name Jezreel.* [The Almighty commanded Hosea to name his son Jezreel.] Although this name depicts the punishment to come upon the Jewish people, as stated below, it nevertheless has no intrinsic connotation of God's loathing of Israel, as do the names of the children that follow. This is because the nation at this time was still primarily loyal to Hashem and their essential relationship with Him was thus still intact (*Malbim*).

Targum renders: *Call their name the scattered ones* — prophesy upon them that they will be exiled and strewn among the nations (*Rashi*).

כִּי־עוֹד מְעַט וּפָקַדְתִּי אֶת־דְּמֵי יִזְרְעֶאל עַל־בֵּית יֵהוּא — *For I will shortly visit the blood of Jezreel upon the house of Jehu.* The name Jezreel symbolizes the destruction I am about to bring upon the house of Jehu for the annihilation of the descendants of Ahab they perpetrated in the Valley of Jezreel.[2] Although I instructed them to do so, they subsequently followed in their predecessors' footsteps and

1. This in fact was the reasoning behind mankind's original inclination to worship idols. The men of that fatal age rationalized: Because God established the stellar bodies as His agents through whom He exerts His will, it is appropriate that they be honored and worshiped for their lofty status as His servants (*Rambam, Hil. Avodas Kochavim* 1:1). Similarly, much of the idolatry which occurred among the Jewish people was based upon reasoning whereby the forces symbolized by the idols were viewed as mediums through which man could become closer to God.

2. The complete story of the annihilation of the house of Ahab at the hands of Jehu is related in *II Kings* chapters 9-10. Following instructions sent him by the prophet Elisha (9:1-7), Jehu eradicated all traces of Ahab's posterity and his idolatrous priests. All this took place in the Valley of יִזְרְעֶאל, *Jezreel*. As a reward for ridding Israel of these evildoers Jehu was promised: *Four generations of your offspring will sit upon the throne of Israel* (10:30). Unfortunately, Jehu only destroyed the Baal-worship of Ahab, while permitting the calf-worship at Beth-el and Dan to continue (10:29).

ה וְהִשְׁבַּתִּי מַמְלְכוּת בֵּית יִשְׂרָאֵל: וְהָיָה בַּיּוֹם
הַהוּא וְשָׁבַרְתִּי אֶת־קֶשֶׁת יִשְׂרָאֵל בְּעֵמֶק
ו יִזְרְעֶאל: וַתַּהַר עוֹד וַתֵּלֶד בַּת וַיֹּאמֶר לוֹ קְרָא
שְׁמָהּ לֹא רֻחָמָה כִּי לֹא אוֹסִיף עוֹד אֲרַחֵם
ז אֶת־בֵּית יִשְׂרָאֵל כִּי־נָשֹׂא אֶשָּׂא לָהֶם: וְאֶת־
בֵּית יְהוּדָה אֲרַחֵם וְהוֹשַׁעְתִּים בַּיהוָה אֱלֹהֵיהֶם

continued the worship of their false gods. I therefore view their slaughter of Ahab's descendants as if it were the shedding of innocent blood, rather than the Divinely ordained destruction of a corrupt monarchy (*Rashi*; *Ibn Ezra*; *Mahari Kara*; *Radak*).

Abarbanel considers it inconceivable that an act of slaughter carried out at the Almighty's behest should later be defined retroactively as a culpable deed. Rather, *the blood of Jezreel* is employed as a symbol of the Almighty's retribution from those who worship false deities.[1] Just as the house of Ahab was wiped out in the Valley of Jezreel for their idolatry, so shall the house of Jehu be annihilated for continuing the same behavior (cf. *Malbim*).

וְהִשְׁבַּתִּי מַמְלְכוּת בֵּית יִשְׂרָאֵל — *And I will terminate the monarchy of the house of Israel.* In addition to eradicating the house of Jehu, I will subsequently destroy the entire kingdom of Israel. Indeed, the destruction and exile of the kingdom followed within a short time [approximately 52 years; see chart] of the former event (*Mahari Kara*; *Radak*; *Metzudos David*).

Others see this phrase as continuing the message of the previous one — referring solely to the destruction of the monarchy of the house of Jehu (*Abarbanel*; *Alshich*; *Malbim*). From that time onward, there were no longer any dynasties that ruled the nation, only a succession of kings who took power by force. Thus the prophet uses the word מַמְלְכוּת — rather than the usual word for kingdom, מַלְכוּת. This is to denote that although there would still be monarchy in Israel it would not be the inherently maintained monarchy of a dynastic line (*Alshich*).

5. וְהָיָה בַּיּוֹם הַהוּא וְשָׁבַרְתִּי אֶת־קֶשֶׁת יִשְׂרָאֵל בְּעֵמֶק יִזְרְעֶאל — *And it will be on that day that I will break the bow of Israel in the Valley of Jezreel.* I will break the might of the kingdom of Jehu, which was conceived in force by the power of the bow in the Valley of Jezreel [where Jehu defeated Jehoram the son of Ahab] (*Malbim*).

On that day, the day in which I will visit upon the house of Jehu the blood shed in the Valley of Jezreel, I will thereby destroy the might and power of the kingdom of Israel, which is concentrated in Samaria and in the Valley of Jezreel (*Radak*). Indeed, from the time that the house of Jehu was destroyed, Assyria began to extend its influence and power over the kingdom of Israel (*R' Eliezer of Beaugency*).

Abarbanel understands the bow of Israel to refer to the entire Jewish nation, including both the kingdom of Israel and that of Judah. Thus: From that day in which I will annihilate the house of Jehu, I will begin the long process of destruction after destruction and defeat after defeat, culminating in the ultimate exile of the citizens of both of the Jewish kingdoms.

6. וַתַּהַר עוֹד וַתֵּלֶד בַּת וַיֹּאמֶר לוֹ קְרָא שְׁמָהּ לֹא רֻחָמָה כִּי לֹא אוֹסִיף עוֹד אֲרַחֵם אֶת־בֵּית יִשְׂרָאֵל כִּי־נָשֹׂא אֶשָּׂא לָהֶם — *And she conceived*

1. יִזְרְעֶאל *Jezreel*, comprises the words זָרוּעַ קֵל, *sown by God*, for it represents the vengeance sown by God to exact retribution from His enemies (*Abarbanel* to v.5).

and I will terminate the monarchy of the house of
Israel. [5] *And it will be on that day that I will break the*
bow of Israel in the Valley of Jezreel. [6] *And she*
conceived again and bore a daughter and He said to
him: Call her name Lo-ruchama, for I will no longer
have mercy [upon] the house of Israel that I should
forebear them. [7] *But [upon] the house of Judah I will*
have mercy and I will save them by H*ASHEM* *their God,*

again and bore a daughter and He said to him: Call her name Lo-ruchama, for I will no longer have mercy [upon] the house of Israel that I should forebear them. Hosea's wife conceived again and bore a daughter. This time, however, it was no longer certain that the child was his, as Gomer had already reverted to her promiscuous ways. Therefore, Hosea was instructed by the Almighty to call the child *Lo-ruchama*, not beloved, for a father of a child born under such circumstances does not relate to her with the same love that he feels for one who is definitely his (*Mahari Kara*; *Malbim*).

Similarly, after the end of the dynasty of Jehu, the monarchies that follow will be weak like women and they will suffer one military defeat after another[1] (*Ibn Ezra*; *Malbim*). This will be due to their straying even further from the ways of the Almighty until they will no longer be identifiable whatsoever as His people (*Malbim*).

כִּי־נָשֹׂא אֶשָּׂא לָהֶם — *That I should forebear them.* I.e., I will no longer have mercy upon them and thereby continue to bear their sins against Me (*Mahari Kara*; *Malbim*). Although I forgave the sins of the people in the time of Jeroboam son of Joash, I will no longer continue to do so in the era depicted. Rather, I shall punish them for their transgressions and send them into exile (*Malbim*).

Others render כִּי to mean as: I will no longer have mercy upon the house of Israel, as I have borne their sins and forgiven them until now (*Radak*; *Metzudos David*; cf. *Ibn Ezra*; *Abarbanel*).

There are other approaches to this phrase which do not render נָשֹׂא אֶשָּׂא to mean bear. *Rashi* renders: I will allot to them the portion of their cup and their deeds. *Ibn Ezra* interprets: I will carry them into exile. According to *Radak*: I will bring upon them the enemy who will exile them and destroy their land (see also *Abarbanel*).

Targum renders: But if they repent I will forgive them — i.e., I will no longer grant clemency to the house of Israel, save for when I will forgive them for their sins when they repent in the end of days (*Abarbanel*).

7. וְאֶת־בֵּית יְהוּדָה אֲרַחֵם — *But [upon] the house of Judah I will have mercy.* Even after the destruction of the kingdom of Israel, I will continue to have mercy to the kingdom of Judah from the time of Hezekiah until that of Zedekiah (*Rashi*).

וְהוֹשַׁעְתִּים בַּה׳ אֱלֹהֵיהֶם — *And I will save them by* H*ASHEM* *their God.* When Sennacherib shall besiege Jerusalem, I will destroy his entire army miraculously

1. Shallum reigned for only one month (*II Kings* 15:13). Menachem became a subject of Pol, king of Assyria (ibid. vs. 19-20). Pechaniah ruled only two years before his own general Pekach assassinated him (ibid. v. 23). During Pekach's reign the Assyrian king Tiglath-Pilnesser made inroads deep into Israel and sliced off large pieces of territory (ibid. v. 29). Finally, Hosea son of Elah was forced to pay tribute to Shalmanesser, king of Assyria, and was eventually exiled, along with all of his subjects, by that king (ibid. 17:3-6).

א/ח־ט וְלֹא אוֹשִׁיעֵם בְּקֶשֶׁת וּבְחֶרֶב וּבְמִלְחָמָה בְּסוּסִים
ח וּבְפָרָשִׁים: וַתִּגְמֹל אֶת־לֹא רֻחָמָה וַתַּהַר וַתֵּלֶד
ט בֵּן: וַיֹּאמֶר קְרָא שְׁמוֹ לֹא עַמִּי כִּי אַתֶּם לֹא עַמִּי
ב/א א וְאָנֹכִי לֹא־אֶהְיֶה לָכֶם: וְהָיָה

without resorting to the weapons of warfare (*Ibn Ezra*; *Radak*; *Malbim*; *Metzudos David*; see *II Kings* 18:35).

Abarbanel interprets these two verses as discussing the return of the exiles of Judah to their land and the restoration of their nation. [This is in accordance with his view, cited above (v. 5), that the destruction of the bow of Israel includes the exile of both Jewish kingdoms.] Thus, the daughter born to Hosea symbolizes the second Jewish commonwealth. She was named *Lo-ruchama* in reference to the members of the ten tribes, who will not be included in Hashem's mercy at that time and will not be returned to their land. *But [upon] the house of Judah I will have mercy and I will save them by HASHEM their God* — I will move Cyrus the king of Persia to allow them to return to the land peacefully, without resorting to the weapons of war in order to accomplish this objective (see *II Chronicles* 36:22,23).

8. וַתִּגְמֹל אֶת־לֹא רֻחָמָה וַתַּהַר וַתֵּלֶד בֵּן — *And she weaned Lo-ruchama and she conceived and bore a son.* Gomer conceived and bore a second son to Hosea. This child represented the kingdom of Judah in the days of Hezekiah and Josiah, when it was strong and secure. [However, the primary symbolism of his birth is the ultimate destruction of that kingdom, as depicted in the following verse.] Thus, this son was not born until after the period of Lo-ruchama's nursing, as the destruction of the kingdom of Judah did not take place until a substantial length of time after the destruction of the ten tribes (*R' Eliezer of Beaugency; Malbim*).

Ibn Ezra interprets this son as representing the ten tribes in their exile and the children who will be born to them there. This follows along the lines of *Targum*, who renders: And that generation that shall be exiled among the nations will be forgotten, for they shall not be beloved, as they will continue to perform evil deeds.

9. וַיֹּאמֶר קְרָא שְׁמוֹ לֹא עַמִּי כִּי אַתֶּם לֹא עַמִּי וְאָנֹכִי לֹא־אֶהְיֶה לָכֶם — *And He said: Call his name Lo-ami, for you are not My nation and I will not be yours.* Call this child *Lo-ami*, not My nation, for you no longer heed My statutes as is befitting the subjects of a king (*Metzudos David*). Furthermore, with the final destruction of the kingdom of Judah there shall no longer be any viable Jewish nation whatsoever (*Malbim*).

Ibn Ezra explains: There [where the ten tribes live in exile] you will remain [for generations] without returning to your land, and you are therefore to be called *Lo-ami*.

Radak, like *Ibn Ezra*, understands this entire chapter to be describing the decline of the kingdom of the ten tribes of Israel. However, he interprets the specifics of the prophecy somewhat differently. The first son, Jezreel, symbolizes Jeroboam himself, who was a powerful monarch and is thus symbolized by a male child. Concerning this child's birth the Almighty states: *I will shortly visit the blood of Jezreel upon the house of Jehu* — i.e., this calamity will not take place in the lifetime of Jeroboam himself but rather under the reign of his son Zechariah. The daughter born to Hosea represents the reign of Zechariah and that of Shallum son of Yavesh who ruled after him. Because their reigns were of such short duration — six months and one month respectively — their monarchies are depicted as a female child. The weakness their monarchies personified continued

and I will not save them with the bow, with the sword,
with battle, with steeds, or with riders. 8 *And she*
weaned Lo-ruchama and she conceived and bore a son.
9 *And He said: Call his name Lo-ami, for you are not My*
nation and I will not be yours.

to plague the nation through the reigns of Menachem son of Gadi and Pekachiah son of Menachem who followed them. Thus, the nursing of this weak child continued throughout their rule. However, they were followed by Pekach son of Remaliyahu, a powerful monarch who restored the might of the kingdom of Israel, as symbolized by the birth of a second son. That son is called *Lo-ami*, not My nation, due to the wickedness of that generation.

Abarbanel interprets this final son as depicting the destruction of the second Jewish commonwealth and the second Temple: Although I will have mercy upon the people of Judah and return them to their land, that, too, shall not last forever. For they will eventually descend again into wickedness until they will no longer be identifiable by their deeds as My nation, and they will then be destroyed once again.

וְאָנֹכִי לֹא־אֶהְיֶה לָכֶם — *And I will not be yours.* I.e., I will no longer be to you for a God [i.e., a protecting God who sees to your welfare and security] (*Mahari Kara*). Alternatively, I will no longer guard and protect you, and you will therefore end up in exile (*Abarbanel*).

In the Midrash this verse is interpreted in a totally different vein: Even though you are not My people for you seek estrangement from Me, nevertheless, I shall not be of the same mind with you in this matter. Indeed, I shall force you to be My people. As it is written: *What enters your thoughts — it will not be! What you say, "Let us be like the nations, like the families of the land, to serve wood and stone* [will not come to pass; what then will happen?]" *As I live — the words of* HASHEM/ELOKIM *— with a strong hand and an outstretched arm and with outpoured fury shall I rule over you!* (*Ezekiel* 20:32,33). [Through the persecution of the nations you will retain your identity as My people.] What a remarkable lesson of the love which the Omnipresent has for Israel! (*Bamidbar Rabbah* 2:16).

II

Having sharply castigated the Jewish nation and depicted their retribution from the Almighty, Hosea now changes his tone to one of mercy, and prophesies words of comfort to the people (*Mahari Kara*), by describing their final redemption and return to the land (*Abarbanel*). Furthermore, as described by the Sages (*Pesachim* 87b; see 1:2), Hosea was filled with remorse for having urged the Almighty to exchange the Jewish nation for another, and therefore changed his tone to words of mercy (*Rashi*).[1]

However, *Ibn Ezra* understands this chapter to be a continuation of the prophecy of doom which was begun in the first chapter. The prophet describes how the

1. The Sages offer a parable of a king who became angry with his wife and sent for a scribe in order to instruct him to write her a *get* (a divorce document). Prior to the scribe's arrival, the king's anger passed and he no longer wished to divorce his wife. However, rather than sending the scribe away bewildered by the king's behavior — who seemingly called for him for no reason — he instructed him instead to write that the king is doubling his wife's *kesubah*, marriage document (*Sifri* to *Numbers* 25:1). [Similarly, after the Almighty revoked His command to Hosea to prophesy that the Jewish nation would be estranged from Him, He instructed him instead to foretell the great fortune and glory that is their ultimate destiny.]

ב/ב מִסְפַּר בְּנֵֽי־יִשְׂרָאֵל֙ כְּחוֹל הַיָּם אֲשֶׁר לֹֽא־יִמַּד
וְלֹא יִסָּפֵר וְֽהָיָה בִּמְקוֹם אֲשֶׁר־יֵאָמֵר לָהֶם֙
ב לֹֽא־עַמִּי אַתֶּם יֵאָמֵר לָהֶם בְּנֵי אֵל־חָֽי׃ וְנִקְבְּצוּ
בְּנֵֽי־יְהוּדָה וּבְנֵֽי־יִשְׂרָאֵל֙ יַחְדָּו וְשָׂמוּ לָהֶם רֹאשׁ
אֶחָד וְעָלוּ מִן־הָאָרֶץ כִּי גָדוֹל יוֹם יִזְרְעֶֽאל׃

members of the ten tribes will bear many sons while in exile, but those children will not fear the Almighty.

1. וְהָיָה מִסְפַּר בְּנֵי־יִשְׂרָאֵל כְּחוֹל הַיָּם אֲשֶׁר לֹא יִמַּד וְלֹא יִסָּפֵר — *And the number of the Children of Israel shall be like [that of] the sand of the sea, which can neither be measured nor counted.*

There, in exile (*Targum; Rashi*), they will increase and multiply until they will be like the sand of the sea, which cannot be counted due to its great quantity.[1] In addition, the sand is held together by the moisture from the sea, and can therefore not be discerned individually in order to be numbered. So, too, shall be the Children of Israel at the dawn of their redemption, bound together as one by their devotion to the Almighty and His Torah (*Abarbanel*; cf. *Radak*).

וְהָיָה בִּמְקוֹם אֲשֶׁר־יֵאָמֵר לָהֶם לֹא־עַמִּי אַתֶּם יֵאָמֵר לָהֶם בְּנֵי אֵל־חָי — *And it shall be that in the place where it was said to them,* "You are not My nation," it shall be said to them, "the children of the living God."

Whereas they had previously been rejected by the Almighty for their wickedness, they will once again regain His favor by returning to His ways (*Radak; Abarbanel*).[1] They will no longer serve false deities, nor will they worship the astrological forces, which function at the behest of the Almighty but have no inherent power. Instead, they will once again serve the true God, Whose existence is intrinsic [and Who is the Source of all life]. At that time, they will earn for themselves the title *the children of the living God* (*Radak*).

Others understand בִּמְקוֹם not in the sense of *instead of*, but more literally as *in the [physical] place*. In that very place to which they will be exiled and thus declared by the Almighty to no longer be His nation, they will repent their wicked deeds and return to Hashem, earning once again the merit to be called in His name (*Targum; Rashi*).[2]

Ibn Ezra interprets that they will continue to pursue their sinful ways while in exile. Thus, although they will call themselves the children of the living God, they will in fact

1. The Sages render: *which shall neither be numbered nor counted.* They thereby derive that it is prohibited to count the Jewish people. However, they elaborate upon this as follows: R' Yonasan asked: It is written, *And the number of the Children of Israel shall be like the sand of the sea* [a definable quantity], and it is written, *which can neither be measured nor counted.* There is no contradiction: The latter refers to a time when Israel fulfills the will of the Omnipresent, and the former to a time when Israel does not fulfill the will of the Omnipresent. R' Yose says: This is by the hand of man [who may not count them] and this is by the hand of Heaven (*Yoma* 22b).

2. *Chida* regards this verse as a lesson in repentance.

Who is the true penitent? One who finds himself in the same situation, in the same place, with the same woman [with whom he previously sinned — but this second time he refrains from repeating his indiscretion] (*Yoma* 86b).

Thus our verse declares, בִּמְקוֹם, *in that very place*, where they previously sinned and which resulted in their being told, *"You are not My people,"* they will repent and He will call them, *"the children of the living God"* (*Tzavarei Shalal*).

[1] *And the number of the Children of Israel shall be*
like [that of] the sand of the sea, which can neither
be measured nor counted; and it shall be that in the
place where it was said to them, "You are not My
nation," it shall be said to them, "the children of the
living God." [2] *And the Children of Judah and the*
Children of Israel shall be assembled together, and they
shall appoint for themselves one head, and they shall
ascend from the land, for the day of Jezreel is great.

remain with their previous status of *Lo-Ami,* not My nation.

2. וְנִקְבְּצוּ בְּנֵי־יְהוּדָה וּבְנֵי־יִשְׂרָאֵל יַחְדָּו — *And the Children of Judah and the Children of Israel shall be assembled together.*

Unlike the renewal in the era of the Second Temple, when the tribes of Judah and Benjamin formed the majority of the populace, the final redemption will see all the tribes of both the kingdom of Judah and that of Israel restored in the land (*Radak*). And whereas the era of the First Temple saw friction and conflict between these two kingdoms, at the time of their redemption they will be united as one in perfect harmony (*Abarbanel*).

וְשָׂמוּ לָהֶם רֹאשׁ אֶחָד וְעָלוּ מִן־הָאָרֶץ — *And they shall appoint for themselves one head, and they shall ascend from the land.*

They shall all follow the leadership of the Messiah, the descendant of King David (*Targum*; *Rashi*; *Radak*), and ascend from the land where they live in exile to *Eretz Yisrael* (*Radak*). Alternatively, their head will be Elijah the prophet, who will lead them out of exile and pave the way for the kingdom of the Messiah (*Radak*).

Mahari Kara notes that from the time of the division of the kingdom of Israel the kings of Israel would ascend on the pilgrimage festivals (Pesach, Shavuos, Succos) to their idols in Dan and Beth-el instead of the Temple in Jerusalem. They did this out of fear that if the people would travel to Jerusalem and offer sacrifices there they would be moved to return to the authority of the Davidic monarchy. Thus, the gatherings of the nation at the time of the festivals were split, with the citizens of Israel traveling to Dan and Beth-el and those of Judah ascending to Jerusalem. However, with the advent of the redemption, they will all gather together under one king in Jerusalem and serve the Almighty there.

כִּי גָדוֹל יוֹם יִזְרְעֶאל — *For the day of Jezreel is great.*

The day of Jezreel in which the kingdom of Israel will be destroyed (see 1:4,5) will be of great magnitude, and the exile it precipitates will last for many centuries. Accordingly, all that they will endure will serve as atonement for their many sins and eventually earn them the merit of returning to the land of their fathers (*Radak*; *Abarbanel*).

Others interpret יִזְרְעֶאל as deriving from the word זֶרַע, *seed*: Thus, *Rashi* renders: *the day of the gathering of their seed* [i.e., at the time of their redemption] *will be great. Radak* cites his father as explaining: *great and long will be the period in which they will be sown,* i.e., among the gentiles,[1] but eventually I

1. Just as a seed is planted in the ground, where it decays and disintegrates but subsequently blooms into the produce which sprouts from the earth, so shall the Jewish people, who are sown [and trampled] in the lands of the gentiles, sprout into a nation of a great multitude (*Malbim*).

ג־ד אִמְרוּ לַאֲחֵיכֶם עַמִּי וְלַאֲחוֹתֵיכֶם רֻחָמָה: רִיבוּ
בְאִמְּכֶם רִיבוּ כִּי־הִיא לֹא אִשְׁתִּי וְאָנֹכִי לֹא
אִישָׁהּ וְתָסֵר זְנוּנֶיהָ מִפָּנֶיהָ וְנַאֲפוּפֶיהָ מִבֵּין

will gather them together (cf. *Mahari Kara*).

Alshich interprets the phrase וְעָלוּ מִן־הָאָרֶץ to mean *they will arise from the land* — i.e., those who have already passed on will travel beneath the earth to the Holy Land and rise from the ground in the Land of Israel at the time of resurrection. Although they were guilty of great sins, the magnitude of their punishment and destruction will earn them the right to be included in the resurrection.

Ibn Ezra interprets this verse as foretelling how Sennacherib, who conquered the kingdom of Israel and exiled its inhabitants, will also capture many cities of the kingdom of Judah and subject them to his rule. All this will occur because of the great magnitude of the day in which the Jewish people will be taken to task for their sinful ways.

3. אִמְרוּ לַאֲחֵיכֶם עַמִּי וְלַאֲחוֹתֵיכֶם רֻחָמָה — *Say to your brothers, "Ami," and to your sisters, "Ruchama."*

[In the previous chapter, the prophet depicted the downfall of the Jewish nation by calling his children the symbolic names of *Lo-ruchama*, not beloved and *Lo-ami*, not My people. Therefore, in portraying the renewal of the Jewish kingdom, he ascribes to the people the titles *Ami*, My people, and *Ruchama*, beloved.]

Members of the tribes of Judah and Benjamin, turn to your brothers and sisters from the ten tribes — who at the time of their exile for their sins were called *Lo-ami* and *Lo-ruchama* (1:6,9). Address them now as *Ami* and *Ruchama* [for they will once again be part of God's nation upon whom He will have mercy] (*Radak* from *R' Saadiah Gaon*).

According to *Abarbanel*, *Lo-ruchama* referred to the kingdom of Israel whereas *Lo-ami* was addressed to the tribes of Judah and Benjamin (see comm. to 1:6,9). Thus, the prophet now depicts the harmony and brotherhood which will be restored between the two portions of the nation when they return together to the Holy Land: Children of Israel, turn to your brothers of the kingdom of Judah, who were once demeaned with the title *Lo-ami*, and call them *Ami*, My people, in an expression of brotherhood. Likewise, Children of Judah, your sister kingdom of Israel — previously called *Lo-ruchama* — has now been restored to her original status. Thus, you may call to her in love and affection and refer to her as *Ruchama.*

Targum renders: *Prophets, say to your brothers, "My nation, return to My Torah and I will have mercy upon your assemblies."*

According to *Ibn Ezra*, the prophet mocks the nation in their demeaned state and challenges them to call each other in terms of their former glory.

4. The prophet changes his tone again from one of mercy to one of castigation (see introduction to v. 1). First he told the Children of Israel that they will no longer be called "not My nation" (v. 1) and now he states that the nation is no longer "My wife." This change can be compared to a man whose wife was unchaste, and he therefore became angry with her and called her a prostitute. When his children heard this they complained to their father that by so proclaiming he was impugning their legitimacy. To this their father responded: Heaven forbid that I should actually maintain that she committed adultery and you may be illegitimate. However, if you will rebuke your mother for her behavior and relate to her that I have pronounced that she is no longer my wife nor I her husband [she will perhaps be shocked into abandoning her wanton ways]. Thus the Almighty instructed His prophets [the children of

3 *Say to your brothers, "Ami," and to your sisters, "Ruchama."*

4 *Remonstrate with your mother, remonstrate, for she is not My wife and I am not her husband, and have her remove her harlotries from her face and her adulteries from*

the metaphor]: Rebuke your nation and tell her that I have declared our relationship null and void, so that she will be moved to mend her ways and abandon her pursuit of idolatry (*Mahari Kara*).

According to *Ibn Ezra*, there is no change in tone (see introduction to 2:1).

Having previously described the fate in store for the Jewish nation if they do not return to Hashem, the prophet now urges them to rectify their deeds and thereby avert their downfall. Alternatively, the following is addressed to the future generations of Jews already in exile, exhorting them to repent so that they may return to their land.

רִיבוּ בְאִמְּכֶם רִיבוּ — *Remonstrate with your mother, remonstrate.*

Prophets and righteous men within the nation, rebuke the people at large for their misdeeds (*Targum*; *Abarbanel*; *Malbim*). Know, too, that although you yourselves are not deserving of the punishment of exile, you will not be spared this misfortune if it is brought down upon the entire nation (*Abarbanel*).

Others understand the mother as representing the nation as a whole and her children to be the specific individuals within the nation. Thus, every individual is exhorted to urge his acquaintances to repent so that together they can ward off the evil decree (*Radak*).

כִּי־הִיא לֹא אִשְׁתִּי וְאָנֹכִי לֹא אִישָׁהּ — *For she is not My wife and I am not her husband.*

She can no longer be described as My wife since she had been disloyal (*Radak*), and I, in turn, will no longer care for her and see to her needs like a devoted husband (*Metzudos David*).

Abarbanel interprets this phrase rhetorically: Can her disloyalty be justified by proclaiming that she is not My wife and I am not her husband? No! This is not the case! For she has already been betrothed to Me and I have given her no *get*, divorce document, to release her. Therefore, it is incumbent upon her to rectify her misdeeds and restore her devotion to Me.

וְתָסֵר זְנוּנֶיהָ מִפָּנֶיהָ וְנַאֲפוּפֶיהָ מִבֵּין שָׁדֶיהָ — *And have her remove her harlotries from her face and her adulteries from between her breasts.*

Exhort her to cease to dress up like a prostitute and to remove the makeup which is painted upon her face, as well as the perfumes which are dabbed between her breasts to arouse the passion of those with whom she strays[1] (*Abarbanel*; *Metzudos David*). I.e., exhort the people to eradicate the worship of idolatry from among them and from within their cities (*Targum*).

Radak interprets *her harlotries from her face* as signifying the false prophets whom the people followed in place of the prophets of Hashem. *Her adulteries from between her breasts* alludes to the pagan statutes which they chose over the two portions of God's Torah — the Written Torah and the Oral Torah.[2]

1. *Rashi* interprets *and her adulteries from between her breasts* to allude to the way she hugs her lovers and squeezes them between her breasts.

2. *Malbim* interprets: Have them remove the harlotry of their straying to false gods, which is done publicly, and is thus comparable to the makeup worn on a prostitute's face. And eradicate, as well, the desires for idolatry and licentiousness which lie within their hearts and are thus concealed between their breasts.

ה שְׁדֶיהָ: פֶּן־אַפְשִׁיטֶנָּה עֲרֻמָּה וְהִצַּגְתִּיהָ כְּיוֹם
הִוָּלְדָהּ וְשַׂמְתִּיהָ כַמִּדְבָּר וְשַׁתִּהָ כְּאֶרֶץ צִיָּה
ו וַהֲמִתִּיהָ בַּצָּמָא: וְאֶת־בָּנֶיהָ לֹא אֲרַחֵם כִּי־בְנֵי
ז זְנוּנִים הֵמָּה: כִּי זָנְתָה אִמָּם הֹבִישָׁה הוֹרָתָם

5. פֶּן־אַפְשִׁיטֶנָּה עֲרֻמָּה וְהִצַּגְתִּיהָ כְּיוֹם הִוָּלְדָהּ — *Lest I strip her bare and stand her as on the day she was born.*

If she will refuse to mend her ways and return to her loyal behavior, I will remove My protective custody from over her and return her to the state in which I found her in Egypt when I first took her as My nation — unclothed and uncared for and wallowing in her own blood (*Rashi; Abarbanel; Malbim;* cf. *Ezekiel* 16:4,5).

וְשַׂמְתִּיהָ כַמִּדְבָּר וְשַׁתִּהָ כְּאֶרֶץ צִיָּה וַהֲמִתִּיהָ בַּצָּמָא — *And I will set her like a wilderness and render her like a parched land and I will cause her to die of thirst.*

I will render her once more like a wilderness, unprotected against any who desire to tread upon her and bereft of any source of sustenance or provisions. In addition, I will destroy her land and turn it into wilderness (*Radak*). Alternatively, I will pronounce upon them that sentence that I decreed upon them in the desert (*Numbers* 14:35): *there they shall cease to be and there they shall die* (*Rashi*).

The hunger and thirst depicted is also symbolic of the intense longing for Torah and *mitzvos*, the Word of Hashem as imparted through His prophets, which will prevail among the Jewish people at that time. However, these will no longer be available to them (*Radak;* cf. *Amos* 8:11).

Targum renders: *Lest I remove My Divine Presence from her and I remove her glory, and I leave her abandoned, as in earlier days before she came near to My worship, and My anger shall fall upon her as it fell upon the generation that transgressed My Torah in the desert, and I will render the land arid and I will kill her with thirst.*

Vilna Gaon interprets this verse as describing the spiritual loss which the Jewish nation will sustain in their exile. *Lest I strip her bare* — lest I send them into exile and strip them of those *mitzvos* — the raiments of their souls — which apply only in the Holy Land. *And stand her as on the day she was born* — While in its mother's womb, a baby is taught the entire Torah. As the newborn infant emerges into the world, an angel taps it above the lip, causing all to be forgotten (*Niddah* 30b). Through the tribulations of exile, the Children of Israel will forget the Torah like a baby on the day of its birth. *And I will set her like a wilderness* — They will be devoid of prophecy in the wilderness of exile. *And render her like a parched land* — even רוּחַ הַקֹּדֶשׁ, *Divine Inspiration*, which is inferior to actual prophecy, will be lacking. *And I will cause her to die of thirst* — The Sages of the nation will lose their Torah knowledge.

6. וְאֶת־בָּנֶיהָ לֹא אֲרַחֵם כִּי־בְנֵי זְנוּנִים הֵמָּה — *And [upon] her children I will not have mercy for they are children of harlotry.*

[I will vent My wrath not only upon her but upon her children as well, for I no longer consider them My own offspring, but rather fruits of her harlotry.]

In Jewish law, the children of a woman who commits adultery are assumed to be from her husband, because of the principle רוֹב בְּעִילוֹת אַחַר הַבַּעַל, *most of her relations are with her husband* — and it is presumed that the children she bears are the product of the majority of her relations. However, if a woman abandons her husband completely and engages publicly in wanton adultery, this assumption is no longer valid and her children are viewed as

between her breasts. 5 *Lest I strip her bare and stand her as*
on the day she was born, and I will set her like a wilderness
and render her like a parched land and I will cause her to
die of thirst. 6 *And [upon] her children I will not have mer-*
cy for they are children of harlotry. 7 *For their mother has*
been promiscuous; she who conceived them has shamed

illegitimate. Thus, Hashem instructs the prophet to relay His message: Since she has gone after her paramours and has relied upon them for the provision of her needs, her children can no longer be assumed to be from Me. Therefore, I will not have mercy upon them and care for them when I banish their mother from My home (*Malbim*).

Even upon the righteous sons of the nation I will have no mercy. Although they themselves are not deserving of this punishment, they are nevertheless included in the nation as a whole and will not be spared its fate (*Abarbanel; Malbim; Metzudos David*).[1]

Alternatively, this alludes to the generations who followed the one that first immersed itself in idolatry [and pursued similar paths] (*Radak*).

7-9. As above, in these verses the aggrieved husband represents the Almighty, and the faithless wife is the Jewish nation. The lovers upon whom she relies symbolize either the false deities and astrological forces that the people chose to worship or the foreign powers to whom they turned for aid.

Thus, the thrust of the following is: The reason My wife has dared to abandon Me and chance My wrath is because she has turned to her lovers for sustenance, and they have indeed provided her with her needs. Therefore, I will prevent her from meeting with them and receiving their gifts so that she will have no recourse other than to return to Me for support.

7. כִּי זָנְתָה אִמָּם הֹבִישָׁה הוֹרָתָם — *For their mother has been promiscuous; she who conceived them has shamed [herself].*

The nation of Israel has strayed from the Almighty and followed instead its false prophets and deities (*Targum; Rashi; Radak; Malbim;* cf. *Abarbanel*). Thus has she shamed herself with her degrading behavior (*Metzudos David*). Alternatively: She should be ashamed of her loathsome deeds (*Radak*).

Alshich interprets הוֹרָתָם as referring to the *Shechinah*, the Divine Presence, which is the source of the people's sustenance. Thus, this phrase describes a pattern of cause-and-effect: The nation has strayed from the ways of Hashem and thereby desecrated the *Shechinah;* Therefore, It will no longer provide for their needs.

Targum renders: *their teachers are shamed* — the wise men who teach them are humiliated before the ignorant, for they say to them, "Do not steal," and they go and steal; "Do not lend with interest," and they go and lend with interest (*Rashi* from *Deuteronomy Rabbah* 2:19).

1. This is based upon the principle of הַשְׁגָּחָה כְּלָלִית, *the general approach of the Almighty to His creations.* When a certain measure of judgment has been decreed on a particular group or locale — or on creation as a whole — those within that grouping are included in that approach even if they themselves are not necessarily deserving of it — and were it only for them it would never have been decreed. The same applies in the reverse: If a particular group is granted an unusual measure of mercy or benevolence, those within the group will benefit from it even if they do not merit to do so (see *Rambam, Hil. Teshuvah* 3:2; *Ramban* to *Genesis* 18:19; *Derashos HaRan, HaDerush HaShlishi*).

כִּי אָמְרָה אֵלְכָה אַחֲרֵי מְאַהֲבַי נֹתְנֵי לַחְמִי וּמֵימַי
ח צַמְרִי וּפִשְׁתִּי שַׁמְנִי וְשִׁקּוּיָי: לָכֵן הִנְנִי־שָׂךְ אֶת־
דַּרְכֵּךְ בַּסִּירִים וְגָדַרְתִּי אֶת־גְּדֵרָהּ וּנְתִיבוֹתֶיהָ לֹא
ט תִמְצָא: וְרִדְּפָה אֶת־מְאַהֲבֶיהָ וְלֹא־תַשִּׂיג אֹתָם
וּבִקְשָׁתַם וְלֹא תִמְצָא וְאָמְרָה אֵלְכָה וְאָשׁוּבָה
י אֶל־אִישִׁי הָרִאשׁוֹן כִּי טוֹב לִי אָז מֵעָתָּה: וְהִיא לֹא
יָדְעָה כִּי אָנֹכִי נָתַתִּי לָהּ הַדָּגָן וְהַתִּירוֹשׁ וְהַיִּצְהָר

כִּי אָמְרָה אֵלְכָה אַחֲרֵי מְאַהֲבַי נֹתְנֵי לַחְמִי וּמֵימַי צַמְרִי וּפִשְׁתִּי שַׁמְנִי וְשִׁקּוּיָי — *For she said, "I will go after my lovers, those who provide my bread and my water, my wool and my flax, my oil and my drink."*[1]

I will turn to the sun and moon and the stars [and all of the other deities that I choose to worship] and through their power, I will be provided with all of my needs (*R' Yosef Kimchi*, cited by *Radak*; *Abarbanel*; *Malbim*).

Alternatively: I will follow the ways of the nations (*Rashi*) and turn to them to provide for my needs (*Targum*). Specifically, I will rely upon Assyria and Egypt, with whom I have forged treaties, and they will both protect me from my enemies and sustain me with provisions (*Mahari Kara*; *Radak*).

Unlike אֹהֲבַי, *My lovers (Exodus* 20:6), מְאַהֲבַי refers to illicit, professed lovers whose love is not real. It is only an outward display [of the conniving attitudes of the self-serving nations] *(Hirsch). Rashi* (*Lamentations* 1:19) renders: Those who make themselves appear as lovers.

וְשִׁקּוּיָי — *My drink.*

I.e., wine and other beverages (*Radak*). The Sages, however, reject this interpretation and explain instead that it means *my desirable possessions* — i.e., my jewelry — stemming from the word תְּשׁוּקָה (*Kesubos* 65a).

8. לָכֵן הִנְנִי־שָׂךְ אֶת־דַּרְכֵּךְ בַּסִּירִים וְגָדַרְתִּי אֶת־גְּדֵרָהּ וּנְתִיבוֹתֶיהָ לֹא תִמְצָא — *Therefore, behold, I will hedge your way with thorns, and I will fence her in, and she shall not find her paths.*

Because you have chosen to follow your paramours (*Metzudos David*), I will hedge your way with thorns so that you will be unable to reach the major roads leading to your lovers, and I will close off the fence so that you cannot communicate with them through its breaches. I will even thwart your efforts to escape to them through the narrow pathways, by covering them up so that you cannot find them (*Malbim*). Thus, I will prevent you from drawing upon the astrological powers of your chosen deities in any manner whatsoever so that you will receive no sustenance from them (*R' Yosef Kimchi*; *Abarbanel*; *Malbim*; *Metzudos David*) and I will likewise cut you off from the nations upon whom you rely for aid and support (*Radak*).

9. וְרִדְּפָה אֶת־מְאַהֲבֶיהָ וְלֹא־תַשִּׂיג אֹתָם וּבִקְשָׁתַם וְלֹא תִמְצָא וְאָמְרָה אֵלְכָה וְאָשׁוּבָה אֶל־אִישִׁי הָרִאשׁוֹן כִּי טוֹב לִי אָז מֵעָתָּה — *And she shall pursue her lovers, but she will*

1. The patriarch Jacob abstained from indulgence in the material and thereby set a standard for his descendants. He was seeking no luxuries, he was satisfied with the necessities of life. Thus he asked for only לֶחֶם לֶאֱכֹל, *bread to eat*, וּבֶגֶד לִלְבֹּשׁ, *and a garment to wear* (*Genesis* 28:20).

When his offspring, however, left the path he had trod, when they sought foreign idols and alien ideals, they acquired an ever greater desire for material possessions. No longer would Jacob's bread to eat (*my food and my water*) and garment to wear (*my wool and my flax*) suffice. Now they also demanded *anointing oil and all my desires* (see below, comm. to וְשִׁקּוּיָי — *My drink*).

[herself]; for she said, "I will go after my lovers, those
who provide my bread and my water, my wool and
my flax, my oil and my drink." 8 *Therefore, behold, I*
will hedge your way with thorns, and I will fence her
in, and she shall not find her paths. 9 *And she shall*
pursue her lovers, but she will not reach them; and she
will seek them, but she will not find [them]; and she will
say, "I will go and return to my first husband for it
was better for me then than it is now." 10 *For she did*
not know that I gave her the grain, the wine, and the oil,

not reach them; and she will seek them, but she will not find [them], and she will say, "I will go and return to my first husband for it was better for me then than it is now."

The people will turn in prayer to all of the deities and forces upon whom they relied, but it will be to no avail. They will pursue all of the avenues available to draw upon these forces and their power in creation, but they will be unsuccessful, for these forces are effective only when it is so willed by the Almighty God (*Abarbanel*).

Similarly, they will turn to their confederates, Assyria and Egypt, for assistance, but the latter will turn their backs on them and offer no aid (*Radak*). Thus, they will finally recognize that they must place their faith in Hashem, for He is the only source of sustenance and assistance that can be relied upon in all circumstances (*Metzudos David*).

This will not occur, however, until after Israel endures a long and bitter exile, when she will finally return to Hashem with a full heart (*Radak*; see *Deuteronomy* 4:30).

Others contend that this statement of the Jewish nation does not represent a wholehearted return to the ways of Hashem, but merely a partial repentance from the extent of their previous decadence. *Abarbanel* explains that upon finding themselves bereft of all of the blessings they previously enjoyed, they will finally recognize that they must make a choice between the Almighty and the worship of Baal. Thus, they will elect to serve the Almighty. However, their favored approach would still be to serve Hashem as the ultimate source of all blessing while simultaneously worshipping the other deities as intermediary in bringing His blessings to fruition.

Malbim contends that when they see that the forces of creation can no longer be relied upon, they will come to the conclusion that these powers are no longer arrayed in their favor. Thus, given no alternative, they will return to Hashem to provide for their needs. However, they will not at this time reject their basic assumption, that when the forces of creation are in their favor it is worthwhile to be involved in their service rather than to pursue that of the Almighty.

10. Having interjected with a depiction of the ultimate future, that the Jewish nation will once again return to Hashem, the prophet now returns to his elaboration of the situation which will prevail before this occurs and the steps that will be taken to bring it about (*Radak* loc. cit.). According to the approach of *Abarbanel* and *Malbim*, the following verses describe the policies the Almighty will pursue after the people have responded only partially to the earlier catastrophes.

וְהִיא לֹא יָדְעָה כִּי אָנֹכִי נָתַתִּי לָהּ הַדָּגָן וְהַתִּירוֹשׁ וְהַיִּצְהָר — *For she did not know that I gave her the grain, the wine, and the oil.*

יא וְכֶסֶף הִרְבֵּיתִי לָהּ וְזָהָב עָשׂוּ לַבָּעַל: לָכֵן אָשׁוּב
וְלָקַחְתִּי דְגָנִי בְּעִתּוֹ וְתִירוֹשִׁי בְּמוֹעֲדוֹ וְהִצַּלְתִּי
יב צַמְרִי וּפִשְׁתִּי לְכַסּוֹת אֶת־עֶרְוָתָהּ: וְעַתָּה אֲגַלֶּה
אֶת־נַבְלֻתָהּ לְעֵינֵי מְאַהֲבֶיהָ וְאִישׁ לֹא־יַצִּילֶנָּה

Until she finally recognized the folly of her ways, Israel had thought that the idols she worshiped were actually capable of providing for her, that they were indeed the source of her sustenance and prosperity while they lasted (*Ibn Ezra*). This misconception was foisted upon her by her leaders and false prophets. However, in truth, any good that Israel enjoyed came only from Me, for I bestowed upon her My blessing and provided her with an abundance of grain, wine, and oil (*Radak*).

Rashi interprets: She did not pay attention, and thus acted as if she did not know. I.e., when she received all of My blessings, she did not give it proper thought to recognize that I am the source of her blessing, but rather [flippantly] attributed her prosperity to her idols (*Mahari Kara*).

וְכֶסֶף הִרְבֵּיתִי לָהּ וְזָהָב עָשׂוּ לַבָּעַל — *And I lavished her with silver and gold, [but] they used [it] for Baal.*

[I even provided Israel with the luxuries of gold and silver, for which she should have served Me with ever-increasing devotion. Instead,] she took the very gold and silver that I gave her and used them to make images of the deities she worshiped, adorning them as well with these precious metals (*Metzudos David*).

They taught in the Academy of R' Yannai: Moses proclaimed before the Holy One, Blessed is He, "Master of the World, it is because of the silver and gold (זָהָב) which You have given Israel in abundance — until they were forced to cry, 'Enough (דַי),' that they made the calf ..." as it is stated (*Deuteronomy* 1:1): וְדִי זָהָב, *and enough gold*[1] — [this] caused the to make the calf. They taught in the Academy of R' Yannai: The lion does not roar from a box of grain, but from a box of meat. Said R' Hoshaya: This is comparable to a person who had a weak cow. He fed it vetch and it kicked him. He said to it, "What caused you to kick me if not the vetch that I fed you?" Said R' Chiya bar Avin in the name of R' Yochanan: It is comparable to a man who had one son and he fed him, gave him drink, clothed and covered him, hung about his neck a purse and placed him at the entrance to a whorehouse. What can the son do that he should not sin?... R' Yonasan taught that the Holy One, Blessed is He, acknowledged Moses' rationalization when He said: *And I lavished them with silver, and gold, [but] they used [it] for Baal* (*Berachos* 32a).

11. לָכֵן אָשׁוּב וְלָקַחְתִּי דְגָנִי בְּעִתּוֹ וְתִירוֹשִׁי בְּמוֹעֲדוֹ וְהִצַּלְתִּי צַמְרִי וּפִשְׁתִּי לְכַסּוֹת אֶת־עֶרְוָתָהּ — *Therefore, I will return and take My grain in its time and My wine in its season,*[2] *and I will remove My wool and*

1. [Among the locations listed in *Deuteronomy* 1:1 as sites where Israel sinned during its forty year sojourn in the wilderness is דִּי זָהָב, *Di-Zahav* (lit., *enough gold*). However, no place with that name is known to exist, nor does any other reference to *Di-Zahav* appear in Scripture. The Talmud explains that the name is both an allusion to, and an alibi for, the Golden Calf.]

2. עֵת, *time*, refers to a point in time dictated by outside forces, whereas מוֹעֵד, *season*, refers to a time designated by choice.

When grain is ripe it must be cut; if left standing it will rot. The farmer cannot arbitrarily decide to postpone the wheat harvest. Conditions external to himself make that determination without ever consulting him. Thus grain is cut בְּעִתּוֹ, *in its* particular *time*.

Grapes, on the other hand, may be cut early when they have just begun to ripen, or left on the vine to ripen fully. The wine, i.e., the grape crop, is harvested בְּמוֹעֲדוֹ, *in its season*, as decided by the farmer (*Malbim*).

and I lavished her with silver and gold, [but] they used
[it] for Baal. 11 *Therefore, I will return and take My*
grain in its time and My wine in its season, and I will
remove My wool and My flax [that I gave her] to cover
her nakedness. 12 *And now I will reveal her shame*
before the eyes of her lovers, and no man shall save her

My flax [that I gave her] to cover her nakedness.

Since they have refused to recognize that all their benefits come from Me, I will withhold from them all of My beneficence. Thus, I will bring a blight upon their crops, so that they will have no grain or wine, and I will annihilate all their flocks, thereby eradicating from their midst all material for clothing (*Radak; Metzudos David*). Then we will see whether the forces to whom they turn are indeed capable of providing for their needs (*Mahari Kara*).

Malbim interprets: Up until now they have been afflicted only by natural disasters. Thus, they have been able to lay the blame for their misfortune on the worsening of their astrological situation. Now, however, I will allow their crops to grow and their wool and flax to be spun, and only then will I set in motion circumstances which will deprive them of the benefits of their food and materials. Thus, they will be forced to acknowledge that I am the source of their misfortune, and I bring it upon them even when the astrological forces work in their favor.

Hosea attributes ownership of the crops to God, *"My" grain ... "My" wine,* whereas Moses says: וְאָסַפְתָּ דְגָנֶךָ וְתִירֹשְׁךָ, *you will gather "your" grain and "your" wine* (*Deuteronomy* 11:14). The latter speaks of a time when Israel fulfills the will of the Omnipresent [then the grain is theirs (*Rashi*)]; the former alludes to a time when Israel flouts the will of the Omnipresent. [At such a time He declares His ownership by confiscating the crops (*Rashi*)] (*Berachos* 35b).

12. וְעַתָּה אֲגַלֶּה אֶת־נַבְלֻתָהּ לְעֵינֵי מְאַהֲבֶיהָ וְאִישׁ לֹא־יַצִּילֶנָּה מִיָּדִי — *And now I will reveal her shame before the eyes of her lovers, and no man shall save her from My hand.*

Until this time, the Jewish nation has enjoyed the benefits of My Divine protection, which has guarded them from any mishap that could be caused by the forces of creation or by the natural cycle of events in the world. Now, however, she will stand naked, bereft of the Divine protection with which she has always been shielded. Until now, she has managed to conceal the extent of her wickedness and the magnitude of her evil deeds. Now, however, I will uncover all of her iniquities and decadence for all to see. In addition, I will bring down upon her punishment from Heaven for her sins, and no force in creation nor any nation on earth will be able to protect her from Me (*Abarbanel; Radak*).

The Sages add: Even the merit of their forefathers shall be depleted and will no longer protect them (*Rashi* from *Shabbos* 55a).[1]

1. *Tosafos* (ad loc.) explain that although the merit of our fathers has lost its potency, the treaty which the Almighty made with them is still intact, and we thus continue to invoke the memory of our forefathers in pleading with the Almighty for salvation. Others add that the Sages do not mean that our forefathers' merit is no longer a factor in God's dealings with us whatsoever, but only that it has lost the potency to ward off destruction in the face of great depravity (*Maharal, Chiddushei Aggados*). Furthermore, it can have effect only when invoked in prayer and activated through repentance, but not within a spiritual vacuum (*Anaf Yosef*).

יג מִיָּדִי: וְהִשְׁבַּתִּי֙ כָּל־מְשׂוֹשָׂ֔הּ חַגָּ֖הּ חָדְשָׁ֣הּ וְשַׁבַּתָּ֑הּ
יד וְכֹ֖ל מוֹעֲדָֽהּ: וַהֲשִׁמֹּתִ֗י גַּפְנָהּ֙ וּתְאֵ֣נָתָ֔הּ אֲשֶׁ֣ר
אָֽמְרָ֗ה אֶתְנָ֥ה הֵ֙מָּה֙ לִ֔י אֲשֶׁ֥ר נָֽתְנוּ־לִ֖י מְאַֽהֲבָ֑י
טו וְשַׂמְתִּ֣ים לְיַ֔עַר וַאֲכָלָ֖תַם חַיַּ֥ת הַשָּׂדֶֽה: וּפָקַדְתִּ֣י
עָלֶ֗יהָ אֶת־יְמֵ֤י הַבְּעָלִים֙ אֲשֶׁ֣ר תַּקְטִ֣יר לָהֶ֔ם
וַתַּ֤עַד נִזְמָהּ֙ וְחֶלְיָתָ֔הּ וַתֵּ֖לֶךְ אַחֲרֵ֣י מְאַֽהֲבֶ֑יהָ
טז וְאֹתִ֥י שָֽׁכְחָ֖ה נְאֻם־יְהוָֽה: לָכֵ֗ן

13. וְהִשְׁבַּתִּי כָּל־מְשׂוֹשָׂהּ חַגָּהּ חָדְשָׁהּ וְשַׁבַּתָּהּ וְכֹל מוֹעֲדָהּ — *And I will terminate all her rejoicing, her festivals, her New Moon, her Sabbath, and all her designated times.*

The rejoicing and tranquility which have always marked the Jewish nation's holidays will be terminated by the terrible straits in which they will find themselves. Thus, they will no longer celebrate their days of Sabbath or the New Moon, nor will they rejoice on their festivals of Pesach, Shavuos and Succos, or the *designated times* of Rosh Hashanah, Yom Kippur and Shemini Atzeres (*R' Saadiah Gaon*, cited by *Radak*).

Radak himself interprets *the festivals* to include all days of festivities — even those not bound to specific times or seasons. *The designated times* refer to any times designated for prearranged events. [Thus, although both terms apply to the Jewish holidays they each include other times and events as well.]

Abarbanel interprets this verse as proclaiming that the fulfillment of the *mitzvos* of these holidays will no longer provide sufficient merit to save the people from disaster. According to *Malbim*, the prophet is discussing those festivals which the people ordained in honor of their idols. These will be turned into days of tragedy and sorrow, in order to indicate beyond the shadow of a doubt that the deities they worship are incapable of providing for their needs.

14. Continuing with his metaphor of the promiscuous wife, the prophet now depicts her husband as describing how he will destroy all of his wife's vines and fig trees which she attributes to her lovers' generosity, but which were actually provided to her by him himself.

וַהֲשִׁמֹּתִי גַּפְנָהּ וּתְאֵנָתָהּ אֲשֶׁר אָמְרָה אֶתְנָה הֵמָּה לִי אֲשֶׁר נָתְנוּ־לִי מְאַהֲבָי וְשַׂמְתִּים לְיַעַר וַאֲכָלָתַם חַיַּת הַשָּׂדֶה — *And I will lay waste her vine and her fig trees [about] which she said, "They are my payment*[1] *that my lovers have given me," and I will render them a forest, and the beast of the field shall devour them.*

I will destroy not only the crops of that specific season but even the very vines and trees which provide them, thereby negating the possibility of future growth (*Malbim*). Thus the Jewish nation will be bereft of those fruits which constitute the staple of their diet — along with the grain already cited as slated for destruction. All this is in retribution for that which they attribute My beneficence to their lovers — i.e., to the false gods to which they have strayed (*Abarbanel*; *Malbim*; *Metzudos David*) and to the nations to whom they turn for assistance (*Targum*). So great will be the destruction that the vineyards and orchards will become like wild forests, whose fruits are trampled and devoured by the beasts of the field — as well as by the hordes of the conquering enemy who are comparable to such beasts (*Radak*).

1. Because the prophet compares the nation to a harlot, its possessions are described as אֶתְנָה — as in אֶתְנַן — the fee paid to a prostitute (*Radak*). *Targum* renders אֶתְנָה to mean something valuable.

from My hand. 13 *And I will terminate all her rejoicing, her festivals, her New Moon, her Sabbath, and all her designated times.* 14 *And I will lay waste her vine and her fig trees [about] which she said, "They are my payment that my lovers have given me," and I will render them a forest, and the beast of the field shall devour them.* 15 *And I will visit upon her the day of the Baal-idols to which she burnt [sacrifices] and [that which] she adorned herself with her earrings and her jewelry and followed after her lovers, and Me she forgot, declares* HASHEM.

Abarbanel understands this latter phrase as offering a second reason for the destruction of the land. Since the Jewish people are to be exiled from there and the land inhabited by the heathen nations, it is not fitting that the fruits of the Holy Land should be left extant to be consumed by these wild hordes.[1]

15. וּפָקַדְתִּי עָלֶיהָ אֶת־יְמֵי הַבְּעָלִים אֲשֶׁר תַּקְטִיר לָהֶם וַתַּעַד נִזְמָהּ וְחֶלְיָתָהּ וַתֵּלֶךְ אַחֲרֵי מְאַהֲבֶיהָ וְאֹתִי שָׁכְחָה נְאֻם־ה׳ — *And I will visit upon her the day of the Baal-idols to which she burnt [sacrifices] and [that which] she adorned herself with her earrings and her jewelry and followed after her lovers, and Me she forgot, declares* HASHEM.

I will exact retribution from them for all of the years in which they offered sacrifices to their false gods, and offered their devotion and service to the celestial forces — just as a prostitute curries favor with her adornments (*Metzudos David*). Thus, their punishment will extend for generations, as did their infidelity. Even their descendants who do not engage in idolatry will continue to bear the burden of their ancestors' wicked ways, so long as they themselves do not serve Me fullheartedly[2] (*Radak*).

The phrase פָּקַד עַל, *to visit upon* [here וּפָקַדְתִּי עָלֶיהָ, *And I will visit upon her*], implies a remembrance of previous misdeeds for the purpose of punishing them. Destruction of the Temple did not come suddenly, as a retribution for a particularly odious sin. Rather, it was the cumulative effect of continual sinfulness — i.e., the remembrance of past iniquities coupled with present ones —

1. Indeed, the Sages state (*Sanhedrin* 98a) that the most certain sign of the imminence of the Messianic era is that the Holy Land will once again produce its fruits generously for the Jewish nation (see *Rashi* ad loc.).

2. The Torah states (*Exodus* 20:5) that the Almighty exacts retribution from sons for the sins of their fathers if they follow in their sinful ways. One explanation given for this policy is that it is incumbent upon the sons to learn the lessons of the punishment meted out to their fathers for their sins. If they do not do so, it compounds the gravity of their own sins and adds to their retribution the culpability of their fathers (*Teshuvos Dvar Avrohom*). [However, this approach would limit the application of this principle to cases in which the original sinners received some measure of punishment for their evil deeds, a condition which does not seem to be indicated by the Torah or the words of the Sages. Perhaps another insight into this phenomenon is that the debt of gratitude owed to one's forebears for his very existence and sustenance extends so far as to include the responsibility of lightening the load of their sins by bearing a portion of the punishment. However, if he rises above their misdeeds by refusing to follow in their wicked ways, he thereby merits being exempted from his share of their misfortune.]

הִנֵּה אָנֹכִי מְפַתֶּיהָ וְהֹלַכְתִּיהָ הַמִּדְבָּר
יז וְדִבַּרְתִּי עַל־לִבָּהּ: וְנָתַתִּי לָהּ אֶת־כְּרָמֶיהָ
מִשָּׁם וְאֶת־עֵמֶק עָכוֹר לְפֶתַח תִּקְוָה

that brought about the destruction (*Daas Sofrim*).

Abarbanel understands the two portions of this verse as depicting two separate eras and the transgressions prevalent during each of them: I will exact retribution for the idolatry which was rampant during the time of the First Temple. And they will answer as well for seeking prosperity and security (during the second commonwealth) by pursuing political alliances with gentile nations rather than by seeking My aid. This will culminate in their treaty with Rome, which will be the beginning of the downfall of the nation. Furthermore, even while in exile they will settle comfortably in foreign lands and endeavor to curry the favor of their neighbors, until they will become deeply rooted in gentile society.

16-17. Having deprived his promiscuous wife of all her worldly goods and benefits, the husband seeks to encourage her to return to his hearth with a new commitment to loyalty and fidelity. Thus, he takes her away from all her lovers so that she will no longer be prey to their allurements, and he tries to win her heart and entice her to return to him.

According to some commentators, this is a metaphor for the exile in which the Almighty will place the Jewish people, and the steps He will take there in order to induce them to repent and to thereby merit their redemption (*Rashi*; *Radak*; *Abarbanel*). Others interpret the husband's seductive words to represent the [closeness to God that will come with the] redemption itself, which will be granted in reward for their repentance (*Targum*; *Ibn Ezra*).

These verses are seen by the commentators as paralleling those in *Ezekiel* (20:35-38), which depict a similar encounter between the Jewish people and the Almighty to be held in a desert. There, as here, there are various views as to the correct interpretation of the encounter and its purpose.

16. לָכֵן הִנֵּה אָנֹכִי מְפַתֶּיהָ וְהֹלַכְתִּיהָ הַמִּדְבָּר וְדִבַּרְתִּי עַל לִבָּהּ — *Therefore, behold, I will seduce her, and I will lead her to the wilderness and I will speak to her heart.*

I will persuade her to follow after Me by taking her out into the wilderness of exile. There, she will [eventually] take to heart the lesson of her banishment — that she is far better off when she follows My will than otherwise (*Rashi*).

Radak interprets the verse as describing a sequence of events: While they are still in exile, I will inspire them to abandon the pursuit of their desires and their evil inclinations and to turn instead to true repentance and the improvement of their ways. When this occurs, I will take them out into a wilderness before bringing them into the Holy Land, and there I will purge them of all those who persist in their evil paths and rebellious ways. At the same time, I will comfort the survivors and quell their fears by reassuring them of their imminent redemption and return to their land.

Alternatively: I will take them out of the lands in which they have settled and taken root — either by inspiring them to leave on their own initiative or through their forced exile at the hand of their host nation. Thus they will wander from one country to the other, through the wilderness of gentile lands in which they will be strangers. However, throughout this ordeal, I will continue to soothe them with words of comfort, so that they will not be completely overwhelmed but will rather continue to follow Me loyally and abide by My laws (*Abarbanel*).

Targum renders: *And thus I will subjugate her to the Torah and I will perform*

[16] *Therefore, behold, I will seduce her, and I will lead her to the wilderness and I will speak to her heart.* [17] *And I will give to her her vineyards from there, and the desolate valley for a portal of hope;*

for her miracles and wonders like I did in the wilderness, and through My servants, the prophets, I will speak words of comfort to her heart. In a similar vein, *Ibn Ezra* explains: Once she recognizes that all of this evil has befallen her because she has forsaken Me, I will seduce her with loving words and take her back to her land, which will have become desolate like a desert [in her absence].

The redemption from Egypt was a prelude to the receiving of the Torah. But the revelation of the Torah was accomplished in three stages. First, [because of its slave mentality] the nation had to be bribed with the booty of Egypt [see *Exodus* 12:35,36] and of the sea [see *Rashi* to *Exodus* 15:22]. After having been induced to follow the true God, the nation was ready to receive His Torah at Mount Sinai. [But only superficial understanding of the Torah was revealed at this time.] Subsequently [during the forty-year sojourn in the wilderness] the people were given a deeper insight and clearer understanding of the Divine wisdom of the Torah. [Indeed, the word מִשְׁנָה, *Mishnah*, which incorporates the body of oral teachings, has been defined as מ׳ שָׁנָה, *forty years.*]

Similarly, when the nation is redeemed from its present exile, *(God) will persuade her* with material enticements; *and lead her into the wilderness* where she will receive the Torah [anew]; *and speak intimately with her*, and teach her the deeper insights and esoteric mysteries of the Torah (*Vilna Gaon*).

17. וְנָתַתִּי לָהּ אֶת־כְּרָמֶיהָ מִשָּׁם — *And I will give to her her vineyards from there.*

As a result of the purification the Jewish nation will undergo in the wilderness — as well as the love of Hashem to which they will be inspired there — they will merit returning to the vineyards and orchards of the Holy Land (*Abarbanel; Metzudos David*; cf. *Radak*).

According to *Mahari Kara*, *from there* refers to *Eretz Yisrael*: I will return to her My grain and wine from [the fields] of the Holy Land.

Targum interprets this phrase metaphorically: *And I will appoint for her her leaders from there* [i.e., from exile].

וְאֶת־עֵמֶק עָכוֹר לְפֶתַח תִּקְוָה — *And the desolate valley for a portal of hope.*

And the Land of Israel, which had been rendered desolate and barren in their absence, will become once more a beautiful, flourishing land which will stand as a portal to their hopes and dreams of a better future (*Mahari Kara; Abarbanel; Metzudos David*).

Alternatively, this refers specifically to the valley of Achor, where Achan was executed for violating the ban on taking anything from the destroyed city of Jericho.[1] Its name shall be changed to פֶּתַח תִּקְוָה, *the portal of hope*, for when the Jewish people enter through there into the

1. After its miraculous conquest of the well-fortified and strongly defended city of Jericho, the Israelite army was beaten by the militarily insignificant inhabitants of Ai. When they had entered the land of Canaan, all the Jewish people were spiritually exalted. God had placed the formidable city of Jericho into their hands, without any of the usual accouterments of war being necessary. Joshua, in thankfulness to the Almighty for giving his nation this victory, sanctified all the material possessions of Jericho to God. But one man, Achan (also called Achar in *I Chronicles* 2:7), could not withstand temptation; he desired the riches which were laid open before him and he took them for himself. This errancy of but one individual caused the defeat of the Israelite army at Ai. When Achan's (Achar's) transgression was discovered and his identity learned, he was put to death and buried under a heap of stones together with the property that he coveted so. The site of his punishment was then called עֵמֶק עָכוֹר, *valley of Achor* (lit., *valley of destruction*), and the heap of stones remained as a reminder of the fruits of greed (see *Joshua* chap. 7). This valley forms part of the northern boundary of the tribal heritage of Judah (*Joshua* 15:7).

וְעָנְתָה שָּׁמָּה כִּימֵי נְעוּרֶיהָ וּכְיוֹם עֲלוֹתָהּ מֵאֶרֶץ־
יח מִצְרָיִם׃ וְהָיָה בַיּוֹם־הַהוּא נְאֻם־
יְהוָה תִּקְרְאִי אִישִׁי וְלֹא־תִקְרְאִי־לִי עוֹד בַּעְלִי׃
יט וַהֲסִרֹתִי אֶת־שְׁמוֹת הַבְּעָלִים מִפִּיהָ וְלֹא־יִזָּכְרוּ
כ עוֹד בִּשְׁמָם׃ וְכָרַתִּי לָהֶם בְּרִית בַּיּוֹם הַהוּא עִם־
חַיַּת הַשָּׂדֶה וְעִם־עוֹף הַשָּׁמַיִם וְרֶמֶשׂ הָאֲדָמָה
וְקֶשֶׁת וְחֶרֶב וּמִלְחָמָה אֶשְׁבּוֹר מִן־הָאָרֶץ

Holy Land they will do so with the secure knowledge that all sinners have already been purged from their midst and they will therefore not be stricken by any calamity such as that brought upon them by the misdeed of Achan (*Radak*; cf. *Ibn Ezra*; see *Radak* to v. 16, cited in comm.).

Rashi renders: The depths of the exile in which they endured great torment will be transferred to a portal of hope, for from those very misfortunes they will be moved to return to Me.

וְעָנְתָה שָּׁמָּה כִּימֵי נְעוּרֶיהָ וּכְיוֹם עֲלוֹתָהּ מֵאֶרֶץ־מִצְרָיִם — *And she will hymn there like in the days of her youth, and like the day of her ascent from the land of Egypt.*

And she will raise a hymn of glory to the Almighty in response to His miracles, as she did in the days of her youth — in the times of the judges and kings of Israel — and [even earlier] when she first ascended from the land of Egypt (*Ibn Ezra*; *Radak*; *Mahari Kara*; *Abarbanel*; *Metzudos David*).

Rashi renders: *She will dwell there,* i.e., like in exile, for many years, *as* she dwelled in the land of Egypt *in the days of her youth.* And just as she cried out to Me there from the depths of her torment and I redeemed her, so shall be the case once again (cf. *Targum*).

The Sages comment: R' Berachiah said in the name of R' Levi: Like the first redeemer shall be the final redeemer; the first redeemer appeared to them and then was hidden from them, so shall be the final redeemer ... To where will he lead them? Some say to the wilderness of Judah and some say to the wilderness of Sichon and Og. This is what is written: *Behold, I will seduce her, and I will lead her to the wilderness.* He who believes shall eat salted foods and berry roots ... and he who does not believe in him, and shall go to the gentiles, shall be killed by them[1] (*Pesikta*, cited by *Yalkut Shimoni*).

18-22. The prophet now goes on to depict the quality of existence which will prevail among the Jewish people after they are finally redeemed. Alternatively, he portrays the perfection awaiting the people, if only they will repent and mend their evil ways (*Ibn Ezra* to v. 25).

18. וְהָיָה בַיּוֹם־הַהוּא נְאֻם־ה׳ תִּקְרְאִי אִישִׁי וְלֹא־תִקְרְאִי־לִי עוֹד בַּעְלִי — *And it shall be*

1. The Sages hereby teach us that the final redemption will follow the format of the first one, and after the Messiah's first appearance the Jewish people will undergo even greater suffering prior to being redeemed.

The two views as to the wilderness to which he will lead them are not discussing geographic locations but are rather describing two different reactions which will be prevalent among the Jewish people. Some will follow in the desert of Judah, i.e., they will retain their identity as members of the Jewish nation and continue to follow the statutes of the Torah despite all their tribulations. They may be reduced by circumstances to eating salted foods and berry roots, but they will nevertheless retain their taste for Hashem. Others, however, will abandon the faith of their fathers and seek to assimilate among the gentiles. However, they will not be successful in this endeavor, for the gentile nations will reject them and wipe them out (*Abarbanel*).

and she will hymn there like in the days of her youth, and
like the day of her ascent from the land of Egypt. 18 *And*
it shall be on that day, declares HASHEM, *you will call*
[Me,]"my husband" and you will no longer call Me, "my
master." 19 *And I will remove the names of the Baal-idols*
from her mouth and they will no longer be remembered
by their name. 20 *And I will seal for them a covenant on*
that day with the beasts of the field and the birds of
the sky and the creeping things of the ground; and the
bow, the sword, and war I will eradicate from the land,

on that day, declares HASHEM, *you will call [Me,]"my husband," and you will no longer call Me, "my master."*

When this great day arrives, you will no longer express a relationship rooted in fear by referring to Me as your master. Rather you will call Me, "my husband" — denoting a bond of love and affection (*Rashi*).

The Sages (*Pesachim* 87a) comment: Like a bride in the house of her father-in-law and not like a bride in her father's house. Thus, the Almighty declares: I will no longer deal with you through intermediaries, for their involvement conceals My presence from you, limiting you to a level of righteousness based solely upon your fear of the consequences of transgressing My dictates. Rather, I will deal with you directly, with My presence openly revealed among you, thereby inspiring you to serve Me out of love. Thus, our relationship will become one of open and total involvement, like a bride already living in the home of her groom (*Malbim*).

Others interpret: Although one of the Hebrew words for husband is *baal*, you will no longer use that term in referring to Me, but will employ instead the word *ish*. For the name of the idol Baal will be removed totally from your lips and you will therefore avoid even its innocent usage (*Ibn Ezra*; *Mahari Kara*; *Radak*; *Abarbanel*).

19. וַהֲסִרֹתִי אֶת־שְׁמוֹת הַבְּעָלִים מִפִּיהָ — *And I will remove the names of the Baal-idols from her mouth.*

Once the Jewish people undertake sincerely to serve Me faithfully, I will assist them in their efforts and inspire them to fear Me alone, and abandon completely all other deities (*Ibn Ezra*; *Radak*; *Abarbanel*) — to the extent that the names of their idols will no longer cross their lips, even innocuously (*Metzudos David*).

וְלֹא־יִזָּכְרוּ עוֹד בִּשְׁמָם — *And they will no longer be remembered by their name.*

The Jewish people will no longer be associated with the idol Baal. Alternatively: The names of the Baal-idols will no longer be mentioned by the Children of Israel. Or possibly: The names of the *Baal*-idols will no longer be remembered whatsoever (*Rashi*). Even the gentile nations will no longer mention them, for they too will abandon all their false gods at that time (*R' Saadiah Gaon*, cited by *Radak*; see ibid.).

20. וְכָרַתִּי לָהֶם בְּרִית בַּיּוֹם הַהוּא עִם־חַיַּת הַשָּׂדֶה וְעִם־עוֹף הַשָּׁמַיִם וְרֶמֶשׂ הָאֲדָמָה וְקֶשֶׁת וְחֶרֶב וּמִלְחָמָה אֶשְׁבּוֹר מִן־הָאָרֶץ — *And I will seal for them a covenant on that day with the beasts of the field and the birds of the sky and the creeping things of the ground; and the bow, the sword, and war I will eradicate from the land.*

I will seal a covenant with the entire animal kingdom, prohibiting them from

כא וְהִשְׁכַּבְתִּים לָבֶטַח׃ וְאֵרַשְׂתִּיךְ לִי לְעוֹלָם
וְאֵרַשְׂתִּיךְ לִי בְּצֶדֶק וּבְמִשְׁפָּט וּבְחֶסֶד
כב וּבְרַחֲמִים׃ וְאֵרַשְׂתִּיךְ לִי בֶּאֱמוּנָה וְיָדַעַתְּ אֶת־
כג יְהוָה׃ וְהָיָה ׀ בַּיּוֹם הַהוּא אֶעֱנֶה נְאֻם־
יְהוָה אֶעֱנֶה אֶת־הַשָּׁמָיִם וְהֵם יַעֲנוּ אֶת־הָאָרֶץ׃

devouring those crops which are meant for human consumption. In addition, I will eradicate from the land all weapons of war (*Radak*) as well as men of battle [who will no longer be involved in such endeavors] (*Targum*).

In a totally different approach, *Abarbanel* connects this verse to the preceding one: The Baal-idols were originally intended as representations of the sun, moon, and other heavenly bodies in their roles as controllers of the forces of nature [see *Rambam, Hil. Avodas Kochavim* 1:1,2] determining man's destiny. *On that day* (see commentary to v. 18) the astrological functions of these bodies will no longer be a factor in the lives of men. All of mankind will be directly under the supervision of the Almighty. However, the forces of nature will not be abolished; rather, *I will seal a covenant with them* — the heavenly bodies and their controlling forces — *on that day* — when they no longer have the power to affect man — *with the beasts of the field, etc.* — i.e., they will retain supervising control over all other living creatures. Similarly, the red star מַאֲדִים, *Mars,* astrologically a sign of bloodshed, will no longer effect war or any other use of weaponry.

וְהִשְׁכַּבְתִּים לָבֶטַח — *And I will lay them down in safety.*

I will allow the Jewish nation to dwell in safety, without fear of attack or persecution (see *Ibn Ezra*; *Mahari Kara*).

Abarbanel interprets this as referring either to the animals of creation, who will dwell in safety together without fear of each other's attack (see *Isaiah* 11:6), or to the nations of the world, who will no longer live in fear of one another, and will never again face each other across lines of battle.

21. וְאֵרַשְׂתִּיךְ לִי לְעוֹלָם וְאֵרַשְׂתִּיךְ לִי בְּצֶדֶק וּבְמִשְׁפָּט וּבְחֶסֶד וּבְרַחֲמִים — *And I will betroth you to Me forever, and I will betroth you to Me with righteousness and with justice, benevolence and mercy.*

Having banished you from My home when you were disloyal, I will renew My betrothal of you[1] when you return to Me faithfully, and I will allow My Divine Presence to dwell among you once more (*Abarbanel*). [This time, however, it shall be established there for eternity, never to be removed.] This renewed betrothal shall be founded upon the righteousness and justice that you will practice and the benevolence and mercy that I in turn will bestow upon you (*Rashi*).

Alternatively, all of the traits cited depict the qualities that will mark the Jewish nation: You will follow the dictates of the Torah with justice and righteousness and you shall go even beyond the letter of the law in pursuing benevolence and mercy (*Abarbanel*; cf. *Ibn Ezra*).

22. וְאֵרַשְׂתִּיךְ לִי בֶּאֱמוּנָה — *And I will betroth you to Me with faith.*

This new, everlasting betrothal will be granted you in reward for your deep and abiding faith in the promises I made to you through My prophets, a faith that you maintained throughout your ordeal in exile (*Rashi*). Alternatively: My betrothal of you will be one in which you can have faith, for it shall last forever (*Radak*).

Abarbanel interprets the three expressions of betrothal as alluding to the three sanctuaries of the Divine Presence (the Tabernacle, plus the two Temples), and its contrast to them: Whereas the Tabernacle built in the wilderness was only temporary, the Third

and I will lay them down in safety. 21 *And I will be-*
troth you to Me forever, and I will betroth you to
Me with righteousness and with justice, benevolence
and mercy. 22 *And I will betroth you to Me with*
faith, and you will know H*ASHEM.* 23 *And it shall be*
on that day, I will answer, declares H*ASHEM; I will*
answer the heavens and they shall answer the earth.

Temple will be permanent, to last forever. Unlike the First Temple, which was marred by the corruption and oppression that was prevalent then among the Children of Israel, the times of the third will be filled with righteousness and with justice, benevolence and mercy. And in contrast to the times of the Second Temple, when the Sadducees and other rebels introduced heresy to the Jewish people, the final redemption will be marked by clarity of faith throughout the nation (cf. *Radak* to v.21).

וְיָדַעַתְּ אֶת־ה׳ — *And you will know* H*ASHEM.*

Every member of the nation, from the greatest to the smallest, shall truly know Me (*Radak*).

Malbim interprets these two verses as describing the unique nature of the new betrothal of the Jewish nation to the Almighty: *I will betroth you to Me forever.* Whereas the first betrothal was only temporary, as it was nullified by your sins, this one will be designated to last forever, never to be abrogated (cf. *Rashi* to *Leviticus* 26:9). The fundaments of this new bond will be your rededication to the ways of the Torah, both in regard to human interaction and to religious devotion. Thus, in exchange for your commitment to righteousness and justice, I will bestow upon you the gifts of benevolence and mercy. For if you act justly with your fellow man, I, in turn, will deal justly with the downtrodden and have mercy upon them. And for acting righteously beyond the letter of the law, I, too, will be benevolent with you to a degree far exceeding that which you earn with your merit. In exchange for your faith in Me and My Torah, upon which is based your commitment to following My statutes, I will reveal My presence to you in a manner that will allow you to actually know Me, beyond the shadow of a doubt, so that you will no longer require blind faith in order to serve Me.

23. In describing the prosperity which will exist at that time (see preface to vs. 18-22), the prophet turns his focus now upon the process of growth which brings about the promised abundance of produce. He depicts that process as if it were achieved by the willful efforts of its factors, with each step in the process turning to the one that precedes it and requesting its support. Thus, the people[1] who benefit from the crops turn to the produce itself and seek the sustenance it provides. The crops, in turn, are dependent upon the earth in which they grow, and they thus seek their subsistence from that land. However, the earth cannot yield its fruits without the rains, so it raises its eyes heavenward and begs for rain. The heavens themselves can only give rain by decree of the Almighty, so they turn to Him in supplication. In order to provide the people with food, each of these factors must respond positively to the one that depends upon it (*Malbim*).

וְהָיָה בַּיּוֹם הַהוּא אֶעֱנֶה נְאֻם־ה׳ אֶעֱנֶה אֶת־הַשָּׁמַיִם וְהֵם יַעֲנוּ אֶת־הָאָרֶץ — *And it shall be on that day, I will answer, declares*

1. This follows the majority of the commentators in their interpretation of the word Jezreel. *Malbim* himself understands it as referring to the seeds, who urge the crops to materialize from within them, the minute seeds in which the latter are contained.

כד וְהָאָרֶץ תַּעֲנֶה אֶת־הַדָּגָן וְאֶת־הַתִּירוֹשׁ וְאֶת־
כה הַיִּצְהָר וְהֵם יַעֲנוּ אֶת־יִזְרְעֶאל: וּזְרַעְתִּיהָ לִּי
בָּאָרֶץ וְרִחַמְתִּי אֶת־לֹא רֻחָמָה וְאָמַרְתִּי לְלֹא־
ג/א א עַמִּי עַמִּי־אַתָּה וְהוּא יֹאמַר אֱלֹהָי: וַיֹּאמֶר
יהוה אֵלַי עוֹד לֵךְ אֱהַב־אִשָּׁה אֲהֻבַת רֵעַ
וּמְנָאָפֶת כְּאַהֲבַת יהוה אֶת־בְּנֵי יִשְׂרָאֵל

HASHEM; I will answer the heavens and they shall answer the earth.

I will answer the plea of the heavens and bestow upon the clouds the capacity to provide rain, and they in turn shall pour their rains upon the earth (*Rashi*). Alternatively: I will direct the dynamics of the heavenly forces which control events here on earth so that they will pour down generously upon the land (*Abarbanel*).

24. וְהָאָרֶץ תַּעֲנֶה אֶת הַדָּגָן וְאֶת־הַתִּירוֹשׁ וְאֶת־הַיִּצְהָר — *And the earth shall answer the grain, the wine, and the oil.*

The earth in turn shall abound with its produce (*Radak*), for it shall no longer be withheld from productivity — not due to lack of rain from above nor for its own inability to produce (*Abarbanel*).

וְהֵם יַעֲנוּ אֶת־יִזְרְעֶאל — *And they shall answer Jezreel.*

With the abundance of produce shall come an abundance of those who consume it, for the land of Israel will be filled with her people. Just as the Jewish nation was called Jezreel in her time of tragedy (1:4), so shall she be called in her hour of redemption, for the people shall be "sown" and planted securely in their land (*Radak*).

Ibn Ezra interprets Jezreel as a specific location in *Eretz Yisrael* by that name, which shall once again be filled with a multitude of inhabitants. According to *Mahari Kara*, it means simply those who will sow the crops.

25. וּזְרַעְתִּיהָ לִּי בָּאָרֶץ — *And I shall sow her to Me in the land.*

In contrast to the years of their exile, when they will be sown throughout the lands of the gentiles (see v.2), I will replant them once more in their own land (*Mahari Kara*; *Metzudos David*) [where they will again be dedicated to Me], and they will multiply and be fruitful like the seeds in the earth (*Ibn Ezra*; *Radak*).

וְרִחַמְתִּי אֶת־לֹא רֻחָמָה וְאָמַרְתִּי לְלֹא־עַמִּי עַמִּי־אַתָּה וְהוּא יֹאמַר אֱלֹהָי — *And I will have mercy upon the unpitied one, and I will say to those who are not My nation, "You are My nation," and he shall say, "[You are] my God."*

The nation whom I called *Lo-ruchama*, the unpitied one[1] — indicating that I would not grant her clemency — I shall once again deal with mercifully. Those whom I declared to be no longer My nation, I will once again accept as My people. They, too, will accept Me as their God and proclaim their faith in Me (*Metzudos David*).

Some commentators explain this as referring back to the two kingdoms among the Jewish nation, which will be destroyed and them redeemed: The nation of Israel, which I called *Lo-ruchama*, will once again be the subject of My mercy. The kingdom of Judah, whom I declared *Lo-ami*, not My people, I will once again accept as My nation, and they will serve Me with a full heart (*Abarbanel*; *Malbim*).[2]

1. [Earlier we translated *Lo-Ruchama* to mean unloved, in accordance with the interpretation of the commentators. Here, however, its literal translation seems more appropriate.]

2. [This follows the approach of *Abarbanel* and *Malbim* to the first chapter, that both Israel and Judah are depicted by the events described there. According to *Ibn Ezra*, the sole subject of these prophecies is the kingdom of Israel, and it is thus to them that the prophecies of redemption are addressed.]

2/24-25 [24] *And the earth shall answer the grain, the wine, and the
oil, and they shall answer Jezreel.* [25] And *I shall sow her to
Me in the land, and I will have mercy upon the unpitied
one, and I will say to those who are not My nation, "You
are My nation," and he shall say, "[You are] my God.'*

3/1 [1] *And HASHEM said to me: Go again, love a woman
who is the beloved of [her] friend yet an adulteress.
[This is] like the love of HASHEM for the Children of Israel,*

III

In the previous chapter, the prophet conveyed to the Jewish nation the Almighty's depiction of the glorious fate that is to be theirs in the end of days. Now, however, he reverts to his castigation of the people of his generation for their misdeeds. This is in line with the practice of the prophets, who often alternate between words of rebuke and those of comfort (*Radak*).

Others contend that this prophecy deals specifically with the fate of the Jewish nation in exile [and not to his generation] (*Abarbanel*; *Malbim*). Although they will continue to be guilty of transgressions, they will no longer indulge in the cardinal sin of idolatry, and the Almighty, too, shall not sever entirely His relationship with them. Thus, the special bond between God and Israel will remain intact until it comes to full fruition with the advent of their redemption (*Abarbanel*).

In this chapter, as in the first, the prophet is commanded by the Almighty to take a woman for himself and endure her promiscuity. Once again, *Targum* interprets the command as an allegorical prophecy concerning the Jewish nation. *Ibn Ezra*, *Malbim*, and *Radak* understand it as an actual command, but contend that both the command and its fulfillment occurred only in a prophetic vision and never really took place (see comm. to 1:2).[1] *Alshich*, however, contends that the events described actually transpired. Having strayed so far from the ways of Hashem, the Children of Israel had despaired of ever returning to Him and restoring their fidelity to His commandment. Therefore, the Almighty directed Hosea to become engaged to a woman who had previously been married and had engaged in promiscuous behavior, and to demand of her that she honor the bond of their engagement by refraining from all sexual activities. Her success in so doing stands as a symbol to the nation that fidelity can be regained even after wanton adultery, and that they, too, will eventually return to Hashem and serve Him faithfully once more.

1. וַיֹּאמֶר ה׳ אֵלַי עוֹד לֵךְ אֱהַב־אִשָּׁה אֲהֻבַת רֵעַ וּמְנָאָפֶת כְּאַהֲבַת ה׳ אֶת־בְּנֵי יִשְׂרָאֵל וְהֵם פֹּנִים אֶל־אֱלֹהִים אֲחֵרִים — *And HASHEM said to me: Go again, love a woman who is the beloved of [her] friend yet an adulteress. [This is] like the love of HASHEM for the*

1. Although *Abarbanel* strongly disputed this approach in the first chapter, in this case he agrees with the premise of these commentators. This is because the prophet describes the events in this chapter in the first person (I went, etc.) rather than in the third person, as he did in the first chapter. Thus, it is possible to interpret his words as depicting a prophetic vision rather than events which actually transpired. Secondly, as portrayed by the Sages, the misstep of Hosea which led to God's decree that he take an adulteress as a wife had already been rectified (see comm. to 1:2) and there is thus no conceivable reason for the Almighty to command him to do so a second time.

וְהֵם פֹּנִים אֶל־אֱלֹהִים אֲחֵרִים וְאֹהֲבֵי אֲשִׁישֵׁי
ב עֲנָבִים׃ וָאֶכְּרֶהָ לִּי בַּחֲמִשָּׁה עָשָׂר כָּסֶף וְחֹמֶר
ג שְׂעֹרִים וְלֶתֶךְ שְׂעֹרִים׃ וָאֹמַר אֵלֶיהָ יָמִים רַבִּים
תֵּשְׁבִי לִי לֹא תִזְנִי וְלֹא תִהְיִי לְאִישׁ וְגַם־אֲנִי

Children of Israel, while they turn to other gods.

Take for a wife a woman who will be the beloved of you, her friend and husband — more beloved to you than any other wife — yet she will abuse that love by engaging in adultery (*Rashi; Radak*; cf. *Ibn Ezra*). This parallels the experience of the Almighty with the Jewish nation; although He has showered them with His boundless love, they have been unfaithful to Him and have pursued the worship of other gods.

וְאֹהֲבֵי אֲשִׁישֵׁי עֲנָבִים — *And love goblets of grapes.*

Instead of loving the Torah of Hashem and its statutes and involving themselves constantly in loving dedication to their study and fulfillment, they have chosen to indulge constantly in physical pleasures, and to party and drink away their days (*Rashi; Radak*).

Targum renders: *But if they will repent, He will forgive them, and view their misdeeds as if they had been committed in a drunken state* — i.e., and they are thus not culpable for them (*Abarbanel*).

As noted in the preface, *Abarbanel* interprets this verse — along with the entire chapter — as depicting the fate of the Jewish people in their exile. This is symbolized by Hosea's taking a wanton adulteress into his home and bestowing his love upon her. Thus does the Almighty maintain His great love for the Children of Israel, notwithstanding that they turned to other gods while still dwelling in the Holy Land and indeed pursued them passionately — as if driven by a state of intoxication from drinking goblets of grape wine.

However, Hosea is not directed to marry this woman, only to love her (*Abarbanel; Malbim*). This represents the plight of the Jewish nation after being spurned by Hashem and called by Him *Lo-ami*, not My nation. Although there is no longer an overt marital bond between God and His people — i.e., they do not enjoy the benefits of His miraculous intervention in their affairs — their basic bond of affection remains intact, and He continues to guide their destiny from behind the veil of natural events (*Malbim*).

In line with this approach, *Malbim* offers the following interpretation to the phrase *and love goblets of grapes*: Whereas they previously mistook their prosperity to be a gift from their false deities instead of acknowledging Me as its source, they now are living in exile with no secure means of sustenance. Nevertheless, they have sold themselves for goblets of grapes, i.e., they have abandoned Me and My statutes for nothing more than the limited pleasures available to them in exile (*Malbim*).

2. וָאֶכְּרֶהָ לִּי בַּחֲמִשָּׁה עָשָׂר כָּסֶף וְחֹמֶר שְׂעֹרִים וְלֶתֶךְ שְׂעֹרִים — *And I acquired her to me for fifteen silver coins and a chomer of barley and a lesech of barley.*

I betrothed her to me with fifteen silver coins,[1] and gave her in addition a *chomer* — which equals ten *eifah* or thirty *se'ah* — and a *lesech* — five *eifah* or fifteen

1. [As cited in the previous verse, *Abarbanel* contends that no marriage was carried out between Hosea and this woman. Accordingly, the acquisition described in this verse refers only to the true subject of the prophecy, the acquisition of the Jewish nation by Hashem, and not to the parable of Hosea's relationship with this woman. Indeed, *Abarbanel* interprets the verse in this manner.]

while they turn to other gods and love goblets of grapes.
2 *And I acquired her to me for fifteen silver coins and a*
chomer of barley and a lesech of barley. 3 *And I said to*
her: You shall wait for me many days [during which] you
shall not be promiscuous nor belong to any man, and also I

se'ah[1] — of barley for her food. Because she indulged in animalistic behavior, I gave her barley, the fodder of beasts, rather than wheat, the staple of human consumption (*Metzudos David*).

Thus, says the Almighty, I acquired the Jewish people on the fifteenth day of the month of Nissan [when I took them out of the land of Egypt] as the word כֶּסֶף is the numerical equivalent of the word נִסָן. The thirty *se'ah* in a *chomer* and the fifteen in a *lesech* represent the thirty days from the exodus until the fifteenth of Iyar, when the manna began to fall, and the next fifteen days until the month of Sivan, when they arrived in the Sinai desert (*Rashi* from *Pesikta*; see comm. to v.3). These are depicted as measures of barley to illustrate how prior to receiving the Torah the bulk of the nation were primitive slaves, schooled only in manual labor, and thus comparable to wild beasts whose diet consists of barley (*Radak*).

Alternatively, the ten *eifah* of the *chomer* and the five of the *lesech* represent together Moses, Aharon, and Miriam and the twelve tribes they led out of Egypt (*Radak*) as well as the three patriarchs and the twelve tribes [i.e., the original sons of Jacob] in whose merit they were delivered (ibid. citing *R' Saadiah Gaon*; cf. *R' Hai Gaon*, cited by *Rashi*; *Ibn Ezra*).

3. וָאֹמַר אֵלֶיהָ יָמִים רַבִּים תֵּשְׁבִי לִי לֹא תִזְנִי וְלֹא תִהְיִי לְאִישׁ וְגַם־אֲנִי אֵלָיִךְ — *And I said to her: You shall wait for me many days [during which] you shall not be promiscuous nor belong to any man, and also I to you.*

Upon betrothing her I commanded that she await the day when our marriage can be consummated, remaining faithful in the meanwhile, uninvolved in promiscuity with any man (*Ibn Ezra*). Thus, five days after the first of Sivan (יָמִים, *days*, equal two: רַבִּים, *many*, signify another three), I gave the Jewish people the Torah, in which I prohibited them from worshiping any other gods (*Rashi* from *Pesikta*).

Alternatively: After she was guilty of adultery I punished her by requiring her to live in abstinence for many days, restrained from further adultery yet uninvolved in conjugal relations with her husband. This represents the experience of the Jews in exile, as depicted in the following verse (*Radak*).

Abarbanel interprets these two verses as the prophet's encouragement to the Jewish people to withstand their tribulations in exile, secure in their awareness that the tragedies of exile along with the ultimate redemption are both predicted in Scripture. Thus: I have already established this with her by means of the fifteen prophets, who foretold the final redemption and for the fulfillment of whose prophecies the Jewish people yearn (כֶּסֶף as in כּוֹסֵף meaning yearning — see *Psalms* 84:3). These are 1) King David (in *Psalms*), 2) Isaiah, 3) Jeremiah, 4) Ezekiel, 5) Hosea, 6) Joel, 7) Amos, 8) Obadiah, 9) Micah, 10) Habakkuk, 11) Zephaniah, 12) Daniel, 13) Haggai, 14) Zechariah, 15) Malachi. In addition, the tribulations you undergo have also been foretold in the Torah itself — in the ninety-eight curses expressed in *Deuteronomy* (ch. 28) and the forty-nine stated in *Leviticus* (ch. 26). These are symbolized by the *chomer* and *lesech* of barley. For the word שְׂעֹרִים, *barley*, begins with שער which can mean a storm of destruction, symbolizing the curses of God's wrath. And like the two

1. A *se'ah* is the quantity of grain produced in a field of 2,500 square cubits.

ג/ד־ה ד אֵלָיִךְ: כִּי ׀ יָמִים רַבִּים יֵשְׁבוּ בְּנֵי יִשְׂרָאֵל אֵין
מֶלֶךְ וְאֵין שָׂר וְאֵין זֶבַח וְאֵין מַצֵּבָה וְאֵין אֵפוֹד
ה וּתְרָפִים: אַחַר יָשֻׁבוּ בְּנֵי יִשְׂרָאֵל וּבִקְשׁוּ אֶת־יהוָה
אֱלֹהֵיהֶם וְאֵת דָּוִיד מַלְכָּם וּפָחֲדוּ אֶל־יהוָה
ד/א א וְאֶל־טוּבוֹ בְּאַחֲרִית הַיָּמִים: שִׁמְעוּ

litanies of curses in the Torah, one of these quantities equals half of the other. Accordingly: Just as your tribulations have befallen you as foretold in Scripture, they will also be followed by your eventual salvation. Therefore, do not despair in your exile or submit to your dire circumstances and abandon the ways of Hashem. Rather, remain faithful and refrain from turning to other gods even as your bond with Him is unfulfilled, and resist as well the pull to other doctrines and faiths that do not include idolatry.

וְגַם־אֲנִי אֵלָיִךְ — *And also I to you.*

Just as you will abstain from conjugal relations, so shall I refrain from relations with you (*Ibn Ezra*; *Radak*). For you shall refrain from idolatry while in exile, even as I withhold from you My Divine Presence (*Abarbanel* to v.4).

Alternatively: And when you repent and return to Me, I, too, will respond in kind and reforge My bond with you (*Targum*; *Mahari Kara*; *Ibn Ezra*).

4. כִּי יָמִים רַבִּים יֵשְׁבוּ בְּנֵי יִשְׂרָאֵל אֵין מֶלֶךְ וְאֵין שָׂר וְאֵין זֶבַח וְאֵין מַצֵּבָה וְאֵין אֵפוֹד וּתְרָפִים — *For many days the Children of Israel shall sit, with no king nor officer and no sacrifice nor pillar and no ephod and teraphim.*

My instructions to her to sit for many days with no man represents a long and bitter exile which you, the Jewish people, shall undergo. During that era, you will have no king from the Davidic dynasty to lead you nor any other independent ruler, and no altar or pillar upon which to offer sacrifices to achieve atonement for your sins. Nor shall you have access to the *ephod*, which contains the *urim vetumim*,[1] nor even to any oracles of idolatry through which to divine future events (*Targum*; *Mahari Kara*). Others interpret *no sacrifice nor pillar* in a manner similar to the final phrase: no sacrifice to Hashem nor any pillar upon which to sacrifice to false deities (*Ibn Ezra*; *Radak*).

Alternatively, this verse describes the loyalty to the Almighty that the Jewish people will retain in their exile: Although the Divine Presence of your Almighty King will not be with you, you will nevertheless not worship the celestial powers through whom events on this world are carried out. Despite the lack of an altar upon which to offer sacrifices to Hashem, you will not raise monuments to worship other gods. And notwithstanding your loss of the *ephod* and the *urim vetumim* it contains, through which you had been able to divine the future, you will not turn instead to the forbidden powers of sorcery in order to do so (*Abarbanel*; *Malbim*; *Metzudos David*; cf. *Alshich*).

5. אַחַר יָשֻׁבוּ בְּנֵי יִשְׂרָאֵל וּבִקְשׁוּ אֶת־ה׳ אֱלֹהֵיהֶם וְאֵת דָּוִיד מַלְכָּם וּפָחֲדוּ אֶל־ה׳ וְאֶל־טוּבוֹ בְּאַחֲרִית הַיָּמִים — *Afterward the Children of Israel shall return and they shall seek* HASHEM *their God and David their king, and they shall tremble for* HASHEM *and for His goodness in the end of days.*

1. This was a parchment with God's Ineffable Name written upon it, which was placed within the fold of the *choshen* — the breast-plate worn by the *Kohen Gadol* in the Temple. It served as a medium of communication with the Almighty, with His responses transmitted by the lighting up of letters carved on the stones in the *choshen*.

to you. [4] *For many days the Children of Israel shall sit,*
with no king nor officer and no sacrifice nor pillar and
no ephod and teraphim. [5] *Afterward the Children of*
Israel shall return and they shall seek HASHEM *their God*
and David their king, and they shall tremble for
HASHEM *and for His goodness in the end of days.*

After many years of exile, when the day of the final redemption arrives (*Radak*; *Metzudos David*), the Children of Israel shall repent their infidelity to Me and devote themselves to My service with a full heart (*Abarbanel*). At the same time, they will seek the kingdom of the Messiah, from the house of David, to whom they will turn for guidance in all their affairs (*Metzudos David*). This will be unlike the other periods of time in which My Divine Presence dwelt among them, when they became comfortable with it and ceased to fear Me. This time, they will continue to tremble before Me and to fear the retribution that will befall them if they are lacking in their devotion, as well as the loss of the great benefits they receive from Me (*Abarbanel*; *Metzudos David*). Alternatively, טובו refers to the glory of the Almighty's presence (*Radak* citing *R' Saadiah Gaon*) [i.e., their appreciation of My Glory will inspire them to tremble from the possibility of transgressing My Will].

It is written in *Isaiah* (33:14): *The sinners will tremble in Zion* [while here it is written: *And they shall tremble for* HASHEM *and for His goodness in the end of days*]. Rabbi Yosi bar Rabbi compared it thus: The chief of the thieves rebelled against the king. Said the king, "Whoever captures him will be rewarded." Indeed, one person succeeded in capturing him. Said the king [to his guards], "Guard both of them overnight." [That night] both of them were trembling; this one in anticipation over how much he would be rewarded, and this one in anticipation over how much he would be punished. So, too, in the future [after the Messiah has arrived] Israel and the idol worshipers will tremble; Israel will *tremble for* HASHEM [in anticipation] *for His goodness* and the idol worshipers *will tremble in Zion* [for the sins they have perpetrated] (*Bereishis Rabbah* 48:7).

The Sages state: R' Shimon bar Yochai said: The Jewish nation despised three things in the days of Rehoboam: the Kingdom of Heaven, the kingdom of David, and the Temple [when they split off into a second kingdom and appointed a separate king, and ceased to come to worship in the Temple]. Said R' Shimon ben Menasheh: The signs of redemption shall not be shown to Israel until they return and seek all three of them, as it is stated: *Afterward the Children of Israel shall return and they shall seek* HASHEM — this is the Kingdom of Heaven; *and David their king* — as implied;[1] *and they shall tremble for* HASHEM *and for His goodness* — this is the Temple, as it says (*Deuteronomy* 3:25): *this good mountain and Lebanon* (*Midrash Samuel* 13:4, cited by *Rashi*, *Radak*).

1. With this statement of the Sages we are given to appreciate how closely the kingdom of David is linked to the sovereignty of the Almighty (because the people of Israel strengthened their attachment to Hashem by subjugating themselves to the Davidic monarchy). Thus, Solomon built the Temple and his royal palace around the same time, and with the destruction of Jerusalem they were both razed together. Similarly, in the time of the Second Temple, when the house of David did not reign, the Divine Presence was also absent from among the Jewish people. Accordingly, in the end of days, they will seek both the Kingdom of Hashem and that of David [as the two are inseparable] (*Abarbanel*).

דְּבַר־יְהוָה בְּנֵי יִשְׂרָאֵל כִּי רִיב לַיהוָה עִם־יוֹשְׁבֵי
הָאָרֶץ כִּי אֵין־אֱמֶת וְאֵין־חֶסֶד וְאֵין־דַּעַת אֱלֹהִים
ב בָּאָרֶץ: אָלֹה וְכַחֵשׁ וְרָצֹחַ וְגָנֹב וְנָאֹף פָּרָצוּ וְדָמִים
ג בְּדָמִים נָגָעוּ: עַל־כֵּן ׀ תֶּאֱבַל הָאָרֶץ וְאֻמְלַל
כָּל־יוֹשֵׁב בָּהּ בְּחַיַּת הַשָּׂדֶה וּבְעוֹף הַשָּׁמָיִם

IV

In this chapter, the prophet again reverts to his castigation of the people of his generation for their sins (*Radak*). His words are directed specifically to the citizens of the kingdom of Israel, and he points a finger particularly at the *Kohanim* and the false prophets who have led the people astray (*Abarbanel*). According to *Rashi*, the *Kohanim* were not the leaders of the revolt against the ways of Hashem but rather its victims (see comm. to v.8).

1. כִּי רִיב לַה׳ עִם־יוֹשְׁבֵי הָאָרֶץ — *For HASHEM has a contention with the inhabitants of the land.*

The Almighty has the following contention to express to the inhabitants of the Land of Israel: I gave you the Land of Israel on condition that you pursue righteousness and justice, and I promised that if you do so I will keep a watchful eye over you throughout the year. However, you have violated the conditions of our agreement, and I will therefore hide My face from you and bring destruction upon the land (*Radak*).

כִּי אֵין־אֱמֶת וְאֵין־חֶסֶד וְאֵין־דַּעַת אֱלֹהִים בָּאָרֶץ — *For there is no truth and no benevolence and no knowledge of God in the land.*[1]

No one acts honestly nor speaks truthfully in the land, and justice and righteousness are thus all but nonexistent. Although there are still righteous people among the nation they are but a small minority, engulfed beneath the tidal wave of corruption, and their presence is not even discernible within the abundance of falsehood. Since the people do not deal with each other honestly, they certainly do not practice benevolence beyond the letter of the law. Thus, there is no knowledge or pursuit of Hashem's ways of justice and righteousness. In addition, no one seeks Hashem and the philosophical knowledge and awareness of His existence (*Radak*).

According to *Abarbanel*, the reference to the people as the *inhabitants of the land* indicates that the failings cited refer to their transgression of the *mitzvos* which are particular to the Holy Land. Adherence to these laws has three purposes: (1) to reinforce the fundaments of our faith which are inherent in them — e.g., the principle of creation which is indicated by the laws of *shemittah*; (2) to provide for the sustenance of the poor and needy; and (3) to fulfill the command-

1. The Sages state that when the time came to create man, there was a great dispute in the Heavens as to the wisdom of this course of action. Benevolence said that he should be created, for the world will be filled with kindness, but Truth took the opposite position since it is filled with falsehood. Righteousness was in favor, for the world contains that in abundance, but Peace was opposed, since mankind is engaged in constant strife. To resolve this dispute, the Almighty took Truth and threw it to the ground — i.e., He gave to the world the Torah, which has the capacity to rectify the effects of falsehood with its eternal truths — thereby leaving a majority of factors in favor of creation.

However, declares the prophet, now the Almighty has a contention with mankind, for there is no truth and no benevolence, and the majority of factors are thus opposed to man's existence. The Torah, which was given to rectify the lack of truth, is of no avail, for no one pursues the knowledge of Hashem and His eternal truths which are found within His Torah (*Alshich*).

[1] *Hear the words of Hashem, Children of Israel, for*
Hashem has a contention with the inhabitants of
the land, for there is no truth and no benevolence and
no knowledge of God in the land. [2] *Swearing, lying,*
murder, robbery, and adultery; they have breached
and blood touches blood. [3] *Therefore shall the land*
be destroyed and all who dwell in it cut off, [along]
with the beasts of the field and the birds of the sky,

ments of the Almighty God, Who instructed us in these precepts, for the sake of following His will. Thus, when the people are lax in the observance of these laws, *there is no truth* — the truth of the fundaments of our faith are not reinforced; *and no benevolence* — there is no source of benevolence to sustain the needy; *and no knowledge of God* — our bond to the Almighty is not strengthened by our fulfillment of His will.

2. אָלֹה וְכַחֵשׁ וְרָצֹחַ וְגָנֹב וְנָאֹף פָּרָצוּ וְדָמִים בְּדָמִים נָגָעוּ — *Swearing, lying, murder, robbery, and adultery; they have breached and blood touches blood.*

[In the place of truth, benevolence, and knowledge of God, you have filled the land with robbery, deceit, adultery, and even murder, thereby totally desecrating the sanctity of the Holy Land, as well as of yourselves.]

I.e., the people swear falsely in My name (*Rashi; Radak*). Others render: *curse and denial* — they have entered into the realm of My curse with their idolatry, as I stated in the Torah (*Deuteronomy* 27:15): *Accursed is the man who shall make a graven image etc.*, and they have denied the God whom they accepted upon themselves as a Lord (*R' Saadiah Gaon*, cited by *Radak*).

פָּרָצוּ וְדָמִים בְּדָמִים נָגָעוּ — *They have breached and blood touches blood.*

They have breached the protective fence of My statutes by their transgressions, and their victims are so numerous that their blood touches and joins together in its abundance (*Mahari Kara; Radak*).

Targum renders: *They bear children from their friends' wives, and they compound transgression upon transgression.*[1]

Others interpret this verse as paralleling the previous one: The Almighty's contention with the people of the land involves two general topics: their lack of truth and benevolence in their dealings with each other, and their refusal to pursue the knowledge of Hashem and His ways. Instead, they desecrate the Name of Hashem by swearing falsely in His name and they oppress each other with murder, robbery, and adultery (*Malbim*; cf. *Abarbanel* to v.3).

3. עַל־כֵּן תֶּאֱבַל הָאָרֶץ וְאֻמְלַל כָּל־יוֹשֵׁב בָּהּ בְּחַיַּת הַשָּׂדֶה וּבְעוֹף הַשָּׁמָיִם וְגַם־דְּגֵי הַיָּם יֵאָסֵפוּ — *Therefore shall the land be destroyed and all who dwell in it cut off, [along]*

1. The Sages of the Talmud (*Kiddushin* 13a) follow this interpretation in a novel approach: Said R' Yehudah in the name of Shmuel: Whoever is not well versed in the laws of marriage and divorce should not become involved with them [i.e., in dealing with them judicially]. Said R' Ashi in the name of R' Yochanan: And [one who does] is harsher upon the world than the generation of the Flood, as it is stated: *Swearing, lying, murder, robbery, and adultery; they have breached and blood touches blood.* What does this imply? As interpreted by R' Joseph: They bear children from their friends' wives and compound transgression upon transgression. And it is stated (v. 3): *Therefore shall the land be destroyed and all who dwell in it cut off, [along] with the beasts of the field and the birds of the sky, and even the fish of the sea shall be annihilated.* Whereas the decree upon the generation of the Flood did not extend to the fish of the sea, as it is stated (*Genesis* 7:22): *of everything that was on dry land died*, i.e., but not the fish of the sea, here even the fish of the sea [were annihilated].

ד וְגַם־דְּגֵי הַיָּם יֵאָסֵפוּ׃ אַךְ אִישׁ אַל־יָרֵב
ה וְאַל־יוֹכַח אִישׁ וְעַמְּךָ כִּמְרִיבֵי כֹהֵן׃
וְכָשַׁלְתָּ הַיּוֹם וְכָשַׁל גַּם־נָבִיא עִמְּךָ לָיְלָה
ו וְדָמִיתִי אִמֶּךָ׃ נִדְמוּ עַמִּי מִבְּלִי הַדָּעַת כִּי־
°וְאֶמְאָסְךָ ק׳ אַתָּה הַדַּעַת מָאַסְתָּ °ואמאסאך מִכַּהֵן לִי

with the beasts of the field and the birds of the sky, and even the fish of the sea shall be annihilated.

Due to these transgressions, you shall be annihilated and the land rendered desolate until the domesticated beasts will be decimated. Alternatively: Even the wild animals will abandon the previously inhabited portions of the land, since there will be no life there whatsoever. The birds of the heavens, too, will no longer be seen, for they inhabit only areas where there is some food available. Indeed, the curse of your destruction shall extend even to the ocean floor, where no vegetation shall grow and the fish who subsist on those plants will thus be wiped out (*Radak*).

Ibn Ezra defines the pattern of cause and effect in the opposite manner: All forms of wildlife will be wiped out, leaving you with no source of sustenance.

Abarbanel interprets this verse allegorically: The land and its inhabitants shall be decimated by the invading hordes of Sennacherib and Nebuchadnezzar — depicted as beasts of the field and birds of the heavens. In later years, the Second Temple will be destroyed and the inhabitants of the land exiled at the hands of the Roman legions, which will consist of soldiers gathered — יֵאָסֵפוּ — from throughout the globe and amassed into large armies like the gatherings of the fish of the sea.

4. אַךְ אִישׁ אַל יָרֵב וְאַל־יוֹכַח אִישׁ — *But no man shall contend nor shall a man rebuke.*

Despite the severity of the fate prophesied upon you, you do not take the rebuke of your true prophets to heart. Rather, you respond to their words by warning them not to contend with you nor admonish you for your misdeeds, as did Amaziah to Amos (*Rashi*; *Mahari Kara*; see *Amos* 7).

Others translate אַךְ to mean *in truth*: In truth there is no point in any man admonishing any other, for his words will not be heard since he, too, is guilty of the same sins (*Radak*). Alternatively: In truth there is no one to rebuke the people since all share in the guilt, and even if someone should try to reprimand them, his life would be endangered. Therefore, as stated above (v. 1), it is left to the Almighty to contend with the nation (*Abarbanel*; cf. *Ibn Ezra*).

וְעַמְּךָ כִּמְרִיבֵי כֹהֵן — *And your nation contends with the Kohen.*

The people quarrel with the *Kohanim*, who are appointed to teach them the word of Hashem, as stated (*Deuteronomy* 33:10): *They shall teach Your ordinances to Jacob etc.* (*Targum*; *Rashi*; *Mahari Kara*). Thus, rather than the *Kohanim* rebuking the people, the multitudes rebuke the *Kohanim* and criticize their every deed — either out of mere contentiousness or because the *Kohanim* are equally sinful and their admonishment is therefore met with a cynical response (*Radak*).

Others interpret: *Your nation is like those who quarreled with the Kohen* — i.e., they are sinful like Korach and his congregation who contested the *Kehunah* of *Aharon* (cited by *Radak*; *Abarbanel*; *Metzudos David*).

5. וְכָשַׁלְתָּ הַיּוֹם וְכָשַׁל גַּם־נָבִיא עִמְּךָ לָיְלָה וְדָמִיתִי אִמֶּךָ — *And you shall stumble by day and the prophet who is with you shall also stumble by night and I will silence your mother.*

and even the fish of the sea shall be annihilated. 4 *But no*
man shall contend nor shall a man rebuke, and your na-
tion contends with the Kohen. 5 *And you shall stumble by*
day and the prophet who is with you shall also stumble
by night and I will silence your mother. 6 *My nation has*
been silenced for lack of knowledge, for you have spurned
knowledge, and I will spurn you from serving Me;

Because of your evil deeds, you shall stumble and fall in misfortune by day and your false prophets will stumble by night, like one who stumbles in the dark (*Targum; Rashi; Radak*). *Radak* renders הַיּוֹם to mean *this day* — i.e., your downfall is imminent.

וְדָמִיתִי אִמֶּךָ — *And I will silence your mother.*

Your nation (see 2:4) shall be stunned into a bewildered silence [by the events that befall them] (*Targum; Rashi*). Others render: *I will cut off your mother* — your nation shall be dispersed and sent into exile and no longer exist as a separate national entity (*Ibn Ezra; Radak*).

R' Eliezer of Beaugency interprets these two verses as directed to the leaders of the nation: No man of stature contends with the people who are sinful nor rebukes them for their misdeeds. Thus, the populace have lost their receptivity to admonition, and on those rare occasions when the *Kohanim* do rebuke them, they respond with hostility and defiance. Therefore, those of you in a position of authority shall stumble and fall in misfortune, along with the false prophets who lead the people astray, for your silence in the face of transgressions is comparable to their willful corruption. Thus, your days shall be turned into nights of darkness and gloom, and your mothers will be silenced — with nowhere to turn for solace or strength — by the magnitude of the calamities that befall you (cf. *Abarbanel; Malbim*).

6. נִדְמוּ עַמִּי מִבְּלִי הַדָּעַת כִּי־אַתָּה הַדַּעַת מָאַסְתָּ וְאֶמְאָסְךָ מִכַּהֵן לִי — *My nation has been silenced for lack of knowledge, for you have spurned knowledge, and I will spurn you from serving Me.*

My nation has been rendered silent (*Rashi; Mahari Kara*) from any words of wisdom, for they are bereft of the knowledge of My ways, which comes from the Torah (*Mahari Kara*).[1] For you, the *Kohanim*, who were entrusted with the responsibility of transmitting My wisdom to the nation, have spurned My knowledge, and refused to learn it yourselves or teach it to others. Therefore, since you have neglected your responsibilities as teachers of the nation, I will spurn you from serving Me in the Temple (*Ibn Ezra; Radak; Abarbanel*).

Others translate נִדְמוּ to mean *cut off* — my nation has been cut off and destroyed due to its lack of knowledge (*Ibn Ezra; Radak; cf. Targum*).

Abarbanel interprets נִדְמוּ from the root דִּמְיוֹן, *imagination*. The nation has turned to the imagined benefits of sorcery and idolatry because they have been left bereft of true knowledge and understanding, as imagination prevails when logic and intellect leave a vacuum. This is

1. Although the Almighty sent prophets to impart His rebuke to the Jewish nation throughout the era of the First Temple, the *Kohanim* — who were designated to guide them — misled them with false teachings. In addition, there were false prophets who claimed to be speaking in Hashem's name but also led them astray. Thus, the people were confused and misguided and they followed the false teachings of these wayward mentors. Therefore, they are portrayed as having been left with no recourse whatsoever to the wisdom of the Torah (*Radak*). [Nevertheless, this portrayal is employed only to emphasize the guilt of the *Kohanim*, not to absolve the people for their sins (see v. 9).]

ז וַתִּשְׁכַּח֙ תּוֹרַ֣ת אֱלֹהֶ֔יךָ אֶשְׁכַּ֥ח בָּנֶ֖יךָ גַּם־אָֽנִי׃ כְּרֻבָּ֖ם
ח כֵּ֣ן חָֽטְאוּ־לִ֑י כְּבוֹדָ֖ם בְּקָל֥וֹן אָמִֽיר׃ חַטַּ֥את עַמִּ֖י
ט יֹאכֵ֑לוּ וְאֶל־עֲוֺנָ֖ם יִשְׂא֥וּ נַפְשֽׁוֹ׃ וְהָיָ֥ה כָעָ֖ם כַּכֹּהֵ֑ן
י וּפָקַדְתִּ֤י עָלָיו֙ דְּרָכָ֔יו וּמַעֲלָלָ֖יו אָשִׁ֥יב לֽוֹ׃ וְאָֽכְלוּ֙ וְלֹ֣א
יִשְׂבָּ֔עוּ הִזְנ֖וּ וְלֹ֣א יִפְרֹ֑צוּ כִּֽי־אֶת־יְהוָ֥ה עָזְב֖וּ לִשְׁמֹֽר׃

the fault of the *Kohanim*, who have spurned knowledge and intellectual pursuit and turned instead to the endeavors of the imagination, and have thus led the nation at large along this misguided path.

וַתִּשְׁכַּח תּוֹרַת אֱלֹהֶיךָ אֶשְׁכַּח בָּנֶיךָ גַּם־אָנִי — *And [as] you have forgotten the Torah of your God, I, too, will forget your children.*

The Torah was entrusted in your hands, *Kohanim*, for you to teach it to the entire nation. Yet you have forgotten and neglected it, refusing to teach it or instruct the people in accordance with its statutes. Therefore, not only shall I spurn you from fulfilling your priestly functions in the Temple by killing you before your time, but I will also turn away from your children as if I had forgotten them. They, too, will be killed or exiled before they even get the chance to carry out the rites of *Kehunah* (*Radak*).

Others interpret this as citing an additional transgression: Not only have many of you refused to study the Torah, but even those who did so have neglected their studies and forgotten what they learned. Therefore, I, too, will act as if I have forgotten your children and I will not protect them with My Divine Providence (*Abarbanel; Malbim*).

Another approach to this verse is that it is directed to the entire nation. Because you have spurned the knowledge of My ways, which is imparted through the Torah, I, too, shall spurn you and prevent you from serving Me (*Mahari Kara*). And because you have chosen to forget My Torah, I will act as if I have forgotten your children. For when the Jewish nation stood at the foot of Mt. Sinai and received the Torah, they offered their children as the guarantors of the Torah, and only on those terms was it granted to them. Therefore, when they abandon the Torah, the Almighty collects from the guarantor, and His wrath is thus poured out on the Jewish children (*Rashi* from *Shir HaShirim Rabbah* 1:24: see ibid.).

7. כְּרֻבָּם כֵּן חָטְאוּ־לִי כְּבוֹדָם בְּקָלוֹן אָמִיר — *As they have increased, so have they sinned against Me; [therefore] I will exchange their honor for disgrace.*

The more they have multiplied in number the more they have sinned against Me, and thus their honor shall be turned into shame (*Rashi*). When Aaron was the *Kohen* he followed My Torah loyally; but now that the tribe of *Kohanim* has grown large, they transgress My statutes and forget My Torah. Therefore, in place of the honor that they have enjoyed as the nobility of the nation, they will be disgraced and despised in the eyes of the people (*Radak*).

Targum renders: *The more I have increased their wealth and possessions, the more they have sinned against Me.*[1]

The Midrash (ibid.) offers another interpretation, understanding כְּרֻבָּם as a reference to the "great ones": Said R' Shmuel Bar Nachmani: For whatever the leaders do, they do. How is this? The prince permits [something actually forbidden], and the chief justice says, "The prince permits it and I should prohibit it?" The rest of the generation then say, "The judges permit it and we should prohibit it?" Thus, who is the cause of the sin of the entire generation? The prince, who sinned first.

1. Said Rabbi: The more I have increased their authority, the more they have sinned against Me. In another vein: The more I have increased their wealth, the more they have sinned against Me (*Yalkut Shimoni* from *Devarim Rabbah* 2:19).

and [as] you have forgotten the Torah of your God I, too, will forget your children. 7 *As they have increased, so have they sinned against Me; [therefore] I will exchange their honor for disgrace.* 8 *The sin-offering of My nation they consume, and to their sins his soul yearns.* 9 *And it shall be, like nation, like Kohen; and I will visit upon him his ways, and his deeds I will requite him.* 10 *And they shall eat but they shall not be sated; they shall be promiscuous but they shall not multiply, for they have abandoned [their] observance of [the ways of]* HASHEM.

8. חַטַּאת עַמִּי יֹאכֵלוּ — *The sin-offering of My nation they consume.*

They fulfill the rites of their *Kehunah* only through consuming the portions of the sin-offerings which are designated for *Kohanim*, but they do not meet their other responsibilities of teaching the nation Torah and instructing them as to the fulfillment of its commandments (*Radak; Abarbanel; Metzudos David*).

וְאֶל־עֲוֹנָם יִשְׂאוּ נַפְשׁוֹ — *And to their sins his soul yearns* [lit., *they lift his soul*].

Their souls yearn for the moment that the Jewish people will sin and thereby be required to bring sacrifices from which they will benefit (*Radak; Metzudos*).

Others interpret *his soul* as referring to the people: *They bear the sins of his soul* — i.e., they comfort the people who sin by convincing them that they can rely on the *Kohanim* to bring them absolution (*Ibn Ezra*).

Rashi interprets this verse as referring to the false prophets among the people: They convince the people to bring their offerings on the altars of idolatry and they, the false prophets, serve as priests, for those deities and eat the portions of the sacrifices which should really belong to the *Kohanim*.[1]

9. וְהָיָה כָעָם כַּכֹּהֵן וּפָקַדְתִּי עָלָיו דְּרָכָיו וּמַעֲלָלָיו אָשִׁיב לוֹ — *And it shall be, like nation, like Kohen; and I will visit upon him his ways, and his deeds I will requite him.*

Just as the nation and the *Kohanim* are equally guilty of transgressing the word of God, so shall they be afflicted equally by His punishment (*Radak; Abarbanel*).

Malbim interprets this verse as describing a pattern of cause and effect: The nation shall emulate the wicked ways of the *Kohanim* and perform sins against Hashem purposely. Therefore, I will punish the *Kohanim* [who are the cause of the peoples' misdeeds] for the baseness of their character and the evil intent behind all their actions, and I will requite them as well for the wicked deeds themselves.

Rashi, following his approach to these verses, interprets as follows: *And the generation shall be like the Kohen* — just as the people disgraced the *Kohanim* and prevented them from serving on their behalf, so shall they themselves be humiliated and disgraced among the gentile nations.

10. וְאָכְלוּ וְלֹא יִשְׂבָּעוּ הִזְנוּ וְלֹא יִפְרֹצוּ כִּי־אֶת־ה׳ עָזְבוּ לִשְׁמֹר — *And they shall eat but they shall not be sated; they shall be promiscuous but they shall not multiply, for they have abandoned [their] observance of [the ways of]* HASHEM.

When the people were righteous and followed the ways of the Torah, even the little food they ate was sufficient to satisfy their hunger. Now, however, that they have debased themselves with their sins, even if they eat in abundance they will not be sated (*Malbim*). Similarly,

1. *Rashi* follows this interpretation because he rejects the notion that the *Kohanim* descended to such a level of depravity (*Abarbanel*).

ד/יא־יד יא־יב זְנוּת וְיַיִן וְתִירוֹשׁ יִקַּח־לֵב: עַמִּי בְּעֵצוֹ יִשְׁאָל
וּמַקְלוֹ יַגִּיד לוֹ כִּי רוּחַ זְנוּנִים הִתְעָה וַיִּזְנוּ מִתַּחַת
יג אֱלֹהֵיהֶם: עַל־רָאשֵׁי הֶהָרִים יְזַבֵּחוּ וְעַל־הַגְּבָעוֹת
יְקַטֵּרוּ תַּחַת אַלּוֹן וְלִבְנֶה וְאֵלָה כִּי טוֹב צִלָּהּ
עַל־כֵּן תִּזְנֶינָה בְּנוֹתֵיכֶם וְכַלּוֹתֵיכֶם תְּנָאַפְנָה:
יד לֹא־אֶפְקוֹד עַל־בְּנוֹתֵיכֶם כִּי תִזְנֶינָה וְעַל־

although they indulge in a great deal of immorality[1] they will not have many children, for because their relations are illicit they will not bear fruit, and even if they do, the children thus conceived will die at a young age (*Radak; Abarbanel*). All this will occur in retribution for their abandonment of the ways of Hashem and His Torah (*Ibn Ezra; Radak*; see below).

11. זְנוּת וְיַיִן וְתִירוֹשׁ יִקַּח־לֵב — *Adultery, wine, and new wine take away the heart.*

Their indulgence in adultery and wine, particularly new wine which intoxicates very quickly (*Radak*), has diverted their hearts from focusing on Me [and My statutes] (*Targum; Rashi; Mahari Kara*). Others interpret: These activities themselves render the heart incapable of concentration and understanding, and the people are thus unable to discern the proper path (*Ibn Ezra; Radak*).

According to another approach, the end of the previous verse continues into this one: *For they have abandoned* HASHEM *to heed [instead] adultery, wine, and new wine, which take away the heart* (*R' Saadiah Gaon*, cited by *Radak; Abarbanel*).

12-14. In the following verses, the prophet describes the extent of the corruption that riddles the nation, and the degree to which the people have allowed the decadence of sorcery, idolatry, and adultery to permeate their lives.

12. עַמִּי בְּעֵצוֹ יִשְׁאָל וּמַקְלוֹ יַגִּיד לוֹ כִּי רוּחַ זְנוּנִים הִתְעָה וַיִּזְנוּ מִתַּחַת אֱלֹהֵיהֶם — *My people consult its wood, and its rod instructs it; for a deviant spirit has misled [them] and they have strayed from under their God.*

If you wish to see clearly that their hearts have been led astray, go and observe how they seek counsel from their wooden idols (*Ibn Ezra; Targum; Rashi*). Note, too, how they hearken to the instructions issued by their false prophets who speak in the name of the rods which they have made into gods (*Rashi*).[2]

Others interpret this verse metaphorically: Just as the blind man relies on his staff to guide him along the way, so have My people turned to its false prophets for leadership (*Radak*, citing his father). In a

1. This translation of the word הִזְנוּ follows the view of *Radak* and *Mahari Kara. Malbim* explains it as causing others to sin. Others interpret it to include both: They themselves have philandered and they have caused others to philander as well (*Ibn Ezra; Abarbanel*).

2. Among the different types of sorcery prohibited by the Torah, *Rambam* (*Sefer HaMitzvos, Mitzvas Lo Taaseh* 45; *Hil. Avodah Zaraah* 11:6) enumerates one who strikes the ground with a rod many times until he evokes an image of the rod speaking to him and describing future events. *Semag* (*Lo Taaseh* 52) describes another use of rod sorcery. Prior to undertaking a journey, a person would peel one side of each of the barks of two pieces of wood and throw them onto the ground. If the first one landed with the unpeeled side on top, and the second the opposite way, it was considered a good omen for success on his journey. Thus, it is possible to interpret this verse as describing both of these processes: *My people consult its wood* — this refers to the method described by *Semag*; *and its rod instructs it* — this is the sorcery depicted by *Rambam* (*Abarbanel*).

[11] *Adultery, wine, and new wine take away the heart.*
[12] *My people consult its wood, and its rod instructs it; for*
a deviant spirit has misled [them] and they have strayed
from under their God. [13] *On the mountaintops they*
slaughter and upon the hills they burn [sacrifices], under
the oak, the styrax, and the elm, for its shade is good.
Therefore, your daughters are promiscuous and your
daughters-in-law commit adultery. [14] *I will not visit*
upon your daughters that they philander [nor] upon

similar vein, the Sages interpret מקל as relating to the word מֵקִיל, *lenient.* Thus: כֹּל הַמֵּקִיל לוֹ יַגִּיד לוֹ, *Whoever is lenient for him, [he allows to] instruct him* (*Pesachim* 52a; see *Abarbanel*).

According to *Alshich*, the prophet comes to explain how the people fell prey to so illogical a premise as the worship of wooden sticks. The answer is that one who sins becomes enveloped by a spirit of *tumah* — spiritual defilement — that propels him even further in the direction of his transgression. Thus, from having indulged in the sin of adultery, the people descended to a level of depravity in which they strayed from their fidelity to the Almighty by serving false gods and wooden idols (*Alshich*).

13. עַל־רָאשֵׁי הֶהָרִים יְזַבֵּחוּ וְעַל־הַגְּבָעוֹת יְקַטֵּרוּ — *On the mountaintops they slaughter and upon the hills they burn [sacrifices].*

They offer sacrifices to their false gods high upon the mountains and hills, where they can be seen [from great distances] (*Ibn Ezra*), in accordance with the prevalent custom among idolaters (*Radak*).

Malbim interprets the duality of this phrase in the following manner: The slaughtering of the sacrifices, which is the primary act of worship, is done in large gatherings upon the mountaintops. The burning, however, is performed privately by each individual and it is done on the hills, which are lower than the mountains.

תַּחַת אַלּוֹן וְלִבְנֶה וְאֵלָה כִּי טוֹב צִלָּהּ — *Under the oak, the styrax, and the elm, for its shade is good.*[1]

All of these trees provide abundant shade, and for this reason they were deemed to be proper settings for the worship of the idols (*Radak*). Alternatively, the phrase *for its shade is good* refers only to the elm. The first two are chosen for the fruits they produce, the elm is used because of its shade (*Abarbanel*).

עַל־כֵּן תִּזְנֶינָה בְּנוֹתֵיכֶם וְכַלּוֹתֵיכֶם תְּנָאַפְנָה — *Therefore, your daughters are promiscuous and your daughters-in-law commit adultery.*

As a result of your involvement with gentile idolaters you intermarry with them, and the children born thereof follow in their ways of adultery (*Targum*; *Rashi*). Alternatively: Because you abandon your homes and go off to offer sacrifices to your idols, your daughters and daughters-in-law are left alone in their homes for long periods of time and eventually turn to adultery (*Ibn Ezra; Radak; Mahari Kara*).

14. לֹא־אֶפְקוֹד עַל־בְּנוֹתֵיכֶם כִּי תִזְנֶינָה וְעַל־כַּלּוֹתֵיכֶם כִּי תְנָאַפְנָה כִּי־הֵם עִם־הַזֹּנוֹת יְפָרֵדוּ וְעִם־הַקְּדֵשׁוֹת יְזַבֵּחוּ וְעָם לֹא־יָבִין יִלָּבֵט — *I will not visit upon your daughters that they philander [nor] upon your daughters-in-law that they commit adultery, for they separate themselves*

1. The translations of אַלּוֹן and אֵלָה are from *Rashi*. He offers no translation for לִבְנֶה other than the fact that it is a tree whose bark is white. *Daas Mikra* identifies it as the styrax.

כַּלּוֹתֵיכֶם֙ כִּ֣י תְנָאַ֔פְנָה כִּי־הֵם֙ עִם־הַזֹּנ֣וֹת יְפָרֵ֔דוּ
טו וְעִם־הַקְּדֵשׁ֖וֹת יְזַבֵּ֑חוּ וְעָ֥ם לֹא־יָבִ֖ין יִלָּבֵֽט׃ אִם־זֹנֶ֤ה
אַתָּה֙ יִשְׂרָאֵ֔ל אַל־יֶאְשַׁ֖ם יְהוּדָ֑ה וְאַל־תָּבֹ֣אוּ הַגִּלְגָּ֗ל
וְאַל־תַּעֲלוּ֙ בֵּ֣ית אָ֔וֶן וְאַל־תִּשָּׁבְע֖וּ חַי־יְהוָֽה׃

with philanderesses and slaughter with prostitutes, and the nation that does not understand shall stumble.

[I will not exact retribution from the womenfolk among you for their licentious ways] for they are not to blame, since they have learned their behavior from the men who are themselves steeped in depravity (*Ibn Ezra; Radak*). For these men separate themselves[1] from the crowd to go off and commit adultery with the wives of other men. In addition, they bring sacrifices to false gods together with prostitutes (*Malbim*), leading up to their fornication together (*Radak; Metzudos David*).

Rashi follows the approach of the Sages (*Sotah* 47a), who interpret this verse to be discussing the procedure of מֵי סוֹטָה, *the waters of the sotah*, which are drunk by a woman suspected of infidelity. As instructed by the Torah (*Numbers* 5:11-31), a woman who is so suspected is required under circumstances described there to drink from a potion of water in which was dissolved a parchment bearing the Name of Hashem. If she was guilty, the potion would miraculously cause her to die in a very degrading manner. Concerning this procedure, the prophet declares: Your daughters and daughters-in-law who are guilty of adultery will no longer be punished in this manner, for it will no longer be effective. This is because the waters of the *sotah* work only if the woman's husband is innocent of any similar wrongdoing. However, now that adultery runs rampant throughout the nation this procedure is no longer viable.

וְעָם לֹא־יָבִין יִלָּבֵט — *And the nation that does not understand shall stumble.*

Since you refuse to focus your minds and hearts to understand [what is required of you by the Almighty], you will stumble and fall in retribution for your sins (*Rashi*).

Alternatively: The nation that does not understand [i.e., that refuses to pursue true understanding] will become totally confused and bereft of comprehension (*Ibn Ezra*).

Abarbanel interprets adultery and prostitution discussed in this verse to refer metaphorically to idolatry — which is the prostitution of the nation from its fidelity to the Almighty. Because the men and women of the nation have indulged extensively in such behavior, your children, too, shall follow in your ways and stumble in the same transgressions.

15. In this verse, the prophet diverts momentarily from his castigation of the kingdom of Israel and focuses upon the people of Judah. According to some, he declares their innocence of the wrongdoings described above and exhorts them to reject the example of their Israelite brothers. Others contend that the Judeans were already involved in these sins and the

1. This is the translation of יְפָרֵדוּ followed by *Radak*, *Malbim*, and *Metzudos David*. *Rashi* cites *Targum* as interpreting it to mean joining — they join together with the prostitutes to drink wine [leading to promiscuity]. He also cites *Menachem*, who translates it *wine barrels*, referring to the drinking of wine which tends to precede such illicit behavior (see *Mahari Kara*).

Radak cites his father as interpreting יְפָרֵדוּ to be derived from the word פֶּרֶד, *mule*: They are steeped in adultery like mules, who stand out among domestic beasts for the extent of their sexual indulgence. Alternatively: They resemble mules because their relations do not lead to propagation, for they perform their act in a manner which does not cause conception.

your daughters-in-law that they commit adultery,
for they separate themselves with philanderesses
and slaughter with prostitutes, and the nation
that does not understand shall stumble. 15 *If you*
have turned astray, Israel, let Judah not become
guilty; do not come to Gilgal and do not ascend to
Beth-aven, and do not swear, "As HASHEM lives."

prophet takes the time to admonish them as well.

אִם־זֹנֶה אַתָּה יִשְׂרָאֵל אַל־יֶאְשַׁם יְהוּדָה וְאַל־תָּבֹאוּ הַגִּלְגָּל וְאַל־תַּעֲלוּ בֵּית אָוֶן וְאַל־תִּשָּׁבְעוּ חַי־ה׳ — *If you have turned astray, Israel, let Judah not become guilty; do not come to Gilgal and do not ascend to Beth-aven, and do not swear, "As HASHEM lives."*

If the kingdom of Israel has succumbed to sin, let the citizens of Judah not emulate their ways and become guilty as well (*Rashi*). [Therefore, people of Judah, do not come to worship the idols situated in Gilgal and Beth-el within the kingdom of Israel.]

This exhortation was especially pertinent at this time, when the kingdom of Israel subjugated Judah, who was thus more prone to enter their cities and emulate their deeds (*Malbim*; see comm. to 1:1).

Alternatively: If you, Israel, are guilty of infidelity to the Almighty, this does not render guilty the people of Judah, and they will thus not be culpable for your sins.[1] However, citizens of Judah, this holds true only as long as you do not emulate the ways of your Israelite brothers and do not come to their cities to worship their false gods (*Rashi*; cf. *Abarbanel*).

Others interpret this verse as an indictment against the people of Judah: If you, Israel, have sinned with your idols, that does not excuse the citizens of Judah for following suit, particularly since they have access to the Temple and have no need to seek other avenues of worship. Thus, citizens of Judah, you should not be going to Gilgal and Beth-aven to worship the idols situated there [and because you have done so you will be punished] (*Ibn Ezra; Radak*).[2]

וְאַל תַּעֲלוּ בֵּית אָוֶן — *And do not ascend to Beth-aven.*

This is Beth-el, the site of one of the golden calves erected by Jeroboam ben Nabot to prevent the people from returning to Jerusalem to worship there. It was dubbed Beth-aven, meaning the house of vanity, by the prophets to indicate the worthlessness of worshiping the idols which stood there. The prophet uses the phrase *do not ascend*, because it was situated in a high place (*Radak*).

וְאַל־תִּשָּׁבְעוּ חַי־ה׳ — *And do not swear, "As HASHEM lives."*

Do not swear falsely in the Name of Hashem (*Targum*). It was customary among the idolaters of Israel to invoke the

1. [This statement seems to be superfluous: Why would one think that the people of Judah should be culpable for the sins of Israel? However, since there is a general principle that the entire nation is culpable for the sins committed in its midst (כָּל יִשְׂרָאֵל עֲרֵבִים זֶה בָּזֶה) one might think that this applies here as well. Furthermore, the majority of the Jewish people of Judah are susceptible to the reaction of the Almighty as caused by the majority of the nation. Therefore, the prophet declares that this is not the case, presumably because the two kingdoms are viewed as two distinct nations and one is not affected by the Almighty's dealings with the other.]

2. *Mahari Kara* follows *Rashi's* interpretation of the first phrase and that of *Ibn Ezra* and *Radak* in the second. Thus, he interprets: If Israel has sinned with her idols, that will not be considered the guilt of Judah. However, the people of Judah are culpable for following the ways of the people of Israel and going to worship idols.

טז כִּי כְּפָרָה סֹרֵרָה סָרַר יִשְׂרָאֵל עַתָּה יִרְעֵם יהוה
יז כְּכֶבֶשׂ בַּמֶּרְחָב: חֲבוּר עֲצַבִּים אֶפְרָיִם הַנַּח־לוֹ:
יח סָר סָבְאָם הַזְנֵה הִזְנוּ אָהֲבוּ הֵבוּ קָלוֹן מָגִנֶּיהָ:

Name of Hashem when swearing falsely and the names of idols when making a valid oath (*Rashi; Mahari Kara*).

Others interpret: If you are not loyal to the Almighty God and observant of His commandments, do not invoke His Holy Name in your oaths, for only those who serve Him righteously have the right to do so (*Ibn Ezra*).

16. כִּי כְּפָרָה סֹרֵרָה סָרַר יִשְׂרָאֵל עַתָּה יִרְעֵם ה׳ כְּכֶבֶשׂ בַּמֶּרְחָב — *For Israel has strayed like a wayward cow; now* HASHEM *shall graze them like a lamb on the range.*

The kingdom of Israel has fallen to dismally low levels of godlessness (*Abarbanel*),[1] and has come to resemble a rebellious cow that avoids the yoke its owner tries to place upon it, straying instead along its own way. So, too, the Jewish nation has thrown off the yoke of Hashem's commandments and strayed from the proper path. For this, the Almighty shall deal with them like one who grazes a lone lamb on a wide range, where the animal wanders around bleating helplessly in confusion and does not even feed from the grass before it (*Ibn Ezra; Radak*).[2]

Alternatively, the prophet conveys the Almighty's regrets over the misbehavior of His people and the results thereof. If only they had not strayed, I would bless them with such abundance, like the shepherd who grazes his lamb upon the broad range (*Ibn Ezra; Radak*, citing his father).[3]

Others interpret: Like a cow that is fattened and then rebels, so have the Children of Israel rebelled against Hashem due to an abundance of food and drink. Therefore, the Almighty shall provide for their needs in a limited fashion — like a lamb that is left to its own devices to graze on the range rather than being fed and fattened on fodder by its owner (*Targum; Rashi; Mahari Kara*).

17. חֲבוּר עֲצַבִּים אֶפְרָיִם הַנַּח־לוֹ — *Ephraim is attached to idols: Leave him be.*

So says the Almighty God to his prophet: Ephraim[4] has become deeply attached to the idols he worships. There-

1. This follows *Abarbanel's* interpretation of the previous verse, that it defends the people of Judah from receiving any blame for the transgressions of the kingdom of Israel. Those who understand that verse to be an indictment of Judah, as well, will interpret this verse to refer to the entire nation of Israel, including both of the kingdoms it comprises.

2. *Abarbanel* suggests that this metaphor is meant to depict the impending exile, in which they will be strewn across the globe and wander from one nation to the next.

3. *Malbim* follows a similar approach, and places it into a historical context. During the reign of Jeroboam ben Joash, the Almighty assisted the kingdom of Israel in expanding its boundaries and recapturing many of its previously lost lands, hoping thereby to awaken in them a sense of gratitude to Him and to arouse them to repentance for their wicked ways. However, they persisted instead in their transgressions, and thereby abused the good they had received. Thus, the prophet proclaims: Israel continues to behave like a wayward cow despite the fact that the Almighty has now expanded their frontiers and grazed them like a lamb on a broad range.

4. The prophet refers to the citizens of the ten tribes as Ephraim because the kingdom was called in his name (*Malbim*) [as its founder, Jeroboam ben Nabot, was from that tribe].

R' Eliezer of Beaugency offers a different interpretation: You citizens of the ten tribes have attached yourselves to the monarchy of Ephraim — i.e., Jeroboam ben Nabot — who rebelled against Me and against the kingdom of Judah. At least leave the people of Judah alone and do not seek to influence them to follow in your wicked ways.

[16] *For Israel has strayed like a wayward cow;*
now HASHEM *shall graze him like a lamb on the*
range. [17] *Ephraim is attached to idols: Leave him*
be. [18] *Their adulterous drinking parties have*
gone astray; her rulers love to invite disgrace.

fore, leave him be and do not seek to reprove him, for it will be to no avail (*Rashi*).[1]

The word עֲצַבִּים is used to describe the idols because such deities bring only sadness and frustration — עֶצֶב — to their worshipers, since they are incapable of providing any benefits (*Ibn Ezra; Abarbanel*).

The Sages interpret this verse as praising the degree of peace that prevailed within the land. Said Rabbi: Great is peace, for even if idolaters are in peace the Almighty is, so to speak, unable to prevail over them, as it is stated: *Ephraim is united;* [therefore, despite his] *idols, leave him alone* (*Yalkut Shimoni*).[2]

18. סָר סָבְאָם הַזְנֵה הִזְנוּ אָהֲבוּ הֵבוּ קָלוֹן מָגִנֶּיהָ — *Their adulterous drinking parties have gone astray; her rulers love to invite disgrace.*

Their parties have strayed from My ways and become strange to me, for they drink wine together with prostitutes [which leads to their sinning with them]. Their officers, and kings in particular, eagerly invite — הֵבוּ — disaster upon themselves with their decadent behavior (*Rashi*; cf. *Mahari Kara*).

Others translate סָר to mean *putrid* and הֵבוּ, *give.* They indulge so excessively in drink that the liquor becomes foul in their mouths. This overindulgence in drinking leads to adultery as well. In addition, their depravity has become so great that their leaders invite the people to give them bribery in order to corrupt justice, which is a great disgrace to the nation (*Radak*; cf. *Ibn Ezra*).

According to another approach, the prophet in this verse depicts the extent of the decadence which riddles the nation: When the wine in which they indulge has worn off, they turn immediately to their other vice of adultery — i.e., their adultery from fidelity to the Almighty by straying instead to other gods. What is the origin of this depravity? The source of their downfall is their leaders, who loved this shameful behavior and gave it to the nation through their example (*Abarbanel; Metzudos David*).

According to *Malbim*, these last two verses are directed to the kingdom of Judah. The king of the nation of Israel is attached to his idols and unwilling to give them up. Therefore, people of Judah, leave him and avoid his company and influence, for the leaders of the nation are involved in excessive drinking, prostitution, and base endeavors — all of which serve only to disgrace them.

1. The intent behind this statement is the subject of a dispute among the commentators:

Radak comments: This is stated in the manner of one who explodes in anger against his friend for refusing to heed his rebuke, and states that he will never again admonish him. Nevertheless, he resumes his rebuke after a short while.

Mahari Kara, however, explains: Now that Ephraim is attached to those who worship idols, leave him alone to act in accordance with his will. [Thus, he understands this to be a measure of retribution: Beyond a certain point, the Almighty will no longer send His prophets to rebuke the people and endeavor to arouse them to repentance.]

2. *Alshich* explains the reasoning behind this principle to be that the merit of the attribute of unity will eventually elevate the people and bring them to repentance. He thus interprets the final verse in this chapter (v. 19) as follows: The spirit of this unity has bound the nation of Israel with its wings — i.e., it has lifted them up and brought them to repentance — until they are ashamed of their [idolatrous] sacrifices, and they will thus cleave only to the Almighty from here on in.

ד/יט יט צָרַר רוּחַ אוֹתָהּ בִּכְנָפֶיהָ וְיֵבֹשׁוּ
ה/א־ב א מִזִּבְחוֹתָם: שִׁמְעוּ־זֹאת הַכֹּהֲנִים
וְהַקְשִׁיבוּ ׀ בֵּית יִשְׂרָאֵל וּבֵית הַמֶּלֶךְ
הַאֲזִינוּ כִּי לָכֶם הַמִּשְׁפָּט כִּי־פַח הֱיִיתֶם
ב לְמִצְפָּה וְרֶשֶׁת פְּרוּשָׂה עַל־תָּבוֹר: וְשַׁחֲטָה
שֵׂטִים הֶעְמִיקוּ וַאֲנִי מוּסָר לְכֻלָּם:

19. צָרַר רוּחַ אוֹתָהּ בִּכְנָפֶיהָ וְיֵבֹשׁוּ מִזִּבְחוֹתָם — *The wind has bound her by her wings, and they shall be ashamed of their sacrifices.*

Like a strong wind which seizes the wings of a bird and prevents it from alighting until it has been carried a great distance, so shall the enemy come and carry them off to a distant land. At that time, they will be deeply ashamed of the sacrifices[1] they offered to their false deities, who will be to no avail in warding off disaster (*Rashi; Metzudos David*).

Others interpret: They are like a person who tries to attach the air to his wings [to enable him to fly] but in truth there is nothing there. So have the people of Israel placed their faith in their idols, but they are like an empty wind which cannot help them whatsoever (*Ibn Ezra; Radak*).[2]

V

When Jeroboam ben Nebot rebelled against Rehoboam and established the separate kingdom of Israel, he was faced with the specter of losing his subjects to the kings of Judah when they would travel to Jerusalem for the Festivals to bring offerings to Hashem in the Temple. He therefore erected two golden calves, one in Dan and one in Beth-el, and commanded the people to worship them rather than ascending to Jerusalem (see *I Kings* 12:25-30). Thus he, and the monarchs who followed in his path, bore the primary responsibility for the pursuit of idolatry which had by now run rampant among the people. Nevertheless, the people who followed were actually happy to do so, and thus the entire nation was subject to Divine punishment.

1. שִׁמְעוּ־זֹאת הַכֹּהֲנִים וְהַקְשִׁיבוּ בֵּית יִשְׂרָאֵל וּבֵית הַמֶּלֶךְ הַאֲזִינוּ כִּי לָכֶם הַמִּשְׁפָּט כִּי־פַח הֱיִיתֶם לְמִצְפָּה וְרֶשֶׁת פְּרוּשָׂה עַל־תָּבוֹר — *Hear this, Kohanim; listen, house of Israel; and hearken, royal house, for the judgment is yours, for you have been a snare to Mizpah and a net extended over Tabor.* Hear my words, *Kohanim*, for you, too, share in the guilt of the nation since you have not taught them properly (*R' Eliezer of Beaugency*).[3] Listen, members of the house of Israel, who have allowed yourselves to be seduced into deviant

1. This follows the translation of the majority of commentators. *Rashi* himself renders זִבְחוֹתָם to mean *their altars*, the places where they offered sacrifices. This follows the approach of *Targum*.

2. Although, according to this interpretation, the first phrase refers to the nation of Israel in both the masculine [צָרַר] and the feminine [אוֹתָהּ] gender, it is the style of Scripture to vary in these things. This course is followed again in the latter half of the verse when the people are described in the plural form, as opposed to the singular form of the first half (*Radak*).

3. *Malbim* interprets the *Kohanim* to be the priests of the false deities whom the people worshiped, who influenced them to follow them in this worship.

4/19 [19] *The wind has bound her by her wings, and they shall*
be ashamed of their sacrifices.

5/1-2 [1] *Hear this, Kohanim; listen, house of Israel; and*
hearken, royal house, for the judgment is yours,
for you have been a snare to Mizpah and a net ex-
tended over Tabor. [2] *And [with] slaughter the deviants*
deepened [their iniquity], and I castigate all of them.

ways (*Malbim*).[1] And hearken to Me, you of the royal house, for you bear the primary responsibility for all that has occurred and are therefore to receive the bulk of the punishment which is to be meted out in judgment. For you have placed guards upon the heights of Mizpah and Tabor to prevent the people of Israel from traveling to Jerusalem and worshiping Me there (*Rashi*).

Radak interprets these words as directed to the kingdom of Judah, whose citizens could have admonished the neighboring nation of Israel and inspired them by example, thereby preventing the tragedy which was to befall them. The prophet addresses the following three groups: *Kohanim* in Judah who serve in the Temple; *the house of Israel* — referring either to the tribe of Judah, which is the primary tribe in the entire house of Israel, or to the Sanhedrin, who judge the house of Israel; and *the royal house* of Judah: You are all guilty of being a stumbling block to the nation of Israel because you did not carry out justice as is incumbent upon you, and you thus served as a poor example for them.

2. וְשַׁחֲטָה שֵׂטִים הֶעְמִיקוּ וַאֲנִי מוּסָר לְכֻלָּם — *And [with] slaughter the deviants deepened [their iniquity], and I castigate all of them.* The sovereigns of the nation deepened their iniquity by imposing the death penalty upon anyone who returned to Jerusalem for the Festivals. Nevertheless, I castigate the entire nation and place the burden of guilt upon all of them, for the people followed willingly in the footsteps of their leaders (*Abarbanel*).

The Sages interpret: They deepened [i.e., they reinforced their decree with the threat of punishment] more than I; for I said that one who does not ascend to Jerusalem for the Festivals transgresses a positive commandment, whereas they declared that anyone who does ascend will be put to death (*Sanhedrin* 102a).[2]

Others translate וְשַׁחֲטָה to mean extent: *The extent of their iniquity they deepened* (*Rashi*; cf. *Mahari Kara*). *Radak* renders: *And the iniquitous deepened [their iniquity] by slaughtering to their false deities.*

וַאֲנִי מוּסָר לְכֻלָּם — *And I castigate all of them. Rashi* understands this to refer to the punishment to be inflicted upon them: *I will prepare castigation for all of them. Radak* renders: *I am castigation for all of them* — referring to the prophet's rebuke: I am a source of castigation for all of them for I rebuke them daily; still, they do not repent.

1. *Mahari Kara* interprets the first portion of this verse as depicting a dialogue between the Almighty and his nation. Said the Almighty to the *Kohanim*: Why do you not offer before Me sacrifices? To which the *Kohanim* respond: Because the people do not bring us any. Hashem then turns to the house of Israel and demands: Why do you not bring sacrifices to be offered on the Altar? The people reply: The royal house does not allow us to do so. At this point, Hashem addresses the royal house and assigns to them the blame for all that has transpired.

2. *Mahari Kara* interprets this contrast a bit differently: Whereas I stated merely that one who does not ascend for the Festivals transgresses a positive commandment, they declared that one who does not join in the worship of the idols they established will be executed.

ג אֲנִי֙ יָדַ֣עְתִּי אֶפְרַ֔יִם וְיִשְׂרָאֵ֖ל לֹא־נִכְחַ֣ד מִמֶּ֑נִּי כִּ֣י
ד עַתָּ֞ה הִזְנֵ֣יתָ אֶפְרַ֔יִם נִטְמָ֖א יִשְׂרָאֵֽל׃ לֹ֤א יִתְּנוּ֙
מַֽעַלְלֵיהֶ֔ם לָשׁ֖וּב אֶל־אֱלֹהֵיהֶ֑ם כִּ֣י ר֤וּחַ זְנוּנִים֙
ה בְּקִרְבָּ֔ם וְאֶת־יְהוָ֖ה לֹ֥א יָדָֽעוּ׃ וְעָנָ֥ה גְאוֹן־
יִשְׂרָאֵ֖ל בְּפָנָ֑יו וְיִשְׂרָאֵ֣ל וְאֶפְרַ֗יִם יִכָּֽשְׁלוּ֙ בַּעֲוֺנָ֔ם
ו כָּשַׁ֥ל גַּם־יְהוּדָ֖ה עִמָּֽם׃ בְּצֹאנָ֤ם וּבִבְקָרָם֙ יֵֽלְכ֔וּ
לְבַקֵּ֖שׁ אֶת־יְהוָ֑ה וְלֹ֣א יִמְצָ֔אוּ חָלַ֖ץ מֵהֶֽם׃

3-4. After laying the lion's share of the blame upon the leaders, Hosea declared in the previous verse, *and I castigate all of them* — the masses, too, were willing participants in this iniquity and not simply innocent victims. In these next two verses, Hosea elaborates further upon that theme.

3. אֲנִי יָדַעְתִּי אֶפְרַיִם וְיִשְׂרָאֵל לֹא־נִכְחַד מִמֶּנִּי כִּי עַתָּה הִזְנֵיתָ אֶפְרַיִם נִטְמָא יִשְׂרָאֵל — *I knew Ephraim, and Israel was not obscured from Me, for now you have strayed, Ephraim; Israel has been defiled.* [Throughout the years when the masses were forced to worship the idols in Dan and Beth-el] I knew the evil that lay in the hearts of Ephraim, who worshiped the false gods set up for them by their kings. Although they claimed to do so only because of the threat of death hanging over them, the truth of the matter — that they followed this course willingly — was not hidden from Me. Now, with the advent of the reign of Hosea ben Elah, their guilt has been revealed. For he ceased to coerce the people to worship the golden calves established by Jeroboam, yet they nevertheless continued to do so of their own volition. Thus, now that they have strayed they shall be punished with exile[1] (*Rashi; Mahari Kara; Metzudos David* from *Seder Olam* ch. 22).

Radak interprets these words as referring to Jeroboam ben Nebot, who was from the tribe of Ephraim: I knew what was in the heart of Jeroboam when he established the golden calves for the people to worship, and the shared guilt of the leaders with whom he took counsel was not hidden from Me. For now, Jeroboam, you have caused the people to stray with your idols and they have thus been defiled.

4. לֹא יִתְּנוּ מַעַלְלֵיהֶם לָשׁוּב אֶל־אֱלֹהֵיהֶם — *They will not abandon their deeds to return to their God.* This follows the translation of *Targum, Rashi, Metzudos David,* and *Malbim. Radak* renders: *Their deeds will not allow them to return to their God* — so steeped are they in their wickedness that even if they are aroused momentarily with thoughts of repentance these are immediately discarded. So great is their guilt that there is no path left open to them which will allow their repentance to be accepted without prior retribution. (See also *Ibn Ezra, Mahari Kara, Abarbanel,* and *Alshich* for other interpretations of this phrase.)

כִּי רוּחַ זְנוּנִים בְּקִרְבָּם — *For a deviant spirit is in their midst.* They are infused with a

1. [This declaration seems puzzling: Why is it necessary for evidence of their wickedness to be revealed before the Almighty exacts retribution for it? Surely He knew from the outset whether they worshiped the idols willingly or only due to coercion. However, as long as they had no choice but to worship the idols they never made the active decision to worship them out of their own volition. Thus, although it was clear to Hashem that they would do so if given the choice, they were not culpable until they actually made that choice (cf. *Ramban* to *Bereishis* 22:1).]

3 I knew Ephraim, and Israel was not obscured from
Me, for now you have strayed, Ephraim; Israel has
been defiled. 4 They will not abandon their deeds to
return to their God for a deviant spirit is in their midst
and HASHEM they do not know. 5 And the pride of
Israel shall be humbled before Him and Israel and
Ephraim shall stumble over their sin, [and] Judah, too,
shall stumble with them. 6 With their sheep and with
their cattle they shall go to seek HASHEM, but they
shall not find [Him]; He has withdrawn from them.

spirit of heresy as well as a hedonistic indulgence in adultery (*Malbim*).

וְאֶת־ה׳ לֹא יָדָעוּ — *And HASHEM they do not know.* They have not sought out the Almighty even one time, so attached are they to their evil deeds (*Radak*). Alternatively: They have not noted and appreciated all of the good He has bestowed upon them (*R' Eliezer of Beaugency*). *Targum* renders: And the teachings of HASHEM they did not seek.

5. וְעָנָה גְאוֹן־יִשְׂרָאֵל בְּפָנָיו — *And the pride of Israel shall be humbled before Him.* [In retribution for all of its evil,] Israel will witness the humbling of its pride (*Targum*). I.e., even before their exile from their land, they will witness and endure their prostration and downfall, in place of the pride and glory which was previously theirs (*Radak*).

Others render עָנָה to mean *testify*: The pride and haughtiness with which they transgressed the will of the Almighty will testify against them when the time of their retribution arrives (*Dunash*, cited by *Rashi*).

וְיִשְׂרָאֵל וְאֶפְרַיִם יִכָּשְׁלוּ בַּעֲוֹנָם כָּשַׁל גַּם־יְהוּדָה עִמָּם — *And Israel and Ephraim shall stumble over their sin, [and] Judah, too, shall stumble with them.* Ephraim — the tribe of Jeroboam ben Navot who instigated the idolatry of the nation — as well as the remainder of the ten tribes shall all stumble and fall as a result of their sins. Even the nation of Judah, which has the Temple in its midst, has abandoned the service of Hashem and worshiped other gods. Thus, they, too, shall face retribution for their deeds (*Radak; Abarbanel*).

6. Having included, at the end of the previous verse, the nation of Judah in the scope of his admonition, the prophet continues in that vein, how Judah's iniquities have caused the loss of their unique closeness with the Almighty.

בְּצֹאנָם וּבִבְקָרָם יֵלְכוּ לְבַקֵּשׁ אֶת־ה׳ וְלֹא יִמְצָאוּ חָלַץ מֵהֶם — *With their sheep and with their cattle they shall go to seek HASHEM, but they shall not find [Him]; He has withdrawn from them.* The people of Judah shall go to the Temple with their sacrifices of sheep and cattle in order to seek the Almighty but they will not find Him, for He has already withdrawn His Glory from them as a result of their sins. Thus, [without the special receptivity to their prayers that His Divine Presence brings] they will be unable to effect the annulment of His decree that they be exiled from their land (*Ibn Ezra; Radak*).

This refers specifically to the reign of Josiah (c. 3285-3316), during which idolatry was abolished in the kingdom of Judah, and the people returned to Hashem and offered a Passover sacrifice in devotion to Him (*Radak*; see *II Kings* 23:22).

Malbim interprets this verse as referring still to the kingdom of Israel. Although the time will come when they

ז בַּיהוָה בָּגָדוּ כִּי־בָנִים זָרִים יָלָדוּ עַתָּה יֹאכְלֵם
ח חֹדֶשׁ אֶת־חֶלְקֵיהֶם׃ תִּקְעוּ שׁוֹפָר
בַּגִּבְעָה חֲצֹצְרָה בָּרָמָה הָרִיעוּ בֵּית אָוֶן
ט אַחֲרֶיךָ בִּנְיָמִין׃ אֶפְרַיִם לְשַׁמָּה תִהְיֶה בְּיוֹם
תּוֹכֵחָה בְּשִׁבְטֵי יִשְׂרָאֵל הוֹדַעְתִּי נֶאֱמָנָה׃

will no longer place guards by the border to prevent the people from ascending to Jerusalem — and, indeed, the populace shall throng to serve Hashem in the Temple — it will be to no avail, for they will no longer find the Divine presence awaiting them there.

The Sages relate that a heretic once commented to Rabban Gamliel: [You are] a nation whose master performed *chalitzah* with him, as it is stated: בְּצֹאנָם וּבִבְקָרָם יֵלְכוּ לְבֵית ה׳ וְלֹא יִמְצָאוּ חָלַץ מֵהֶם. He said to him: Fool! Does it say חָלַץ לָהֶם — *he performed chalitzah to them?* It says חָלַץ מֵהֶם — *He received chalitzah from them.* If a *yevamah* performs *chalitzah* to the brothers, does it have any significance (*Yevamos* 102b)?[1]

7. בַּה׳ בָּגָדוּ כִּי־בָנִים זָרִים יָלָדוּ — *They broke faith with* HASHEM *for they begot alien children.* They violated the decree of the Almighty forbidding them to intermarry, and they thereby begot children from gentile women, whose offspring are themselves gentiles (*Rashi; Metzudos David*). Alternatively: They raised children who followed the ways of the idolatrous gentiles (*Radak*).

Abarbanel interprets this as referring specifically to the generation of Hezekiah, who, under his leadership, were righteous and true to the Almighty but nevertheless raised a generation of children who became alienated from serving Hashem.

R' Eliezer of Beaugency understands this phrase metaphorically: They strayed so far from the ways of Hashem that they became like a woman who betrays her husband and bears children from other men, and is thus unable to deny her wrongdoing.

עַתָּה יֹאכְלֵם חֹדֶשׁ אֶת־חֶלְקֵיהֶם — *Now the month shall devour them with their portions.* The enemy shall come in Av, the month which has long been designated for the suffering of the Jewish nation,[2] and he will conquer them and consume the produce of their fields (*Rashi; Radak; Abarbanel; Metzudos David*). Alternatively: He will come then and destroy the goodly portion of the Jewish people — i.e., the Temple (*Mahari Kara*).

According to *Malbim*, this verse depicts the destruction of the royal house of Jehu, whose descendant Zechariah ben Jeroboam was overthrown by Shallum ben Yavesh, who wiped out the entire royal family (see *II Kings* 15). Thus: *They begot alien children* — referring to Zechariah, the descendant of Jehu, who was alienated from the Almighty

1. If a man dies without children, his wife is a *yevamah*, who must either marry her husband's brother or else receive *chalitzah* from him — in which they undergo a specific ritual as described in the Torah (*Deuteronomy* 25:5ff). Until this is done, she is forbidden to any other man; once the brother has granted her *chalitzah*, she is permitted to everyone else but prohibited to him. Thus, the heretic sought to prove from this verse that the Almighty had rejected the Jewish people and severed his special relationship with them. To this Rabban Gamliel replied that the prophet states only that he received *chalitzah* — i.e., the process was performed by the Jewish nation. Just as a *yevamah* who rejects her *yavam* nevertheless remains bound to him as before, so, too, the Jewish nation. Although they rebelled against the Almighty, no act of severance was performed on His part and their unique bond remains intact (*Maharasha*, ad loc.).

2. *Radak* explains the verse to refer to the two months of Tamuz and Av.

[7] *They broke faith with HASHEM for they begot alien children, now the month shall devour them with their portions.* [8] *Sound a shofar in Gibeah, a trumpet in Ramah; shout in Beth-aven, "After you, Benjamin."* [9] *Ephraim shall be bewildered on the day of contention; among the tribes of Israel I made known [that which is] true.*

by his deeds. *Now the month shall devour them* — Shallum ben Yavesh, who will rule for a period of only one month, will devour them and wipe out the royal family in that short time.

8. תִּקְעוּ שׁוֹפָר בַּגִּבְעָה חֲצֹצְרָה בָּרָמָה הָרִיעוּ בֵּית אָוֶן אַחֲרֶיךָ בִּנְיָמִין — *Sound a shofar in Gibeah, a trumpet in Ramah; shout in Beth-aven, "After you, Benjamin."* Sound the shofar in Gibeah and Ramah to warn the people to watch out for the invading enemy and to hide themselves and their livestock from the destructive hordes. Shout out in the town of Beth-aven, "The invading forces are after you, Benjamin" (*Rashi; Radak; Metzudos David*).

Targum renders: Prophets, raise up your voices like the sound of the shofar and prophesy that a murdering nation is coming upon them because they crowned Shaul from Gibeah. Cry out like trumpets and say that kings are coming against them with their weapons for not heeding the statements of Samuel from Ramah. Give them tidings of the cry of warriors because they were false to My words and they turned back from My service, as they did not serve Me in the Temple which lies in the land of the tribe of Benjamin (see *Rashi*).

Others interpret all of this verse as a preface to the following one (*Ibn Ezra*). Thus: Sound the shofar in Gibeah and Ramah to announce the following proclamation: People of Benjamin, shout out [your rebuke] to the citizens of the tribe of Ephraim who live among you in the border-town of Beth-aven[1] and perhaps they will be moved to repent (*R' Eliezer of Beaugency*).

9-15. Although there was a time when the people of Judah were steadfast in their loyalty to Hashem and His commandments, and were thus a people apart from the decadent nation of Israel, they, too, plunged themselves into the spiritual abyss of idolatry and immorality. Thus, the prophet shifts the focus of his words back and forth from Ephraim to Judah and from Judah to Ephraim, rebuking them severely for their misdeeds and foretelling of the misfortune that awaits them.

9. אֶפְרַיִם לְשַׁמָּה תִהְיֶה בְּיוֹם תּוֹכֵחָה בְּשִׁבְטֵי יִשְׂרָאֵל הוֹדַעְתִּי נֶאֱמָנָה — *Ephraim shall be bewildered on the day of contention; among the tribes of Israel I made known [that which is] true.* When that day comes, in which I will present My quarrel to the people of Ephraim, they shall be "confused and bewildered" with nothing to answer. For I long made known to them — along with all of the tribes of Israel — the dictates of My true Torah, and they have willfully transgressed it (*Rashi*).

Others understand לְשַׁמָּה to mean *desolation* — Ephraim will be laid waste because they transgressed My Torah (*Metzudos*). The word תּוֹכֵחָה is also subject to other interpretations. *Targum* translates it as the day of the payment of retribution. *Mahari Kara* renders it to mean silence. *Radak* explains the structure of the verse in a different manner: *On the day of warning — among the tribes of Israel I made known the truth* — when all of the tribes were together I

1. He thus maintains that Beth-aven was within the boundaries of the tribe of Benjamin. *Abarbanel*, too, follows this view. *Radak*, however, contends that it was a town in the portion of Ephraim which bordered that of Benjamin.

י הָיוּ֙ שָׂרֵ֣י יְהוּדָ֔ה כְּמַסִּיגֵ֖י גְּב֑וּל עֲלֵיהֶ֕ם
יא אֶשְׁפּ֥וֹךְ כַּמַּ֖יִם עֶבְרָתִֽי׃ עָשׁ֥וּק אֶפְרַ֖יִם רְצ֣וּץ
יב מִשְׁפָּ֑ט כִּ֣י הוֹאִ֔יל הָלַ֖ךְ אַחֲרֵי־צָֽו׃ וַאֲנִ֥י
כָעָ֖שׁ לְאֶפְרָ֑יִם וְכָרָקָ֖ב לְבֵ֥ית יְהוּדָֽה׃
יג וַיַּ֨רְא אֶפְרַ֜יִם אֶת־חָלְי֗וֹ וִיהוּדָה֙ אֶת־מְזֹר֔וֹ

warned them of the truth, that if they would not heed my commandments they would be subject to severe punishment.

The Sages offer the following interpretation: Said R' Abahu in the name of R' Yose bar Chanina: On the day that the Holy One, Blessed is He, will contend with them in judgment, they will have no basis for argument, for among the tribes I made known that the judgment is true. You find that when the ten tribes were exiled, Judah and Benjamin were not, and the ten tribes were saying that because they are members of His palace He did not exile them; there is favoritism in the matter. [However] there is not, God forbid, any favoritism; rather, only their [Judah's] measure [of sin] was not yet filled. Once they sinned, they were exiled. Then the ten tribes were bewildered with no answer in their mouths, and they proclaimed: Behold God! Behold the Mighty One! Behold the Just One! For even to the members of His household He did not turn His face, to fulfill that which is stated: *Among the tribes of Israel I made known the truth* (*Rashi* from *Eichah Rabbah*).

In a novel approach, *Abarbanel* interprets these last two verses as recalling the event hundreds of years earlier in the days of the judges, when members of the tribe of Benjamin sexually assaulted a concubine in the town of Gibeah and thereby murdered her (see *Judges* chs. 19-21). At that time, the other tribes waged war against the tribe of Benjamin in retaliation for this terrible deed and for the refusal of the members of that tribe to avenge it. However, in the initial two days of battle, the united tribes suffered greater casualties than did Benjamin, and only afterward did they succeed in destroying the defending forces.

The prophet sees in that sequence of events a symbol of what was to transpire centuries later. He thus recounts the call which went out among the other tribes: *Sound the shofar in Gibeah, Ramah, and Beth-aven* — all towns within the province of Benjamin, to call together the united forces of the nation. *After you, Benjamin* — they are joining together to pursue you in response to the great offense which you have condoned by your refusal to punish it.

Nevertheless, on that day of castigation, in which the combined tribes came to punish the tribe of Benjamin, I made known the truth of what will occur in subsequent times. For because the people of the other tribes were more sinful than those of Benjamin, they had to undergo a measure of affliction in these battles which, at the outset, exceeded the casualties inflicted upon the Benjaminites. This heralded the future in store for the two nations, when the ten tribes would undergo greater retribution and a longer exile than the tribe[s] of [Judah and] Benjamin (cf. *Alshich*).

10. הָיוּ שָׂרֵי יְהוּדָה כְּמַסִּיגֵי גְּבוּל עֲלֵיהֶם אֶשְׁפּוֹךְ כַּמַּיִם עֶבְרָתִי — *The officers of Judah were like those who shift the boundaries; upon them I will pour out My wrath like water.* Despite the affliction I imposed upon the people of Ephraim, the leaders of Judah did not take heed (*Metzudos David*). Rather, they extended themselves into the spiritual terrain of the kingdom of Israel by following in their wicked ways — much as one extends the boundaries of his properties into those of his neighbor (*Rashi; Mahari Kara; Abarbanel*). Therefore, they, too, shall be included in the suffering that will be endured when I pour out My wrath.

Radak offers several other interpretations of this verse. At face value, it describes how the princes of Judah would extend their

10 *The officers of Judah were like those who shift
the boundaries; upon them I will pour out My
wrath like water.* 11 *Ephraim is plundered, shattered
by [his] judgment, for he has willingly followed
after their bidding.* 12 *And I am like a moth to
Ephraim, like a worm to the house of Judah.*
13 *And Ephraim saw his ailment and Judah his wound*

boundaries into the properties of their neighbors who were weaker than they. *Radak* cites his father, who notes that the verse describes them merely as *like those who shift the boundaries*, i.e., they ignored the cries of the victims of those who actually extended their boundaries and were thus considered partners in their oppression. *R' Saadiah Gaon* explains this metaphorically: They violated the boundaries of Hashem's commandments by transgressing them.

Malbim explains these three verses from a historical perspective. As stated earlier (see comm. to 1:1) at the time of the initial prophecies of Hosea, the kingdom of Judah was subjugated to Israel, and remained so until twenty-seven years into the reign of Jeroboam ben Joash. Similarly, Pekach ben Remaliahu (c. 3166-3187) king of Israel subjugated the kingdom of Judah in the latter portion of his reign. Thus, during these periods of time, the tribe of Benjamin, which bordered that of Ephraim, was subject to the latter's authority.

The prophet addresses himself to these circumstances and proclaims: Sound the shofar and trumpet in the towns of the tribe of Benjamin, and proclaim to the populace that they should follow after you, Benjamin, and not after the ruling nation of Ephraim. For the cities of Ephraim are destined to be devastated on the day of their rebuke, when the Almighty comes to castigate them for their misdeeds and exact retribution from them. Indeed, I have made known to the ten tribes of Israel — who have made themselves officers over Judah as well, and have thus violated the boundaries between themselves and the kingdom of the Davidic dynasty — that I shall soon pour out My wrath upon them and they will cease to exist as an independent nation.

11. עָשׁוּק אֶפְרַיִם רְצוּץ מִשְׁפָּט כִּי הוֹאִיל הָלַךְ אַחֲרֵי־צָו — *Ephraim is plundered, shattered by [his] judgment, for he has willingly followed after their bidding.* Why do the officers of Judah follow in the ways of Ephraim, when they see for themselves (*Metzudos David*) how the latter have been plundered by foreign nations and broken with suffering in retribution for following the bidding of the prophets of Baal (*Rashi; Mahari Kara*)? Alternatively: for they have followed the bidding of Jeroboam ben Navot — who established golden calves of idolatry on their frontier — not only because they were coerced into doing so but willingly, of their own volition (*Radak; Abarbanel; Metzudos David*).

Targum renders *for their judges turned to go after money* [acquired through] *falsehood*.

12. וַאֲנִי כָעָשׁ לְאֶפְרָיִם וְכָרָקָב לְבֵית יְהוּדָה — *And I am like a moth to Ephraim, like a worm to the house of Judah.* I am to Ephraim like a moth that devours clothing (*Mahari Kara*) and to the children of Judah like a worm that eats wood and grinds it up (*Rashi*), I, too, am bringing their retribution upon them little by little — beginning with the invasion of foreign forces and culminating with their total expulsion from the land (*Abarbanel; Alshich*).

Others render: I am like a moth, which devours from without, to Ephraim where I do not dwell. And I am like internal decay, which develops from within, to the children of Judah, among whom My Divine Presence resides (*Malbim*; cf. *R' Eliezer of Beaugency*).

13. וַיַּרְא אֶפְרַיִם אֶת־חָלְיוֹ וִיהוּדָה אֶת־מְזֹרוֹ — *And Ephraim saw his ailment and*

וַיֵּלֶךְ אֶפְרַיִם אֶל־אַשּׁוּר וַיִּשְׁלַח אֶל־מֶלֶךְ
יָרֵב וְהוּא לֹא יוּכַל לִרְפֹּא לָכֶם וְלֹא־יִגְהֶה
יד מִכֶּם מָזוֹר׃ כִּי אָנֹכִי כַשַּׁחַל לְאֶפְרַיִם וְכַכְּפִיר
לְבֵית יְהוּדָה אֲנִי אֲנִי אֶטְרֹף וְאֵלֵךְ אֶשָּׂא
טו וְאֵין מַצִּיל׃ אֵלֵךְ אָשׁוּבָה אֶל־מְקוֹמִי עַד
אֲשֶׁר־יֶאְשְׁמוּ וּבִקְשׁוּ פָנָי בַּצַּר לָהֶם יְשַׁחֲרֻנְנִי׃

Judah his wound.[1] When Ephraim and Judah saw how they were constantly subject to invasion and plundering by enemy forces, they turned to the king of Assyria for protection rather than turning to Me for salvation (*Radak; Abarbanel*).

One who does not recognize his illness or its source, and therefore does not take the necessary steps to eradicate it, is not completely blameworthy for his subsequent downfall. However, if he recognizes the nature of his misfortune as well as the cause which brought it about, and nonetheless refrains from taking corrective measures, he is fully responsible for the results of his actions. Thus, the Jewish people are highly culpable for their misdeeds, for Ephraim recognized the nature and cause of his malady as did Judah the essence of his lesser wound. Both are aware that the reason for their misfortune is their abandonment of My ways and their embrace of idolatry. Nevertheless, they turned to Assyria for aid rather than rectifying their deeds, and their behavior therefore warrants severe punitive measures (*Alshich*; cf. *Malbim*).

וַיֵּלֶךְ אֶפְרַיִם אֶל־אַשּׁוּר וַיִּשְׁלַח אֶל־מֶלֶךְ יָרֵב — *And Ephraim went to Assyria and sent to the king of Yarev*. Hosea ben Elah, king of Israel, submitted himself to the authority of Assyria, but eventually rebelled (*Rashi; Abarbanel; Metzudos David;* see *II Kings* 17:4). Ahaz, king of Judah, paid tribute to Tiglath-Pilnesser, king of Assyria,[2] to invoke his aid against Retzin, king of Aram, and Pekach ben Remaliahu, king of Israel (ibid.).

Others interpret *Ephraim went to Assyria* to refer to Menachem ben Gadi who sent one thousand talents of silver to Pul, king of Assyria, to strengthen his hand against the insurrection which took place under his rule[3] (*Mahari Kara; Radak; Malbim*).

וְהוּא לֹא יוּכַל לִרְפֹּא לָכֶם וְלֹא־יִגְהֶה מִכֶּם מָזוֹר — *But he will not be able to cure you nor to heal your wound*. The king of Assyria shall be of no help in rescuing Israel, nor will he be of any assistance in ridding Judah of its invaders (*Mahari Kara; Malbim*).

Rashi interprets both phrases as referring to the plight of Judah: He will not be

1. *Rashi* translates מָזוֹר to mean illness; at the end of this verse it is used to mean a cure. Thus, it is one of a number of words which are used to describe two opposite phenomena. Others contend that the primary meaning of מָזוֹר is a medicine which heals. It is also used to refer to a wound, which is subject to treatment by such medicine (*Ibn Ezra; Radak; Abarbanel; Malbim; Metzudos David*).

2. *Rashi* interprets Yarev as being another name for Assyria. According to *Radak*, it was the name of a city within Assyria. *Targum* renders it as battle — he sent to Tiglath-Pilnesser to wage war against Aram and Israel. Alternatively, it refers to Sennacherib, who waged war against the entire world (*Abarbanel*). [See also 10:6 comm. ibid.]

3. The term חוֹלִי applies to an internal illness which develops within in the body, whereas מָזוֹר refers to a wound inflicted externally. Thus, the insurrection against Menachem ben Gadi which took place within his nation is referred to as מָזוֹר, and the invasion of Judah from without is called a חוֹלִי (*Malbim*).

and Ephraim went to Assyria and sent to the king of
Yarev, but he will not be able to cure you nor to heal
your wound. 14 *For I am like a lion to Ephraim and like*
a lion's whelp to the house of Judah. I, I will mangle,
and I will go; I will carry off and no one will rescue. 15 *I*
will go and return to My place until they will
acknowledge their guilt and seek My face; in their
hardship they will seek Me.

able to cure you of the many troops of Philistines and Arabs which have risen against you (see *II Chronicles* 28:21).

14. כִּי אָנֹכִי כַשַּׁחַל לְאֶפְרַיִם וְכַכְּפִיר לְבֵית יְהוּדָה — *For I am like a lion to Ephraim and like a lion's whelp*[1] to the house of Judah. How could the king of Assyria possibly be of any assistance to you, when it is not the natural might of foreign armies that you face but My Divine Power, which I have unleashed against you like a raging lion (*Radak; Malbim*)?

Others see this as following a chronological sequence: Now that you have recognized your plight and have nevertheless refused to mend your ways and repent, I will no longer punish you piecemeal like a moth or a worm causing decay, but I will rather befall you like a raging lion, attacking mercilessly and devouring totally (*Abarbanel; Alshich*).

אֲנִי אֲנִי אֶטְרֹף וְאֵלֵךְ אֶשָּׂא וְאֵין מַצִּיל — *I, I will mangle, and I will go; I will carry off and no one will rescue.* I will tear apart Ephraim and mangle Judah, like a lion who destroys its prey and carries it off, with no one to rescue the victim from its clutches (*Mahari Kara*). *Alshich* interprets: I will mangle Judah and then go away, without having wreaked total destruction upon them, but Israel I shall carry off to distant lands, for there is no Temple in their midst to provide the merit to mitigate their punishment.

15. אֵלֵךְ אָשׁוּבָה אֶל־מְקוֹמִי עַד אֲשֶׁר־יֶאְשְׁמוּ וּבִקְשׁוּ פָנָי בַּצַּר לָהֶם יְשַׁחֲרֻנְנִי — *I will go and return to My place until they will acknowledge their guilt and seek My face; in their hardship they will seek Me.* I will withdraw My Divine Presence from their midst and return it to its place in the heavens until the time will come when they will recognize and admit to their guilt[2] and seek My countenance and My pardon (*Rashi; Radak; Metzudos David*). Do not think that this will never occur, for eventually they will be moved by the wretchedness of their plight to seek Me[3] (*Abarbanel*).

Alternatively: My presence will be withdrawn until the advent of one of two events. Either they will recognize their guilt on their own and will seek Me in repentance, or else they will encounter misfortune upon misfortune until they are forced by their plight to return to Me (*Alshich; Malbim,* cf. *Sanhedrin* 96b).

1. There are various views concerning the difference between the words שַׁחַל and כְּפִיר. *Targum* translates שַׁחַל as a lion and כְּפִיר as a בַּר אוּרְיָן — a lion's whelp. According to *Mahari Kara,* שַׁחַל is a young lion and כְּפִיר an adult. *Malbim* maintains the exact opposite: שַׁחַל is an adult lion and כְּפִיר a younger one. According to *Alshich*, a שַׁחַל is a larger lion and a כְּפִיר a smaller one. Because the kingdom of Ephraim experienced a greater degree of destruction, the Almighty's wrath upon it is depicted as a larger, and thus more dangerous, beast than that which devoured Judah.

2. *Ibn Ezra* offers an alternative interpretation of יֶאְשְׁמוּ: *until they will be rendered desolate.*

3. *Ibn Ezra* renders: *until they will seek Me like the dawn.*

א לְכוּ וְנָשׁוּבָה אֶל־יהוה כִּי הוּא טָרָף
ב וְיִרְפָּאֵנוּ יַךְ וְיַחְבְּשֵׁנוּ: יְחַיֵּנוּ מִיֹּמָיִם בַּיּוֹם
ג הַשְּׁלִישִׁי יְקִמֵנוּ וְנִחְיֶה לְפָנָיו: וְנֵדְעָה
נִרְדְּפָה לָדַעַת אֶת־יהוה כְּשַׁחַר נָכוֹן מֹצָאוֹ

VI

This chapter is a continuation of the previous one. Having noted in the final verse that the Children of Israel will ultimately be moved to return full-heartedly to Hashem, the prophet now goes on to depict the spirit of repentance which will prevail at that time and the words with which it will be expressed by the people (*Targum; Rashi; Mahari Kara; Malbim; Metzudos David*). [And having described their tendency to turn for aid to foreign powers rather than to the Almighty, he now describes how they will finally recognize that only through Hashem can they achieve salvation.]

Abarbanel suggests that these may be the words of the prophet to the populace rather than those uttered among the people themselves. Having declared to the nation that their only recourse to salvation is through returning to the ways of the Torah, Hosea goes on to exhort them to repent.

Radak interprets this specifically as a depiction of the return to the ways of the Almighty that occurred in the days of Josiah, king of Judah. According to *Alshich*, this is not a prediction of future events at all, but rather a description of the spirit of repentance which took hold among the people in reaction to the admonitions of the previous chapter.

1. לְכוּ וְנָשׁוּבָה אֶל־ה׳ כִּי הוּא טָרָף וְיִרְפָּאֵנוּ יַךְ וְיַחְבְּשֵׁנוּ — *Come, let us return to* HASHEM *for He has mangled and He shall heal us; He has smitten and He shall bandage us.* Let us return once more to the service of the Almighty in order to seek salvation. Since He is the One Who rendered us asunder, it is to Him that we must turn for a cure, for only He knows the means to heal us. And as it is He Who smote us, He is the One Who will know how to bandage our wounds (*Mahari Kara*).

Malbim interprets רְפוּאָה to mean the curing of internal ailments and חֲבִישָׁה the bandaging of bodily wounds. Thus, the people will declare: All of our misfortune is not due to natural causes but rather to Divine intervention. Therefore, our internal diseases can be cured only by Him, and our external wounds, as well, require His care.

2. יְחַיֵּנוּ מִיֹּמָיִם בַּיּוֹם הַשְּׁלִישִׁי יְקִמֵנוּ וְנִחְיֶה לְפָנָיו — *He will heal us after two days; on the third day He will raise us up and we will live before Him.* Rather than seeking relief and salvation from the king of Assyria, we must turn to the Almighty for help. For whereas Assyria is powerless to assist us in any way, the Almighty will cure us quickly and effectively. Over two days our cure will take effect and by the third we will be back on our feet — in contrast to the natural flow of events, in which the third day of illness is the most severe (*Mahari Kara; Ibn Ezra; R' Eliezer of Beaugency;* cf. *Radak*).

Others render: *He will heal us from the two days:* He will revive and strengthen us from the two waves of affliction which passed over us — i.e., for the destruction of the two Temples — and He will raise us up forever with the erection of the third (*Rashi; Metzudos David;* cf. *Radak; Malbim*).

3. וְנֵדְעָה נִרְדְּפָה לָדַעַת אֶת־ה׳ — *And let us know, let us strive to know* HASHEM. Let us join in unison and set our minds to pursue the knowledge of Hashem (*Ibn Ezra; Radak*). Although it is impossible for the human mind to fully fathom the

[1] *Come, let us return to* HASHEM *for He has mangled
and He shall heal us; He has smitten and He
shall bandage us.* [2] *He will heal us after two days; on
the third day He will raise us up and we will live
before Him.* [3] *And let us know, let us strive to
know* HASHEM *like the dawn whose emergence is true,*

nature and greatness of the Almighty, we can nevertheless pursue that knowledge and understanding to the best of our ability and achieve whatever levels are within our reach (*Abarbanel*).

Alshich cites the words of the Sages (*Sotah* 3a) that a person sins only if a spirit of foolishness enters within him. Thus, the people implore the Almighty: Help us to be men of intellect, unaffected nor distracted by that spirit of foolishness, and we will thereby be certain to continuously pursue the knowledge of Hashem.

Another approach to this phrase is that it expresses the determination of those who seek to develop a deep, heartfelt bond with the Almighty, but do not experience the emotions which such a bond requires. However, by performing the external manifestations of such devotion they slowly effect the emotions within their heart, until their goal of true attachment to God is realized (*Mesillas Yesharim* ch. 7).

The Sages translate נִרְדְּפָה literally to mean chase — *let us pursue the knowledge of* HASHEM. They derive from here that it is forbidden to leave hurriedly from a synagogue, but to run to the synagogue is highly commendable (*Berachos* 6b).

לָדַעַת אֶת־ה׳ — *To know* HASHEM. To know the fear of Hashem (*Targum*) and to know His ways of justice and righteousness and follow them (*Radak*). *Mahari Kara* explains: To seek Hashem through repentance and supplication. *Alshich* interprets: To know Hashem through delving into the secrets of His Holy Torah (see *Ibn Ezra* cited below).[1]

כְּשַׁחַר נָכוֹן מֹצָאוֹ — *Like the dawn whose emergence is true.* We will pursue that knowledge truly and wholeheartedly, like the dawn whose emergence is true and sure (*Rashi*; cf. *Mahari Kara*).

Others interpret: and that knowledge will eventually become clear to us like the light of dawn when it is unimpeded by clouds and fog (*Radak*, citing his father; *Malbim*). Alternatively: Just as the emerging dawn is a sure sign of the impending light of day, so will our pursuit of the knowledge of Hashem be a guarantee of our ultimate success in that endeavor (*Abarbanel; Metzudos David*).

1. The various approaches to this verse reflect a fundamental dispute among Torah scholars concerning the pursuit of philosophical recognition and understanding of God. *R' Saadiah Gaon* (*Emunos VeDeos* sec. 3), *Rambam* (*Hil. Yesodei Torah* ch. 2; *Moreh Nevuchim* 3:51), and *Chovos HaLevavos* (sec. 1) are among the most notable proponents of this pursuit, maintaining that therein lies the true fulfillment of the *mitzvah* of *emunah*, faith in God. This is the approach followed by *Ibn Ezra* in his interpretation of this verse.

Others dispute this notion, contending that the dangers inherent in such a pursuit outweigh its merits. To their mind, the exhortation to know Hashem refers to the achievement of Godliness — with differing views as to the specific aspect of His service being stressed — as reflected by the various interpretations cited above.

It is important to note that even according to the former view, one is permitted to undertake this pursuit only if he has first filled his mind with the study of Mishnah and Gemara (*Rambam, Hil. Yesodei HaTorah* 2:13; *Rama, Yoreh Deah* 246:5).

For further elaboration upon this issue, see the introduction to *Shaar HaYichud* of *Chovos HaLevovos* by the author of the *Lev Tov* commentary to that work.

ד וְיָבוֹא כַגֶּשֶׁם לָנוּ כְּמַלְקוֹשׁ יוֹרֶה אָרֶץ׃ מָה
אֶעֱשֶׂה־לְּךָ אֶפְרַיִם מָה אֶעֱשֶׂה־לְּךָ יְהוּדָה
ה וְחַסְדְּכֶם כַּעֲנַן־בֹּקֶר וְכַטַּל מַשְׁכִּים הֹלֵךְ׃ עַל־כֵּן
חָצַבְתִּי בַּנְּבִיאִים הֲרַגְתִּים בְּאִמְרֵי־פִי וּמִשְׁפָּטֶיךָ
ו אוֹר יֵצֵא׃ כִּי חֶסֶד חָפַצְתִּי וְלֹא־זָבַח וְדַעַת

וְיָבוֹא כַגֶּשֶׁם לָנוּ כְּמַלְקוֹשׁ יוֹרֶה אָרֶץ — *And He will come to us like the rain, like the late rain that satiates the earth.* He will bestow His blessing upon us in abundance like the rain that saturates the earth with water (*Targum; Abarbanel*) — specifically, like the late rain, which falls at the end of the growing season and brings about the actual growth of the fruits of the earth (*R' Eliezer of Beaugency*). Thus, He will heal us at that time of all our wounds and maladies (*Mahari Kara*) and He will revive those who are so broken in spirit that they are comparable to one who is already dead (*Radak*).

Ibn Ezra interprets the verse in the following manner: Let us strive to know the Almighty, for that is the basis of all wisdom and for this alone was man created. In the beginning, we will recognize Hashem from His handiwork in creation, and little by little we will ascend the ladder of wisdom to reach lofty levels of knowledge of God. Thus, we will be like the emerging dawn, that brightens slowly through the early morning until achieving full daylight. When we will thus be immersed in that pursuit, the Almighty Himself will assist us in our endeavor and bestow upon us true knowledge and understanding, which He will pour down upon us as He does the rains.

4. Having depicted the total repentance of the Jewish nation which will take place when they finally decide to return to the ways of Hashem, the prophet now returns to his castigation of them for their present failure to do so, and presents the Almighty's declaration of the limits to His mercy and patience with them under such conditions (*Abarbanel*). According to *Radak*, these verses follow in the wake of the previous ones. Although the nation abandoned to a great degree their sinful ways, their repentance was not long-lasting. Thus, the edict of retribution hanging over them could not be repealed. In the approach to this chapter suggested by *Abarbanel*, that it comprises the words of the prophet who cajoles the people to mend their ways, he now goes on to depict the fate in store for them if they do not do so (*Abarbanel*).

מָה אֶעֱשֶׂה־לְּךָ אֶפְרַיִם מָה אֶעֱשֶׂה־לְּךָ יְהוּדָה וְחַסְדְּכֶם כַּעֲנַן־בֹּקֶר וְכַטַּל מַשְׁכִּים הֹלֵךְ — *What can I do for you, Ephraim? What can I do for you, Judah? When your benevolence is like the morning cloud and like the dew that departs early.* Children of Israel, how can I possibly forgive your sins (*Mahari Kara*) and heal your wounds (*Radak*)? With what can I appease the Attribute of Justice that is extended over you, so that your judgment should turn out in your favor (*Targum Rashi*)? For all of your goodness and righteousness[1] is of no substance (*Rashi*), like the morning cloud that produces no rain (*Malbim; Metzudos David*),[2] and your repentance is of short duration, like the morning dew that evaporates with

1. The word חֶסֶד, which is translated literally to mean kindness or benevolence, is actually applicable to both the realm of human interaction and that of man's relationship with God. For whatever a person does beyond the measure required of him flows from the same source within him as his benevolence to others — the broadness of character which motivates him to give of himself beyond that which is demanded (*Malbim*).

2. Others interpret the entire second half of the verse to be describing the transience of their

and He will come to us like the rain, like the late rain
that satiates the earth. 4 *What can I do for you,*
Ephraim? What can I do for you, Judah? When your
benevolence is like the morning cloud and like the dew
that departs early. 5 *Therefore I have hewn through*
the prophets, I have slain them with the words of
My mouth, and your judgment shall emerge in light.
6 *For I desire benevolence, not sacrifices, and knowledge*

the rising sun. Although Hezekiah followed loyally in the ways of Hashem, Menasseh his successor was wicked. Whereas Josiah returned to the Almighty with all his heart, his sons rebelled against his righteousness (*Abarbanel*).

5. עַל־כֵּן חָצַבְתִּי בַּנְּבִיאִים הֲרַגְתִּים בְּאִמְרֵי־פִי וּמִשְׁפָּטֶיךָ אוֹר יֵצֵא — *Therefore I have hewn through the prophets, I have slain them with the words of My mouth, and your judgment shall emerge in light.* I have therefore hewn out My words for you through My prophets in order to induce you to repent. However, it has been to no avail, and My words have caused instead the death of My prophets, such as Zechariah and Uriah, who were murdered for transmitting My message. Thus, My judgment upon you will emerge in the light of truth and righteousness, for it shall be undeniably just (see below).

עַל־כֵּן — *Therefore.* This follows the translation of *Radak, Abarbanel,* and *Metzudos* — as well as *R' Eliezer of Beaugency* who interprets it somewhat differently. Others render it: *because — because I have hewn out my words to you through My prophets and they have not been heeded, the punishment stated below shall befall you* (*Rashi; Mahari Kara;* cf. *Targum*).

חָצַבְתִּי בַּנְּבִיאִים הֲרַגְתִּים בְּאִמְרֵי־פִי — *I have hewn through the prophets, I have slain them with the words of My mouth.* The explanation given above for the first of these phrases follows *Rashi, Abarbanel,* and *Metzudos*; that of the latter phrase is in accordance with the view of *Radak's* father, *Abarbanel,* and *Metzudos*. *Radak* himself interprets, as does *R' Eliezer of Beaugency*: I have coerced the prophets to arise daily and exhort you to return to the proper path, and have thus worn them out almost to the point of death.

Others understand the phrase *I have slain them* to refer to the populace rather than to the prophets: Because they have not heeded My warning, I have slain them in retribution (*Targum; Rashi; Mahari Kara*).

וּמִשְׁפָּטֶיךָ אוֹר יֵצֵא — *And your judgment shall emerge in light.* This follows *Ibn Ezra, Mahari Kara,* and *Radak*. Others see this as a rhetorical question: Under such conditions, can your judgment possibly come to light in your favor (*Rashi; Abarbanel; Metzudos*)?

Ibn Ezra interprets this verse as referring to the false prophets among the Jewish nation. I have hewn out among these prophets by killing some of them for encouraging the people to continue their wicked acts, and I have slain them for the false words they have uttered with their mouths.

6. כִּי חֶסֶד חָפַצְתִּי וְלֹא־זָבַח וְדַעַת אֱלֹהִים מֵעֹלוֹת — *For I desire benevolence, not sacrifices, and knowledge of God over burnt offerings.* Do not think that the

righteousness: It is like the morning cloud and the early dew, neither of which last for very long (*Ibn Ezra; Mahari Kara; Radak*).

ז אֱלֹהִים מֵעֹלוֹת׃ וְהֵמָּה כְּאָדָם עָבְרוּ בְרִית
ח שָׁם בָּגְדוּ בִי׃ גִּלְעָד קִרְיַת פֹּעֲלֵי אָוֶן
ט עֲקֻבָּה מִדָּם׃ וּכְחַכֵּי אִישׁ גְּדוּדִים חֶבֶר
כֹּהֲנִים דֶּרֶךְ יְרַצְּחוּ־שֶׁכְמָה כִּי זִמָּה עָשׂוּ׃

sacrifices you offer in the Temple will suffice to ward off My retribution for your deeds. For I seek from you benevolence in your dealings with each other, as well as knowledge of Me and fidelity to My statutes, not merely the ritual acts of bringing sacrifices (*Abarbanel*).[1] Indeed, the whole point of bringing sacrifices is that they inspire a person to rededicate himself to serving Me devoutly (*Malbim*).

Radak, following his approach to these verses, interprets: Although the people returned to the service of Hashem in the days of Hosea ben Elah, who removed the guards that restrained the populace from ascending to Jerusalem, and Josiah king of Judah, who abolished the private altars upon which the people offered sacrifices illicitly, they remained lacking in their benevolence and knowledge of God. For this the prophet takes them to task.

The Sages comment: Said the Holy One, Blessed is He: The kindness you perform with one another is more dear to Me than all of the burnt offerings offered to Me by King Solomon . . . R' Yochanan ben Zakai was going to Jerusalem and R' Yehoshua was following him. He saw the Temple in its destruction and said: Woe is to us for the House which was destroyed, the place in which our sins were forgiven. [R' Yochanan] said to him: My son, do not despair. For we have for ourselves a different source of atonement equal to it. What is this? This is benevolence (*Yalkut*).

Malbim interprets these last two verses as expressing one joint idea, as if they read: *Therefore I have hewn out my prophets, whom I have slain with the words of My mouth, that I desire benevolence, and not sacrifices, and knowledge of God over burnt offerings.* Because, as stated above, your benevolence is like the morning cloud etc., I have sent My prophets to declare to you that I desire benevolence above sacrifices, and burnt offerings must be accompanied by knowledge of God. For bearing this message the prophets were murdered by the people — and it is thus as if I Myself have slain them with the words of My mouth which I imparted through them. However, their work has not been in vain, for their supreme sacrifice on behalf of this message has caused it to be inscribed in the collective memory of the nation, as if it had been carved out upon those very bodies which were forfeited in conveying it. *And your judgment shall emerge in light* is a parenthetical phrase: If your sword has devoured your prophets, how can your judgment possibly come out in your favor?

7. It is not only the absence of benevolence and knowledge of God that has aroused My anger. You have also violated the covenant that bound you to Me as My nation, and you have become steeped in corruption and robbery, murder and adultery, as you relentlessly pursue the decadent ways you have chosen for yourselves.

וְהֵמָּה כְּאָדָם עָבְרוּ בְרִית שָׁם בָּגְדוּ בִי — *But they, like Adam, transgressed the covenant; there they broke faith with Me.* Just like Adam, who was privileged to be placed in the Garden of Eden yet transgressed the word of the Almighty by eating from the Tree of Knowledge, so, too, have they betrayed My trust by violating My covenant in the very land that I gave to them as a heritage (*Rashi; Abarbanel; Metzudos David* from *Bereishis Rabbah* 19:9; cf. *Targum*).

Others translate the word אָדָם to mean *man*, rather than Adam: They take My covenant lightly and violate it, as one violates a treaty drawn up with another man. Thus, there in the very land where

1. This follows the translation of *Targum* as well. *Radak* interprets *knowledge of God* to refer to the following of His ways, which is a further reference to human interaction. (See also above, comm. to v. 3 and fn. 1 to v. 4.)

of God over burnt offerings. 7 *But they, like Adam,*
transgressed the covenant; there they broke faith
with Me. 8 *Gilead is a city of evildoers, filled with*
those who waylay for blood. 9 *And like gangs*
await a man, a band of Kohanim murders on
the road with one will, for they devised a plot.

I have bestowed upon them so much blessing, they have broken faith with Me (*Radak*). Alternatively: They deal with Me as if I were a mere man, and thus do not hesitate to violate My covenant (*R' Eliezer of Beaugency*).

8. גִּלְעָד קִרְיַת פֹּעֲלֵי אָוֶן עֲקֻבָּה מִדָּם — *Gilead is a city of evildoers, filled with those who waylay for blood.* This follows the translation of most commentators. *Radak* cites *Yerushalmi* (*Avodah Zarah* 5:10) as rendering עֲקֻבָּה מִדָּם to mean *sullied with blood.*

The Sages derive from this verse that the city of Gilead was noted for a disproportionally large number of murderers. For this reason, the smaller region of the Land of Israel east of the Jordan River — where Gilead is located — contained the same number of cities of refuge for those who kill inadvertently as did the larger area on the other side (*Makkos* 9b).

According to *Abarbanel*, these last two verses form two parts of a total picture: The people of the kingdom of Judah, in whose midst was the Temple, sought to fulfill their requirements by offering sacrifices, without pursuing kindness and knowledge of God. The northern kingdom of Israel is castigated for tolerating the presence of murderers in its midst.

9. וּכְחַכֵּי אִישׁ גְּדוּדִים חֶבֶר כֹּהֲנִים דֶּרֶךְ יְרַצְּחוּ־שֶׁכְמָה כִּי זִמָּה עָשׂוּ — *And like gangs await a man, a band of Kohanim murders on the road with one will, for they devised a plot.* Just as gangs of bandits lie in ambush along the roads, waiting to waylay passers-by, so do the *Kohanim*[1] gather in groups with the unanimous intent[2] to kill anyone who will resist their efforts to rob them (*Radak; Metzudos David; R' Eliezer of Beaugency;* cf. *Abarbanel*).

R' Saadiah Gaon (cited by *Radak*) translates חַכֵּי to mean fishhooks and גְּדוּדִים to refer to riverbanks: As fishermen stand by the riverbanks and cast their hooks [into the water to catch the fish], so, too, etc. *Mahari Kara* interprets: As the fishermen assemble in groups to catch the fish with their hooks, so do the Jewish people join together in gangs. And like a group of *Kohanim* that gathers to receive their tithes, the people collect in bands and, in this manner, murder those who pass along the road.

Rashi renders: *When they have a group of people gathered together, it is a band of Kohanim who are assembled in order to commit murder.*[3]

כִּי זִמָּה עָשׂוּ — *For they devised a plot.* This is the plot they devised together before

1. *Ibn Ezra* interprets *Kohanim* to refer to the false prophets among the people. *Radak* understands it to mean the priests of the private altars [assumedly those of idolatry]. He cites his father as explaining it to mean princes and men of stature. [However, the silence of the remainder of the commentators on this issue would seem to indicate that they consider *Kohanim* to be meant literally: The decadence reached so low a level that even the *Kohanim* were involved in such horrible acts.]

2. *Abarbanel* suggests that the word שֶׁכְמָה refers to the city of Shechem — *they murdered people on the road to Shechem.* This follows the view of the Sages (*Maakos* 10a), who derive from this verse that Shechem, too, was a city steeped in the blood of murder (v. 8).

3. *Rashi* cites another interpretation from R' Meir Shaliach Tzibbur, that the prophet compares these groups of *Kohanim* to bands of fishermen who gather fish upon their fishhooks. According to his rendition, the word גְּדוּדִים is joined with the words that follow: *Like the*

ו/י־יא י בְּבֵית֙ יִשְׂרָאֵ֔ל רָאִ֖יתִי שערוריה שָׁ֚ם זְנ֣וּת
°שַׁעֲרוּרִיָּה ק׳ יא לְאֶפְרַ֔יִם נִטְמָ֖א יִשְׂרָאֵֽל׃ גַּם־יְהוּדָ֕ה שָׁ֥ת קָצִ֛יר
ז/א א לָ֑ךְ בְּשׁוּבִ֖י שְׁב֥וּת עַמִּֽי׃ כְּרָפְאִ֣י
לְיִשְׂרָאֵ֗ל וְנִגְלָ֞ה עֲוֺ֤ן אֶפְרַ֙יִם֙ וְרָע֣וֹת שֹׁמְר֔וֹן
כִּ֥י פָעֲל֖וּ שָׁ֑קֶר וְגַנָּ֣ב יָב֔וֹא פָּשַׁ֥ט גְּד֖וּד בַּחֽוּץ׃

they assembled to travel in one group (*Rashi*; cf. *Mahari Kara*).

Radak translates זִמָּה to mean abomination: In addition to these sordid deeds, they have performed all sorts of abominable acts. Others see this as qualifying the previous statement. They have not actually murdered with their own hands, but have rather indulged in such heinous acts so as to bring down retribution upon the nation, even including death (*Abarbanel; Metzudos David*).

10. בְּבֵית יִשְׂרָאֵל רָאִיתִי שַׁעֲרוּרִיָּה שָׁם זְנוּת לְאֶפְרַיִם נִטְמָא יִשְׂרָאֵל — *In the house of Israel I have seen an abomination; there [is found] the adultery of Ephraim; Israel has been defiled.* Within the nation of Israel, in the towns of Dan and Beth-el, I have seen the golden calves that they established as idols, which are a great abomination[1] in their midst. These idols are primarily the adultery of Ephraim; Jeroboam ben Nebot, from that tribe, established them in an act of infidelity to Me. However, the remainder of the nation of Israel has defiled itself as well with their worship of those calves (*Ibn Ezra; Radak; Metzudos David*).

R' Eliezer of Beaugency renders: *I have seen something baffling* — normally an individual tends to follow the direction of the masses but in this case the entire nation emulated the misdeeds of one individual and thereby strayed from their fidelity to Me.

Targum interprets שַׁעֲרוּרִיָּה to mean deviation — they have deviated from their [proper] path (*Rashi*).

11. גַּם יְהוּדָה שָׁת קָצִיר לָךְ בְּשׁוּבִי שְׁבוּת עַמִּי — *Judah, too, has planted a branch for you when I [sought to] revoke*[2] *the captivity of My nation.* Not only have you yourselves sinned, citizens of Israel, but you have also served as a poor example for your brothers in Judah. For they have followed in your evil ways and have thus planted an offshoot from the body of your decadence. And they did so at a time when I sought to deal with you mercifully and return you from your captivity in response to your cry, *"Let us return to Hashem."* Now, however, I cannot do so, for the wrath which has been aroused can no longer be restrained (*Ibn Ezra; Metzudos David*; cf. *Radak*).

Alternatively: *they set a branch to you* — they extended to you their roots by arranging marriages between the two royal families, thus defiling the sanctity of the House of David with the decadence of your misdeeds (*R' Eliezer of Beaugency*).

Rashi renders: *Judah, too, He has set a harvest for you, when I return the deviance of My nation* — since you, too, have indulged in sin, He who designates all things has designated a time for your retribution, in which I will castigate you in order to impel you to return from your

gatherings of fish by the fishermen upon their hooks, so are the gatherings of gangs. Bands of Kohanim, who gather together to travel on the road, murder there with one will. [However, in citing this view, *Rashi* seems to translate the word חַכֵּי in various ways, and it is thus difficult to clarify the precise translation intended.]

1. *Mahari Kara* and *Abarbanel* render: *Something bitter and harsh.*

2. Literally, בְּשׁוּבִי means *when I returned.* However, in this verse, it is used as a transitive verb, with the *captivity of My nation* as its object, and has therefore been translated *I sought to revoke.*

6/10-11 [10] *In the house of Israel I have seen an abomination; there [is found] the adultery of Ephraim; Israel has been defiled.* [11] *Judah, too, has planted a branch for you when I [sought to] revoke the captivity of My nation.*

7/1 [1] *When I would heal Israel, the iniquity of Ephraim is revealed along with the evils of Samaria, for they have wrought falsehood, and a thief comes; a gang extends itself outside.*

deviance (cf. *Mahari Kara*).[1]

Radak sees this verse as being directed to the people of Judah. It refers to the incident when Jeroboam ben Joash king of Israel recaptured Damascus and Hamath from Aram (see *II Kings* 14:28) and returned them to Judah. Thus: *You too, Judah* [benefited from My kindness], *for Jeroboam planted a branch for you* — i.e., by returning those regions to you, *when I returned the captives of My nation* — through the conquests of Jeroboam. Nevertheless, neither you nor Israel has shown any inclination toward repentance in recognition of this kindness (see also *Abarbanel*).

VII

1. כְּרָפְאִי לְיִשְׂרָאֵל וְנִגְלָה עֲוֹן אֶפְרַיִם וְרָעוֹת שֹׁמְרוֹן כִּי פָעֲלוּ שָׁקֶר וְגַנָּב יָבוֹא פָּשַׁט גְּדוּד בַּחוּץ — *When I would heal Israel, the iniquity of Ephraim is revealed along with the evils of Samaria, for they have wrought falsehood, and a thief comes; a gang extends itself outside.* In reaction to the call of the populace (6:1): *for He has mangled and He shall heal us,* the Almighty proclaims[2] (*Ibn Ezra*): Whenever I seek to save the Jewish people and heal them of their wounds, their iniquities stand revealed before Me and prevent Me from doing so. For they are constantly guilty of engaging in falsehood and committing acts of robbery (*Rashi; Metzudos David;* cf. *Ibn Ezra*).

Others interpret this as continuing the previous chapter: *When I seek to heal Israel their sins become revealed* — when I tried to help them by returning to them their previous boundaries through conquests of Jeroboam ben Joash, they began to indulge in sins even more openly than before. Ephraim strayed from My faith and the inhabitants of Samaria, the capital city of the kingdom of Israel, became steeped in their oppression of one another (*Radak* to 6:11; *Malbim*).

Alternatively, the revelation of the sin of Ephraim etc. is part of the healing process: When I come to cure the nation of Israel I do so like an expert physician, who opens up the wound in order to reveal the infection within and remove it, rather than merely covering it over with bandages. Thus, those iniquities which they have hitherto managed to keep hidden — thereby allowing them to profess their righteousness in public — shall soon be brought out into the open for all to see, in order to ultimately bring about their repentance and subsequent salvation (*R' Eliezer of Beaugency; Abarbanel*).

וְגַנָּב יָבוֹא פָּשַׁט גְּדוּד בַּחוּץ — *And a thief comes; a gang extends itself outside.* By

1. As in many places in Scripture, the prophet changes from the third person to the first within the same verse in referring to Hashem.

2. Alternatively, the speaker in this verse is Hosea himself: When I sought to heal Israel by pleading with the Almighty that He have mercy upon them, my efforts were impeded by the sins of Ephraim and Samaria (*Alshich,* see ibid.).

ב וּבַל־יֹאמְרוּ לִלְבָבָם כָּל־רָעָתָם זָכָרְתִּי עַתָּה
ג סְבָבוּם מַעַלְלֵיהֶם נֶגֶד פָּנַי הָיוּ׃ בְּרָעָתָם יְשַׂמְּחוּ־
ד מֶלֶךְ וּבְכַחֲשֵׁיהֶם שָׂרִים׃ כֻּלָּם מְנָאֲפִים כְּמוֹ תַנּוּר
בֹּעֵרָה מֵאֹפֶה יִשְׁבּוֹת מֵעִיר מִלּוּשׁ בָּצֵק עַד־

night the thieves rob stealthily in people's homes, and by day they form marauding gangs that extend their reach beyond the city limits (*Targum; Ibn Ezra; Radak;* cf. *Mahari Kara*). *Rashi* renders: They constantly come and steal the money of their acquaintances, and they even form bands of robbers that spread out to rob the people.

Malbim follows his approach to the first half of the verse, and interprets: Whereas solitary thieves would previously rob stealthily when no one saw, they now form gangs who [are not afraid or ashamed] to pursue their banditry publicly and in broad daylight.

2. וּבַל־יֹאמְרוּ לִלְבָבָם כָּל־רָעָתָם זָכָרְתִּי עַתָּה סְבָבוּם מַעַלְלֵיהֶם נֶגֶד פָּנַי הָיוּ — *And they do not say in their hearts that I remember all their evils; now their deeds have surrounded them; they were before My face.* They do not take to heart that all of their evil is inscribed in My memory (*Rashi*), [and they therefore feel free to pursue their corrupt ways without constraint. Indeed,] they have immersed themselves in sin so completely that they are totally surrounded by their transgressions (*Mahari Kara*). Accordingly, when their punishment shall befall them, they will finally recognize that their wicked deeds were done before My face and it is I Who is requiting them for their sins (*Radak*).

Malbim sees this as flowing from the previous verse, in accordance with his commentary there (see above): As long as times were difficult for them, they took heed of the fact that I witness all of their deeds and thus restrained themselves to some degree in their wanton ways. However, once I extended their boundaries in order to inspire them to return to Me they took it as a sign that I no longer make note of their actions. They therefore began to commit their transgressions in public. In truth, however, even if I were to forget their previous sins, those which they have committed since then are sufficient grounds to surround them with evil and bring about their retribution.

3. בְּרָעָתָם יְשַׂמְּחוּ־מֶלֶךְ וּבְכַחֲשֵׁיהֶם שָׂרִים — *With their evil they gladden the king; and with their falsehoods, officers.* With their oppression and robbery they gladden the heart of their wicked king, for he, too, shares in their spoils. And the falsehood with which they deal with each other brings joy to their officers, for they are also enriched thereby (*Rashi; Mahari Kara; Radak*).

Others see this as describing the cheer brought to the kings and officers when they observe these heinous deeds: Rather than implementing justice in accordance with their responsibilities, they mock and jeer the impoverished victims of oppression when these individuals turn to them for aid (*R' Eliezer of Beaugency*). Alternatively: The people cheer the king and his officers by entertaining them with tales of their acts of persecution (*Abarbanel*).

Radak interprets this verse as recalling the people's descent into idolatry when Jeroboam ben Nebot established the two golden calves in Dan and Beth-el: They gladdened the heart of their king when they supported him in establishing his idols. And when they denied the Almighty by declaring these calves as their god, they cheered as well the officers with whom Jeroboam took counsel.

4. כֻּלָּם מְנָאֲפִים כְּמוֹ תַנּוּר בֹּעֵרָה מֵאֹפֶה — *They are all adulterers, like an oven fired by a baker.* All of them, the king and his officers as well as the populace (*Radak*), are filled with a passionate lust that inflames their hearts like a

[2] *And they do not say in their hearts that I remember all their evils; now their deeds have surrounded them; they were before My face.* [3] *With their evil they gladden the king; and with their falsehoods, officers.* [4] *They are all adulterers, like an oven fired by a baker. The arouser rests from the kneading of the dough until*

burning oven heated by the baker (*Rashi*).

יִשְׁבּוֹת מֵעִיר מִלּוּשׁ בָּצֵק עַד־חֻמְצָתוֹ — *The arouser rests from the kneading of the dough until its leavening.* The evil inclination that arouses them to adultery rests from his incitement only for the short while *from the kneading of the dough* — from the time they formulate a plan for carrying out their desires — *until its leavening* — until it is actually brought to fruition (*Abarbanel; Metzudos David;* cf. *Radak* citing his father). Others render: *He rests and then awakens* — the people themselves rest from the pursuit of their desires only as long as they sleep; the moment they awaken they continue in their wickedness (*Rashi;*[1] *Mahari Kara*).

Some commentators interpret this latter phrase as continuing the metaphor of the first half of the verse. According to *Radak*, it comes to describe the intensity of the flame of desire that burns inside them: The baker *rests from exhorting* his employees to stoke the oven *from the kneading of the dough until its leavening,* when they are busy with the dough. Once the dough has risen they return to the oven to place the loaves in to bake. Thus, the oven is at its hottest during that period of time, when it is fired up and empty of any bread baking within it. This is the flame to which the people's burning passion is compared.

Others see this as depicting the consistency of their adultery: The baker does not rest or nap except for the short period of time from when the dough is kneaded until it leavens — during which the oven stands idle and does not require stoking. Similiarly, the people are so immersed in their adulteries that they are left with only a similar minute duration of time for sleep (*Alshich*).[2]

Alternatively, the subject of the parable is the urgings of their desires, which incite them throughout the day and stops to "rest" only for the short while from when they satisfy their lust until it awakens anew (*Malbim*).

Targum interprets the verse in the following manner: They all desire to commit adultery with their friends' wives. They burn like an oven that the baker has heated. Therefore, they will be exiled quickly from their cities in the same manner they think to carry out their evil desires [i.e., they seek to carry them out immediately]. [Additionally, they will be exiled] not remembering the miracles and mighty deeds that were done for them on the day of their exodus from Egypt, from the time of the kneading of the dough until it did not leaven.[3]

1. This is the implication of *Rashi*, s.v., מלוש בצק. However, immediately prior to this he interprets: *Their evil inclination who arouses them rests,* identifying the evil inclination as the one who rests. His true intent is thus unclear.

2. *Alshich* himself interprets this as referring back to the previous verse: They gladden the king with their involvement in adultery because they thereby produce more people to populate his kingdom.

3. *Rashi* cites *Targum* and comments: I am unable to reconcile it with the wording of the Scripture.

ה חֲמִצָתוֹ: יוֹם מַלְכֵּנוּ הֶחֱלוּ שָׂרִים חֲמַת מִיָּיִן
ו מָשַׁךְ יָדוֹ אֶת־לֹצְצִים: כִּי־קֵרְבוּ כַתַּנּוּר לִבָּם
בְּאָרְבָּם כָּל־הַלַּיְלָה יָשֵׁן אֹפֵהֶם בֹּקֶר הוּא בֹעֵר
ז כְּאֵשׁ לֶהָבָה: כֻּלָּם יֵחַמּוּ כַּתַּנּוּר וְאָכְלוּ אֶת־
שֹׁפְטֵיהֶם כָּל־מַלְכֵיהֶם נָפָלוּ אֵין־קֹרֵא בָהֶם אֵלָי:

5. After rebuking the people for their adultery, the prophet now goes on to chastise them for their indulgence in wine and drunkenness (*Abarbanel*).

יוֹם מַלְכֵּנוּ הֶחֱלוּ שָׂרִים חֲמַת מִיָּיִן — *The day of our king, the officers became ill from the heat of the wine.* On the day of the coronation of our king (*Targum; Rashi; Ibn Ezra; Radak*), when it would be appropriate for him and his officers to discuss matters of state and justice, they involved themselves instead in their indulgence in food and drink (*Radak*), until the officers became sick from too much wine (*Rashi*).

Alternatively: On the day of rejoicing with our king, whether in honor of his birthday or his coronation (*Abarbanel; Metzudos David*). *R' Eliezer of Beaugency* renders: On the day designated for the king to sit in judgment over the people and to try the cases brought before him.

Others render הֶחֱלוּ to mean *they make ill* — i.e., they ply the king with drink until they cause him to become ill, as each one comes with his own flask —חֵמֶת — of wine and offers the king to partake of it (*Radak; Ibn Ezra*).

מָשַׁךְ יָדוֹ אֶת־לֹצְצִים — *He withdrew his hand [to be] with scoffers.* At that time, the king withdrew his hand from those who are good and righteous and joined instead with the scoffers (*Rashi*). Alternatively: He withdrew his hand from being involved in matters of state and joined instead in the activities of the cynics (*Metzudos David*).

Radak adds that the scoffers are those very officers described above. Before they begin to drink, the prophet refers to them as officers; once they have become drunk, they are called scoffers.

The Sages interpret *the king* as referring to the King of kings, and render: He withdrew His hand from scoffers. They thereby derive that scoffers are among those people who do not merit to receive the Divine Presence (*Sotah* 42; *Sanhedrin* 103).

6. כִּי־קֵרְבוּ כַתַּנּוּר לִבָּם בְּאָרְבָּם כָּל הַלַּיְלָה יָשֵׁן אֹפֵהֶם בֹּקֶר הוּא בֹעֵר כְּאֵשׁ לֶהָבָה — *For they have prepared their hearts with their plot like an oven; all night their baker sleeps [and in the] morning he burns like a blazing fire.* The baker places logs into his oven at night and then goes to sleep while it heats up — awakening in the morning to an oven ready for baking. So, too, their evil designs lie dormant at night when they cannot be pursued, but awaken in the morning to inflame them with a burning passion to commit evil deeds (*Rashi; Radak*).[1]

Ibn Ezra contrasts their evil designs with the activities of the baker: *They prepare their hearts with their plots throughout the night like an oven; whereas their baker sleeps [at night] and [only] in the morning makes the oven burn with a blazing flame.*

1. *Rashi's* actual wording is somewhat difficult to interpret with certainty, but it seems to read as follows: *All night their baker sleeps* — [this refers to] their baker who heats up the oven. [The intent of the metaphor is as follows:] After they have prepared their hearts and considered how to bring about the completion of the evil, *their baker sleeps* — i.e., until morning they sleep, and with morning they burn like fire [until] they have completed their evil.

its leavening. [5] *The day of our king, the officers became*
ill from the heat of the wine; he withdrew his hand
[to be] with scoffers. [6] *For they have prepared their*
hearts with their plot like an oven; all night their
baker sleeps [and in the] morning he burns like a
blazing fire. [7] *They have all become heated like an*
oven and they have devoured their judges, all their
kings have fallen, [yet] no one among them calls Me.

Abarbanel understands this verse to be describing their murder of the very kings and officers with whom they rejoiced with wine, as described in the previous verse. Thus: They prepared their hearts like an oven with their secret plots. Just as the oven stands cold the entire night while the baker sleeps, and is stoked into flame in the morning, so do they quell the fires of their evil designs while they are with the kings and officers and only later allow them to materialize.

7. כֻּלָּם יֵחַמּוּ כַּתַּנּוּר וְאָכְלוּ אֶת־שֹׁפְטֵיהֶם — *They have all become heated like an oven and they have devoured their judges.* They are all aflame with passion for the pursuit of their evil desires — like an oven heated for baking (*Metzudos David*) — and they have even murdered the judges of the Sanhedrin who dared rebuke them for their misdeeds (*Rashi*). Alternatively: Through their misdeeds they have caused their judges to be devoured. For the preponderance of evildoers has made the judges afraid to render justice, and has even led them to pander to the wicked. Thus, they judge only on behalf of those who have the power to [help or harm them] and ignore the needs of the powerless, thereby bringing down upon themselves the wrath of the Almighty (*Radak*).

Targum renders: *And with their false tongue they cause their judges to become guilty* [of incorrect judgments].

כָּל־מַלְכֵיהֶם נָפָלוּ אֵין־קֹרֵא בָהֶם אֵלָי — *All their kings have fallen, [yet] no one among them calls Me.* Time after time the kings of Israel have been the victims of murder. Sometimes they were murdered by those who wrested the crown from their heads[1] and at other times they were killed at the hand of the enemy. As such, it would behoove the people to recognize that their salvation does not lie within the hands of their monarchs, and to thus return to Hashem and seek his protection. Nevertheless, no one calls to Me in repentance and prayer (*Radak*).

Alternatively: Despite the continuous fall of these kings at the hands of their enemies, none of them are moved to return to Me and invoke My protection (*Radak*). Thus, the house of Jeroboam has fallen as has the house of Baasha, along with those of Zimri and Ahab, yet their successors do not take this to heart (*R' Eliezer of Beaugency*).

Others render: All their kings have fallen because none of them calls to Me (*Rashi; Mahari Kara*).

The Sages interpret these three verses as describing the descent of the people to idolatry under Jeroboam ben Nebot. As noted above (preface to chapt. 5), Jeroboam introduced idolatry to the nation in order to protect his monarchy from dissolution. As interpreted by the Sages: *On the day of our king* — on the day they crowned Jeroboam, *the officers became ill from the heat of wine* — they came to him and said to him, "Arise and make idols for us." He said to them,

1. Indeed, this occurred many times throughout the history of the northern kingdom of Israel (*Abarbanel*). Thus, Zechariah ben Jeroboam was murdered by a revolt, as were Shallum ben Yavesh, Pekachiah ben Menachem and Pekach ben Remaliahu. In addition, Hosea ben Elah was taken captive by those who rebelled against him (*Malbim*).

ח אֶפְרַיִם בָּעַמִּים הוּא יִתְבּוֹלָל אֶפְרַיִם הָיָה עֻגָה
ט בְּלִי הֲפוּכָה: אָכְלוּ זָרִים כֹּחוֹ וְהוּא לֹא יָדָע
י גַּם־שֵׂיבָה זָרְקָה בּוֹ וְהוּא לֹא יָדָע: וְעָנָה גְאוֹן־
יִשְׂרָאֵל בְּפָנָיו וְלֹא־שָׁבוּ אֶל־יהוה אֱלֹהֵיהֶם
יא וְלֹא בִקְשֻׁהוּ בְּכָל־זֹאת: וַיְהִי אֶפְרַיִם כְּיוֹנָה
פוֹתָה אֵין לֵב מִצְרַיִם קָרָאוּ אַשּׁוּר הָלָכוּ:

"Now is the time of evening and all the people are drunk," — i.e., it is a time of drunkenness; perhaps now you are drunk [and therefore make such demands] but tomorrow you will change your minds. They went and returned in the morning. This is what is written: *For they have prepared like an oven.* He said to them, "I fear your Sanhedrin." They said to him, "We will murder them." This is what is written: *And they have devoured their judges. He withdrew his hand* etc. — When he would see a righteous man he would place two scoffers next to him and they would say to him, "Which generation is the most beloved of all generations?" and he would say to them, "The generation of the desert." They said to him, "And did they not worship idols?" And he said to them, "Since they were beloved they were not punished." And they would say to him, "Silent! For the king wishes to do that [i.e., to establish idol worship]." [*Rashi* from *Yerushalmi Avodah Zarah* 1:1; cf. *Mahari Kara* to v. 5.]

8. אֶפְרַיִם בָּעַמִּים הוּא יִתְבּוֹלָל — *Ephraim is intermingled with the nations.* What brought about all of this decadence to which the Jewish nation has descended? Their intermingling with the gentile nations, from whom Hashem separated them; they have assimilated into their society and emulated their deeds (*Radak; Abarbanel; Metzudos David*).

Alternatively: They turn to the gentile nations for aid in their times of need rather than seeking My salvation (*Ibn Ezra; R' Eliezer of Beaugency*).

Others see this as a depiction of their punishment for the aforementioned misdeeds: *They shall be exiled to dwell among the nations* (*Rashi; Alshich*).

אֶפְרַיִם הָיָה עֻגָה בְּלִי הֲפוּכָה — *Ephraim was [like] a cake which was not turned over.* Because of their misdeeds Ephraim has been rendered like a cake that is devoured before it is even turned over on the flame (*Targum; Rashi*). Thus, even before they could carry out their desire to [fully] intermingle with the gentiles, strangers came and devoured their strength [as stated in the following verse] (*Mahari Kara*).

Alternatively: A cake which is not turned over on the coals becomes burnt on one side and remains raw on the other — and is thus not fit for consumption. So, too, the counsel taken by the people of Ephraim to pursue idolatry was a half-baked idea not thoroughly thought through, for they did not discern correctly between good and evil (*Ibn Ezra; Radak; Abarbanel; Metzudos David*).

9. אָכְלוּ זָרִים כֹּחוֹ וְהוּא לֹא יָדָע — *Strangers have consumed his strength but he did not know.* Foreign nations have come and plundered his wealth (*Targum; Alshich*), and Assyria and Egypt have consumed the riches with which he bribed them (*Ibn Ezra; Abarbanel*). But he has not taken his plight to heart, nor has he come to recognize that it has occurred as a result of wickedness. Thus he is not moved to repent his evil ways and return to Me (*Rashi; Radak*). Alternatively: Despite his misfortune, he has not come to know Hashem (*Mahari Kara*).

Rashi interprets the first phrase as referring to the kings of Aram who conquered and devoured Israel in the day of King Jehoahaz (see *II Kings* 13:7).

[8] *Ephraim is intermingled with the nations, Ephraim was [like] a cake which was not turned over.* [9] *Strangers have consumed his strength but he did not know, also old age was cast upon him but he did not know.* [10] *And the glory of Israel was humbled before him, but they did not return to* HASHEM *their God and they did not seek Him despite all this.* [11] *And Ephraim was like the foolish dove with no understanding; they have called to Egypt; they have gone to Assyria.*

גַּם־שֵׂיבָה זָרְקָה בּוֹ וְהוּא לֹא יָדָע — *Also old age was cast upon him but he did not know.* He was weakened to a point of helplessness, as if overtaken by old age, and thus could not rise up to fend off his enemies (*Rashi; Targum; Mahari Kara;* cf. *Ibn Ezra*).

Radak interprets: Normally, when a person approaches old age there is a tendency for him to repent his past misdeeds and return to the proper path prior to his death. However, although Ephraim has been rendered old and infirm by a long period of afflictions — and is approaching as well the final days of the kingdom — he nevertheless refuses to abandon his wicked ways.

Chovos HaLevavos (*Shaar Cheshbon HaNefesh* ch. 3, s.v. והאחד עשר) interprets: He has gone for a long period of time without examining his deeds and coming to know them.

10. וְעָנָה גְאוֹן־יִשְׂרָאֵל בְּפָנָיו וְלֹא־שָׁבוּ אֶל־ה׳ אֱלֹהֵיהֶם וְלֹא בִקְשֻׁהוּ בְּכָל־זֹאת — *And the glory of Israel was humbled before him, but they did not return to* HASHEM *their God and they did not seek Him despite all this.* The people of Israel have witnessed the fall of their pride and glory; yet they continue to refuse to mend their ways (*Targum; Rashi*).

Others render וְעָנָה to mean *witness*: His fall from the heights of power and glory to his present lowly status bore testimony before him to his transgressions; nevertheless, he remained steadfast in his wicked ways (*R' Eliezer of Beaugency;* cf. *Abarbanel*; see also 5:5 and commentary ibid.).

11. וַיְהִי אֶפְרַיִם כְּיוֹנָה פוֹתָה אֵין לֵב מִצְרַיִם קָרָאוּ אַשּׁוּר הָלָכוּ — *And Ephraim was like the foolish dove with no understanding; they have called to Egypt; they have gone to Assyria.* Ephraim is like the foolish dove, who rushes eagerly to the snare to eat the seeds placed there for him without comprehending that he will thereby become entrapped. So has the Jewish nation plunged recklessly into its treaties with Egypt and Assyria without realizing that I have laid a trap for them,[1] and that this very course will lead to their downfall (*Ibn Ezra; Radak; Metzudos David*).

Others interpret: Ephraim has been like the foolish dove, who does not discern between the beneficial and the harmful (*Rashi*). Whereas other birds avoid their nests if they discover their offspring have been captured, the dove takes no heed of this and continues to dwell in it (*Mahari Kara*). So, too, has Ephraim foolishly and recklessly turned for aid and security to Egypt and Assyria — the very nations who have long been their oppressors — rather than turning to

1. When Jerusalem was besieged by the armies of Aram, King Ahaz invoked the aid of Assyria to drive them off. Upon doing so, Assyria proceeded to turn upon Israel, and turned it into a vassal state, prompting King Hosea to turn to Egypt for assistance. This incited Shalmanesser, king of Assyria, to besiege Samaria (*II Kings* chs. 16, 17).

יב כַּאֲשֶׁר יֵלֵכוּ אֶפְרוֹשׂ עֲלֵיהֶם רִשְׁתִּי כְּעוֹף הַשָּׁמַיִם
יג אוֹרִידֵם אַיְסִרֵם כְּשֵׁמַע לַעֲדָתָם׃ אוֹי
לָהֶם כִּי־נָדְדוּ מִמֶּנִּי שֹׁד לָהֶם כִּי־פָשְׁעוּ בִי
יד וְאָנֹכִי אֶפְדֵּם וְהֵמָּה דִּבְּרוּ עָלַי כְּזָבִים׃ וְלֹא־
זָעֲקוּ אֵלַי בְּלִבָּם כִּי יְיֵלִילוּ עַל־מִשְׁכְּבוֹתָם

the Almighty, their true source of support (*Rashi; Mahari Kara; Abarbanel*).

Mahari Kara renders: *Egypt has called* [as well as] *Assyria* [and] *they have gone* — when these nations call to them they follow [blindly].

12. כַּאֲשֶׁר יֵלֵכוּ אֶפְרוֹשׂ עֲלֵיהֶם רִשְׁתִּי — *When they go, I will spread My net over them.* Indeed, when they will go to Egypt and Assyria for aid I will spread My net over them, and their move in that direction will thus prove to be their downfall (*Radak; R' Eliezer of Beaugency; Metzudos David*).

Alternatively: When they will go to Egypt to escape the Assyrians I will spread My net over them, and there they will be decimated by hunger and the sword (*Rashi; Mahari Kara*).[1]

כְּעוֹף הַשָּׁמַיִם אוֹרִידֵם — *Like the birds of the heaven I will bring them down.* Just as the birds of the heaven are caught in nets which hang in the air upon poles and are then dragged down to earth, so shall I bring them down to disaster (*Rashi; Mahari Kara*). Alternatively: Just as the birds of the heaven — such as the eagle and the hawk — soar higher than the dove to capture and bring her down to earth, so shall I bring down the Jewish people through Nebuchadnezzar, even in the land of Egypt (*Rashi*).

אַיְסִירֵם כְּשֵׁמַע לַעֲדָתָם — *I will afflict them, as has been heard by their congregation.* I will bring upon them suffering like all that I have made known to their congregation through the prophet Jeremiah (*Rashi; Mahari Kara*).[2] Alternatively: I will afflict those who go down to Egypt, which will serve as a source of castigation to be heard by their brothers still residing in their land (*Ibn Ezra*).

Others translate אַיְסִרֵם to mean *bound* (*Menachem* cited by *Rashi; Radak*) — I will incarcerate them in the bonds of the gentile nations, as I disclosed to them yet in the desert through the warning and curses issued in the Torah for those who do not heed My word (*Radak*).

Abarbanel renders: *I will afflict them in heed of their congregation* — I will follow the course they set for themselves and thereby bring about their downfall. Just as they sought out Assyria so shall I

1. When Nebuchadnezzar king of Babylon conquered Judah and exiled its inhabitants, he appointed Gedaliah ben Ahikam governor of those who remained in the Holy Land. When Gedaliah was murdered (*Jeremiah* 41), the people, led by Yochanan ben Kareiah, felt themselves very vulnerable to the Chaldeans living nearby and beseeched Jeremiah to plead with the Almighty on their behalf and to transmit to them His instructions. The prophet returned with the message from Hashem that they should remain in the Land of Israel where He would protect them. In their terror the people rejected Jeremiah's words and fled to Egypt — forcing the prophet to accompany them. At that time, the Almighty declared through His prophet that Egypt would be conquered and the Jewish settlement there wiped out (see *Jereremiah* chs. 42-44).

2. *Rashi* and *Mahari Kara* themselves follow their approach to the entire verse, that it refers to those who disregarded Jeremiah's admonitions and sought refuge in Egypt. They thus cite the dialogue between Jeremiah and the people that is recorded in the Book of *Jeremiah* (42:2-6). Nevertheless, their interpretation of this phrase is plausible even according to the other commentators.

12 When they go, I will spread My net over them, like
the birds of the heaven I will bring them down, I
will afflict them, as has been heard by their congrega-
tion. 13 Woe is to them for they have moved away
from Me; plunder to them for they have rebelled
against Me; and I would redeem them but they have
spoken lies about Me. 14 And they did not cry out to
Me in their hearts when they wailed on their beds,

hand them over to Assyria, who will offer them not the open hand of a friendly power but the iron fist of the conquering enemy. Thus, they will plummet from the heights of their former glory to the depths of exile and enslavement.

13. אוֹי לָהֶם כִּי־נָדְדוּ מִמֶּנִּי שֹׁד לָהֶם כִּי־פָשְׁעוּ בִי וְאָנֹכִי אֶפְדֵּם וְהֵמָּה דִּבְּרוּ עָלַי כְּזָבִים — *Woe is to them for they have moved away from Me; plunder to them for they have rebelled against Me; and I would redeem them but they have spoken lies about Me.* Woe is to them, for they have moved away from their fear of Me (*Targum*) and from their service of Me in the Temple, and have turned instead to the worship of other deities (*Radak*). Therefore, the plundering nation of Assyria shall fall upon them (*Abarbanel; Metzudos David*). I wished to redeem them from their tragic plight, but they have made this impossible, for they utter lies about Me, denying that I observe their deeds and respond to their good and evil. Therefore, I have hidden My face from them and left them to their misery and sorrow (*Radak; Abarbanel; Metzudos David*). Alternatively: They have lied about Me and proclaimed that all I seek is to harm them (*Ibn Ezra*).

Rashi interprets this, too, as referring to the dispute between the people and Jeremiah whether to seek refuge in Egypt. He thus interprets: They said to Jeremiah (*Jeremiah* 43:2), *You speak falsely;* H*ASHEM did not send you to say, "You should not go to Egypt."*[1]

Another approach to this verse is that it refers to the plight of the Jewish nation after their banishment from the Holy Land: Woe is to them for they have wandered into exile. And because they continue to transgress My word and do not repent, they will continue to be plundered and persecuted there in foreign lands. I would have redeemed them from the exile imposed upon them by Assyria, but they have spoken lies about Me and denied My faith [and I have therefore left them to their bitter fate] (*Abarbanel*).

14. וְלֹא־זָעֲקוּ אֵלַי בְּלִבָּם כִּי יְיֵלִילוּ עַל־מִשְׁכְּבוֹתָם — *And they did not cry out to Me in their hearts when they wailed on their beds.* As they lie in their beds bewailing their bitter fate, they refuse to recognize that I am the source of their misfortune. Thus, they do not turn to Me in repentance in order to improve their lot, but rather continue to insist that I do not hear their cries nor take heed of their bitter plight (*Radak; Abarbanel; Metzudos David*). Even on those rare occasions when they turn to Me in prayer, they offer only lip service, with their hearts far removed from any feelings of devotion (*Alshich; Malbim*).

Others interpret: *They did not cry out to Me in their hearts; therefore they will wail on their beds* — i.e., from the misfortune which will overtake them and the exile that will be their lot (*Targum; Rashi; Mahari Kara*).

1. [Although they rejected only Jeremiah, denying his legitimacy as Hashem's spokesman, this is described by Scripture as being directed at God Himself — *they have spoken lies about Me.* Since Jeremiah was an established prophet, they had no valid basis for their denial of his validity, and it therefore indicated a lack of faith in the Almighty.]

ז/טו־טז טו עַל־דָּגָן וְתִירוֹשׁ יִתְגּוֹרָרוּ יָסוּרוּ בִי: וַאֲנִי
יִסַּרְתִּי חִזַּקְתִּי זְרוֹעֹתָם וְאֵלַי יְחַשְּׁבוּ־רָע:
טז יָשׁוּבוּ ׀ לֹא עָל הָיוּ כְּקֶשֶׁת רְמִיָּה יִפְּלוּ
בַחֶרֶב שָׂרֵיהֶם מִזַּעַם לְשׁוֹנָם זוֹ לַעְגָּם
ח/א א בְּאֶרֶץ מִצְרָיִם: אֶל־חִכְּךָ שֹׁפָר כַּנֶּשֶׁר עַל־בֵּית
יְהוָה יַעַן עָבְרוּ בְרִיתִי וְעַל־תּוֹרָתִי פָּשָׁעוּ:

עַל־דָּגָן וְתִירוֹשׁ יִתְגּוֹרָרוּ יָסוּרוּ בִי — *For grain and wine they gather; they turn away from Me.* So great is the famine that pervades that land that when grain and wine are brought into the city, people swarm to them in their hunger. Nevertheless, despite the dire straits in which they find themselves, they continue to turn away from Me (*Radak*). Alternatively: They gather to indulge in food and drink and speak ill of Me (*Ibn Ezra; Abarbanel*).[1] Others render: They gather stores of grain and wine; [therefore] they rebel against Me (*Targum; Rashi*).

Another translation of the word יִתְגּוֹרָרוּ is *wander*: They wander from place to place to seek grain and wine (*Malbim*; cf. *Metzudos David*).

15. וַאֲנִי יִסַּרְתִּי חִזַּקְתִּי זְרוֹעֹתָם וְאֵלַי יְחַשְּׁבוּ־רָע — *And I afflicted; I strengthened their arms, but they attribute evil to Me.* I have afflicted the Children of Israel — not for the sake of tormenting them but only in order to get them to repent and thereby be strengthened. They, however, refuse to recognize this; rather, they impugn My motives and maintain that I seek only their harm (*Targum; Ibn Ezra; Alshich; Malbim*).

Rashi renders: *I admonished* — I admonished them through My prophets and sought to inspire them with fear so that they would heed the words of the prophets and their arms would thereby be strengthened.[2]

Radak interprets the word יִסַּרְתִּי to be derived from the root אסור — *bound*: When they were blessed with prosperity, it was I Who girded their arms and strengthened them. However they did not acknowledge My beneficence but rather attributed their prosperity to happenstance.[3]

16. יָשׁוּבוּ לֹא עָל הָיוּ כְּקֶשֶׁת רְמִיָּה יִפְּלוּ בַחֶרֶב שָׂרֵיהֶם מִזַּעַם לְשׁוֹנָם זוֹ לַעְגָּם בְּאֶרֶץ מִצְרָיִם — *They turn not to the One Above; they were like a deceitful bow; their officers shall fall by the sword from the fury of their tongues; this was their derision in the land of Egypt.* They respond to their

1. *Alshich* interprets this phrase as continuing the thought of the beginning of the verse: When the leaders of the nation come to visit those who are bedridden with their illness, they do not come to comfort them and to encourage them to repent and thereby be healed. Rather, they stand before the victims and dwell upon how they will divide their possessions [after they have passed on].

2. *Mahari Kara* interprets this verse as still referring to the dialogue between the prophet Jeremiah and the people after the Holy Land had been conquered by the Babylonians. I sent my prophet Jeremiah to admonish them and to exhort them to strengthen their arms before the king of Babylonia. I reassured them that they need not fear his might, for I would be with them. However, they spurned My words and rejected Jeremiah's urgings, claiming that he spoke falsely in My Name.

3. *R' Eliezer of Beaugency* follows an approach similar to *Ibn Ezra*, but interprets the phrase, *I strengthened their arms*, to refer to the Almighty's actions rather than merely describing His intent: Due to My great love for them, I have afflicted them as a father punishes his son, making sure to strengthen their arms [in other ways] at the same time. Accordingly, they should have realized that all the misfortune I brought upon them was to arouse them to repentance. Nevertheless, they attributed to Me the intention and desire to harm them maliciously.

7/15-16 *for grain and wine they gather; they turn away from Me.* [15] *And I afflicted; I strengthened their arms, but they attribute evil to Me.* [16] They *turn not to the One Above; they were like a deceitful bow; their officers shall fall by the sword from the fury of their tongues; this was their derision in the land of Egypt.*

8/1 [1] *To your palate a shofar; like an eagle upon the House of* HASHEM, *because they have violated My covenant, and they have rebelled against My Torah.*

plight by turning not to the Almighty Who dwells Above but only to the natural courses of action open to them [particularly to the gentile nations whose aid they seek (*Radak*)]. By so doing, they show a total lack of appreciation for all the blessings I have bestowed upon them. In this manner, they have distorted the straight and upright path like a crooked bow, that shoots its arrows in an entirely different direction than the one in which it is aimed. With the fury invoked by their spurious tongues and words of heresy, they have brought about the demise of their kings and officers. In this, they have followed the paths they took in Egypt prior to their exodus, where they were also steeped in heresy and in the denial of Divine Providence (*Abarbanel; Metzudos David*).

Alternatively: *They were like a deceitful bow* — i.e., a deceitful archer, whose perfidy is expressed through his bow, when he indicates his intention to shoot in one direction and turns to a different one at the last moment. So, too, have the Children of Israel been turned aside from their commitment to improve their deeds — when such commitments have been forthcoming at all — by the false prophets who encourage them in their wicked ways. These leaders who guide them along wayward paths shall be smitten by the sword for exhorting the people with tongues of fury — i.e., tongues that arouse the fury of the Almighty. They glibly declare, "If the enemy comes we will turn to Egypt for aid." However, the Egyptians will mock the Jewish people contemptuously for turning to them for salvation (*Radak*).

Rashi interprets this verse as referring to the people's disregard of Jeremiah's admonitions and their flight to Egypt: *They will return but to no avail* — they will return to Egypt but it will not help them. Rather they will be like a deceitful bow which is aimed to the north but shoots toward the south. So shall Yochanan ben Kareiah [see footnote to v. 12] and all who follow him be felled by the sword in Egypt for the harsh words and tongue of fury with which they responded to Jeremiah. Indeed, this shall be their derision in Egypt, for the Egyptians will say to them, "Why have you come to us to bring affliction upon us? Is it not written (*Exodus* 14:13) *and you shall no longer continue to see them?*" (cf. *Mahari Kara*).

VIII

Hosea is instructed to continue his castigation of the Children of Israel for their misdeeds, with special focus on the sin of idolatry. He also foretells of the disaster which is to befall them in retribution. According to the majority of the commentators, these verses record the words of the Almighty that were stated to Hosea. *Radak* interprets the first verse as the prophet's words to the nation.

1. אֶל־חִכְּךָ שֹׁפָר כַּנֶּשֶׁר עַל־בֵּית ה׳ יַעַן עָבְרוּ בְרִיתִי וְעַל־תּוֹרָתִי פָּשָׁעוּ — *To your palate a shofar; like an eagle upon the House of* HASHEM, *because they have violated My*

ב־ג לִי יִזְעָקוּ אֱלֹהַי יְדַעֲנוּךָ יִשְׂרָאֵל: זָנַח יִשְׂרָאֵל טוֹב
ד אוֹיֵב יִרְדְּפוֹ: הֵם הִמְלִיכוּ וְלֹא מִמֶּנִּי הֵשִׂירוּ וְלֹא
יָדָעְתִּי כַּסְפָּם וּזְהָבָם עָשׂוּ לָהֶם עֲצַבִּים לְמַעַן

covenant, and they have rebelled against My Torah. Raise your voice loudly and call out like a shofar. Do so speedily, as if the shofar were attached to your palate, and the wind coming from your throat thus blows through it very quickly (*Rashi*; *Abarbanel*). In this manner, proclaim to the nation that the enemy shall swoop down like an eagle upon the House of Hashem for having violated My covenant and rebelled against My Torah (*Targum; Yefes*, cited by *Ibn Ezra; Abarbanel; Metzudos David*). This alludes to Nebuchadnezzar king of Babylonia, who conquered the nation of Judah and destroyed the Temple (*Abarbanel*).

Alternatively: Raise your voice like a shofar to the enemies of the Jewish nation, and exhort them in the name of the Almighty: Hurry and fly like an eagle and swoop down upon the House of Hashem (*Rashi; Mahari Kara*).

Others interpret the phrase *like an eagle upon the House of HASHEM* as referring still to the prophet: *Place a shofar to your palate and swoop like an eagle upon the House of HASHEM* (*Ibn Ezra*) — Ascend upon the Holy Mountain and admonish the people for their transgressions when they come up to visit the Temple (*R' Eliezer of Beaugency* cf. *Malbim*).

וְעַל־תּוֹרָתִי פָּשָׁעוּ — *And they have rebelled against My Torah.* According to the majority of the commentators, this is a repetition of the previous phrase. *Alshich* interprets it as referring specifically to the study of the Torah. This follows the statement of the Sages (*Yerushalmi, Chagigah* 1) that the Almighty was willing to countenance even the cardinal sins of idolatry, adultery, and murder but not that of the cessation of Torah study [for without the latter there is no more hope for improvement].

2-3. לִי יִזְעָקוּ אֱלֹהַי יְדַעֲנוּךָ יִשְׂרָאֵל. זָנַח יִשְׂרָאֵל טוֹב אוֹיֵב יִרְדְּפוֹ — *To Me Israel*[1] *will cry out, "My God, we know You." Israel has forsaken good; the enemy shall pursue him.* When misfortune shall befall the nation, the people of Israel will call out to Me and proclaim their fidelity. However, I will no longer hearken to their pleas, for they have totally forsaken good and must therefore be pursued by the enemy (*Rashi; Mahari Kara*).

Others interpret: To Me they should have cried out in their time of trouble, and proclaimed, "We know you, O God, and recognize that You are our only source of salvation." However, they have not done so, but have rather abandoned good; therefore the enemy shall pursue them (*Radak; Metzudos David*). *Metzudos David* adds: All of Israel, both the northern kingdom and that of Judah, have abandoned good, and they shall therefore all be conquered by the enemy.

Abarbanel suggests an alternative interpretation to these three verses: The prophet is referring to the invasion of Sennacherib king of Assyria, who invaded the kingdom of Judah as well as that of Israel. Soon after conquering the latter and exiling its inhabitants, he swooped down speedily like an eagle to attack the Temple — which no doubt occurred in retribution for the sins of the nation under the reign of Ahaz. However, unlike their Israelite brethren, the people of Judah cried out to the Almighty in repentance and prayer and were miraculously saved from the invading hordes. Thus, proclaims the Almighty: The people of Judah

1. This follows the approach of most commentators, that the word *Israel* at the end of the verse should be interpreted as if it were in the middle. *Targum*, however, renders: *Every time misfortune befalls them they pray before Me and say, "Now we know that we have no other God save You. Save us, for we are Your nation Israel."*

2 To Me Israel will cry out, "My God, we know You."
3 Israel has forsaken good; the enemy shall pursue him.
4 They have enthroned kings but not from Me; they have ordained officers but I did not know. [From] their silver and gold they made themselves idols for it

cried out to Me and declared their fidelity, unlike those of Ephraim, who abandoned Me. Therefore, the former will be spared My wrath, whereas the latter will be pursued and conquered by the enemy. The prophet refers to both nations as *Israel* in order to emphasize how far they diverged in their deeds despite originating from the same forebears.

זָנַח יִשְׂרָאֵל טוֹב — *Israel has forsaken good.* According to most of the commentators, the word *good* refers to the Almighty.

Radak explains: This is Hashem Who is the only Being that is totally good, with no aspect of evil. According to *Ibn Ezra*: The God Who has been good to him. Alternatively: The God Who is good to all His creations (*Abarbanel*).

Others, however, interpret this literally: *Israel has abandoned good for they have not returned to Me* (*R' Eliezer of Beaugency*). Alternatively: *They have abandoned that which is good for them* (*Metzudos David*). *Targum* renders: *Israel has strayed from after My service, for which I bring good upon them.*

The Sages offer a different view: Said R' Pazi: There is no good save the Torah, as it is stated (*Proverbs* 4:2), *for a good purchase [I have given them].* And so it is stated (*Jeremiah* 9:12), *for abandoning My Torah* [the land was destroyed] (*Yalkut Shimoni*).

4. הֵם הִמְלִיכוּ וְלֹא מִמֶּנִּי הֵשִׂירוּ וְלֹא יָדָעְתִּי — *They have enthroned kings but not from Me; they have ordained officers but I did not know.* The people of Israel have anointed officers without My knowledge [i.e., consent] (*Targum; Rashi; Ibn Ezra; Radak; Metzudos David*). Even their original monarch, Jeroboam ben Nebot, was enthroned without My involvement.

Although Hashem sent Ahiyah Hashiloni to inform Jeroboam that the Almighty intended to crown him, the populace acted without ever having been commanded to do so. Furthermore, when they saw how he abandoned the ways of Hashem and prohibited them from ascending to Jerusalem — establishing his two golden calves instead — they should have removed him from office. The remainder of the kings of Israel were also anointed without consultation with the Almighty, with the exception of Yehu ben Nimshi (*Radak*).

Others translate הֵשִׂירוּ to mean *they remove*, as in הֵסִירוּ: They deposed one king from office and replace him with another, all without My instructions (*Rashi*, in second version; *Mahari Kara; Malbim*). Indeed, twice in the history of the Israelite kingdom, the people deposed of a monarch for ceasing to support or sanction idolatry. This occurred to Shalom ben Yavesh, about whom it is not written that he did what was evil in the eyes of Hashem. Apparently, in his battle for the throne with Menachem ben Gadi, he stood for the abolition of idolatry, whereas the latter favored it and was supported by those of the same mind. Similarly, Hosea ben Elah abolished the sentries who prevented the people from ascending to Jerusalem. Consequently, those in support of idolatry informed upon him to the king of Assyria when he made a treaty with Egypt, and he was therefore placed in prison (*Malbim*).

כַּסְפָּם וּזְהָבָם עָשׂוּ לָהֶם עֲצַבִּים לְמַעַן יִכָּרֵת — *[From] their silver and gold they made themselves idols for it to be cut off.* The very gold and silver that I bestowed upon them, they turned around and used to make idols in defiance of My will. Therefore, that same gold and silver will be cut off from them (*Radak; R' Eliezer of*

ה יִכָּרֵת: זָנַח֙ עֶגְלֵ֣ךְ שֹׁמְר֔וֹן חָרָ֥ה אַפִּ֖י בָּ֑ם עַד־מָתַ֕י
ו לֹ֥א יוּכְל֖וּ נִקָּיֹֽן: כִּ֤י מִיִּשְׂרָאֵל֙ וְה֔וּא חָרָ֣שׁ עָשָׂ֔הוּ
וְלֹ֥א אֱלֹהִ֖ים ה֑וּא כִּֽי־שְׁבָבִ֣ים יִֽהְיֶ֔ה עֵ֖גֶל שֹׁמְרֽוֹן:
ז כִּ֛י ר֥וּחַ יִזְרָ֖עוּ וְסוּפָ֣תָה יִקְצֹ֑רוּ קָמָ֣ה אֵֽין־ל֗וֹ צֶ֚מַח
בְּלִ֣י יַעֲשֶׂה־קֶּ֔מַח אוּלַ֣י יַעֲשֶׂ֔ה זָרִ֖ים יִבְלָעֻֽהוּ:

Beaugency). Alternatively: That gold and silver will be the cause of the loss of their idols, for the enemy will seize them for their inherent value (*Metzudos David*).

The reading of others has the people themselves as the object of the verb: For using gold and silver to make idols, their name shall be cut off and they will be exiled from their land (*Radak;* cf. *Targum*).

Abarbanel interprets this verse —along with the next (see below) — as expressing the Almighty's rejoinder to the excuse of the nation that only their leaders are responsible for their transgressions and they themselves are free of blame. To this the Almighty responds: They appointed their kings and officers without consulting Me, and they are thus to blame for the corruption incurred thereby. Furthermore, they willingly donated their own gold and silver for the construction of the idols they served, and thus they cannot claim innocence of that abomination.

5. In place of the Almighty, whose service they abandoned, the Children of Israel turned to the worship of the golden calves of Jeroboam. In truth, however, these are not deities at all, but merely the handiwork of human beings, and they are thus incapable of providing aid in a time of crisis.

זָנַח עֶגְלֵךְ שֹׁמְרוֹן חָרָה אַפִּי בָּם עַד מָתַי לֹא יוּכְלוּ נִקָּיֹן — *Your calf has forsaken [you] Samaria,*[1] *My anger burns against them; until when will they be incapable of cleansing?* The golden calf that you worship has forsaken you, Samaria, for it did not come to your aid when you suffered the effects of My wrath. Now that you have seen for yourselves the uselessness of your chosen deities, how long will it take until you act upon this knowledge and cleanse yourselves from the corruption of idolatry (*Ibn Ezra; Abarbanel; Metzudos David*)?

Radak renders: *Your calf has distanced [you]* — i.e., because of your service to it, you have been exiled from your land. Alternatively: *Your calf has been distanced [from you]* — for when the king of Assyria came and conquered the land he destroyed the golden calves and confiscated the gold from which they were made (ibid.).

Others understand Hashem to be the unstated subject of this verse: *[Hashem] has forsaken [you], people of Samaria, [because of your sin of worshiping] the golden calves* (*Rashi; Mahari Kara*).

6. כִּי מִיִּשְׂרָאֵל וְהוּא חָרָשׁ עָשָׂהוּ וְלֹא אֱלֹהִים הוּא — *For [it is] from Israel and it was made by a craftsman and it is not a god.* The gold and silver from which the idols were made were donated by all of the members of the nation of Israel (*Rashi*) and the idols were constructed at their behest. It is therefore the collective responsibility of the people and not just that of the leaders (*Abarbanel;* cf. *Ibn Ezra*). From that gold, the idols were formed by a mortal craftsman; thus it cannot possibly be a true god, for how could the product be greater than its creator (*Radak*)?

Metzudos David sees this entire phrase as conveying the latter message: The calf was made by Israelites, mere human

1. Although the golden calf was in Beth-el rather than in Samaria, it is nevertheless referred to as the idolatry of Samaria, for from the time of Ahab the city of Samaria was the seat of royalty from which the worship of the calf was supported and encouraged (*Radak*).

8/5-7
to be cut off. [5] *Your calf has forsaken [you] Samaria,*
My anger burns against them; until when will they
be incapable of cleansing? [6] *For [it is] from Israel and*
it was made by a craftsman and it is not a god, for
the calf of Samaria shall be splinters. [7] *For they sow*
wind and they shall reap a tempest; it has no stand-
ing stalks; what sprouts will produce no flour; [and] if
it should somehow produce, strangers will devour it.

beings, and not by the heavenly angels. It was formed by a craftsman with the tools of his trade, and not through some magical process. Therefore it could not possibly be any more than a mere construction of metal.

Radak interprets: *For it is from Israel* — they did not duplicate the deeds of some gentile nation, but rather drew upon their own original concept of idolatry that they devised in the desert when they worshiped the golden calf.

Others interpret the word וְהוּא as belonging to the first phrase — *For it is of Israel*. The "*vav*" is superfluous and does not mean *and* in this case — as is found in other places in Scripture (*Rashi; Dunash*, cited by *Mahari Kara*). Alternatively: the "*vav*" — meaning *and* — is added in order to emphasize that this calf is not the first such idol constructed by the Jewish nation but is rather an addition to the one that they worshiped in the desert (*Rashi*). *Mahari Kara* offers the following interpretation: for [this calf that was made at the behest of Jeroboam] is of Israel, *and it* — i.e., in addition to the original calf that you made in the desert, with which you distanced yourselves from Me and pursued courses of vanity.

כִּי־שְׁבָבִים יִהְיֶה עֵגֶל שֹׁמְרוֹן — *For the calf of Samaria shall be splinters.* You will soon see how ineffective your idol is in helping you, for not only will it not protect you, but it will not even manage to defend itself. Rather, it shall be smashed into smithereens and confiscated — not for its stature as a deity but merely for the value of its gold (*Radak; Abarbanel*).

Others interpret שׁוֹבֵב to mean straying: The calf of Samaria was made by Israel for the purpose of straying (*Yefes*, cited by *Ibn Ezra*). Alternatively: For the straying hearts of the Israelites produced the calf of Samaria (*R' Eliezer of Beaugency*).

7. כִּי רוּחַ יִזְרָעוּ וְסוּפָתָה יִקְצֹרוּ קָמָה אֵין־לוֹ צֶמַח בְּלִי יַעֲשֶׂה־קֶּמַח אוּלַי יַעֲשֶׂה זָרִים יִבְלָעֻהוּ — *For they sow wind and they shall reap a tempest; it has no standing stalks; what sprouts will produce no flour; [and] if it should somehow produce, strangers will devour it.* They pursue the service of their idols for naught, like one who seeks to sow the wind, for they will receive no benefit from their worship. Rather, they shall harvest only sorrow, like that which is brought on by a roaring tempest. Indeed, they will not even reach the point at which their anticipated benefit seems within reach, comparable to the standing stalks of grain in the fields. Perhaps, on rare occasions, they will manage to enjoy some slight measure of success in their endeavors — like the grain that sprouts from the ground. However, it will never materialize into flour — i.e., into the full measure of possible blessing or any benefit that is long-lasting. And if by some remote chance they should actually achieve the anticipated fruits of their labors, these will quickly be devoured by strangers (*Rashi; Radak; Abarbanel*).

R' Eliezer of Beaugency interprets the second half of the verse literally: Their idols cannot provide them with sustenance; thus their sprouted grain will never become flour, and even that which does grow will be consumed by the enemy.

ח נִבְלַע יִשְׂרָאֵל עַתָּה הָיוּ בַגּוֹיִם כִּכְלִי אֵין־חֵפֶץ
ט בּוֹ: כִּי־הֵמָּה עָלוּ אַשּׁוּר פֶּרֶא בּוֹדֵד לוֹ אֶפְרַיִם
י הִתְנוּ אֲהָבִים: גַּם כִּי־יִתְנוּ בַגּוֹיִם עַתָּה אֲקַבְּצֵם
יא וַיָּחֵלּוּ מְּעָט מִמַּשָּׂא מֶלֶךְ שָׂרִים: כִּי־הִרְבָּה
אֶפְרַיִם מִזְבְּחוֹת לַחֲטֹא הָיוּ־לוֹ מִזְבְּחוֹת לַחֲטֹא:

Others interpret this verse as referring back to the entire scope of the previous ones. Having described the decadence of the Israelite nations, the prophet now goes on to depict the punishment they will endure: They shall harvest in accordance with that which they have sown. Thus their pursuit of valueless activities, which are empty of substance like the wind, will produce results that are similar but of increased dimension, like the damaging winds of a roaring tempest (*Metzudos David; Malbim;* cf. *Alshich*).

8-9. Along with their neglect of My commandments has come an abandonment of My faith. Thus, in their hour of need, they seek their salvation from foreign nations rather than from Me. However, their efforts are to no avail, for they are continuously spurned and rejected by the gentile world.

8. נִבְלַע יִשְׂרָאֵל עַתָּה הָיוּ בַגּוֹיִם כִּכְלִי אֵין־חֵפֶץ בּוֹ — *Israel has been devoured; now they have become among the nations like a useless vessel.* Gentiles have come and devoured not only the produce of Israel, but the entire nation as well, with all that they possess (*Ibn Ezra; Radak*). When they turn to other nations for aid they are spurned and rejected, like a vessel that has no use and is thus undesired by all (*Radak*). Alternatively: They have been exiled among the nations [where they are viewed like a useless vessel] (*Radak;* cf. *Abarbanel*).

Alshich interprets: Now that they have been left with no source of sustenance in their land, they have perforce been devoured by the gentile nations and sent into exile, in order to allow for their survival.[1]

9. כִּי־הֵמָּה עָלוּ אַשּׁוּר פֶּרֶא בּוֹדֵד לוֹ אֶפְרַיִם הִתְנוּ אֲהָבִים — *For they ascended*[2] *to Assyria like a wild donkey on his own; Ephraim has paid tribute for friendship.* They have turned to Assyria for assistance on their own initiative — without seeking counsel from Me or My prophets — like a wild donkey that travels alone and pursues his own course and direction. Indeed, they have gone so far as to offer payment to Assyria and Egypt in order to earn their friendship and support (*Radak; Abarbanel; Metzudos David*). Thus, they have cheapened themselves and lowered their esteem in the eyes of the nations, until — as stated above — they have become like a useless vessel that no one desires (*R' Eliezer of Beaugency*).

Alternatively: Just as a wild ass cannot be tamed or domesticated but rather

1. [Although the Almighty is obviously capable of providing for their needs in the Land of Israel as well as elsewhere, their exile is nevertheless necessary for their sustenance. For without the necessary merit they cannot be granted their own source of sustenance, but this does not preclude their inclusion in the Divine Providence bestowed upon humanity at large (cf. *Rashi* to *Numbers* 23:9, s.v. ובגוים). Furthermore, the Heavenly Wrath is not aroused to the same degree outside the Land of Israel as within, and they are thus safer in exile so long as they do not perfect their deeds (cf. *Ramban* to *Leviticus* 18:28).]

2. Although the Land of Israel is [referred to by the Sages as the highest of lands (see *Rashi* to *Genesis* 45:9) and is thus] higher than Assyria, the word עָלוּ is not used literally, but means merely that they withdrew from their land to go to Assyria. *R' Saadiah Gaon* interprets it to mean *they came*. However, it is possible that the literal meaning is actually correct here. For when Pul king of Assyria visited Israel during the reign of Menachem ben Gadi, the latter went to visit him and pay him a tribute of one thousand talents of silver. It is thus possible that the place where Pul was staying was higher than the palace of Menachem and he thus actually ascended to visit him (*Radak*).

[8] *Israel has been devoured; now they have become*
among the nations like a useless vessel. [9] *For they*
ascended to Assyria like a wild donkey on his own;
Ephraim has paid tribute for friendship. [10] *Although*
they pay tribute to the nations, now I will gather
them, but they will [first] be somewhat humbled
from the burden of the king [and] the officers. [11] *For*
Ephraim has increased altars to sin; he had altars to sin.

follows in his own independent path, so have the Children of Israel refused the guidance of My prophets, and have turned instead to Assyria and followed in their decadent ways (*Mahari Kara*).

Targum renders: *For they will be exiled to Assyria for following their base desires; like a wild lizard, the house of Israel has been given over to friendly nations* — i.e., they wander in the wilderness like a lizard that sniffs the air [for the smell of friendly animals], seeking to purchase strange lovers (*Rashi*).[1]

10. גַּם כִּי־יִתְנוּ בַגּוֹיִם עַתָּה אֲקַבְּצֵם וַיָּחֵלּוּ מְּעָט מִמַּשָּׂא מֶלֶךְ שָׂרִים — *Although they pay tribute to the nations, now I will gather them, but they will [first] be somewhat humbled from the burden of the king [and] the officers.* Nevertheless, despite their infidelity to Me in seeking the support and friendship of the gentile nations, I will not turn away from them forever. Rather, when the time for their redemption eventually arrives, I shall gather them together [and return them to their land]. However, they will first undergo a period of exile in which they will be humbled due to their fear of the burdens imposed upon them by the kings and officers of the gentile nations (*Rashi*).

Alternatively: וַיָּחֵלּוּ is translated *they will be made ill.* I have sent them into exile so that they should experience the ill effects of subjugation to the gentile nations. This will bring them to recognize the vast difference that exists between worshiping Me and serving other gods (*Mahari Kara*).

The Sages see an allusion in this verse. They state that the word יתנו is meant to be understood by its Aramaic meaning — *to learn.* Thus: If they will learn Torah, I will gather them from among the nations. However, if only a minority shall do so, then they will be relieved only partially from the burden of kings and officers. From this the Sages derive that Torah scholars are exempt from taxes imposed upon the people for defense purposes, for their study of Torah is the greatest defense available to the Jewish nation (*Bava Basra* 8a).

Others explain these words to be continuing the castigation of the nation of Ephraim: Although they have paid tribute to the gentile nations, I shall nevertheless gather these nations together to conquer the Jewish people and send them into exile. First, however, the latter will begin to complain about the burden imposed upon them by the gentile kings and officers, but their complaints will be minor compared to the scope of their misfortune when they are actually exiled (*Ibn Ezra; Radak*).

Alternatively: וַיָּחֵלּוּ refers to a duration of time. They will enjoy a brief hiatus from their misfortune, during which time they will have kings and officers who will carry the burden and lead them. However, soon thereafter they will be conquered (*R' Eliezer of Beaugency*).

Abarbanel sees in this verse a reference to the plight of the Jews in exile, in which they suffer only partially at the hands of the kings and officers but much more so from the hordes of the populace.

11. כִּי־הִרְבָּה אֶפְרַיִם מִזְבְּחוֹת לַחֲטֹא הָיוּ־לוֹ מִזְבְּחוֹת לַחֲטֹא — *For Ephraim has increased altars to sin; he had altars to sin.* Why will I first impose hardship upon

1. This is the way *Rashi* interprets the words of *Targum*. *Radak* understands the phrase *like a wild* ערד to be part of *Targum's* interpretation of the first half of the verse. Accordingly, ערד would be translated by its other meaning, a wild donkey, and the phrase would read: *for that which they followed their desires like a wild donkey.*

°אֶכְתָּב
°רֻבֵּי ק'

°אכתוב־לוֹ °רבּוֹ תּוֹרָתִי כְּמוֹ־זָר נֶחְשָׁבוּ׃ זִבְחֵי
הַבְהָבַי יִזְבְּחוּ בָשָׂר וַיֹּאכֵלוּ יהוה לֹא רָצָם עַתָּה
יִזְכֹּר עֲוֹנָם וְיִפְקֹד חַטֹּאותָם הֵמָּה מִצְרַיִם יָשׁוּבוּ׃

them and then redeem them (*Rashi*)? For despite their access to the altars[1] of idolatry that they received from their fathers, they found it necessary to add to them and increase even further the extent of their sinful worship [thus indicating the depth of their commitment to their false gods] (*Ibn Ezra; Radak; Abarbanel*).

Targum renders: *For the house of Ephraim has increased altars to sin; they had altars to their idols for a pitfall.* [I.e., the altars bequeathed to them by previous generations were pitfalls leading them to sin, but their existence was not due to the iniquity of that generation. However, the building of additional altars was in itself a transgression of the will of Hashem; thus these are defined as being inherently sinful.] *Radak* comments to this: *And he has interpreted nicely.*

Malbim interprets: *Ephraim increased altars for sin* — i.e., for idolatry; *the altars they had from before* — i.e., those which were dedicated for offerings to Hashem — *were sinful in their eyes.*

12. אֶכְתָּב־לוֹ רֻבֵּי תּוֹרָתִי כְּמוֹ־זָר נֶחְשָׁבוּ — *I write for them the great things of My Torah; they are regarded as something alien.* I constantly send My prophets to admonish them and to seek to inscribe [in their hearts] the great and noble laws and principles which are written in My Torah (*Rashi; Metzudos David*).[2] But their words elicit no response and inspire no repentance, for the people have come to view these laws and principles as something alien, to which they do not relate. Indeed in the days of Josiah, the discovery of a Sefer Torah was considered something out of the ordinary (*Radak*).

Alternatively: They viewed My Torah as something strange and illogical, not fitting to be followed (*R' Eliezer of Beaugency*). *Metzudos* translates: They considered it as the words of a stranger whom they did not recognize; therefore they quickly forgot it.

Mahari Kara interprets the verse a bit differently: I wrote for them many prophecies and admonitions to teach them the proper way, but they viewed them as something alien, as if they had never heard any prophecies or rebuke.

Abarbanel understands this verse as depicting the contrast between the attitude of the Jewish people to their chosen idols and their attitude toward the Torah of the Almighty: Whereas — as stated in the previous verse — they continuously increased and multiplied their altars to their false gods, the words of My Torah were strange and alien to them. Thus, if I were to write over the many laws of My Torah, it would be in their eyes like something new and alien to which they had no previous exposure.

13. In this verse, the prophet addresses the people of Judah, who eventually followed in the wicked ways of the ten

1. *Radak* points out that the form of the word מִזְבְּחוֹת is actually one of סְמִיכוּת, in which the noun is used as a descriptive phrase for the following word. In this case, the object of the phrase is unspoken; it may be understood to refer either to the altars of the golden calves or the altars of the idols in general.

2. The verse is written רֻבּוֹ תּוֹרָתִי but reads רֻבֵּי תּוֹרָתִי. The text as written means the precepts that exist in multitude in My Torah. As read, however, it is rendered: the great and noble precepts which are found in My Torah. The word אֶכְתּוֹב is written in the future tense but actually refers to the past. It is written in this form to indicate that it is as if Hashem rewrites the Torah for them every day, as He sends them His prophets to remind them of its precepts and to admonish them to follow them (*Radak*).

12 *I write for them the great things of My Torah;*
they are regarded as something alien. 13 *The sacri-*
fices of My burnt offerings let them slaughter for
flesh and eat [it]; HASHEM does not desire them.
Now He will remember their transgressions and
punish their sins, and they will return to Egypt.

tribes, and relied upon the merit of their sacrifices in the Temple to protect them from punishment (*Abarbanel; Metzudos David*).

זִבְחֵי הַבְהָבַי יִזְבְּחוּ בָשָׂר וַיֹּאכֵלוּ ה׳ לֹא רָצָם — *The sacrifices of My burnt offerings let them slaughter for flesh and eat [it]; HASHEM does not desire them.* You offer עולות — offerings burnt in their entirety — before Me upon My Altar [seeking thereby to evoke My good will]. But it would be better if you would simply slaughter those animals and eat them yourselves, for I have no desire for such offerings and I am not at all appeased by them (*Rashi; Abarbanel; Metzudos David*).[1]

Others understand הַבְהָבַי to refer to sacrifices that are partially burnt on the Altar and partially eaten. Thus, they interpret as follows: The sacrifices that you burn before Me are slaughtered merely for the purpose of consuming their meat, since they are not accompanied by your repentance. Therefore, they are not desirable to Me (*Radak; R' Eliezer of Beaugency*).[2]

Mahari Kara offers a third approach: Your *olos*, burnt offerings, that are consumed entirely upon the Altar, as well as your *shelamim*, peace offerings, from which the owners also partake — let them all be eaten together. For due to the corruption of your deeds, the Almighty does not desire your sacrifices.

Malbim offers a unique interpretation to this phrase: The burnt offerings, which have been designated to be consumed upon the Altar, you use instead for private consumption. You do so because you claim that the Almighty does not involve Himself in the affairs of mankind — even to the point of accepting their sacrifices. Therefore, you bring offerings instead to your false gods and idols.

עַתָּה יִזְכֹּר עֲוֹנָם וְיִפְקֹד חַטֹּאותָם הֵמָּה מִצְרַיִם יָשׁוּבוּ — *Now He will remember their transgressions and punish their sins, and they will return to Egypt.* [Due to all this decadence,] the Almighty shall remember[3] their transgressions and punish them for all their sins in the near future, and they will be forced to flee to Egypt in the course of their exile (*Abarbanel; Metzudos David*).

Alternatively: This refers to the party of Jews led by Yochanan ben Kareiah who defied the instructions of Hashem as issued through Jeremiah and fled to Egypt (see comm. to 7:13). For this — declares the Almighty — I will remember

1. Others interpret הַבְהָבַי to mean *gifts* — the gifts that they think they are giving Me by offering sacrifices on the Altar (*Radak*).

2. *Radak* supports this interpretation and rejects that of *Rashi* on the basis of that which the word ויאכלו is written with a *"patach"* under the *"vuv"* (וַיאכלו) rather than a *"sheva"* (וְיאכלו). It is therefore rendered *and they eat* rather than *let them eat*. However, *Minchas Shai* notes that in other editions to the text it is actually written with a *"sheva."*

3. [Although the Almighty obviously does not forget anything and thus has no need of subsequent remembering, all descriptions of the Almighty actually refer to His interactions with creation. Thus, when He responds to their deeds it is depicted as if He remembers them at that time.]

יד וַיִּשְׁכַּח יִשְׂרָאֵל אֶת־עֹשֵׂהוּ וַיִּבֶן הֵיכָלוֹת וִיהוּדָה
הִרְבָּה עָרִים בְּצֻרוֹת וְשִׁלַּחְתִּי־אֵשׁ בְּעָרָיו
א וְאָכְלָה אַרְמְנֹתֶיהָ׃ אַל־תִּשְׂמַח
יִשְׂרָאֵל ׀ אֶל־גִּיל כָּעַמִּים כִּי זָנִיתָ מֵעַל
אֱלֹהֶיךָ אָהַבְתָּ אֶתְנָן עַל כָּל־גָּרְנוֹת דָּגָן׃
ב גֹּרֶן וָיֶקֶב לֹא יִרְעֵם וְתִירוֹשׁ יְכַחֶשׁ בָּהּ׃

their transgressions and punish them for their sins, and those who flee there will be wiped out to the last soul (*Radak* cf. *Ibn Ezra; Mahari Kara*).

14. וַיִּשְׁכַּח יִשְׂרָאֵל אֶת־עֹשֵׂהוּ וַיִּבֶן הֵיכָלוֹת וִיהוּדָה הִרְבָּה עָרִים בְּצֻרוֹת וְשִׁלַּחְתִּי־אֵשׁ בְּעָרָיו וְאָכְלָה אַרְמְנֹתֶיהָ — *And Israel has forgotten his Maker and he has built temples, and Judah has increased fortified cities, and I will send a fire into his cities and it will consume his palaces.* The people of the nations of Israel have forgotten the Almighty Who elevated them and glorified them. They have built great fortifications for protection rather than placing their faith in the Almighty (*Mahari Kara; Radak; Abarbanel*). However, all their efforts will be to no avail, for I will send against them the enemy who will conquer their land and set fire to all of their palaces and fortifications — even the Temple of Hashem (*Radak*). Alternatively: I will bring down upon them such total destruction that it will seem as if their land had been consumed by a great fire (ibid.).

Others interpret the first phrase as also describing the great fortifications erected for protection in place of relying on Hashem (*Mahari Kara; Radak*).

IX

1. אַל־תִּשְׂמַח יִשְׂרָאֵל אֶל־גִּיל כָּעַמִּים כִּי זָנִיתָ מֵעַל אֱלֹהֶיךָ — *Rejoice not, Israel, like the exultation of the nations, for you have strayed from your God.* Do not allow yourselves to rejoice, Israel, even for those things over which all nations exult — such as weddings and similar celebrations. For you have strayed from Hashem your God, and it is therefore fitting that you be totally wrapped up in mourning. When Moshe castigated the Jewish nation in the desert for worshiping the golden calf, they hearkened to his words and mourned for their misdeeds. But you are rebuked daily by My prophets for your transgressions, yet no one takes their words to heart (*Ibn Ezra; Radak; Metzudos David*).

Mahari Kara interprets: Do not rejoice over your worship of false gods, as do the other nations. For although they, too, have come to realize that their idols do not contain the power to help or harm them, they nevertheless continue to serve them out of loyalty to the faith of their fathers. But you have strayed from your own faith and sought the strange gods of other people.

Others see this as the prophet's advice to the people concerning their behavior while in exile: When blessing is bestowed upon the nations among whom you live, do not join with them in their rejoicing, for you have strayed from your God [and must always remain aware of your sorry plight] (*Abarbanel;* cf. *Alshich*).

Malbim understands this verse to be the foretelling of future events: You will not be able to rejoice along with the other nations, Israel. For they are under the protection of the heavenly forces that control events here on earth, and their fortunes thus rise with the ascension of their angels. You, however, were not allotted such benefactors, since I took

8/14 14 *And Israel has forgotten his Maker and he has*
built temples, and Judah has increased fortified
cities, and I will send a fire into his cities and it
will consume his palaces.

9/1-2 1 *Rejoice not, Israel, like the exultation of the*
nations, for you have strayed from your God.
You have loved a harlot's fee on all threshing
floors of grain. 2 *The threshing floor and wine pit*
shall not feed them and wine shall deny her.

you as My personal portion in creation. Therefore, when you rebuff the sanctuary of My love, you are left unprotected and thus vulnerable to all misfortune.[1]

אָהַבְתָּ אֶתְנָן זוֹנָה עַל כָּל־גָּרְנוֹת דָּגָן — *You have loved a harlot's fee on all threshing floors of grain.* You have desired and chosen to be like a prostitute, who appears at the threshing floor to receive her fee in grain (*Rashi*). So have you prostituted yourself before all the nations and degraded yourself by turning to them in search of assistance [instead of seeking your protection from the Almighty] (*Metzudos David; Malbim*).

Radak renders: *when upon all threshing floors was grain.* When I bestowed My blessing upon them and filled their threshing floors with grain, they were unfaithful to Me like a harlot, and pursued the service of other gods. Alternatively: They worshiped their idols there in the threshing houses, in their belief that the gods who dwelt there were responsible for their prosperity (ibid.).

Another interpretation is: *You loved to pay a harlot's fee on all threshing floors of grain* — rather than fulfilling My commandments to tithe your grain to give to the Levite and offer a second tithe to Me, you prostituted yourselves to the idols and offered portions of your produce to them instead (*Ibn Ezra; Abarbanel*).

2. גֹּרֶן וָיֶקֶב לֹא יִרְעֵם וְתִירוֹשׁ יְכַחֶשׁ בָּהּ — *The threshing floor and wine pit shall not feed them and wine shall deny her.*[2] They refuse to acknowledge that I am the source of their sustenance, and

1. In this vein, *R' Meir Simchah of Dvinsk* (*Meshech Chachmah, Leviticus* 26:44), using our verse, explained the awesome devastation that was to overtake European Jewry a full twelve years before World War II! He wrote: Soon they will be saying, *Our fathers inherited falsities* (*Jer.* 16:19). The Israelite will altogether forget his heritage and will be considered a new, inexperienced citizen. He will leave the study of his own law to study languages which do not belong to him. He will learn from the worthless, rather than from the worthwhile — believing that "Berlin is Jerusalem"; imitating the words of [the gentiles] . . . *Rejoice not, Israel, like the exultion of the nations.* Then will come a rushing stormwind, uprooting him from his source, carrying him to a distant nation whose language he has not learned. Then he will know that he is a stranger, that his language is our holy tongue . . . that his heritage is the root of Israel, and his consolations are those of Hashem's prophets . . .

2. The prophet uses the phrase *shall deny her*, referring to the nation of Ephraim, which is sometimes referred to in the plural form — referring to the people, and sometimes in the singular — referring to the nation as a whole. The use of the feminine gender is appropriate in reference to the congregation [which is a feminine word]. However, some versions to the text read יְכַחֶשׁ בָּם, *shall deny them* (*Radak*). [Indeed, *Targum* seems to have had such a version.] *Abarbanel* understands the use of the singular feminine form to relate to the previous verse, in which the nation is compared to a prostitute.

ג לֹא יֵשְׁבוּ בְּאֶרֶץ יהוה וְשָׁב אֶפְרַיִם מִצְרַיִם
ד וּבְאַשּׁוּר טָמֵא יֹאכֵלוּ: לֹא־יִסְּכוּ לַיהוה ׀ יַיִן וְלֹא
יֶעֶרְבוּ־לוֹ זִבְחֵיהֶם כְּלֶחֶם אוֹנִים לָהֶם כָּל־
אֹכְלָיו יִטַּמָּאוּ כִּי־לַחְמָם לְנַפְשָׁם לֹא יָבוֹא בֵּית
ה יהוה: מַה־תַּעֲשׂוּ לְיוֹם מוֹעֵד וּלְיוֹם חַג־יהוה:

that it is I who blesses them with their grain and wine. They have abandoned My service, worshiping instead the false deities they have chosen for themselves. Therefore, I will bring down upon them blight and decay as well as the sword of the enemy, eradicating all of their produce. Thus, their grain and the grapes[1] that are placed in their wine pits will no longer feed them, and their wine shall deny them the benefits that they seek from it (*Radak*).

Other commentators offer different interpretations to the word יְכַחֶשׁ. *Ibn Ezra* renders: *It will deny them recognition* — as if it does not know them [i.e., and it will thus refuse to provide for them]. *Mahari Kara* translates: *It shall cease. Targum* renders: *wine will not provide them.*

Alshich interprets: *The granary and wine pit will not feed them* — for they will provide no food. And even if there will be wine in the wine pits, *wine will deny them* — i.e., it will spoil in the barrel.

3. לֹא יֵשְׁבוּ בְּאֶרֶץ ה׳ — *They shall not dwell in the land of* HASHEM. Because they have defiled their land with their abominations, they shall no longer be permitted to dwell there, for the Holy Land does not abide idolatry in its midst for any length of time (*Rashi; Radak;* see *Leviticus* 18:28, *Ramban* ad loc.).

Abarbanel sees this as referring back to the beginning of the chapter: There is yet another reason that you should not rejoice among the nations, for it is appropriate for one who is banished from his own homeland to constantly mourn his loss and refrain from indulgence in celebrations and exultation.

וְשָׁב אֶפְרַיִם מִצְרַיִם — *But Ephraim shall return to Egypt.* [Ephraim shall flee to Egypt to escape its bitter plight.]

Although the Torah promises (*Exodus* 14:13): *You shall no longer continue to see them,* it also states (*Deuteronomy* 28:68): *And* HASHEM *shall return you to Egypt* [i.e., in punishment for your sins. This was carried out with the people of Ephraim]. Despite the fact that it was the Assyrians who exiled the nation of Israel, many of its citizens had already fled to Egypt prior to the exile in order to escape the hunger and oppression that plagued the land. In addition, there were some members of the ten tribes who fled to Egypt together with the citizens of Judah against the orders of Jeremiah (*Radak*).

וּבְאַשּׁוּר טָמֵא יֹאכֵלוּ — *And in Assyria they shall eat that which is defiled.* While in exile in Assyria they will be forced to eat bread which has become ritually defiled, for it will no longer be possible to maintain the level of purity and cleanliness that precludes the partaking of such foods (*Radak*). This will come in retribution for their wanton consumption in the Holy Land, where they indulged in food and drink without first offering their tithes to the Almighty (*Ibn Ezra*).

4. Now the prophet changes his focus once again and addresses his words to the people of Judah, in whose land was the Temple (*Abarbanel*).

לֹא־יִסְּכוּ לַה׳ יַיִן וְלֹא יֶעֶרְבוּ־לוֹ — *They should not pour out wine to* HASHEM *[for] they will not be pleasing to Him.* Let them

1. The word יֶקֶב, meaning *wine pit*, can be used in reference to the wine and/or to the grapes from which it is made. In this case, since wine is discussed in the following phrase, the wine pits must be understood as referring to the grapes (*Radak*).

[3] *They shall not dwell in the land of HASHEM, but
Ephraim shall return to Egypt and in Assyria they
shall eat that which is defiled.* [4] *They should not pour
out wine to HASHEM [for] they will not be pleasing to
Him; their sacrifices will be to them like the bread
of mourners; all who partake of it shall be defiled;
for their bread is for their soul, not to come to the
House of HASHEM.* [5] *What will you do for the designated day, and for the day of Hashem's slaughter?*

no longer pour libations of wine upon the altar of Hashem. These no longer please Him, since the people continue to transgress His commandments (*Radak; R' Eliezer of Beaugency*).

Alternatively: *They will not pour libations of wine to HASHEM and they will not please Him* — i.e. with their *menachos* (flour-offerings), about which it is stated (*Malachi* 3:4): *And the minchah of Judah shall be pleasing to Hashem* (*Rashi; Mahari Kara*). According to *Ibn Ezra*, this refers to those who will remain behind in the Holy Land after the bulk of the nation is exiled: They will [generally] not have wine to pour libations, and even if they do, these will not be pleasing to the Almighty.

Alshich interprets this portion of the verse in the following manner: Because they have not offered libations to Hashem, their own wine will no longer be sweet for them but will rather spoil in their possession, since it lacks the blessing evoked by the libations.

זִבְחֵיהֶם כְּלֶחֶם אוֹנִים לָהֶם כָּל־אֹכְלָיו יִטַּמָּאוּ — *Their sacrifices will be to them like the bread of mourners; all who partake of it shall be defiled.* As long as they fulfilled My will, the sacrifices they brought before Me were pleasant to Me (*Mahari Kara*). Now, however, these have become comparable to the bread of mourners — which is ritually defiled because of the mourners' contact with the deceased. They are thus unacceptable upon the altar (*Rashi; Ibn Ezra; Radak*). Alternatively, לֶחֶם אוֹנִים means *bread of robbery* — bread that they have procured by employing their power — אוֹנִים — to steal from others (*Rashi; Metzudos David*), which defiles him who eats it (*Metzudos David*).

כִּי־לַחְמָם לְנַפְשָׁם לֹא יָבוֹא בֵּית ה׳ — *For their bread is for their soul, not to come to the House of HASHEM.*

For the bread of the sacrifices that they offer is solely for the purpose of feeding their own soul, and not in order to honor the Almighty with their offerings (*R' Eliezer of Beaugency*).[1]

Others interpret: Let them consume their bread themselves and not bring it to the House of Hashem for sacrifices — since they are in any case not pleasing to Me (*Rashi; Abarbanel; Metzudos David*). *Radak* renders: Let them not bring to the House of Hashem those sacrifices that they bring to achieve forgiveness for their souls. Since they commit their transgressions willfully, their offerings will be to no avail [as sacrifices are effective only for sins committed in error].

5. מַה־תַּעֲשׂוּ לְיוֹם מוֹעֵד וּלְיוֹם חַג־ה׳ — *What will you do for the designated day, and for the day of Hashem's slaughter?* What will you do to save yourselves (*Metzudos David*) on the day designated for the invasion of the enemy? [And how will you protect yourselves] from the day in

1. [Although he is the only commentator to interpret the verse in this manner, the translation follows his approach because it is the only one that explains the use of the word כִּי.]

ו כִּֽי־הִנֵּ֤ה הָֽלְכוּ֙ מִשֹּׁ֔ד מִצְרַ֥יִם תְּקַבְּצֵ֖ם מֹ֣ף תְּקַבְּרֵ֑ם
מַחְמַ֣ד לְכַסְפָּ֗ם קִמּוֹשׂ֙ יִֽירָשֵׁ֔ם ח֖וֹחַ בְּאָהֳלֵיהֶֽם׃
ז בָּ֣אוּ ׀ יְמֵ֣י הַפְּקֻדָּ֗ה בָּ֚אוּ יְמֵ֣י הַשִּׁלֻּ֔ם יֵדְע֖וּ יִשְׂרָאֵ֑ל
אֱוִ֣יל הַנָּבִ֗יא מְשֻׁגָּע֙ אִ֣ישׁ הָר֔וּחַ עַ֚ל רֹ֣ב עֲוֺנְךָ֔
ח וְרַבָּ֖ה מַשְׂטֵמָֽה׃ צֹפֶ֥ה אֶפְרַ֖יִם עִם־אֱלֹהָ֑י נָבִ֞יא פַּ֤ח
יָקוֹשׁ֙ עַל־כָּל־דְּרָכָ֔יו מַשְׂטֵמָ֖ה בְּבֵ֥ית אֱלֹהָֽיו׃

which Hashem shall bring about the wanton slaughter that He has decreed upon you[1] (*Rashi;* cf. *Metzudos David*)?

Others interpret: What will you do when the days of your Festivals arrive and you are banished to foreign lands? How will you bring your many offerings required on the Festivals at that time (*Abarbanel; Alshich*)? (See 2:3 for discussion of the difference between מוֹעֵד and חַג.)

6. כִּי־הִנֵּה הָלְכוּ מִשֹּׁד מִצְרַיִם תְּקַבְּצֵם מֹף תְּקַבְּרֵם — *For behold they have gone from plunder; Egypt shall gather them in; Moph shall bury them.* Behold they have fled their homes in the face of the great degree of plunder[2] that has befallen the land with the arrival of the hordes of Nebuchadnezzar (*Rashi*). Egypt shall gather them in when they flee there under the leadership of Yochanan ben Kareiah (see comm. to 7:12), but Moph shall bury them, for they will perish there by the sword and from famine (*Metzudos David; Radak*).

Abarbanel suggests that this verse may refer to the Jewish settlement of Alexandria which existed during and after the era of the Second Temple. It was eventually wiped out by the forces of the Roman emperor Trajan.

Moph was situated in Egypt (*Rashi*). It is also referred to in Scripture as Noph (*Radak*). *Targum* identifies it as Memphis, which was the capital city of southern Egypt. It was situated approximately twenty-five kilometers south of modern Cairo and was also used as a major site for burial grounds (*Daas Mikra*). *Abarbanel* postulates that it may refer to the western portion of Egypt, where many Jews fled after the destruction of both the First and Second Temples.

מַחְמַד לְכַסְפָּם קִמּוֹשׂ יִירָשֵׁם חוֹחַ בְּאָהֳלֵיהֶם — *The treasure houses of their silver — thistles shall inherit them; briars [will grow] in their tents.* The treasure houses which once contained their silver will be destroyed and laid waste, until thorns and thistles will overrun them, along with the tents in which they dwelled (*Radak; Metzudos David*). Alternatively: קִמּוֹשׂ and חוֹחַ are species of wild animals (*Targum; Rashi*).

Abarbanel interprets this phrase metaphorically: Jerusalem, which was the focus of their desires like a treasure house of silver, will be laid waste and overrun.

Although the people continue to insist that the prophecies of doom are false and the calamities foretold will not come to pass, the prophet declares that their arrival is now imminent (*Abarbanel; Malbim*).

7. בָּאוּ יְמֵי הַפְּקֻדָּה בָּאוּ יְמֵי הַשִּׁלֻּם יֵדְעוּ יִשְׂרָאֵל אֱוִיל הַנָּבִיא מְשֻׁגָּע אִישׁ הָרוּחַ עַל רֹב עֲוֹנְךָ וְרַבָּה מַשְׂטֵמָה — *The days of visitation have come; the days of requital have arrived; Israel shall know [that] the prophet is insane; the man of spirit mad; [all] because of the abundance of your iniquity, and the enmity is great.* The days of visitation, in which your sins will be recounted in order to be visited upon you,

1. *Rashi* thus translates חַג to mean slaughter. *Radak* follows the same approach to the verse but translates חַג in the usual manner: the day in which Hashem has declared a *festival* for all of the enemies, who will gather together to destroy the Temple and slaughter the inhabitants of the land.

2. *Radak* renders שֹׁד to mean *famine.* The majority of commentators, however, follow *Rashi's* view.

6 *For behold they have gone from plunder; Egypt shall
gather them in; Moph shall bury them. The treasure
houses of their silver — thistles shall inherit them;
briars [will grow] in their tents.* 7 *The days of visitation
have come; the days of requital have arrived; Israel
shall know [that] the prophet is insane; the man of spirit
mad; [all] because of the abundance of your iniquity,
and the enmity is great.* 8 *The prophet of Ephraim is
with My God; the prophet is a net that ensnares [him] in
all his ways and causes enmity in the House of his God.*

have finally come. The days of requital, in which your debts to the Almighty will be exacted from you, have finally arrived (*Rashi; Malbim, Beur HaMilos*). As your retribution befalls you, Children of Israel, you will finally know and recognize — and even acknowledge — the error of your ways in following the false prophets who led you astray. Then you will declare: Those false prophets and spurious men of spirit, who continuously reassured us that all will be well, are nothing but lunatics and madmen (*Radak; Abarbanel; Metzudos David*).

Others interpret this phrase as referring to the true prophets of Hashem: Israel — those very people who had previously said, "The prophet is insane; the man of spirit is mad" — will finally come to recognize the authenticity of the prophets and the veracity of their words (*Mahari Kara; Malbim;* cf. *Ibn Ezra*).

Rashi renders: Even the true prophets among them will become wayward, such as Chananiah ben Azzur [who disputed the prophecy of Jeremiah concerning the oncoming destruction of the kingdom of Judah and proclaimed in the name of Hashem that the yoke of Babylonia upon them would be broken] (cf. *Jeremiah* 28; *Sanhedrin* 89a).

עַל רֹב עֲוֹנְךָ וְרַבָּה מַשְׂטֵמָה — *[All] because of the abundance of your iniquity, and the enmity is great.* All this shall befall you because of the abundance of iniquity which you have perpetrated and the enmity the Almighty has for you as a result (*R' Eliezer of Beaugency; Abarbanel*). Alternatively: Your following of the false prophets was caused by the great degree of your iniquity [which led you astray]. Therefore, the Almighty has come to hate you (*Radak*).

Ibn Ezra interprets *the enmity is great* as referring to the hatred for Hashem which lies in the hearts of the people.

8. צֹפֶה אֶפְרַיִם עִם־אֱלֹהָי — *The prophet of Ephraim is with My God.* The prophet chosen by Ephraim declares his false prophecies in the name of Hashem (*Mahari Kara; Abarbanel*). Alternatively: Hosea declares: *He speaks against my God*; the Almighty has proclaimed that calamity will befall the Jewish nation, but the [false] prophet denies the truth of that declaration and claims that all is well (*R' Eliezer of Beaugency*).

Others interpret the phrase as referring to the idols: Ephraim has established for himself a prophet who speaks in the name of his false gods (*Radak; Metzudos David*). Alternatively: They have established prophets who steer them towards the service of their false gods (*Rashi*).[1]

נָבִיא פַּח יָקוֹשׁ עַל־כָּל־דְּרָכָיו מַשְׂטֵמָה בְּבֵית אֱלֹהָיו — *The prophet is a net that ensnares [him] in all his ways and causes enmity in the House of his God.* That false

1. *Rashi* apparently had a version to the text which states עִם אֱלֹהָיו *with "his" god* (*Abarbanel;* see ibid.). The same applies to *Radak* (*Parshandatha*).

ט הֶעְמִיקוּ שִׁחֵתוּ כִּימֵי הַגִּבְעָה יִזְכּוֹר עֲוֹנָם
י יִפְקוֹד חַטֹּאותָם: כַּעֲנָבִים
בַּמִּדְבָּר מָצָאתִי יִשְׂרָאֵל כְּבִכּוּרָה בִתְאֵנָה
בְּרֵאשִׁיתָהּ רָאִיתִי אֲבוֹתֵיכֶם הֵמָּה בָּאוּ בַעַל־
פְּעוֹר וַיִּנָּזְרוּ לַבֹּשֶׁת וַיִּהְיוּ שִׁקּוּצִים כְּאָהֳבָם:

prophet is like a net to the people of Ephraim, for he ensnares and entraps them in the evil of his words (*Ibn Ezra; Radak; Abarbanel*), and thus arouses enmity between them and the Almighty in the Temple where the Divine Presence resides (*Radak; Abarbanel*). Alternatively: The false prophet dwells in the house of his false gods and from there generates enmity between the Jewish people and Hashem (*Radak; Metzudos David*).

Others render: *[for the] prophet — a net that ensnares [him] in all his ways* — for they lay traps for the true prophets of Hashem in order to ensnare them and bring about their downfall (*Rashi; Mahari Kara*). Indeed, they are filled with enmity and loathing for the prophets of Hashem, who dwell in His house in order to receive His word (*Mahari Kara*). *Rashi* comments: In the Temple they murdered Zechariah and sought to kill Jeremiah.[1]

9. הֶעְמִיקוּ שִׁחֵתוּ כִּימֵי הַגִּבְעָה יִזְכּוֹר עֲוֹנָם יִפְקוֹד חַטֹּאותָם — *They deepened [and] corrupted [their ways] as in the days of Gibeah; He will remember their iniquities: He will visit their sins.* They deepened the extent of their transgressions and corrupted their ways until they reached the decadence of the people of Gibeah. Just as those sinners tolerated the mistreatment of the concubine in their midst and went so far as to support the perpetrators of that misdeed (see *Judges* 19 above, comm. to 5:8,9), so have these false prophets supported and encouraged the idolaters within the nation. Therefore, the Almighty shall bring down upon them retribution for their wickedness (*Metzudos David*).[2] *R' Eliezer of Beaugency* comments: Just as the people of Israel who attacked Benjamin sought counsel from the Almighty before they attacked but were nevertheless defeated [in the initial battle], so shall the people who rely on the comforting words of their false prophets be vanquished for continuing in their corrupt ways.

The infidelity of this nation to Me is not a new phenomenon; even in the first flush of our loving relationship, when I redeemed them from the land of Egypt, they shortly thereafter succumbed to the lure of promiscuity and idolatry (see *Abarbanel*). And just as I punished them at that time, despite the intensity of My affection, so shall I certainly exact retribution for their present misdeeds (*Malbim*).

10. כַּעֲנָבִים בַּמִּדְבָּר מָצָאתִי יִשְׂרָאֵל כְּבִכּוּרָה בִתְאֵנָה בְּרֵאשִׁיתָהּ רָאִיתִי אֲבוֹתֵיכֶם הֵמָּה בָּאוּ בַעַל־פְּעוֹר וַיִּנָּזְרוּ לַבֹּשֶׁת וַיִּהְיוּ שִׁקּוּצִים כְּאָהֳבָם — *Like grapes in the desert I found Israel; like a ripe fig on a fig tree in its beginning I viewed your fathers; they came to Baal Peor and they separated*

1. *Radak* cites this comment from the *midrash*, but notes that this verse is discussing the nation of Ephraim, whereas Zechariah was murdered in the Temple by the people of Judah. [Thus, this comment is not to be understood as the basic meaning of the verse but merely as bringing out an allusion to that occurrence.]

2. This follows the approach of most of the commentators. *Rashi*, however, adds: And some say that this refers to Givat Shaul, where the people demanded of Samuel that he provide them with a king (see *I Samuel* 15).

[9] *They deepened [and] corrupted [their ways] as in
the days of Gibeah; He will remember their iniquities:
He will visit their sins.* [10] *Like grapes in the desert I
found Israel; like a ripe fig on a fig tree in its beginning I viewed your fathers; they came to Baal Peor
and they separated themselves to [follow] shamefulness; and they became loathsome when they loved.*

themselves to [follow] shamefulness; and they became loathsome when they loved. When I first encountered the Jewish nation they were precious to Me like grapes in the desert, and I rejoiced over them like one rejoices over the first ripe fruits which sprout from his fig tree. Indeed, I was comparable then to one who travels in an arid desert bereft of fruit or refreshment and suddenly discovers grapes and figs from which he can partake. In this manner I found the Children of Israel in the desert and I fed them and cared for their needs (*Radak*). They were precious to Me like grapes, which is a fruit of great stature [since it is used to make wine], for they carried the stature of their illustrious forefathers. Their charm was further enhanced because *I found them in the desert* — i.e., they followed Me unquestioningly into the wilderness, without having any notion of how they would survive. And they were yet more beloved to Me like the first ripe fig, as they were the first and only nation upon whom I placed My name and in whom I entrusted My service (*Abarbanel;* cf. *Malbim*).

However, they did not appreciate My kindness to them (*Radak*) [nor repay Me in kind]. For when they came within the domain of the idol Baal Peor, they separated themselves from their fidelity to Me and turned instead to the shamefulness of an idol[1] whose worshipers are shamed and disgraced. Thus did they become loathsome[2] to Me when they defiled themselves through their promiscuity with the daughters of Moab and their worship of their idols (*Rashi; Ibn Ezra; Radak*).

Others render: *And they were loathsome like their love* — with the same intensity that I had loved them when they followed Me loyally so did I loathe them when they worshiped Baal Peor (*Radak* citing his father; *Metzudos David*).

According to *Abarbanel*, the entire focus of this verse is the promiscuity itself; the prophet is not yet dealing with the sin of idolatry. Thus, they came to Baal Peor and separated themselves from their chastity and sanctity to turn to the shame of adultery with

1. The Sages relate that when Balaam was unsuccessful in his attempt to place a curse upon the Jewish nation, he advised Balak, king of Moab, to overcome their invincible power by seducing them into promiscuity. Thus, the Moabites placed stands along the path of the Jewish nation in which prostitutes sat and sold linens. An older woman would sit outside and a younger one inside. When a Jew would be drawn to the store to buy linen, the older woman would quote him a price and the younger one would then offer him a better deal from inside. Thus, the Israelite would be drawn inside the store with the young prostitute. [As he would be involved in purchasing,] she would offer him to sit down while he perused her stock and she would then offer him a drink of wine. With this, he would be aroused and seek her favors, through which she induced him to worship her idols (*Sanhedrin* 106).

2. *Malbim* explains that the word כְּאָהֳבָם, *when they loved*, refers back to the entire phrase: *They separated themselves to shamefulness and became loathsome when they loved the daughters of Moab.* Through their promiscuity with the daughters of Moab, they were led to the even greater abomination of idolatry. *Radak* suggests that perhaps שקוצים refers to the idols they worshiped — *they [served] abominations when they loved.*

יא אֶפְרַיִם כָּעוֹף יִתְעוֹפֵף כְּבוֹדָם מִלֵּדָה וּמִבֶּטֶן
יב וּמֵהֵרָיוֹן: כִּי אִם־יְגַדְּלוּ אֶת־בְּנֵיהֶם וְשִׁכַּלְתִּים
יג מֵאָדָם כִּי־גַם־אוֹי לָהֶם בְּשׂוּרִי מֵהֶם: אֶפְרַיִם
כַּאֲשֶׁר־רָאִיתִי לְצוֹר שְׁתוּלָה בְנָוֶה וְאֶפְרַיִם
יד לְהוֹצִיא אֶל־הֹרֵג בָּנָיו: תֵּן־לָהֶם יהוה מַה־
תִּתֵּן תֵּן־לָהֶם רֶחֶם מַשְׁכִּיל וְשָׁדַיִם צֹמְקִים:

the daughters of Moab, and they themselves thus became loathsome just as their love for these women was an abomination.

The Sages offer the following insights into this verse: When they stood by Mt. Sinai the Jewish people were comparable to grapes: Just as grapes are beautiful on the outside but ugly within, so was Israel. When they said (*Exodus* 24:7): כֹּל אֲשֶׁר דִּבֶּר ה׳ נַעֲשֶׂה וְנִשְׁמָע, *We will do and we will hear all that* HASHEM *says*, this was with their mouths, but their hearts were not proper, as it is stated (*Psalms* 78:36,37): *And they fooled Him with their mouths and with their tongues they lied to Him, but their heart was not proper with Him.*

Another point [is as follows]: *like grapes in the desert* — Why the desert and not a settlement? Because [they were] like a man traveling in the desert, who is parched. If he is given bread to eat he seeks drink. If he is given water or wine to drink he seeks food. But if he is given grapes he eats them and lacks nothing, for they contain both food and drink. Thus, Israel in the desert received the Torah [which contains the qualities of both food (halachah) and drink (aggadah)] as it is stated (*Proverbs* 9:5): *Go partake of My bread and drink from the wine that I mixed*, and it is stated (*Isaiah* 55:1): *Whoever is thirsty go to water; go procure and eat* (*Yalkut Shimoni*).

11-12. אֶפְרַיִם כָּעוֹף יִתְעוֹפֵף כְּבוֹדָם מִלֵּדָה וּמִבֶּטֶן וּמֵהֵרָיוֹן: כִּי אִם־יְגַדְּלוּ אֶת־בְּנֵיהֶם וְשִׁכַּלְתִּים מֵאָדָם כִּי־גַם־אוֹי לָהֶם בְּשׂוּרִי מֵהֶם — *Ephraim — their honor will fly like a bird from [the time of] birth or from the womb or from conception. For if they shall rear their children I will bereave them from manhood, for woe is to them as well when I turn away from them.* The honor of Ephraim shall desert them speedily, like the flight of a swift bird (*Ibn Ezra*), for the true honor of the people is their children, and these will be decimated from among them. Some will die at birth; others will be the victims of miscarriages; and still others will never be created — i.e., the women will remain barren, unable to conceive (*Radak*).[1] But even this will be preferable to the alternative (*Abarbanel*). If there will be those who manage to bear children and raise them, these will die in their youth, without ever achieving adulthood and the status of "man." Yet, as great and terrible as this punishment may be, it alone will not suffice as retribution for their sins. Rather, I will bring misfortune down upon them until their suffering is all-encompassing, and the only fitting commentary to their plight will be "woe is to them." All this shall occur when I turn away from them [because of their wickedness] (*Radak; Abarbanel; Metzudos David*).

Rashi offers two alternative interpretations to this verse: In the first, he renders: *Let the honor of Ephraim fly like a bird* — Would that they be like a bird that flies from its nest and abstains from procreation. Thus would it be preferable

1. Others interpret: *from birth* — They will die shortly after birth and their parents will not achieve the honor that normally comes with the feast that accompanies the circumcision (*Abarbanel; Metzudos David*).

11 *Ephraim — their honor will fly like a bird from*
[the time of] birth or from the womb or from con-
ception. 12 *For if they shall rear their children I will*
bereave them from manhood, for woe is to them as
well when I turn away from them. 13 *Ephraim is as I*
saw Tyre, implanted in [her] dwelling place; but
Ephraim [seeks] to take his children out to the slayer.
14 *Give to them, HASHEM, what You will give; give*
to them a bereaving womb and shriveled breasts.

for them to lose their children from birth, from the womb, or from conception. For what good is their childbirth when I intend to prevent the offspring from ever achieving manhood?

Alternatively: All of the honor [that is the due result] of all that they will undergo through childbirth, pregnancy, and conception will disappear like a fleeting bird, for their children will be wiped out in their youth.

13. אֶפְרַיִם כַּאֲשֶׁר־רָאִיתִי לְצוֹר שְׁתוּלָה בְנָוֶה וְאֶפְרַיִם לְהוֹצִיא אֶל־הֹרֵג בָּנָיו — *Ephraim is as I saw Tyre, implanted in [her] dwelling place; but Ephraim [seeks] to take his children out to the slayer.* Just as I witnessed Tyre in her glory and prosperity, securely implanted in her dwelling place, so have I seen Ephraim [enjoying the blessings of My beneficence]. Yet how do they repay Me for My kindness? They involve themselves in taking their children to be sacrificed and slaughtered to [the idol worship known as] Molech (*Targum; Rashi*).[1]

Others render: *Ephraim [is set] to take out his children to the slayer* — I have seen Ephraim in peace and tranquility just as I once saw Tyre implanted securely in her dwelling place. However, just as Tyre was subsequently engulfed by the sea, so shall Ephraim be conquered and destroyed. Thus, when the enemy comes upon them and their cities, they will send their sons out to battle, but the enemy shall be victorious and their sons will be slain (*Ibn Ezra; Radak*).

Abarbanel understands this verse as defining a contrast: I have seen the contrast between Ephraim and the neighboring nation of Tyre. Whereas Tyre sits implanted securely in her dwelling place, Ephraim is busy sending her children to be slain by the conquering enemy.

14. Having foretold the horrible fate in store for the nation of Ephraim, and particularly for her children, the prophet is unable to restrain himself. He interjects with a prayer to the Almighty to spare them this awful calamity. Destroy the children at birth, or even earlier, rather than killing them in their youth, when the pain and anguish of their parents is so much greater (*Rashi; R' Eliezer of Beaugency*).

תֵּן־לָהֶם ה׳ מַה־תִּתֵּן תֵּן־לָהֶם רֶחֶם מַשְׁכִּיל וְשָׁדַיִם צֹמְקִים — *Give to them, HASHEM, what You will give; give to them a bereaving womb and shriveled breasts.* Give to them immediately, Hashem, that which You have decreed to inflict upon them at a later date (*Rashi; Abarbanel; Metzudos David*). *Give to them a bereaving womb* — that they should perish while still in their mother's womb, or at least bestow upon them shriveled breasts that will cause them to starve to death

1. This follows the rendition of the majority of the commentators. *Rashi* himself translates the phrase *implanted in her dwelling place* as referring to Ephraim — *Ephraim, as I saw Tyre, is implanted in her dwelling place.*

ט/טו־יז טו כָּל־רָעָתָם בַּגִּלְגָּל כִּי־שָׁם שְׂנֵאתִים עַל רֹעַ
מַעַלְלֵיהֶם מִבֵּיתִי אֲגָרְשֵׁם לֹא אוֹסֵף אַהֲבָתָם
טז כָּל־שָׂרֵיהֶם סֹרְרִים: הֻכָּה אֶפְרַיִם שָׁרְשָׁם יָבֵשׁ
°בַּל־ק׳ פְּרִי °בלי־יַעֲשׂוּן גַּם כִּי יֵלֵדוּן וְהֵמַתִּי מַחֲמַדֵּי
יז בִטְנָם: יִמְאָסֵם אֱלֹהַי כִּי לֹא שָׁמְעוּ לוֹ וְיִהְיוּ
י/א א נֹדְדִים בַּגּוֹיִם: גֶּפֶן בּוֹקֵק
יִשְׂרָאֵל פְּרִי יְשַׁוֶּה־לּוֹ כְּרֹב לְפִרְיוֹ הִרְבָּה

while they are still tiny infants. For both of these fates are preferable to their dying when in their youth (*Ibn Ezra; Mahari Kara; Radak; R' Eliezer of Beaugency*).

Rashi interprets *a bereaving womb* to mean that they should die at the moment that they emerge from the womb and enter the world. *Abarbanel* and *Metzudos David* understand *shriveled breasts* to imply that the mothers should not conceive whatsoever. Their breasts will thus be dry and shriveled from the lack of milk, which enters a woman's body only when she is pregnant.

15. כָּל־רָעָתָם בַּגִּלְגָּל כִּי שָׁם שְׂנֵאתִים עַל רֹעַ מַעַלְלֵיהֶם — *All their evil is in Gilgal where I hated them for the evil of their deeds.* All of their evil was revealed and exposed in Gilgal (*Targum*), where they established idols and worshiped them extensively. They chose this site for their idolatry because it was there that the Tabernacle was set up when the Jewish nation first entered into the Holy Land. The prophets of Baal therefore instructed them that it was a provident site for religious service (*Rashi; Radak; Metzudos David*). Thus, in this place I hated and loathed their presence due to this evil (*Metzudos David*).

Others relate that Gilgal was singled out because the nation gathered there in the times of Samuel and demanded a king like all other nations. Because they thereby expressed their animosity to Me and My direct rule over them, I too, came to loathe them in turn (*Radak; Abarbanel*). *Ibn Ezra* interprets: In Gilgal they should have been especially loyal to Me, since that was the place where they first entered the Land through My great blessings.

מִבֵּיתִי אֲגָרְשֵׁם — *From My house I will banish them.* Because they have thus spurned Me and My worship, and have chosen instead the service of other gods, I will banish them from My House and raze it to the ground, so that even if they choose to pursue My service it will no longer be possible (*Radak*).

Abarbanel interprets *My House* to refer to all of *the Land of Israel.*

Mahari Kara offers the following commentary: In every place where there had originally been sanctity, there they established their idolatries. Thus, in Gilgal, where the Tabernacle stood throughout the fourteen years of conquering and settling the land, they erected idols. And in My House, which had been designated for holiness, they placed an idol in the Sanctuary.

לֹא אוֹסֵף אַהֲבָתָם כָּל שָׂרֵיהֶם סֹרְרִים — *I will not continue to love them; all their officers are rebellious.* I will no longer shower love upon them, for now that their leaders and officers are rebellious against Me there is no hope of their being rebuked and returning to the proper path (*Radak*).

Abarbanel comments: *Their officers* refers to the kings who ruled over Israel [i.e., the kingdom of the ten tribes] after the split of the kingdom, all of whom were wayward and rebellious against the Almighty.

16. הֻכָּה אֶפְרַיִם שָׁרְשָׁם יָבֵשׁ פְּרִי בַל־יַעֲשׂוּן גַּם כִּי יֵלֵדוּן וְהֵמַתִּי מַחֲמַדֵּי בִטְנָם — *Ephraim had*

9/15-17 [15] *All their evil is in Gilgal where I hated them for the
evil of their deeds; from My House I will banish them;
I will not continue to love them; all their officers are
rebellious.* [16] *Ephraim had been smitten; their root is
withered; they will not produce fruit; even if they gave
birth I will slay the treasures of their wombs.* [17] *My God
shall spurn them for they have not obeyed Him, and
they shall wander among the nations.*

10/1 [1] *Israel is a vine that has eliminated the fruit that is fitting for it; when his fruits were plentiful he increased*

been smitten; their root is withered; they will not produce fruit; even if they gave birth I will slay the treasures of their wombs. Ephraim had been smitten by his enemies, and has become analogous to a tree whose roots have withered, and thus gives no fruit. Therefore, as a general rule, the people of Ephraim will bear no offspring. In the rare case when they do have children, the treasured and most desirable among them will be slain in their youth (*Radak; Metzudos David*). *Targum* renders: The house of Israel is comparable to a tree whose root is smitten from below and its branches are withered from above; [thus] it provides no fruit. Even if they will abound with children, I will slay the treasures of their womb. *Ibn Ezra* adds: The smiting of the tree [and the withering of the fruits] is a parable for the fathers and the children. *Rashi* interprets: They should not bear fruit, for to do so will not be to their benefit, since I will slay the treasures of their womb.

17. יִמְאָסֵם אֱלֹהַי כִּי לֹא שָׁמְעוּ לוֹ וְיִהְיוּ נֹדְדִים בַּגּוֹיִם — *My God shall spurn them for they have not obeyed Him, and they shall wander among the nations.* The prophet declares: The Almighty — Who is My God but no longer theirs, since they have spurned Him and refused to heed His words — shall spurn them in turn and banish them from before Him. Thus, they will be exiled from the Holy Land and sent off to wander among the gentiles (*Radak*; cf. *Rashi; Ibn Ezra*).

Others see this as a plea from the prophet before the Almighty: It is indeed proper that Hashem should spurn them, since they have not heeded His word. However, please let them wander among the nations in penitence for their sins rather than annihilating them entirely (*R' Eliezer of Beaugency; Abarbanel*).

X

Having foretold the great tragedies that were to befall the nation of Israel, including even the annihilation of her children, the prophet now goes on to describe the iniquitous acts which caused this terrible decree[1] (*Abarbanel*) [interjecting a depiction (v. 3) of the remorse the people will experience at that time for their misdeeds].

1. גֶּפֶן בּוֹקֵק יִשְׂרָאֵל פְּרִי יְשַׁוֶּה־לּוֹ כְּרֹב לְפִרְיוֹ הִרְבָּה לַמִּזְבְּחוֹת כְּטוֹב לְאַרְצוֹ הֵיטִיבוּ מַצֵּבוֹת — *Israel is a vine that has eliminated the fruit that is fitting for it; when his fruits were plentiful he increased altars; when his land was bountiful they improved*

1. Following his approach to the previous verses — that they refer specifically to the sin of promiscuity (see comm. to 9:10) — *Abarbanel* adds that in this chapter the prophet continues on to the other cardinal sin of which they were guilty — idolatry.

ב לַמִּזְבְּחוֹת כְּטוֹב לְאַרְצוֹ הֵיטִיבוּ מַצֵּבוֹת׃ חָלַק
לִבָּם עַתָּה יֶאְשָׁמוּ הוּא יַעֲרֹף מִזְבְּחוֹתָם
ג יְשֹׁדֵד מַצֵּבוֹתָם׃ כִּי עַתָּה יֹאמְרוּ אֵין מֶלֶךְ
לָנוּ כִּי לֹא יָרֵאנוּ אֶת־יהוה וְהַמֶּלֶךְ מַה־
ד יַּעֲשֶׂה־לָּנוּ׃ דִּבְּרוּ דְבָרִים אָלוֹת שָׁוְא כָּרֹת
בְּרִית וּפָרַח כָּרֹאשׁ מִשְׁפָּט עַל תַּלְמֵי שָׂדָי׃

pillars. Israel is similar to a vine that eliminates its own fruit, i.e., by withholding it yield or, alternately, by causing its fruits to drop. What is the fruit which the vine of Israel has eliminated? The fruit of the Divine Service (*Rashi*); the ways of righteousness (*Malbim*); wealth and progeny (*Radak*); actual produce of the fields (*Mahari Kara*).

Indeed, the more I bestowed upon them My blessing of plenty,[1] the more they prepared calves for their idolatrous altars (*Rashi*). And the more I blessed their land with an abundance of produce, the more they improved, strengthened (*Radak*), and increased (*Mahari Kara*) the pillars that they erected to their false gods.

Others render: *Israel is an empty vine; is he fitting for fruit? When his fruits etc.* — i.e., Israel has become like a vine that is devoid of all moisture and potency, for he has been plundered of all his possessions by the enemy. But I cannot bless him with prosperity and restore his wealth, since the more I bestowed upon him in the past, the more he used it to rebel against My will (*Radak; Abarbanel;* cf. *Metzudos David*).

2. חָלַק לִבָּם עַתָּה יֶאְשָׁמוּ הוּא יַעֲרֹף מִזְבְּחוֹתָם יְשֹׁדֵד מַצֵּבוֹתָם — *Their hearts are divided, now they shall be desolate. That shall destroy their altars; it shall plunder their pillars.* Their hearts have parted from Me and from My Torah (*Rashi; Radak*); therefore they shall now be rendered desolate (*Ibn Ezra; Radak; Abarbanel; Metzudos*). Their turning away from Me shall bring about the destruction of their altars and the plunder of the very pillars into which they have invested so much energy and wealth (*Rashi; Ibn Ezra; Radak*). This will take place at the time of the destruction [of their land] (*Radak*).

Ibn Ezra explains the parting of their hearts to mean that they have split their loyalty between Hashem and other deities. The word יֶאְשָׁמוּ is rendered by some to mean *guilt* — now they have become guilty and culpable to Me (*Targum; R' Eliezer of Beaugency*).

Rashi cites *Midrash Aggadah:* Great is peace, for even when Israel worships idols, if there is peace among them Satan cannot prosecute against them, as it is stated (above, 4:17): *Ephraim is united [therefore, despite his] idols, leave him be* (see comm. ibid.). Strife is hateful, as it is stated: *Their hearts are divided; now they shall be desolate* — Satan has an opening to prosecute.

3. כִּי עַתָּה יֹאמְרוּ אֵין מֶלֶךְ לָנוּ כִּי לֹא יָרֵאנוּ אֶת־ה׳ וְהַמֶּלֶךְ מַה־יַּעֲשֶׂה לָּנוּ — *For now they shall say, "We have no king, for [since] we did not fear* HASHEM, *what can the king do for us?"* Now, when the evil befalls them, they will finally realize and proclaim: The king whom we so urgently demanded to lead us in battle and save us

1. Among those who translate the first phrase in the same manner, there are various approaches to the words פְּרִי יְשַׁוֶּה־לוֹ. *Ibn Ezra* interprets: He thought to produce his fruits but he has been left level like an empty vine [with no fruit to break the evenness of the land]. *Radak* cites others who render: *Fruit has lied to him* [i.e., has not fulfilled its promise of growth]. *Abarbanel* suggests that the fruit refers to the offspring, whose behavior follows that of their fathers. Thus: *Israel is a desolate vine; its fruit is similar to it.*

10/2-4 *altars; when his land was bountiful they improved*
pillars. [2] *Their hearts are divided, now they shall be*
desolate. That shall destroy their altars; it shall plun-
der their pillars. [3] *For now they shall say, "We have*
no king, for [since] we did not fear H*ASHEM*, *what*
can the king do for us?" [4] *They have spoken words,*
swearing falsely, executing a covenant, and judgment
shall sprout like hemlock on the furrows of the field.

from our enemies is of no use to us; it is as if he was non-existent. For our abandonment of the fear of Hashem and His commandments has caused His wrath to pour out against us, and there is no recourse to any source of salvation (*Rashi; Radak; Metzudos David*).

R' Eliezer of Beaugency interprets: For now, at the time of their misfortune, they should recognize and proclaim that their king cannot help them if they do not fear Hashem. Nevertheless, they still refuse to do so.

Abarbanel suggests two novel interpretations of these two verses. In the first, he explains that the prophet is describing the remorse that the people will feel for their worship of the two calves of idolatry. Thus, when the evil befalls them, their hearts will finally part from these abominations. And with a cry, "We have been guilty," they will destroy the altars of idolatry that they constructed. Why will this occur?[1] For now, at the time of destruction, they will declare, "We have no king, for the king whom we accepted upon ourselves was not a legitimate monarch since we did not fear Hashem and anoint a ruler in accordance with His instructions."

Alternatively, these verses refer to the original split in the kingdom of Israel under the leadership of Jeroboam ben Nebot. Concerning this, the prophet declares: Now they will recognize their guilt for parting their hearts from the kingdom of David and dividing the nation in two. For that division is the true cause for the destruction of their altars by the conquering enemy [since it led to their involvement in idolatry and their subsequent overall decadence]. Therefore, now, in their hour of destruction, they will proclaim, "We no longer have any king at all. Had we feared Hashem and remained loyal to the Davidic dynasty none of this would have befallen us, but now, what can the kings we appointed possibly do to help us avert catastrophe?"

4. דִּבְּרוּ דְבָרִים אָלוֹת שָׁוְא כָּרֹת בְּרִית וּפָרַח כָּרֹאשׁ מִשְׁפָּט עַל תַּלְמֵי שָׂדָי — *They have spoken words, swearing falsely, executing a covenant, and judgment shall sprout like hemlock on the furrows of the field.* They utter whichever words enter their minds, with no judgment or discrimination whatsoever; thus do they swear falsely and conclude pacts with their idols. Therefore, a judgment of punishment and affliction shall sprout up against them, as the poisonous hemlock sprouts over the furrows of the field (*Rashi; Metzudos David*).

Alternatively: The judgment mentioned here is the corrupt justice that pervaded the nation. Thus: *They speak false words and make false oaths and establish false covenants* — all their dealings with one another are steeped in falsehood. And their false justice has bred harm and misfortune for the poor and powerless among them, with results that are poisonous like the hemlock that

1. [With this approach, the flow of the two verses is clear: Upon recognizing their mistake they will destroy their idolatrous altars, because they will say, "We have no king." According to the other interpretations, the word כִּי, *because*, is puzzling; the appropriate conjunction would seem to be *therefore*.]

י/ה־ז

ה לְעֶגְלוֹת֙ בֵּ֣ית אָ֔וֶן יָג֖וּרוּ שְׁכַ֣ן שֹׁמְר֑וֹן כִּֽי־אָבַ֨ל
עָלָ֜יו עַמּ֗וֹ וּכְמָרָיו֙ עָלָ֣יו יָגִ֔ילוּ עַל־כְּבוֹד֖וֹ כִּֽי־גָלָ֥ה
ו מִמֶּֽנּוּ׃ גַּם־אוֹתוֹ֙ לְאַשּׁ֣וּר יוּבָ֔ל מִנְחָ֖ה לְמֶ֣לֶךְ
יָרֵ֑ב בָּשְׁנָה֙ אֶפְרַ֣יִם יִקָּ֔ח וְיֵב֥וֹשׁ יִשְׂרָאֵ֖ל מֵעֲצָתֽוֹ׃
ז נִדְמֶ֥ה שֹׁמְר֖וֹן מַלְכָּ֑הּ כְּקֶ֖צֶף עַל־פְּנֵי־מָֽיִם׃

sprouts upon the furrows of the field (*Rashi*).[1]

According to *Radak*, this verse refers to Jeroboam and his advisers, who convened discussions to decide what to do to maintain the kingdom. At that time they proclaimed that the people should not ascend to Jerusalem for the festivals, and they established an oath and a covenant instead with the calves that they erected in Dan and Beth-el.

Others interpret this as the continuation of the words of the Children of Israel concerning their leaders:[2] The kings of Israel have led us astray, for they have coerced us into speaking and even swearing falsely and to compact covenants with their idols (*Mahari Kara*).

5. לְעֶגְלוֹת בֵּית אָוֶן יָגוּרוּ שְׁכַן שֹׁמְרוֹן — *Because of the calves of Beth-aven the inhabitants of Samaria shall be frightened.* When the people of Samaria shall see the destruction of the calves of idolatry in Beth-el, they will be overcome with fear. They will then think to themselves, "If the deities we worshiped could not protect even themselves, how will they deliver us from the hands of the enemy?" (*Radak; Abarbanel; Metzudos David*).

Beth-aven is the city of Beth-el [where one of the two calves erected by Jeroboam was placed]. It is called Beth-aven, as in the Book of *Joshua* (7:2) (*Rashi*). Alternatively, this is a pejorative nickname — *city of iniquity* — given to it by the prophets because of the activities that took place there (*Radak; Abarbanel*).

Although only one of the two calves was placed in Beth-el, the prophet uses the plural term here. Perhaps they eventually made many replicas of the original idol in the town where it was worshiped (*Abarbanel*). Alternatively, the plural refers to both of Jeroboam's idols, the one in Dan as well as the one in Beth-el. However, since the primary center of worship was in Beth-el it is described as the primary location of the idols (*Radak*). The feminine form of the word calves — עֶגְלוֹת — is used to indicate that the calves themselves were not the actual deities that the people worshiped but rather mere symbols of the gods they represented (*Radak*).

The prophet ascribes the idolatry to Samaria because that was the capital city of the kingdom and the heart of the culture of idolatry that pervaded it (*Radak*). *Mahari Kara* renders: the neighbors of Samaria — i.e., the ten tribes of Israel who lived in the vicinity of Samaria.

כִּי־אָבַל עָלָיו עַמּוֹ וּכְמָרָיו עָלָיו יָגִילוּ עַל־כְּבוֹדוֹ כִּי־גָלָה מִמֶּנּוּ — *For its people shall mourn over it, as well as its priests [who] rejoiced over its glory, for it has withdrawn from it.* The people who believed in the divinity of these idols shall mourn bitterly over their destruction. So, too, shall the priests who served them, who once rejoiced over their stature and glory in times of peace and prosperity. Now

1. *R' Eliezer of Beaugency* also follows this approach. However, he interprets the first half of the verse as describing the falseness of the words of the Children of Israel to the Almighty and of the covenant they sealed with Him. Thus, the Almighty declares: I am like a person who has sown his field. He eagerly awaits the growth of its fruit and is bitterly disappointed if the crop is blighted. So have I vigorously sought righteousness and justice from the Jewish nation, but have reaped instead the poisonous hemlock of their corruption.

2. [According to this interpretation, the word שָׂדָי is translated literally as *my field*, since it is the owners of the fields in question who are speaking.]

[5] *Because of the calves of Beth-aven the inhabitants
of Samaria shall be frightened; for its people shall
mourn over it, as well as its priests [who] rejoiced
over its glory, for it has withdrawn from it.* [6] *It,
too, shall be brought to Assyria, a gift to the king
of Yareb; Ephraim shall take shame and Israel
shall be shamed for his counsel.* [7] *Samaria's king
has been silenced; he is like foam upon the water.*

they shall bemoan the fate of their gods, whose glory withdrew from them when they were taken into captivity (*Radak; Ibn Ezra; Metzudos David*).

Others render: *Its people and its priests, who [all] rejoiced over its glory, shall mourn it, for it* [i.e., its glory] *has withdrawn from it* (*Mahari Kara; Abarbanel; Malbim*).

6. גַּם־אוֹתוֹ לְאַשּׁוּר יוּבָל מִנְחָה לְמֶלֶךְ יָרֵב — *It, too, shall be brought to Assyria, a gift to the king of Yareb.* Not only the people will be taken into captivity but also their god in whom they placed their faith (*Abarbanel; Metzudos David*). For after dismantling the idols, the Assyrians will sequester the gold from which they were made (*Radak; Abarbanel*) and present them in tribute to Sennacherib their king (*Rashi*).[1] Alternatively: Not only the aforementioned idol of Beth-el, but also the calf situated in Dan, will be seized by the enemy (*R' Saadiah Gaon*, cited by *Radak*).

בָּשְׁנָה אֶפְרַיִם יִקָּח וְיֵבוֹשׁ יִשְׂרָאֵל מֵעֲצָתוֹ — *Ephraim shall take shame and Israel shall be shamed for his counsel.* Jeroboam ben Nebot, of the tribe of Ephraim, shall be subject to shame and disgrace for establishing these idols and proclaiming them gods. Israel, too, shall be humiliated for the counsel they rendered when Jeroboam deliberated over their erection (*Rashi; Mahari Kara*). Alternatively: for their counsel in deciding to worship them (*Abarbanel*). *R' Eliezer of Beaugency* understands the shame and disgrace to be for the faith which the tribe of Ephraim and the nation of Israel placed in these idols, turning to them for blessing and security.

7. נִדְמֶה שֹׁמְרוֹן מַלְכָּהּ כְּקֶצֶף עַל־פְּנֵי־מָיִם — *Samaria's king has been silenced; he is like foam upon the water.* The king of [Ephraim who dwells in] Samaria has been silenced[2] [by the dire straits in which he finds himself and his kingdom]. He is like the foam which bubbles upon the water and then disappears; so, too, shall he soon pass from the pages of history (*Rashi; R' Eliezer of Beaugency*).

Others translate נִדְמֶה to mean similar: *The king of Samaria is similar to foam upon the water* (*Mahari Kara; Abarbanel; Malbim; Metzudos*); just as bubbles appear in the water and then disperse in all directions, so shall he and

1. [Although *Rashi* identifies מֶלֶךְ יָרֵב as Sennacherib, he may be merely identifying the king of Yareb, not translating Yareb to mean Sennacherib.] Indeed, *Mahari Kara* identifies Yareb as Assyria, citing *Seder Olam* as his source. [It is not found in our editions of *Seder Olam*.] *Radak*, however, states that this refers to a king of Assyria named Yareb. According to *Targum* it is a description rather than a name — the king who is destined to exact retribution from them (see 5:13, comm.).

2. *Abarbanel* cites *Rashi* as translating: *Samaria has been silenced and its king has been silenced.* [In our editions, this approach is given by *Ibn Ezra*, not by *Rashi*. It seems likely that a printer's error crept into the texts of *Abarbanel's* commentary.]

ח וְנִשְׁמְדוּ בָּמוֹת אָוֶן חַטַּאת יִשְׂרָאֵל קוֹץ וְדַרְדַּר
יַעֲלֶה עַל־מִזְבְּחוֹתָם וְאָמְרוּ לֶהָרִים כַּסּוּנוּ
ט וְלַגְּבָעוֹת נִפְלוּ עָלֵינוּ: מִימֵי
הַגִּבְעָה חָטָאתָ יִשְׂרָאֵל שָׁם עָמָדוּ לֹא־
תַשִּׂיגֵם בַּגִּבְעָה מִלְחָמָה עַל־בְּנֵי עַלְוָה:

his nation be exiled and strewn across the face of the earth (*Mahari Kara*). Alternatively: Just as bubbles remain in existence for only a short period of time, so are the days of Israel's king numbered, for the enemy is soon to vanquish him and his kingdom (*Abarbanel; Metzudos David*).

Radak renders: *In Samaria its king has been cut off. He is like bark upon the water.* After being a virtual prisoner within his capital city under the siege of Assyria, he will soon be captured and sent into exile.

8. וְנִשְׁמְדוּ בָּמוֹת אָוֶן חַטַּאת יִשְׂרָאֵל קוֹץ וְדַרְדַּר יַעֲלֶה עַל־מִזְבְּחוֹתָם וְאָמְרוּ לֶהָרִים כַּסּוּנוּ וְלַגְּבָעוֹת נִפְלוּ עָלֵינוּ — *And the shrines of Aven shall be destroyed, the sin of Israel; thorns and thistles shall ascend upon their altars, and they will say to the mountains, "Cover us!" and to the hills, "Fall upon us!"* The shrines of the false gods of Beth-el [i.e., Aven, see comm. to v. 5], which are the sin of Israel, shall be destroyed, and thorns and thistles will rise up over their altars, for they will be left abandoned with no one to worship upon them (*Rashi; Radak*).[1] And in their hour of great humiliation, the people will cry out to the mountains, "Cover us!" and they will beg of the hills, "Fall upon us [and thereby conceal us]!" — so that no one should see their shame and disgrace (*Rashi; Metzudos David*).

Others interpret: In their dire straits and great misfortune, they will beg of the mountains and hills to cover them over and bury them, so that they will thereby avoid the tragic circumstances of their plight (*Radak; Abarbanel*). *R' Eliezer of Beaugency* comments: It would be better they die beneath the hills and mountains than the enemy should come and rule over them harshly and sell them for slaves and maidservants.

Others interpret the verse as portraying the imaginary call of the desecrated altars of the idols: They will call out to the hills and mountains and beseech them to bury them so that they should no longer be seen (*Ibn Ezra* citing *R' Moshe; cf. Malbim*).

9-11. The prophet recalls how the iniquity of the Jewish nation is not a new phenomenon but rather hearkens back to its earlier past (cf. comm. to 9:10). Even in the early years of the Jewish settlement in the Land of Israel, idolatry and sinfulness were to be found among the people. Thus, throughout their history, the Almighty sent His prophets to rebuke them and His agents to punish them, seeking always to return them to His righteous ways. But His efforts were often unsuccessful, as Israel continuously deviated to paths of indulgence and decadence. They thereby forced the hand of Hashem, necessitating that He punish and oppress them severely in order to exact retribution for their evil deeds.

9. מִימֵי הַגִּבְעָה חָטָאתָ יִשְׂרָאֵל שָׁם עָמָדוּ לֹא־תַשִּׂיגֵם בַּגִּבְעָה מִלְחָמָה עַל־בְּנֵי עַלְוָה — *From the days of Gibeah you have sinned, Israel; there they stood. The war against men of iniquity did not overtake*

1. *Alshich* explains that the sin of Israel itself is that which has destroyed the shrines and altars of the idols, for every transgression — particularly one of idolatry — generates a wave of spiritual defilement whose nature it is to wreak destruction upon the sinners.

[8] *And the shrines of Aven shall be destroyed, the sin of*
Israel; thorns and thistles shall ascend upon their altars,
and they will say to the mountains, "Cover us!" and to
the hills, "Fall upon us!" [9] *From the days of Gibeah you*
have sinned, Israel; there they stood. The war against
men of iniquity did not overtake them in Gibeah.

them in Gibeah. Your sin of idolatry[1] hearkens back to the early years of the Jewish settlement in the Holy Land, to the tragic event of the concubine in Gibeah. At that time, when Asnial ben Kenaz was yet the judge of Israel, you introduced idolatry into your midst with the פֶּסֶל מִיכָה, the graven image erected by Michah and worshiped by him (see *Judges* 17). And you have remained in that state of ignominy since that time, for you have continued to grasp that trait of pursuing idolatry (*Rashi; Mahari Kara; Metzudos David*). Because of that sin, you were unable to [expediently] conquer the iniquitous tribe of Benjamin when you attacked them for harboring vicious criminals. Since you allowed idolatry to fester in your midst [the blessings of the Almighty were not with you even in your righteous efforts] (*Rashi*).

Radak renders: *From the days of Gibeah,* when the tribe of Benjamin allowed a heinous deed to be perpetrated in its midst and harbored the wicked men who carried it out — and the nation at large allowed idolaters to exist among them, *there they stood* — it seems as if the evildoers of our day stood among the wicked men of that generation, for they have continued in their evil ways. They convince themselves that *war and destruction shall not overtake them as it did the iniquitous men* in the tribe of Benjamin *when they were overrun by the nation of Israel in Gibeah.* But in truth, they too shall answer for their sins, and the sword of the enemy shall soon overtake them as well.

Targum interprets the reference to Gibeah as alluding to the time when the Jewish nation gathered in Gibeah and demanded from Samuel that he provide them with a king like all other nations. However, *Rashi* and *Radak* both contend that this does not sit well with the literal meaning of the text.

Abarbanel[2] renders: *More than the days of Gibeah you have sinned, Israel* — your level of corruption exceeds even that of the infamous generation of Gibeah. For at that time, the entire nation rose up in anger against the perpetrators of that heinous deed and waged war against the tribe of Benjamin that harbored them. But if *they had stood there* — if the sinners of today had lived at that time — *they would not have overtaken the men of iniquity with war in Gibeah* — for no one wages war to eradicate a sin of which he himself is guilty.

בְּנֵי עַלְוָה — *Men of iniquity.*

This follows the translation of the bulk of the commentators, who render the word עַלְוָה to be the same as if it were written עַוְלָה. *Rashi,* however, translates: *sons of haughtiness.*

1. In *Rashi's* version to this verse, the word חָטָאת was written without the *kamatz* under the *tav*. *Rashi* thus comments on the feminine gender of the word and takes pains to explain that it is the feminine form of the verb "you sinned" and not the noun חַטָּאת, *sin.*

2. *Abarbanel* takes issue with *Rashi's* interpretation of the verse, rejecting the contention that throughout the period of Samuel and the kingdoms of Saul and David, idolatry ran rampant through the land. [Perhaps *Rashi's* intention is that the roots of this sin lay dormant throughout that period, as the tendency in that direction was not eradicated from the Jewish psyche entirely. This allowed the transgression itself to eventually recur within the nation (cf. *Ramban* to *Deuteronomy* 29:17).]

י בְּאַוָּתִי וְאֶסֳּרֵם וְאֻסְּפוּ עֲלֵיהֶם עַמִּים בְּאָסְרָם
עוֹנֹתָם ק׳ יא לִשְׁתֵּי °עינתם׃ וְאֶפְרַיִם עֶגְלָה מְלֻמָּדָה אֹהַבְתִּי
לָדוּשׁ וַאֲנִי עָבַרְתִּי עַל־טוּב צַוָּארָהּ אַרְכִּיב
אֶפְרַיִם יַחֲרוֹשׁ יְהוּדָה יְשַׂדֶּד־לוֹ יַעֲקֹב׃

10. בְּאַוָּתִי וְאֶסֳּרֵם וְאֻסְּפוּ עֲלֵיהֶם עַמִּים — *By My will I afflicted them, and the nations gathered against them.* In accordance with My will, I have always brought affliction upon the Jewish nation [when they sinned] (*Rashi; R' Eliezer of Beaugency*). Indeed [through My intervention], nations have [now] gathered together to ascend upon them and [exact retribution for their misdeeds] (*R' Eliezer of Beaugency*).

Another translation renders וְאֶסֳּרֵם to mean *rebuke*: In the past, as a result of My great desire to return them to My service, I would chastise them with words of rebuke. Now, however, I [am forced] to send against them an assembly of nations who will bring about their retribution, as they refuse to heed My admonition (*Mahari Kara*).

Abarbanel sees this as a continuation of the theme of the previous verse: Since they are even more decadent than the people of Gibeah (see above), it is appropriate that I bring down upon them [at least] the same punishment suffered by the latter. Therefore, I shall gather against them an assembly of nations.

Others interpret this verse in the future tense: It is My will and desire to afflict them, for they refuse to heed My rebuke and the admonition of My prophets. Therefore, I shall bring about the assembly of nations who will gather against them (*Radak;* cf. *Metzudos David*).

בְּאָסְרָם לִשְׁתֵּי עוֹנוֹתָם — *When they bound them [to plow] two furrows.* These nations will conquer and subdue them like one subdues a cow and places it under the yoke of the plow. They will force them to plow two furrows — i.e., each of the two Jewish nations will suffer this fate (*Ibn Ezra*). Alternatively: They will be subjected to a double burden of misfortune, as if forced to plow two furrows simultaneously (*Metzudos David; Malbim*).

Mahari Kara also interprets the verse in this manner. However, he understands ענתם to mean plowshares rather than the furrows that they plow.

Abarbanel interprets ענתם to be from the root עָוֹן, *iniquity. They bound themselves to two sins* — i.e., to the two calves of idolatry they erected; therefore they will be overrun by the enemy.

Another rendition is: *When they were bound to their two eyes*[1] (*Targum; Rashi*). They were rendered comparable to a cow which is bound to the yolk of the plowshare, and the pegs of the yoke are connected to the plowshare on each side of the animal alongside his eyes (*Rashi*).

Others render: *When they were bound to two furrows* — i.e., when Judah and Ephraim were both attached to the plow and directed to plow properly and well, but instead they plowed crookedly. Thus, these two nations joined together to pursue a path of decadence and corruption, rather than following the ways in which they were directed by Hashem. This refers specifically to when Jehoshaphat king of Judah allied himself through marriage with Ahab king of Israel, and his son Jehoram was thereby led to follow in Ahab's wicked ways (*Radak*).

R' Eliezer of Beaugency renders: *When they bound themselves to two plows* — i.e., when they attached themselves to two faiths simultaneously, serving Hashem as well as the Baal-idols.

11. וְאֶפְרַיִם עֶגְלָה מְלֻמָּדָה אֹהַבְתִּי לָדוּשׁ — *And Ephraim is a trained heifer who*

1. [This phrase has a קְרִי וּכְתִיב; it is written עֵינֹתָם but read עוֹנוֹתָם. *Rashi's* interpretation would seem to be consistent with the כְּתִיב rather than with the קְרִי.]

10 By My will I afflicted them, and the nations
gathered against them when they bound them [to
plow] two furrows. 11 And Ephraim is a trained
heifer who loves to thresh; and I passed over
the superbness of her neck; I will place Ephraim
astride; Judah shall plow; Jacob shall harrow.

loves[1] *to thresh.* Ephraim resembles a heifer, who is taught to plow in order to eventually bring about the growth of the crop and benefit from it, but instead seeks only to thresh the fruit from its husks and enjoy its benefits immediately. So, too, with Ephraim. I taught them in the youth of their nationhood to fulfill the statutes of the Torah and thereby earn their ultimate reward. But they seek to forgo their responsibilities and to pursue the immediate pleasures available to them (*Radak; Metzudos David*).

Abarbanel interprets: *Ephraim is accustomed to calves* — i.e., to the worship of the golden calves. However, she has not learned the lesson of the calf — to submit herself to the yoke; rather, she loves only to thresh the fruit and to be constantly in the vicinity of the fruits and its pleasures.

Rashi renders: *Ephraim is a goaded calf.* She has been subject to many misfortunes — like a calf that has often been placed under the yoke. Nevertheless she refuses to humble herself before Me and submit herself to My will. Rather, she seeks only the pleasures and benefits of the threshing floor.

וַאֲנִי עָבַרְתִּי עַל־טוּב צַוָּארָהּ — *And I passed over the superbness of her neck.* I inspected her neck and found it superb, capable of withstanding the yoke of the enemy. Therefore, I shall bring upon her the conquering enemy who will weaken and subdue her (*Rashi; Abarbanel*).

Alternatively: When I passed over her neck to place the yoke upon it, I did so in a manner that would leave her neck upright and in superb condition, rather than imposing so heavy a yoke that it would bend and weaken her neck. Thus, when I commanded the Jewish nation in My *mitzvos,* I did not demand of them more than they were capable of fulfilling (*Radak*).

Radak suggests as well the following interpretation: When I passed over them to split the kingdom in two — i.e., when I sent Ahiyah Hashiloni to anoint Jeroboam as king — *I passed over the superbness of her neck* — i.e., I did so at a time when the nation of Israel was prosperous and secure, every man under his fig tree and grapevine.

אַרְכִּיב אֶפְרַיִם יַחֲרוֹשׁ יְהוּדָה יְשַׂדֶּד־לוֹ יַעֲקֹב — *I will place Ephraim astride; Judah shall plow; Jacob shall harrow.* If you wish Me to [restore Ephraim to his former glory and] place him astride the gentile nations, [the nation of] Judah must plow a furrow of righteous deeds and [the remaining ten tribes from the children of] Jacob must follow suit by harrowing further the clumps of ground — i.e., by continuing the process of filling the land with righteousness and justice (*Rashi*).

Others see this phrase as a continuation of the prophecy of Ephraim's retribution: I will place the aforementioned nations astride Ephraim and humble them with exile. Upon witnessing this cataclysmic event, Judah will be moved to return to righteousness and to plow good deeds throughout the land. Even those members of the other tribes who dwell within the Judaic kingdom will follow in this path and clear their ways of all foreign objects and prohibited deeds, thus returning to Me wholeheartedly. Indeed, for two of the three generations following the destruction of Samaria, the nation of Judah was

1. Although written אֹהַבְתִּי, the word means *loves,* as if it were written אֹהֶבֶת, without the *yud* (*Rashi; Radak*).

יב זִרְעוּ לָכֶם לִצְדָקָה קִצְרוּ לְפִי־חֶסֶד נִירוּ לָכֶם
נִיר וְעֵת לִדְרוֹשׁ אֶת־יהוה עַד־יָבוֹא וְיֹרֶה
יג צֶדֶק לָכֶם׃ חֲרַשְׁתֶּם־רֶשַׁע עַוְלָתָה קְצַרְתֶּם
אֲכַלְתֶּם פְּרִי־כָחַשׁ כִּי־בָטַחְתָּ בְדַרְכְּךָ בְּרֹב
יד גִּבּוֹרֶיךָ׃ וְקָאם שָׁאוֹן בְּעַמֶּךָ וְכָל־מִבְצָרֶיךָ יוּשַּׁד

a paragon of righteousness (*Abarbanel*).

Metzudos David interprets the yoke as that of the Torah and *mitzvos:* Having determined that the neck of Ephraim is strong and capable, I placed upon him the yoke of My Torah. Judah too shall plow furrows of good deeds, and the entire nation of Jacob will remove the clods in the ground and thereby produce its fruits — i.e., they will remove all remaining limits to their righteousness and thus the barriers to their reward.

Radak sees this as a flashback to the time of the division of the kingdom of Israel: I placed Jeroboam from the tribe of Ephraim astride the Jewish nation, and directed him to command the people to serve Me and to submit to My will. [The leaders of] Judah, who already had a kingdom, needed only to plow — i.e., to command the nation to follow in My ways. If both kingdoms would thus plow the soil [and lay the groundwork for the nation's righteousness], it would be left to the people of Jacob to harrow the ground. They would break the remaining clumps of earth [i.e., the remaining pockets of resistance within their own hearts] — by directing their ears and hearts to heed My dictates, and they would thereby come to sow the seeds of righteousness with their deeds [as stated in the following verse]. (See *Mahari Kara* and *Malbim* for alternative approaches to this verse.)

12. Having stressed in the end of the previous verse that only through repentance can the Jewish people achieve salvation, the prophet goes on to elaborate upon the type of behavior that is required in order to bring this about.

זִרְעוּ לָכֶם לִצְדָקָה קִצְרוּ לְפִי־חֶסֶד — *Sow for yourselves righteousness; reap according to benevolence.* Sow for yourselves seeds of righteousness and you will thereby reap the rewards of My benevolence to you — far beyond the scope of that which you actually earn with your deeds (*Abarbanel; Malbim; Metzudos David*). Alternatively: All the rewards you reap in this world will be pure benevolence from the Almighty, for He will withhold the true fruits of your righteousness until the world to come (*Radak* citing his father).

Others interpret *reap according to benevolence* as part of the directive to the Jewish nation: *Targum* renders: House of Israel, do for yourselves good deeds; go in the ways of truth, and fulfill the teachings of the Torah (נִירוּ לָכֶם נִיר) (cf. *Mahari Kara*).

The Sages, too, interpret the verse in this manner, and thus comment: Said R' Elazar: Benevolence is greater than charity, as it is stated: *Sow for yourselves charity* [an alternative translation of צְדָקָה] *and reap according to benevolence.* [When] a person sows, he remains in doubt as to whether he will eat, but once he harvests, he is certain to eat (*Succah* 49b).

נִירוּ לָכֶם נִיר — *Till for yourselves a tilling.* Involve yourselves in the study of Torah, and from that you will learn how to follow in the proper path and overcome your evil inclination — just as one tills the soil to overturn all the remaining roots of grass and weeds that would otherwise be an obstacle to the growth of his produce (*Rashi*).

Others interpret: Till the soil of your souls and remove from them the thorns and weeds that obstruct the planting — i.e., all of the burning desires, faulty character traits, and misguided beliefs that impede the desired results of your righteousness and benevolence (*Ibn Ezra; Metzudos David; Malbim*).

According to *Radak:* Even after you reap, go back and plow again, and then

[12] *Sow for yourselves righteousness; reap according*
to benevolence; till for yourselves a tilling and [set] a
time to seek HASHEM *until He shall come and teach*
you righteousness. [13] *You have plowed wickedness;*
you have reaped iniquity; you have eaten the fruit of
denial; for you relied on your way, on your many
mighty men. [14] *And there shall arise a din among your*
peoples, and all your fortresses shall be plundered,

plant further — i.e., do not suffice with your past achievements but rather continue relentlessly to pursue ever greater heights of righteousness.

וְעֵת לִדְרוֹשׁ אֶת־ה׳ עַד־יָבוֹא וְיֹרֶה צֶדֶק לָכֶם — *And [set] a time to seek* HASHEM *until He shall come and teach you righteousness.* Designate a set time for the study of Torah — rather than merely learning whenever the chance arises. With your toil over His wisdom, He will guide your understanding and teach you the secrets of His Torah with righteousness [i.e., accurately, without distortion] (*Rashi; Metzudos David*).

Others interpret יוֹרֶה to mean *rain* (*Ibn Ezra; Radak*); He shall rain down benevolence upon you. *Malbim* follows this translation but interprets the intent of the verse similarly to *Rashi*: After you have plowed with righteousness and tilled the soil of your souls to eradicate all obstacles to spirituality, it will then be appropriate to turn to the Almighty in supplication and request His assistance. He, in turn, shall pour down upon you a shower of righteousness — i.e., He will water your souls, that are thirsting for the rain of His holiness, and satiate them with the flow of His Divine Blessing.

Rashi offers a second interpretation as well: *Till yourselves a tilling* — perform good deeds [in abundance] before the oppressor befalls you, and this will cause your prayers at that time to be heard. Thus, when the time comes for you to seek Hashem and His protection, He will answer your prayers and pour down upon you His righteousness and blessing.

Targum renders: *At all times the prophets say to you, "Return to the fear of Hashem; now He will reveal Himself and bring merit to you." Radak* contends that this is the basic meaning of the verse.

13. חֲרַשְׁתֶּם־רֶשַׁע עַוְלָתָה קְצַרְתֶּם אֲכַלְתֶּם פְּרִי־כָחַשׁ כִּי־בָטַחְתָּ בְדַרְכְּךָ בְּרֹב גִּבּוֹרֶיךָ — *You have plowed wickedness; you have reaped iniquity; you have eaten the fruit of denial; for you relied on your way, on your many mighty men.* Whereas I exhorted you to sow righteousness, you opted to plow wickedness and sow its seeds. You will therefore reap the results of your iniquity and eat the fruits of your denial of Me. Alternatively: You will eat the fruits that deny you their benefits. How did this terrible situation and the dire consequences it has caused come about? Because you relied upon the validity of the wicked ways and aberrant beliefs that you adopted for yourselves, and you placed your faith in your mighty warriors, along with those of your Egyptian allies, to protect you from invasion (*Radak*).

Others interpret the phrase *you reaped iniquity* to be part of the crime rather than its punishment (*R' Eliezer of Beaugency; Metzudos David*). Thus: You plowed the soil and laid the groundwork for your wickedness with your evil plots, and you carried out your plans with iniquitous deeds (*Metzudos*).

14. וְקָאם שָׁאוֹן בְּעַמֶּךָ וְכָל־מִבְצָרֶיךָ יוּשַּׁד — *And there shall arise a din among your peoples, and all your fortresses shall be plundered.* Although you dwell now in peace and tranquility, unafraid of any

י/טו כְּשֹׁד שַׁלְמַן בֵּית אַרְבֵאל בְּיוֹם מִלְחָמָה
טו אֵם עַל־בָּנִים רֻטָּשָׁה׃ כָּכָה עָשָׂה לָכֶם בֵּית־
אֵל מִפְּנֵי רָעַת רָעַתְכֶם בַּשַּׁחַר נִדְמֹה נִדְמָה
יא/א א מֶלֶךְ יִשְׂרָאֵל׃ כִּי נַעַר יִשְׂרָאֵל וָאֹהֲבֵהוּ

invader or attacker (*Mahari Kara*), your sense of security shall prove to be misguided. For the enemy shall soon befall you and conquer your land, and nothing you do will avail to fend him off (*Abarbanel*). The din of an assembly of many nations shall arise in the midst of your nation, as these powerful forces attack and invade you (*Mahari Kara; Radak*), and all of your mighty fortresses that you deemed impregnable shall be plundered by these hordes (*Radak*).

Rashi interprets the mighty din as alluding to the voices of the vanquished Israelite nation crying, "Flee, flee!"

כְּשֹׁד שַׁלְמַן בֵּית אַרְבֵאל בְּיוֹם מִלְחָמָה — *Like the surprise attack and plunder of a people at peace on the day of war.* The invasion will resemble the total rout and overrunning of a nation living in peace, unprepared for war, by the sneak attack of an invading enemy who takes them unawares and plunders all that is to be found (*Targum; Rashi; Mahari Kara; Abarbanel*).

These commentators understand both שַׁלְמַן and אַרְבֵאל to be common nouns rather than proper nouns: שַׁלְמַן derives from the word שָׁלוֹם, *peace*, and אַרְבֵאל is from the word אָרַב, *ambush*, or *surprise attack* (see *Rashi; Mahari Kara*). *R' Eliezer of Beaugency* follows the same approach, but interprets בֵּית אַרְבֵאל to mean a deep valley, where an invader could descend in sudden surprise without being previously detected.

Others interpret בֵּית אַרְבֵאל as referring to a place by that name (*Dunash*, cited by *Rashi*)[1] or the home of a prominent person who lived at that time (*Radak*). Thus, the prophet alludes to an event which was well known, in which a mighty warrior named Shalmon had befallen Beis Arbael in a surprise attack and annihilated its inhabitants and plundered its wealth (*Radak*). Some contend that Shalmon is actually Shalmanesser, the king of Assyria (*Ibn Ezra; Radak*, citing his father).[2]

אֵם עַל־בָּנִים רֻטָּשָׁה — *A mother has been torn asunder along with [her] children.* Mother and child have been dashed to the ground and thus torn to pieces. This came as a result of the great mercy a mother has for children. When the enemy would befall the children, their mothers would throw themselves in front of them to protect them, and they would thereby share their fate (Radak).

Alternatively — as interpreted by the Sages (*Bava Metzia* 39a) — רֻטָּשָׁה means *abandoned.* The men would abandon their wives and children and flee before the enemy, as well as from the hunger of the famine (ibid.).

15. כָּכָה עָשָׂה לָכֶם בֵּית אֵל מִפְּנֵי רָעַת רָעַתְכֶם — *So has Beth-el done to you because of the evil of your evil.* Thus has your worship of the idols in Beth-el been the ultimate cause of all the misfortune that has already befallen you and all that is yet to come upon you (*Rashi; Radak*). The willful evil (of your idolatry) led to the many wicked deeds that you have per-

1. *Daas Mikra* offers several possibilities as to the identification of that place. Some say that it was the name of a city in Assyria. Others identify it as a town in lower Galilee north of Tiberias. Still others contend that it alludes to a town in northern Gilead. Yet another town of that name is known to exist from the time of the Talmud; this one lies in the Valley of Jezreel, near Afula.

2. *Radak* cites his father as interpreting that the attack in question is Shalmanesser's conquest of the city of Samaria. However, *Abarbanel* rejects this theory, since the subject of these prophecies is the destruction that was to befall Samaria but had not yet occurred.

10/15 *like the surprise attack and plunder of a people at peace on the day of war; a mother has been torn asunder along with [her] children.* 15 *So has Beth-el done to you because of the evil of your evil; at dawn, the king of Israel is silenced.*

11/1 1 *For [when] Israel was a lad I loved him and*

formed and for which you are now being punished (*Rashi; R' Eliezer of Beaugency*).

Others interpret: *the utmost evil from among all of your evil* — i.e., your worship of the golden calves and declaration that they are your god (*Ibn Ezra; Radak*). Alternatively: *from the evil which is your evils* — i.e., from the golden calf in Beth-el, which follows the course you have taken before and to which you have become accustomed, dating back to the idol you erected in the wilderness (*Abarbanel; Metzudos David*).

בַּשַּׁחַר נִדְמֹה נִדְמָה מֶלֶךְ יִשְׂרָאֵל — *At dawn, the king of Israel is silenced.* Even in the daylight of dawn, the king of Israel remains as if in a deep sleep, as he is totally silenced and bereft of any energy to respond to the enemy (*Rashi*; see *Parshandasa*; cf. *Mahari Kara*). *R' Eliezer of Beaugency* interprets: One who is still asleep at dawn is caught by surprise by the invading enemy with no recourse to flight or defense. So has the king of Israel been silenced [from any effective response] when the enemy has befallen him.

Others render נִדְמָה to mean *cut off* (*Ibn Ezra; Radak; Metzudos*). They shall be plundered by night, and by morning their king will already be cut off (*Ibn Ezra*). Alternatively, this refers to the dawn of the kingdom of Hosea ben Elah — in the sixth year of his reign. At that time, he was imprisoned by the king of Assyria, who then went on to besiege Samaria for three years and to finally conquer it. In fact, even prior to this, Hosea was vanquished by Assyria and made a vassal of the latter, who demanded an annual tribute from him. Thus, from that time, he was already cut off from the full powers of his monarchy (*Radak; Metzudos David*).

XI

Having described the severity of the punishment about to befall the Jewish nation, the Almighty now sends His prophet to explain the reason for this harsh treatment (*Rashi; Radak*): Because I singled them out for special attention and love from the outset of their very existence, I therefore deal with them more strictly than I do with other nations. Since I have designated them as "My children," it is incumbent upon Me to reprimand and even punish them as a father does his offspring (*Radak; Mahari Kara*). Accordingly, now that they have consistently sinned against Me, they have no cause for complaint when I punish them (*Abarbanel*).

1. כִּי נַעַר יִשְׂרָאֵל וָאֹהֲבֵהוּ — *For [when] Israel was a lad I loved him.* When Israel was but a young lad in the land of Egypt I loved him dearly [and brought him close to Me] (*Ibn Ezra; Radak; Abarbanel; Metzudos David*).[1] Indeed, his youth enhanced his endearment to Me, since he had not yet tasted the flavor of

1. *Abarbanel* suggests that the word *Israel* may refer to the patriarch Jacob — also called Israel — who was the beloved of the Almighty, as stated by the prophet *Malachi* (1:2): *For is not Esau the brother of Jacob? And I loved Jacob.*

ב וּמִמִּצְרַיִם קָרָאתִי לִבְנִי: קָרְאוּ לָהֶם כֵּן הָלְכוּ
מִפְּנֵיהֶם לַבְּעָלִים יְזַבֵּחוּ וְלַפְּסִלִים יְקַטֵּרוּן: וְאָנֹכִי
ג תִרְגַּלְתִּי לְאֶפְרַיִם קָחָם עַל־זְרוֹעֹתָיו וְלֹא יָדְעוּ

sin[1] (*Yalkut* to *Jeremiah* 1:5, §262). In addition, his relative innocence allowed Me to look away to some degree from his transgressions, for less can be expected from a mere child (*Yalkut* here).

Alshich detects a contrary theme: Although they were still in the foolish stage of youth, undeveloped and untrained by the wisdom of Torah, I nevertheless loved them and brought them close to Me.

Rashi translates נַעַר differently than do all of the other commentators, stating at the end of the previous chapter: *And why [has] all this [been decreed upon you]? For when Israel was young, devoid of all good, I loved him* [yet — as described in this chapter — he nevertheless continued to sin against Me].

וּמִמִּצְרַיִם קָרָאתִי לִבְנִי — *And from Egypt I called My son.* When they were still in the land of Egypt, I called to them through My prophet Moses to attach themselves to Me and My Torah (*Rashi; Metzudos David*).

Others render: *and from Egypt I called [him] My son* — since the days when they were exiled in the land of Egypt I have referred to the nation of Israel as *My son* (*Targum; Mahari Kara; Radak*), as when I declared to Pharaoh through My spokesman Moses (*Exodus* 4:22): *My son, My firstborn, is Israel* (*Mahari Kara;* see *Radak*).

2. קָרְאוּ לָהֶם כֵּן הָלְכוּ מִפְּנֵיהֶם לַבְּעָלִים יְזַבֵּחוּ וְלַפְּסִלִים יְקַטֵּרוּן — *They called to them, so did they turn away from them; to the Baal-idols they slaughtered and to graven images they burnt [sacrifices].*

The more My prophets called out to the Children of Israel to teach them My ways, the more the people turned their backs and withdrew from them to pursue the worship of other gods (*Targum; Rashi; Mahari Kara; Radak*).

Others interpret the subject and object of the phrase *they called to them* as the people and their idols: Whereas I called to them in Egypt to come serve Me, *they called* out instead *to them* — the *Baal-idols* and graven images — and sought their worship (*Ibn Ezra; Abarbanel; Malbim*).

According to *Alshich*, these two verses come to answer an unspoken but compelling question: Why does Hashem not make the first move towards reconciliation with His people and thereby inspire them to follow suit? To this the Almighty responds: I brought you close to Me in a miraculous manner in Egypt when you were still untrained in the ways of the Torah, yet you responded by pursuing the worship of other gods. It is thus clear that you are incapable of responding properly to My overtures unless you first elevate and discipline yourselves. Therefore, it is up to you to initiate our reconciliation by abandoning your wicked ways, and only then will I relent from the retribution I have decreed upon you (cf. *Abarbanel* to v. 7, 9 cited in comm. ibid.).

3. וְאָנֹכִי תִרְגַּלְתִּי לְאֶפְרַיִם קָחָם עַל־זְרוֹעֹתָיו — *And I sent to Ephraim [a leader] who took them upon his arms.* Why have the people treated Me so ignobly? How has the tribe of Ephraim come to install idols in the land (*Radak*)? [This is certainly not in response to any mistreatment they suffered at My hands.] For

1. [Although the Jewish nation was steeped in the decadence of Egyptian society prior to their redemption, they are nevertheless depicted as being untainted by sin. Apparently, since they had not yet received the Torah nor been instructed by the Almighty in His commandments, they were comparable to a child who has not yet come of age and is not held responsible for his misdeeds — and indeed is viewed by the Torah as innocent of all sin. Accordingly, the two statements cited from *Yalkut* explaining the endearment of Israel's youth are actually two aspects of the same principle.]

from Egypt I called My son. [2] *They called to them, so*
did they turn away from them; to the Baal-idols
they slaughtered and to graven images they burnt
[sacrifices]. [3] *And I sent to Ephraim [a leader] who*
took them upon his arms and they did not know

when I took them out of the land of Egypt, I sent before them a leader who would guide them gently (*Rashi; Abarbanel*) — i.e., Moses, who took them upon his arms and led them [as described by the Torah (*Numbers* 11:12)] like a nursing father carries a suckling child (*Rashi; Radak*).

Mahari Kara interprets this verse as referring to the leadership of Joshua, who took the Jewish people into the Land of Israel: After forty years in the desert I led them into the Holy Land through Joshua ben Nun from the tribe of Ephraim, and he took them upon his arms and brought them into the land.

Others understand this phrase to be describing the leadership of the Almighty Himself: *I conducted Ephraim* — I escorted them out of Egypt as one guides a young child whose steps are still wavering. Thus, I led them from station to station without great difficulties and I provided them with clouds of glory and fire to assist them along the way (*Radak; R' Eliezer of Beaugency*).

Alternatively: *I sent to Ephraim [a leader]* — In addition to the many benefits I bestowed upon them, I was also careful not to overburden them with too heavy a load. Thus, when I took them out of Egypt I conditioned them piecemeal to the requirements of My service rather than overwhelming them immediately with the entire range of My commandments (*Ibn Ezra; Radak*).

Among those following this approach — that the Almighty is describing the nature of His leadership — some interpret the second phrase in the same manner as *Rashi* — that it refers to Moses. Thus, they render *He took them upon his arms* (*Radak*).

Others explain this, too, as describing the gentle guidance provided by Hashem: I conducted their unsteady steps, treating them like a child who is taken upon the arms of one who escorts him (*Ibn Ezra*). Alternatively: I led them like a woman conducting a child as he takes his wavering steps; when he falters she takes him upon her arms (*R' Eliezer of Beaugency*).[1]

וְלֹא יָדְעוּ כִּי רְפָאתִים — *And they did not know that I healed them.* They did not take heed of the obvious fact that their redemption and survival was by My hand (*Rashi; Metzudos David*). Others explain that they did not even recognize that fact (*Radak*).

Malbim, too, makes this assumption, in accordance with his unique interpretation of the entire verse: I became the foot and pedestal [תִרְגַּלְתִּי — from the root רֶגֶל, *foot*] of Ephraim upon which he was supported, even as he carried his false deities upon his arms. For I support and carry My creations, whereas the idols are borne by those who serve them. Nevertheless, he did not attribute his recovery from illness to Me but rather to the false gods that he carried.

The Sages interpret this verse as alluding to the blessing of Ephraim and Manasseh at the hand of Jacob in the land of Egypt. When Joseph brought them before his father, Jacob discerned that Ephraim was destined to be the forebear of wicked men — e.g., Jeroboam and Ahab — and the Holy Spirit left him, rendering him unable to bless them. At this, Joseph prayed for mercy. The Divine Presence returned to Jacob and he

1. According to his approach, the verse concludes: *And when he was wounded I healed him, but even this they did not recognize.*

ד כִּי רְפָאתִים: בְּחַבְלֵי אָדָם אֶמְשְׁכֵם בַּעֲבֹתוֹת
אַהֲבָה וָאֶהְיֶה לָהֶם כִּמְרִימֵי עֹל עַל לְחֵיהֶם
ה וְאַט אֵלָיו אוֹכִיל: לֹא יָשׁוּב אֶל־אֶרֶץ מִצְרַיִם
ו וְאַשּׁוּר הוּא מַלְכּוֹ כִּי מֵאֲנוּ לָשׁוּב: וְחָלָה
חֶרֶב בְּעָרָיו וְכִלְּתָה בַדָּיו וְאָכָלָה מִמֹּעֲצוֹתֵיהֶם:

blessed them. Thus, says the prophet, I conducted My spirit [to rest] upon Jacob for the sake of Ephraim, and he took them upon his arms [and blessed them] (*Rashi* from *Tanchuma* to *Genesis.* 48:1).

4. בְּחַבְלֵי אָדָם אֶמְשְׁכֵם בַּעֲבֹתוֹת אַהֲבָה — *With the cords of man I drew them, with bonds of love.* Although I have compared Ephraim to a calf (10:11), I nevertheless do not pull him with heavy ropes — as one does a calf — when I wish him to follow My will (*Radak*). Rather, I have drawn him lovingly and mercifully with the cords of man — with the light cords one employs when he needs to pull his son — tugging gently and slowly without imposing undue pressure and hardship (*Targum; Rashi; Ibn Ezra; Radak*).[1]

Mahari Kara comments: When I drew Jacob and his sons to Egypt, I did so with cords and bonds of love; I first led Joseph to Egypt and elevated him to rule over the entire land and only then brought the entire family to a situation in which they were able to live securely in prosperity. Why [was this necessary at all]? Because of the covenant I made with Abraham when I told him that his seed would be strangers in a foreign land.[2]

וָאֶהְיֶה לָהֶם כִּמְרִימֵי עֹל עַל לְחֵיהֶם — *And I have been to them like those who lift the yoke upon their pegs.* I have treated them in the manner of a merciful farmer, who lengthens the pegs to which the yoke of the plow is fastened in order to loosen it from upon the animal's neck. So have I stood by them through their every tribulation, lightening the load of their misfortune (*Targum; Rashi*). Alternatively: like the farmer who raises the yoke through the bridles with his hands in order to lighten the load (*Rashi*).

Others render: *I have been to them like those who lift the yoke [from] upon the jaw* of their animals, to lighten the load

1. According to this approach, the phrase *with bonds of love* is merely a repetition of the previous phrase. Indeed, *Metzudos David* states this explicitly. However, others interpret the two phrases as expressing independent thoughts. *Abarbanel* interprets: *With the leadership of a man* — i.e., Moses — *I drew them.* This constituted *bonds of love,* because the people were not yet ready to receive My blessing without the aid of an intermediary. *Alshich* understands this as alluding to the two types of punishments which the Almighty brings upon man. There are those that are meted out to bring forgiveness for sins already committed and those given to the sinless, which are meant to draw them ever closer to Hashem (see *Berachos* 5a). Thus: In order to rectify their sins I brought upon them the *cords of man* — i.e., those punishments brought about by the wicked acts of man. Once they had been cleansed, I added *bonds of love* — those tribulations which are wrought with love, in order to bring them closer to Me.

2. Said R' Berachiah in the name of R' Judah the son of Simon: It would have been appropriate for our forefather Jacob to descend to Egypt imprisoned in chains [as the Jewish nation was destined to be enslaved there]. Said the Holy One, Blessed is He: He is My son, My firstborn, and I should take him down in humiliation? Behold I shall bring down his son before him. [This is comparable to] a cow that is being taken to market but refuses to go. What do they do? They pull its son before it and it perforce follows along (*Bereishis Rabbah* ch. 86, cited by *Yalkut Shimoni*).

that I healed them. [4] *With the cords of man I drew them,*
with bonds of love, and I have been to them like those
who lift the yoke upon their pegs, and I extended food to
them. [5] *He shall not return to the land of Egypt, but As-*
syria is his king, for they have refused to repent. [6] *And*
the sword shall alight upon his cities and it shall destroy
his branches and devour [them] because of their designs.

[from] upon them (*Abarbanel; Metzudos*).[1]

Alshich sees a contrary theme in this phrase. *I was in their eyes like one who raises the yoke upon their jaws* — i.e., instead of accepting the rebuke inherent in the punishment I brought upon them, they interpreted it as a hostile blow and spurned the admonition to be derived from it.

וְאַט אֵלָיו אוֹכִיל — *And I extended food to them.* I was to them like the farmer, who feeds his animal in its place even after lightening its load, and does not impose upon it the hardship of going to seek its own food. So did I feed them miraculously with manna in the desert after redeeming them from the land of Egypt, without requiring them to exert themselves in order to eat (*Targum; Ibn Ezra; Radak; Abarbanel*).

Rashi renders: *I extended to him* the strength *to withstand* the yoke of his suffering. Alternatively: I extended to him the yoke of Egypt in a manner that enabled him to withstand it (*Mahari Kara*).

5. לֹא יָשׁוּב אֶל־אֶרֶץ מִצְרַיִם וְאַשּׁוּר הוּא מַלְכּוֹ כִּי מֵאֲנוּ לָשׁוּב — *He shall not return to the land of Egypt, but Assyria is his king, for they have refused to repent.* I promised him concerning Egypt, *You shall no longer continue to see them* (Exodus 14:13). But it was to no avail, as [I had to place] Assyria over them instead because they sinned and refused to repent their evil deeds (*Rashi*).

Others interpret: They should not have returned to the land of Egypt — where I have forbidden them to go — in order to seek assistance, nor would they have found it necessary if they had only returned to My ways. Now, however, that they have sinned and refuse to repent, they will suffer the burden of Assyria's rule and be forced to pay them tribute (*Radak*).

Others interpret the phrase וְאַשּׁוּר הוּא מַלְכּוֹ to be a rhetorical question: Is, then, Assyria his king? Will he wage their wars and pursue their interests? [Apparently, that is their assumption, for] they have refused to return to Me and rely instead upon the support of the kingdom of Assyria (*Abarbanel; Metzudos David*).

6. וְחָלָה חֶרֶב בְּעָרָיו וְכִלְּתָה בַדָּיו וְאָכָלָה מִמֹּעֲצוֹתֵיהֶם — *And the sword shall alight upon his cities and it shall destroy his branches and devour [them] because of their designs.* The sword [of the enemy] shall alight upon Israel and destroy his mighty warriors and devour them (*Targum; Rashi*). All of this will occur as a result of the evil designs of the people, who decided to worship idols, abandon the Almighty, and seek aid from Assyria and Egypt (*Abarbanel*). *Mahari Kara* renders: *because of their counsel* — for the counsel they took together with Jeroboam to establish the golden calves in Dan and Beth-el.

1. According to them, the word עַל is interpreted as if it were written מֵעַל לְחֵיהֶם, *from upon their jaws.* See *Abarbanel* who cites similar instances in Scripture. *Radak*, however, concurs with their translation of the word לְחֵיהֶם but interprets it literally: like those who lift the yoke from upon the necks of their animals and place it upon their jaws in order to lessen their burden. [It is unclear, however, how placing a yoke on an animal's jaw would be helpful to it.]

ז וְעַמִּי תְלוּאִים לִמְשׁוּבָתִי וְאֶל־עַל יִקְרָאֻהוּ יַחַד
ח לֹא יְרוֹמֵם: אֵיךְ אֶתֶּנְךָ אֶפְרַיִם אֲמַגֶּנְךָ יִשְׂרָאֵל
אֵיךְ אֶתֶּנְךָ כְאַדְמָה אֲשִׂימְךָ כִּצְבֹאיִם נֶהְפַּךְ
ט עָלַי לִבִּי יַחַד נִכְמְרוּ נִחוּמָי: לֹא אֶעֱשֶׂה חֲרוֹן
אַפִּי לֹא אָשׁוּב לְשַׁחֵת אֶפְרָיִם כִּי אֵל אָנֹכִי
וְלֹא־אִישׁ בְּקִרְבְּךָ קָדוֹשׁ וְלֹא אָבוֹא בְּעִיר:

Radak interprets בַּדָּיו, *his branches*, to refer to the suburban villages which branch off from the major cities.

7. וְעַמִּי תְלוּאִים לִמְשׁוּבָתִי — *And My people waver [as] to [their] return to Me.* When the prophets teach them and exhort them to mend their ways they vacillate in their decision, unsure whether to undertake the difficult effort of returning to Me. Thus, even when they do repent, they do so with great reluctance and hesitation (*Targum; Rashi; Mahari Kara*).

Others render מְשׁוּבָה to mean *deviation*: My people waver in their fulfillment of My commandments. Although they are aware of their obligations, they nevertheless persist in deviating from My paths and in rebelling against Me (*Radak*, citing his father). *Radak* himself explains: My nation wavers between calamity and deliverance; at times one prevails and at times the other. This is due to their deviance from My ways and their rebellion against Me.

Abarbanel understands מְשׁוּבָה to mean the refusal to repent or change one's ways. The Jewish nation is guilty of this in their refusal to repent their wicked ways, and the Almighty, in turn, resists their supplications and refuses to rescind His evil decrees. The people thus contend that if the Almighty would only retract His decree and restore them to peace and prosperity, they too would repent from their evil ways. Accordingly, the Almighty states: And My people make themselves dependent upon My resistance and My refusal to abrogate their punishment — stating that if only I will compromise My position they too will mend their ways (see comm. to v. 9).

וְאֶל־עַל יִקְרָאֻהוּ — *And to the One Above they call them.* The prophets all call out to the nation and exhort them to return to the Almighty Who dwells on high (*Ibn Ezra; Radak; Abarbanel; Metzudos David*).

Targum renders: *A strong* [i.e. harsh] *occurrence will befall them.* He thus renders אֵל to mean strong (cf. *Genesis* 31:29) (*Rashi*).[1]

יַחַד לֹא יְרוֹמֵם — *Together they do not exalt [Him].* From among the entire nation there is no one who returns to Hashem and exalts Him in word and thought (*Radak; Abarbanel; Metzudos David*). Alternatively: *Together they shall not raise their heads* (*Ibn Ezra*) — i.e., they shall not succeed (*Abarbanel*).

Others interpret these last two phrases as one: *And to that upon which they call them, together they do not uphold it* — the matter for which the prophets call to the people and exhort them, they unanimously refuse to uphold (*Rashi; Mahari Kara*).

8. Despite your lack of appreciation for the special treatment I have accorded you, and in spite of your constant rebelliousness and infidelity to Me, I will nevertheless withhold the full force of the retribution you have earned, as My great love for you prevents Me from carrying it out.

1. *Rashi* and *Radak*, however, both contest this interpretation, contending that if it were correct the word וְאֶל would be vowelized with a *tseireh* — אֵל — rather than a *segol*.

7 *And My people waver [as] to [their] return to Me; and to the One Above they call them; together they do not exalt [Him].* 8 *How can I give you over Ephraim [or] deliver you, Israel; how can I render you like Admah [or] make you like Zeboyim? My heart has been turned over; My mercies have been kindled.* 9 *I will not carry out My wrath; I will not renege to destroy Ephraim, for I am God and not a man; the Holy One is in your midst and I will not enter a city.*

אֵיךְ אֶתֶּנְךָ אֶפְרַיִם אֲמַגֶּנְךָ יִשְׂרָאֵל אֵיךְ אֶתֶּנְךָ כְאַדְמָה אֲשִׂימְךָ כִּצְבֹאיִם נֶהְפַּךְ עָלַי לִבִּי יַחַד נִכְמְרוּ נִחוּמָי — *How can I give you over Ephraim [or] deliver you, Israel; how can I render you like Admah [or] make you like Zeboyim? My heart has been turned over; My mercies have been kindled.* How can I possibly give you over to the enemy, Ephraim? How can I deliver you, the remaining tribes of Israel, to the oppressor? Although you are deserving of the same fate as met by the cities of Admah and Zeboyim, which were overturned and destroyed along with Sodom and Gemorrah,[1] I find Myself "unable" to carry out such a decree. For My heart has been turned over and My decision rescinded (*Radak*) [due to My great love for the Jewish nation], and My mercies for you have been kindled and set aflame (*Targum; Mahari Kara*).

Others render נִחוּמָי to mean *My remorse* (*Ibn Ezra*) [i.e., My remorse over My decision to destroy you completely has been aroused]. Alternatively: *My remorse has been stirred* — for I have regretted the evil that I had decreed upon you and I shall thus not carry it out (*Radak; Abarbanel*).[2]

9. לֹא אֶעֱשֶׂה חֲרוֹן אַפִּי לֹא אָשׁוּב לְשַׁחֵת אֶפְרָיִם כִּי אֵל אָנֹכִי וְלֹא־אִישׁ בְּקִרְבְּךָ קָדוֹשׁ וְלֹא אָבוֹא בְּעִיר — *I will not carry out My wrath; I will not renege to destroy Ephraim, for I am God and not a man; the Holy One is in your midst and I will not enter a city.* [Since I have been moved to deal with you mercifully,] I will not carry out the decree of total annihilation which I rendered in My wrath. Nor will I renege on My vow that I proclaimed in the Torah (*Leviticus* 26:44): *I have not spurned them nor have I loathed them* — and destroy Ephraim totally (*Rashi*). For I am the Almighty God and not a man. I do not rescind any commitment I have made to benefit mankind (*Rashi; Radak*). Nor am I compelled to carry out My decree immediately [without allowing time for repentance] (*Mahari Kara*) for fear that I will not have the opportunity to do so at a later date (*Metzudos David*). In addition, being God, I am capable of bearing the burden of My anger if I so desire, and I

1. The prophet uses Admah and Zeboyim as examples, rather than the better-known cities of Sodom and Gemorrah, in order to differentiate between the kingdom of Israel and that of Judah, who had been compared by Isaiah (1:9,10) to Sodom and Gemorrah (*Abarbanel*). Alternatively, the two cities cited were annihilated completely, whereas Lot and his daughters were saved from the city of Sodom (*Alshich*).

2. Although it is obvious that an omniscient God does not change His mind or regret His decisions, the annulment of His decree is depicted as such in order to describe it in terms that the human mind can comprehend (*Ibn Ezra*). [In actuality, the wrath described is the response to their misdeeds that would be appropriate in accordance with a standard of strict justice. However, by virtue of the Almighty's attribute of mercy, that severe punishment is withheld.]

י אַחֲרֵי יהוה יֵלְכוּ כְּאַרְיֵה יִשְׁאָג כִּי־הוּא יִשְׁאַג
יא וְיֶחֶרְדוּ בָנִים מִיָּם: יֶחֶרְדוּ כְצִפּוֹר מִמִּצְרַיִם וּכְיוֹנָה
מֵאֶרֶץ אַשּׁוּר וְהוֹשַׁבְתִּים עַל־בָּתֵּיהֶם נְאֻם־

do not find it necessary to translate it into action (*Ibn Ezra; Radak*).

Radak renders לֹא אָשׁוּב לְשַׁחֵת אֶפְרָיִם to mean: Even if I have afflicted them for their iniquities, I will not return to them to destroy them completely.

Abarbanel renders: *I will not renege from destroying Ephraim.* Herein lies the Almighty's rejoinder to the argument of the people (v. 7) that if He will only take the initial steps towards reconciliation they will follow suit and repent. To this Hashem responds: I cannot follow such a course of action. For I am God, not a man, and it is not appropriate for Me to compromise My honor in this manner.

בְּקִרְבְּךָ קָדוֹשׁ וְלֹא אָבוֹא בְּעִיר — *The Holy One is in your midst and I will not enter a city.* I have already vowed to make My Divine Presence reside in your midst in Jerusalem and I will not enter with My Presence into any other city in its stead (*Targum; Rashi*). Alternatively: I have caused My Glory to reside in your midst, which I have not done with any other nation (*Radak*).

Rashi cites a second translation: *and I will not come with hatred. Mahari Kara* interprets: As long as there is Holiness in your midst, *I will not enter the city* to destroy it.

The Sages comment: Said R' Yochanan: Said the Holy One, Blessed is He: I will not enter Jerusalem above until I enter Jerusalem below. Is there a Jerusalem above? Yes; as it is stated (*Psalms* 122:3): *Jerusalem which is built like a city that is joined together with it* (*Taanis* 5a).[1]

Alshich sees this verse as referring back to verse 7, which he interpreted as lauding and encouraging the attribute of unity. יַחַד לֹא יְרוֹמֵם, *together He shall not cause* — i.e., if there will only be unity among the Jewish people, the Almighty will not raise His Presence and remove It from their midst. Here He declares: When I see the Jewish people uniting to plead with Me for salvation, I am immediately moved to rescind My decree and spare them. For, in truth, it is My will that My Presence have a place here on earth, not only in the heavens. However, since I am God and not a man, a geographical location does not suffice to contain My Presence. Rather, I can only find a "home" in your midst — i.e., in the hearts and souls of My people, and only in unity are you able to house My Presence among you.

10. The prophet ends this chapter with a glimpse into the (then) distant future, depicting the final redemption of the Jewish people and their permanent return to the Holy Land.

אַחֲרֵי ה׳ יֵלְכוּ כְּאַרְיֵה יִשְׁאָג כִּי־הוּא יִשְׁאַג וְיֶחֶרְדוּ בָנִים מִיָּם — *After* HASHEM *they will follow; like a lion He shall roar; for He shall roar and the children shall stir from the west.* [Although I have responded to their iniquities with restraint,] the magnitude of their sins nevertheless compels Me to remove My Divine Presence from their midst and to banish them from their land. However, the day shall yet arrive when they will seek out Hashem and follow after Him while still in their exile (*Radak*).

1. Know that Jerusalem, Zion, and the Temple are all symbols of very sublime spiritual entities. In fact, this applies to all of the land of Israel [apparently to a lesser degree]. For this reason the Land is referred to as נַחֲלַת ה׳, the legacy of God, and it is also the cause for the many *mitzvos* that are unique to the Holy Land. [Thus, when the Sages mention the heavenly Jerusalem, they refer to those entities which the physical Jerusalem symbolizes] (*Rashba*, cited by *Ein Yaakov*).

11/10-11 [10] *After* HASHEM *they will follow; like a lion He shall roar; for He shall roar and the children shall stir from the west.* [11] *They will stir like a bird from Egypt and like a dove from the land of Assyria, and I will settle them in their homes, declares* HASHEM.

When that occurs, they will earn the right to follow Him out of exile back to their homeland (*Rashi*). For at that time, the Almighty shall roar like a lion — who emits his mighty roar to gather together all the beasts of the jungle where he reigns supreme. So shall Hashem reveal Himself to His people through a prophet or through a miraculous sign of His Presence (*Radak*). This will move them to stir from the west where they are exiled (*Targum; Rashi*) and to return to His Holy Land to experience once again His Divine Presence there — like a son responding to his father's call to return home (*Radak*).

Ibn Ezra specifies *the west* as referring to Egypt, which is southwest of Israel, as well as Assyria. *Radak* comments: They will stir from the east and the west. [His intent is unclear; where does he see a reference to the east in this verse?] According to *R' Eliezer of Beaugency*, the word מִיָּם is translated *from the sea*: They shall stir in response to His roar just as all are shaken and stirred by the roar of the lion. However, the lion is feared only by those standing nearby on dry land, but not by those safely away at sea. The roar of the Almighty, on the other hand, will shake and stir even those in the distant sea.

Others interpret: When the Children of Israel shall follow after Hashem and His ways and seek Him out in their exile, He will roar like a lion against the gentile nations who have subjugated them. At that time, the Jewish people will stir from the west in their exile [and return to their land] (*Mahari Kara; Ibn Ezra*).

Malbim sees this as a depiction of their relationship with Hashem while in exile: Even when they will be banished from their cities they will find the Almighty ready to lead them into exile and maintain His Divine Presence in their midst. However, they will no longer experience His overt involvement in their affairs. Rather, *He will roar like a lion* — He will express Himself not with His own voice, but with that of the lion, carrying out His will covertly by influencing the decisions of the monarchies of Assyria and Babylon — symbolized in Scripture by the lion — and thereby guiding the destiny of His nation. Nevertheless, the day shall yet arrive when He will once again emit His own mighty roar and lead His children with His overt Divine Providence. At that time, they will stir from the west where they are exiled and return to the Holy Land.

11. יֶחֶרְדוּ כְצִפּוֹר מִמִּצְרַיִם וּכְיוֹנָה מֵאֶרֶץ אַשּׁוּר וְהוֹשַׁבְתִּים עַל־בָּתֵּיהֶם נְאֻם־ה׳ — *They will stir like a bird from Egypt and like a dove from the land of Assyria, and I will settle them in their homes, declares* HASHEM. Those who are exiled in Egypt will stir like a bird, who embarks on a journey to return to his home (*Radak*). Even those banished to distant Assyria shall set their sights on the Holy Land and embark on their long journey — like homing pigeons who find their way even from great distances (*Malbim*). When this occurs, I will return them to the Land of Israel (*Malbim*) and settle them safely and securely in their homes (*Metzudos David*).

Abarbanel suggests that this verse may be an exhortation to the people of the prophet's generation rather than a depiction of the future redemption: If only the people of Israel would tremble like a bird aflutter in fear of transgressing the will of the Almighty by turning to Egypt for aid; if only they would quake like a dove from placing their faith in Assyria, then surely the Almighty would accept their repentance and revoke the decree of exile from upon them, settling them safely in their homes.

א יְהוָה: סְבָבֻנִי בְכַחַשׁ אֶפְרַיִם וּבְמִרְמָה
בֵּית יִשְׂרָאֵל וִיהוּדָה עֹד רָד עִם־אֵל וְעִם־
ב קְדוֹשִׁים נֶאֱמָן: אֶפְרַיִם רֹעֶה רוּחַ וְרֹדֵף קָדִים
כָּל־הַיּוֹם כָּזָב וָשֹׁד יַרְבֶּה וּבְרִית עִם־אַשּׁוּר יִכְרֹתוּ
ג וְשֶׁמֶן לְמִצְרַיִם יוּבָל: וְרִיב לַיהוָה עִם־יְהוּדָה
וְלִפְקֹד עַל־יַעֲקֹב כִּדְרָכָיו כְּמַעֲלָלָיו יָשִׁיב לוֹ:

XII

The prophet now reverts to his previous theme of relaying the Almighty's contentions with the Jewish people for their misdeeds — seeking once more to inspire them to repent. In so doing, he draws a distinction between the sinful nation of Israel and the people of Judah, who were still loyal to Hashem. Although the latter were also eventually exiled for their sinful ways, the following verses refer to a point in time when this was not yet the case. Some interpret this to be the time when the kingdom of Israel was first split in two. Whereas Jeroboam shortly thereafter introduced idolatry to the nation of the ten tribes and led the people astray, Judah still remained faithful to Hashem and continued to cling to His ways (*Radak*). Alternatively, this prophecy depicts the generation of the destruction of the kingdom of Israel, at which time Hezekiah ruled over the land of Judah and led them in a renaissance of Torah scholarship and spiritual growth (*Malbim*).

1. סְבָבֻנִי בְכַחַשׁ אֶפְרַיִם וּבְמִרְמָה בֵּית יִשְׂרָאֵל — *Ephraim has surrounded Me with falsehood and the house of Israel with deceit.* Ephraim and the tribes of Israel allied with him surround My Divine Presence in Jerusalem with their wicked provinces that are filled with idolatry and corruption (*Rashi; Radak*). *Malbim* renders: Ephraim, the ruling tribe among the Israelite nation, surrounds Me with denial and heresy, and the remaining tribes of the house of Israel are steeped in corruption in their dealings with their fellow man.

Others interpret: Although they surround Me like subjects who surround their king, they do so deceitfully, for they are actually steeped in the depravity of their idolatry (*Ibn Ezra; Abarbanel; Metzudos David*).

וִיהוּדָה עֹד רָד עִם־אֵל וְעִם־קְדוֹשִׁים נֶאֱמָן — *But Judah yet rules with God and with the Holy One he is faithful.* The monarchy of Judah still rules with the fear of Hashem, and his kings are still faithful to the Holy One Blessed is He. In this manner they lead their people and thus set the tone for the entire nation (*Rashi; Radak*). Others render רָד to mean *cleave* — they still cleave to the service of the Almighty (*Mahari Kara; R' Eliezer of Beaugency*).

Abarbanel renders: *And Judah in his descent* (רָד) *is yet with God, and is with the holy ones in faith.* Despite having been lowered from ruling over the entire nation to a monarchy encompassing only the two tribes of Judah and Benjamin, Judah nevertheless remains loyal to the Almighty and continues to pursue the faith of his holy patriarchs.

Ibn Ezra (v. 3) rejects this entire approach and contends that Judah is also included in the rebuke expressed in this chapter. [However, he provides no explanation of this verse, which is the basis for the view of the other commentators. Perhaps he understands this chapter to be describing a historical sequence: Originally, only Ephraim strayed from the ways of Hashem, but Judah remained loyal to Him. Eventually, however,

[1] *Ephraim has surrounded Me with falsehood and
the house of Israel with deceit, but Judah yet rules
with God and with the Holy One he is faithful.*
[2] *Ephraim embraces the wind and pursues the east
wind; all day he increases falsehood and plunder,
and they execute a pact with Assyria and oil is carried to Egypt.* [3] *And the contention of* H*ASHEM is with
Judah and to visit upon Jacob according to his ways;
in accordance with his deeds He will requit him.*

both nations fell prey to their evil desires, and the Almighty thus has a contention with both of them.]

2. אֶפְרַיִם רֹעֶה רוּחַ וְרֹדֵף קָדִים כָּל־הַיּוֹם כָּזָב וָשֹׁד יַרְבֶּה וּבְרִית עִם־אַשּׁוּר יִכְרֹתוּ וְשֶׁמֶן לְמִצְרַיִם יוּבָל — *Ephraim embraces the wind and pursues the east wind; all day he increases falsehood and plunder, and they execute a pact with Assyria and oil is carried to Egypt.* Ephraim befriends and embraces the empty winds of idolatry, which, in truth, are devoid of substance (*Rashi*). He pursues even the east wind, which is strong and violent and harms those who embrace it — as his idolatry has brought upon him only pain and misfortune (*Radak*). Nevertheless, the people do not repent their evil ways. Rather, they continuously expand the scope of their devotion to the falsehood and vanity of idolatry, bringing upon themselves ever-increasing plunder and destruction in retribution for their sins (*Radak; R' Eliezer of Beaugency*). Even as their straits become further imperiled, they do not return to Me and thereby bring salvation. Instead they turn to the foreign powers of Egypt and Assyria. They invoke their aid with treaties and seek to cement their friendship with tribute by sending fine oils to the land of Egypt (*Radak; R' Eliezer of Beaugency*).

Others translate רֹעֶה רוּחַ to mean *grazing from the wind* — they open their mouths to the empty winds of idolatry in the hope of thereby receiving benefit, but it is to no avail (*Radak*). Alternatively: They graze and cultivate the wind, seeking to draw benefits from it (*Metzudos David*).

Malbim interprets: They involve themselves in faiths that are merely empty winds, with no substance. In their dealings with each other, they increase falsehood and robbery throughout the day.

Alshich sees this verse as describing the process whereby Jeroboam ben Nebot from the tribe of Ephraim descended into idolatry and brought the nation down with him: Initially he grazed and cultivated his wind — i.e., the hot air of his haughtiness. He saw his position as monarch threatened by the specter of the people ascending to Jerusalem on the Festivals, and reaffirming their loyalty to the Davidic dynasty. As a result he pursued the harsh winds of idolatry by establishing two golden calves as deities for the nation. From this he continued to increase falsehood and plunder, as he convinced the people to follow his path. Eventually his monarchy was weakened and threatened in retribution for his evil, and he was forced thereby to seek alliances with Egypt and Assyria in order to survive.

3. וְרִיב לַה׳ עִם־יְהוּדָה וְלִפְקֹד עַל־יַעֲקֹב כִּדְרָכָיו כְּמַעֲלָלָיו יָשִׁיב לוֹ — *And the contention of* H*ASHEM is with Judah and to visit upon Jacob according to his ways; in accordance with his deeds He will requit him.* The Almighty shares his contention against the people of Israel with His loyal nation of Judah. He explains to them the evil the former have committed so that they should not be

ד בַּבֶּטֶן עָקַב אֶת־אָחִיו וּבְאוֹנוֹ שָׂרָה אֶת־אֱלֹהִים:
ה וַיָּשַׂר אֶל־מַלְאָךְ וַיֻּכָל בָּכָה וַיִּתְחַנֶּן־לוֹ בֵּית־אֵל
ו יִמְצָאֶנּוּ וְשָׁם יְדַבֵּר עִמָּנוּ: וַיהוָה אֱלֹהֵי הַצְּבָאוֹת

perplexed [and dismayed] when He exacts from Israel in accordance with its wicked deeds (*Rashi; Mahari Kara*).

Alternatively, the subject of this verse is the nation of Ephraim, who was continuously involved in conflict with the nation of Judah as a result of their basic ideological disagreement. Thus: *He has a dispute with Judah due to and concerning* HASHEM — i.e., whether to remain loyal to the Almighty. In bitter sarcasm, the prophet adds: The ten tribes remember the ways of their ancestor Jacob and follow in his footsteps, as he, too, was involved in contention with his brother (*Abarbanel; Malbim*).

Others interpret this verse in accordance with its literal translation — HASHEM *has a dispute with Judah.* Although they were once steadfast in their loyalty to Him, they too eventually succumbed to the lures of idolatry. Thus He now has a contention to pick with them as well. Now that this is so, the entire nation descending from Jacob shall be requited in accordance with its wicked deeds (*Radak; R' Eliezer of Beaugency; Metzudos David*).

As cited above, *Ibn Ezra* rejects the approach to these verses that sees in them words of praise for the loyalty of Judah. He thus interprets this verse as a continuation of the castigation of both Jewish kingdoms.

[Having mentioned the patriarch Jacob in the previous verse, the Almighty recalls the special relationship He had with him and the miracles He performed on his behalf, seeking to inspire the people to dedicate themselves to recovering that close bond.]

4. בַּבֶּטֶן עָקַב אֶת־אָחִיו וּבְאוֹנוֹ שָׂרָה אֶת־אֱלֹהִים — *In the womb he seized his brother's heel, and with his strength he struggled*[1] *with an angel.* Look at all that I have granted Jacob [and how his descendants repay My kindness]! While yet in his mother's womb, he seized the heel of his brother Esau [in an effort to prevent him from emerging first and earning for himself the birthright], displaying thereby the superhuman strength that I bestowed upon him (*Rashi*). Indeed, such a feat is nothing short of miraculous. A fetus while still in the womb has no power or control over its limbs, and it is certainly not capable of piercing its placenta as well as that of its twin and grasping the latter's heel. Obviously, then, this was a sign from above that in the end of days, the descendants of Jacob will conquer and subjugate those of Esau (*Ibn Ezra; Radak*).

But My wonders with their father Jacob did not end there. Years later, I enabled him to struggle with an angel of God and, indeed, to prevail over him (*Genesis* 32:25-31). This, too, was not a natural event. One angel was sufficient to destroy the entire camp of the mighty armies of Assyria [when they besieged Jerusalem in the days of Hezekiah]. Even [so holy an individual as] King David was seized by trembling when he encountered an angel. Yet Jacob managed to struggle and even to subdue him (*Ibn Ezra*). This, too, was a sign of the destiny of the Jewish nation. They will be the portion of Hashem Himself in creation, and thereby rise above the power and reach of all of the heavenly forces and angels. Certainly, then, they may rest assured that as long as they fulfill My will they need not fear any power in creation, for their attachment to the Almighty renders them impervious to its strength (*Radak*). Why, then, do the children of

1. This follows the translation of *Targum.* Others render שָׂרָה to mean *he conquered* (*Radak; Metzudos*).

[4] *In the womb he seized his brother's heel, and with his strength he struggled with an angel.* [5] *And he struggled with an angel and prevailed; he wept and beseeched him. [In] Beth-el He will find us and there He will speak with us.* [6] *And* HASHEM *the God of Hosts,*

Jacob not remember these facts and take them to heart? Why do they not turn to Me for salvation rather than relying on alliances with heathen nations (*Ibn Ezra; Metzudos David* to v. 5)?

5. וַיָּשַׂר אֶל־מַלְאָךְ וַיֻּכָל בָּכָה וַיִּתְחַנֶּן־לוֹ בֵּית־אֵל יִמְצָאֶנּוּ וְשָׁם יְדַבֵּר עִמָּנוּ — *And he struggled with an angel and prevailed; he wept and beseeched him. [In] Beth-el He will find us and there He will speak with us.* Emphasizing his words through repetition, the prophet again reminds the Jewish nation how their ancestor Jacob struggled miraculously with an angel and even managed to prevail. Indeed, the angel was forced to cry before Jacob[1] and to implore him to allow him to return to the heavens so that he could take his place among the angels who sing the praises of the Almighty with the rising of the morning star. All this was meant to demonstrate [to Israel] how Hashem sends His angels to assist the truly righteous and to submit to their will; thus that angel could return only with Jacob's consent (*Radak*).

בֵּית־אֵל יִמְצָאֶנּוּ וְשָׁם יְדַבֵּר עִמָּנוּ — *[In] Bethel He will find us and there He will speak with us.* Thus pleaded the angel with Jacob: Allow me to depart at this moment, for in due time the Almighty will reveal Himself to you in Beth-el [and bestow upon you the name Israel (*Rashi* to *Genesis* 32:26)]. There He will find us and speak to us, for I, too, the guardian angel of Esau,[2] will be present, and I will there acknowledge your right to the blessings of Isaac (*Rashi*).

Others interpret this phrase as two separate statements. *[In] Beth-el he found him* — the angel encountered Jacob in the city of Beth-el a second time and there he blessed him. [The prophet uses the future tense in place of the past, as is found often in Scripture.]

And there he will speak with us — these are the words of the prophet to the nation: Because the town of Beth-el was thus established as one in which heavenly encounters occur, it was here that Amos and myself were directed by Hashem to prophesy to the nation, and to rebuke them for their worship of the golden calves that takes place there (*Ibn Ezra; Radak*).

6. וַה׳ אֱלֹהֵי הַצְּבָאוֹת ה׳ זִכְרוֹ — *And* HASHEM *the God of Hosts,* HASHEM *is His appellation.* Just as He was then the God of Hosts, ruling over all that exists in the heavens above and on the earth below, so is He still the Almighty God. And His appellation [lit. *His remembrance* — the Name by which He is remembered] is יהוה which denotes that He is the master of all existence (*Rashi; Mahari Kara; Metzudos David*). Therefore, if you will only go with Him wholeheartedly as did

1. The Sages expound: *And he struggled with an angel and he prevailed* — I would not know who prevailed over whom. However, since it is stated (*Genesis* 32:29), *for you struggled with angels and with men and you prevailed,* it may be assumed that Jacob achieved supremacy over the angel. *He cried and beseeched him* — I do not know who cried to whom. Since it says (*Genesis* 32:27), *send me, for the morning star has risen . . . and he blessed him there,* it may be assumed that the angel cried to Jacob (*Yalkut Shimoni* from *Bereishis Rabbah* 32).

2. This follows the view of *Bereishis Rabbah* (78). *Radak* cites the Sages as identifying this angel as Michael. About him Jacob later stated (*Genesis* 48:16), *The angel who redeemed me, etc.*

ז יְהוָה זִכְרוֹ: וְאַתָּה בֵּאלֹהֶיךָ תָשׁוּב חֶסֶד וּמִשְׁפָּט
ח שְׁמֹר וְקַוֵּה אֶל־אֱלֹהֶיךָ תָּמִיד: כְּנַעַן בְּיָדוֹ מֹאזְנֵי
ט מִרְמָה לַעֲשֹׁק אָהֵב: וַיֹּאמֶר אֶפְרַיִם אַךְ עָשַׁרְתִּי
מָצָאתִי אוֹן לִי כָּל־יְגִיעַי לֹא יִמְצְאוּ־לִי עָוֺן

your father Jacob, He will deal with you in the same miraculous manner that He did with the latter (*Rashi; Mahari Kara*).

Radak interprets: Although He appeared to your forefathers by the title אֵל שַׁדַּי [the Lord Who rules over the forces of nature], He revealed the Name of His true Glory — that He is the Lord of Hosts Who rules over all of the angels and forces in Heaven — to Moses (*Exodus* 6:3). He disclosed this aspect of His Godliness to him in order to import that you, the Jewish nation, have been granted the capacity to attach yourselves to that Name if only you will fulfill His will and follow in His ways.

According to *Malbim*, these last two verses depict an imaginary dialogue between Jeroboam and the prophet. Jeroboam's designating Beth-el as a site of idolatry was based on his assumption that it was an appropriate place for sanctified deeds, since it had been rendered such by the angel's revelation there to Jacob. There, too, the angel cried to Jacob and beseeched him to release him, promising him at that time that he would join him in Beth-el and consent to his acquisition of the blessings of Isaac. Similarly, *there he shall speak with us* — i.e., that angel has remained in that site and will serve there as a medium between us and the Almighty.

To this the prophet responds: The Jewish nation does not receive its Divine Blessing through any medium whatsoever. Rather, *HASHEM is the God of Hosts* — Who rules over all angels and mediums — *HASHEM is the Name by which He is remembered* — i.e., by which He is remembered by us, as we have a direct link to His Godliness without the need for any intermediary.

7. Because He is the Almighty God, and because He has granted you the ability to cleave to Him, your sinful deeds and corrupt ways can still be rectified and the punishment in store for you can still be avoided, if only you will repent and return to His ways.

וְאַתָּה בֵּאלֹהֶיךָ תָשׁוּב חֶסֶד וּמִשְׁפָּט שְׁמֹר וְקַוֵּה אֶל־אֱלֹהֶיךָ תָּמִיד — *And you may return by your God; keep benevolence and justice and you may always hope for your God.* If only you will practice benevolence and justice you may rely on the promise[1] and support of Hashem, your God, Who will enable you to return to Him. Thus you will be guaranteed the right to realistically hope for His salvation at all times [in reward for your fidelity to Him] (*Rashi; Metzudos David*).

Others render בֵּאלֹהֶיךָ as if it were written לֵאלֹהֶיךָ, *to your God*. They interpret the entire verse as a challenge issued to the Jewish nation: You must return to your God and practice benevolence and justice, and place your faith and hopes in the Almighty God rather than in any other forces in Heaven or on earth (*Targum; Mahari Kara; R' Eliezer of Beaugency*).[2]

Radak translates תָשׁוּב as tranquility: *And you, Israel, be tranquil by your God* — i.e., if you will appease your God, you will rest in peace and tranquility. But to

1. [*Rashi* does not elaborate upon the nature of this promise. Presumably, it refers to the Almighty's guarantee that one who sincerely attempts to repent and improve himself will receive Divine assistance in his efforts.]

2. As stated in *Jeremiah* (9:23), the traits by which the Almighty describes His actions on this world are benevolence, justice, and righteousness and — as noted there — these are the qualities He seeks from His creations. Thus, the prophet here exhorts the Children of Israel to practice these traits. Benevolence and justice he cites explicitly, and righteousness is included in the connotation of the final phrase — *and hope to HASHEM always* (*Radak*).

HASHEM is His appellation. [7] *And you may return by your God; keep benevolence and justice and you may always hope for your God.* [8] *A trader with scales of deceit in his hand; he loves to rob.* [9] *And Ephraim said: But I have become rich; I have found power for myself, [for] all my toil they will not find to me iniquity*

accomplish this you must follow in His ways of benevolence and justice. You must also place your hopes and faith in the Almighty God, attributing to Him all your success and prosperity and keeping Him constantly in your heart and mind (cf. *Ibn Ezra*).

Abarbanel suggests that these last three verses may be interpreted as an exhortation to the nation of Ephraim to return to their fidelity to Hashem and to abandon their worship of the idols of Dan and Beth-el: Having recalled the encounter between Jacob and the angel, the prophet challenges the people with the rhetorical question: Will He speak with us there? Will the Almighty communicate with us through our calves as He did with Jacob through His angel? No! Certainly not! Our only recourse to direct interaction with the Almighty is in the Temple, where the Divine Presence of Hashem is to be found and where He has established Himself as the God of His Hosts — i.e., of the tribes of Judah and Benjamin [and the Levites] who are yet loyal to Him. Therefore, Ephraim, return to Hashem and practice benevolence and justice. For although you are guilty of great iniquity He will yet accept your sincere repentance. Thus, you may always turn to Him with the realistic hope for salvation.

8. Continuing his pattern of alternating between rebuke and encouragement, the prophet once again reverts to his castigation of the Children of Israel for their corruption and dishonesty.

כְּנַעַן בְּיָדוֹ מֹאזְנֵי מִרְמָה לַעֲשֹׁק אָהֵב — *A trader with scales of deceit in his hand; he loves to rob.* However, Ephraim, you have not followed this course, but rather that of the errant trader, who carries dishonest weights to cheat his customers. Instead of seeking justice and righteousness, he loves to rob and cheat in pursuit of his livelihood (*Radak; Metzudos David*).

Others render: *Do not be like the trader with scales of deceit in his hand* (*Targum; Mahari Kara*).

Abarbanel suggests that כְּנַעַן may also mean the nation of Canaan, whom the prophet accuses Israel of having come to resemble in its behavior. He suggests as well an alternative translation to the phrase לַעֲשֹׁק אָהֵב, *Due to [his] robbery he loves [him].* The dishonest trader should be shunned and despised due to his deceitful practices, but Ephraim in his corruption chooses to love [and emulate] him instead.

9. וַיֹּאמֶר אֶפְרַיִם אַךְ עָשַׁרְתִּי מָצָאתִי אוֹן לִי כָּל־יְגִיעַי לֹא יִמְצְאוּ־לִי עָוֹן אֲשֶׁר־חֵטְא — *And Ephraim said: But I have become rich; I have found power for myself, [for] all my toil they will not find to me iniquity which [contains] sin.* In their decadence, the people of Ephraim do not turn to Hashem as urged, but rather seek to attribute their prosperity to themselves, while spuriously claiming innocence of any wrongdoing. Thus, they declare, "I, with my efforts, have made myself wealthy; it is not the Almighty's doing but rather my own. And it is I, as well, who has found the means to increase my power."[1] Furthermore, I have done so

1. This is one translation of אוֹן offered by *Radak*. It is also the one employed by *Rashi* and *Metzudos*. Another possibility is that it means wealth (*Radak; Abarbanel*). *Metzudos* sees this first half of the verse as one thought: I became rich through the power and energy I found to amass wealth.

י אֲשֶׁר־חֵטְא: וְאָנֹכִי יְהוָה אֱלֹהֶיךָ מֵאֶרֶץ מִצְרָיִם
יא עֹד אוֹשִׁיבְךָ בָאֳהָלִים כִּימֵי מוֹעֵד: וְדִבַּרְתִּי
עַל־הַנְּבִיאִים וְאָנֹכִי חָזוֹן הִרְבֵּיתִי וּבְיַד
יב הַנְּבִיאִים אֲדַמֶּה: אִם־גִּלְעָד אָוֶן אַךְ־שָׁוְא הָיוּ

without indulging in any wrongdoing whatsoever. No one can point to any iniquity among my actions — at least none in which I was guilty of sin. For if perchance there was theft or dishonesty involved, I was totally unaware of that fact and remain innocent and blameless[1] (*Radak*).

Others interpret the second half of this verse as the prophet's response to the spurious claim of the people: All of your wealth will not stand up for you on the day of the payment of your debt (*Targum*). I.e., it would be to your benefit to recognize and proclaim: All of my wealth [for which I toiled] will not suffice to achieve atonement for my iniquities that I have sinned (*Rashi*).[2]

Rashi cites R' Shimon (father of *Mahari Kara*) as offering a metaphorical interpretation to this verse, that it refers to Jeroboam ben Nebot, the first king of the ten tribes, who was from the tribe of Ephraim. In attempting to validate his reign over Israel, he declares, "I have found a bill of indebtedness — און — from the nation of Israel. For [when my forefather Joseph ruled over Egypt,] his brothers said to him (*Genesis* 50:18): *Behold, we are to you like slaves.* And [the *halachah* is that] whatever is acquired by a slave belongs to his master. Thus, all of the wealth of Israel really belongs to me. Therefore, I am not guilty of any iniquity or sin if I confiscate all that they possess." In response to this, the next verse begins: *And I am HASHEM your God from the land of Egypt.* I.e., all of the greatness you ascribe to your ancestors in Egypt came from Me. [Furthermore,] that which was stated, *behold, we are to you like slaves,* you recall, but that which was stated, *I am HASHEM your God,* you do not recall. Thus, you have erected two golden calves of idolatry in Dan and Beth-el.

10. וְאָנֹכִי ה׳ אֱלֹהֶיךָ מֵאֶרֶץ מִצְרָיִם עֹד אוֹשִׁיבְךָ בָאֳהָלִים כִּימֵי מוֹעֵד — *And I am HASHEM your God from the land of Egypt; I will yet settle you in tents like [early] times.* Why do you persist in pursuing your rebellious ways, refusing to take note of the kindness I have bestowed upon you and the wonders I have shown you since the dawn of your existence, as well as those I have in store for you if you will only heed My words and repent? For I am the very God Whom your ancestors came to recognize in the land of Egypt. There I delivered you with miracles and overt manifestations of My power, and there I dealt with you directly through My Divine Providence rather than

1. *Radak* suggests two other possible translations for the final phrase, לֹא יִמְצְאוּ־לִי עָוֹן אֲשֶׁר־חֵטְא: One is that אֲשֶׁר is used here to mean *and.* They will not find in Me iniquity, or even the lesser fault of sin — which oftentimes refers to inadvertent wrongdoing. Alternatively, it is rendered *they will not find in me iniquity [or that] which contains sin.*

Ibn Ezra sees this as a response to the prophet's analogy to the dishonest trader: Why do you compare me to the errant trader when no one can find any wrongdoing among my efforts? *Malbim,* too, follows this approach, but specifies the response as being the age-old rationalization for corruption: I have not been a thief or a criminal; rather, I have accumulated all this wealth through my energy and efforts in my business dealings. If my weights and measures have been dishonest, that is not robbery, merely smart business practices. Indeed, in all of my actions in pursuit of my fortune, you will find not a shred of robbery or crime.

2. *Mahari Kara,* too, interprets this phrase in this manner, but he understands it as part of the flow of the entire verse: *And Ephraim said* — this is what Ephraim should have recognized and expressed when they sinned against Me: Why do we transgress the Will of the Almighty, when all of the riches we have acquired and all of our possessions for which we have toiled will not suffice to redeem our souls on the day of Hashem's wrath for our iniquities and sins?

which [contains] sin. 10 *And I am* H*ASHEM your God from*
the land of Egypt; I will yet settle you in tents like [early]
times. 11 *And I spoke with the prophets and I increased*
visions, and through the prophets I used imagery. 12 *If*
Gilead [suffered] destruction they were but vanity;

through any celestial intermediary. In this manner I fed you and housed you in tents [in the wilderness], and I have dealt with you similarly whenever you have hearkened to My voice. So, too, shall I yet deliver you from the lands of the gentiles in which you will be dispersed. At that time I will house you in tents in the wilderness and show you My miracles, just as I did when I delivered you from Egypt, until I eventually return you to the land of your fathers (*Radak; Metzudos David;* see 2:16; *Radak*, comm. ibid.; cf. *Ibn Ezra; Mahari Kara*).

Rashi interprets the two halves of this verse as being independent of each other. *And I am* H*ASHEM your God from the land of Egypt* — You say that you have found power through your false weights and measures, but I am the Almighty God from the land of Egypt. There I discerned between the drop [of sperm from which was conceived] a firstborn and that of those not firstborn [when I passed over Egypt and killed all their firstborn]. So, too, do I take note of those who rob My people with false weights and measures and I (eventually) exact retribution from them (cf. *Bava Metzia* 61b).

I will yet settle you in tents like [early] times — I will eventually excise from your midst all corrupt merchants, and I will set up among you tent dwellers — students involved in the study of Torah — just as in ancient times, when your forefather Jacob was a dweller in tents.

11. וְדִבַּרְתִּי עַל־הַנְּבִיאִים וְאָנֹכִי חָזוֹן הִרְבֵּיתִי וּבְיַד הַנְּבִיאִים אֲדַמֶּה — *And I spoke with the prophets and I increased visions, and through the prophets I used imagery.* What have I not done; what course have I not pursued — in an attempt to inspire you to remember Me and return to My ways? I spoke consistently with your prophets, instructing them to rebuke you for your misdeeds and to exhort you to repent, and I increased their prophetic visions [to intensify My efforts]. Indeed, I have even employed imagery, in the form of parables and metaphors — conveying it to the prophets in order to enhance your receptivity to My words (*Rashi; Ibn Ezra; Radak; Malbim; Metzudos David*). [And yet, with all this, you persist in ignoring My warnings and spurning My rebuke.]

Another rendition is: *I have assumed likenesses* (*Rashi*). I appeared to My prophets in many different images and forms. At times I appeared before them like a mighty warrior and at times like an elderly sage (*Pesikta Rabbasi* 33).

Abarbanel offers a unique interpretation to these two verses, which he sees as the Almighty's response to the statement of Ephraim in verse 9: You, Ephraim, persist in taking credit for the accumulation of your wealth. Know, however, that I am the God from the land of Egypt Who first made you wealthy with the plunder of Egypt [and it is I Who am responsible for any prosperity you attained since that time]. However, since you persist in denying My benevolence to you I will strip you of your wealth and banish you from your land, leaving you to wander barefoot and naked into exile and to settle in the tents of the hostile forces of Edom and Ishmael. This will take place in the time that I have designated for its occurrence (בִּימֵי מוֹעֵד). I have instructed My prophets to inform you time and time again of this fate that is in store for you and I shall continue to do so in the future through the prophets whom I will yet send to you.

12. אִם־גִּלְעָד אָוֶן אַךְ־שָׁוְא הָיוּ — *If Gilead [suffered] destruction they were but vanity.* If the province of Gilead, in the kingdom of Israel, has suffered destruction and oppression, they brought it upon themselves, for they have filled their lives with deeds containing nothing but

בַּגִּלְגָּל שְׁוָרִים זִבֵּחוּ גַּם מִזְבְּחוֹתָם כְּגַלִּים
יג עַל תַּלְמֵי שָׂדָי: וַיִּבְרַח יַעֲקֹב שְׂדֵה אֲרָם
וַיַּעֲבֹד יִשְׂרָאֵל בְּאִשָּׁה וּבְאִשָּׁה שָׁמָר:
יד וּבְנָבִיא הֶעֱלָה יהוה אֶת־יִשְׂרָאֵל מִמִּצְרָיִם
טו וּבְנָבִיא נִשְׁמָר: הִכְעִיס אֶפְרַיִם תַּמְרוּרִים
וְדָמָיו עָלָיו יִטּוֹשׁ וְחֶרְפָּתוֹ יָשִׁיב לוֹ אֲדֹנָיו:

vanity and emptiness (*Rashi; Metzudos;* cf. *R' Eliezer of Beaugency*).

Radak renders: *If Gilead [practices] iniquity* — Although Gilead began the practice of evil deeds, and thus they were the first to be exiled, Gilgal has managed to increase their iniquity, as described in the remainder of the verse.[1]

בַּגִּלְגָּל שְׁוָרִים זִבֵּחוּ — *In Gilgal they slaughtered oxen.* On the hallowed ground of Gilgal, where the Tabernacle stood when the Jewish nation first crossed into the Land of Israel (*Radak; Metzudos David*), the people have slaughtered oxen to their idols (*Rashi*). They learned this practice from their brothers in Gilead, from whom they were separated by only the narrow waters of the Jordan River (*Radak*).

גַּם מִזְבְּחוֹתָם כְּגַלִּים עַל תַּלְמֵי שָׂדָי — *Indeed, their altars are like heaps upon the furrows of the field.* They have not limited their idolatry to the altars within the town of Gilgal itself. Rather, they have expanded their idolatry throughout the land (*Mahari Kara*) until they have become as numerous and noticeable as the heaps of earth along the furrows which are plowed in the fields (*Rashi; Ibn Ezra*). Alternatively: They have extended their idolatry to every field and every furrow, where they stand like piles of stones along the furrows of the field (*Mahari Kara; Radak*). Indeed, the Sages comment: There is no furrow throughout the Land of Israel upon which King Ahab did not erect false gods and bow to them (*Sanhedrin* 102b).

R' Eliezer of Beaugency sees this phrase as a prophecy of the destruction of Gilgal: In Gilgal they slaughtered oxen [to idolatry]; their altars upon which they thus slaughtered will yet be laid waste and rendered like heaps of stones and rubble.

13. Having recalled earlier (vs. 4, 5) the kindness He performed with Jacob, the Almighty — speaking through His prophet — reverts to that theme, and continues with further aspects of His kindness with Jacob and with his descendants after him (*Rashi*).

וַיִּבְרַח יַעֲקֹב שְׂדֵה אֲרָם וַיַּעֲבֹד יִשְׂרָאֵל בְּאִשָּׁה וּבְאִשָּׁה שָׁמָר — *And Jacob fled to the field of Aram, and Israel worked for a wife, and for a wife he guarded.* My kindness with Jacob continued when he fled from his brother Esau to the fields of his uncle Laban in Aram, where I continued to protect him and hold him close to Me. There he worked for Laban [for seven years] for the sake of a wife, and he continued to guard Laban's sheep for another seven for the second wife he took there. Throughout this time, I continued to guard him and — indeed — I raised him from poverty to prosperity even while in these trying straits (*Rashi; Radak*).

Mahari Kara interprets: Why do you not heed the lesson of your forefather Jacob, who kept the command of his

1. *Radak* is uncertain as to the correct interpretation of the phrase אַךְ־שָׁוְא הָיוּ. It may be a mere repetition of the first phrase, or it might be part of the next thought: *they were but vanity in Gilgal; they slaughtered oxen etc.*

in Gilgal they slaughtered oxen; indeed, their altars are
like heaps upon the furrows of the field. [13] *And Jacob*
fled to the field of Aram, and Israel worked for a wife,
and for a wife he guarded. [14] *And through a prophet*
HASHEM brought Israel up from Egypt, and through a
prophet he was guarded. [15] *Ephraim angered bitterly,*
and He shall spread his blood upon him, and his Lord
shall requit upon him his disparagement.

mother (*Genesis* 27:45) and remained in the house of Laban for twenty years after having gone with the intention of dwelling there for a short time and taking for himself a wife?

14. וּבְנָבִיא הֶעֱלָה ה׳ אֶת־יִשְׂרָאֵל מִמִּצְרָיִם וּבְנָבִיא נִשְׁמָר — *And through a prophet HASHEM brought Israel up from Egypt, and through a prophet he was guarded.* The Almighty's kindness with the Children of Israel continued in the land of Egypt, where He sent His prophet Moses to take them out of slavery and emerge as a mighty nation with great wealth. This benevolence continued through forty years in the wilderness, where the nation was guarded through Hashem's prophet and did not lack anything that they required. Thus — declares the Almighty — time and time again, I have bestowed upon you My blessing. Yet you refuse to remember these events and appreciate them, and you turn instead to the alien gods with which you arouse My wrath (*Ibn Ezra; Radak*). *Metzudos* adds: All this came about through My Divine Providence. How, then, do you continue to deny the existence of that providence and claim that I neither see nor respond to the deeds of mankind?

Others underscore the verse's emphasis that they were redeemed and guarded through a prophet: Nevertheless you continue to humiliate My prophets and disregard their words, ignoring the fact that signs and miracles come through them, and it is thus incumbent upon you to hearken to their words (*Rashi; Mahari Kara*).

Malbim interprets these two verses as the response of the Jewish nation to the Almighty's criticism of their heresy and corruption. Concerning the latter, they retort: Our dishonesty is the heritage of our father Jacob, who fled the wrath of his brother Esau after having deceived their father Isaac and thereby received the blessings that were rightfully the birthright of the firstborn. He, in turn, was subject to similar treatment in the house of Laban, where he worked for two seven-year periods in order to receive the wife he desired because Laban deceived him and first gave him Leah instead of Rachel. Thus, this approach to life is the heritage we have received from our ancestors.

In regard to our heresy, it is not that at all, but merely our recognition of the fact that we require an intermediary in our relationship with the Almighty in order to receive His blessing. When He redeemed us from the land of Egypt He did so through an intermediary — His prophet Moses — and He continued this policy when He sustained us for forty years in the wilderness by means of Moses' leadership (see comm. to 13:4 for the response to this argument).

15. הִכְעִיס אֶפְרַיִם תַּמְרוּרִים וְדָמָיו עָלָיו יִטּוֹשׁ וְחֶרְפָּתוֹ יָשִׁיב לוֹ אֲדֹנָיו — *Ephraim angered bitterly, and He shall spread his blood upon him, and his Lord shall requit upon him his disparagement.* The people of Ephraim have provoked their Creator to bitter anger through their incessant idolatry and their wicked ways (*Radak; Abarbanel; Metzudos*). [They have even gone so far as to become steeped in murder,] and the blood they have spilled shall be spread out over them by their

א כְּדַבֵּר אֶפְרַיִם רְתֵת נָשָׂא הוּא בְּיִשְׂרָאֵל
ב וַיֶּאְשַׁם בַּבַּעַל וַיָּמֹת: וְעַתָּה ׀ יוֹסִפוּ לַחֲטֹא
וַיַּעֲשׂוּ לָהֶם מַסֵּכָה מִכַּסְפָּם כִּתְבוּנָם

Lord, who shall requit them as well for the scorn and disgrace they have heaped upon Him (*Ibn Ezra; Radak; Abarbanel; Metzudos*). For although they refuse to recognize and accept the Almighty's authority, He is nevertheless their Lord and master, and He shall exact retribution for all their evil deeds (*Radak; Metzudos David*).

Ibn Ezra translates תַּמְרוּרִים to mean *openly*. *Radak* suggests that it may mean *signposts*, referring to the altars of idolatry which were like signposts [pointing out the availability of idol worship]. Others interpret this word as describing the result of the anger with which Ephraim angered the Almighty — i.e., therefore they shall suffer bitterness (*Rashi; Abarbanel*).

Rashi interprets this verse as referring specifically to Jeroboam ben Nebot, the first monarch of the northern kingdom of Israel, who was from the tribe of Ephraim. He angered Hashem by scorning His prophets and by rebelling against His word; therefore he shall reap the bitter results of the wickedness he has sown. He is deemed as having spilled the blood of the Jewish nation, and so shall he be judged, for one who causes another to sin harms him worse than one who kills him.[1] In addition, he shall suffer requital for scorning King Solomon, the anointed of Hashem, with his brazen rebuke,[2] as his own guilt of much greater misdeeds leaves him in no position to offer admonition.

Mahari Kara follows a similar approach, but understands the prophet's words to be directed to the general populace: You do not learn the lessons of Jacob your father, but rather follow in the sinful ways of Jeroboam and his cohorts from Ephraim, who have angered the Almighty with the calves they erected. Therefore, you have been visited with harsh decrees (תַּמְרוּרִים).

XIII

1. כְּדַבֵּר אֶפְרַיִם רְתֵת נָשָׂא הוּא בְּיִשְׂרָאֵל וַיֶּאְשַׁם בַּבַּעַל וַיָּמֹת — *When Ephraim spoke there was trembling; he was exalted in Israel, but he became guilty through Baal and he died.* In the days before the people of Ephraim began to sin, their words evoked trembling throughout the region, due to the fear they inspired in the neighboring nations. At that time, they were exalted and respected as well within the kingdom of Israel, among whose tribes they occupied the predominant position. However, once they succumbed to the temptations of the idol Baal their stature plummeted

1. This is derived by *Sifri* (cited by *Rashi*) from the law that Egyptians may marry into the Jewish nation after two generations have passed subsequent to conversion, whereas members of the tribes of Ammon and Moab are never allowed to enter into the congregation of Israel through marriage with them (*Deuteronomy* 23:4, 23:8). Although Egyptians were guilty of physical mistreatment and even murder they are treated more leniently than the descendants of Ammon and Moab, who led Israel to sin with the idol Baal Peor. This is because one who murders another harms him only in this world, but one who causes him to sin detracts from his share in the World to Come.

2. The Sages relate that King David made breaches in the walls of Jerusalem in order to facilitate access to the city for the עוֹלֵי רֶגֶל — the pilgrims who came to celebrate the three Festivals there. King Solomon closed off one of those walls and built a palace for the daughter of Pharaoh — who was his wife — called the Millo. For this, he was rebuked publicly by Jeroboam. For his rebuke, Jeroboam was rewarded with monarchy, but for doing so publicly he was punished (*Sanhedrin* 101b, based upon *I Kings* 11:27).

1 *When Ephraim spoke there was trembling; he was
exalted in Israel, but he became guilty through
Baal and he died.* 2 *And now they have continued
to sin and they have made for themselves a molten
image from their silver according to their form,*

so low that it resembled that of a dead man. Their power and prosperity were lost and they were decimated before their enemies (*Targum; Ibn Ezra; Radak; Abarbanel*).

Others interpret this as referring to Jeroboam: When Jeroboam was zealous on behalf of the honor of the Almighty he rebuked King Solomon [see comm. above] with great trembling, as Solomon was a powerful monarch. For this he was elevated to become a king of the ten tribes of Israel. However, once he turned to the idolatry of [Baal and other false gods], it was decreed upon him that his entire house would be wiped out (*Rashi; Mahari Kara*).

The Sages offer a slightly different interpretation to the phrase וַיֶּאְשַׁם בַּבַּעַל וַיָּמֹת: The Almighty said to him: Why do you rebuke him? He is a *Nasi* [a term of leadership, referring here to his monarchy] in Israel. [I swear by] your life that I will give you a taste of his position and you will be unable to withstand the test. As soon as he became king, "he became guilty with Baal" (*Yalkut Shimoni* to *Jeremiah* 32:31).

2. וְעַתָּה יוֹסִפוּ לַחֲטֹא — *And now they have continued to sin.* Despite having witnessed the destruction of the sinful houses of Jeroboam and Ahab, the house of Jehu has continued to pursue its wicked ways (*Rashi*), and has even increased iniquity beyond that of its predecessors (*Mahari Kara*). Others understand the subject of this verse to be the entire generation of Hosea — the populace at large along with their rulers (*Ibn Ezra; Abarbanel; Metzudos David*).

Radak interprets this as a flashback to the days of Jeroboam: Now that Jeroboam has taken power, they have increased the scope of their sins. For in the days of the judges, even if they strayed after idolatry, they would return to the service of the Almighty with the rebuke of their judges. Now, however, they have abandoned the worship of Hashem entirely. For the monarchy has prohibited the ascent to Jerusalem on the Festivals and replaced His service with the golden calves in Dan and Beth-el.

וַיַּעֲשׂוּ לָהֶם מַסֵּכָה מִכַּסְפָּם כִּתְבוּנָם — *And they have made for themselves a molten image from their silver according to their form.* Following in the footsteps of their wicked leaders, the people have made their own silver copies of the golden images erected by Jeroboam, according to the form of those idols (*Abarbanel; Metzudos David*).

The Sages interpret: Every one of them had his own private idol which he carried in his breast. Whenever he would remember, he would take it out and hug it and kiss it (*Sanhedrin* 63b).

Others render כִּתְבוּנָם to be derived from תְּבוּנָה — i.e., their *understanding* (*Ibn Ezra; Radak*): They contemplated the question of the proper form for their idols and concluded that they should follow in the footsteps of their forefathers in the wilderness and make golden calves (*Radak*).[1] This was based on the following argument presented by Jeroboam. Since I have been anointed by Ahiyah Hashiloni to become king, it is obvious that the Almighty no longer desires the kingdom of David nor the capital of Jerusalem. It is thus incumbent upon us to establish a new capital in which to center our service to Him. Just as Aaron erected a golden calf in the desert to replace Moses as an intermediary, when he thought that Moses had died, so must we erect golden calves in our religious centers to replace the Divine Presence in Jerusalem (*Radak* to *I Kings* 12:28).

1. According to this approach, the idols they erected were of gold, not silver. Thus, the phrase *they made for themselves molten images from their silver* must be understood to refer to the silver which they donated in order to purchase the gold for the idols (*Radak*).

עֲצַבִּים מַעֲשֵׂה חָרָשִׁים כֻּלֹּה לָהֶם הֵם אֹמְרִים
ג זֹבְחֵי אָדָם עֲגָלִים יִשָּׁקוּן: לָכֵן יִהְיוּ כַּעֲנַן־
בֹּקֶר וְכַטַּל מַשְׁכִּים הֹלֵךְ כְּמֹץ יְסֹעֵר מִגֹּרֶן
ד וּכְעָשָׁן מֵאֲרֻבָּה: וְאָנֹכִי יהוה אֱלֹהֶיךָ מֵאֶרֶץ
מִצְרָיִם וֵאלֹהִים זוּלָתִי לֹא תֵדָע וּמוֹשִׁיעַ אַיִן
ה בִּלְתִּי: אֲנִי יְדַעְתִּיךָ בַּמִּדְבָּר בְּאֶרֶץ תַּלְאֻבוֹת:

עֲצַבִּים מַעֲשֵׂה חָרָשִׁים כֻּלֹּה — *Idols, wholly the work of craftsmen.* All of these duplicate idols were made by expert craftsmen, in order to resemble as much as possible the primary idols of Dan and Beth-el (*Abarbanel; Metzudos David*). *Radak* notes: They were all the work of mere craftsmen, with no spiritual essence whatsoever.

לָהֶם הֵם אֹמְרִים זֹבְחֵי אָדָם עֲגָלִים יִשָּׁקוּן — *To them they say, "Those who slaughter man shall kiss the calves."* The priests of the idols proclaim to the people, "Whoever slaughters his children to our god shall be privileged to kiss the golden calf, for he has thereby offered a sacrifice of great substance" (*Rashi* from *Sanhedrin* 63b).

Others interpret the kissing of the calf to be part of its worship. The priests of the idols would declare, "Whoever seeks to offer the sacrifice of human beings — i.e., those offered by human beings — to our god must kiss the calves on their lips, for their worship is not complete without that act" (*Radak*). Alternatively: "Whoever kisses the calf in his worship will receive great reward for his service, as if he had made the supreme sacrifice of offering his children to the idol" (*Abarbanel; Metzudos David*).

Ibn Ezra sees this phrase as the prophet's depiction of the ridicule incurred by these idolaters: People mock them for kissing the idols and stooping to human sacrifice. These observers exclaim, "They slaughter people and kiss calves, in place of the normal human behavior of kissing other people and slaughtering calves for food."

Mahari Kara interprets this verse as depicting the clever fraud that the priests of idolatry would perpetrate in order to authenticate their worship: They would make a form of one of the officers of the town, and then choose a calf and feed it consistently before that form, thus causing it to view that form as the source of its benefits. When the time would come for human sacrifice, they would gather all the people and proclaim that whomever the calf shall kiss will be chosen for that sacrifice. They would then release the calf, who would immediately go to that person whose form he had seen and begin to nuzzle him. Thus, declares the prophet: *They slaughtered the man whom the calf kisses.*

Malbim explains it to be portraying the hypocrisy of the people, who would remove their wicked rulers and execute them because of their corruption and then go on to indulge in the very decadence against which they had rebelled. Thus: *Now,* after having murdered their king for his wicked deeds, *they increase their sin* — they indulge in behavior worse than that of their deposed monarchs. For *they have made [their own] idols from their own silver* — rather than sufficing with those of gold erected by the rulers. Indeed, *[they have made them] with understanding,* in accordance with their own contemplation into the proper form for such deities. Therefore, the prophet depicts the molten images they have made as if they were the work of such great craftsmen that they were able to open their mouths and speak. And these deities say to the people, *"Those who slaughter man shall kiss the calves?"* I.e., is it not ludicrous that the same people who executed their monarchs for their idolatry shall then turn around and kiss the images of those very idols?

3. לָכֵן יִהְיוּ כַּעֲנַן־בֹּקֶר וְכַטַּל מַשְׁכִּים הֹלֵךְ כְּמֹץ יְסֹעֵר מִגֹּרֶן וּכְעָשָׁן מֵאֲרֻבָּה — *Therefore, they shall be like the morning cloud and like the dew that rises early and departs; like chaff that is blown from the threshing*

idols, wholly the work of craftsmen; to them they say,
"Those who slaughter man shall kiss the calves."
3 Therefore, they shall be like the morning cloud and
like the dew that rises early and departs; like chaff
that is blown from the threshing floor, and like
smoke from a skylight. 4 And I am HASHEM *your*
God from the land of Egypt, and you shall not know
any god besides Me, and there is no savior but Me.
5 I knew you in the wilderness in a parched land.

floor, and like smoke from a skylight. Because of their decadence, the people shall quickly be destroyed. [So quickly, in fact, that] they will be compared to a morning cloud that dissipates rapidly (*Metzudos David*), and to the dew that rises early and departs from the ground upon which it lies, as it melts into the air with the emergence of the morning sun. And just as the chaff is blown by the wind from the threshing floor, so shall they be speedily banished from their land — indeed, like the smoke that rises quickly through the skylight and is seen no more (*Radak*).

Malbim explains the verse to be describing increasing levels of misfortune: You will be bereft of all blessing and beneficence, as symbolized by the morning cloud, which first seems to be bringing rain but soon dissipates and disappears. Even on the rare occasion that you do receive some measure of blessing, it will be like the transient dew, for it will shortly thereafter be taken from you. In addition to your lack of blessing, you will also undergo catastrophe and misfortune in retribution for your misdeeds. Thus, a foreign nation will ascend upon your land and carry you away into exile. At first he will carry off only the wicked among you, leaving the righteous to dwell in the land — just as the wind sweeps away the chaff from the threshing floor. Eventually, however, your entire population shall be exiled, like smoke that departs in its entirety through the skylight of the building in which it appeared.

4. Indeed, the people have sinned and shall therefore be punished, but their guilt is compounded by its contrast to the loving care and kindness they have received from the Almighty throughout their history.

וְאָנֹכִי ה׳ אֱלֹהֶיךָ מֵאֶרֶץ מִצְרָיִם וֵאלֹהִים זוּלָתִי לֹא תֵדָע וּמוֹשִׁיעַ אַיִן בִּלְתִּי — *And I am* HASHEM *your God from the land of Egypt, and you shall not know any god besides Me, and there is no savior but Me.* You should not have rebelled against Me (*Rashi*) and sought out other gods (*Ibn Ezra*). For I am the Almighty God Whom you came to know in Egypt through My miracles that I performed on your behalf (*Radak;* see comm. to 12:10) and Whose authority you accepted upon yourselves there (*R' Eliezer of Beaugency*). Indeed, there can be no excuse for your acknowledgment and service of your false gods. Only I am your savior, and none of the deities that you have chosen are capable of offering you any support or protection (*Radak*).

Alshich offers the following interpretation: I am Hashem your God with Whom you are already familiar from My miracles that I performed in the past in the land of Egypt. In the future, too, you shall not know any other gods besides Me, and in the present, as well, there is no savior but Me.

5. אֲנִי יְדַעְתִּיךָ בַּמִּדְבָּר בְּאֶרֶץ תַּלְאֻבוֹת — *I knew you in the wilderness in a parched land.* Indeed, it is incumbent upon you to recognize and acknowledge Me as your God (*Radak*), for I am also the God Who

ו כְּמַרְעִיתָם֙ וַיִּשְׂבָּ֔עוּ שָׂבְע֖וּ וַיָּ֣רָם לִבָּ֑ם עַל־כֵּ֖ן
ז שְׁכֵחֽוּנִי׃ וָאֱהִ֥י לָהֶ֖ם כְּמוֹ־שָׁ֑חַל כְּנָמֵ֖ר עַל־דֶּ֥רֶךְ
ח אָשֽׁוּר׃ אֶפְגְּשֵׁם֙ כְּדֹ֣ב שַׁכּ֔וּל וְאֶקְרַ֖ע סְג֣וֹר לִבָּ֑ם
וְאֹכְלֵ֥ם שָׁם֙ כְּלָבִ֔יא חַיַּ֥ת הַשָּׂדֶ֖ה תְּבַקְּעֵֽם׃

paid attention to your plight and your needs in the wilderness (*Rashi*), in a parched and arid land [where, without My Divine Providence, you could not possibly have survived] (*Ibn Ezra; Radak; Abarbanel*).

Others render תַּלְאֻבוֹת to mean תֵּל שֶׁאוֹבִין בּוֹ, *a heap in which one longs for all good but does not find it* (*Targum; Rashi; Mahari Kara*). *Ibn Ezra* cites this interpretation but contends that it is homiletic in nature and not the literal meaning of the verse. *R' Eliezer of Beaugency* states that the *"lamed"* is extra and the word is the same as תְּאוּבוֹת — which means *longing*.

Abarbanel interprets these two verses as explaining why the Almighty's wrath is so aroused by the idolatry of the Jewish nation: I am the God Who took you out of slavery in Egypt on condition that you accept My authority as your God. No one else could have redeemed you; only I am your savior. [Thus, it is incumbent upon you to fulfill your side of the covenant between us.] Furthermore, I provided for you for forty years in the wilderness and saw to your every need there. Thus, I have acquired you eternally as My servants, and there can be no exchanging Me for another deity.

According to *Malbim*, these verses are the Almighty's response to the contention of the people that He can be served only through a medium (see comm. to 12:14): I Myself took you out of the land of Egypt without any intermediary; I Myself was your only savior there. And I, too, personally saw to all of your needs in the wilderness, in a parched land where, without My Divine Providence, you could not possibly have survived.[1]

6. כְּמַרְעִיתָם וַיִּשְׂבָּעוּ שָׂבְעוּ וַיָּרָם לִבָּם עַל־כֵּן שְׁכֵחוּנִי — *With their grazing they were sated; they were sated and their hearts grew haughty; therefore they forgot Me.* When they arrived [at last] to the land of their grazing, they were sated (*Rashi*). I.e., when I brought them into the Land of Israel they were well provided for by the abundant fruits of the land (*Mahari Kara*). But with their satiation they became haughty and soon forgot Me, just as I foretold in the Torah (*Deuteronomy* 8:14), *and your heart [shall] grow haughty and you will forget HASHEM your God* (*Radak*).

Alshich emphasizes the word *their grazing* — they perceived it as being their own rather than the result of My blessing; therefore it led them to become haughty and forget Me.

7. Because they have forsaken Me and forgotten all My kindness to them, I too shall abandon them to their fate at the hands of the gentile nations. [But My retribution shall not be merely passive. Rather, I will actively pursue their downfall, as do wild beasts on a rampage destroying all that is in their path.] Thus,

1. [This approach requires elaboration, for as specified by the nation in their contention, the Almighty's dealings with Israel in Egypt and the wilderness came through Moses. However, although Moses was Hashem's spokesman in Egypt he was not empowered to bring about the plagues or the Exodus itself, merely to invoke the Divine intervention of the Almighty. Similarly, it was the Almighty who provided manna, water, and protective clouds in the wilderness; none of these were within the capabilities of Moses himself. Thus, Moses' leadership consisted only of relaying the word of Hashem to the nation, instructing and exhorting them in its fulfillment, and invoking His aid and mercy on their behalf. This is in stark contrast to the idolatry of the people, in which they viewed their deities as having been granted the power and authority to provide for their needs and respond to their worship, with the Almighty relegating Himself to the background.]

[6] *With their grazing they were sated; they were
sated and their hearts grew haughty; therefore they
forgot Me.* [7] *And I shall be to them like a lion; like
a leopard I will lurk on the way.* [8] *I will encounter
them as a bereaving bear, and I will rend the enclosure of their heart, and I will devour them there like
a lion; the beast of the field shall split them open.*

I will enable their enemies to subdue and conquer them, and only through their repentance will they be able to prevail (*Radak*).

וָאֱהִי לָהֶם כְּמוֹ־שָׁחַל כְּנָמֵר עַל־דֶּרֶךְ אָשׁוּר — *And I shall be to them like a lion; like a leopard I will lurk on the way.* I will be to them like a lion, who slashes and mangles his prey (*Metzudos David*), and I will lurk in waiting, watching for their arrival, like a leopard lying in ambush for its victim (*Rashi; Mahari Kara; Abarbanel*).[1] Others translate אָשׁוּר to mean *I will tread* — I will be to them like a leopard who mangles all upon which it treads while walking on its way.

8. אֶפְגְּשֵׁם כְּדֹב שַׁכּוּל — *I will encounter them as a bereaving bear.* I will deal with them as if I were a bear whose entire being is bent upon bereaving those whom it encounters (*Rashi; Mahari Kara; R' Eliezer of Beaugency*). Others render: *like a bereaved bear* — like a bear whose young have been slain, and it is thus bereaved and bitter. In such a state, it destroys any person or animal that it encounters (*Ibn Ezra; Radak; Abarbanel*). The prophet specifies a bear, rather than a lion or leopard, because when a bear gives birth the cub comes out encased in a thick placenta which the mother removes slowly in order to avoid harming the cub. Having thus toiled to give life to its young, it is that much more embittered if the cub is then killed (*Radak*).

וְאֶקְרַע סְגוֹר לִבָּם — *And I will rend the enclosure of their heart.* I will thereby tear through the enclosure in which they have hidden their hearts and shielded them from any feelings of repentance (*Targum; Rashi; Radak; Abarbanel*) — like the bear, who pierces its victim's chest with its claws and rips through to the heart (*Rashi*).[2] *Mahari Kara* adds that this refers back to verse 6, in which the prophet described how the people had become sated and thereby come to forget Hashem. This is the covering that they have placed over their hearts.

וְאֹכְלֵם שָׁם כְּלָבִיא חַיַּת הַשָּׂדֶה תְּבַקְּעֵם — *And I will devour them there like a lion; the beast of the field shall split them open.* Like a lion who hunts its prey without mercy, I will devour them in their cities through plague and the sword of the enemy. Outside the towns, as well, the beasts of the field shall attack them and split them open (*Radak; Abarbanel*).

Malbim interprets the beasts portrayed here as representing the various nations that conquered the Jewish people. He explains

1. Whenever the word אשור is written it has a *dagesh* — a dot — in the *shin* [and a *patach* under the *aleph*]. In this instance, however, [the *aleph* is punctuated with a *kametz*] and there is no *dagesh* in the *shin*. It is thus evident that it does not refer here to the nation of Assyria [but is rather a verb in the first person and the future tense] (*Rashi*).

2. *Radak* states that this is a metaphor for the actions of the lion, who, when killing its prey, rips open the body until the heart and then devours the flesh and drinks the blood. [Apparently, he sees this phrase as connected to the following one, *and I will devour them there like a lion.*]

ט־י שִׁחֶתְךָ יִשְׂרָאֵל כִּי־בִי בְעֶזְרֶךָ: אֱהִי מַלְכְּךָ אֵפוֹא
וְיוֹשִׁיעֲךָ בְּכָל־עָרֶיךָ וְשֹׁפְטֶיךָ אֲשֶׁר אָמַרְתָּ תְּנָה־
יא לִּי מֶלֶךְ וְשָׂרִים: אֶתֶּן־לְךָ מֶלֶךְ בְּאַפִּי וְאֶקַּח
יב בְּעֶבְרָתִי: צָרוּר עֲוֹן אֶפְרָיִם צְפוּנָה חַטָּאתוֹ:

these two verses to be the Almighty's portrayal of how the Jewish nation has come to view Him, in their mistaken notion that He is responsible for the evil that has befallen them — rather than they themselves with their misdeeds. He is thus symbolized in their eyes by these beasts of prey through whom He carried out His — to their minds — malicious intentions.

The lion represents the kingdoms of Assyria and Babylonia, who are thus depicted by Daniel (7:4). The leopard (mentioned in *Daniel* 7:6) is the Hellenist kingdom of Greece, who tread upon them in their land but did not send them into exile. Persia is depicted by the bear — also as by Daniel (7:5) — under whose domain the Almighty will rend through to the Jewish people's hearts and arouse them to repentance by means of the evil decree of Haman. Finally comes the second lion, that of Rome, who will devour them without mercy. Regarding all of these, the Almighty proclaims: *the beast of the field shall split them open* — it is not I who brings misfortune upon you but rather the gentile nations themselves. Because of your misdeeds and your heresy I have withdrawn My Divine Providence from over you and left you to your natural fate (cf. *Alshich*).

9. שִׁחֶתְךָ יִשְׂרָאֵל כִּי־בִי בְעֶזְרֶךָ — *[You] have destroyed yourself, Israel, for [you rebelled] against Me, your help.* You have wrought your own destruction, Israel, by means of your iniquities, for you have rebelled against Me. This is a very grievous offense, since it is I who am your help [and protection] (*Rashi; Mahari Kara*). Alternatively: For your help has always lain with Me [and your rebellion against Me is thus the cause of your misfortune] (*Abarbanel*).

Radak renders: [The calves cited above] *have destroyed you, for* [were it not for them] *your help would lie with Me.* According to *R' Eliezer of Beaugency: For you should have placed your faith in Me for your help.*

Abarbanel (to v. 10) cites *Rabbeinu Nissim*[1] as offering a somewhat different interpretation: Your destruction has been brought about because you presumed I would always be your help, no matter how far you strayed, just as I was with you when I delivered you from Egypt.

10. The prophet now refers back to the time when the Jewish people came to Samuel with the contention that they required a king to lead them, just as enjoyed by all other nations. Samuel rebuked them severely for this request. Since they were hitherto led by the word of Hashem through His prophets, their request for a king at that time was seen as a degree of rejection of God's sovereignty. Nevertheless, the Almighty commanded him to accede to their request, and Saul was anointed king (see *I Samuel* chap. 7). Now, hundreds of years later, the Almighty challenges them to produce evidence of having improved their lot through their demand.

אֱהִי מַלְכְּךָ אֵפוֹא וְיוֹשִׁיעֲךָ בְּכָל־עָרֶיךָ וְשֹׁפְטֶיךָ אֲשֶׁר אָמַרְתָּ תְּנָה־לִּי מֶלֶךְ וְשָׂרִים — *I shall be; where is your king that he may save you in all your cities, and your judges about whom* [lit. *that*] *you said, "Give me a king and officers"?* I Myself shall be — I shall exist forever. But where is the king

1. *Abarbanel's* source is unclear. In *Derashos HaRan, Haderush Hashishi, Rabbeinu Nissim* presents the following explanation: I am your help, and I assist you generously when you seek to return to My ways — that in itself is a source of destruction for the wicked, as they are left with no viable excuse for their sinful ways.

9 *[You] have destroyed yourself, Israel, for [you re-*
belled] against Me, your help. 10 *I shall be; where is*
your king that he may save you in all your cities,
and your judges about whom [lit. *that*] *you said, "Give*
me a king and officers"? 11 *I give you a king in My*
wrath and take [him] away in My fury. 12 *Ephraim's*
iniquity is bound up; his sin is hidden away.

for whom you spurned My sovereignty and requested a monarch so that he would protect and save you? Where is he when he is needed to save you in your cities when the enemy attacks them (*Radak; Metzudos David*)? If he cannot protect you in the fields, let him at least provide security within the walls of the cities themselves (*Alshich*). And where, indeed, are your judges, whom you appointed on your own [without consulting Me], at the time that you demanded a king and officers? Do you not see that your salvation is in My hands, and by My hand alone can security be found (*Radak; Metzudos*)?

Others interpret: *I will be* — i.e., I will be standing by and watching to see how you fare with the kings you have demanded and where they will be when you need them to save you (*Rashi;* cf. *Mahari Kara*).[1] Others render אֱהִי to mean *where,* as if it were written אַיֵּה. Where is your king now (אֵפוֹא) that he may save you (*Targum; Abarbanel*)?

11. אֶתֶּן־לְךָ מֶלֶךְ בְּאַפִּי וְאֶקַּח בְּעֶבְרָתִי — *I give you a king in My wrath and take [him] away in My fury.* When I gave you Saul as a king I did so in anger, since your demand that I do so was in effect a rejection of My rule over you. Accordingly, when I took him away from you, that too was done in fury, as I killed him at the hands of the Philistines after only two years of rule. It should thus be clear that your true monarchy is in My hands, and the kings I appoint over you shall lead and protect you successfully only if they are loyal to Me (*Radak; Metzudos David*).

Alternatively: *In My fury I shall take away your last monarch* — referring to Zedekiah, who was led away into captivity and blinded by Nebuchadnezzar (*Mahari Kara*).

Others see this verse as referring specifically to the kingdom of the ten tribes: In My wrath with the house of David I gave you your own sovereignty and your own king. In My fury I shall take it away when I send Assyria to conquer Hosea ben Elah (cited by *Radak, Abarbanel; Malbim*). Malbim adds that the word עֶבְרָה denotes an anger that is all-encompassing, including even those who were not responsible for inciting it but were nevertheless caught up in its wake. This is particularly appropriate to the conquest of Hosea ben Elah, who was himself a righteous king seeking to follow the will of Hashem [but was unable to effect a degree of repentance that would have annulled the decree already hanging over the nation].

12. צָרוּר עֲוֹן אֶפְרָיִם צְפוּנָה חַטָּאתוֹ — *Ephraim's iniquity is bound up; his sin is hidden away.* Do not think that I have pardoned Ephraim for his sins (*Rashi*), for his iniquities are bound up and kept in My possession (*Radak*). His sins are hidden away, waiting for the day when I will exact retribution for them (*Mahari Kara*).

Mahari Kara interprets this as referring to all the sins and iniquities of the Jewish nation. *Radak* contends that it refers specifically to the golden calves

1. *R' Eliezer of Beaugency* translates אֱהִי to mean *he will be* — where will your king be in order to save you? (see also comm. to v. 14).

יג חֶבְלֵי יוֹלֵדָה יָבֹאוּ לוֹ הוּא־בֵן לֹא חָכָם כִּי־עֵת
יד לֹא־יַעֲמֹד בְּמִשְׁבַּר בָּנִים: מִיַּד שְׁאוֹל אֶפְדֵּם
מִמָּוֶת אֶגְאָלֵם אֱהִי דְבָרֶיךָ מָוֶת אֱהִי קָטָבְךָ
טו שְׁאוֹל נֹחַם יִסָּתֵר מֵעֵינָי: כִּי הוּא בֵּין אַחִים יַפְרִיא
יָבוֹא קָדִים רוּחַ יהוה מִמִּדְבָּר עֹלֶה וְיֵבוֹשׁ מְקוֹרוֹ
וְיֶחֱרַב מַעְיָנוֹ הוּא יִשְׁסֶה אוֹצַר כָּל־כְּלִי חֶמְדָּה:

that they worshiped. [Apparently, for some the guilt was greater and it was deemed an iniquity; for others, it is viewed merely as חֵטְא — a lesser sin, bordering on the inadvertent.] *R' Eliezer of Beaugency* maintains that the prophet is still discussing the rebellion against Hashem that was inherent in their demand for a king.

Malbim interprets this verse in an entirely different manner: Ephraim does not abandon his sins; rather, he binds them up and hides them away, holding on to them tenaciously and refusing to repent.

13. חֶבְלֵי יוֹלֵדָה יָבֹאוּ לוֹ הוּא־בֵן לֹא חָכָם כִּי־עֵת לֹא־יַעֲמֹד בְּמִשְׁבַּר בָּנִים — *The pangs of childbirth shall come upon him; he is an unwise son, for it is the time when he shall not stand at the children's birthstool.* Calamity shall come upon him like the pangs of childbirth, for he is an unwise son who does not foresee the results of his deeds (*Metzudos David*). Thus, he does not recognize that he will soon experience misfortune that will bring him to his knees, unable to stand and endure, just as a woman in childbirth sits upon the birthstool because she is no longer able to stand in her agony (*Rashi; Metzudos*).

Radak understands the unwise son to represent the subsequent generations: Having witnessed the downfall of their fathers, and having noted that it was caused by their sins, they nevertheless do not have sufficient wisdom to abandon their fathers' wicked ways and return to Hashem. For if the son were wise, *he would not stand for [even] one moment on the children's birthstool* — i.e., the womb. Rather, he would extricate himself from his predicament by repenting, like a zealous child who emerges quickly from the womb (cf. *Abarbanel*). *Ibn Ezra* interprets: The son to be born will be foolish like his fathers and not wise; therefore he will not stand long on the birthstool for he shall die immediately.

Alshich interprets this verse and the one preceding it as referring specifically to Jeroboam ben Nebot, who was appointed by the Almighty to rule over the ten tribes, but then led them to idolatry. The prophet addresses himself to the obvious question: If Jeroboam was so wicked and so despised by Hashem, why then did his reign endure and his power prosper? To this he responds: Fear not. His iniquities and sins have not been forgotten. Rather, they have been hidden away to compile until their aggregate weight shall bring total destruction down upon his house.

14. מִיַּד שְׁאוֹל אֶפְדֵּם מִמָּוֶת אֶגְאָלֵם — *From the clutches of the grave I would ransom them; from death I would redeem them.* [In the past,] it was I Who would ransom the Children of Israel from the clutches of the grave and it was I Who would redeem them from death (*Targum; Rashi; Ibn Ezra*). For when they fulfilled My will, I ransomed them from the hands of heathen nations — who are comparable to the grave — and I redeemed them from death [at the latter's hands] (*Mahari Kara*).

Others render: Had they but been wise, *I would have ransomed them from the grave and redeemed them from death* (*Radak*). Had they only repented, I would have saved them from[1] exile at the hands

1. Exile is depicted as the grave to indicate its permanence — an exile from which there is no return [i.e., until the final redemption] (*Malbim*).

13 The pangs of childbirth shall come upon him; he is an
unwise son, for it is the time when he shall not stand at
the children's birthstool. 14 From the clutches of the
grave I would ransom them; from death I would redeem
them; I will be your words of death; I will be the One
Who decrees upon you the grave; change of heart shall
be hidden from My eyes. 15 For [though] he flourishes
among the marshes, an east wind shall come, a wind of
HASHEM ascending from the wilderness, and his foun-
tainhead shall be parched and his spring shall dry up; it
shall plunder the treasure of all desirable vessels.

of the king of Assyria, as well as from the slaughter and death he brought upon them (*Malbim*).

Abarbanel understands this phrase to be a question: Given their misdeeds, should I ransom them from the grave and redeem them from death?

אֱהִי דְבָרֶיךָ מָוֶת — *I will be your words of death.* But now that you have not been wise but rather foolish and despicable, spurning all My benefits (*Radak*), your "measure of evil" has thus been filled (*Metzudos David*). Therefore, I will appoint Myself to speak of you words of death (*Rashi*) [i.e., I will cause Myself to be the one whose words are of your death].

Radak renders: Not only shall I not redeem you from death, but I will actually bring it upon you through pestilence and the sword; thus My word that I sent to you and you refused to heed shall be the cause of your slaughter. Alternatively: *I will be your plague of death* (ibid.).

R' Eliezer of Beaugency understands this as still referring to the Jewish nation's demand for a king: As long as I was your king, I would redeem you from destruction, but now that you have demanded a human monarch, that itself will be the cause of your death and downfall (cf. comm. to v. 10).

אֱהִי קָטָבְךָ שְׁאוֹל — *I will be the One Who decrees upon you* [lit. *cuts for you*] *the grave.* I will cut [i.e., conclude] My decree, imposing the grave upon you (*Rashi*). Alternatively: I will bring about your being cut off to the grave (*Radak*). *Abarbanel* interprets: *I will confine you to the pit*[1] *of purgatory.*

Others interpret אֱהִי to mean *where*, as if it were written אַיֵּה. *Where are your words [concerning] death* — in which you claimed to have made a treaty [enabling you to avoid it]? *And where is the covenant you made with the grave* [guaranteeing you protection from its clutches]? (cited by *Ibn Ezra; Mahari Kara*).

נֹחַם יִסָּתֵר מֵעֵינָי — *Change of heart shall be hidden from My eyes.* The possibility that I might change My mind and revoke this decree shall be hidden from My eyes [as if it did not exist], for I shall not rescind My judgment from upon you (*Rashi; Radak*).

15. כִּי הוּא בֵּין אַחִים יַפְרִיא יָבוֹא קָדִים רוּחַ ה׳ מִמִּדְבָּר עֹלֶה וְיֵבוֹשׁ מְקוֹרוֹ וְיֶחֱרַב מַעְיָנוֹ הוּא יִשְׁסֶה אוֹצַר כָּל־כְּלִי חֶמְדָּה — *For [though] he flourishes among the marshes, an east wind shall come, a wind of HASHEM ascending from the wilderness, and his fountainhead shall be parched and his spring shall dry up; it shall plunder the treasure of all desirable vessels.* Al-

1. [Although שְׁאוֹל is generally rendered to mean the grave, its literal translation is a hole in the ground.]

א תֶּאְשַׁם שֹׁמְרוֹן כִּי מָרְתָה בֵּאלֹהֶיהָ בַּחֶרֶב יִפֹּלוּ
ב עֹלְלֵיהֶם יְרֻטָּשׁוּ וְהָרִיּוֹתָיו יְבֻקָּעוּ׃ שׁוּבָה
יִשְׂרָאֵל עַד יהוה אֱלֹהֶיךָ כִּי כָשַׁלְתָּ בַּעֲוֺנֶךָ׃

though he flourishes like the wildlife that grows among the marshes, a force that is harsh and powerful like the east wind shall soon come from Assyria to the east. This, force shall be driven by the power of the Almighty, Who shall set it in motion against the nation of Israel. The wind will ascend through the wilderness that lies between Israel and Assyria — and it shall dry up the spring of Ephraim and plunder all of his desirable possessions (*Radak*).

This wind represents the armies of Assyria, a powerful force led by a mighty king and driven by the incitement of the Almighty (see *I Chronicles* 5:26). These armies shall ascend upon Ephraim, who was once compared to a tree flourishing by the water (see *Genesis* 49:22), and they shall cause all of his springs and sources of water to dry up — i.e., all of his potency shall wither. In addition, they will plunder all of the treasures of the nation (*Targum; Rashi; Radak*).

כִּי הוּא בֵּין אַחִים יַפְרִיא — *For [though] he flourishes among the marshes.* אַחִים is rendered either as *marshes* (*Rashi, Mahari Kara,* cf. *Ramban, Genesis* 41:2) or *brothers* (*Radak, Abarbanel*). Thus, according to the latter understanding, the verse is understood as follows: *For he flourishes among his brothers* — as foretold by Jacob (*Genesis* 48:19): *But his younger brother* [i.e., Manasseh's younger brother Ephraim] *shall become greater than he and his seed shall become the fill of the nations* (*Radak*). Alternatively: *When he was among his brothers* — joined and united with the tribe of Judah — *he flourished in his righteousness* (*Abarbanel*).

Other translate בֵּין to mean *son: For they were called sons, but they abounded with decadent deeds* (*Targum*). Alternatively: *Jeroboam was the son* [of the nation] *who rent the brotherhood of the nation* (*Rashi; Abarbanel*).

מִמִּדְבָּר עֹלֶה — *Ascending from the wilderness.* According to *Radak*, the analogy to a wilderness is based on the phenomenon that winds generally develop in the wilderness. He suggests as well that a wilderness lies between the lands of Israel and Assyria. *R' Eliezer of Beaugency* interprets: Just as a wind develops in all its fury in the wilderness, where there is nothing to break its flow and limit its force.

וְיֵבוֹשׁ מְקוֹרוֹ וְיֶחֱרַב מַעְיָנוֹ — *And his fountainhead shall be parched and his spring shall dry up. Abarbanel* interprets: Ephraim, who is compared to a flowing fountain, shall be parched, and the spring — i.e., the remaining tribes of the nation — shall dry up. Alternatively: The land of Israel, which is the primary source of Israel's sustenance, shall become parched, and the springs which flow from that source — i.e., the springs of heavenly providence that provide for them — shall be dried up as well. For the dispersal of the people to the four corners of the earth shall sever their link as a nation to those springs (*Malbim*).

XIV

Even after the remainder of the Northern Kingdom of Israel had been conquered, the capital city of Samaria still stood (*Radak*). However, the peace they enjoyed was to be short-lived; soon the sword of the enemy would befall them and bring death and destruction to the city. Thus, the prophet directs his words to Samaria to foretell its terrible fate.

14/1-2 [1] *Samaria shall be laid waste for she has rebelled against her God; they shall fall by the sword; their infants shall be shattered and their pregnant women shall be split open.* [2] *Return, Israel, to* H*ASHEM* *your God, for you have stumbled in your iniquity.*

1. תֶּאְשַׁם שֹׁמְרוֹן כִּי מָרְתָה בֵּאלֹהֶיהָ בַּחֶרֶב יִפֹּלוּ עֹלְלֵיהֶם יְרֻטָּשׁוּ וְהָרִיּוֹתָיו יְבֻקָּעוּ — *Samaria shall be laid waste for she has rebelled against her God; they shall fall by the sword; their infants shall be shattered and their pregnant women shall be split open.* Samaria shall be laid waste and rendered desolate (*Ibn Ezra; Radak; Abarbanel; Metzudos*), for she has been the primary culprit in the decadence and idolatry of Israel — as the leaders residing there have set the tone for the entire nation (*Radak*). Therefore, her inhabitants shall die by the sword (*Ibn Ezra*); her infants will be cruelly dashed against the rocks to shatter their bodies; and her pregnant women will be split open [by the enemy] (*Rashi; Radak*).

Others render תֶּאְשַׁם to mean *shall be rendered guilty* (*Targum*) — i.e., her guilt shall be revealed (*Rashi*).

2. In the following verses, the prophet Hosea issues the clarion call to the Jewish nation to repent their evil deeds and return to the Almighty with all their hearts. Appropriately, these words are read throughout the congregations of Israel on the Sabbath between Rosh Hashanah and Yom Kippur, when awareness of one's obligations to God and his deficiencies therein — as well as sensitivity to the Divine and involvement in true repentance — are at their height.

שׁוּבָה יִשְׂרָאֵל עַד ה׳ אֱלֹהֶיךָ כִּי כָשַׁלְתָּ בַּעֲוֹנֶךָ — *Return, Israel, to* H*ASHEM* *your God, for you have stumbled in your iniquity.* Take heed of my words of rebuke and return to the Almighty God, for you have stumbled in misfortune due to your sins, and only Hashem can raise you up again (*Rashi; Ibn Ezra; Radak*).

There are various views among the commentators as to whom is being addressed with these words. According to some, they are directed to the citizens of Samaria, in continuation of the previous verse. Since it has been decreed upon you that you will be destroyed, it is an absolute necessity that you immediately repent and return to the ways of Hashem, so that you can still be saved (*Mahari Kara; Metzudos David*).

The Sages offer a parable of a wayward prince who was sentenced to imprisonment by his father. One of the king's advisers warned the prince of his father's intention and advised him as follows: Your father is going to imprison and punish you until you come and plead before him, at which time he will have mercy and accept you. If you will only listen to me, you will reverse the procedure and go plead with him immediately, for he will surely accept your repentance and you will thereby avoid your punishment. So says the prophet to the Jewish nation: Know that the Almighty plans to punish you and oppress you [until you finally repent and return to Him]. Return to Him now and you will avoid your bitter fate (*Yalkut Shimoni*).

Others perceive this verse as being directed to the nation of Judah, who witnessed the downfall of neighboring Samaria. The prophet exhorts them to repent the evil in their own lives lest they too succumb to a similar fate. This is comparable to a king of a nation, one of whose provinces rebelled against him, who sent a general to destroy them. Being wise and deliberate, the general exhorted the members of the province to reassert their fidelity to their monarch. "If not," he declared, "I will do to you what I did to

ג קְחוּ עִמָּכֶם דְּבָרִים וְשׁוּבוּ אֶל־יְהוָה אִמְרוּ אֵלָיו כָּל־תִּשָּׂא עָוֹן וְקַח־טוֹב וּנְשַׁלְּמָה פָרִים שְׂפָתֵינוּ׃

such-and-such a province." Thus, having foretold the destruction of Samaria, the prophet turns to Judea and warns them to repent (*Rashi* from *Sifri* to *Num.* 25:11).

In yet another approach, the prophet is speaking to the kingdom of Israel prior to its destruction — i.e., to those dwelling beyond the confines of the capital city of Samaria, who were led into idolatry by the ruling class dwelling within: If Samaria refuses to repent, let her be laid waste, since she has actually rebelled against the Almighty. But you, Israel, who have merely stumbled and been misled into iniquity, if only you will return to Hashem your destruction can still be avoided (*Malbim*).

עַד ה׳ אֱלֹהֶיךָ — *To* HASHEM *your God.* Said R' Levi: Great is repentance for it reaches until the Almighty's throne of glory, as it is stated, *Return, Israel, to* HASHEM *your God.* Said Reish Lakish: Great is repentance, for [through it] intentional sins are turned to inadvertent sins, as it is stated: *for you have stumbled in your iniquities.* עָוֹן, *iniquity*, indicates willful transgression; yet the prophet calls it stumbling [indicating inadvertence]. Is this so? Did not Reish Lakish say: Great is repentance, for iniquities become like merits, etc.? There is no contradiction; this [refers to repentance performed] from love [of Hashem] and this to [repentance from] fear (*Yoma* 86b).

R' Meir learned: Return, Israel, while He still [deals with you as] יהוה — with the attribute of mercy. For if not, He will change to אֱלֹהֶיךָ — the attribute of strict justice (*Rashi* from *Pesikta D'Rav Kahana*).

Ibn Ezra comments: Return little by little to Hashem. In a similar vein, the Sages offer a parable of a high rock on a crossroads upon which passersby would stumble. Said the king: Shave it little by little until the day will come when I can remove it from the world. So said the Holy One, Blessed is He: My children, the evil inclination is a great stumbling block; shave it little by little[1] and eventually I will remove it from the world, as it is stated (*Ezekiel* 36:26): *And I will remove the heart of stone from your midst* (*Yalkut Shimoni*).

3. קְחוּ עִמָּכֶם דְּבָרִים וְשׁוּבוּ אֶל־ה׳ — *Take with you words and return to* HASHEM. I do not demand of you gold and silver; nor do I ask for burnt offerings, only the words of your lips admitting your sins to Me, accompanied by your full-hearted remorse and repentance (*Ibn Ezra; Radak; Metzudos David*).

Others interpret: Take my words and place upon your hearts exhortations for you to return to Hashem (*Mahari Kara*).

The Midrash sees implied in the word קְחוּ the use of verbal persuasion (*Bereishis Rabbah* 16:5; *Bamidbar Rabbah* 18:2). Indeed, it characterizes Hosea as the first one to [verbally] urge others to repentance (*Bereishis Rabbah* 84:19).

אִמְרוּ אֵלָיו כָּל־תִּשָּׂא עָוֹן — *Say to Him, "Forgive all iniquity.* This follows the rendition of most commentators. *Ibn Ezra* renders: *All iniquity that you will bear we will repent.* Alternatively: *For all* [i.e., For all of Israel] *bear sin* (*Radak*).

וְקַח־טוֹב — *And accept good.* Accept the few good deeds in our hands

1. [A person cannot eradicate the evil inclination from his heart by merely willing it to disappear. However, every time he resists its enticements and overcomes his instincts and desires, he weakens the power that it has over him until it eventually ceases to affect him (cf. *Sefer Hachinuch, mitzvah* 16).]

[3] *Take with you words and return to HASHEM;
say to Him, "Forgive all iniquity and accept good,
and we will pay [for] bulls [with] our lips."*

and judge us in accordance with them (*Rashi*).[1] Alternatively: Accept a good heart [i.e., our intention to improve] (*Radak*). Another interpretation is: Accept our confession, which is referred to in Scripture as good, as it is stated (*Psalms* 2:2): *It is good to confess to HASHEM* (*Rashi; Ibn Ezra*).

Another translation of קַח is *teach:* Teach us the good ways (*Rashi;* cf. *Targum, Rashi* to 1:2).

וּנְשַׁלְּמָה פָרִים שְׂפָתֵינוּ — *And we will pay [for] bulls [with] our lips."* Those sacrifices which we should be offering to You we will replace with the appeasing words of our lips (*Rashi*). Indeed, our words of repentance are preferable to You over our sacrifices, as evidenced by the fact that even sacrifices are of no value if they are not accompanied by words of confession (*Radak*).

In the Siddur, these words are understood to serve as the basis for the substitution of prayer in place of sacrifices as the focal point of the Jew's service to Hashem: Master of the Universe! You commanded us to sacrifice the daily offering ... Now, the daily offering is abolished, and we have neither *Kohen* serving, Levite performing, nor Israel in attendance. However, You have declared: *and we will pay [for] bulls [with] our lips.* [Although we long for the day when the Temple will be rebuilt and we can once more serve You with our prayers and our sacrifices, we know that the utterance of our lips alone can be as pleasing to You as even the Yom Kippur service (cf. *Shir Hashirim Rabbah* 4:9).

Israel had said: "Master of the Universe! When the princes sin they bring a sacrifice and are forgiven; when the anointed ones sin they bring sacrifices and are forgiven. But we have no sacrifice!" Hashem replied: "*And if the whole congregation of Israel shall make a mistake ... then the assembly shall offer a young bullock for a sin offering*" (*Leviticus* 4:13, 14). They replied: "But we are poor and do not have the resources to bring sacrifices." Hashem said: "I desire words, as it says, *Take with you words and return to HASHEM,* and I will pardon your sins." The "words" here refer to words of Torah ... They then replied to God: "We know no Torah." "Then weep and pray to Me and I will accept [you] ... I do not seek at your hands either sacrifices or offerings, only 'words' " (*Shemos Rabbah* 38:4).

Malbim interprets these two verses as describing the process of total repentance: First, perform the basic fundamentals of repentance by regretting your past misdeeds and committing yourselves to improvement. This will bridge the vast chasm that separates you from the Almighty due to your sins. Afterward, carry the process further by bearing forth those things (דְּבָרִים) that will stand in your merit — i.e., *mitzvos* and good deeds — and then repent once more — this time out of love for Hashem. At that point, it will no longer be necessary to view

1. [This request is somewhat puzzling, as a person is judged and requited for all his deeds, both good and bad. However, the Sages state that whoever judges his friend to the side of merit — i.e., he gives him the benefit of the doubt in assessing his deeds — is judged in that manner by the Almighty. Although Hashem knows the true nature of one's deed, the fact is that a person is multifaceted, and most — if not all — of his actions contain many aspects of intent and motivation. One who views others from the perspective of the good that is within them is dealt with accordingly by Hashem, and his deeds are viewed in Heaven from the perspective of the loftier aspects included in them. Similarly, we ask of the Almighty that He view our more meritorious deeds as those that personify our being and that He judge us in that light with regard to all of our acts.]

ד אַשּׁוּר ׀ לֹא יוֹשִׁיעֵנוּ עַל־סוּס לֹא נִרְכָּב וְלֹא־
נֹאמַר עוֹד אֱלֹהֵינוּ לְמַעֲשֵׂה יָדֵינוּ אֲשֶׁר־בְּךָ
ה יְרֻחַם יָתוֹם׃ אֶרְפָּא מְשׁוּבָתָם אֹהֲבֵם נְדָבָה כִּי שָׁב
ו אַפִּי מִמֶּנּוּ׃ אֶהְיֶה כַטַּל לְיִשְׂרָאֵל יִפְרַח כַּשּׁוֹשַׁנָּה
ז וְיַךְ שָׁרָשָׁיו כַּלְּבָנוֹן׃ יֵלְכוּ יֹנְקוֹתָיו וִיהִי כַזַּיִת הוֹדוֹ

your sins as inadvertent transgressions, for they will be transformed to merit by virtue of your repentance from love. Thus, you will be able to request of the Almighty that He bear all your sins, and take the merit into which they have been transformed in their stead.

4. אַשּׁוּר לֹא יוֹשִׁיעֵנוּ עַל־סוּס לֹא נִרְכָּב וְלֹא־נֹאמַר עוֹד אֱלֹהֵינוּ לְמַעֲשֵׂה יָדֵינוּ אֲשֶׁר־בְּךָ יְרֻחַם יָתוֹם — *Assyria shall not save us; upon horses we will not ride, and we will no longer say to our handiwork, "our gods," for with You an orphan finds pity.* They will further confess to Him and proclaim: The Assyrians in whom we have placed our trust cannot save us from our plight, for no one but You has the ability to help us (*Radak*). Nor will we turn to Egypt to supply us with horses as we have done in the past (*Rashi*). And we [certainly] shall no longer attribute Godliness to the idols that we made with our own hands (*Metzudos David*). For it has become clear to us that only You have mercy upon an orphan and You alone can aid one who is weak and broken and supply him with the strength he needs (*Radak; Malbim*).

Radak interprets עַל־סוּס לֹא נִרְכָּב to mean: We will no longer ride on horseback to Egypt to seek their aid. According to *Metzudos David:* We will no longer place our faith in the might of warrior steeds.

Targum renders: You took pity on our forefathers in Egypt where they were like orphans.

5. Having exhorted the people to repent and return wholeheartedly to Hashem, the prophet now goes on to depict the reaction such a course will evoke from the Almighty (*Rashi; Radak*).

אֶרְפָּא מְשׁוּבָתָם אֹהֲבֵם נְדָבָה כִּי שָׁב אַפִּי מִמֶּנּוּ — *I will remedy their deviance; I will love them gratuitously; for My anger has turned away from them.* I will provide a remedy for their deviance and rebellion, which is a sickness to the soul as illness is to the body (*Ibn Ezra; Radak*). And despite the fact that they had made themselves My enemies — and even an enemy who makes peace does not immediately establish a relationship of love (*Abarbanel*) — I will nevertheless love them graciously from the generosity of My heart (*Rashi*). For My anger has totally subsided and turned away from them (*Abarbanel*), and all that is left is the basic love I feel for them (*Metzudos David*).

Metzudos understands His gratuitous love to mean that even a repentance that is not complete will be accepted.

Others interpret: I will heal the misfortune brought upon them by their deviance, and I will love them for the graciousness of their hearts in their repentance before Me (*Mahari Kara; R' Eliezer of Beaugency*).[1]

6. אֶהְיֶה כַטַּל לְיִשְׂרָאֵל יִפְרַח כַּשּׁוֹשַׁנָּה וְיַךְ שָׁרָשָׁיו כַּלְּבָנוֹן — *I will be to Israel like the dew; he shall blossom like the rose, and his roots shall strike out like the*

1. The Talmud (*Yoma*) teaches that Hashem not only views heartfelt repentance as better than obligatory sacrifices but actually deems repentance as a voluntary offering. אֹהֲבֵם נְדָבָה is thus interpreted: I will love them as [if they had brought] a voluntary offering.

⁴ Assyria shall not save us; upon horses we will not
ride, and we will no longer say to our handiwork,
"our gods," for with You an orphan finds pity. ⁵ I will
remedy their deviance; I will love them gratuitously;
for My anger has turned away from them. ⁶ I will be to
Israel like the dew; he shall blossom like the rose, and
his roots shall strike out like the Lebanon. ⁷ His branches
shall go forth, and his beauty shall be like [that of]

Lebanon. Their fountainhead shall not be parched, nor shall their spring dry up (see 13:15), for I will be to them like the dew [that provides moisture] consistently, never neglecting to appear (*Radak; Abarbanel*). And they will thereby blossom quickly like the rose (*Ibn Ezra*) and bloom into other similarly beautiful flowers (*Metzudos David*).[1] However, although the roots of a rose are very fine and fragile, Israel's will be strong and thick, and they will spread outward like those of the trees of Lebanon (*Ibn Ezra; Radak; Abarbanel; Metzudos David*). Alternatively: *The dew I send will strike the roots [and render them] like the roots of the trees of Lebanon* (*Rashi*).

The Sages explain the metaphor of the rose to be expressing Hashem's exhortation to the Jewish nation: Just as the rose looks upward, so must you repent with your hearts turned heavenward. When this will take place, I will redeem you (*Yalkut*).

Unlike rain which is a gift of sustenance, dew functions to elicit minerals etc. which lie under the surface of the earth. Similiarly, Hashem will act as dew awakening the dormant spiritual inherent in man that awaits release and actualization (*Avnei Nezer*).

7. יֵלְכוּ יֹנְקוֹתָיו וִיהִי כַזַּיִת הוֹדוֹ — *His branches shall go forth, and his beauty shall be like [that of] the olive.* Their children shall multiply and emerge in abundance (*Targum; Rashi; Mahari Kara; Abarbanel*), and they will shine with a beauty like that of the olive, whose oil gives light when kindled (*Malbim*). Indeed, they will glow like the very light of the menorah in the Temple (*Targum; Rashi*). Alternatively: The name of Israel shall shine in glory and beauty, acclaimed and appreciated by the entire world (*Mahari Kara*).

Radak interprets: Their branches — i.e., the benefits which will emerge anew on a daily basis — will spread out and expand in all directions. Alternatively: Knowledge and fulfillment of Torah will be firm and steadfast in their midst, and its branches — i.e., the ever-increasing knowledge of God — will expand continuously. Indeed, their freshness and vitality will be constant — like the leaves of the olive tree that remain throughout the year — for their benefits will be showered upon them ceaselessly.

Alshich perceives this verse as describing the situation of the Jewish nation while still in exile, once they have returned to Hashem with all their hearts: Although the branches are spread out over the world and far from the home of their father, they will nevertheless glow with the light of their righteousness and Torah, reflecting the light of the Almighty Himself.

1. *Radak* notes that Israel is compared elsewhere in Scripture to the rose (*Song of Songs* 2:1) and is therefore depicted so by the prophet here as well.

ח וְרֵיחַ לוֹ כַּלְּבָנוֹן: יָשֻׁבוּ יֹשְׁבֵי בְצִלּוֹ יְחַיּוּ דָגָן
ט וְיִפְרְחוּ כַגָּפֶן זִכְרוֹ כְּיֵין לְבָנוֹן: אֶפְרַיִם מַה־לִּי עוֹד
לָעֲצַבִּים אֲנִי עָנִיתִי וַאֲשׁוּרֶנּוּ אֲנִי כִּבְרוֹשׁ רַעֲנָן

וְרֵיחַ לוֹ כַּלְּבָנוֹן — *And his fragrance like [that of] Lebanon.* Their good name will spread out across the globe, acclaimed and appreciated like the fragrance of the diverse trees and flowers of Lebanon (*Radak*). Alternatively: Their lives will be filled with benefits and pleasures, like the sweet aroma of those fragrant trees (*Metzudos David*).

Others interpret the reference to Lebanon to mean the Temple, which is referred to in the Torah as Lebanon (see *Deuteronomy* 3:25, *Sifri, Rashi* ad loc.).[1] The Jewish people will be fragrant with the flavor of sanctity and holiness, like the holiness of the Temple (*Targum; Rashi; Malbim*).

8. יָשֻׁבוּ יֹשְׁבֵי בְצִלּוֹ — *Those who dwell in his shade shall return.* Those who dwell in the shade of that tree — i.e., of the nation of Israel — will return to that shade, unable to part from it due to its lovely fragrance and fruits (*Ibn Ezra; Mahari Kara; R' Eliezer of Beaugency*). This refers to the slaves, who will attach themselves to the Jewish nation and be the farmers and vinedressers (*Ibn Ezra*).

Many commentators interpret the shade as being that of the Almighty: The Jewish nation will return to their land and dwell under the protection of Hashem (*Radak*). Alternatively, this refers to the proselytes, who will come to place themselves under the shade of the Almighty (*Yalkut*).

Others translate יָשֻׁבוּ to mean *serenity*: Those who return to dwell in the shade of the Almighty will enjoy peace and serenity in their lives (*Abarbanel; Metzudos David*).

Yet another approach understands the shade to be that of the aforementioned Lebanon (*Rashi; Yafes,* cited by *Ibn Ezra; Malbim*). Those who previously dwelled in the shade of Lebanon — to which the prophet compared both Israel and the Temple — will return once more to that shade (*Rashi*).

יְחַיּוּ דָגָן וְיִפְרְחוּ כַגָּפֶן — *They shall revive like the grain and sprout like the vine.* The Jewish people will revive themselves and renew their energy, like the grain that gives strength to its consumers. They will sprout in great abundance as well, like the vine that grows masses of flowers with its grapes (*Abarbanel; Metzudos David*). *Radak* interprets: They will revive themselves constantly with the *mitzvos* of Hashem which they will fulfill, and which, in turn, will sustain them as grain sustains man. In addition, they will sprout like the vine, for their benefits will continue without stop like the vine that renews itself annually and requires no new planting.

Others render: *The grain shall revive and shall sprout like the vine.* Whereas the land was previously cursed with the destructions of its crops of grain (9:2), when the Almighty's favor shines once more upon Israel, the land shall revive and be restored to its vitality and it shall once again give forth its grain (*Mahari Kara; Ibn Ezra*). Indeed, the fields of grain will not require sowing from year to year. Rather, the roots will miraculously be revitalized and produce their yield with no further planting, just as the vineyard need not be resown from year to year (Commentators cited by *Radak; R' Eliezer of Beaugency*).

Targum renders this first half of the verse as follows: *They will gather from their exile and dwell in the shade of their*

1. *Why is it called Lebanon? Based on* [the words] (*Deuteronomy* loc. cit.): *This good mountain and Lebanon. Said R' Shimon bar Yochai: Because it whitened —* מְלַבִּין *— the sins of Israel like snow. R' Tavyumi said: Because all hearts —* לְבָבוֹת *— rejoiced with it* (*Yalkut*).

the olive and his fragrance like [that of] the Lebanon.
8 Those who dwell in his shade shall return; they shall
revive like the grain and sprout like the vine; its men-
tion [shall be] like the wine of Lebanon. 9 Ephraim [says]:
"What further [use] are the idols to me?" I will respond
and I will gaze upon him; I am like the fresh cypress;

Messiah, and their dead will be resurrected and they will enjoy an abundance of good.

זִכְרוֹ כְּיֵין לְבָנוֹן — *Its mention [shall be] like the wine of Lebanon.* The mention of their name shall be like that of the highly lauded wines of Lebanon, for it shall be acclaimed throughout the land (*Abarbanel; Metzudos David*). Others interpret this as referring to the vines that the land will produce: The mention and fame of their vines will spread far and wide, as does the fame of the wines of Lebanon (*Yafes*, cited by *Ibn Ezra*).

According to *Targum* and *Rashi*, Lebanon refers again to the Temple: The remembrance of their good shall ascend [to the Heavens] without stop, like the remembrance of the blasts of the trumpets over the old wine that was poured for libations in the Temple — for they would blow trumpets as they poured libations and the Levites recited their song.

R' Eliezer of Beaugency interprets: The remembrance of Ephraim — i.e., that which they will remember Me constantly [and take pleasure in Me] as they do in the wines of Lebanon [will be expressed in the manner described in the following verse].

Others render זִכְרוֹ to mean *its fragrance.* The fragrance of the vine to which Israel will be compared will be like that of the wines of Lebanon, which are renowned for their sweet aroma. Indeed, it is written in the works of Assaf the Healer that the wines of Lebanon are most outstanding in their taste and fragrance — along with those of Hermon, Carmel, the hills of Israel and Jerusalem, Samaria and the Caphtarian mountains in Egypt (*Radak*).[1]

9. אֶפְרַיִם מַה־לִּי עוֹד לָעֲצַבִּים — *Ephraim [says]: "What further [use] are the idols to me?"* [At that time] Ephraim will declare, "What purpose is there to my continued pursuit of idolatry? When I worshiped them, I was plagued with misfortune, whereas when I serve Hashem all conceivable good is bestowed upon me." He will thus abandon his idols and return to Hashem (*Rashi; Ibn Ezra; Radak;* cf. *Abarbanel*, cited below).

אֲנִי עָנִיתִי וַאֲשׁוּרֶנּוּ — *I will respond and I will gaze upon him.* [To this the Almighty responds:] I will respond generously to all of his prayers and requests, and I will place My eyes — i.e., My Divine Providence — upon him, bestowing upon him all of My blessing (*Targum; Ibn Ezra; Metzudos David*). Alternatively: I will respond with the answer that is stated in the following words (*Radak; Malbim*).

Rashi interprets this phrase as referring still to the time of Israel's suffering: I will answer him in his suffering and I will gaze upon his sorry plight [i.e., to focus My Divine Providence upon redeeming him from his misfortune].

אֲנִי כִּבְרוֹשׁ רַעֲנָן — *I am like the fresh cypress.* I will be to him like the fresh cypress, whose branches are easily bent down to be grasped. So shall I be readily available to him (*Rashi*) — particularly

1. [According to this interpretation as well,] the fragrance is a metaphor for the good name Israel will enjoy throughout the world (ibid.).

י מִ֥י חָכָם֙ וְיָ֣בֵן אֵ֔לֶּה נָב֖וֹן וְיֵדָעֵ֑ם
כִּֽי־יְשָׁרִ֞ים דַּרְכֵ֣י יהוה וְצַדִּקִים֙ יֵ֣לְכוּ בָ֔ם וּפֹשְׁעִ֖ים
יִכָּ֥שְׁלוּ בָֽם׃

to those who are bent in their humility or their broken spirit (*Radak*). *Mahari Kara* adds: Just like a cypress, which one can bend down and thus climb upon its branches, so shall I be there to support them.

Others see the reference to the cypress as alluding to its vast shade: So shall I provide succor and shelter to them in all circumstances (*Abarbanel; Malbim*).

מִמֶּנִּי פֶּרְיְךָ נִמְצָא — *Your fruit is provided* [lit. *found*] *from Me.* Lest you note that a cypress gives shade and support but provides no fruit, know that I will be the source of your fruit as well, for all good which you enjoy shall come directly from Me (*Rashi; Ibn Ezra; Radak*).

R' Eliezer of Beaugency sees the entire verse, with the exception of this final phrase, as being part of the words of Ephraim: Ephraim shall say, "What further use do I have with my idols? While I served them I suffered — עָנִיתִי — constantly; indeed I have looked carefully — וַאֲשׁוּרֶנּוּ — and noted that I was bent like the cypress due to my false gods. Therefore, I will return to my first Master, for my plight was far better under Him." This you shall recall — declares the Almighty — for all of your fruits are provided from Me.

Abarbanel, on the other hand, understands the entire verse as being the words of the Almighty: Ephraim, why should I continue to castigate you for your idols and to show you their uselessness? For I have spoken to you and told you about them — עָנִיתִי — and I have looked — i.e., I have focused My Divine Providence — to see if you will abandon them or merely continue to return to them and worship them. Know that I Myself am constant and unchanging like the mighty cypress, but My ways of dealing with you are the fruits of your deeds and the results of your actions. If you will improve I will bestow blessing upon you, but if you sin I shall punish you.

10. [Having reproved the Jewish nation for its misdeeds, as well as depicting the ultimate fate which is theirs as soon as they repent,] Hosea closes his words of prophecy by issuing this final challenge (*Radak*).

מִי חָכָם וְיָבֵן אֵלֶּה נָבוֹן וְיֵדָעֵם — *Who is wise and will understand these; understanding and will know them?* Who will be wise enough to contemplate my words and to thereby be moved to return to Hashem (*Rashi*)?

Malbim explains that the term חָכְמָה refers to the wisdom one receives from outside sources, whereas בִּינָה applies to that which one deduces from his own wisdom. Knowledge — דַּעַת — means the clarity of knowledge which one has attained through his understanding. A person is capable of achieving a great deal of understanding in many areas through his own intelligence. However, when dealing with matters beyond human comprehension, he must first acquire the necessary wisdom and only then can he deepen his understanding through his logical prowess. This applies particularly to the knowledge of the ways of Hashem, along with all matters of Godliness. Thus: Who is wise, having acquired the wisdom of Hashem's ways, and can thereby build upon that wisdom

your fruit is provided from Me. [10] *Who is wise and will*
understand these; understanding and will know them?
For the ways of H*ASHEM* *are straight, and the righteous*
shall walk with them and the wayward shall stumble
over them.

to achieve understanding? Furthermore, all matters of wisdom require contemplation and evaluation to achieve full understanding; they cannot be attained through superficial glimpses. Therefore, the one who has applied himself to these matters sagaciously will come to a full knowledge of them.

כִּי־יְשָׁרִים דַּרְכֵי ה׳ וְצַדִּקִים יֵלְכוּ בָם וּפֹשְׁעִים יִכָּשְׁלוּ בָם — *For the ways of* H*ASHEM* *are straight, and the righteous shall walk with them and the wayward shall stumble over them.* I have placed before you a choice between two ways of life: good and evil (*Mahari Kara*). The righteous choose good and thereby prosper; those who deviate from the proper path stumble and fall in their deviance (*Targum; Rashi; Ibn Ezra; Mahari Kara*).

Alternatively: Because the ways of Hashem are straight and upright, those who lean to good and righteousness rejoice over these ways and follow them faithfully. Those, however, who are corrupt and deviant see only difficulties and obstructions in Hashem's dictates and they therefore end up distorting them and stumbling over them (*Abarbanel; Metzudos David*). *R' Eliezer of Beaugency* interprets: The wayward see the ways of Hashem as being the source of their downfall, for their sole interest in life is fulfilling their whims and desires, and the ways of the Torah stand in their way.

Radak cites his father as explaining that when the wayward seek to return to Hashem's ways they stumble often, since they are not accustomed to them. This is in contrast to the righteous, who follow the Torah smoothly. However, this applies only to those who are still deviant in their hearts even as they seek to repent; those who return with a full heart will be aided generously by the Almighty and will therefore not stumble in their path.

Radak himself understands this verse as referring to the ways of Hashem's Divine Providence and his dealing with humanity — specifically the age-old puzzle that the righteous are often plagued with misfortune whereas the wayward are many times blessed with prosperity. The righteous are unfazed by this phenomena, for they trust implicitly in the Almighty and recognize that His plans and policies are beyond human comprehension. Thus, when they see a righteous man suffer, they assume that either he is not as righteous as he seems or Hashem is punishing him for his sins on this world so as to enhance his reward in the world to come. Similarly, when they observe the wicked enjoying prosperity, they recognize that the latter may be receiving their reward for their good deeds in this world. The wayward, however, [presumptuously assume to truly understand what is right and what is wrong and therefore set themselves up as the judges of Hashem's ways]. Thus, when they see these phenomena, they declare that there is no judge and no justice, and there is no Supreme Being who oversees events in this world.

yoel

א דְּבַר־יהוה אֲשֶׁר הָיָה אֶל־יוֹאֵל בֶּן־פְּתוּאֵל:
ב שִׁמְעוּ־זֹאת הַזְּקֵנִים וְהַאֲזִינוּ כֹּל יוֹשְׁבֵי הָאָרֶץ
הֶהָיְתָה זֹּאת בִּימֵיכֶם וְאִם בִּימֵי אֲבֹתֵיכֶם:
ג עָלֶיהָ לִבְנֵיכֶם סַפֵּרוּ וּבְנֵיכֶם לִבְנֵיהֶם וּבְנֵיהֶם
ד לְדוֹר אַחֵר: יֶתֶר הַגָּזָם אָכַל הָאַרְבֶּה וְיֶתֶר
הָאַרְבֶּה אָכַל הַיָּלֶק וְיֶתֶר הַיֶּלֶק אָכַל הֶחָסִיל:

I

1. דְּבַר־ה׳ אֲשֶׁר הָיָה אֶל־יוֹאֵל בֶּן־פְּתוּאֵל — *The word of HASHEM that came to Joel the son of Pethuel.*

Scripture offers no information concerning the identity of this prophet nor the period of time in which he lived. There are various theories among the Sages concerning this question.

The *Gemara* (*Taanis* 5a) places him in the times of Yehoram, the son of Ahab, king of Israel (c. 3043-3055). During his reign, Elisha prophesied that there would be a famine in the Land of Israel that would last for seven years (*II Kings* 8:1). This is the famine described at length by Joel (*Rashi*). Each of the four species of locust mentioned below (v. 4) decimated one year's crops, and the land was stricken by drought for three years thereafter (*Radak*; cf. comm. to v. 4).

Another view identifies him as the eldest son of the prophet Samuel (2830-2883), who was named Joel (*I Samuel* 8:2). Samuel is referred to here as Pethuel because he placated the Almighty — פִּתָּה אֵל — with his prayers (*Rashi* from *Midrash Shmuel* 1:6; see *I Samuel* 7:6). Although the sons of Samuel are described in Scripture as evildoers (*I Samuel* 8:3), they eventually repented, and the eldest of them achieved the level of prophecy (*Yalkut Shimoni* II:77).

A third opinion places him in the times of Manasseh, king of Judah (c. 3228-3283), along with the prophets Nahum and Habakkuk (*Seder Olam* 20). According to this view, the reigning king is not noted here [unlike the general practice of Scripture when introducing a prophet] because his wicked ways rendered him unworthy of such an honor (*Radak*).

בֶּן־פְּתוּאֵל — *The son of Pethuel.*

Scripture's identification of the prophet's father indicates that he, too, was a prophet (*Abarbanel*), or at least an honored individual (*Ibn Ezra*).

2. Starting here until the end of chapter 2, the prophet foretells of a great plague of locusts which was to sweep the Land of Israel and destroy all vegetation, causing a devastating famine throughout the land. This was decreed by the Almighty in retribution for the sins of the Jewish nation, and the prophet urges the people to repent from their evil ways and thereby bring about the annulment of the decree. He begins his prophecy by emphasizing the unique scale of the impending plague.

Abarbanel contends that the entire prophecy concerning the swarms of locusts is actually a parable for the invading armies which are destined to conquer the Holy Land. The prophet exhorts his listeners to remember this prophecy and relate it to future generations, because it accurately describes the future fate of the Jewish nation. *R' Eliezer of Beaugency* follows a similar approach.

שִׁמְעוּ־זֹאת הַזְּקֵנִים וְהַאֲזִינוּ כֹּל יוֹשְׁבֵי הָאָרֶץ — *Hear this, you elders, and hearken, all you inhabitants of the land.*

You, *elders*, who keep your distance, *hear* [from a distance] what I am about

[1] *The word of HASHEM that came to Joel the son of*
Pethuel. [2] *Hear this, you elders, and hearken, all*
you inhabitants of the land: Was there such a thing
in your days or in the days of your fathers? [3] *Tell*
your children about it, and your children to their
children, and their children to another generation.
[4] *The remnant from the gazam-locust the arbeh-locust*
has devoured; and the remnant from the arbeh-locust
the yelek-locust has devoured; and the remnant
from the yelek-locust the chasil-locust has devoured.

to say. Because you have witnessed and experienced so much in your lifetimes, you are unmoved by the news of impending events and thus do not approach to listen to my words. [However, the disaster I am about to describe will be of unparalleled dimensions, beyond anything you or your ancestors have endured.] Those *inhabitants of the land* who are younger, come close and *hearken* [from nearby] to my words [and you will hear of a catastrophe of unimaginable scope and magnitude] (*Alshich*).

הֲהָיְתָה זֹּאת בִּימֵיכֶם וְאִם בִּימֵי אֲבֹתֵיכֶם — *Was there such a thing in your days or in the days of your fathers?*

Has a plague of locusts such as described below ever occurred in the past (*Rashi*)?

This would seem to contradict the statement of the Torah (*Exodus* 10:14) that there will never be a plague of locusts like that which was inflicted upon the Egyptians. However, that swarm consisted of one species, *arbeh*,[1] the scope of which was never equaled by a single swarm. The plague described here included four different waves, each of a different species, which followed one after the other (*Radak; Rashi* to *Exodus* ad loc.). [The total scale of these swarms exceeded even that of the plague in Egypt (cf. *Ramban* to *Exodus* loc. cit.).]

3. עֲלֶיהָ לִבְנֵיכֶם סַפֵּרוּ וּבְנֵיכֶם לִבְנֵיהֶם וּבְנֵיהֶם לְדוֹר אַחֵר — *Tell your children about it, and your children to their children, and their children to another generation.*

This plague will be so awesome that it will be discussed for generations to come (*Radak*).

4. יֶתֶר הַגָּזָם אָכַל הָאַרְבֶּה וְיֶתֶר הָאַרְבֶּה אָכַל הַיָּלֶק וְיֶתֶר הַיֶּלֶק אָכַל הֶחָסִיל — *The remnant from the gazam-locust the arbeh-locust has devoured; and the remnant from the arbeh-locust the yelek-locust has devoured; and the remnant from the yelek-locust the chasil-locust has devoured.*

Four different species of locusts shall overrun the land of Israel, consuming between them every last vestige of vegetation (*Rashi*). Contrary to their natural tendencies, the *gazam, arbeh,* and *yelek* will each leave over substantial quantities of growth to allow for the next wave of invading locusts. It will thus be clearly evident that the destruction is the result of a Divine decree and not merely a natural disaster (*Alshich*).

Alternatively, this plague will have a duration of four years [unlike the above explanation which understands the plague to have occurred all in one year]. Each year, one of these species will

1. Although Scripture (*Psalms* 78:46, 105:34) describes the locust plague in Egypt as including the species of *chasil* and *yalek* as well, these were merely supplementary swarms which accompanied those of *arbeh*, but they were not sufficiently noteworthy even to be mentioned in the Torah (*Radak*).

ה הָקִיצוּ שִׁכּוֹרִים וּבְכוּ וְהֵילִלוּ כָּל־שֹׁתֵי יָיִן
ו עַל־עָסִיס כִּי נִכְרַת מִפִּיכֶם׃ כִּי־גוֹי עָלָה עַל־
אַרְצִי עָצוּם וְאֵין מִסְפָּר שִׁנָּיו שִׁנֵּי אַרְיֵה
ז וּמְתַלְּעוֹת לָבִיא לוֹ׃ שָׂם גַּפְנִי לְשַׁמָּה וּתְאֵנָתִי
לִקְצָפָה חָשֹׂף חֲשָׂפָהּ וְהִשְׁלִיךְ הִלְבִּינוּ שָׂרִיגֶיהָ׃
ח אֱלִי כִּבְתוּלָה חֲגֻרַת־שַׂק עַל־בַּעַל נְעוּרֶיהָ׃

descend upon the land and devour all of its crops (*Radak;* see comm. to v. 1).

According to some, the names signed to these different species are actually descriptions of their characteristics. *Gazam* derives its name from the word גוזז, *to cut*, because it cuts the produce. *Arbeh* comes from the word רב, *many*, because it is the most numerous species. *Yelek* is derived from לוקק, *lick*, because it nibbles and licks up vegetation from the ground. The *chasil* finishes off the final vestiges of any remaining produce. A similar usage of the word is found in the phrase (*Deuteronomy* 28:38): יַחְסְלֶנּוּ הָאַרְבֶּה, *the arbeh shall totally destroy it* (*Radak*).

As interpreted by *Abarbanel*, the four species of locusts symbolize the four kingdoms which subsequently conquered the Land of Israel. *Gazam* refers to Babylonia, whose king, Nebuchadnezzar, was so noteworthy in both power and wickedness that [his description sounds like] an exaggeration (גוּזְמָה). Alternatively, it relates to the word גוֹזֵז, as he *cut* away all of the nations in existence. *Arbeh* — meaning many — represents the kingdom of Persia, which consisted of a great multitude of people since it included the nations of both Persia and Media. *Yelek* are the people of Greece, who *lapped* with their tongues like dogs.[1] *Chasil*, the finishing locusts, symbolize the Roman Empire, which wreaked the final destruction upon the Jewish nation, destroying the Temple and exiling the inhabitants of the land.

The prophet now proceeds to depict in vivid detail the extent of the destruction which the plague will cause and the sadness and mourning among the people which will follow in its wake. He employs the past tense rather than the future [a common device in Scriptural prophecy]. Alternatively, this is done in order to vividly portray the grief which will be expressed by the land's inhabitants after the calamity has actually occurred (*Radak* to v. 7).

5. הָקִיצוּ שִׁכּוֹרִים וּבְכוּ — *Awaken, you drunkards, and weep.*

Those of you who are accustomed to indulging in drink — awaken from your drunken stupor (*Malbim*) — and weep for your vineyards that the locusts shall destroy (*Radak*).

וְהֵילִלוּ כָּל־שֹׁתֵי יָיִן — *And wail all you wine-drinkers.*

Those who drink in moderation for pleasure — you, too, may wail over the fact that no more wine will be forthcoming (*Malbim*).

The Sages state (*Eruvin* 65a) that wine was primarily created for two purposes: (a) to allow the wicked a source of pleasure in order to repay them in this world for their few good deeds, and (b) to help mourners drown out the sorrow of their loss. Thus the prophet addresses these two categories of people and proclaims: Those wicked people who were previously repaid for their good with wine should cry over this loss, since they no longer have access to their reward. Those who partake in it to drown their sorrows will now have to wail in mourning, as there shall be no wine available to distract them (*Alshich*).

עַל־עָסִיס — *For wine.*

The root עסס, *to crush*, is used in reference to wine, which is produced by the crushing of grapes (*Radak, Malbim;* cf.

1. [*Abarbanel* offers no further elaboration on this point. Perhaps it refers to the total involvement of the Greeks in hedonistic self-indulgence — like a dog thirstily lapping water.]

5 Awaken, you drunkards, and weep, and wail all you
wine-drinkers — for wine has been cut off from your
mouths. 6 For a nation has ascended upon my land,
mighty and without number; its teeth are the teeth of
a lion, and it has the molars of a young lion. 7 He has
rendered my vine desolate and my fig tree a source
of despair; he has stripped its bark and discarded [it];
its branches have turned white. 8 Lament like a virgin
girt with sackcloth for the husband of her youth.

Ibn Ezra). *Rashi* renders: superior wine.

6. כִּי־גוֹי עָלָה עַל־אַרְצִי עָצוּם וְאֵין מִסְפָּר שִׁנָּיו שִׁנֵּי אַרְיֵה וּמְתַלְּעוֹת לָבִיא לוֹ — *For a nation has ascended upon my land, mighty and without number; its teeth are the teeth of a lion, and it has the molars of a young lion.*

A gathering of living creatures — described as a "nation"[1] — has invaded the Land of Israel. So destructive are these creatures that it is as if they had the fangs of mighty lions (*Radak*).

The translation for לָבִיא ("young lion") follows the view of *Targum Yonasan*. *Radak* contends that it refers to a larger species of lion.

7. שָׂם גַּפְנִי לְשַׁמָּה — *He has rendered my vine desolate.*

The invading swarms have totally consumed the fruit of my vine (*Targum Yonasan*). Alternatively, the locusts have destroyed not only the grapes but even the vines themselves. Thus, there will be no more wine until new vines are planted and left uneaten for three years, in accordance with the laws of *orlah* (*Alshich*).

וּתְאֵנָתִי לִקְצָפָה — *And my fig tree a source of despair.*

[Rather than providing pleasure and sustenance, the fig trees have been rendered a source of despair due to their desolation.]

This follows the translation of *Targum* and *Rashi*. According to *Ibn Ezra*, לִקְצָפָה refers to the froth on waves, something which has no substance. *Radak* translates it as a curse or, alternatively, as a peeling off (see below).

חָשֹׂף חֲשָׂפָהּ וְהִשְׁלִיךְ הִלְבִּינוּ שָׂרִיגֶיהָ — *He has stripped its bark and discarded [it]; its branches have turned white.*

He has peeled the bark of the tree and thrown it away and consumed the sap which lies between the bark and the wood (*Radak*), thus leaving over only the naked white branches (*Rashi*; *Radak*). Alternatively: He has discarded the budding plants themselves, thereby destroying them (*Radak*).

Abarbanel understands the previous verse (v. 6) literally, referring to the nation of Babylon which will ascend and conquer the Land of Israel. The vines and fig trees discussed in this verse are symbolic of the Jewish people — portrayed as the vineyard of the Almighty — who will suffer the wrath of the oppressor. Thus, the words of this verse are those of the Almighty, Who is depicted as lamenting the loss of His nation at the hand of the enemy.

8. אֱלִי כִּבְתוּלָה חֲגֻרַת־שַׂק עַל־בַּעַל נְעוּרֶיהָ — *Lament like a virgin girt with sackcloth for the husband of her youth.*

Lament in sorrow over this tragedy, like a young maiden who dons sackcloth in place of her ornaments when her husband dies while they are still in their youth at the height of their enjoyment of each other (*Radak*).

1. Scripture elsewhere (*Proverbs* 30:25,26) refers to a gathering of living creatures as an עַם, a people or nation (*Radak*).

ט הָכְרַ֥ת מִנְחָ֛ה וָנֶ֖סֶךְ מִבֵּ֣ית יְהוָ֑ה אָֽבְלוּ֙ הַכֹּ֣הֲנִ֔ים
י מְשָׁרְתֵ֖י יְהוָֽה׃ שֻׁדַּ֣ד שָׂדֶ֔ה אָבְלָ֖ה אֲדָמָ֑ה כִּ֚י
שֻׁדַּ֣ד דָּגָ֔ן הוֹבִ֥ישׁ תִּיר֖וֹשׁ אֻמְלַ֥ל יִצְהָֽר׃
יא הֹבִ֣ישׁוּ אִכָּרִ֗ים הֵילִ֙ילוּ֙ כֹּֽרְמִ֔ים עַל־חִטָּ֖ה
יב וְעַל־שְׂעֹרָ֑ה כִּ֥י אָבַ֖ד קְצִ֥יר שָׂדֶֽה׃ הַגֶּ֣פֶן הוֹבִ֔ישָׁה
וְהַתְּאֵנָ֖ה אֻמְלָ֑לָה רִ֠מּוֹן גַּם־תָּמָ֤ר וְתַפּ֙וּחַ֙ כָּל־
עֲצֵ֤י הַשָּׂדֶה֙ יָבֵ֔שׁוּ כִּֽי־הֹבִ֥ישׁ שָׂשׂ֖וֹן מִן־בְּנֵ֥י
יג אָדָֽם׃ חִגְר֨וּ וְסִפְד֜וּ הַכֹּהֲנִ֗ים הֵילִ֙ילוּ֙
מְשָׁרְתֵ֣י מִזְבֵּ֔חַ בֹּ֚אוּ לִ֣ינוּ בַשַּׂקִּ֔ים מְשָׁרְתֵ֖י אֱלֹהָ֑י

Alternatively: Lament like a young maiden whose intended groom dies suddenly when all is prepared and the wedding is about to take place. Similarly, just as the crops are ready for harvest they will be eradicated from your midst (*R' Eliezer of Beaugency*).

Others interpret this exhortation to be directed to the land, which will lose its crops and be left desolate like a young wife who loses her husband (*Ibn Ezra*). In a similar vein, *Malbim* explains it to refer to the vines and fig trees whose fruits will be destroyed. A tree which has never been picked is referred to in Talmud as a virgin tree; the branches which cover it can thus be depicted as its husband. Accordingly, the vines and fruit trees which have been stripped of their branches and left naked — thereby necessitating that they be covered with sacks to protect them from the elements — are depicted as wailing over their tragic fate.

According to *Abarbanel*, the prophet addresses the virgin nation of Israel, which had hitherto never been conquered: Lament the loss of the Divine Presence which ceased to dwell among you after you were exiled, just as a young maiden bemoans the premature death of her husband.

9. הָכְרַת מִנְחָה וָנֶסֶךְ מִבֵּית ה׳ אָבְלוּ הַכֹּהֲנִים מְשָׁרְתֵי ה׳ — *Meal-offering and libation have been cut off from the House of* HASHEM; *the Kohanim, the ministers of* HASHEM, *mourn.*

So extensive is the destruction caused by the invading locusts that no wine or grain is available for the offerings in the Temple. Thus, the *Kohanim*, who rely on their share of the Temple offerings for sustenance, are left to mourn their destitution (*Radak*).

This also reemphasizes the exhortation to the drunkards stated earlier. If there is not even wine available for necessities such as the Temple offerings, there certainly are no supplies for the indulgence of drunkards. They are therefore urged to mourn this great calamity (*Ibn Ezra*).

In another interpretation of these two verses, the prophet instructs the nation of Israel in the proper reaction to this great tragedy: Be like a newly married maiden, whose husband dies before they can consummate their marriage. Although it would be understandable for her to bemoan the denial of her awaited pleasure, she cries instead over the loss of her intended mate and partner for life. You, too, must focus your grief not on the negation of your personal enjoyment, but rather on the more momentous calamity of the cessation of the offerings in the Temple (*Alshich*).

10. שֻׁדַּד שָׂדֶה אָבְלָה אֲדָמָה כִּי שֻׁדַּד דָּגָן הוֹבִישׁ תִּירוֹשׁ אֻמְלַל יִצְהָר — *The field has been robbed, the land destroyed; for the grain has been robbed, the wine had dried up, and the oil has been cut off.*

The fields have been robbed of their grain, and the land has been rendered

9 *Meal-offering and libation have been cut off from the*
House of HASHEM; the Kohanim, the ministers of
HASHEM, mourn. 10 *The field has been robbed, the land de-*
stroyed; for the grain has been robbed, the wine has dried
up, and the oil has been cut off. 11 *Be ashamed, farmers;*
wail, vinedressers — over wheat and over barley, for the
harvest of the field has been lost. 12 *The vine has dried up*
and the fig tree has been cut off; the pomegranate tree as
well as the date tree and the apple tree — all the trees of
the field — have dried up, because rejoicing has dried up
from among the sons of man. 13 *Gird yourselves and*
lament, Kohanim; wail, ministers of the altar; come
spend the night in sackcloth, ministers of my God —

desolate from its wine and oil (*Mahari Kara; Malbim*), thereby denying the people the staples of their diet (*Radak*).

The translation of the word אָבְלָה follows *Targum* and *Radak*. *Ibn Ezra* interprets it as "mourning," referring to the inhabitants of the land who mourn the loss of their crops. The phrase הוֹבִישׁ תִּירוֹשׁ may also be translated *the wine is ashamed*; the wine is portrayed figuratively as being shamed by its negation (*Radak*).

11. הֹבִישׁוּ אִכָּרִים הֵילִילוּ כֹּרְמִים עַל־חִטָּה וְעַל־שְׂעֹרָה כִּי אָבַד קְצִיר שָׂדֶה — *Be ashamed, farmers; wail, vinedressers — over wheat and over barley, for the harvest of the field has been lost.*

Be ashamed, you farmers, over the loss of your wheat and barley (*Rashi*), for all of your efforts in cultivating them have come to naught (*Radak*). Wail, you vinedressers, for the loss of your vineyards, as depicted in the following verse (*Rashi*).

The translation of אִכָּרִים as farmers follows the majority of the commentators; others render it *those who guide the plow* (*Rashi; Mahari Kara*).

12. הַגֶּפֶן הוֹבִישָׁה וְהַתְּאֵנָה אֻמְלָלָה רִמּוֹן גַּם־תָּמָר וְתַפּוּחַ כָּל־עֲצֵי הַשָּׂדֶה יָבֵשׁוּ כִּי־הֹבִישׁ שָׂשׂוֹן מִן־בְּנֵי אָדָם — *The vine has dried up and the fig tree has been cut off; the pomegranate tree as well as the date tree and the apple tree — all the trees of the field — have dried up, because rejoicing has dried up from among the sons of man.*

In addition to the staples of life which have been eradicated from your midst, the various trees of the field have lost their fruit as well. True, these are not necessities, and their loss does not warrant sorrow and mourning. Nevertheless, they are basic sources of pleasure (*Alshich*), which have been destroyed by the Almighty to abolish rejoicing from among the people in retribution for their misdeeds (*Metzudos David*).

Others translate this verse figuratively: Be ashamed, all you different types of trees, for the fact that your productivity has ceased due to the plague of locusts. The spirit of rejoicing is nowhere to be found, for it, too, is embarrassed to appear among the populace in such circumstances (*Ibn Ezra; Radak*).

13. חִגְרוּ וְסִפְדוּ הַכֹּהֲנִים הֵילִילוּ מְשָׁרְתֵי מִזְבֵּחַ בֹּאוּ לִינוּ בַשַּׂקִּים מְשָׁרְתֵי אֱלֹהָי — *Gird yourselves and lament, Kohanim; wail, ministers of the altar; come spend the night in sackcloth, ministers of my God.*

Gird yourselves in sackcloth, *Kohanim* (*Ibn Ezra*), and wail in sorrow. Even by night do not remove your garments of

יד כִּי נִמְנַע מִבֵּית אֱלֹהֵיכֶם מִנְחָה וָנָסֶךְ׃ קַדְּשׁוּ־
צוֹם קִרְאוּ עֲצָרָה אִסְפוּ זְקֵנִים כֹּל יֹשְׁבֵי הָאָרֶץ
טו בֵּית יהוה אֱלֹהֵיכֶם וְזַעֲקוּ אֶל־יהוה׃ אֲהָהּ
לַיּוֹם כִּי קָרוֹב יוֹם יהוה וּכְשֹׁד מִשַּׁדַּי יָבוֹא׃
טז הֲלוֹא נֶגֶד עֵינֵינוּ אֹכֶל נִכְרָת מִבֵּית אֱלֹהֵינוּ
יז שִׂמְחָה וָגִיל׃ עָבְשׁוּ פְרֻדוֹת תַּחַת מֶגְרְפֹתֵיהֶם
נָשַׁמּוּ אֹצָרוֹת נֶהֶרְסוּ מַמְּגֻרוֹת כִּי הֹבִישׁ
יח דָּגָן׃ מַה־נֶּאֶנְחָה בְהֵמָה נָבֹכוּ עֶדְרֵי בָקָר כִּי
אֵין מִרְעֶה לָהֶם גַּם־עֶדְרֵי הַצֹּאן נֶאְשָׁמוּ׃

mourning; perhaps the Almighty will be moved to have mercy upon you (*Radak*).

Alternatively: All of the *Kohanim* should don sackcloth and mourn. However, those whose turn it is to minister to the altar at the time this calamity takes place must wail even more intensely over the disaster. You Levites, who administer the Temple, should also don sackcloth in mourning, and try to placate the Almighty by singing His praises throughout the night (*Alshich;* cf. *Malbim*).

כִּי נִמְנַע מִבֵּית אֱלֹהֵיכֶם מִנְחָה וָנָסֶךְ — *For meal-offering and libation have been withheld from the House of your God.*

You must undertake these actions in order to appeal to the Almighty, since your normal method of approaching him — by means of Temple offerings — has been rendered impossible due to the destruction of the crops (*Ibn Ezra*).

Alternatively: Focus your prayers on the negation of the means to serve Hashem rather than on your own personal losses. By doing so, you increase the likelihood of your pleas being answered (*Alshich*).

Abarbanel cites this verse in support of his approach that the prophet refers to the conquest of Israel and its destruction, as the offerings in the Temple were never interrupted prior to that time.

14. קַדְּשׁוּ־צוֹם קִרְאוּ עֲצָרָה אִסְפוּ זְקֵנִים כֹּל יֹשְׁבֵי הָאָרֶץ בֵּית ה׳ אֱלֹהֵיכֶם וְזַעֲקוּ אֶל־ה׳ — *Decree a fast; call an assembly; gather the elders [and] all the inhabitants of the land to the House of* HASHEM, *your God, and cry out to* HASHEM.

Gather all of the people together in fast and prayer to beg the Almighty to repeal the decree of the locust plague. This course of action will certainly be necessary once the invading swarms have descended upon the land. If you follow it immediately, you may even be able to prevent their arrival (*Radak*).

The translation of עֲצָרָה ("assembly") follows the view of *Targum, Rashi,* and *Malbim.* Others interpret it to refer to a prohibition against labor (*Ibn Ezra; Radak; Alshich;* cf. *Taanis* 12b).

15. אֲהָהּ לַיּוֹם כִּי קָרוֹב יוֹם ה׳ וּכְשֹׁד מִשַּׁדַּי יָבוֹא — *Woe is to the day, for the day of* HASHEM *is near and like robbery it shall come from the Almighty.*

Children of Israel, express your anguish over this impending day of disaster, for the plague of the Almighty shall come upon you suddenly — like a robbery which befalls its victim without warning (*Radak*) — and there shall thus be no escape (*Ibn Ezra*).

Malbim renders: *like robbery from the Almighty it shall come* — even if the laws of nature do not allow for this destruction it shall be triggered by שַׁדַּי — the Name of God which indicates the negation of the laws of nature — and there will thus be no way to escape it.

for meal-offering and libation have been withheld
from the House of your God. [14] *Decree a fast; call an*
assembly; gather the elders [and] all the inhabitants
of the land to the House of HASHEM*, your God, and*
cry out to HASHEM. [15] *Woe is to the day, for the day*
of HASHEM *is near and like robbery it shall come*
from the Almighty. [16] *Is not food cut off before our*
eyes; from the House of our God, happiness and
exultation? [17] *Casks of wine have become moldy under*
their lids; storehouses are laid desolate [and] silos
destroyed, for the grain has dried up. [18] *How the beasts*
groan; herds of cattle are bewildered, for there is not
pasture for them; also flocks of sheep are desolated.

Abarbanel interprets these two verses to refer to the ninth of Av — the day of the destruction of both Temples — which would be ordained as a day for the Jewish people to gather together in fast and mourning over their destruction. It is referred to as *the day of Hashem* because it was already designated by the Almighty as a day of mourning when He decreed that they wander forty years in the desert. Woe is to that day, declares the prophet, because the calamity which is drawing near will arrive on that same day.

16. הֲלוֹא נֶגֶד עֵינֵינוּ אֹכֶל נִכְרָת מִבֵּית אֱלֹהֵינוּ שִׂמְחָה וָגִיל — *Is not food cut off before our eyes; from the House of our God, happiness and exultation?*

The locusts have appeared before our very eyes and consumed all of our produce until there is no food. Thus, as the Festival of Succos arrives, there is no harvest over which to rejoice and for which to offer thanksgiving to the Almighty (*Radak*).

Alternatively: The prophet describes the vision of prophecy as being so clear that even now, before it takes place, it is as if it is occurring before his eyes (*Malbim*).

17. עָבְשׁוּ פְרֻדוֹת תַּחַת מֶגְרְפֹתֵיהֶם — *Casks of wine have become moldy under their lids.*

Wine casks sit empty for lack of wine with which to fill them; they have begun to rot and turn moldy from disuse.

This follows the translation of *Targum* and *Rashi*. Others render: *The seeds have shriveled beneath their clods* (*Ibn Ezra; Radak*). Even the seeds which lie beneath the ground and are thus untouched by the swarms of locusts will be smitten by a plague that will arrest their growth (*Radak*). Thus, not only will this year's crops be decimated, but there will be no potential for future growth either (*Alshich*).

נָשַׁמּוּ אֹצָרוֹת נֶהֶרְסוּ מַמְּגֻרוֹת כִּי הֹבִישׁ דָּגָן — *Storehouses are laid desolate [and] silos destroyed, for the grain has dried up.*

Storehouses of oil and wine (*Rashi*) lay desolate for lack of anything with which to fill them. Silos, too, are empty of any grain. Alternatively: The silos themselves have been in disuse for years until they have decayed from neglect (*Radak*).

Abarbanel renders מַמְּגֻרוֹת, *"from terror"* — because of terror from the invading enemy no one will harvest the crops, and the storehouses will thus be left desolate.

18. מַה נֶּאֶנְחָה בְהֵמָה נָבֹכוּ עֶדְרֵי בָקָר כִּי אֵין מִרְעֶה לָהֶם גַּם־עֶדְרֵי הַצֹּאן נֶאְשָׁמוּ — *How the beasts groan; herds of cattle are bewildered, for there is not pasture for them; also flocks of sheep are desolated.*

How the beasts of the field groan in anguish over their sorry plight (*Radak*)!

א/יט־כ יט אֵלֶיךָ יְהוָה אֶקְרָא כִּי אֵשׁ אָכְלָה נְאוֹת מִדְבָּר
כ וְלֶהָבָה לִהֲטָה כָּל־עֲצֵי הַשָּׂדֶה: גַּם־בַּהֲמוֹת שָׂדֶה
תַּעֲרוֹג אֵלֶיךָ כִּי יָבְשׁוּ אֲפִיקֵי מָיִם וְאֵשׁ אָכְלָה
ב/א־ב א נְאוֹת הַמִּדְבָּר: תִּקְעוּ שׁוֹפָר בְּצִיּוֹן וְהָרִיעוּ
בְּהַר קָדְשִׁי יִרְגְּזוּ כֹּל יֹשְׁבֵי הָאָרֶץ כִּי־בָא יוֹם־
ב יְהוָה כִּי קָרוֹב: יוֹם חֹשֶׁךְ וַאֲפֵלָה יוֹם עָנָן וַעֲרָפֶל

The cattle are lost and confused, for they are trapped in the forests and deserts into which they have strayed (*Rashi*). Even the sheep, who have access to pasture high upon the mountains [have been devastated by the plague] (*Radak*).

Others interpret this verse as a question. Even if people were wicked, what sins did the beasts do that the herds of cattle and sheep suffer so (*Malbim*)?

19. אֵלֶיךָ ה׳ אֶקְרָא כִּי אֵשׁ אָכְלָה נְאוֹת מִדְבָּר וְלֶהָבָה לִהֲטָה כָּל־עֲצֵי הַשָּׂדֶה — *To You, HASHEM, I call, for fire has consumed the dwellings of the desert, and flame has scorched the trees of the field.*

So great is the destruction, so all-encompassing — like a land consumed by a raging fire — that there are no avenues of endeavor available whatsoever. Thus I turn to You, Hashem — to the God of my fathers — as the only recourse of salvation (*Abarbanel*).

There are several different interpretations of the nature of the fire described in this verse. *Targum* explains it to mean an eastern wind, powerful like a fire, which destroyed all growth. Others maintain that along with the swarms of grasshoppers the fields were plagued with drought as well (*Ibn Ezra*). A third view is that it refers to the locusts themselves, who wreaked such total destruction that it appeared as if the earth had been scorched by fire (*Radak*). *Abarbanel* follows his general approach and interprets this to refer to the flames of destruction brought by the enemy.

20. גַּם־בַּהֲמוֹת שָׂדֶה תַּעֲרוֹג אֵלֶיךָ כִּי יָבְשׁוּ אֲפִיקֵי מָיִם וְאֵשׁ אָכְלָה נְאוֹת הַמִּדְבָּר — *Also the beasts of the field cry out to you, for the springs of water have dried up and fire has consumed the dwellings of the desert.*

Even the wild animals who find their sustenance far from civilization cry out to You in their thirst (*Radak*) [for the effects of the destruction have spread to the fields and deserts far beyond human habitation].

According to the allegorical approach, the prophet describes how after destroying the land of Judah, Nebuchadnezzar will continue to conquer other nations as well, symbolized in this verse by the beasts of the field (*Abarbanel*).

II

According to some commentators, this chapter begins a new phase of the prophet's exhortations. In the previous chapter, the people were urged to fast and assemble prior to the advent of the plague; now the locusts have actually begun to descend upon the land, and there is one last chance to inspire the people to repentance (*Ibn Ezra; Malbim;* cf. *Abarbanel*). Others see in it nothing more than an intensification of the prophet's previous urgings for repentance as a means of avoiding the plague of locusts (*Rashi; Alshich*).

תִּקְעוּ שׁוֹפָר בְּצִיּוֹן וְהָרִיעוּ בְּהַר קָדְשִׁי יִרְגְּזוּ כֹּל יֹשְׁבֵי הָאָרֶץ כִּי־בָא יוֹם־ה׳ כִּי קָרוֹב — *Sound a shofar in Zion and trumpet upon My holy mountain; let all the inhabitants of the land tremble. For the day of HASHEM has come; it is near.*

1/19-20 [19] *To You, HASHEM, I call, for fire has consumed the
dwellings of the desert, and flame has scorched the trees
of the field.* [20] *Also the beasts of the field cry out to you,
for the springs of water have dried up and fire has
consumed the dwellings of the desert.*

2/1-2 [1] *Sound a shofar in Zion and trumpet upon My holy
mountain; let all the inhabitants of the land tremble.
For the day of HASHEM has come; it is near —* [2] *a day of
darkness and pitch-darkness, a day of cloud and fog,*

Sound a shofar to alert the people of Israel to repent, before it is too late and the evil decree befalls them (*Rashi*). They have already been exhorted to declare a fast and gather in prayer in the hope that they would thereby repent (1:14). Now that this has proven ineffective, the situation calls for further measures. It is therefore time for the sounding of the shofar, which has the capacity to instill fear in all those who hear it. Hopefully this will arouse the populace to recognize their faults and improve their deeds (*Alshich*).

תִּקְעוּ שׁוֹפָר . . . וְהָרִיעוּ — *Sound a shofar . . . and trumpet.*

These phrases are synonymous; the prophet repeats himself to enhance the effect of his words (*Radak*). Alternatively, he is outlining two distinct steps which must be taken to avoid catastrophe: First *sound a shofar in Zion* — throughout the city of Jerusalem — to call the populace to gather together in the Temple area. Once they are assembled there, *trumpet upon My holy mountain* [with shofar blasts] to arouse them to repentance (*Malbim*).

כִּי־בָא יוֹם־ה׳ כִּי קָרוֹב — *For the day of HASHEM has come; it is near.*

The day of the Almighty's vengeance (*Metzudos*) mentioned earlier (1:15) has arrived [and the plague of locusts which has been foretold is imminent] (*Rashi*).

The impending decree of a mortal being cannot yet be described as having been fulfilled, since there is always the possibility that it will somehow be averted. However, a decree issued by the Almighty cannot be repulsed; therefore, now that it is imminent the prophet rightly proclaims that its time has come (*Malbim*).

Abarbanel, continuing his metaphorical interpretation of the prophecy of the locust swarm, explains that this chapter deals specifically with the destruction of the two Temples. In this verse, the prophet focuses on that of the first. He directs his words to the kingdom of Judah and declares: *Sound a shofar* throughout Jerusalem to proclaim its fall, *trumpet* in the Temple itself to declare its destruction; *all the inhabitants* of the entire kingdom shall *tremble,* for the sound of the shofar will alert them that *the day of Hashem is near.* Just as the shofar in the year of Jubilee heralds the return of the inhabitants to their land (see *Leviticus* 25:9), so will it be employed to announce the reverse — the exile of the Jewish nation from the Land of Israel.

2. יוֹם חֹשֶׁךְ וַאֲפֵלָה יוֹם עָנָן וַעֲרָפֶל — *A day of darkness and pitch-darkness, a day of cloud and fog.*

[This *day of Hashem* will be] a day of great tragedy and suffering — symbolized by darkness, in contrast to joy which is symbolized by light (*Radak*). [So great will be the suffering that it cannot be depicted merely as] *darkness and pitch-darkness,* referring to the absence of light. Rather, it will be a day of *cloud and fog* as well, consisting of a tangible blackness brought about by dark clouds (*Malbim*).

כְּשַׁחַר פָּרֻשׂ עַל־הֶהָרִים עַם רַב וְעָצוּם כָּמֹהוּ
לֹא נִהְיָה מִן־הָעוֹלָם וְאַחֲרָיו לֹא יוֹסֵף עַד־
ג שְׁנֵי דּוֹר וָדוֹר׃ לְפָנָיו אָכְלָה אֵשׁ וְאַחֲרָיו
תְּלַהֵט לֶהָבָה כְּגַן־עֵדֶן הָאָרֶץ לְפָנָיו וְאַחֲרָיו
מִדְבַּר שְׁמָמָה וְגַם־פְּלֵיטָה לֹא־הָיְתָה לּוֹ׃
ד כְּמַרְאֵה סוּסִים מַרְאֵהוּ וּכְפָרָשִׁים כֵּן יְרוּצוּן׃

Alternatively, the verse refers to actual darkness. The swarms of locusts will be so massive that they will block the light of the sun (*Radak*).

כְּשַׁחַר פָּרֻשׂ עַל־הֶהָרִים — *Like the dawn, spread over the mountains.*

The locusts will spread over the mountains, just as the dawn blankets the entire world (*Rashi*). Others explain the phrase *spread over the mountains* to refer to the dawn; the locusts will descend upon you rapidly, just as the dawn appears suddenly over the mountaintops where it is first seen (*Ibn Ezra; Radak*). *Malbim* offers a third interpretation: Just as the dawn first appears above the mountaintops as a distant light amidst the darkness, so will the locusts be viewed as a glimmer of light in the distance when they first approach over the mountains (cf. *Abarbanel*).

עַם רַב וְעָצוּם כָּמֹהוּ לֹא נִהְיָה מִן־הָעוֹלָם וְאַחֲרָיו לֹא יוֹסֵף עַד שְׁנֵי דּוֹר וָדוֹר — *A people numerous and mighty; its like has never been and after it there shall never again be [its like], until the years of generation upon generation.*

[The swarm will be] a united multitude (*Ibn Ezra*) worthy of note due both to its numbers and strength (*Malbim*; cf. 1:6). Indeed the different species will combine to form a multitude so great that it will be unique in history (*Rashi*; cf. comm. to 1:2), not to be equaled even until the end of all generations (*Metzudos David*).

According to *Abarbanel*, this verse continues the description of the events surrounding the destruction of the First Temple. *The day of HASHEM* — the ninth day of the month of Av — was *a day of darkness* for the Jews in the desert, for on that day it was decreed that they would not enter the Land of Israel. That same day will now be a *day of clouds and fog* as well, due to the destruction of the Temple which will take place then. At that time, a great blackness will descend upon the Jewish nation, similar to the blackness that covers the earth before dawn. This will be the invading forces of Nebuchadnezzar, so numerous and mighty that they will not be equalled until generations later[1] by the Imperial Legions of the Roman Empire.

3. לְפָנָיו אָכְלָה אֵשׁ וְאַחֲרָיו תְּלַהֵט לֶהָבָה כְּגַן־עֵדֶן הָאָרֶץ לְפָנָיו וְאַחֲרָיו מִדְבַּר שְׁמָמָה וְגַם־פְּלֵיטָה לֹא־הָיְתָה לּוֹ — *Before it the fire consumed and after it the flame shall scorch; before it the land was like the Garden of Eden and after it a desolate desert; and neither was there any remnant of it.*

So great will be the destruction caused by the locusts that it will far exceed the ravages of a natural locust plague (*Metzudos David*). Rather, it will seem as if the locusts were preceded by a fire which consumed all in its path and followed again by a flame (*Rashi*) which further extended the destruction by destroying even the roots of all vegetation (*Malbim*).

Others interpret the first phrase to be describing units of space rather than of time: The locusts will amass in one area and spread from there to consume the surrounding vegetation, causing such devastation that the land on either side of

1. [Whereas *Metzudos* interprets the phrase *until the years of generation upon generation*, as the end of all generations, *Abarbanel* understands it to mean merely until many generations afterward.]

like the dawn, spread over the mountains — a people
numerous and mighty; its like has never been and
after it there shall never again be [its like], until the
years of generation upon generation. 3 *Before it the*
fire consumed and after it the flame shall scorch;
before it the land was like the Garden of Eden and
after it a desolate desert; and neither was there any
remnant of it. 4 *Their appearance is like the appear-*
ance of horses, and like horsemen so shall they run.

them will appear as if scorched by a fire. The actual area in which they will alight is not described here, because it will be rendered invisible by their mass presence (*Radak*).

וְגַם־פְּלֵיטָה לֹא־הָיְתָה לּוֹ — *And neither was there any remnant of it.*

There will be no vegetation whatsoever left over by the locusts. *Targum Yonasan* interprets: There will be no remnant of the wicked [left over from this hunger caused by this plague][1] (*Radak*).

According to *Abarbanel* this refers to the remnant of the Jewish nation, which was left in the Holy Land under the stewardship of Gedaliah ben Ahikam after the destruction of the First Temple. At the behest of the king of Ammon, Yishmael ben Nethaniah murdered Gedaliah and thereby caused the dispersal of this last vestige of Jewish society in Judah (see *Jeremiah* chs. 40,41).

Alshich interprets these last two verses, as well as the five that follow, to be describing how each of the different species of locusts will consume that which the previous one leaves behind. The *gazam*, symbolized by darkness, will consume like fire all that is in their path. They will be followed by the dark clouds of the *arbeh* — swarms who will render the land like the scorched earth caused by a blazing flame (cf. *Malbim*, cited above). However, these two swarms will not descend everywhere; there will still be areas of growth left untouched. Those regions will be destroyed by the *yelek*, which will spread over the entire land like the dawn, and render desolate that which had previously bloomed like the Garden of Eden. Finally, there shall come a horde of unprecedented number and might — the *chasil*, which will enter into people's homes and destroy all vegetation to be found even there, as will be described.

4-10. [In the following verses, the prophet describes the oncoming plague of locusts in terms which are more familiar to the people (in order that his words should have greater effect). He employs the metaphor of horses and chariots to depict the mighty force of the locusts and portrays their invasion as the overpowering onslaught of a conquering army. According to *Abarbanel*, the opposite is true: What follows is the true description of that which was depicted metaphorically by the prophecy of the locust-swarms.]

4. כְּמַרְאֵה סוּסִים מַרְאֵהוּ וּכְפָרָשִׁים כֵּן יְרוּצוּן — *Their appearance is like the appearance of horses, and like horsemen so shall they run.*

[The swarms of locusts will resemble in some ways the gallop of racing horses.] They will approach rapidly, like horses running swiftly to their destination (*Rashi; Ibn Ezra; Radak*), and the noise they generate will be similar to the din of mighty steeds rushing to battle (*Malbim*). Furthermore, just as the pace of the horses is accelerated by the prodding of the horsemen riding them, so will the flight

1. [The implication here is that only the wicked will be destroyed by the famine, but the righteous will somehow survive. However, no explanation is given as to how this will be made to happen.]

ה כְּקוֹל מַרְכָּבוֹת עַל־רָאשֵׁי הֶהָרִים יְרַקֵּדוּן
כְּקוֹל לַהַב אֵשׁ אֹכְלָה קָשׁ כְּעַם עָצוּם עֱרוּךְ
ו מִלְחָמָה׃ מִפָּנָיו יָחִילוּ עַמִּים כָּל־פָּנִים קִבְּצוּ
ז פָארוּר׃ כְּגִבּוֹרִים יְרֻצוּן כְּאַנְשֵׁי מִלְחָמָה יַעֲלוּ
חוֹמָה וְאִישׁ בִּדְרָכָיו יֵלֵכוּן וְלֹא יְעַבְּטוּן
ח אֹרְחוֹתָם׃ וְאִישׁ אָחִיו לֹא יִדְחָקוּן גֶּבֶר בִּמְסִלָּתוֹ
ט יֵלֵכוּן וּבְעַד הַשֶּׁלַח יִפֹּלוּ לֹא יִבְצָעוּ׃ בָּעִיר
יָשֹׁקּוּ בַּחוֹמָה יְרֻצוּן בַּבָּתִּים יַעֲלוּ בְּעַד
י הַחַלּוֹנִים יָבֹאוּ כַּגַּנָּב׃ לְפָנָיו רָגְזָה אֶרֶץ רָעֲשׁוּ
שָׁמָיִם שֶׁמֶשׁ וְיָרֵחַ קָדָרוּ וְכוֹכָבִים אָסְפוּ נָגְהָם׃

of the locusts be hastened by the decree of the Almighty urging them forward (*Malbim*).

Abarbanel interprets this to refer to the Babylonian soldiers. They will be so large and mighty as to resemble horses, and [even] the foot-soldiers will travel as fast as cavalrymen on their steeds.

5. כְּקוֹל מַרְכָּבוֹת עַל־רָאשֵׁי הֶהָרִים יְרַקֵּדוּן כְּקוֹל לַהַב אֵשׁ אֹכְלָה קָשׁ כְּעַם עָצוּם עֱרוּךְ מִלְחָמָה — *[With a noise] like the noise of chariots they shall leap upon the mountaintops, like the sound of a flame of fire consuming chaff; like a mighty people arrayed for battle.*

The flight of the locusts will raise such a clamor as to rival that of chariots in motion. But their range will extend even further, for they will leap to the tops of the mountains where the chariots are unable to go (*Ibn Ezra; Radak*). The noise caused by their consumption will be like the crackling of a flame consuming chaff (*Malbim*), and their overall din will resemble that of a nation poised for battle (*Radak*). Alternatively, they shall be poised to descend from the mountaintops like an army arrayed for battle (*Malbim*).

Abarbanel explains this verse as depicting the overwhelming fearsomeness of the Babylonian armies. They will generate a great deal of noise, like chariots traveling on a mountaintop where the sounds are highly resonant. In addition, they will not be unseasoned soldiers, but rather an army of experienced warriors well prepared for battle.

6. מִפָּנָיו יָחִילוּ עַמִּים כָּל־פָּנִים קִבְּצוּ פָארוּר — *From before it peoples shall tremble; all faces have gathered blackness.*

[The onslaught of locusts will inspire such fear] that the faces of the people will become black, like the bottom of (פרור) a pot (*Rashi*).

This translation follows the majority of commentaries. An alternative view is that פָּארוּר derives from the word פְּאֵר, *beauty;* all faces will withdraw their beauty [due to the fear of these invaders] (*Ibn Ezra;* cf. *Radak*).

7. כְּגִבּוֹרִים יְרֻצוּן כְּאַנְשֵׁי מִלְחָמָה יַעֲלוּ חוֹמָה וְאִישׁ בִּדְרָכָיו יֵלֵכוּן וְלֹא יְעַבְּטוּן אֹרְחוֹתָם — *Like mighty men they shall run; like men of war they shall ascend the wall, and each man in his ways shall go, and they will not impede their paths.*

The locusts will overwhelm your towns in a manner reminiscent of a conquering army. They will rush upon the city like mighty men, breaking through the resistance at its fortifications. They will then scale the walls, like experienced warriors who are well versed in the ways of battle. When taking the town, an army divides into separate battalions, each of which maps out a primary route of invasion as well as a secondary path to be employed if necessary. The locusts, too, will attack in similar waves, none of which

5 [With a noise] like the noise of chariots they shall leap
upon the mountaintops, like the sound of a flame of fire
consuming chaff; like a mighty people arrayed for bat-
tle. 6 From before it peoples shall tremble; all faces have
gathered blackness. 7 Like mighty men they shall run;
like men of war they shall ascend the wall, and each
man in his ways shall go, and they will not impede their
paths. 8 No man shall press his fellow, [each] man in his
path shall go, and on the sword they shall fall [but]
they will not be wounded. 9 They stride in the city; they
run on the walls; they ascend into the houses; through
the windows they come like a thief. 10 Before it the
land trembled, the heavens quaked; the sun and moon
have blackened and stars have withdrawn their shine.

will be impeded by defenders (*Malbim*).

The translation of יְעַבְּטוּן follows the view of *Targum Yonasan* and *Radak*. Others render *they will not make their ways crooked* [i.e., they will not be forced by the town's defenders to deviate from their intended routes] (*Rashi; Ibn Ezra*).

8. וְאִישׁ אָחִיו לֹא יִדְחָקוּן גֶּבֶר בִּמְסִלָּתוֹ יֵלֵכוּן וּבְעַד הַשֶּׁלַח יִפֹּלוּ לֹא יִבְצָעוּ — *No man shall press his fellow, [each] man in his path shall go, and on the sword they shall fall [but] they will not be wounded.*

Like the mighty warriors of a conquering army (*Ibn Ezra; Radak*), the invading locusts will have no need to crowd each other when attacking, as each one will be free to maintain his designated route (*Metzudos David*). Furthermore, being locusts, they will not be hampered by the normal means of defense, for even if they fall upon the sword their light weight will ensure that they are not harmed (*Radak*).

Targum Yonasan translates the latter half of the verse differently: *To the place where they are sent they are killed; they do not accept money.* They lay down their lives for the sake of the mission given to them by the Almighty and they cannot be bought off (*Rashi*).

According to *Abarbanel*, this verse describes the valor of the Babylonian soldiers, who were not deterred by the enemy's sword, and therefore often fell before it. Alternatively, when they were unarmed and accosted by an enemy soldier wielding a sword, they would overwhelm him and take away his weapon. Such an approach, however, is very dangerous, and oftentimes they were *cut down for the sword*, i.e., when trying to take the sword.

9. בָּעִיר יָשֹׁקּוּ בַּחוֹמָה יְרֻצוּן בַּבָּתִּים יַעֲלוּ בְּעַד הַחַלּוֹנִים יָבֹאוּ כַּגַּנָּב — *They stride in the city; they run on the walls; they ascend into the houses; through the windows they come like a thief.*

The locusts stride incessantly with their long legs, with barely a break to rest. Even houses which were built high up to resist enemy invasion are not safe from their attack. Nor are they deterred by doors and gates, for they enter like thieves through the windows of the houses (*Radak*).

This translation follows *Ibn Ezra* and *Radak*. *Targum Yonasan* explains the word יָשֹׁקּוּ to be derived from the word נֶשֶׁק, *they are armed.* Others maintain that it means noise — they raise a clamor in the streets of the city (*Rashi; Malbim*).

10. לְפָנָיו רָגְזָה אֶרֶץ רָעֲשׁוּ שָׁמָיִם שֶׁמֶשׁ וְיָרֵחַ קָדָרוּ וְכוֹכָבִים אָסְפוּ נָגְהָם — *Before it the land trembled, the heavens quaked; the*

יא וַיהוָה נָתַן קוֹלוֹ לִפְנֵי חֵילוֹ כִּי רַב מְאֹד מַחֲנֵהוּ
כִּי עָצוּם עֹשֵׂה דְבָרוֹ כִּי־גָדוֹל יוֹם־יְהוָה
יב וְנוֹרָא מְאֹד וּמִי יְכִילֶנּוּ: וְגַם־עַתָּה נְאֻם־
יְהוָה שֻׁבוּ עָדַי בְּכָל־לְבַבְכֶם וּבְצוֹם וּבִבְכִי
יג וּבְמִסְפֵּד: וְקִרְעוּ לְבַבְכֶם וְאַל־בִּגְדֵיכֶם
וְשׁוּבוּ אֶל־יְהוָה אֱלֹהֵיכֶם כִּי־חַנּוּן וְרַחוּם
הוּא אֶרֶךְ אַפַּיִם וְרַב־חֶסֶד וְנִחָם עַל־הָרָעָה:

sun and moon have blackened and stars have withdrawn their shine.

The coming plague will make life so bleak that it will seem as if all of creation has ceased to function (*Radak*). Alternatively, the inhabitants of the land will tremble [in fear] (*Ibn Ezra*), and even the heavens will quake and quiver from the punishment brought upon the Jewish nation (*Rashi*). In addition, the massive swarms will block the light of the stellar bodies, causing them to blacken and withdraw their shine (*Mahari Kara*).

Others explain this verse to refer to the astrological influence of the celestial bodies upon events in this world. These forces will be harnessed to bring punishment upon Israel (*Abarbanel*). Alternatively, their natural effect will be negated entirely, as the destruction will be completely the work of the Almighty (*Malbim*).

11. וַה׳ נָתַן קוֹלוֹ לִפְנֵי חֵילוֹ כִּי רַב מְאֹד מַחֲנֵהוּ כִּי עָצוּם עֹשֵׂה דְבָרוֹ כִּי־גָדוֹל יוֹם־ה׳ וְנוֹרָא מְאֹד וּמִי יְכִילֶנּוּ — *And HASHEM emitted His voice before His army that His camp is very numerous [and] he who performs His word is mighty, for the day of HASHEM is great and very fearsome, and who will be able to bear it?*

[Having once again vividly depicted the oncoming onslaught of locusts (vs. 4-10), the prophet reverts to words of exhortation, seeking to inspire the Jewish people to abandon their wicked ways and thereby avert — or at least minimize — this great calamity.]

The Almighty has announced through His prophets the coming of His army [of locusts] in order to arouse the populace to repent (*Rashi; Mahari Kara; Radak*). He has proclaimed (*Metzudos David*) that the hosts He has employed to carry out His will are both numerous and mighty, and no one will be capable of withstanding their onslaught (*Abarbanel*).

Alternatively, the army of locusts is a very formidable force, but it is surpassed by the might of those who will follow the will of the Almighty and repent. Such people succeed in driving the locusts from their midst (*Malbim*).

According to *Alshich*, this verse offers three reasons why the Almighty sends His prophets to forewarn the nation of the coming calamity. He does so out of compassion for the large numbers of His nation who will be affected, and also in honor of the truly righteous of His people, whose merit provides a measure of protection for the entire generation. In addition, the harshness of the punishment would be impossible for anyone to endure without previous warning.

12. וְגַם־עַתָּה נְאֻם־ה׳ שֻׁבוּ עָדַי בְּכָל־לְבַבְכֶם וּבְצוֹם וּבִבְכִי וּבְמִסְפֵּד — *And even now — declares HASHEM — return to Me with all your heart and with fasting and with weeping and with lamentation.*

Even now, proclaims the Almighty, after the swarms of locusts have descended upon you due to your wicked ways, catastrophe can still be averted and the locusts banished from your midst if only you will return to Me with all your hearts (*Radak*). Therefore, repent within your hearts by truly regretting your misdeeds, engage in fasting and other acts of penitence; lament and weep as you confess your sins to Me and plead for forgiveness (*Ibn Ezra*).

11 *And* H*ASHEM* *emitted His voice before His army that*
His camp is very numerous [and] he who performs
His word is mighty, for the day of H*ASHEM* *is great*
and very fearsome, and who will be able to bear it?
12 *And even now — declares* H*ASHEM* *— return to Me*
with all your heart and with fasting and with weep-
ing and with lamentation. 13 *And rend your hearts*
and not your garments, and return to H*ASHEM* *your*
God, for He is gracious and merciful, slow to anger
and of great kindness, and He relents of the evil.

The Sages comment to the previous verse as follows: *And* H*ASHEM* *emitted His voice* — on Rosh Hashanah, when the clarion call of the Almighty to repentance is sounded by the shofar, and on *the great day of Hashem* — Yom Kippur, when the final judgment is pronounced (*Pesikta d'Rav Kahana* 157b). Nevertheless — declares the prophet — even if you have not repented by that time, all is not lost. As long as you return to the Almighty with all your heart your repentance will be accepted *even now*, after Yom Kippur (*Alshich*).

13. וְקִרְעוּ לְבַבְכֶם וְאַל־בִּגְדֵיכֶם וְשׁוּבוּ אֶל־ה׳ אֱלֹהֵיכֶם כִּי־חַנּוּן וְרַחוּם הוּא אֶרֶךְ אַפַּיִם וְרַב־חֶסֶד וְנִחָם עַל־הָרָעָה — *And rend your hearts and not your garments, and return to* H*ASHEM* *your God, for He is gracious and merciful, slow to anger and of great kindness, and He relents of the evil.*

Do not attempt to appease Me with superficial acts of righteousness such as the rending of your garments to manifest your remorse (*Rashi*). Rather, you must rend your very hearts and totally eradicate the evil which has taken root within them (*Radak*). Tear away the coverings which have grown around them that prevent My admonition from having any effect (*Ibn Ezra*). Rebuke and shame yourselves within your hearts over your failure to properly fulfill your responsibilities to your Creator (*Chovos HaLevavos, Shaar HaTeshuvah*, ch. 5). And commit yourselves irrevocably to improve your deeds, girding yourselves with strength to bear the anguish you may endure when you abandon the evil ways to which you have become accustomed (ibid. ch. 3).

Alternatively, rend your hearts and repent so that you will not need to rend your garments in mourning for your children [who will die in the plague] (*Pesikta d'Rav Kahana* 161b; *Rashi*). If you seek inspiration to overcome the resistance which prevents you from changing your ways, contemplate the fact that if you do not do so, the wrath of the Almighty will bring death to your children. This will certainly motivate you to subdue your evil inclination (*Alshich*).

כִּי־חַנּוּן וְרַחוּם הוּא אֶרֶךְ אַפַּיִם וְרַב־חֶסֶד וְנִחָם עַל־הָרָעָה — *For He is gracious and merciful, slow to anger and of great kindness, and He relents of the evil.*

The Almighty is merciful and kindly and He will surely forgive you and retract His evil decree if only you will return to Him (*Radak*). If you suspect that you have faults which will prevent Hashem from accepting your repentance, know that *He is gracious and merciful* and will forgive even those who are not truly worthy. Although your actions are a cause not only for loss of blessing but for punishment as well, the Almighty is *slow to anger*, and will allow you time to change your ways. If the scales of justice remain equally balanced [even after your

יד מִי יוֹדֵעַ יָשׁוּב וְנִחָם וְהִשְׁאִיר אַחֲרָיו בְּרָכָה
טו מִנְחָה וָנֶסֶךְ לַיהוָה אֱלֹהֵיכֶם: תִּקְעוּ
טז שׁוֹפָר בְּצִיּוֹן קַדְּשׁוּ־צוֹם קִרְאוּ עֲצָרָה: אִסְפוּ־
עָם קַדְּשׁוּ קָהָל קִבְצוּ זְקֵנִים אִסְפוּ עוֹלָלִים
וְיֹנְקֵי שָׁדָיִם יֵצֵא חָתָן מֵחֶדְרוֹ וְכַלָּה מֵחֻפָּתָהּ:

repentance], do not despair; God is of *great kindness,* and in such circumstances, he tips the scales to the side of merit. Even if you have not yet responded to His call before the decree is rendered, the Almighty *relents of evil* even after it has been decreed, as long as there is sincere repentance (*Alshich*).

In the phrase אֶרֶךְ אַפַּיִם, *slow to anger,* the word אַפַּיִם is written in the plural form. The Sages explain that there are two distinct facets to the Almighty's patience. Firstly, He is forbearing of the righteous in that He exacts retribution for their misdeeds little by little in this world so as to enhance their reward in the World to Come. In addition, He bestows peace on evildoers in this world, in order to exact total retribution for their evil in the next (*Pesikta* loc. cit.).

14. מִי יוֹדֵעַ יָשׁוּב וְנִחָם וְהִשְׁאִיר אַחֲרָיו בְּרָכָה מִנְחָה וָנֶסֶךְ לַה׳ אֱלֹהֵיכֶם — *Whoever knows should repent and regret, and it will leave after it a blessing, [for] meal-offering and libation to HASHEM your God.*

Whoever among you knows that he has sinned, repent your evil ways and express remorse for your misdeeds. If you would only do so, the locusts would leave blessing in their wake — the blessing which the Almighty will bestow upon your crops due to your repentance (*Rashi;* cf. *Radak*). Even if only individuals among you repent, it will still evoke some measure of God's mercy and allow some crops to be left untouched (*Alshich; Malbim*). Thus, you will still be left with sufficient produce to bring meal-offerings and libations to the Almighty (*Radak*).

Ibn Ezra renders: *Who knows? Perhaps Hashem will rescind* [His decree]. Who knows to what extent your repentance can have effect? True, your misdeeds were great, and it is therefore impossible to predict the degree to which His mercy can be evoked (*Radak*). [Nevertheless, the possibility exists that your repentance will cause Him to actually rescind the decree.]

Abarbanel understands these last three verses as foretelling the reestablishment of the Jewish commonwealth after the destruction of the First Temple and the exile to Babylonia. *Even now, declares HASHEM* — even after having been exiled into Babylonia — *return to Me with all your heart* etc. Although your return to Jerusalem seems an impossible dream, *who knows* the ways of the Almighty? There are many ways open to Him, and even what seems to be impossible can be brought about, if only you will repent.

Since the second Commonwealth included only a portion of the Jewish nation, it is described by the prophet with the phrase *and He will leave after Him blessing,* i.e., the blessing foretold will affect only a remnant of the people. In addition, the Second Temple did not contain the Holy Ark nor the *Urim VeTumim*; the *Shechinah,* the Divine Presence, did not reside there; and there was no prophecy among the Jewish people during its existence. Therefore, the blessing of its establishment was limited to the fact that offerings and libations were once again brought before the Almighty.

15. As explained by the commentators, a major shift of focus takes place at this point in the chapter. Until now, Scripture has recorded the prophecies which preceded the plague of locusts and those which were uttered during their invasion. None of these succeeded in arousing the populace to repent, and the locusts

[14] *Whoever knows should repent and regret, and it will leave after it a blessing, [for] meal-offering and libation to* HASHEM *your God.* [15] *Sound a shofar in Zion; decree a fast; call an assembly.* [16] *Gather the people; prepare the congregation; assemble the elders, gather the children and sucklings; let the bridegroom go out from his chamber and the bride from her canopy.*

ravaged the land and consumed its crops. Now the destruction is finished and the land is barren, but the prophet's words of exhortation are not finished. Rather, he once again urges the people to repent, promising that if they do so the Almighty will banish the locusts which still sit upon the land (*Malbim*) and allow new crops to grow (*Alshich*).

תִּקְעוּ שׁוֹפָר בְּצִיּוֹן קַדְּשׁוּ־צוֹם קִרְאוּ עֲצָרָה — *Sound a shofar in Zion; decree a fast; call an assembly.*

Sound a shofar in Zion to arouse the populace to repentance; declare a fast and call an assembly (see 1:4, comm. ibid.) so that they will reflect upon their deeds and cleanse themselves of all evil (*Alshich*).

According to *Abarbanel* this verse begins Joel's prophecy concerning the destruction of the Second Temple and Commonwealth. There will yet be another enemy who will come upon you at a future date. At that time, you will sound a shofar to alert the populace to his presence and you will decree a fast and call an assembly for the purpose described in the following verse.

16. אִסְפוּ־עָם קַדְּשׁוּ קָהָל קִבְצוּ זְקֵנִים אִסְפוּ עוֹלָלִים וְיוֹנְקֵי שָׁדָיִם יֵצֵא חָתָן מֵחֶדְרוֹ וְכַלָּה מֵחֻפָּתָהּ — *Gather the people; prepare the congregation; assemble the elders, gather the children and sucklings; let the bridegroom go out from his chamber and the bride from her canopy.*

[Let every individual from every segment of society come join in this fast and assembly: old and young; men and women; even the innocent children and infants.] Although these have no sins for which to atone, they are nevertheless required to participate, for when they will cry out in hunger it will move the adults to humble their hearts before the Almighty and repent. In addition, the weeping of the children will itself evoke a merciful response from Hashem and He will hopefully eradicate the plague from your midst. Not even a bride and bridegroom, who should rightfully be involved in rejoicing with each other, are exempt from this gathering. Rather, they must come out from their wedding chamber and take part in the assembly (*Radak*).

The chamber of the groom and the canopy (חֻפָּה) of the bride both refer to the same wedding chamber. Alternatively: The חֻפָּה is not a canopy but the jewelry that adorns the bride's head on the day of her wedding, which she must leave behind when she goes to join the mourning (ibid.).

The Mishnah (*Taanis* 2:1) states that during a communal fast which is declared due to drought, the ark containing the Torah scroll is to be brought out in the town square for the prayers and that both the *Nassi* — the prince of the Jewish nation — and the chief justice of the court must participate, as described there. The Sages cite this verse as a source for that ruling. "*Let the bridegroom go out from his chamber* — this is the Ark [which is concealed in its chamber like a bridegroom (*Korban HaEdah*)] — *and the bride from her canopy* — this is the Torah [which is compared to a bride (ibid.)]. Alternatively: *Let the bridegroom go out from his chamber* — this is the *Nassi* [who resides in his house in splendor like a groom (ibid.)] — *and the bride from her canopy* — the chief of the court [for the Torah which he judges by is compared to a bride (ibid.)]" (*Yerushalmi, Taanis* ad loc.).

יז בֵּין הָאוּלָם֙ וְלַמִּזְבֵּ֔חַ יִבְכּוּ֙ הַכֹּ֣הֲנִ֔ים מְשָׁרְתֵ֖י
יהוה וְיֹֽאמְר֞וּ ח֧וּסָה יהוה עַל־עַמֶּ֗ךָ וְאַל־
תִּתֵּ֨ן נַחֲלָתְךָ֤ לְחֶרְפָּה֙ לִמְשָׁל־בָּ֣ם גּוֹיִ֔ם לָ֚מָּה
יח יֹאמְר֣וּ בָֽעַמִּ֔ים אַיֵּ֖ה אֱלֹהֵיהֶֽם׃ וַיְקַנֵּ֥א יהוה
יט לְאַרְצ֑וֹ וַיַּחְמֹ֖ל עַל־עַמּֽוֹ׃ וַיַּ֨עַן יהוה וַיֹּ֜אמֶר
לְעַמּ֗וֹ הִנְנִ֨י שֹׁלֵ֤חַ לָכֶם֙ אֶת־הַדָּגָן֙ וְהַתִּיר֣וֹשׁ
וְהַיִּצְהָ֔ר וּשְׂבַעְתֶּ֖ם אֹת֑וֹ וְלֹֽא־אֶתֵּ֨ן אֶתְכֶ֥ם ע֛וֹד
כ חֶרְפָּ֖ה בַּגּוֹיִֽם׃ וְֽאֶת־הַצְּפוֹנִ֞י אַרְחִ֣יק מֵעֲלֵיכֶ֗ם
וְהִדַּחְתִּיו֮ אֶל־אֶ֣רֶץ צִיָּ֣ה וּשְׁמָמָה֒ אֶת־פָּנָ֗יו
אֶל־הַיָּם֙ הַקַּדְמֹנִ֔י וְסֹפ֖וֹ אֶל־הַיָּ֣ם הָאַחֲר֑וֹן וְעָלָ֣ה
בָאְשׁ֗וֹ וְתַ֙עַל֙ צַחֲנָת֔וֹ כִּ֥י הִגְדִּ֖יל לַעֲשֽׂוֹת׃

17. בֵּין הָאוּלָם וְלַמִּזְבֵּחַ יִבְכּוּ הַכֹּהֲנִים מְשָׁרְתֵי ה׳ — *Between the antechamber and the altar let the Kohanim, the ministers of* H*ASHEM*, *weep.*

Let the *Kohanim* leave the Temple proper — where involvement in weeping would not be suitable (*Ibn Ezra*) — and enter the area of the courtyard which lies between the antechamber to the Temple and the altar upon which the sacrifices are offered. There, where they used to perform the Temple service before supplies ran out, let them weep and plead with the Almighty to have mercy on His nation (*Radak*).

וְיֹאמְרוּ חוּסָה ה׳ עַל־עַמֶּךָ וְאַל תִּתֵּן נַחֲלָתְךָ לְחֶרְפָּה לִמְשָׁל־בָּם גּוֹיִם לָמָּה יֹאמְרוּ בָעַמִּים אַיֵּה אֱלֹהֵיהֶם — *And let them say, "Have mercy,* H*ASHEM*, *upon Your nation, and do not place Your heritage in disgrace for peoples to rule over them. Why should they say among the nations, 'Where is their God?' "*

[Take pity, O God, upon the Children of Israel and relieve them of the suffering brought upon them by the plague.] Have mercy upon those who are Your heritage, who dwell in disgrace in other lands where they have been forced to wander in order to seek sustenance (*Radak;* cf. *Ibn Ezra*). Above all, defend the honor of Your Holy Name, which lies in desecration before all who witness Your people in misery and disgrace, and who thereby conclude that You are unable to see to their needs (*Alshich*).

This follows the translation of *Targum Yonasan. Rashi* translates לִמְשָׁל בָּם, *to make them an example,* rather than *to rule over them.* [Do not allow Your nation to be disgraced and humiliated by the fact that other nations use them as a symbol of misery and tragedy.]

18. וַיְקַנֵּא ה׳ לְאַרְצוֹ וַיַּחְמֹל עַל־עַמּוֹ — *And* H*ASHEM defended His land and He took pity on His people.*

If you will only repent, the Almighty will take action immediately[1] to serve the needs of His land and His nation (*Mahari Kara*). The cause of His land He will champion zealously and unstintingly, since it has done no wrong to warrant the devastation brought upon it by the invading swarms. To save His nation, however, He will have to employ the attribute of mercy, since their misfortune is the result of their own misdeeds (*Alshich*).

Rashi, quoting *Sotah* 3a, mentions an interpretation which translates וַיְקַנֵּא as

1. [The verse is written in the past tense to convey this immediacy] (cf. *Ibn Ezra*).

17 *Between the antechamber and the altar let the*
Kohanim, the ministers of HASHEM*, weep, and let*
them say, "Have mercy, HASHEM*, upon Your nation,*
and do not place Your heritage in disgrace for peoples
to rule over them. Why should they say among the
nations, 'Where is their God?' " 18 *And* HASHEM *de-*
fended His land and He took pity on His people. 19 *And*
HASHEM *replied and He said to His people: "Behold I*
am sending to you the grain, the wine, and the oil and
you shall be sated from it, and I will no longer place
you in disgrace among the nations. 20 *And the northern*
one I will distance from you and I will banish it to a
land arid and desolate; its face to the eastern sea and
its end to the western sea, and its stink will ascend
and its stench will go out, for it has achieved greatly.

"He warned." The Almighty acted on behalf of His land and nation, and He *warned* the locusts against causing further destruction.

19. וַיַּעַן ה׳ וַיֹּאמֶר לְעַמּוֹ הִנְנִי שֹׁלֵחַ לָכֶם אֶת־הַדָּגָן וְהַתִּירוֹשׁ וְהַיִּצְהָר וּשְׂבַעְתֶּם אֹתוֹ וְלֹא־אֶתֵּן אֶתְכֶם עוֹד חֶרְפָּה בַּגּוֹיִם — *And* HASHEM *replied and He said to His people: "Behold I am sending to you the grain, the wine, and the oil, and you shall be sated from it, and I will no longer place you in disgrace among the nations.*

[From this verse onward, the remainder of this chapter describes] God's positive response as communicated through His prophets to the supplications of His people (*Radak*).

[If the Jewish people will repent,] I will heed their plea and act — not only to uphold My honor, but for their sake and in their merit as well. Thus, I shall provide them miraculously with wine, grain, and oil despite the fact that the vines and olive trees have been destroyed (see 1:10,12). Furthermore, the blessing will come in great abundance rather than merely sufficing to save them from starvation. In addition, since I shall champion their honor, they will no longer be subject to humiliation at the hands of the gentiles (*Malbim*).

20. וְאֶת־הַצְּפוֹנִי אַרְחִיק מֵעֲלֵיכֶם וְהִדַּחְתִּיו אֶל־אֶרֶץ צִיָּה וּשְׁמָמָה אֶת־פָּנָיו אֶל־הַיָּם הַקַּדְמֹנִי וְסֹפוֹ אֶל־הַיָּם הָאַחֲרוֹן וְעָלָה בָאְשׁוֹ וְתַעַל צַחֲנָתוֹ כִּי הִגְדִּיל לַעֲשׂוֹת — *And the northern one I will distance from you and I will banish it to a land arid and desolate; its face to the eastern sea and its end to the western sea, and its stink will ascend and its stench will go out, for it has achieved greatly.*

I will distance from you the locusts (*Rashi; Radak*), which come from the north,[1] and I will drive them to an arid and desolate land. These great swarms, which extended from the Sea of Galilee and the Dead Sea on the eastern side of the Land of Israel all the way to the

1. According to *Daas Mikra*, it is known from experience that the locusts which invade the Land of Israel do not come from the north. However, he quotes an eyewitness to the locust swarm of 1915 as stating that the locusts constantly turned their faces northward. He thus suggests that perhaps for this reason they are referred to by the prophet as northern ones.

כא אַל־תִּירְאִי אֲדָמָה גִּילִי וּשְׂמָחִי כִּי־הִגְדִּיל יְהֹוָה
כב לַעֲשׂוֹת׃ אַל־תִּירְאוּ בַּהֲמוֹת שָׂדַי כִּי דָשְׁאוּ
נְאוֹת מִדְבָּר כִּי־עֵץ נָשָׂא פִרְיוֹ תְּאֵנָה וָגֶפֶן
כג נָתְנוּ חֵילָם׃ וּבְנֵי צִיּוֹן גִּילוּ וְשִׂמְחוּ בַּיהֹוָה
אֱלֹהֵיכֶם כִּי־נָתַן לָכֶם אֶת־הַמּוֹרֶה לִצְדָקָה
וַיּוֹרֶד לָכֶם גֶּשֶׁם מוֹרֶה וּמַלְקוֹשׁ בָּרִאשׁוֹן׃

Mediterranean to the west, shall all die of thirst, and their stench will invade the nostrils of all passers-by (*Radak*).

וְעָלָה בָאְשׁוֹ וְתַעַל צַחֲנָתוֹ — *And its stink will ascend and its stench will go out.*

The prophet repeats the description of the smell caused by the dead locusts [for emphasis] (*Radak*). Alternatively, the term בָּאְשׁוֹ applies to the smell caused by something which decays — in this case the bodies of the locusts. צַחֲנָה is the stench of something which has a foul odor from its inception. In addition to the stink of the locusts themselves, the air will be fouled from the stench of their seed, which they will leave in their wake (*Malbim*).

כִּי הִגְדִּיל לַעֲשׂוֹת — *For it has achieved greatly.*

The invader has fulfilled its function of sowing great destruction throughout the land (*Radak*) and it has also achieved its ultimate purpose of arousing the people to repent (*Malbim*). [It is therefore time that it be banished from the midst of the Jewish nation and destroyed.]

The Sages (*Succah* 52a) interpret this verse to refer to the times of the Messiah: *I will distance the hidden one* (הַצְּפוֹנִי) *from you* — this is the *yetzer hara*, the evil inclination, which is hidden within the heart of a person. *I will banish him etc.* — when the Messiah comes, he will be banished to a place void of inhabitants and people will no longer be subject to his influence. *His face to the eastern* (קַדְמֹנִי) *sea and his end to the western* (אַחֲרוֹן) *sea* — he set his eyes upon the First (קַדְמֹנִי) Temple and caused its destruction as well as the death of the Torah scholars, and then did likewise to the Second (אַחֲרוֹן) Temple and its scholars. [The Temples are depicted as seas because all of the people would gather there (to celebrate the festivals) just as all the rivers stream to the sea (*Rashi* ad loc.).] *His stench has ascended* — [he has caused great calamity] by attaching himself to the Jewish people and ignoring the other nations. *For he has achieved greatly* — [i.e., great evil, for he reached out his arm to great people (*Rashi*)]. Said Abaye: And to the Torah scholars more than to anyone [i.e., when seeking to seduce Torah scholars the evil inclination intensifies his efforts and temptations more than in any other of his endeavors].

Targum Yonasan interprets this verse as referring to the invasion of the Holy Land by the Assyrian empire, which lay to the north of *Eretz Yisrael*. They divided their troops for the invasion, with some approaching from the east and some from the west (*Rashi;* cf. *Abarbanel*).

21. אַל־תִּירְאִי אֲדָמָה גִּילִי וּשְׂמָחִי כִּי־הִגְדִּיל ה׳ לַעֲשׂוֹת — *Fear not, O land; exult and be happy, for* HASHEM *has achieved greatly.*

You inhabitants of the Land of Israel (*Radak*), who previously quaked from the fearsome day of the Almighty's wrath (*Ibn Ezra* from v. 11) — once you have repented you will no longer have anything to fear (*Rashi*). In place of assembling for prayer and mourning, you will now indulge in celebration and exultation. For the great achievements of the locusts in destroying the crops will be replaced by the great achievements of the Almighty Who will restore them (*Radak*).

The word גִּיל applies to the exultation evoked by an unexpected source of rejoicing; שִׂמְחָה refers to happiness for a continuous situation (*Malbim*).

22. אַל־תִּירְאוּ בַּהֲמוֹת שָׂדַי כִּי דָשְׁאוּ נְאוֹת מִדְבָּר כִּי־עֵץ נָשָׂא פִרְיוֹ תְּאֵנָה וָגֶפֶן נָתְנוּ חֵילָם

[21] *Fear not, O land; exult and be happy, for* HASHEM
has achieved greatly. [22] *Fear not, beasts of the field, for*
the dwelling places of the desert have become covered
with grass, for the tree has borne its fruit; the fig
tree and the vine have given forth their potency. [23] *And*
children of Zion, exult and be happy with HASHEM
your God, for He has given you a teacher for righteous-
ness, and He has brought down for you the rain —
the early rain and the late rain in the first [month].

— *Fear not, beasts of the field, for the dwelling places of the desert have become covered with grass, for the tree has borne its fruit; the fig tree and the vine have given forth their potency.*

The beasts of the field, who previously cried out in hunger (1:20), will now have nothing to fear, for the dwelling places of the wilderness will abound with vegetation instead of their being consumed by fire (1:19), and the trees will produce their fruits instead of their being scorched by flame (*Ibn Ezra; Radak*).

According to *Abarbanel,* this verse is directed to the nations of the world — depicted as beasts of the field — who were also subjugated by the four kingdoms that conquered the Jewish nation. After having foretold how the Land of Israel will flourish in the care of the Almighty during the times of the Messiah, the prophet goes on to reassure the rest of the nations that peace will prevail throughout the world as well, and no nation will need fear the invasion of another.

23. וּבְנֵי צִיּוֹן גִּילוּ וְשִׂמְחוּ בַּה׳ אֱלֹהֵיכֶם כִּי־נָתַן לָכֶם אֶת־הַמּוֹרֶה לִצְדָקָה וַיּוֹרֶד לָכֶם גֶּשֶׁם מוֹרֶה וּמַלְקוֹשׁ בָּרִאשׁוֹן — *And children of Zion, exult and be happy with* HASHEM *your God, for He has given you a teacher for righteousness, and He has brought down for you the rain — the early rain and the late rain in the first [month].*

[Rejoice, children of Zion, in your closeness with the Almighty, a closeness engendered by] the prophets He has sent you, who teach you the ways of righteousness (*Ibn Ezra;* cf. *Rashi*).

Others explain: Rejoice over the fact that the Almighty sent swarms of locusts which served as your teachers by compelling you to reexamine your deeds and repent. Focus your joy upon the closeness to God which you thereby achieved (*Alshich; Malbim*).

Another rendition is: *for He has given you the early rain in charity* — i.e., he forgave your iniquities and provided you with rain in its proper time (*Radak*).

וַיּוֹרֶד לָכֶם גֶּשֶׁם מוֹרֶה וּמַלְקוֹשׁ בָּרִאשׁוֹן — *And He has brought down for you the rain — the early rain and the late rain in the first [month].*

[Rejoice in the miraculous salvation wrought by the Almighty, Who sent down two showers of rain in the month of Nissan — rather than one in Cheshvan and one in Nissan as usual — and they nevertheless bore fruit.]

Normally, if no rain has fallen in Israel by the month of Nissan, all supplication for rain ceases, because from that point on it is too late for the water to be of any benefit (*Taanis* 1:7). In the time of Joel, however, the first rain of the year did not arrive until the first of Nissan, after which the prophet instructed the people to go out and plant their crops. They planted on the second, third, and fourth of the month, and a second shower fell on the fifth. Miraculously, the land bore fruit in this short time, and the Omer sacrifice — which is usually the product of six months of growth — was brought in the Temple on the fifteenth of Nissan (*Radak* citing *Taanis* 5a).

כד וּמָלְאוּ הַגֳּרָנוֹת בָּר וְהֵשִׁיקוּ הַיְקָבִים תִּירוֹשׁ
כה וְיִצְהָר: וְשִׁלַּמְתִּי לָכֶם אֶת־הַשָּׁנִים אֲשֶׁר אָכַל
הָאַרְבֶּה הַיֶּלֶק וְהֶחָסִיל וְהַגָּזָם חֵילִי הַגָּדוֹל
כו אֲשֶׁר שִׁלַּחְתִּי בָּכֶם: וַאֲכַלְתֶּם אָכוֹל וְשָׂבוֹעַ
וְהִלַּלְתֶּם אֶת־שֵׁם יהוה אֱלֹהֵיכֶם אֲשֶׁר־
עָשָׂה עִמָּכֶם לְהַפְלִיא וְלֹא־יֵבֹשׁוּ עַמִּי
כז לְעוֹלָם: וִידַעְתֶּם כִּי בְקֶרֶב יִשְׂרָאֵל אָנִי וַאֲנִי
יהוה אֱלֹהֵיכֶם וְאֵין עוֹד וְלֹא־יֵבֹשׁוּ עַמִּי

24. וּמָלְאוּ הַגֳּרָנוֹת בָּר וְהֵשִׁיקוּ הַיְקָבִים תִּירוֹשׁ וְיִצְהָר — *And the granaries shall be filled with grain, and the pits shall overflow with wine and oil.*

Due to My blessings, says the Almighty, the silos will miraculously abound with grain (*Malbim*) and the pits containing wine and oil will be so full that their produce will flow over the top (*Radak*). Even if there is insufficient produce to fill the silos and pits to capacity, it will continue to increase while in storage until all the granaries are full and the wine and oil pits are overflowing (see *Bava Metzia* 42a). Furthermore, only בָּר, *pure grain,* will develop this way, with none of the usual chaff found within it (*Alshich; Malbim*).

Rashi renders וְהֵשִׁיקוּ, *they will roar:* So much wine and oil will flow from the presses into the pits that it will cause great clamor.

25. וְשִׁלַּמְתִּי לָכֶם אֶת־הַשָּׁנִים אֲשֶׁר אָכַל הָאַרְבֶּה הַיֶּלֶק וְהֶחָסִיל וְהַגָּזָם חֵילִי הַגָּדוֹל אֲשֶׁר שִׁלַּחְתִּי בָּכֶם — *And I will repay you for the years that the arbeh, yelek, chasil, and gazam consumed — My great army that I sent among you.*

Once you have earned My mercy by repenting your sins, not only shall I prevent the locusts from causing further destruction, but I will repay you as well for all their previous damage. Because the *gazam* came first, before there were any stirrings of repentance whatsoever, their consumption was the most fully deserved of the four. Therefore that will be the last to be repaid — only after your penitence is completed (*Malbim*).

The Sages cite this verse as an example of the practice of the prophets — learned from Moses — to follow harsh words of rebuke with reassurances of comfort and God's mercy (*Sifri to Vzos Habrachah* 33:1).

26. וַאֲכַלְתֶּם אָכוֹל וְשָׂבוֹעַ וְהִלַּלְתֶּם אֶת־שֵׁם ה׳ אֱלֹהֵיכֶם אֲשֶׁר־עָשָׂה עִמָּכֶם לְהַפְלִיא וְלֹא־יֵבֹשׁוּ עַמִּי לְעוֹלָם — *And you shall eat — eating and being satisfied — and you shall praise the Name of* HASHEM *your God Who has acted with you wondrously, and My people shall not be ashamed evermore.*

You will eat to satiation, with no fear of hunger whatsoever. Not only will there be an abundance of provisions, but the crops will also be blessed within your bodies, and you will thus be satiated by small quantities of food (*Alshich; Malbim*).

וְהִלַּלְתֶּם אֶת־שֵׁם ה׳ אֱלֹהֵיכֶם אֲשֶׁר־עָשָׂה עִמָּכֶם לְהַפְלִיא — *And you shall praise the Name of* HASHEM *your God Who has acted with you wondrously.*

You will praise the Almighty for the wondrous nature of His beneficence, for He will replace the product of four years of famine in one year, and provide the entire crop miraculously in the month of Nissan (*Radak*). You will exalt Him, as well, for the plague of locusts itself, for it brought you to repent and to thereby achieve the level of sanctity which earned you these miraculous benefits (*Alshich*).

וְלֹא־יֵבֹשׁוּ עַמִּי לְעוֹלָם — *And My people shall not be ashamed evermore.*

Never again shall the Jewish people

24 *And the granaries shall be filled with grain, and the
pits shall overflow with wine and oil.* 25 *And I will repay
you for the years that the arbeh, yelek, chasil, and gazam
consumed — My great army that I sent among you.*
26 *And you shall eat — eating and being satisfied — and
you shall praise the Name of HASHEM your God Who has
acted with you wondrously; and My people shall not be
ashamed evermore.* 27 *And you shall know that I am in
the midst of Israel, and I am HASHEM and there is no
other; and My people shall not be ashamed evermore.*

suffer humiliation among the family of nations due to famine (*Radak;* see v. 17). No longer will you need be ashamed of the misdeeds which caused this catastrophe, for your repentance out of love of God will completely eradicate them (*Malbim*).[1]

27. וִידַעְתֶּם כִּי בְקֶרֶב יִשְׂרָאֵל אָנִי וַאֲנִי ה׳ אֱלֹהֵיכֶם וְאֵין עוֹד וְלֹא־יֵבֹשׁוּ עַמִּי לְעוֹלָם — *And you shall know that I am in the midst of Israel, and I am HASHEM and there is no other; and My nation shall not be ashamed evermore.*

You will recognize clearly that I alone am your God, and I reside in your midst hearkening to your cries (*Radak*), for without My glory in your midst none of the wonders described above would have been possible (*Ibn Ezra*). Accordingly, as stated in the previous verse, you will never again be ashamed, since you will now be certain of My presence among you (*Abarbanel*).

Alternatively: You will know that My presence is actually in your midst, i.e., that the body of a Jew is not a barrier to the Divine Presence as long as he achieves his potential for sanctity. Thus, your bodies will be satiated miraculously from minute amounts of food, due to My presence within them. [You will also comprehend in retrospect that the punishment you endured was in reality a source of great benefit,] and you will thereby recognize that I am both Hashem — the dispenser of mercy — and *Elokim* — the dispenser of justice, and there is no other source for either of these Divine attributes. Finally, the quality of life you will enjoy at this time will allow you a glimpse of the lofty level of existence which will be attained with the ultimate redemption, and you will thereby perceive with great clarity that once the Messianic era arrives you will never again be ashamed (*Alshich*).

Others contend that this final phrase is more than merely a reiteration of the parallel statement in the previous verse: [Before, the prophet was discussing the immediate future,] and promised the people that they would no longer be ashamed of their evil deeds (*Malbim*). Now he is depicting the situation in the Messianic era (*Mahari Kara*). He

1. [*Malbim's* explanation avoids a serious question that *Radak's* approach raises: Since these events took place during the era of the First Temple, and were thus followed by both exiles and all of the suffering and degradation that they wrought, how can the prophet proclaim that they will never again undergo similar humiliation? According to *Malbim*, however, he is discussing the specific humiliation caused by those particular sins. Concerning *Radak's* interpretation, we can only theorize. Perhaps the humiliation of a nation in exile is not comparable to one that suffers famine while in its own land. In the former case, the situation is viewed as temporary, for ultimately, the Jewish people will be redeemed and restored to their previous status. While in its homeland, however, a nation's situation defines its status, and destitution and hunger in these circumstances are degrading to the entire nation.]

א לְעוֹלָם׃ וְהָיָה אַחֲרֵי־כֵן אֶשְׁפּוֹךְ אֶת־
רוּחִי עַל־כָּל־בָּשָׂר וְנִבְּאוּ בְּנֵיכֶם וּבְנוֹתֵיכֶם
זִקְנֵיכֶם חֲלֹמוֹת יַחֲלֹמוּן בַּחוּרֵיכֶם חֶזְיֹנוֹת יִרְאוּ׃
ב וְגַם עַל־הָעֲבָדִים וְעַל־הַשְּׁפָחוֹת בַּיָּמִים הָהֵמָּה
ג אֶשְׁפּוֹךְ אֶת־רוּחִי׃ וְנָתַתִּי מוֹפְתִים בַּשָּׁמַיִם וּבָאָרֶץ
ד דָּם וָאֵשׁ וְתִימֲרוֹת עָשָׁן׃ הַשֶּׁמֶשׁ יֵהָפֵךְ לְחֹשֶׁךְ
וְהַיָּרֵחַ לְדָם לִפְנֵי בּוֹא יוֹם יהוה הַגָּדוֹל וְהַנּוֹרָא׃

guarantees that in the end of days they will enjoy the full measure of Divine Presence in their midst and will thus not be disgraced by even its partial absence. Accordingly, those things which were missing in the Second Temple due to the absence of His presence will be replaced with the coming of the Messiah (*Malbim*).

III

This chapter begins an entirely new phase of the prophecy of Joel, in which he foretells of the Messianic era that will take place in the end of days (*Rashi*). In the final verse of the previous chapter, he described how the Jewish people will recognize the presence of the Almighty in their midst. He now goes on to depict how that recognition will increase in the end of days to a level which will preclude further sin (*Radak;* see below). [In the first three verses he speaks in the name of Hashem, referring to the Almighty in the first person.]

1. וְהָיָה אַחֲרֵי־כֵן — *And it will be after this.*

The following shall occur in the end of days [in the times of the Messiah] (*Rashi; Radak;* et al.).

Others contend that the Messianic era is always alluded to in prophecy specifically as the "end of days." The phrase *it will be after this* denotes a period of time significantly prior to the final redemption. In this case, it seems to refer to the times of Jehoshafat, during which prophets and prophecy abounded among the Jewish people (*Ibn Ezra,* citing *R' Moshe HaKohen*).

אֶשְׁפּוֹךְ אֶת־רוּחִי עַל־כָּל־בָּשָׂר — *I will pour out My spirit upon all flesh.*

I will bestow upon all flesh a spirit of wisdom and understanding as well as fear of God (*Radak*) along with all of the spiritual qualities which rightfully accompany these attributes (*Malbim*).

According to some, this refers only to members of the Jewish nation (*Radak*). Others contend that all of mankind will achieve this clear recognition of the Almighty, but only the Children of Israel will reach the level of prophecy, as described below (*Abarbanel*). *Rashi* presents a third view: *All flesh* denotes all who have within them hearts of flesh that are receptive to the presence of the Almighty.

וְנִבְּאוּ בְּנֵיכֶם וּבְנוֹתֵיכֶם זִקְנֵיכֶם חֲלֹמוֹת יַחֲלֹמוּן בַּחוּרֵיכֶם חֶזְיֹנוֹת יִרְאוּ — *And your sons and daughters shall prophesy; your elders shall dream dreams, your young men shall see visions.*

When My spirit shall pervade the consciousness of mankind, the gift of prophecy will descend upon all who are qualified to receive it, each according to his level (*Radak*).[1] Your sons and daughters who will be born in that era will be so infused with the glory of My presence that they will attain the highest levels of prophecy — called נְבוּאָה. Your elders, on the other hand, who will have reached

1. As explained by *Rambam* (*Moreh Nevuchim* 2:36), not every person is capable of experiencing prophecy. Even with the proper training and preparation, it is only attainable by those who were granted the natural propensity for its achievement (*Radak*).

[1] "*And it will be after this, I will pour out My spirit*
upon all flesh, and your sons and daughters
shall prophesy; your elders shall dreams, your young
men shall see visions. [2] *Also upon the slaves and upon*
the maidservants in those days I will pour out My
spirit. [3] *And I shall set portents in the heavens and on*
earth; blood, fire, and pillars of smoke. [4] *The sun shall*
turn to darkness and the moon to blood before the
coming of the day of HASHEM Who is great and awesome.

maturity prior to the redemption, will be limited to the experience of prophetic dreams. Above the level of such dreams but still below full prophecy is the intermediate degree of prophetic visions. These will be achieved by your youth, who will be born before the redemption but will reach adulthood during the Messianic era (*Malbim*).

2. וְגַם עַל־הָעֲבָדִים וְעַל־הַשְּׁפָחוֹת בַּיָּמִים הָהֵמָּה אֶשְׁפּוֹךְ אֶת־רוּחִי — *Also upon the slaves and upon the maidservants in those days I will pour out My spirit.*

Even those gentile servants and maidservants who will serve the Jewish people in the Land of Israel will be elevated by the spirit of holiness which I will bestow upon the land. However, only the Jewish people themselves will achieve the level of prophecy (*Radak; Malbim*).

3. The prophet now goes on to describe the signs that the Almighty will place in heaven and earth to herald the destruction of the enemies of Israel. This will occur during the wars of Gog and Magog, a series of cataclysmic battles that will be fought prior to the final redemption (see *Ezekiel* chs. 38, 39, *Zechariah* ch. 14).

[Since these battles will precede the redemption, it seems that the verse is somewhat of a flashback, i.e., the full relationship with the Almighty described above will come after the following great events. Alternatively, the lofty levels described in the previous verses will be attained in the beginning of the Messianic era, with the first steps of redemption — even before the great wars of Gog and Magog and the total redemption that will follow them.]

וְנָתַתִּי מוֹפְתִים בַּשָּׁמַיִם וּבָאָרֶץ — *And I shall set portents in the heavens and on earth.*

At that time, I will produce omens in the heaven and on earth to foretell of future events (*Radak*).

דָּם וָאֵשׁ וְתִימְרוֹת עָשָׁן — *Blood, fire, and pillars of smoke.*

A sign of blood will appear on earth to symbolize the great bloodshed which will occur, and lightning from heaven will strike the land, causing fires, and, with them, pillars of smoke.[1] These will portend the impending destruction of those nations who join with Gog and Magog in attacking Jerusalem (*Radak*).

Others interpret this verse as describing how the Almighty will provide a clear sign of His presence through the wondrous manner in which He will destroy the enemies of Israel. The sword which smites them here on earth will cause their blood to flow, while fire will descend upon them from heaven and consume them in a pillar of smoke (*Abarbanel; Malbim*).

4. הַשֶּׁמֶשׁ יֵהָפֵךְ לְחֹשֶׁךְ וְהַיָּרֵחַ לְדָם לִפְנֵי בּוֹא יוֹם ה׳ הַגָּדוֹל וְהַנּוֹרָא — *The sun shall turn to darkness and the moon to blood before the coming of the day of HASHEM Who is great and awesome.*

Prior to the advent of the day of God's judgment (*Malbim*), the sun will cease to

1. The word תִּימְרוֹת is derived from תָּמָר, *a palm tree,* as the smoke will rise in pillars which are high and straight like a palm tree (ibid.).

ג/ה ה וְהָיָה כֹּל אֲשֶׁר־יִקְרָא בְּשֵׁם יהוה יִמָּלֵט °כִּי בְּהַר־
צִיּוֹן וּבִירוּשָׁלַםִ תִּהְיֶה פְלֵיטָה כַּאֲשֶׁר אָמַר יהוה
ד/א א וּבַשְּׂרִידִים אֲשֶׁר יהוה קֹרֵא: כִּי הִנֵּה בַּיָּמִים הָהֵמָּה
אָשִׁיב ק׳ וּבָעֵת הַהִיא אֲשֶׁר °אשוב אֶת־שְׁבוּת יְהוּדָה

give forth its light and the moon will turn blood-red,[1] thereby humiliating all those who worship these celestial bodies (*Rashi; Mahari Kara*). Alternatively: These afflictions will portend the cataclysmic events which shall befall the nations of Gog and Magog and their allies when they attack the Jewish nation in the end of days (*Ibn Ezra; Radak*).

Others interpret this verse allegorically: The smiting of the sun and moon described will not actually occur, they merely symbolize impending disasters. According to some, they represent the punishment which will befall the enemies of Israel (*Rambam, Moreh Nevuchim* 2:29 as cited by *Radak; Alshich*) — alluding specifically either to the army of Sennacherib or to the enemies in the times of the Messiah (*Rambam* ad loc.). Others understand them to depict the destruction which will occur to the Jewish people themselves prior to their final redemption (*Radak*).

Alshich interprets this to be a continuation of the previous verse: Blood, fire, and pillars of smoke are the omens which will appear on earth, whereas the blackening of the sun and the reddening of the moon are those which will be seen in the heavens. These wonders will foretell the destruction of the historic enemies of the Jewish people. Blood is the sign of Edom, the nation that lives by the sword. Fire symbolizes the Babylonians, who decreed upon those who served Hashem that they be thrown into a furnace of fire. The Persians and the Greeks, who oppressed the Jews to a lesser degree than the first two — as they did not destroy the Temple [nor send the Jewish people into exile] — are symbolized as one unit. Their retribution has actually already begun — the Greeks in the times of the Maccabees, and the Persians in the times of Mordechai and Esther. Their final destruction, however, as depicted by a pillar of smoke, will take place in the end of days.

Beyond any of these nations, the ultimate nemesis of the Jewish people is Amalek. Their destruction is symbolized by wonders in Heaven. Yaakov, as represented by the sun, will cover Amalek with darkness; Rachel, as depicted by the moon, will spill their blood — as stated by the Sages (*Pesikta Rabbasi* ch. 13), that Amalek will fall into the hands of the descendants of Rachel.

5. וְהָיָה כֹּל אֲשֶׁר יִקְרָא־בְּשֵׁם ה׳ יִמָּלֵט — *And it shall be [that] all who call in the Name of HASHEM shall escape.*

All those who turn to the Almighty in sincerity will be saved from the great destruction described above (*Radak*). Some maintain that this will include the entire Jewish nation, who will return to God and thus be spared (see *Abarbanel*). Others contend that only those individuals who will be outstanding in their sanctity and fear of God will escape these cataclysmic events (*Radak*).

The Sages interpret this phrase homiletically to mean *all who will be called by the Name of Hashem.* The Midrash explains: Is it possible for a human being to be called by God's Name? However, the Omnipresent is called merciful, as it is stated: *Merciful and benevolent is HASHEM* (*Psalms* 145:8); you, too, must bestow favors even if undeserved. The Omnipresent is called righteous, as it is stated: *HASHEM is righteous; He loves righteousness* (ibid. 11:7); you, too, must

1. When the moon is fully eclipsed it is blackened; when it is only partially covered it appears red like blood (*Radak*).

3/5 [5] *And it shall be [that] all who call in the Name of*
HASHEM shall escape, for on the mountain of Zion and in
Jerusalem there shall be refuge as HASHEM said, and
among the survivors whom HASHEM calls.

4/1 [1] *"For behold in those days and at that time, when*
I will bring back the captivity of Judah and

be righteous. The Omnipresent is called a *chassid* [one who is righteous beyond the letter of the law], as it is stated: *for I am a chassid* (*Jeremiah* 3:12); you, too, must be a *chassid*. Therefore, it says: *All who are* **called** *in the Name of HASHEM will escape* (*Yalkut*).

כִּי בְּהַר־צִיּוֹן וּבִירוּשָׁלַם תִּהְיֶה פְלֵיטָה — *For on the mountain of Zion and in Jerusalem there shall be refuge.*

The salvation of the Jewish people will occur only if they return to the Holy Land and to Jerusalem, for there alone refuge will be granted (*Abarbanel;* see below).

כַּאֲשֶׁר אָמַר ה׳ — *As HASHEM said.*

This special treatment of the Jewish people is already foretold in the Torah (*Deuteronomy* 28:10), where it is stated: *And all the nations of the land will see that the Name of HASHEM is called upon you* (*Rashi;* cf. *Abarbanel*).

וּבַשְּׂרִידִים אֲשֶׁר ה׳ קֹרֵא — *And among the survivors whom HASHEM calls.*

Those individuals of special merit, whom the Almighty will invite to serve Him and reap the fruit of His blessing (*Rashi,* cf. *Ibn Ezra, Radak*) [shall be saved from this great destruction], as stated above (*Ibn Ezra*).

Another view perceives this phrase as elaborating upon the terms of the salvation described above. According to some, it states that even in Jerusalem not everyone will be spared, only those who will be singled out by the Almighty due to their unique merit (*Abarbanel*). Others contend that Jerusalem will be a haven from the calamities described for all who dwell there, even for those with no singular merit, as described in the previous phrase. In addition, the truly righteous shall be saved by the Almighty wherever they may be found, even if they are in the very midst of the destruction (*Alshich; Malbim*).

IV

In this chapter, the prophet describes how the enemies of Israel will amass to attack Jerusalem, in the end of days, and will be annihilated. This is part of the wars of Gog and Magog, which are also foretold by the prophets Ezekiel (chs. 32,38,39) and Zechariah (ch. 14).

Ibn Ezra, however, suggests that as in the previous chapter, this prophecy is discussing not the Messianic era, but rather an occurrence which took place during the reign of Jehoshafat, king of Judah. At that time the fear of the Almighty fell upon the nations surrounding Jerusalem and they came to offer tribute to Jehoshafat (*Ibn Ezra,* citing *R' Moshe HaKohen*; see *II Chronicles* 17:10ff; cf. comm. to 3:1).

1. כִּי הִנֵּה בַּיָּמִים הָהֵמָּה וּבָעֵת הַהִיא אֲשֶׁר אָשִׁיב אֶת שְׁבוּת יְהוּדָה וִירוּשָׁלָםִ — *For behold in those days and at that time, when I will bring back the captivity of Judah and Jerusalem.*

[That which is described in the following verses] will take place in the times of the Messiah, when I will redeem the captives of the Jewish nation and allow them to live in peace forever after (*Radak*).

ב וִירוּשָׁלָֽםִ׃ וְקִבַּצְתִּי֙ אֶת־כָּל־הַגּוֹיִ֔ם וְה֣וֹרַדְתִּ֔ים
אֶל־עֵ֖מֶק יְהוֹשָׁפָ֑ט וְנִשְׁפַּטְתִּ֨י עִמָּ֜ם שָׁ֗ם עַל־עַמִּ֨י
וְנַחֲלָתִ֤י יִשְׂרָאֵל֙ אֲשֶׁ֣ר פִּזְּר֣וּ בַגּוֹיִ֔ם וְאֶת־אַרְצִ֖י
ג חִלֵּֽקוּ׃ וְאֶל־עַמִּ֖י יַדּ֣וּ גוֹרָ֑ל וַיִּתְּנ֤וּ הַיֶּ֙לֶד֙ בַּזּוֹנָ֔ה
ד וְהַיַּלְדָּ֥ה מָכְר֖וּ בַיַּ֥יִן וַיִּשְׁתּֽוּ׃ וְגַ֨ם מָה־אַתֶּ֥ם לִי֙ צֹ֣ר
וְצִיד֔וֹן וְכֹ֖ל גְּלִיל֣וֹת פְּלָ֑שֶׁת הַגְּמ֗וּל אַתֶּם֙ מְשַׁלְּמִ֣ים

Although all of the twelve tribes of Israel will be redeemed at that time, the prophet singles out that of Judah, the tribe of the Messiah, and Jerusalem, which will be the site of the restored monarchy of Israel as well as of the battles described below (*Radak*). Alternatively: Since all of his other prophecies concern Judah and Jerusalem, the prophet specifies them even when discussing that which applies to the entire Jewish nation (*Abarbanel; Metzudos David*).

The word אָשִׁיב has a dual connotation. It is written with a *"vav,"* which translates *I will make rest*. However, it is read with [a *"chirik,"* as if it were spelled with] a *"yud,"* which means *I will bring back* (*Radak*).

2. וְקִבַּצְתִּי אֶת־כָּל־הַגּוֹיִם — *And I will gather all of the nations.*

At that time I will incite all of the nations to join with Gog and Magog and ascend against Jerusalem, as described by the prophet Ezekiel (39:2) (*Radak*).

וְהוֹרַדְתִּים אֶל־עֵמֶק יְהוֹשָׁפָט — *And I will bring them down to the Valley of Judgment.*

I shall bring all of these nations together to a valley in Jerusalem (*Radak*) where they will stand for judgment (*Targum; Rashi*). עֵמֶק יְהוֹשָׁפָט can be understood as the Valley of Jehoshafat, referring to the king of Judah by that name, who apparently built some edifice or performed some deed within the valley for which it was called in his name (*Radak*).

Ibn Ezra [in accordance with the view of *R' Moshe HaKohen* cited above] explains this to refer to the Valley of Berachah, where the armies of Jehoshafat battled the combined might of Ammon, Moab, and Seir. [The Almighty commanded the Jewish army to refrain from battle, and He incited the attacking armies against each other, thereby causing their decimation (*II Chronicles* 20).]

וְנִשְׁפַּטְתִּי עִמָּם שָׁם עַל־עַמִּי וְנַחֲלָתִי יִשְׂרָאֵל — *And I will indict them there concerning Israel, My people and My heritage.*

I will bring them to judgment and castigate them for the evil they perpetrated against the Jewish people, when they were exiled among them (*Radak*). Alternatively: I will punish them for their evil (*Targum*), and that punishment will serve them as a reprimand for their deeds (*Metzudos David*).

אֲשֶׁר פִּזְּרוּ בַגּוֹיִם וְאֶת־אַרְצִי חִלֵּקוּ — *Which they dispersed among the peoples, and My land they divided up.*

Particularly, I shall exact retribution from the nation of Rome, who, under the leadership of Titus, conquered the Land of Israel and scattered its inhabitants among the nations (*Radak*).

Alternatively, this phrase responds to the likely defense of these nations: that they were merely carrying out God's will in punishing His people for their misdeeds. To this point the prophet replies that they abused that mission in three ways. First, although the exile was Divinely ordained, these nations allowed the Jews no rest even in exile, causing them so much suffering that they continued to be dispersed to all ends of the world. In addition, the nations assumed ownership over the Land of Israel as if it were allocated to them. Finally, they enslaved the Jewish people themselves, as described in the following verse (*Malbim*).

Some commentators interpret the war of Gog and Magog to refer to a war which will be fought between the armies of Edom — i.e.,

Jerusalem, [2] *And I will gather all of the nations and I*
will bring them down to the Valley of Judgment and I
will indict them there concerning Israel, My people
and My heritage, which they dispersed among the
peoples, and My land they divided up. [3] *And upon My*
people they cast lots, and they gave a boy for a har-
lot, and a girl they sold for wine and they drank.
[4] *And also, what are you to Me, Tyre and Sidon and*
all the districts of Philistia; are you paying requital

the Christian nations — and Yishmael — the Arab peoples. The Almighty will incite them to meet in battle in the vicinity of Jerusalem, where they will both be decimated in punishment for their persecutions of the Jewish people (*Abarbanel; Malbim*).

3. וְאֶל־עַמִּי יַדּוּ גוֹרָל וַיִּתְּנוּ הַיֶּלֶד בַּזּוֹנָה וְהַיַּלְדָּה מָכְרוּ בַיַּיִן וַיִּשְׁתּוּ — *And upon My people they cast lots, and they gave a boy for a harlot, and a girl they sold for wine and they drank.*

They drew lots concerning the captives they took from My people to decide who would receive whom as a slave (*Radak*). The degradation of the Jewish prisoners was so great that a Jewish boy would serve merely as payment for the services of a prostitute, and a girl was offered in exchange for a cask of wine (*Malbim*). *Ibn Ezra* interprets: for the price of wine to drink together with the prostitute.

Others render זוֹנָה to mean food — from the word מָזוֹן (*R' Eliezer of Beaugency;* cf. *Joshua* 2:1, *Rashi* ad loc.). [Thus: *they exchanged a boy for food and a girl for drink.*][1]

4. [The prophet now addresses himself to those who have allied themselves with the armies attacking the Jewish nation, such as *Tyre and Sidon,* etc.] Speaking in the name of the Almighty, he first challenges them to produce evidence of any provocation that would warrant such behavior, and then goes on to specify the acts of hostility for which they are being taken to task. Finally, he describes the retribution to be exacted from them for their wickedness.

מָה־אַתֶּם לִי — *What are you to Me?*

What is there between us that you have entered My land for hostile purposes, rather than coming to My aid as would befit neighboring countries (*Radak*)? The nations in whose hands I placed My people were sent here by My word; only their excesses were sinful (see comm. to v. 2). You, however, had no business entering into the fray whatsoever (*Malbim*).

Targum renders: *Of what importance are you to Me?*

הַגְּמוּל אַתֶּם מְשַׁלְּמִים עָלָי — *Are you paying requital to Me?*

Are you coming to avenge previous wrongs that I have done to you (*Ibn Ezra, Radak, Malbim*)? If that is your claim, I challenge you to cite any action I have taken to harm you (*Radak*).

1. The Talmud (*Gittin* 6b) interprets this as a castigation of the practice of Torah students who left their wives in Babylonia and traveled to the Land of Israel for extended periods of study. In this fashion they demonstrated a lack of importance for their marital relationship and towards their obligation to father and raise children (see *Rashi* ad loc.).

Tosafos interprets זוֹנָה as *sustenance,* since the children left in Babylonia had to financially fend for themselves. Wine is a commonly used metaphor for Torah (see *Rashi, Shir Hashirim* 1:2).

The end — even one as exalted as Torah study — does not justify the means.

עָלָי וְאִם־גֹּמְלִים אַתֶּם עָלַי קַל מְהֵרָה אָשִׁיב
ה גְּמֻלְכֶם בְּרֹאשְׁכֶם׃ אֲשֶׁר־כַּסְפִּי וּזְהָבִי לְקַחְתֶּם
ו וּמַחֲמַדַּי הַטֹּבִים הֲבֵאתֶם לְהֵיכְלֵיכֶם׃ וּבְנֵי יְהוּדָה
וּבְנֵי יְרוּשָׁלַםִ מְכַרְתֶּם לִבְנֵי הַיְּוָנִים לְמַעַן
ז הַרְחִיקָם מֵעַל גְּבוּלָם׃ הִנְנִי מְעִירָם מִן־הַמָּקוֹם
אֲשֶׁר־מְכַרְתֶּם אֹתָם שָׁמָּה וַהֲשִׁבֹתִי גְמֻלְכֶם
ח בְּרֹאשְׁכֶם׃ וּמָכַרְתִּי אֶת־בְּנֵיכֶם וְאֶת־בְּנוֹתֵיכֶם
בְּיַד בְּנֵי יְהוּדָה וּמְכָרוּם לִשְׁבָאיִם אֶל־גּוֹי רָחוֹק כִּי
ט יְהוָה דִּבֵּר׃ קִרְאוּ־זֹאת בַּגּוֹיִם קַדְּשׁוּ מִלְחָמָה
הָעִירוּ הַגִּבּוֹרִים יִגְּשׁוּ יַעֲלוּ כֹּל אַנְשֵׁי הַמִּלְחָמָה׃

Rashi translates: *Is this the payment you render Me,* i.e., is this how you repay the kindness shown to you by King Solomon, who gave Hiram, king of Tyre, a gift of twenty cities (see *I Kings* 9:11)?

וְאִם־גֹּמְלִים אַתֶּם עָלַי קַל מְהֵרָה אָשִׁיב גְּמֻלְכֶם בְּרֹאשְׁכֶם — *And if you are initiating action against Me, swiftly and soon will I return your action upon your head.*

If your attack is not due to any past grievances but is rather an unprovoked act of aggression (*Radak*), I will exact retribution in a swift manner and within a short period of time (*Abarbanel, Malbim*). For I view any action taken against the Jewish people as if the hostilities were directed against Myself (*Radak*).

The word גְּמוּל applies to any act that benefits or harms someone else which is done as a result of passion — whether love or hatred. When it is done in reaction to a previous deed of the other party, it is referred to as תַּשְׁלוּם גְּמוּל, *payment of requital.* When it is an initial action, it is referred to simply as גְּמוּל (*Malbim*).

5. The prophet now specifies the acts of hostility performed by these neighboring nations.

אֲשֶׁר־כַּסְפִּי וּזְהָבִי לְקַחְתֶּם וּמַחֲמַדַּי הַטֹּבִים הֲבֵאתֶם לְהֵיכְלֵיכֶם — *That My silver and gold you have taken and My desirable and good possessions you have brought to your palaces.*

You looted (*Abarbanel, Malbim*) the treasures of the Jewish people, which in reality are Mine, since I gave them these possessions (*Radak*). Alternatively: You exacted payment from the Jews for tribute and for the redemption of captives (*Ibn Ezra*).

6. וּבְנֵי יְהוּדָה וּבְנֵי יְרוּשָׁלַםִ מְכַרְתֶּם לִבְנֵי הַיְּוָנִים לְמַעַן הַרְחִיקָם מֵעַל גְּבוּלָם — *And the children of Judah and the children of Jerusalem you sold to the children of the Jevanim in order to distance them from their border.*

When the Jewish people were still in their own land, you would kidnap them from their homes and sell them to far-off lands in order to make sure they would not return. Alternatively, this refers to the time of exile: You came with the enemies of the Jewish people and took their children captive and sold them (*Radak*).

Malbim adds: This is even worse than your theft of their gold and silver; that was done for the sake of profit, whereas you sold the children to distant lands purely out of hatred and cruelty.

7. הִנְנִי מְעִירָם מִן הַמָּקוֹם אֲשֶׁר־מְכַרְתֶּם אֹתָם שָׁמָּה וַהֲשִׁבֹתִי גְּמֻלְכֶם בְּרֹאשְׁכֶם — *Behold I will rouse them [to come] from the place to where you sold them, and I will visit your action upon your head.*

Although you have sent them off to

to Me? And if you are initiating action against Me,
swiftly and soon I will return your action upon your
head — 5 that My silver and gold you have taken and
My desirable and good possessions you have brought to
your palaces. 6 And the children of Judah and the chil-
dren of Jerusalem you sold to the children of the Jevanim
in order to distance them from their border. 7 Behold I
will rouse them [to come] from the place to where you
sold them, and I will visit your action upon your head.
8 And I will sell your sons and daughters into the hands
of the children of Judah and they shall sell them to She-
baites, to a distant nation, for HASHEM has spoken. 9 An-
nounce this among the nations; prepare for war; arouse
the mighty; let all the men of war approach and ascend.

distant lands, I will yet arouse them or their children — or perhaps both them and their children; them after resurrection and their descendants at the time of redemption — to return to their homes (*Radak*), and exact retribution from you for your evil (*Ibn Ezra, Metzudos David*).

8. וּמָכַרְתִּי אֶת־בְּנֵיכֶם וְאֶת־בְּנוֹתֵיכֶם בְּיַד בְּנֵי יְהוּדָה וּמְכָרוּם לִשְׁבָאִים אֶל־גּוֹי רָחוֹק — *And I will sell your sons and daughters into the hands of the children of Judah and they shall sell them to Shebaites, to a distant nation.*

I will deliver your children into the hands of the returning children of Israel, who, in turn, will sell them to the Shebaites, a nation even more distant than the Jevanim (*Radak*). This punishment will include not only your sons, but your daughters as well, despite the fact that women do not wage war [and they were thus not actively involved in your misdeeds] (*Ibn Ezra*).

The land of Sheba lies far to the southeast of Israel, and is also very distant from Tyre and Sidon (*Radak*).

כִּי ה׳ דִּבֵּר — *For HASHEM has spoken.*

[This is the promise of the Almighty,] and no one can annul or prevent it (*Metzudos David*). Alternatively: With this, I shall fulfill My ancient prophecy concerning their ancestor Ham (*Genesis* 9:25): *A slave of slaves he shall be to his brother* (*Rashi*, from *Mechilta* to *Exodus* 12:25).

9. The prophet now returns to the topic of the great gathering of armies which will take place in the Valley of Judgment [Jehoshafat] (*Malbim*).

קִרְאוּ־זֹאת בַּגּוֹיִם קַדְּשׁוּ מִלְחָמָה הָעִירוּ הַגִּבּוֹרִים יִגְּשׁוּ יַעֲלוּ כֹּל אַנְשֵׁי הַמִּלְחָמָה — *Announce this among the nations; prepare for war; arouse the mighty; let all the men of war approach and ascend.*

[All of you hostile nations,] gather together for battle and let us see whether you are capable of waging war against Me (*Rashi*). Unlike a mortal monarch, who seeks to limit the size of his opposing forces, the Almighty urges them to gather in force so that He can punish all of them together for their sins (*Alshich*).

Alternatively: The prophet depicts the clarion call to arms which will be issued among these nations to gather them for war against Jerusalem (*Radak*). [As explained earlier, there are various opinions

י כֹּתּוּ אִתֵּיכֶם לַחֲרָבוֹת וּמַזְמְרֹתֵיכֶם לִרְמָחִים
יא הַחַלָּשׁ יֹאמַר גִּבּוֹר אָנִי: עוּשׁוּ וָבֹאוּ כָל־
הַגּוֹיִם מִסָּבִיב וְנִקְבָּצוּ שָׁמָּה הַנְחַת יהוה
יב גִּבּוֹרֶיךָ: יֵעוֹרוּ וְיַעֲלוּ הַגּוֹיִם אֶל־עֵמֶק יְהוֹשָׁפָט
כִּי שָׁם אֵשֵׁב לִשְׁפֹּט אֶת־כָּל־הַגּוֹיִם מִסָּבִיב:
יג שִׁלְחוּ מַגָּל כִּי בָשַׁל קָצִיר בֹּאוּ רְדוּ כִּי־
מָלְאָה גַּת הֵשִׁיקוּ הַיְקָבִים כִּי רַבָּה רָעָתָם:

as to the specifics of the battle under discussion (see comm. to v. 2).]

Abarbanel contends that this alludes to the resurrection of [some of] the dead, which will take place at the time of this war. Among these will be individuals from the Jewish people who will be brought to life to witness the downfall of the nations that persecuted them. Additionally, it will include the leaders of these nations, who will be reawakened to be punished along with their descendants and to witness their destruction.

10. כֹּתּוּ אִתֵּיכֶם לַחֲרָבוֹת וּמַזְמְרֹתֵיכֶם לִרְמָחִים — *Beat your plowshares into swords and your pruning forks into spears.*

So great will be the scope of this battle that you will need to change your farming tools into weapons in order to supply for the needs of this great army (*Radak, Abarbanel*). However, once this battle is over the process will be reversed, as foretold by Isaiah (2:4): *And they will beat their swords into plowshares and their spears into pruning forks* (*Radak*).

הַחַלָּשׁ יֹאמַר גִּבּוֹר אָנִי — *The weak one shall say, 'I am mighty.'*

The inspiration to join in this great battle will be so pervasive that even the weak will gather their courage and claim to be fit to enter the fray (*Abarbanel*).

Alshich interprets this phrase as an extension of the Almighty's challenge: All your efforts will be to no avail, for although you can change your tools of peace into weapons of war, can the weak one say I am mighty — i.e., can mere mortals, who are so weak compared to the Almighty, change that fact simply by declaring themselves mighty?

11. עוּשׁוּ וָבֹאוּ כָל־הַגּוֹיִם מִסָּבִיב — *Gather and come, all the nations from around.*

Having foretold the fate of the distant nations, the prophet redirects his words to the neighboring states of Tyre, Sidon, and Philistia (*Alshich*) [and challenges them to gather together for battle].

וְנִקְבָּצוּ — *And they shall gather.*

Even those who are seemingly unable to come to the Valley of Judgment will be brought there by Divine decree (*Alshich*) [in order to annihilate them].

שָׁמָּה הַנְחַת ה׳ גִּבּוֹרֶיךָ — *There* HASHEM *shall break your mighty ones.*

There, in the Valley of Judgment, your might shall be crushed (*Rashi*).

Others translate הַנְחַת as bringing down, and interpret this phrase in the imperative mode: *Bring down your mighty angels,* HASHEM [to participate in this battle] (*Ibn Ezra, Radak*).

12. יֵעוֹרוּ וְיַעֲלוּ הַגּוֹיִם אֶל־עֵמֶק יְהוֹשָׁפָט כִּי שָׁם אֵשֵׁב לִשְׁפֹּט אֶת־כָּל־הַגּוֹיִם מִסָּבִיב — *The nations shall rouse themselves and go up to the Valley of Judgment, for there I will sit to judge all the nations from around.*

All of the nations shall be aroused to come to the Valley of Judgment where this great battle shall take place, and there they will be judged for their persecutions of the Jewish people (*Metzudos David*).

Alshich cites the words of the Sages (*Avodah Zarah* 2b) that in the end of days,

[10] *Beat your plowshares into swords and your prun-*
ing forks into spears; the weak one shall say, 'I am
mighty.' [11] *Gather and come, all the nations from*
around; and they shall gather; there HASHEM *shall*
break your mighty ones. [12] *The nations shall rouse*
themselves and go up to the Valley of Judgment, for
there I will sit to judge all the nations from around.
[13] *Extend the sickle for the harvest has ripened;*
come descend, for the wine press has been filled;
the vats have overflowed; for their evil is great.

when the Almighty will judge the nations for their actions against the Jewish people, He will first deal with Rome, then with Persia, and finally with the others. Although the Persians will see that the Romans are judged harshly, they will nevertheless ascend to be judged and to argue their case, for the fact that they rebuilt the Temple, whereas the Romans destroyed it, will lead them to believe that they will be vindicated in judgment. Even after they too are sentenced, the other nations will present their cases, for the first two conquered and subjugated the Jewish nation whereas the others did not.

This is alluded to by the seemingly contradictory phrase: *shall "go up" to the Valley of Judgment*. They will present their case with the assumption that their judgment will be in their favor and will thus be an ascension for them. In reality, however, they will be descending into an abyss, for the Almighty will find them all guilty of persecuting the Jewish people.

13. The Almighty has a plan for history which includes a final date for His vengeance against His enemies and the redemption of His nation. Verse 13 depicts that time as the harvesting of ripe grain and the collection of pressed wine, symbolizing that the nations will be ripe for punishment at that time due to the magnitude of their crimes (*Abarbanel*).

שִׁלְחוּ מַגָּל כִּי בָשַׁל קָצִיר — *Extend the sickle for the harvest has ripened.*

Stretch out your swords, those who go on My mission to destroy the enemies of the Almighty (*Rashi*). Just as one extends a sickle to his crop when it is ripe for harvest, so shall your sword be stretched out against the nations when their time has arrived (*Radak*).

בֹּאוּ רְדוּ כִּי־מָלְאָה גַּת — *Come descend, for the wine press has been filled.*

Go down into the Valley [of Judgment] and destroy the nations assembled there, for they are like a wine press filled with grapes, which are ready to be trodden (*Radak*).

Rashi translates רְדוּ as *rule*: Come subjugate these nations, for their measure [of evil] is filled like a wine press filled with grapes [and ready to be trodden].

הֵשִׁיקוּ הַיְקָבִים כִּי רַבָּה רָעָתָם — *The vats have overflowed; for their evil is great.*

Due to the extent of the evil which the nations have perpetrated against the Jewish nation, their blood is ready to be spilled, like wine which fills the vat to the top and spills out all around it (*Radak*; cf. *Rashi*; comm. to 2:24).

Targum renders this phrase as a command: *Spill their blood for their evil is great.*

Malbim interprets these last few verses to be describing a series of battles which will take place between the forces of Edom — the Christian nations — and those of Yishmael — the Arab world (cf. comm. to v.2). In the first battle, depicted in verse 9, the mighty warriors who are experienced in the ways of war will meet and decimate each other's forces. Afterwards, when there are no warriors left to wage war, the farmers and

יד הֲמוֹנִים הֲמוֹנִים בְּעֵמֶק הֶחָרוּץ כִּי קָרוֹב יוֹם יהוה
טו בְּעֵמֶק הֶחָרוּץ׃ שֶׁמֶשׁ וְיָרֵחַ קָדָרוּ וְכוֹכָבִים אָסְפוּ
טז נָגְהָם׃ וַיהוה מִצִּיּוֹן יִשְׁאָג וּמִירוּשָׁלַםִ יִתֵּן קוֹלוֹ
וְרָעֲשׁוּ שָׁמַיִם וָאָרֶץ וַיהוה מַחֲסֶה לְעַמּוֹ וּמָעוֹז
יז לִבְנֵי יִשְׂרָאֵל׃ וִידַעְתֶּם כִּי אֲנִי יהוה אֱלֹהֵיכֶם
שֹׁכֵן בְּצִיּוֹן הַר־קָדְשִׁי וְהָיְתָה יְרוּשָׁלַםִ קֹדֶשׁ
יח וְזָרִים לֹא־יַעַבְרוּ־בָהּ עוֹד׃ וְהָיָה

the workers of the fields will beat their tools into weapons and engage in combat. Once these too have been annihilated, the untrained masses of both sides will gather and fight each other.

In this verse, the prophet summarizes the destruction of these three waves of forces. At first, the armies will be compared to standing grain ready to be reaped, since they were all hitherto living in peace in their lands. The second group, coming after partial destruction, is compared to grapes which are already harvested and are sitting in the press waiting to be crushed into wine. After even these are destroyed, the remaining forces will be like grapes which have already been crushed into wine, but the wine has not yet been separated from the grapes and placed into vats. Each of these levels of destruction will take place because of the great magnitude of the evil that was perpetrated by these peoples.

14. הֲמוֹנִים הֲמוֹנִים בְּעֵמֶק הֶחָרוּץ כִּי קָרוֹב יוֹם ה׳ בְּעֵמֶק הֶחָרוּץ — *Groups upon groups in the Valley of the Decision, for the day of* HASHEM *is near in the Valley of the Decision.*

Many groups of people will gather in the Valley of Judgment, where their final judgment will be decided and carried out (*Rashi; Mahari Kara*). Others translate: *the Valley of the Cutting* — for the nations will be decimated there (*Radak*).

Malbim explains that when referring to the time in which the nations will be judged and their fate pondered, the valley is called the Valley of Judgment. Once the decision has been made and their fate sealed, it is referred to as the Valley of the Decision.

כִּי קָרוֹב יוֹם ה׳ — *For the day of* HASHEM *is near.*

[The reason they will all gather in that valley is because[1] the day of Hashem — in which He will take vengeance from these nations (*Ibn Ezra*) — is near.]

15. שֶׁמֶשׁ וְיָרֵחַ קָדָרוּ וְכוֹכָבִים אָסְפוּ נָגְהָם — *The sun and moon have blackened, and the stars have withdrawn their shine.*

The misfortune which befalls these nations will be so overwhelming that it will seem as if the stellar bodies have ceased to shed light upon the earth (*Metzudos David*). Alternatively: The astrological influence of these celestial bodies upon worldly events will be negated in order to allow for the colossal scale of God's punishment (*Abarbanel; Malbim;* cf. 2:10).

16. וַה׳ מִצִּיּוֹן יִשְׁאָג וּמִירוּשָׁלַםִ יִתֵּן קוֹלוֹ — *And* HASHEM *shall roar from Zion, and shall emit His voice from Jerusalem.*

From Zion and Jerusalem, the dwelling place of the Divine Presence, shall come out the mighty roar of the Almighty, which will cause the nations to tremble violently in fear (*Radak*). According to some, this is the roar of God's judgment which will be passed upon these nations. [Since this judgment will manifest His rulership over creation it is depicted as a

1. [*Ibn Ezra,* followed by *Metzudos David,* interprets *groups upon groups in the Valley of the Decision* to refer to their downfall there. Accordingly, the second half of the verse seems redundant. Perhaps it means to explain the term חָרוּץ — that the valley is called such because of the decision of the Almighty which will take place there.]

14 Groups upon groups in the Valley of the Decision, for
the day of HASHEM *is near in the Valley of the Decision.*
15 The sun and moon have blackened, and the stars
have withdrawn their shine. 16 And HASHEM *shall roar*
from Zion, and shall emit His voice from Jerusalem;
and the heavens and earth shall tremble, and HASHEM
[shall be] a shelter for His people and a fortification
for the Children of Israel. 17 And you shall know that
I am HASHEM *your God, Who dwells in Zion, My holy*
mountain; and Jerusalem shall be holy, and stran-
gers shall no longer pass through her. 18 And it will be

proclamation of that rulership.] In Zion, where His Presence is more intense, that proclamation will be like a mighty roar; in the rest of Jerusalem it will be of lesser intensity, comparable to a quieter sound (*Malbim*).

Others translate: *because of Zion* — the Almighty will let out a roar in reaction to that which the nations did to Zion and Jerusalem (*Rashi; Abarbanel*). Specifically, He will roar mightily in response to the voice of Torah that goes out from Zion, which they stilled, and He will emit His voice over their destruction of the Holy Temple in Jerusalem (*Alshich*).

וְרָעֲשׁוּ שָׁמַיִם וָאָרֶץ — *And the heavens and earth shall tremble.*

All of creation will be gripped by an overwhelming fear of the Almighty, as if the heavens and earth themselves will be trembling (*Ibn Ezra; Radak*). Alternatively, a great trembling shall seize the heavenly princes of the nations — i.e., the angels (*Abarbanel*), as well as their leaders here on earth (*Rashi*).

Radak adds: A great earthquake will occur at that time, as depicted in the prophecies of Ezekiel (ch. 38) and Zechariah (ch. 14).

וַה׳ מַחֲסֶה לְעַמּוֹ וּמָעוֹז לִבְנֵי יִשְׂרָאֵל — *And* HASHEM *[shall be] a shelter for His people and a fortification for the Children of Israel.*

The Almighty will protect the Jewish people from the assembled nations as well as from the earthquake (*Radak*). In addition, He will fortify and strengthen them further, beyond their natural limits (*Malbim*).

Alshich interprets his phrase as referring to the lengthy exile of the Jewish nation. During this time, the Almighty shall be a shelter for the Jews in their exile, for His presence among them will prevent the righteous from indulging in sin. In addition, He will be a source of strength for the entire nation, for the fact that the Divine Presence is in exile along with them is a guarantee that they will eventually be redeemed.

17. וִידַעְתֶּם כִּי אֲנִי ה׳ אֱלֹהֵיכֶם שֹׁכֵן בְּצִיּוֹן הַר־קָדְשִׁי — *And you shall know that I am* HASHEM *your God, Who dwells in Zion, My holy mountain.*

When you will witness the Divine retribution exacted from your enemies, you will finally achieve an absolute level of faith in Me, along with full recognition of the fact that I am indeed the God Who oversees and controls all that happens here on earth. In addition, with the return of My Divine Presence to Jerusalem, you will become fully aware of the concentration of My presence there (*Abarbanel*).

וְהָיְתָה יְרוּשָׁלַםִ קֹדֶשׁ וְזָרִים לֹא־יַעַבְרוּ־בָהּ עוֹד — *And Jerusalem shall be holy, and strangers shall no longer pass through her.*

בַיּ֨וֹם הַה֜וּא יִטְּפ֧וּ הֶהָרִ֣ים עָסִ֗יס וְהַגְּבָעוֹת֙ תֵּלַ֣כְנָה
חָלָ֔ב וְכָל־אֲפִ֥יקֵי יְהוּדָ֖ה יֵ֣לְכוּ מָ֑יִם וּמַעְיָ֗ן מִבֵּ֤ית
יט יהוה֙ יֵצֵ֔א וְהִשְׁקָ֖ה אֶת־נַ֥חַל הַשִּׁטִּֽים׃ מִצְרַ֙יִם֙
לִשְׁמָמָ֣ה תִהְיֶ֔ה וֶאֱד֕וֹם לְמִדְבַּ֥ר שְׁמָמָ֖ה תִּֽהְיֶ֑ה
מֵחֲמַס֙ בְּנֵ֣י יְהוּדָ֔ה אֲשֶׁר־שָׁפְכ֥וּ דָם־נָקִ֖יא
כ בְּאַרְצָֽם׃ וִֽיהוּדָ֖ה לְעוֹלָ֣ם תֵּשֵׁ֑ב וִירוּשָׁלִַ֖ם לְד֥וֹר
כא וָדֽוֹר׃ וְנִקֵּ֕יתִי דָּמָ֖ם לֹא־נִקֵּ֑יתִי וַֽיהוָ֖ה שֹׁכֵ֥ן בְּצִיּֽוֹן׃

Never again will invading nations be able to enter Jerusalem to harm the Jewish people. Alternatively: In that time the sanctity of Jerusalem will reach such a high level that it will be off limits to all but the Jewish people — just as the sanctuary of the Temple is prohibited to all but *Kohanim* (*Radak*).

18. וְהָיָה בַיּוֹם הַהוּא יִטְּפוּ הֶהָרִים עָסִיס וְהַגְּבָעוֹת תֵּלַכְנָה חָלָב — *And it will be on that day [that] the mountains shall drip wine, and the hills shall flow with milk.*

After the defeat of the enemies of Israel, the Jewish nation will be further blessed with plenty. This will come to them without any effort on their part, as if the mountains and hills themselves surge with wine and milk (*Radak*).

וְכָל־אֲפִיקֵי יְהוּדָה יֵלְכוּ מָיִם — *And all the springs of Judah shall flow with water.*

Until now, there was no water in Judah except for that which flowed from the spring of Shiloah. Far from Jerusalem, therefore, water was very expensive to purchase. However, when the Jewish nation shall finally bask in the full blessing of the Almighty, there will be plenty of water available for all (*Mahari Kara*).

The translation of אֲפִיקֵי follows *Rashi*. According to *Ibn Ezra*, it means the strong places. *Radak* renders: the deep valleys where the water is noticeable.

וּמַעְיָן מִבֵּית ה׳ יֵצֵא וְהִשְׁקָה אֶת־נַחַל הַשִּׁטִּים — *And a well from the House of* HASHEM *shall go out and water the Valley of Shittim.*

The waters from the well which lies in the Temple will flow all the way to the Valley of Shittim, outside the Land of Israel (*Mahari Kara*). R' Saadiah Gaon maintains that this refers to the Jordan River, which flows near the area called Shittim (*Radak*).

The Midrash explains that different springs of water have the tendency to nurture different character traits: Some develop mighty warriors and others weaklings; some produce beautiful people and others ugly ones; some produce modest people and others promiscuous ones. The waters of Shittim had the tendency to produce promiscuity. In fact, these are the waters which fed the people of Sodom [and caused their wanton behavior]. Thus, when the Jewish nation camped in Shittim they too [were affected by these waters] and fell prey to promiscuity (see *Numbers* 25:1-3). Therefore, in future times, the Almighty promises to dry up that spring forever (*Tanchuma, Balak* 17).

This verse is also interpreted metaphorically: The word of Torah, which is symbolized by water, will go forth from Jerusalem to the entire world (*Abarbanel; Malbim*).

19. מִצְרַיִם לִשְׁמָמָה תִהְיֶה וֶאֱדוֹם לְמִדְבַּר שְׁמָמָה תִּהְיֶה מֵחֲמַס בְּנֵי יְהוּדָה אֲשֶׁר־שָׁפְכוּ דָם־נָקִיא בְּאַרְצָם — *Egypt will become desolate, and Edom will become a desert waste because of the robbery of the children of Judah [and] because they shed [their] innocent blood in their land.*

At that time, in the end of days, the Almighty shall wreak the final destruction upon the Arab world — represented by Egypt, the homeland of the wife of Ishmael, who was the mother of the Arab peoples — and the Roman nation, who descended primarily from Edom (cf.

on that day [that] the mountains shall drip wine, and the
hills shall flow with milk, and all the springs of Judah
shall flow with water, and a well from the House of
HASHEM shall go out and water the Valley of Shittim.
19 *Egypt will become desolate, and Edom will become a*
desert waste because of the robbery of the children of Ju-
dah [and] because they shed [their] innocent blood in their
land. 20 *And Judah shall exist forever, and Jerusalem*
from generation to generation. 21 *And I will cleanse, [but]*
their blood I will not cleanse, and HASHEM dwells in Zion.

ArtScroll *Daniel* 2:40). These two nations were most prominent in their mistreatment of the Jewish people [and will therefore be singled out for punishment] (*Radak*).

Others contend that the prophet singles out Egypt specifically because they were the first people to enslave the Jewish nation. Therefore, they and the Romans, who brought the final destruction on the Holy Land, will be utterly destroyed. The Christian nations will initiate this action by attacking Egypt on their way to invading the Land of Israel. This will provoke a massive retaliation by the Arab people, who will annihilate the Roman kingdom (*Abarbanel;* cf. *Malbim*).

Rashi explains that the prophet mentions Egypt together with Edom because only through Egypt was the Edomite nation maintained. This occurred in the time of King David, when the armies of the Jewish nation conquered Edom and wiped out their entire male population. A few individuals escaped and fled to Egypt where they were granted sanctuary by the pharaoh. From these individuals arose the Edomite nation which eventually became the nemesis of the Jewish people (see *I Kings* 11:16-25).

[According to *R' Moshe HaKohen,* that this prophecy refers to events which occurred in Biblical times,] the Egyptian nation existing today is not that of ancient Egypt, which — as described in this verse — was destroyed (*Ibn Ezra*).

20. וִיהוּדָה לְעוֹלָם תֵּשֵׁב וִירוּשָׁלַיִם לְדוֹר וָדוֹר — *And Judah shall exist forever, and Jerusalem from generation to generation.*

In contrast to Edom and Egypt, which will be destroyed, *Judah* will remain in existence forever (*Radak*).

21. וְנִקֵּיתִי דָּמָם לֹא־נִקֵּיתִי — *And I will cleanse, [but] their blood I will not cleanse.*

Even if I will forgive them for the other sins they committed — such as the gold and silver they looted and robbed (*Radak*) — I will not exonerate them from the crime of spilling the blood of the children of Judah (*Rashi*). Rather, I shall exact retribution, a soul for a soul, from them or from their descendants (*Radak*).

Targum interprets נִקֵּיתִי to mean retribution [i.e., one is cleansed of his sins when he has paid for them]. Although the war of Gog and Magog will include primarily the Edomites, Ishmaelites, and those who are allied with them, all other nations who have mistreated the Jews will also be punished at that time (*Malbim*). The verse would thus be translated: I will then exact retribution from those nations from whom I have not yet exacted retribution.

Another translation is: *Have I cleansed their blood? I have not cleansed.* The punishment described above will be meted out because there can be no forgiveness for the Jewish blood which these nations have shed as if it were water (*Abarbanel*).

וַה׳ שֹׁכֵן בְּצִיּוֹן — *And HASHEM dwells in Zion.*

When will this take place? When the Almighty will dwell in Zion (*Rashi*). Alternatively, this refers back to the previous verse. Just as Judah shall exist forever, so shall the Divine Presence dwell in Zion forever once it returns there with the coming of the Messiah (*Radak*).

amos

א דִּבְרֵי עָמוֹס אֲשֶׁר־הָיָה בַנֹּקְדִים מִתְּקוֹעַ אֲשֶׁר
חָזָה עַל־יִשְׂרָאֵל בִּימֵי ׀ עֻזִּיָּה מֶלֶךְ־יְהוּדָה
וּבִימֵי יָרָבְעָם בֶּן־יוֹאָשׁ מֶלֶךְ יִשְׂרָאֵל שְׁנָתַיִם
ב לִפְנֵי הָרָעַשׁ׃ וַיֹּאמַר ׀ יהוה מִצִּיּוֹן יִשְׁאָג

I

1. [This verse introduces the prophecies of Amos, who lived in the end of the era of the kingdom of the ten tribes of Israel.] The introductory phrase, *The words of* . . ., is an uncommon one, which is used only for three prophets: Koheles, Jeremiah, and Amos. It is meant to indicate that the prophet discusses within his prophecies events which occurred to him himself [as דִּבְרֵי means *things of* as well as *words of* — the things which involve Amos] (see 7:10-17). Indeed, the Sages state that these three prophets rebuked the people of Israel very sharply and therefore included themselves in their prophecies — i.e., they related events in which they themselves were involved (*Radak*). [Apparently, they could not bear to castigate Israel so harshly in a manner which implied that they stood outside the people.]

אֲשֶׁר־הָיָה בַנֹּקְדִים — *Who was among the herders.* He was the owner of herds (*Targum; Rashi*) of sheep (*Mahari Kara*). Alternatively, he was a shepherd (*Ibn Ezra; Radak*). The word נָקוֹד is used to refer to sheep because they are by and large spotted (נָקוֹד) (*Radak*).

The prophet's use of the phrase *who was among the herders* — rather than simply stating that he was a herder — indicates that Amos was the most prominent shepherd in his town (*Radak*). Others assume the opposite: He was merely a shepherd hired to care for the herds of others but he did not own any sheep of his own (*Abarbanel; Malbim*).

מִתְּקוֹעַ — *Of Tekoa.* This was a large city within the province of the tribe of Asher[1] (*Radak*).

1. *Abarbanel* maintains that Tekoa was a town of simple people, among whom the pursuit of wisdom was not a prevalent trait. Thus, in his view, Scripture emphasizes the simple roots and station of this prophet in order to indicate his apparent unworthiness of being granted the gift of prophecy. Amos himself remarks in a similar vein (7:14), *I am not a prophet nor am I the son of a prophet* [the latter term referring to one who involves himself in preparation for prophetic vision (see *Rambam, Hil. Yesodei HaTorah* 7:4,5)]. Accordingly, contends *Abarbanel*, this contradicts the opinion of *Rambam* (ibid. 7:1; *Moreh Nevuchim* 2:32) that only one who is outstanding in all of the spiritual, intellectual, and physical attributes is capable of attaining the lofty level of prophecy. Here we see that this is not the case: As long as one is imbued with fear of Hashem, the spirit of prophecy may descend upon him. This is because prophecy is in any case not a natural phenomenon but rather an act of miraculous Divine providence, and is thus not bound by the limits of human endeavor.

Malbim, however, defends *Rambam*'s position. He explains that although prophecy is indeed a miraculous occurrence, the Almighty, as a general rule, bestows it only upon someone who has developed the capacity to receive it. However, in instances when the needs of the Jewish nation require prophetic communication, the Almighty allows for exceptions to this rule. In such cases, if there is no one available who is worthy of prophecy, He chooses the individual who is closest to that level and speaks through him.

Alshich interprets this verse in a manner that precludes the entire discussion. According to his view, Scripture specifies Amos's means of livelihood to explain that the reason he achieved the level of prophecy was because his trade allowed him plenty of time for solitude and contemplation. In addition, he came from Tekoa, a town that was known for its wise inhabitants (see *II Samuel* 14:2; *Menachos* 85b). Amos's statement that he was not a נָבִיא means merely that his prophecy achieved only the lower level of חִזָּיוֹן and not the higher level of נְבוּאָה (*Alshich* ad loc.).

[1] *The words of Amos, who was among the herders of
Tekoa, who saw visions concerning Israel in the
days of Uzziah king of Judah and in the days of Jeroboam son of Joash king of Israel, two years before the
earthquake.* [2] *And he said:* HASHEM *from Zion shall roar*

אֲשֶׁר חָזָה עַל־יִשְׂרָאֵל בִּימֵי עֻזִּיָּה מֶלֶךְ־יְהוּדָה וּבִימֵי יָרָבְעָם בֶּן־יוֹאָשׁ מֶלֶךְ יִשְׂרָאֵל — *Who saw visions concerning Israel in the days of Uzziah king of Judah and in the days of Jeroboam son of Joash king of Israel.* The majority of Amos's prophecies concerned the kingdom of Israel and not that of Judah. They were uttered during the reign of these two kings, whose regimes coincided with each other (*Radak*).

The Sages state that four prophets prophesied during the same period of time: Hosea, Isaiah, Amos, and Michah (*Pesachim* 87a). Of these, Hosea and Amos directed the majority of their words to the kingdom of Israel, whereas the latter two focused on the kingdom of Judah (*Malbim*).

Alshich contends that the sole subject of the prophecies of Amos is the kingdom of Israel. Although he goes on to describe the punishment wrought upon other nations, he does so only for the sake of the contrast he draws between them and Israel. The others merited the devastation of only some of their cities but not the total destruction of the nations [as interpreted in the following verses by *Alshich*]. Israel alone was deserving of such great retribution that they were sent into exile for long centuries.[1]

שְׁנָתַיִם לִפְנֵי הָרָעַשׁ — *Two years before the earthquake.* During his reign, Uzziah entered the Temple illicitly to burn incense on the altar [a task reserved for *Kohanim*], and was therefore smitten with leprosy (*II Chronicles* 26:16ff). The Sages state that this caused the great earthquake mentioned by Zechariah (14:5): *as you fled before the earthquake in the days of Uzziah king of Judah,* and referred to as well by Isaiah (6:4). Two years before this occurrence, the prophecies of Amos began (*Rashi*). The event is noted here because Amos foretold it at this time, as alluded to in the verse (3:15): *And I will smite the winter house along with the summer house* (*Radak*; cf. *Malbim* to v. 2).[2]

2. וַיֹּאמַר ה׳ מִצִּיּוֹן יִשְׁאָג וּמִירוּשָׁלַםִ יִתֵּן קוֹלוֹ — *And he said:* HASHEM *from Zion shall roar and from Jerusalem shall emit His voice.* From the Holy of Holies in Jerusalem (*Rashi*), the Almighty makes His voice heard to His prophets and communicates to them His prophecies (*Radak*).

This is part of the introduction to the prophecies of Amos. Although he lives amidst a nation steeped in sin, his attainment of prophecy is nevertheless possible because it is transmitted via the Holy of Holies which contains the Holy Ark and houses the *Shechinah* (*Abarbanel*).

Others interpret the roar as depicting

1. [This comment would seem to indicate that the Jewish nation descended more deeply into depravity than did the heathen nations that neighbored them. Indeed, such an assumption is apparently borne out by the prophet's words below (3:9), as interpreted by *Abarbanel* (see comm. ibid.). However, the majority of the commentators do not indicate so. Furthermore, the words of the prophet in 3:2 and the commentaries thereon would appear to contradict this theory. Rather, they maintain that the Jewish people's standard of behavior far exceeded that of the other nations. However, much more was expected of them due to their lofty heritage. Thus, because they somewhat emulated the heathen nations in their actions they were punished very severely.]

2. Others contend that this is not the meaning of that verse, and, as such, there is no prophecy from Amos concerning the earthquake. Rather, due to the magnitude of that event it was well remembered and was therefore used as a frame of reference with which to date the prophecies of Amos; they were all uttered within the two years preceding the earthquake (*Abarbanel*).

וּמִירוּשָׁלַ֫ם יִתֵּ֣ן קוֹל֑וֹ וְאָֽבְלוּ֙ נְא֣וֹת הָרֹעִ֔ים וְיָבֵ֖שׁ
ג רֹ֥אשׁ הַכַּרְמֶֽל׃ כֹּ֚ה אָמַ֣ר יהוה עַל־
שְׁלֹשָׁה֙ פִּשְׁעֵ֣י דַמֶּ֔שֶׂק וְעַל־אַרְבָּעָ֖ה לֹ֣א אֲשִׁיבֶ֑נּוּ
ד עַל־דּוּשָׁ֛ם בַּחֲרֻצ֥וֹת הַבַּרְזֶ֖ל אֶת־הַגִּלְעָֽד׃ וְשִׁלַּ֥חְתִּי
אֵ֖שׁ בְּבֵ֣ית חֲזָאֵ֑ל וְאָֽכְלָ֖ה אַרְמְנ֥וֹת בֶּן־הֲדָֽד׃

the great punishment which the Almighty shall bring down upon the nations cited below (*Ibn Ezra*).

Alshich notes the contrast between this verse and a parallel verse in *Joel* (4:16). There it states: וַה׳, *And HASHEM*, which, as taught by the Sages, refers to the Almighty *and* His celestial court which dispenses strict and total justice (see *Rashi* to *Genesis* 19:24). In our verse, *Hashem* is written without the preface *and* indicating that HASHEM would be acting alone. In addition, in *Joel* this phrase is used to portend a total upheaval, while it alludes here merely to a drought. This is because Joel is depicting the final day of judgment at the end of the exile, whereas Amos is describing calamities which occurred during the time of the Holy Temple, when the anger of the Almighty was not yet as great.

וְאָבְלוּ נְאוֹת הָרֹעִים וְיָבֵשׁ רֹאשׁ הַכַּרְמֶל — *And the dwellings of the shepherds shall perish and the summit of the Carmel shall wither.* [A great drought shall befall the nation of Israel in punishment for its sins.] This drought will bring about the destruction of the dwellings of the shepherds, for all of their sheep will perish from thirst (*Ibn Ezra*). In its wake, as well, the trees which appear at the top of Mt. Carmel shall wither and die. Alternatively, ראש refers here to the best: The choice areas of the Carmel, which is a prime location for planting fields and orchards, will dry up from lack of rain (*Radak*).

This phrase can also be understood metaphorically to refer to the destructions foretold in the following verses (*Radak*). Thus, *Targum* renders: *And the dwellings of the kings shall become desolate and the might of their walled cities shall be destroyed.*

Abarbanel translates מִצִּיּוֹן and מִירוּשָׁלַם to mean *because of Zion and Jerusalem*. Amos prefaces his words foretelling the punishment of Israel as well as of her neighboring nations by explaining that the punishment of the gentiles will be due to their oppression of Zion, whereas that of Israel is because of their own sins. Thus the *dwelling places of the grazers* (הָרֹעִים) — those who came to Israel to consume it — shall be destroyed, and *the top of the Carmel* — referring to Jerusalem and the entire Holy Land — *will be made to wither.*

According to *Malbim*, this verse is a continuation of the previous ones. Having acknowledged that he was an unusual candidate for prophecy (see comm. to v. 1), Amos explains the reason for his acceptance by the populace as a legitimate spokesman of the Almighty. This occurred because he accurately foretold the great earthquake in the times of Uzziah as well as the drought that came with it, two years prior to their occurrence.

3. This verse begins the actual prophecy of Amos (*Malbim*). He first directs his words to six countries neighboring Israel, and foretells the punishment that is destined to befall them for their persecution of the Jewish people. He then addresses the Jewish people themselves and castigates them for their evil deeds (*Radak*). The proximity of these nations to the Land of Israel guaranteed that the Jewish people would witness their downfall. As such, it was incumbent upon them to draw the following conclusion: If all of these nations were punished so severely for their misdeeds, surely we — who were chosen by Hashem from among all the nations to be His servants — will suffer great misfortune if we do not repent (*Alshich*).

The first nation cited by the prophet is Aram — or Syria — whose capital city was Damascus. As stated below, the people of Syria were often involved in conflict with the Jewish nation. Amos

and from Jerusalem shall emit His voice, and the
dwellings of the shepherds shall perish and the sum-
mit of the Carmel shall wither. 3 *So said* HASHEM: *For*
three transgressions of Damascus. . . but for four I will
not acquit them: for their threshing the Gilead with
rods of iron. 4 *And I will send fire into the house of*
Hazael and it shall consume the palaces of Ben-hadad.

castigates them here for this and foretells their eventual downfall at the hands of the Assyrian army.

עַל־שְׁלֹשָׁה פִּשְׁעֵי דַמֶּשֶׂק וְעַל־אַרְבָּעָה לֹא אֲשִׁיבֶנּוּ — *For three transgressions of Damascus. . . but for four I will not acquit them.* I have already borne three sins from the people of Damascus without exacting retribution; with the advent of the fourth I can no longer allow them to go unrequited for their evil deeds. This is as stated in Scripture (*Job* 33:29): *All these the Almighty will work twice [or] thrice with a man, but with the fourth [time] He will punish him* (*Rashi*, cf. *Yoma* 86a).

Others translate this phrase as a rhetorical question: *For three transgressions of Damascus as well as for the fourth, should I not repay them* (*Abarbanel*; *Malbim*)?

Rashi adds: And certainly now that he has many sins I will punish him. *Abarbanel* explains *Rashi's* words as follows: Although it is implausible that all of these nations were guilty of exactly four transgressions, the prophet means to say that their guilt for four infractions or more will be repaid.

The prophet does not specify the three sins, indicating that they are well-known transgressions. It is therefore apparent that this refers to the three cardinal transgressions of idolatry, murder, and promiscuity (*Abarbanel*). Others insist that the Almighty does not respond to the deeds of the gentiles if they do not affect the Jewish nation unless they threaten the viability of society — e.g., the sins of Sodom or those of the generation of the flood.[1] Thus, the three transgressions cited by the prophet, they explain, are the three times that the Jewish nation was oppressed by Damascus: in the time of Baasha king of Israel (*I Kings* 15:18-20), during the reign of Ahab (ibid. ch.22), and in the days of Jehoahaz, son of Jehu (*II Kings* 13:7). With the advent of the fourth persecution, in the times of Ahaz (*II Kings* 16:5), Syria was punished for all of these and was conquered by Assyria (*Radak*).

עַל־דּוּשָׁם בַּחֲרֻצוֹת הַבַּרְזֶל אֶת־הַגִּלְעָד — *For their threshing the Gilead with rods of iron.* They have tortured the settlers of Gilead with the serrated iron rods which are used for cutting stalks of grain in order to make straw (*Rashi*). Others explain that they would run over their bodies with iron plows, just as was done earlier by Hazael (*II Kings* 10:32ff) (*Radak*). [For their great cruelty in this fourth iniquity the Syrians will finally be punished for all of their sins.]

4. וְשִׁלַּחְתִּי אֵשׁ בְּבֵית חֲזָאֵל וְאָכְלָה אַרְמְנוֹת בֶּן־הֲדָד — *And I will send fire into the house of Hazael and it shall consume the palaces of Ben-hadad.* The consuming

1. The Sages state (*Yevamos* 63a) that punishment comes upon the world only because of the Jewish people. This is based on the principle that the Almighty exacts retribution for misdeeds on an ongoing basis only from the Children of Israel. In dealing with the gentile nations, he allows them to follow their chosen paths until they [either repent or] exceed the limits of His tolerance, at which time He destroys them completely (*Avodah Zarah* 4a; see comm. to 3:2). When He sometimes deviates from this policy and exacts retribution from the nations, it is solely for the sake of the Jews (*Iyun Yaakov* to *Yevamos* loc. cit.; *Kovetz Maamarim* p. 84) [i.e., for their mistreatment of the Jewish people (cf. *Rashi* to *Yevamos* ad loc.)].

ה וְשָׁבַרְתִּי בְּרִיחַ דַּמֶּשֶׂק וְהִכְרַתִּי יוֹשֵׁב מִבִּקְעַת־אָוֶן
וְתוֹמֵךְ שֵׁבֶט מִבֵּית עֶדֶן וְגָלוּ עַם־אֲרָם קִירָה אָמַר
ו יְהוָה׃ כֹּה אָמַר יְהוָה עַל־שְׁלֹשָׁה פִּשְׁעֵי
עַזָּה וְעַל־אַרְבָּעָה לֹא אֲשִׁיבֶנּוּ עַל־הַגְלוֹתָם
ז גָּלוּת שְׁלֵמָה לְהַסְגִּיר לֶאֱדוֹם׃ וְשִׁלַּחְתִּי אֵשׁ
ח בְּחוֹמַת עַזָּה וְאָכְלָה אַרְמְנֹתֶיהָ׃ וְהִכְרַתִּי יוֹשֵׁב
מֵאַשְׁדּוֹד וְתוֹמֵךְ שֵׁבֶט מֵאַשְׁקְלוֹן וַהֲשִׁיבוֹתִי יָדִי

fire of the enemy (or of HASHEM's wrath) shall descend upon Syria and destroy the houses of Hazael and Ben-hadad, kings of Aram (*Radak*, cf. *Abarbanel*). This event occurred in the time of Rezin, their descendant, whose kingdom was conquered by Sennacherib (*Abarbanel*; cf. *Ibn Ezra*). Indeed, all of the prophecies concerning the downfall of heathen nations which were uttered prior to the times of Sennacherib refer to his conquests; those which were prophesied afterward apply to the conquests of Nebuchadnezzar (*Rashi* to v. 5).

5. After predicting the downfall of the kings of Aram and the destruction of their palaces, the prophet foretells the conquest of their land (*Abarbanel*).

וְשָׁבַרְתִּי בְּרִיחַ דַּמֶּשֶׂק — *And I will break the bolt of Damascus.* I will render the doors and bolts to the city of Damascus totally ineffectual in defending it (*Radak*), as if the bolts were broken and the gates left open (*Metzudos David*).

וְהִכְרַתִּי יוֹשֵׁב מִבִּקְעַת־אָוֶן וְתוֹמֵךְ שֵׁבֶט מִבֵּית עֶדֶן — *And I will cut off any inhabitant from Bikath-aven and one who holds the scepter from Beth-eden.* I will render desolate the prominent Syrian city of Bikath-aven, and I will eradicate from the city of Beth-eden any vestige of the royal family — who hold the scepter as a sign of the authority — residing there (*Radak*).

Daas Mikra suggests that Bikath-aven is in reality the valley of Lebanon, mentioned elsewhere (*Joshua* 11:17). It is given the degrading name Bikath-aven — Valley of Sin — because of the idol Baal Gad which was situated there. Beth-eden he identifies as Bit-adini, a town near the Euphrates river. Thus, the prophet specifies cities on the two ends of Aram to indicate that the entire kingdom will be destroyed.

Abarbanel differs with the majority of the commentators in interpreting Bikath-aven and Beth-eden. He contends that the former is the valley around Damascus, which is outstandingly fertile. Due to its fertility, it was home to multitudes of the people of Damascus, who were then driven from there by the invading enemy. The prophet calls it Valley of Sin because of the wickedness of its inhabitants. Beth-eden is Damascus itself, called such because of the wealth of pleasures it offered its inhabitants. Indeed, he writes, Arab legend has it that Mohammed refused to enter there, stating that one who does so enjoys the Garden of Eden in this world and will therefore not enter there after death.

וְגָלוּ עַם־אֲרָם קִירָה — *And the nation of Aram will be exiled to Kir.* I will exile the people of Aram to the Assyrian city of Kir. This was fulfilled in the times of Ahaz, king of Judah (c. 3183-3199), as described in *II Kings* 16:8 (*Ibn Ezra*; *Radak*).

According to another approach to these two verses, the prophet foretells how the downfall of Damascus will not follow the natural pattern of foreign conquest. Normally, an invading power first conquers the outlying suburbs and only then the major cities. In this case, the enemy will begin his conquest with the royal palace of Hazael, followed by the adjoining palaces built by his son, Ben-hadad. Next, the bolt of the fortified city of Damascus will be broken, followed by the destruction of Bikath-aven, which surrounds it. Beth-eden was the home of a semi-autonomous tribe within the kingdom

5 *And I will break the bolt of Damascus and I will cut*
off any inhabitant from Bikath-aven and one who holds
the scepter from Beth-eden, and the nation of Aram will
be exiled to Kir, said HASHEM. 6 *So said* HASHEM: *For*
three transgressions of Azzah... but for four I will not
acquit them: for their effecting a total exile by
delivering to Edom. 7 *And I will send fire into the wall*
of Azzah and it shall consume its palaces. 8 *And I will*
cut off any inhabitant from Ashdod and one who holds
the scepter from Ashkelon, and I will return My hand

of Aram. It, too, will be exiled to Kir along with the nation of Aram (*Malbim*).

6. The prophet now turns to the people of Philistia, and foretells the retribution to be exacted from them for their oppression of the Jewish people. According to the majority of commentators, the oppression cited, as well as the retribution thereof, occurred centuries after the times of Amos, during the Roman invasion of the Land of Israel. Nevertheless, the prophet alludes to these events in the past tense, in the style of prophetic writings.

עַל־שְׁלֹשָׁה פִּשְׁעֵי עַזָּה וְעַל־אַרְבָּעָה לֹא אֲשִׁיבֶנּוּ — *For three transgressions of Azzah... but for four I will not acquit them.* I have borne the three cardinal transgressions of idolatry, murder, and adultery without responding; the fourth — their persecution of the Jewish nation — cannot be left unavenged (*Abarbanel; Malbim;*[1] see comm. to v. 3).

עַל־הַגְלוֹתָם גָּלוּת שְׁלֵמָה לְהַסְגִּיר לֶאֱדוֹם — *For their effecting a total exile by delivering to Edom.* They cannot be forgiven for having assisted the Roman conqueror (Rome is identified with Edom) in exiling the Jewish people when they destroyed the Second Temple. At that time, the Philistines from Azzah guarded the roads in order to abduct any Jews who escaped and return them to their captors. This was actually done by enemies from all four directions: Azzah to the south, Tyre to the north, Damascus from the east, and the Arabs from the west (*Rashi* from *Sifri* to *Deuteronomy* 32:27).

Others explain that there were Jews who succeeded in escaping the Romans and fled to the neighboring land of Philistia, seeking refuge. Rather than protecting them, the Philistines delivered them into the hands of the enemy (*Ibn Ezra; Radak*).

A third view ascribes this event to the times of the First Temple, when Edomites persecuted the Jews, and the Philistines would deliver them into their hands (*R' Eliezer of Beaugency*).

7. וְשִׁלַּחְתִּי אֵשׁ בְּחוֹמַת עַזָּה וְאָכְלָה אַרְמְנֹתֶיהָ — *And I will send fire into the wall of Azzah and it shall consume its palaces.* I will send the war-fires of the invading enemy to conquer Azzah and destroy its palaces (*Ibn Ezra*; see comm. to v. 4).

8. וְהִכְרַתִּי יוֹשֵׁב מֵאַשְׁדּוֹד וְתוֹמֵךְ שֵׁבֶט מֵאַשְׁקְלוֹן וַהֲשִׁיבוֹתִי יָדִי עַל־עֶקְרוֹן וְאָבְדוּ שְׁאֵרִית פְּלִשְׁתִּים אָמַר ה׳ אֱלֹהִים — *And I will cut off any inhabitant from Ashdod and one who holds the scepter from Ashkelon, and I will return My hand upon Ekron, and the remnant of Philistines shall be lost, says* HASHEM ELOHIM. I will destroy the principal cities of Philistia. Ashdod

1. *Rashi* and *Radak*, who interpret the three sins of Damascus borne by the Almighty in a different vein, offer no explanation here. Perhaps they agree in this case with those who interpret it to mean the cardinal sins.

עַל־עֶקְרוֹן וְאָבְדוּ שְׁאֵרִית פְּלִשְׁתִּים אָמַר אֲדֹנָי
ט יֱהוִה׃ כֹּה אָמַר יהוה עַל־
שְׁלֹשָׁה פִּשְׁעֵי־צֹר וְעַל־אַרְבָּעָה לֹא אֲשִׁיבֶנּוּ
עַל־הַסְגִּירָם גָּלוּת שְׁלֵמָה לֶאֱדוֹם וְלֹא זָכְרוּ
י בְּרִית אַחִים׃ וְשִׁלַּחְתִּי אֵשׁ בְּחוֹמַת צֹר וְאָכְלָה
יא אַרְמְנֹתֶיהָ׃ כֹּה אָמַר
יהוה עַל־שְׁלֹשָׁה פִּשְׁעֵי אֱדוֹם וְעַל־אַרְבָּעָה
לֹא אֲשִׁיבֶנּוּ עַל־רָדְפוֹ בַחֶרֶב אָחִיו וְשִׁחֵת
רַחֲמָיו וַיִּטְרֹף לָעַד אַפּוֹ וְעֶבְרָתוֹ שְׁמָרָה נֶצַח׃

will be left void of inhabitants and Ashkelon shall lose its seat of royalty (*Malbim*). *I will return My hand upon Ekron* — I will smite it once and again (*Rashi*) — i.e., it shall be destroyed twice (*Malbim*). [Indeed, My wrath shall wreak destruction throughout Philistia,] so that no remnant of that nation shall remain extant (*Metzudos David*).

Gath, the fifth major Philistine city, is not cited here, because it was annexed by the kings of Judah and most of its inhabitants converted to Judaism. Those who did not are included in the phrase *the remnant of Philistines* (*Radak* to v. 6).

Radak interprets the phrase *return My hand* somewhat differently: After Ashdod and Ashkelon shall be destroyed, I will yet return My Hand upon Ekron to destroy it, and, with it, those remaining Philistines [from after the first wave of destruction].

Abarbanel maintains that the prophecies of Amos were rendered after those of Joel, and were sometimes said with Joel's prophecies in mind. Thus, having heard Joel's prophecies concerning the downfall of Tyre and Sidon, which were Philistine cities, Amos foretold the destruction of the remainder of that nation.

9. The city of Tyre in Phoenicia enjoyed harmonious relations with the Jewish people during the era of the First Temple. However, they too were destined to persecute the Jewish people during the time of the destruction of the Second Temple, and would in turn be punished for their treachery.

כֹּה אָמַר יהוה . . . עַל־הַסְגִּירָם גָּלוּת שְׁלֵמָה לֶאֱדוֹם — *So said* HASHEM: *. . . for their delivering a total exile to Edom.* The people of Tyre will not be forgiven for the sin, at the time of the destruction of the Second Temple (*Radak*; cf. comm. to v. 6), of capturing Jewish refugees who escaped the Romans and delivering them into their hands (*Rashi* to v. 6). Alternatively, this refers to those Jews who escaped to Tyre, assuming they would find refuge there, only to be handed over to the Romans (*Malbim*).

וְלֹא זָכְרוּ בְּרִית אַחִים — *And they did not remember the covenant of brothers.* Their treachery was particularly heinous in light of the fact that it violated the treaty drawn between Solomon and Hiram, King of Tyre (*I Kings* 5:26), concerning which Hiram said (ibid. 9:13): *What are these cities that you have given me, my brother?* (*Rashi*; *Mahari Kara*).

Alternatively, the brothers cited are Jacob and Esau, the propagators of the Jewish and Roman nations respectively. The Tyrians delivered Jewish exiles into the hands of the Romans, despite the fact that the Romans violated basic humanistic principles by persecuting their Jewish brothers (*Ibn Ezra*; *Radak*).

10. וְשִׁלַּחְתִּי אֵשׁ בְּחוֹמַת צֹר וְאָכְלָה אַרְמְנֹתֶיהָ — *And I will send fire in the wall of Tyre and it shall consume its palaces.* I will

upon Ekron, and the remnant of Philistines shall be lost, says HASHEM ELOHIM. 9 *So said* HASHEM*: For three transgressions of Tyre... but for four I will not acquit them: for their delivering a total exile to Edom... and they did not remember the covenant of brothers.*
10 *And I will send fire in the wall of Tyre and it shall consume its palaces.* 11 *So said* HASHEM*: For three transgressions of Edom but for four I will not acquit them: for pursuing his brother with the sword and destroying his mercy; and his anger has slaughtered incessantly and he has guarded his fury forever.*

destroy Tyre by the hand of Nebuchadnezzar and once again through Alexander the Great (*Malbim*).

11. Next to be castigated is the nation of Edom, the historical nemesis of the Jewish people. Time and again they have been involved in the persecution of the Children of Israel, and they too will receive their just punishment. Some commentators understand the retribution described to refer to the ultimate annihilation of Edom in the times of the Messiah. *Alshich* contends that only partial destruction is discussed by the prophet (see below).

עַל־שְׁלֹשָׁה פִּשְׁעֵי אֱדוֹם וְעַל־אַרְבָּעָה לֹא אֲשִׁיבֶנּוּ — *For three transgressions of Edom... but for four I will not acquit them.* Despite Edom's indulgence in the three cardinal sins, I have restrained My anger, but for the fourth transgression of persecuting the Jewish nation I will not return him empty-handed (*Abarbanel*; *Malbim*; cf. comm. to v. 6).

עַל־רָדְפוֹ בַחֶרֶב אָחִיו וְשִׁחֵת רַחֲמָיו — *For pursuing his brother with the sword and destroying his mercy.* These descendants of Esau have totally destroyed the feelings of mercy they should naturally feel towards their brothers, the Children of Israel, and have responded to them instead with hatred and cruelty (*Radak*). Thus, when the Jewish nation sought to pass through the land of Edom on the way to the Land of Israel, the Edomites met them at the border, refusing them entry, and threatening them with war (*Rashi* from *Numbers* 20:18).

Others explain this to refer to the original hatred of Esau for his brother Jacob (*Mahari Kara*). In this vein, *Ibn Ezra* notes that the word רַחֲמָיו is related to רֶחֶם, the *womb*; although they shared the same womb, he nevertheless sought to kill him.

A third view relates Esau's lack of mercy to the destruction of the Jewish Commonwealth and the Second Temple by Rome (*Radak*).

וַיִּטְרֹף לָעַד אַפּוֹ — *And his anger has slaughtered incessantly.* Throughout the generations he has slaughtered the Jewish people in his anger at every opportunity (*Radak*).

Rashi renders: *he has grasped his anger always* — and never let go.

וְעֶבְרָתוֹ שְׁמָרָה נֶצַח — *And he has guarded his fury forever.* So intense is his fury that it extends to every member of the nation, even those who have done him no harm whatsoever. Thus, throughout history, Edom has seized every opportunity to oppress the Jewish people (*Malbim*).

According to *Radak*, this phrase is merely a reiteration of the previous one.

Abarbanel offers an alternative interpretation to this verse, that the four descriptions of Esau's hatred for Jacob refer to the three transgressions for which the Almighty withheld punishment and the fourth, which sealed their fate. *He pursued his brother with the*

א/יב־טו

יב וְשִׁלַּחְתִּי אֵשׁ בְּתֵימָן וְאָכְלָה אַרְמְנוֹת
יג בָּצְרָה: כֹּה אָמַר יהוה עַל־שְׁלֹשָׁה פִּשְׁעֵי
בְנֵי־עַמּוֹן וְעַל־אַרְבָּעָה לֹא אֲשִׁיבֶנּוּ עַל־בִּקְעָם
יד הָרוֹת הַגִּלְעָד לְמַעַן הַרְחִיב אֶת־גְּבוּלָם: וְהִצַּתִּי
אֵשׁ בְּחוֹמַת רַבָּה וְאָכְלָה אַרְמְנוֹתֶיהָ בִּתְרוּעָה
טו בְּיוֹם מִלְחָמָה בְּסַעַר בְּיוֹם סוּפָה: וְהָלַךְ מַלְכָּם
ב/א א בַּגּוֹלָה הוּא וְשָׂרָיו יַחְדָּו אָמַר יהוה: כֹּה
אָמַר יהוה עַל־שְׁלֹשָׁה פִּשְׁעֵי מוֹאָב וְעַל־

sword when Esau himself sought to murder his brother Jacob. *He destroyed his mercy* by his refusal to allow the Jewish people to pass through his land. *He grasped his anger always* when, in the times of the First Temple, the people of Edom encouraged its destruction, as described in *Psalms* (137:7; cf. Ovadiah 1:11-14). *He has guarded his fury forever* until he finally destroyed the Second Temple, for which there can be no forgiveness.

As noted earlier (comm. to v. 1; preface), *Alshich* contends that the prophecies of Amos concerning all of these nations refer not to their ultimate downfall but only to the partial destruction which occurred to them in Biblical times. Accordingly, the sins of Edom cited here do not include their destruction of the second Temple, since that will only be avenged by their final annihilation.

In line with this approach, he interprets the four phrases of this verse as follows: The first sin was Esau's plan to murder Jacob when the latter was returning from the house of Laban. In so doing he also negated his mercy for his father Isaac, which had prevented him from pursuing his brother before he fled. A third transgression was the attack of Amalek, the descendant of Esau, against the Jewish nation immediately following the exodus from Egypt. That hatred remained in his heart forever, as evidenced by the fact that he tried once again to annihilate the Jews after the death of Aaron, and he subsequently refused the Jews entry into his land. For these four transgressions, the Almighty promises to punish the nation of Edom.

12. וְשִׁלַּחְתִּי אֵשׁ בְּתֵימָן וְאָכְלָה אַרְמְנוֹת בָּצְרָה *— And I will send fire into Taiman and it shall consume the palaces of Bozrah.* Taiman was the son of Elifaz, son of Esau (see *Genesis* 36), and his name was apparently given to a major city in Edom. This should not be confused with present-day Taiman — Yemen — on the Arabian Peninsula (*Daas Mikra*). Bozrah was a city situated between Moab and Edom, which originally belonged to Moab but became aligned with Edom and, in fact, provided them with their second king (*Rashi*; see *Genesis* 36:33). It is mentioned in Scripture as a major city of Edom (*Daas Mikra;* see *Isaiah* 63:1).

Abarbanel contends that Taiman was a city in Biblical Edom, but Bozrah refers to Rome, which was settled by the Edomites. It is called Bozrah — fortified city — because it was the outstanding stronghold of the nation. Thus, the Almighty declares: I will punish contemporary Edom with the destruction of the city of Taiman. But the fires of My vengeance will smolder for centuries to come until they will ultimately consume the city of Rome in the times of the Messiah — just as the Edomites have guarded their hatred for Israel and maintained it throughout the generations.

13. Ammon and Moab were the two nations that descended from Lot, the nephew of Abraham (see *Genesis* 19:30-38). Despite this relationship, Ammon eventually pursued policies of aggression against the Jewish nation, and retribution is therefore forthcoming.

כֹּה אָמַר ה׳ עַל־שְׁלֹשָׁה פִּשְׁעֵי בְנֵי־עַמּוֹן וְעַל־אַרְבָּעָה לֹא אֲשִׁיבֶנּוּ עַל־בִּקְעָם הָרוֹת הַגִּלְעָד

1/12-15 [12] *And I will send fire into Taiman and it shall consume
the palaces of Bozrah.* [13] *So said HASHEM: For three
transgressions of the Ammonites... but for four I will
not acquit them: for their splitting open the pregnant
women of the Gilead in order to extend their border.*
[14] *And I will kindle a fire in the wall of Rabbah and it
shall consume its palaces, amidst trumpeting on the day
of battle, with a hurricane on the day of the tempest.*
[15] *And their king shall go into exile, he and his officers
together, said HASHEM.*

2/1 [1] *So said HASHEM: For three transgressions of Moab...*

לְמַעַן הַרְחִיב אֶת־גְּבוּלָם — *So said HASHEM: For three transgressions of the Ammonites... but for four I will not acquit them: for their splitting open the pregnant women of the Gilead in order to extend their border.* I have borne the indulgence of the children of Ammon in the three cardinal sins (see comm. to vs. 3, 6). However, I will not tolerate their sin upon conquering the cities of Gilead. They split open the pregnant women living there so that they should not produce heirs to the land who would contest the legitimacy of the Ammonite occupation (*Rashi*).

Others translate: *they split the mountains of Gilead* — i.e., they leveled mountains which were in Gilead and illegally extended their borders to include those areas. This type of theft, הַשָּׂגַת גְּבוּל — the extension of one's boundaries to steal someone else's land — is a grave transgression, as evidenced by the fact that it is included in the curses of the Torah [*Deuteronomy* 27:17] (*Radak*).

Alternatively, הָרוֹת refers to the fortified cities — depicted as mountains to symbolize their strength — which were conquered and razed by the people of Ammon (ibid.).

14. וְהִצַּתִּי אֵשׁ בְּחוֹמַת רַבָּה .... — *And I will kindle a fire in the wall of Rabbah ...* I will send the invading enemy against the nation of Ammon. He shall descend upon them suddenly and conquer them swiftly — like the sudden destruction wrought by a powerful storm (*Radak*; *Abarbanel*) — and he will set fire to the capital city of Rabbah (*Abarbanel*).

15. וְהָלַךְ מַלְכָּם בַּגּוֹלָה הוּא וְשָׂרָיו יַחְדָּו אָמַר ה׳ — *And their king shall go into exile, he and his officers together, said HASHEM.*

Not only will the land be conquered, but the king and his officers will also be sent into exile (*Abarbanel*). *Malbim* adds that the word מַלְכָּם can also refer to their idol — which is pronounced *Milkam* (*Daas Mikra* from *I Kings* 11:5).

II

In this chapter, Amos continues his list of nations to be punished for their wrongdoings. The final gentile nation cited is Moab, which, unlike the others, was not involved in the persecution of the Jewish people but is nonetheless culpable for the act of iniquity described below.

1. כֹּה אָמַר ה׳ עַל־שְׁלֹשָׁה פִּשְׁעֵי מוֹאָב וְעַל־אַרְבָּעָה לֹא אֲשִׁיבֶנּוּ עַל־שָׂרְפוֹ עַצְמוֹת מֶלֶךְ־אֱדוֹם לַשִּׂיד — *So said HASHEM: For three transgressions of Moab... but for four I will not acquit him: for his burning the bones of the king of Edom for lime.* Although I have ignored the evil deeds of the nation of Moab, I will not tolerate the

אַרְבָּעָה לֹא אֲשִׁיבֶנּוּ עַל־שָׂרְפוֹ עַצְמוֹת מֶלֶךְ־
ב אֱדוֹם לַשִּׂיד: וְשִׁלַּחְתִּי־אֵשׁ בְּמוֹאָב וְאָכְלָה
אַרְמְנוֹת הַקְּרִיּוֹת וּמֵת בְּשָׁאוֹן מוֹאָב בִּתְרוּעָה
ג בְּקוֹל שׁוֹפָר: וְהִכְרַתִּי שׁוֹפֵט מִקִּרְבָּהּ וְכָל־שָׂרֶיהָ
ד אֶהֱרוֹג עִמּוֹ אָמַר יהוה: כֹּה אָמַר
יהוה עַל־שְׁלֹשָׁה פִּשְׁעֵי יְהוּדָה וְעַל־אַרְבָּעָה לֹא
אֲשִׁיבֶנּוּ עַל־מָאֳסָם אֶת־תּוֹרַת יהוה וְחֻקָּיו לֹא
שָׁמָרוּ וַיַּתְעוּם כִּזְבֵיהֶם אֲשֶׁר־הָלְכוּ אֲבוֹתָם
ה אַחֲרֵיהֶם: וְשִׁלַּחְתִּי אֵשׁ בִּיהוּדָה וְאָכְלָה אַרְמְנוֹת
ו יְרוּשָׁלִָם: כֹּה אָמַר יהוה עַל־
שְׁלֹשָׁה פִּשְׁעֵי יִשְׂרָאֵל וְעַל־אַרְבָּעָה לֹא אֲשִׁיבֶנּוּ

fact that their king murdered the king of Edom, burned his bones, and used the ashes to color the walls of his house. This degradation of royalty cannot go unpunished (*Rashi; Targum*), and the grave affront to the honor of Isaac, Edom's ancestor, must be avenged (*Ibn Ezra*).

Others explain this as alluding to the verse in *II Kings* 3:27: *And he took his first-born son who would reign after him and he brought him up for a burnt-offering and there was a great anger against Israel.* This took place during a war in which the kings of Judah, Israel, and Edom were allied against the forces of Moab. At that time, the king of Moab, who had taken captive the crown prince of Edom — referred to here by the position of king for which he was designated — brought him up for a burnt-offering to his god on the wall of the city. Because this loss was brought about through the nations of Israel and Judah, it incited the king of Edom in hatred against them, eventually causing them much suffering. For this iniquitous deed, and the Edomite anger against Israel that it precipitated, the nation of Moab is taken to task by the Almighty (*Radak*; *Abarbanel*; see *Radak* to *II Kings* ad loc.).

2. וּמֵת בְּשָׁאוֹן מוֹאָב.. — *And Moab shall die in tumult. . .* Moab will be annihilated in the tumult of battle while the enemy trumpets and sounds the shofar (*Metzudos David*). *Malbim* interprets: Moab will die of fright from the din of battle, without even entering into the fray.

3. וְהִכְרַתִּי שׁוֹפֵט מִקִּרְבָּהּ וְכָל־שָׂרֶיהָ אֶהֱרוֹג עִמּוֹ אָמַר ה׳ — *And I will cut off the ruler from its midst, and all its officers I will kill along with him, said* HASHEM. I will kill the king of Moab as well as his officers (*Ibn Ezra*), cutting them off from amidst the city of Kerioth, the seat of the Moabite royalty (*Radak*).

4. At this point, the prophet shifts his focus from the gentile nations to the Children of Israel, castigating them for their misdeeds and describing the impending catastrophes they have brought upon themselves. He begins with the southern kingdom of Judah, to which he addresses himself briefly, and then continues on to the primary subject of his prophecies, the northern kingdom of the ten tribes of Israel.

כֹּה אָמַר ה׳. . . — *So said* HASHEM. . . I have remained patient with the people of Judah even as they indulged in the three cardinal sins (*Abarbanel*; *Alshich*; *Malbim*). [However, their behavior can no longer be tolerated] for they despise the Torah and its statutes, and do not even bother to include Me in their worship along with their other gods. Rather, they are steeped

but for four I will not acquit him: for his burning the
bones of the king of Edom for lime. 2 *And I will send fire*
into Moab and it shall consume the palaces of Kerioth,
and Moab shall die in tumult, amidst trumpeting and
the sound of the shofar. 3 *And I will cut off the ruler*
from its midst, and all its officers I will kill along with
him, said HASHEM. 4 *So said* HASHEM: *For three trans-*
gressions of Judah. . . but for four I will not acquit them:
for their despising the Torah of HASHEM *and His*
statutes they did not heed, and their falsehoods that
their fathers followed have corrupted them. 5 *And I will*
send fire into Judah and it shall consume the palaces
of Jerusalem. 6 *So said* HASHEM: *For three transgres-*
sions of Israel. . . but for four I will not acquit them:

entirely in the deceptive teachings of their false prophets and the service of their idols (*Abarbanel*).

Alternatively, their transgressions are not the result of powerful urges to which they succumb but are rather due to their denial of the legitimacy of the Torah and its precepts, brought about by the distorted beliefs and ideas transmitted to them by their fathers (*Malbim*).

Alshich understands the emphasis of this verse differently: For their indulgence in idolatry, bloodshed, and promiscuity I would withhold punishment. However, they have rejected the study of the Torah and [their commitment] to the fulfillment of its precepts and thus My hand can no longer be stayed.[1]

According to *Radak*, this verse describes the regimes of the four wicked kings of Judah who reigned after the death of Hezekiah. Prior to that time, although there were periods of sinful behavior, the Almighty exacted retribution little by little, rather than castigating the people for all of their sins with one major punishment. However, this approach ended with the reign of Manasseh, who exceeded all previous monarchs in the scope of his evil deeds. Still, Hashem stayed His hand from destruction, as He continued to do through the iniquitous reign of Ammon and that of Jehoachaz. However, when Zedekiah, too, followed in their wicked ways (*II Kings* 24:19; cf. *Malbim* ad loc.), the attribute of justice could no longer be restrained, and the wrath of the Almighty was poured over Jerusalem. Thus: Through the iniquitous reigns of three monarchs I have stayed My hand from punishment, but with the advent of the fourth I can no longer acquit them.

5. וְשִׁלַּחְתִּי אֵשׁ בִּיהוּדָה וְאָכְלָה אַרְמְנוֹת יְרוּשָׁלִָם — *And I will send fire into Judah and it shall consume the palaces of Jerusalem.* The roaring "flames" of the armies of Nebuchadnezzar will descend upon the people of Judah (*Ibn Ezra; Radak*), along with actual fires which shall consume the Temple and the royal palaces of Jerusalem (*Abarbanel*).

6. כֹּה אָמַר ה׳ . . . — *So said* HASHEM: *For three transgressions of Israel. . . but for four I will not acquit them: for their*

1. This follows the statements of the Sages (*Midrash Eichah, Pesichta* 2): If only they would abandon Me and yet keep My Torah, the light within it would guide them back to righteousness.

עַל־מִכְרָם בַּכֶּסֶף֙ צַדִּ֔יק וְאֶבְי֖וֹן בַּעֲב֥וּר נַעֲלָֽיִם׃
ז הַשֹּׁאֲפִ֤ים עַל־עֲפַר־אֶ֙רֶץ֙ בְּרֹ֣אשׁ דַּלִּ֔ים וְדֶ֥רֶךְ
עֲנָוִ֖ים יַטּ֑וּ וְאִ֣ישׁ וְאָבִ֗יו יֵֽלְכוּ֙ אֶל־הַֽנַּעֲרָ֔ה לְמַ֥עַן
ח חַלֵּ֖ל אֶת־שֵׁ֥ם קָדְשִֽׁי׃ וְעַל־בְּגָדִ֤ים חֲבֻלִים֙
יַטּ֔וּ אֵ֖צֶל כָּל־מִזְבֵּ֑חַ וְיֵ֤ין עֲנוּשִׁים֙ יִשְׁתּ֔וּ בֵּ֖ית
ט אֱלֹהֵיהֶֽם׃ וְאָנֹכִ֗י הִשְׁמַ֤דְתִּי אֶת־הָאֱמֹרִי֙ מִפְּנֵיהֶ֔ם

selling a righteous man for silver, and a poor man for shoes. I can tolerate the guilt of the nation of Israel even for their transgression of the three cardinal sins. However, their involvement in a fourth sin as well has sealed their fate that they be conquered and exiled by the Assyrians (*Radak*). This sin is that of corruption, which is so rampant in their society that even the judges are totally steeped in graft, and they sell their verdict to the highest bidder. A decision against a man of means, who has the capacity to retaliate, can be acquired with silver. To rule against a poor man, who is helpless against the judges, all they demand is a pair of shoes (*Alshich*).

This is considered to be the height of iniquity, as evidenced by the fact that the fate of Sodom and Gemorrah was sealed because of their involvement in the sin of robbery (*Sanhedrin* 108a). Certainly when the culprits are the judges themselves, who are responsible for maintaining law-and-order, such practices cannot be tolerated (*Radak*).

Targum interprets: *and a poor man in order to inherit*. A judge would bend the law against a poor man who owned property between his own fields so that he would need to sell his field in order to pay. Thus, the judge effectively locked in [from the word לִנְעֹל, *to lock*] all the fields within his property lines (*Rashi*; cf. *Radak*).

7. הַשֹּׁאֲפִים עַל־עֲפַר־אֶרֶץ בְּרֹאשׁ דַּלִּים — *Who aspire upon the dust of the earth for the head of the poor.* As they tread upon the dust of the earth, all their thoughts and aspirations concern the poor man and how they will rob him of his possessions (*Rashi*; *Mahari Kara*).

Others render: *Who aspire to [crush to] the dust of the earth the heads of the poor* — by appointing officers who beat them to the ground if they resist the false judgments rendered against them (*Ibn Ezra*; *Radak*).

וְדֶרֶךְ עֲנָוִים יַטּוּ — *And the way of the humble they divert.* They cause the weak and humble to veer from their path in order to avoid encountering these judges, whom they so rightly fear (*Rashi*; *Mahari Kara*). Alternatively: They pervert the judgment of the humble for the sake of the bribery they receive (*Targum*; *Radak*).

וְאִישׁ וְאָבִיו יֵלְכוּ אֶל־הַנַּעֲרָה — *And a man and his father go to a maiden.* [A father and son go together to have promiscuous relations with] a betrothed maiden[1] (*Rashi*), with no shame from each other for their wicked deed (*Radak*).

Ibn Ezra explains this as connected to the previous phrase: *they diverged from the path of humility to such a degree that a father and son go together to visit a prostitute.*

לְמַעַן חַלֵּל אֶת־שֵׁם קָדְשִׁי — *In order to desecrate My Holy Name.* This behavior is a grave desecration of My Holy Name, for the Jewish people have been called in My Name and are obligated to act in accordance with the sanctity it confers upon them (*Radak*). Such brazen wicked-

1. Having relations with a betrothed girl who has only recently attained her legal majority (נַעֲרָה מְאוֹרָסָה) is singled out by the Torah (*Devarim* 22:23) as a particularly heinous form of adultery.

for their selling a righteous man for silver, and a poor
man for shoes. [7] *Who aspire upon the dust of the earth*
for the head of the poor, and the way of the humble they
divert, and a man and his father go to a maiden in order
to desecrate My Holy Name. [8] *And on pledged gar-*
ments they recline beside every altar, and the wine of
the penalized they drink in the house of their gods.
[9] *And I destroyed the Emorite from before them —*

ness indicates so great a disrespect for My Honor that it is tantamount to acting for the express purpose of desecrating My Name (*Abarbanel*; *Metzudos David*).

8. וְעַל־בְּגָדִים חֲבֻלִים יַטּוּ אֵצֶל כָּל־מִזְבֵּחַ — *And on pledged garments they recline beside every altar.* They confiscate the clothing of the poor as security for the payments they impose upon them [in their false judgments], and they recline upon those garments as they feast (*Rashi*; *Mahari Kara*; *Radak*) by the altars of their idols (*Mahari Kara*).

Ibn Ezra translates: Not only do they pervert justice in order to confiscate the clothing of the poor as securities, but they are brazen enough to do this publicly, in the places where they gather together by the altars of Baal.

וְיֵין עֲנוּשִׁים יִשְׁתּוּ בֵּית אֱלֹהֵיהֶם — *And the wine of the penalized they drink in the house of their gods.* With the money from the fines which they impose upon the people [unjustly (*Ibn Ezra*)], they go and buy wine, which they drink in their temples of idolatry (*Rashi*).

Abarbanel interprets these three verses to be describing how the fourth sin of the people of Israel duplicates all of the iniquities of the nations cited above, and they therefore merit special punishment. Just as the people of Tyre and Gaza betrayed the trust of the Jewish refugees who turned to them for help, so did the judges of Israel betray the trust placed in them by perverting the judgment of the innocent for the sake of bribery. Just as the people of Damascus were taken to task for their cruel treatment of the inhabitants of Gilead, so were the judges of Israel cited for their cruelty to the poor, whom they ground into degrading submission. Just as Edom betrayed the bonds of brotherhood by their treatment of their Jewish cousins, so did the Israelites profane their family ties and the constraints they impose by father and son going together to commit adultery. Just as the Ammonites manifested their corruption by extending their borders into the hills of Gilead, so did the people of Israel indulge in robbery by taking for security the garments of the poor and using them for their own purposes. And just as the king of Moab brought the son of the king of Edom, whom he had abducted, as a sacrifice to his idol, so did the people of Israel drink wine bought with stolen money in the worship of their false gods.

Malbim contends that all of the transgressions cited are extensions of the three cardinal sins. In addition to murder, they would accept graft to judge or testify falsely and thereby cause innocent people to be executed. In the realm of adultery, they became so immoral that a father and son were not embarrassed to go together to sin with a betrothed maiden. In addition to worshiping false gods, they also stole the money and possessions of others to use in their worship. Thus, all of these are included in the statement: *and for four I will not acquit them* — the fourth sin being their extension of the other three.

9. Prior to describing the retribution to be exacted for the wickedness cited above, the Almighty first elaborates upon His unique relationship with the Jewish nation and the lessons He has provided them to encourage righteousness. In the light of this unique bond with Hashem, their decadent ways are particularly reprehensible and they are thus deserving of extremely harsh punishment.

וְאָנֹכִי הִשְׁמַדְתִּי אֶת־הָאֱמֹרִי . . . — *And I destroyed the Emorite . . .* I destroyed the

אֲשֶׁר כְּגֹבַהּ אֲרָזִים֙ גָּבְה֔וֹ וְחָסֹ֥ן ה֖וּא כָּֽאַלּוֹנִ֑ים
י וָאַשְׁמִ֤יד פִּרְיוֹ֙ מִמַּ֔עַל וְשָׁרָשָׁ֖יו מִתָּֽחַת׃ וְאָנֹכִ֛י
הֶעֱלֵ֥יתִי אֶתְכֶ֖ם מֵאֶ֣רֶץ מִצְרָ֑יִם וָאוֹלֵ֨ךְ אֶתְכֶ֜ם
בַּמִּדְבָּר֙ אַרְבָּעִ֣ים שָׁנָ֔ה לָרֶ֖שֶׁת אֶת־אֶ֥רֶץ הָאֱמֹרִֽי׃
יא וָאָקִ֤ים מִבְּנֵיכֶם֙ לִנְבִיאִ֔ים וּמִבַּחוּרֵיכֶ֖ם לִנְזִרִ֑ים
יב הַאַ֥ף אֵין־זֹ֛את בְּנֵ֥י יִשְׂרָאֵ֖ל נְאֻם־יְהוָֽה׃ וַתַּשְׁק֥וּ
אֶת־הַנְּזִרִ֖ים יָ֑יִן וְעַל־הַנְּבִיאִים֙ צִוִּיתֶ֣ם לֵאמֹ֔ר לֹ֖א

Emorites — the most powerful of the seven Canaanite nations — from before the Jewish nation when the latter entered the Land of Israel (*Radak*). The double metaphor of the mighty trees is explained by *Malbim* as follows: The Emorites' heavenly benefactor, the angel appointed to guide their destiny, was lofty like the cedar trees (due to his prominent position among the Heavenly hosts). Their rulers, too, enjoyed a very high stature [among the nations], their military strength as formidable as the mighty oak (*Malbim*). Nevertheless, I annihilated them completely due to their wicked ways (*Mahari Kara; Radak*) and due to the desecration of My Holy Land caused by their misdeeds (*Ibn Ezra*). This should have served as a warning to you, Israel, who, as My Holy nation, are expected to adhere to a higher standard of behavior (*Metzudos David*). Nevertheless, you did not take heed of this lesson, but rather emulated the deeds of the Emorites and followed in their evil ways (*Mahari Kara; Radak*).

וָאַשְׁמִיד פִּרְיוֹ מִמַּעַל וְשָׁרָשָׁיו מִתָּחַת — *And I destroyed his fruit from above and his roots from below.* They were not destroyed by your might, but rather by Mine (*Radak*), as evidenced by the miraculous manner in which they were defeated (*Malbim*). Both their heavenly protectors (*Rashi*) (who had provided them with sustenance and are thus symbolized by fruit — *Abarbanel*) and their human princes (*Rashi*) — along with all other aspects of natural power which they enjoyed (*Abarbanel*) — were destroyed.

Alternatively, this phrase refers to the צִרְעָה, *tzirah*, an insect employed by the Almighty in defeating the Canaanite nations (see *Devarim* 7:20), This creature would emit a poison at them which blinded their eyes [*destroyed his fruit*] and rendered them sterile [*destroyed . . . his roots below*] (*Rashi*).

Mahari Kara interprets: The son is the fruit of the father and the father the root of the son — i.e., he destroyed father and son together.

The Sages comment: Sichon (the mighty king of the Emorites) was mighty like a tower and no human being could conquer him. What did the Almighty do? He tied up his heavenly benefactor and threw him from his place [in Heaven] and handed him over to the Jewish people (*Tanchuma, Yalkut Shimoni*).

10. וְאָנֹכִי הֶעֱלֵיתִי אֶתְכֶם מֵאֶרֶץ מִצְרָיִם וָאוֹלֵךְ אֶתְכֶם בַּמִּדְבָּר אַרְבָּעִים שָׁנָה לָרֶשֶׁת אֶת־אֶרֶץ הָאֱמֹרִי — *And I brought you up from the land of Egypt and I led you through the wilderness forty years to inherit the land of the Emorites.* [You have followed in your evil ways despite the fact that] I secluded you in the desert for forty years in order to accustom you to My statutes so that you would not emulate the depravities of the Canaanites when you came to the Land of Israel.

Alternatively, the final phrase, *to inherit the land of the Emorites,* refers back to the beginning of the verse (*Radak*): I took you out of Egypt to become My sanctified nation and rise above the Canaanite level of behavior so that you would be worthy of inheriting their land.

whose height was like the height of cedar trees and
who was mighty like oaks — and I destroyed his
fruit from above and his roots from below. 10 *And I*
brought you up from the land of Egypt and I led
you through the wilderness forty years to inherit the
land of the Emorites. 11 *And I raised up some of your*
sons as prophets and some of your young men as
nazirites; is this also not so, Children of Israel? says
HASHEM. 12 *And you gave the nazirites wine to drink*
and to the prophets you commanded, saying, 'Do not

However, you did not live up to My expectations but rather steeped yourself in the depravities of the heathen nations (*Mahari Kara*).

11. וָאָקִים מִבְּנֵיכֶם לִנְבִיאִים וּמִבַּחוּרֵיכֶם לִנְזִרִים הַאַף אֵין־זֹאת בְּנֵי יִשְׂרָאֵל נְאֻם־ה׳ — *And I raised up some of your sons as prophets and some of your young men as nazirites;*[1] *is this also not so, Children of Israel? says HASHEM.*

I made you unique among all the nations of the world by bestowing upon you alone the spirit of My prophecy (*Radak*) in order to teach you My statutes (*Ibn Ezra*) and infuse you with My holiness (*Radak*). So great was My beneficence that even your young sons were blessed with the gift of prophecy (*Ibn Ezra; Radak*) [without the years of self-development which would seem to be necessary for so great an achievement]. Furthermore, even the youth among you, whose nature it is to follow their every whim and seek to satisfy all their desires, were moved to elevate themselves above these pursuits and undertake nazirite vows (*Ibn Ezra; Radak*).

Targum renders נְזִרִים to mean teachers — referring to those who turn away from all mundane endeavors and devote themselves solely to the study [and teaching] of Torah (*Rashi*; cf. *Mahari Kara*).

הַאַף אֵין־זֹאת — *Is this also not so.* Would you deny the truth of this claim (*Rashi*)?

Others explain this as linked to the following verse: Is it not sufficient that you do not heed My statutes? Must you also deter others from pursuing the levels of prophecy and *nezirus* (*Abarbanel*)?

12. וַתַּשְׁקוּ אֶת־הַנְּזִרִים יָיִן וְעַל־הַנְּבִיאִים צִוִּיתֶם לֵאמֹר לֹא תִּנָּבְאוּ — *And you gave the nazirites wine to drink and to the prophets you commanded, saying, 'Do not prophesy.'* Your wickedness did not end with ignoring My commandments and refusing to appreciate My benevolence. Rather, you even deterred those who sought to achieve the levels of prophecy and *nezirus*, which were the marks of the sanctity of the Jewish nation (*Radak*). You coerced (*Ibn Ezra*) or persuaded (*Radak*) the nazirites to drink wine [in violation of their nazirite vows], and you forcefully prevented the prophets among you from prophesying and admonishing you in My name (*Radak*).

Amos himself was a victim of this behavior, when Amaziah, the priest of

1. A nazirite is someone who vows to abstain from wine, avoid *tumah* (spiritual contamination), and refrain from cutting his hair for a specified period of time. The Torah (*Numbers* ch. 6) grants such a person the status of a nazirite and dictates a series of laws which are unique to him alone. Such a person is considered to be crowned with a lofty level of sanctity comparable to that of a prophet (*Ramban*, ad loc. v. 14).

יג תְּנַבְּאוּ: הִנֵּה אָנֹכִי מֵעִיק תַּחְתֵּיכֶם כַּאֲשֶׁר
יד תָּעִיק הָעֲגָלָה הַמְלֵאָה לָהּ עָמִיר: וְאָבַד מָנוֹס
מִקָּל וְחָזָק לֹא־יְאַמֵּץ כֹּחוֹ וְגִבּוֹר לֹא־יְמַלֵּט
טו נַפְשׁוֹ: וְתֹפֵשׂ הַקֶּשֶׁת לֹא יַעֲמֹד וְקַל בְּרַגְלָיו
טז לֹא יְמַלֵּט וְרֹכֵב הַסּוּס לֹא יְמַלֵּט נַפְשׁוֹ: וְאַמִּיץ
לִבּוֹ בַּגִּבּוֹרִים עָרוֹם יָנוּס בַּיּוֹם־הַהוּא נְאֻם־
ג/א א יהוה: שִׁמְעוּ אֶת־הַדָּבָר הַזֶּה
אֲשֶׁר דִּבֶּר יהוה עֲלֵיכֶם בְּנֵי יִשְׂרָאֵל עַל כָּל־
הַמִּשְׁפָּחָה אֲשֶׁר הֶעֱלֵיתִי מֵאֶרֶץ מִצְרַיִם לֵאמֹר:

Beth-el, enjoined him from prophesying (*Rashi*; see 7:12).

As cited above (comm. to v. 11), *Targum* interprets the mention of nazirites to refer to the Torah scholars. The people would force these scholars to drink wine and thereby prevent them from issuing decisions in Torah law, since this is prohibited to one who is inebriated (*Rashi*).

13. The prophet now foretells the punishment which will befall the nation of Israel because of the sins cited above. Since the primary focus of his prophecies is the kingdom of Israel, he goes into much greater detail in describing their punishment than he did with the other nations (*Abarbanel*).

הִנֵּה אָנֹכִי מֵעִיק תַּחְתֵּיכֶם כַּאֲשֶׁר תָּעִיק הָעֲגָלָה הַמְלֵאָה לָהּ עָמִיר — *Behold I will oppress [you] in your place just as the wagon full of sheaves is oppressed.* I will oppress you in your dwelling places until you will be like a wagon filled with bundles of grain, which — figuratively speaking — is oppressed by its heavy load and by the foul air of the sheaves (*Radak*). [Furthermore,] I will enclose you in your place allowing you no escape, just as a wagon filled with sheaves is encircled with a fence to prevent the grain from spilling out (*Malbim*).

14. וְאָבַד מָנוֹס מִקָּל וְחָזָק לֹא־יְאַמֵּץ כֹּחוֹ וְגִבּוֹר לֹא־יְמַלֵּט נַפְשׁוֹ — *And escape shall be lost to the swift; the strong shall not strengthen himself; and the mighty one shall not save his soul.* The enemy's presence will be so pervasive that even the swift of foot will be unable to flee him (*Metzudos David*). Even those with great natural strength will be unable to stand up to the enemy forces, for the overwhelming fear that he inspires will weaken their might (*Malbim*) and render them unable to concentrate enough to gather their strength (*Radak*). Not only will the mighty be unable to turn the tide of battle, but their strength will not even suffice to save their own lives (*Malbim*).

Abarbanel approaches these two verses in a different manner: Just as a wagon filled with sheaves squeaks and groans from the weight of its burden as it travels along, so shall you be unable to contain your cries of anguish from the oppression of the enemy.

Generally, when the tide of battle turns against an army, they seek the appropriate means to escape death or captivity. The swift of foot simply flee. The strong warriors, laden with armor, harness their superior energy and find the means to escape their pursuers. Those who are mighty — but less so than the former group — are left with no alternative but to fight for their lives. In any event, all three of these groups are totally involved in seeking the means to escape with their lives. In your case, however, none of these courses of action will be open to you, and you will be left with no recourse save to cry out in anguish.

2/13-16 *prophesy.' 13 Behold I will oppress [you] in your place*
just as the wagon full of sheaves is oppressed. 14 And
escape shall be lost to the swift; the strong shall not
strengthen himself; and the mighty one shall not save
his soul. 15 And he who holds the bow shall not stand;
the swift of foot shall not escape; the rider of the horse
shall not save his soul. 16 And *the bold-hearted among*
the mighty shall flee naked on that day, says HASHEM.

3/1 1 *Hear this word which* HASHEM *has spoken to you,*
Children of Israel, concerning the entire family
which I brought up from the land of Egypt, saying:

15. וְתֹפֵשׂ הַקֶּשֶׁת לֹא יַעֲמֹד וְקַל בְּרַגְלָיו לֹא יְמַלֵּט וְרֹכֵב הַסּוּס לֹא יְמַלֵּט נַפְשׁוֹ — *And he who holds the bow shall not stand; the swift of foot shall not escape; the rider of the horse shall not save his soul.* The archer will be unable to exercise his skill, for he will not have the strength to draw his bow (*Radak*). He will therefore abandon his position and flee in fear from the enemy (*Ibn Ezra*). Nor shall the swift make use of their speed, for they will not have the energy to take flight. Even the cavalry will be unable to escape, for the horse offers no salvation when the Almighty does not will it (*Radak*).

Malbim interprets this verse as describing a pattern of cause and effect. The archer, who usually holds off the enemy long enough for others to escape, will not maintain his position but will rather flee immediately. Therefore, even those who are swift of foot or riding on horses will not have the opportunity to flee.

16. וְאַמִּיץ לִבּוֹ בַּגִּבּוֹרִים עָרוֹם יָנוּס בַּיּוֹם־הַהוּא נְאֻם־ה׳ — *And the bold-hearted among the mighty shall flee naked on that day, says* HASHEM. Even the brave and mighty warriors will flee empty-handed ("naked") without their weapons of war (*Targum*; *Rashi*; *Mahari Kara*). Alternatively, they will shed even their clothing in order to speed their flight (*Ibn Ezra*; *Radak*; *Abarbanel*).

Malbim comments: If there will be one warrior who is mightier and more courageous than the rest, his superior prowess may enable him to flee with his life. However, he will not manage to salvage his money or clothing, and he will [certainly] not be victorious in battle.

III

1. The prophet relates to the ten tribes of the kingdom of Israel (*Children of Israel*) the word of the Almighty which was actually intended for the entire Jewish people (*the entire family...*) (*Alshich*). [In this verse, he touches again upon the theme of Israel's unique relationship with the Almighty and the high level of morality in which it obligates them.]

כָּל־הַמִּשְׁפָּחָה — *The entire family.* The entire nation is referred to as one great family (*Radak*).

אֲשֶׁר הֶעֱלֵיתִי מֵאֶרֶץ מִצְרַיִם — *Which I brought up from the land of Egypt.* I took you out of Egypt and established you as My 'portion' in creation, to be dealt with directly and solely by Divine Providence without any medium of heavenly benefactors and astrological forces between us (*Malbim*).

ב רַק אֶתְכֶם יָדַעְתִּי מִכֹּל מִשְׁפְּחוֹת הָאֲדָמָה עַל־
ג כֵּן אֶפְקֹד עֲלֵיכֶם אֵת כָּל־עֲוֹנֹתֵיכֶם׃ הֲיֵלְכוּ שְׁנַיִם
ד יַחְדָּו בִּלְתִּי אִם־נוֹעָדוּ׃ הֲיִשְׁאַג אַרְיֵה בַּיַּעַר וְטֶרֶף
אֵין לוֹ הֲיִתֵּן כְּפִיר קוֹלוֹ מִמְּעֹנָתוֹ בִּלְתִּי אִם־
ה לָכָד׃ הֲתִפֹּל צִפּוֹר עַל־פַּח הָאָרֶץ וּמוֹקֵשׁ אֵין
לָהּ הֲיַעֲלֶה־פַּח מִן־הָאֲדָמָה וְלָכוֹד לֹא יִלְכּוֹד׃

2. רַק אֶתְכֶם יָדַעְתִּי מִכֹּל מִשְׁפְּחוֹת הָאֲדָמָה עַל־כֵּן אֶפְקֹד עֲלֵיכֶם אֵת כָּל־עֲוֹנֹתֵיכֶם — *You alone did I know from among all of the families of the earth; therefore I will visit upon you all of your sins.* I have made your suffering known to Me more than that of any other people and I have manifested that knowledge by saving you from your persecutors. Because of this, your sins against Me are of greater magnitude than the iniquities of other nations and are thus more cause for retribution (*Mahari Kara; Ibn Ezra*). *Targum* and *Rashi* translate יָדַעְתִּי to mean *I loved* — in return for the love I showed you, you have rebelled against Me.

Alternatively: It is common practice for kings to be more strict in dealing with those who are close to them than with those who are distant, as more is expected from the former (*Ibn Ezra; Radak*). Similarly, because I have blessed you with Divine providence in every aspect of your lives — and I am thereby intimately involved in all that you do — you are obliged to adhere to a higher standard of behavior. Your failure to do so cannot go unrequited and I will therefore visit upon you all of your sins (*Abarbanel*).

The Sages interpret this verse in a different light. They offer a parable of a person who lends money to two people, one whom he loves and one whom he despises. From his friend he exacts payment little by little so that it should not have too great an effect upon his finances. From his enemy he demands the entire payment at one time; and when time for payment arrives, he collects it mercilessly. So, too, the Almighty grants the other nations the freedom to act as they choose until they reach the 'limits of His endurance,' at which time He exacts retribution mercilessly. From the Jews, however, He exacts partial payment on an ongoing basis so that the scope of their punishment should be limited (*Avodah Zarah* 4a; *Alshich*). [Thus, whereas other nations have achieved great prosperity and prestige and then passed from this stage of history, the Jewish people have undergone one cataclysm after the other but remain extant after so many centuries (cf. fn to 1:1).]

3. The prophet now goes on to pose seven rhetorical questions to preface his subsequent prophecy. All of these questions are meant to emphasize how every event that takes place can be properly understood only in the light of its true cause. Similarly, the calamities that have befallen the Jewish nation must be viewed as their punishment from the Almighty for their sins.

Along with the basic flow of these verses, these questions convey additional points metaphorically. These messages have been added to the interpretation in smaller print.

הֲיֵלְכוּ שְׁנַיִם יַחְדָּו בִּלְתִּי אִם־נוֹעָדוּ — *Do two walk together unless they [so] arranged?* If two people arrive in the same place at the same time for the same purpose, is it not evident that their meeting was pre-arranged (*Ibn Ezra*; cf. *Rashi*)?

Similarly, the fact that the words of the prophets all come true is ample evidence that the events they predict are predestined and they themselves are My emissaries. Accordingly, your protestations to them that they should cease to prophesy [about coming calamities] are senseless (ibid.).

[2] *You alone did I know from among all of the families of the earth; therefore I will visit upon you all of your sins.* [3] *Do two walk together unless they [so] arranged?* [4] *Does the lion roar in the forest if it has no kill? Does the young lion send forth its voice from its lair unless it has captured?* [5] *Does a bird fall on the net on the ground if it does not have a snare? Does the net rise from the ground without entrapping?*

Another interpretation is as follows: The fact that the separate nations of Judah and Israel both transgressed the word of Hashem and turned to idolatry simultaneously is evidence that they support each other's wickedness, much as if they had planned their deviation together. Similarly, the gentile nations will seem to have plotted together to bring about their destruction — an allusion to the invasion of Israel by Sennacherib and that of Judah by Nebuchadnezzar (*Abarbanel*).

4. הֲיִשְׁאַג אַרְיֵה בַּיַּעַר וְטֶרֶף אֵין לוֹ — *Does the lion roar in the forest if it has no kill?* Does the lion let out its mighty roar of victory if it has not yet killed its prey (*Rashi*)?

Similarly, Nebuchadnezzar's cry of triumph will be evidence of his success in conquering the Jewish nation (ibid. to v. 6).

Ibn Ezra understands it to refer to the Almighty: [Do you think] that My roar is any less significant than the lion's? [I.e., are My words of warning through My prophets to be taken so lightly?] Even as the lion's roar betokens conquest, would I roar for nothing?

הֲיִתֵּן כְּפִיר קוֹלוֹ מִמְּעֹנָתוֹ בִּלְתִּי אִם־לָכָד — *Does the young lion send forth its voice from its lair unless it has captured?* Does the young lion emit a jubilant roar from its lair if it has not succeeded in capturing its prey (*Metzudos David*)?

Alternatively: *Does the young lion come out from its lair and raise its voice without capturing?* Just as one who is attacked by a lion is unable to flee because its mighty roar paralyzes him with terror, so, too, will it be impossible for you to escape the judgment that I shall wreak upon you (*Ibn Ezra*).

Rashi offers a second interpretation to this verse, that it refers to the spirit of prophecy which descends upon a prophet. Thus, the prophet poses the questions: Does the Almighty send His prophets to prophesy evil unless he has prey — i.e., unless there is a decree of evil in Heaven? Does He emit His voice to speak harshly unless He has caught you with iniquity?

5. הֲתִפֹּל צִפּוֹר עַל־פַּח הָאָרֶץ וּמוֹקֵשׁ אֵין לָהּ — *Does a bird fall on the net on the ground if it does not have a snare?* Does a bird alight upon the net if there is no snare inside to lure it (*Metzudos David*)?

Alternatively: Does a bird fall upon the net without being trapped by the snare? Similarly, do you think you can commit transgressions without being trapped in the web of punishment caused by your misdeeds (*Rashi*)?

הֲיַעֲלֶה־פַּח מִן־הָאֲדָמָה וְלָכוֹד לֹא יִלְכּוֹד — *Does the net rise from the ground without entrapping?* Does a net lying on the ground suddenly rise from its place unless there is a bird caught within struggling to escape (*Rashi*)?

Similarly, will your sins rise to the Heavens without ensnaring you in their grasp (ibid.)?[1]

Ibn Ezra interprets this verse in the following manner: A bird which flies above in the sky would seem to be impervious to human attack. Nevertheless, the human being is

1. [This metaphor is best understood in the light of the words of *Nefesh HaChaim*. He explains that the system of creation is so designed that every *mitzvah* performed sets in motion dynamics that bring reward to the one who performed it, and every transgression works in the opposite manner. Thus, the sin itself is the net which ensnares the sinner in his punishment.]

ו אִם־יִתָּקַע שׁוֹפָר בְּעִיר וְעָם לֹא יֶחֱרָדוּ אִם־
ז תִּהְיֶה רָעָה בְּעִיר וַיהוָה לֹא עָשָׂה: כִּי לֹא
יַעֲשֶׂה אֲדֹנָי יֱהוִה דָּבָר כִּי אִם־גָּלָה סוֹדוֹ
ח אֶל־עֲבָדָיו הַנְּבִיאִים: אַרְיֵה שָׁאָג מִי לֹא
ט יִירָא אֲדֹנָי יֱהוִה דִּבֶּר מִי לֹא יִנָּבֵא: הַשְׁמִיעוּ
עַל־אַרְמְנוֹת בְּאַשְׁדּוֹד וְעַל־אַרְמְנוֹת בְּאֶרֶץ
מִצְרָיִם וְאִמְרוּ הֵאָסְפוּ עַל־הָרֵי שֹׁמְרוֹן וּרְאוּ
מְהוּמֹת רַבּוֹת בְּתוֹכָהּ וַעֲשׁוּקִים בְּקִרְבָּהּ:

capable of devising means whereby the bird is lured from the heavens and trapped. Certainly then, says the Almighty, I, Who am above you, am capable of defeating you, and you will not be able to defend yourselves against Me. Accordingly, I will send the enemy to conquer the Jewish people and he will not rise to depart until My vengeance has been taken (*Does the net rise from the ground until it has entrapped?*).

Radak interprets these three verses to be discussing the perils of a nation under siege: *Do two go together unless they arranged?* See what your rebellion against Me has wrought, that it is not safe to go out alone without accompaniment due to fear of the enemy. *Does the lion roar*, etc? Just as the lion does not return from the hunt empty-handed, because the other animals are paralyzed by fear, so too shall you be paralyzed from fear of the enemy, and he will plunder you at will. Finally, just as the bird is trapped by the snare, so shall you be trapped by your enemy, who will not depart from you empty-handed.

6. אִם־יִתָּקַע שׁוֹפָר בְּעִיר וְעָם לֹא יֶחֱרָדוּ — *Can the shofar be blown in a city and the people not tremble?* Will the sentries sound the shofar to announce that the enemy is approaching without the populace trembling in fear (*Metzudos David*)? [Here, too, the sound of the shofar clearly indicates its cause, the approach of the enemy.]

Similarly, when the prophets — who keep watch to alert you of oncoming catastrophe — warn you of impending disaster, you should be trembling with fear (*Rashi*), rather than casually ignoring their words.

Targum adds: *Does the shofar sound in the city **not in its time** and the people not tremble?* There are many occasions when the shofar is a signal of joy or a call to congregate. However, if its sound is heard when none of these reasons are appropriate, it causes fear and trembling (*Radak*).

אִם־תִּהְיֶה רָעָה בְּעִיר וַה׳ לֹא עָשָׂה — *Can there be evil in a city that HASHEM has not caused?* [Can evil come upon a city other than at the behest of the Almighty? With this phrase, the prophet arrives at the point of all of the previous metaphors:] Just as each of the phenomena cited above could occur only as a result of its appropriate cause, so, too, can punishment come upon you only if decreed so by Hashem (*Metzudos David*). Accordingly, you must cease to attribute your misfortune to coincidence. Recognize once and for all that the evil which has befallen you is by design of the Almighty, as evidenced [further] by the fact that it was foretold by His prophets (*Radak*).[1]

1. It is a positive commandment to cry out and to blow trumpets for every misfortune which comes upon the community, as it is stated (*Numbers* 10:9): *For the oppressor who oppresses you shall blow upon the trumpets* — meaning anything which oppresses you. This procedure is one of the means of repentance, for when misfortune comes and they cry out over it and blow the trumpet, all will know that it is because of their evil deeds that evil has befallen them . . . (*Rambam, Hil. Taanis* 1:12).

6 Can the shofar be blown in a city and the people
not tremble? Can there be evil in a city that HASHEM
has not caused? 7 For HASHEM/ELOHIM *will not do a*
thing unless He has revealed His secret to His ser-
vants the prophets. 8 The lion has roared; who will
not fear? HASHEM/ELOHIM *has spoken; who will not*
prophesy? 9 Announce in the palaces of Ashdod and
in the palaces in the land of Egypt; and say: Gather
on the mountains of Samaria and observe the great
turmoil within it and the oppressed people in its midst.

Rashi comments: When the evil comes upon you, know that the Almighty is doing this to you because you have not hearkened to his prophets.

7. כִּי לֹא יַעֲשֶׂה ה׳ אֱלֹהִים דָּבָר כִּי אִם־גָּלָה סוֹדוֹ אֶל־עֲבָדָיו הַנְּבִיאִים — *For* HASHEM/ELOHIM *will not do a thing unless He has revealed His secret to His servants the prophets.* [Prior to precipitating any major event, the Almighty discloses His plans to His servants, the prophets.] Accordingly, now that He has revealed His secrets to them and commanded them to warn you of the oncoming disaster, why do you not take heed and repent your evil ways (*Radak*)?

Others understand the phrase that precedes this verse as a statement rather than a question: *If there will be evil in a city it is not the Almighty's doing* but rather that of its sinful inhabitants. For Hashem does not bring punishment suddenly but only after He has issued a warning, *revealing His secret to His servants the prophets*, and thereby offering the populace an opportunity to repent (*Mahari Kara*; *Abarbanel*).

8. אַרְיֵה שָׁאָג מִי לֹא יִירָא ה׳ אֱלֹהִים דִּבֶּר מִי לֹא יִנָּבֵא — *The lion has roared; who will not fear?* HASHEM/ELOHIM *has spoken; who will not prophesy?* Just as there is no one who can ignore the roar of the lion, so too is it unreasonable to demand of the prophets that they ignore the Almighty's call to them to prophesy (*Rashi*; *Radak*).

Alternatively: Do not claim that the calamities are the fault of the prophets because they did not convey the warnings of the Almighty, as it is clear to everyone that a prophet is unable to ignore the prophetic call of Hashem (*Abarbanel*).

9-10. These two verses are directed to the peoples of Philistia and Egypt, countries which neighbored the kingdom of Israel. They are meant to convey the pervasiveness of evil within the Jewish nation, and are thus an appropriate preface to the description of their impending misfortune that follows.

9. הַשְׁמִיעוּ עַל־אַרְמְנוֹת בְּאַשְׁדּוֹד ... — *Announce in the palaces of Ashdod ...* Members of the nobility of Ashdod and Egypt, spread the word from your palaces to the general populace that they should gather upon the mountains of Samaria to witness the great chaos that pervades the kingdom of Israel. Instruct them to note, as well, that this has come upon the Jewish people in retribution for the acts of oppression of which they are guilty (*Radak*; cf. *Malbim*). Although Ashdod itself is filled with robbery and oppression and the Egyptians are steeped in idolatry and licentiousness, even they will be struck by the extent of the corruption that exists among the people of Israel (*Abarbanel*; cf. fn to 1:1).

Others explain this verse to refer to a declaration of war: Call the people to assemble together in order to invade Samaria, because the Almighty has granted permission

י וְלֹא־יָדְעוּ עֲשׂוֹת־נְכֹחָה נְאֻם־יְהוָה הָאוֹצְרִים
יא חָמָס וָשֹׁד בְּאַרְמְנוֹתֵיהֶם׃ לָכֵן
כֹּה אָמַר אֲדֹנָי יֱהוִה צַר וּסְבִיב הָאָרֶץ
יב וְהוֹרִד מִמֵּךְ עֻזֵּךְ וְנָבֹזּוּ אַרְמְנוֹתָיִךְ׃ כֹּה אָמַר
יְהוָה כַּאֲשֶׁר יַצִּיל הָרֹעֶה מִפִּי הָאֲרִי שְׁתֵּי
כְרָעַיִם אוֹ בְדַל־אֹזֶן כֵּן יִנָּצְלוּ בְּנֵי יִשְׂרָאֵל
הַיֹּשְׁבִים בְּשֹׁמְרוֹן בִּפְאַת מִטָּה וּבִדְמֶשֶׁק עָרֶשׂ׃

to conquer it (*Ibn Ezra*).[1] Do not be afraid of its inhabitants, for they are undergoing great turmoil due to their wickedness and they will therefore be delivered into the hand of the enemy (*Metzudos David*).

10. וְלֹא־יָדְעוּ עֲשׂוֹת־נְכֹחָה — *And they do not know [how] to do right.* So immersed have they become in their evil ways that they are no longer capable of righteous behavior even for short periods of time (*Radak*). Therefore, I will certainly not assist them [if they are invaded] (*Metzudos David*; see comm. to v. 9).

הָאֹצְרִים חָמָס וָשֹׁד בְּאַרְמְנוֹתֵיהֶם — *Those who store rapine and plunder in their palaces.* They rob not only to meet their needs but even to store the stolen goods in their palaces — thereby compounding the transgression (*Metzudos David*).

Only the princes and officers had palaces in which to store their plunder. Thus, the prophet emphasizes that even they, whose responsibility it was to protect the populace from robbery and oppression, were themselves involved in such activities (*Alshich*).

11. The prophet reverts again to addressing the nation of Israel and depicting the great calamities to come upon them.

לָכֵן כֹּה אָמַר ה׳ אֱלֹהִים צַר וּסְבִיב הָאָרֶץ וְהוֹרִיד מִמֵּךְ עֻזֵּךְ וְנָבֹזּוּ אַרְמְנוֹתָיִךְ — *Therefore, so said HASHEM/ELOHIM: The oppressor [shall] surround the land, and he will take down from you your might, and your palaces shall be plundered.* The oppressor shall come and surround the land so that you will have no means of escape (*Radak*; *Abarbanel*; cf. *Rashi*). He will raze your citadels to the ground and plunder all the stolen treasures found within them (*Ibn Ezra*).

Alternatively, *your might* refers to the strength of the city of Samaria, in which the people placed their trust. This might will be felled by the enemy, who will conquer the city and plunder the palaces within it (*Abarbanel*; see also *Radak*).

12. כַּאֲשֶׁר יַצִּיל הָרֹעֶה מִפִּי הָאֲרִי שְׁתֵּי כְרָעַיִם אוֹ בְדַל־אֹזֶן — *Just as the shepherd rescues from the mouth of the lion two legs or the cartilage of the ear.* When the lion comes and steals a sheep from the herd, it is unafraid of the shepherd who chases him with only his staff, and it thus continues on with its plunder. Therefore, the shepherd is able to save only small portions of the sheep — such as the legs, which the lion eats last, and the cartilage of the ear, which he does not consume at all (*Radak*). These he brings as evidence of the disaster that occurred (*Mahari Kara*) [and of his innocence of any negligence].

1. *Abarbanel* rejects this interpretation because it was Assyria that invaded Israel not Philistia or Egypt. However *Malbim* (to v. 11) explains that not every attack on the Jews is necessarily recorded in Scripture. As such, it is likely that Philistia, which attacked Israel in the time of Ahaz (see *II Chronicles* 29), continued their oppression when the Jews were weakened by Assyria. Similarly, Egypt had a measure of freedom to enter the cities of Israel at that time, as indicated by the prophecies of Hosea (see *Hosea* 7:11; 8:9; 9:6; 11:5 and comm. of *Malbim* ad loc.).

10 *And they do not know [how] to do right, says* H*ASHEM,*
those who store rapine and plunder in their palaces.
11 *Therefore, so said* H*ASHEM/*E*LOHIM: The oppressor*
[shall] surround the land, and he will take down from you
your might, and your palaces shall be plundered. 12 *So*
said H*ASHEM: Just as the shepherd rescues from the*
mouth of the lion two legs or the cartilage of the ear, so
shall be saved from the Children of Israel who dwell in
Samaria the corner of a bed and the edge of a bed.

כֵּן יִנָּצְלוּ בְּנֵי יִשְׂרָאֵל הַיֹּשְׁבִים בְּשֹׁמְרוֹן — *So shall be saved from the Children of Israel who dwell in Samaria.* Similarly, only a small portion of the nation of Israel will be saved from the conquering invader (*Rashi*). The prophet specifies Samaria because it was the capital city of the kingdom and was not conquered until last (*Radak*).

בִּפְאַת מִטָּה וּבִדְמֶשֶׁק עָרֶשׂ — *The corner of a bed and the edge of a bed.* Only the bedridden, who will cringe in fear in the corners of their beds, will be saved from the enemy (*Abarbanel; Ibn Ezra; Radak*). Since they are not capable of doing battle (*Abarbanel*), the enemy will not concern himself with them (*Radak*).

Although the word דְמֶשֶׁק is not found elsewhere in Scripture, it apparently means the edge or corner (*Ibn Ezra; Radak*). According to some, the 'dalet' in the word is a prefix; the root is שק — thigh, as the leg of the bed is on its edge (*Radak*; cf. *Abarbanel*). *Alshich* interprets the word as deriving from מַשְׁקֶה — a liquid — referring to all of the secretions of the person who is so ill that he is confined to his bed.

Targum interprets: With the might of rulership and trusting in Damascus.[1] He understands the corner of the bed to allude to its strongest part — symbolizing some of the borders of Israel which were reclaimed by Jeroboam, son of Joash (see *II Kings* 14:25,27). דַמֶּשֶׂק עָרֶשׂ refers to when Pekach ben Remaliahu, king of Israel, allied himself with Rezin, king of Aram [whose capital was Damascus], thus rendering Damascus the primary foundation of his trust (*Rashi*).

Seder Olam (ch. 22) states: *So shall be saved the Children of Israel who dwell in Shomron* — these are the ten tribes who relied upon Hezekiah, king of Judah, and upon Judah and escaped with them. *The corner of the bed* — this teaches that only one out of eight of them were saved, as there are four corners to a bed and a portion of a corner, as intimated by the word בִּפְאַת, *of a corner*, is thus an eighth (*Rashi*). וּבְדַמֶּשֶׂק עָרֶשׂ — And the remainder of the bed was where? — in Damascus. [This refers to] the many Jews who found refuge in Damascus at the beginning of the Assyrian conquest. However, they, too, were eventually exiled by the King of Assyria to distant lands — even those who were sick and bedridden (*Malbim*).

Rashi cites an additional interpretation of this verse, quoting *R' Meir*, who comments as follows: *With the corner of the bed* — due to the sin of Ahaziah son of Ahab, who sent [from his sickbed] to inquire of Baal Zevuv, the god of Ekron, whether he would recover from his illness. *And in Damascus is the bed* — Ben Hadad, king of Aram, sent to inquire of the God of Israel [in contrast to the above case]. [Due to these events, only a small portion of the Jewish kingdom will be saved from the enemy.]

1. This follows an alternative reading which has דַּמֶּשֶׂק with a *"sin,"* rather that with a *"shin."* Apparently, in ancient texts both versions are to be found, although most texts contain a *"shin"* (*Abarbanel*).

יג שִׁמְעוּ וְהָעִידוּ בְּבֵית יַעֲקֹב נְאֻם־אֲדֹנָי יֱהוִה
יד אֱלֹהֵי הַצְּבָאוֹת: כִּי בְּיוֹם פָּקְדִי פִשְׁעֵי־יִשְׂרָאֵל
עָלָיו וּפָקַדְתִּי עַל־מִזְבְּחוֹת בֵּית־אֵל וְנִגְדְּעוּ
טו קַרְנוֹת הַמִּזְבֵּחַ וְנָפְלוּ לָאָרֶץ: וְהִכֵּיתִי בֵית־
הַחֹרֶף עַל־בֵּית הַקָּיִץ וְאָבְדוּ בָּתֵּי הַשֵּׁן וְסָפוּ
א בָּתִּים רַבִּים נְאֻם־יְהוָה: שִׁמְעוּ
הַדָּבָר הַזֶּה פָּרוֹת הַבָּשָׁן אֲשֶׁר בְּהַר שֹׁמְרוֹן
הָעֹשְׁקוֹת דַּלִּים הָרֹצְצוֹת אֶבְיוֹנִים הָאֹמְרֹת
ב לַאֲדֹנֵיהֶם הָבִיאָה וְנִשְׁתֶּה: נִשְׁבַּע אֲדֹנָי יֱהוִה
בְּקָדְשׁוֹ כִּי הִנֵּה יָמִים בָּאִים עֲלֵיכֶם וְנִשָּׂא
אֶתְכֶם בְּצִנּוֹת וְאַחֲרִיתְכֶן בְּסִירוֹת דּוּגָה:

13. שִׁמְעוּ וְהָעִידוּ בְּבֵית יַעֲקֹב נְאֻם־ה׳ אֱלֹהִים אֱלֹהֵי הַצְּבָאוֹת — *Hearken and testify in the house of Jacob, says HASHEM/ELOHIM, the Lord of Hosts.* Hearken, My prophets — says the Almighty — to that which I have decreed, and relate it to the Jewish nation prior to its occurrence (*Radak*) [thereby attesting that the tragedies about to befall them are the result of My punishment rather than mere coincidence].

14. כִּי בְּיוֹם פָּקְדִי פִשְׁעֵי־יִשְׂרָאֵל עָלָיו וּפָקַדְתִּי עַל־מִזְבְּחוֹת בֵּית־אֵל — *For on the day that I visit the transgressions of Israel upon him, I will wreak judgment upon the altars of Beth-el.* [When the day of My retribution from the nation of Israel arrives, not only shall I punish the people themselves, but I will also destroy their altars of idolatry.] This occurred in the times of Uzziah, when Israel was smitten by a major earthquake (*Ibn Ezra*; *Radak*; see 1:1). Alternatively, it alludes to the conquest of the kingdom of Israel by the Assyrians (*Ibn Ezra*; *Abarbanel*).

וְנִגְדְּעוּ קַרְנוֹת הַמִּזְבֵּחַ — *And the corners of the altar will be cut off.* The corners of the altar, where the blood from your offerings is placed, will shatter and fall — thereby causing the destruction of the entire altar which is supported by those corners (*Radak*).

Alternatively: When the corners of the altar of idolatry in Beth-el will miraculously shatter and fall off, with no apparent cause, this will be a sign from Above that My retribution from you is imminent (*Alshich*).

15. וְהִכֵּיתִי בֵית־הַחֹרֶף עַל־בֵּית הַקָּיִץ וְאָבְדוּ בָּתֵּי הַשֵּׁן וְסָפוּ בָּתִּים רַבִּים נְאֻם־ה׳ — *And I will smite the winter house along with the summer house, and the houses of ivory shall be lost, and many houses shall be destroyed, says HASHEM.* [I will eradicate from your midst the comforts and luxuries in which you indulge yourselves.] The separate homes for summer and winter which the wealthy among you — particularly the kings and princes (*Radak*) — have built for themselves will be destroyed. The houses paneled with ivory (*Targum*; *Rashi*) — first initiated by King Ahab (*Ibn Ezra*; *Radak* from *II Kings* 22:39) and subsequently emulated by many others (*Ibn Ezra*) — I will remove from your midst.

Malbim interprets these last three verses as describing the events which led to the conquest of Israel by Assyria. As he explains in his commentary to *Hosea* (7:11), this was precipitated by the request of Hosea the son of Elah, king of Israel, for aid from Egypt against Assyria. Because he tried to eradicate idolatry from the midst of Israel, the popu-

3/13-15 13 *Hearken and testify in the house of Jacob, says*
HASHEM/ELOHIM, the Lord of Hosts. 14 *For on the day that*
I visit the transgressions of Israel upon him, I will wreak
judgment upon the altars of Beth-el, and the corners of
the altar will be cut off and they shall fall to the ground.
15 *And I will smite the winter house along with the*
summer house, and the houses of ivory shall be lost, and
many houses shall be destroyed, says HASHEM.

4/1-2 1 *Hear this word, cows of Bashan that are on Mt. Samar-*
ia, who rob the poor, who crush the destitute, who
say to their lords, 'Bring and we will drink.' 2 *HASHEM/*
ELOHIM has sworn in His Holiness that behold there are
days coming upon you, and the [nations] will carry you
off upon their shields and your posterity in fishing boats.

lace rose against him and informed the king of Assyria of his plans, thereby inciting his invasion. Thus, the root of all that transpired was the involvement of the Jewish nation in idolatry. The prophet here depicts in advance this sequence of events: When the time for My retribution from you arrives, King Hosea shall destroy the corners of your altars of idolatry in order to render them unfit for blood-offerings. In response, you will incite against him the king of Assyria, who will come and destroy the summer home and winter home of the king, and the ivory houses belonging to him and his officers. In the course of this violence, the homes of many of the people will be destroyed as well.

IV

After having castigated the men of the kingdom of Israel for their evil ways, the prophet now goes on to describe the misdeeds of the women (*Alshich*).

1. שִׁמְעוּ הַדָּבָר הַזֶּה פָּרוֹת הַבָּשָׁן אֲשֶׁר בְּהַר שֹׁמְרוֹן הָעֹשְׁקוֹת דַּלִּים הָרֹצְצוֹת אֶבְיוֹנִים הָאֹמְרֹת לַאֲדֹנֵיהֶם הָבִיאָה וְנִשְׁתֶּה — *Hear this word, cows of Bashan that are on Mt. Samaria, who rob the poor, who crush the destitute, who say to their lords, 'Bring and we will drink.'* Hearken to My words, O wives of the princes and officers, who are steeped in self-indulgence, and are sleek and beautiful from pampering — like the cows who graze in the bountiful fields of Bashan (*Radak; Abarbanel*). You are responsible for the oppression of the poor and needy by your husbands, for they pursue those paths in order to satisfy your incessant demands for more luxuries and pleasures (*Radak*).

Targum translates the *cows of Bashan* to mean those who are wealthy with possessions.

2. נִשְׁבַּע ה׳ אֱלֹהִים בְּקָדְשׁוֹ כִּי הִנֵּה יָמִים בָּאִים עֲלֵיכֶם וְנִשָּׂא אֶתְכֶם בְּצִנּוֹת וְאַחֲרִיתְכֶן בְּסִירוֹת דּוּגָה — *HASHEM/ELOHIM has sworn in His Holiness that behold there are days coming upon you, and the [nations] will carry you off upon their shields and your posterity in fishing boats.* The Almighty has sworn from His holy abode in the heavens (*Ibn Ezra; Radak*) — i.e., He has decreed in His Divine Wisdom (*Abarbanel*) — that the day of your destruction

ג וּפְרָצִים תֵּצֶאנָה אִשָּׁה נֶגְדָּהּ וְהִשְׁלַכְתֶּנָה
ד הַהַרְמוֹנָה נְאֻם־יְהוָה: בֹּאוּ בֵית־אֵל וּפִשְׁעוּ
הַגִּלְגָּל הַרְבּוּ לִפְשֹׁעַ וְהָבִיאוּ לַבֹּקֶר זִבְחֵיכֶם
ה לִשְׁלֹשֶׁת יָמִים מַעְשְׂרֹתֵיכֶם: וְקַטֵּר מֵחָמֵץ תּוֹדָה
וְקִרְאוּ נְדָבוֹת הַשְׁמִיעוּ כִּי כֵן אֲהַבְתֶּם בְּנֵי יִשְׂרָאֵל
ו נְאֻם אֲדֹנָי יֱהוִה: וְגַם־אֲנִי נָתַתִּי לָכֶם נִקְיוֹן

is drawing near. At that time, the enemy soldiers shall carry you away upon their shields, in the manner that those who are victorious carry away their plunder (*Daas Mikra*; cf. *Abarbanel*, *Metzudos David*). Furthermore, your daughters shall be led away in small fishing boats (*Targum*; *Rashi*) — a means of transportation usually reserved for captive prostitutes, and totally unbefitting the daughters of princes and noblemen (*Abarbanel*).

Others translate צִנּוֹת and סִירוֹת to mean various types of thorns or hooks. They will carry you away on thorns and your posterity on fishhooks, in the manner which one carries fish that he has caught. [This is a figurative depiction of the degrading manner with which the captive Israelites will be dealt] (*Radak*).

Abarbanel offers a third interpretation: Instead of the warm and comfortable homes in which you were protected against the elements, you will be placed by your captors in the cold (צִנּוֹת) of winter without any shelter. In place of the delicious foods with which you indulged yourselves, your end will be a bitter exile in which you will be forced to subsist on pots of fish.

3. וּפְרָצִים תֵּצֶאנָה אִשָּׁה נֶגְדָּהּ — *And [through] the breaches they shall go out, each woman directly before her.* So many breaches will be made by the enemy in the walls of the city that a woman will not need to seek out the city gates in order to flee. Rather, she will escape through the opening in the wall which lies directly opposite the place where she is standing (*Rashi*; *Mahari Kara*; *Radak*).

Alternatively: The women will be forced to flee through breaches in the wall because all of the proper openings will be closely guarded by the enemy (*Abarbanel*).

וְהִשְׁלַכְתֶּנָה הַהַרְמוֹנָה נְאֻם־ה׳ — *And you shall be expelled beyond the mountains of darkness.* [You shall be exiled to beyond the distant mountains known as הָרֵי חֹשֶׁךְ, *the mountains of darkness.*] This follows the rendition of *Targum*. *Rashi* interprets: You will cast down the haughtiness and dominion which you took for yourselves.

Alternatively: You will cast yourselves into the royal palaces on the outskirts of the city in order to escape the clutches of the invader (*Abarbanel*; see also *Ibn Ezra*; *Radak*; *Alshich*).

Others interpret this verse as depicting the plight of the women of Israel after they are taken captive. Wanton women will come out to take the Jewish women from their captors, where they will be thrown degradingly into the harem to be designated for service or prostitution (*Malbim*).

4. בֹּאוּ בֵית־אֵל וּפִשְׁעוּ הַגִּלְגָּל הַרְבּוּ לִפְשֹׁעַ וְהָבִיאוּ לַבֹּקֶר זִבְחֵיכֶם לִשְׁלֹשֶׁת יָמִים מַעְשְׂרֹתֵיכֶם — *Come to Beth-el and rebel, in Gilgal increase rebellion; and bring your sacrifices in the morning, your tithes for three days.*

Go ahead and pursue your idolatrous ways, until your measure of transgressions is filled [and My wrath is poured out upon you] (*Rashi*; *Kara*). Alternatively: Now that you have been warned

3 *And [through] the breaches they shall go out, each
woman directly before her, and you shall be expelled
beyond the mountains of darkness, says* HASHEM. 4 *Come
to Beth-el and rebel, in Gilgal increase rebellion; and bring
your sacrifices in the morning, your tithes for three days.*
5 *And burn a thanksgiving-offering of leavened bread,
and announce and publicize voluntary offerings, for so
you have loved [to do], O Children of Israel, says*
HASHEM/ELOHIM. 6 *And also I have given you cleanness*

of the evil which is to befall you, go ahead and continue to serve your false gods; let us see if they will be of any help to you (*Abarbanel*).

The prophet now jeeringly refers to the lenient practices allowed by the idolatrous priests in their rituals. *Bring your sacrifices for the morning* — whereas the Torah stipulates that you may not leave offerings overnight, our gods are more lenient, and they allow you to leave them overnight and consume them the next morning. *For three days your tithes* — the Torah demands that you consume the tithe-offerings of your livestock within two days, but these idols allow you three days in which to eat them. *And burn a thanksgiving-offering of leavened bread* — the Torah prohibits the offering of leavened bread upon the altar, but our altars accept thanksgiving-offerings consisting of leaven. *And announce and publicize voluntary offerings* — the Torah states that you may not delay the fulfillment of your vows, but we allow you to bring your pledged offerings whenever you are able (*Rashi* from *Yerushalmi Avodah Zarah* 1:1).

Radak interprets the verse as follows: *Go to Beth-el* and worship the idol [set up there by Jeroboam]; *increase your rebellion in Gilgal,* where you serve your chosen deities in place of the service in the Tabernacle which once took place there. *Bring your sacrifices* to those gods every morning, instead of the daily sacrifice you should be offering in My Temple. Take all your tithes which accrue over time and offer them there every three years (taking יָמִים to mean 'years,' as in *Vayikra* 25:29, rather than the usual meaning of 'days'), in place of fulfilling your obligation to empty your homes at that time of all the offerings and tithes which are due to be brought to the Temple in Jerusalem.

5. וְקַטֵּר מֵחָמֵץ תּוֹדָה וְקִרְאוּ נְדָבוֹת הַשְׁמִיעוּ כִּי כֵן אֲהַבְתֶּם בְּנֵי יִשְׂרָאֵל נְאֻם ה׳ אֱלֹהִים — *And burn a thanksgiving-offering of leavened bread, and announce and publicize voluntary offerings, for so you have loved [to do], O Children of Israel, says* HASHEM/ELOHIM. Continue to bring your thanksgiving-offerings, accompanied by loaves of leavened bread, to your idols in Beth-el and Gilgal rather than to Me. Declare festivals to serve these false deities, and exhort the people to volunteer offerings in celebration (*Radak; Abarbanel*). For this is the path you have chosen and these are the ways you love, but you will yet be requited for your deeds (*Abarbanel*).

Targum translates חָמֵץ as oppression: Offer thanksgiving-offerings from that which you have extorted.

6. The prophet now goes on to describe five different calamities which the Almighty brought upon the Jewish nation in order to alert them to His displeasure with their sinful ways, and to thereby warn them to repent before they are destroyed. The depiction of each of the five ends with the statement: *but you have not returned to Me, says* HASHEM

שִׁנַּיִם בְּכָל־עָרֵיכֶם וְחֹסֶר לֶחֶם בְּכֹל מְקוֹמֹתֵיכֶם
ז וְלֹא־שַׁבְתֶּם עָדַי נְאֻם־יְהוָה: וְגַם אָנֹכִי מָנַעְתִּי
מִכֶּם אֶת־הַגֶּשֶׁם בְּעוֹד שְׁלֹשָׁה חֳדָשִׁים לַקָּצִיר
וְהִמְטַרְתִּי עַל־עִיר אֶחָת וְעַל־עִיר אַחַת לֹא
אַמְטִיר חֶלְקָה אַחַת תִּמָּטֵר וְחֶלְקָה אֲשֶׁר־לֹא־
ח תַמְטִיר עָלֶיהָ תִּיבָשׁ: וְנָעוּ שְׁתַּיִם שָׁלֹשׁ עָרִים
אֶל־עִיר אַחַת לִשְׁתּוֹת מַיִם וְלֹא יִשְׂבָּעוּ וְלֹא־
ט שַׁבְתֶּם עָדַי נְאֻם־יְהוָה: הִכֵּיתִי אֶתְכֶם בַּשִּׁדָּפוֹן
וּבַיֵּרָקוֹן הַרְבּוֹת גַּנּוֹתֵיכֶם וְכַרְמֵיכֶם וּתְאֵנֵיכֶם
וְזֵיתֵיכֶם יֹאכַל הַגָּזָם וְלֹא־שַׁבְתֶּם עָדַי נְאֻם־
י יְהוָה: שִׁלַּחְתִּי בָכֶם דֶּבֶר בְּדֶרֶךְ מִצְרַיִם הָרַגְתִּי
בַחֶרֶב בַּחוּרֵיכֶם עִם שְׁבִי סוּסֵיכֶם וָאַעֲלֶה בְּאֹשׁ
מַחֲנֵיכֶם וּבְאַפְּכֶם וְלֹא־שַׁבְתֶּם עָדַי נְאֻם־יְהוָה:

— for their purpose was to evoke a response of repentance (*Abarbanel*).[1]

וְגַם־אֲנִי נָתַתִּי לָכֶם נִקְיוֹן שִׁנַּיִם בְּכָל־עָרֵיכֶם וְחֹסֶר לֶחֶם בְּכֹל מְקוֹמֹתֵיכֶם וְלֹא־שַׁבְתֶּם עָדַי נְאֻם־ה׳ — *And also I have given you cleanness of teeth in all your cities and lack of bread in all your places, but you have not returned to Me, says* HASHEM. Just as you left My Temple bereft of your sacrifices, so have I withheld from you the provisions that you require (*Radak*; *Abarbanel*). I have rendered your teeth clean from all meat, which tends to get stuck between one's teeth (*Rashi*), and your dwelling places empty of all bread, leaving you in hunger (*Abarbanel*). This has been brought about by the invading enemy, who has occupied your land and confiscated all of its produce (*Abarbanel*). [Despite this, you refuse to take heed of My warning and return to Me.]

Malbim interprets: I have emptied your cities of any food whatsoever, leaving your teeth completely clean. In your rural areas, where fruits and vegetables can be found, I have nevertheless destroyed all crops of grain so that there can be no bread.

Targum renders נִקְיוֹן to mean *pungency*: I have brought a pungent sensation to your teeth by withholding food from them (*Radak*).

7. וְגַם אָנֹכִי מָנַעְתִּי . . . — *And also I have withheld* . . . I brought the rain in the early months of the year, so that you could take your seeds from storage and plant them in the ground (*Abarbanel*). However, I will withhold the rains during the three months prior to the harvest, when they are crucial to the growth of the crops (*Radak*), thereby destroying the crops and causing the loss of your seeds as well (*Abarbanel*). In order to ensure that you do not attribute this

1. [The continuous alternation in these verses between the future tense and the past leads to confusion as to whether these punishments had already occurred or were being foretold by the prophet. Based on the prophecy in the beginning of chapter 7, as interpreted by *Abarbanel* and *Malbim*, it appears that the following verses refer to disasters which had not yet materialized. Nevertheless, since there is still room for doubt, the translation and commentary will follow the literal tenses of the verses themselves.]

of teeth in all your cities and lack of bread in all your
places, but you have not returned to Me, says HASHEM.
7 *And also I have withheld from you the rain yet three*
months before the harvest, and I will bring down rain up-
on one city, and upon another city I will not; one portion
will receive rain and the portion which will not receive
rain will wither.
8 *And two or three cities will travel to a*
single city to drink water but they will not be sated, and
you have not returned to Me, says HASHEM.
9 *I have smit-*
ten you with blight and mildew; the increased produce
of your gardens, your vineyards, your fig trees, and your
olive trees the locusts shall consume, and you have not
returned to Me, says HASHEM.
10 *I have sent against you*
pestilence on the way to Egypt; I have killed your youth
with the sword along with the capture of your horses, and
I have raised the stench of your camps even into your
nostrils, and you have not returned to Me, says HASHEM.

drought to natural causes, I will bring rain upon one city but not upon its neighbor, indicating clearly that the lack of rain is Divinely ordained as a punishment which I have brought upon you (*Radak; Abarbanel*). Even within one town, there will be areas which will receive rain due to the merit of their owners (*Abarbanel; Malbim*), and other areas which will remain dry.

The Sages interpret the entire prophecy in this verse as depicting catastrophe: Some cities will receive no rain and will therefore go dry; others will be hit with a great deluge which will destroy all of their crops (*Rashi* from *Taanis* 20a).

8. וְנָעוּ שְׁתַּיִם שָׁלֹשׁ עָרִים . . . — *And two or three cities will travel* . . . The residents of those towns which suffer from the drought will travel to the cities blessed with rain in order to quench their thirst (*Radak*) but there will not be sufficient water to satisfy their needs (*Metzudos David*). Alternatively: They will be cursed by the Almighty to remain unsated by the water they procure (*Abarbanel; Malbim*). Despite all this, you have not accepted My rebuke and repented of your evil ways.

9. הִכֵּיתִי אֶתְכֶם בַּשִּׁדָּפוֹן וּבַיֵּרָקוֹן . . . — *I have smitten you with blight and mildew* . . . In a subsequent year, in which the rains would fall and your crops would grow, you will nevertheless be left without provision (*Radak*), for your grain shall be smitten with disease and your fruits and vegetables will be consumed by locusts (*Abarbanel; Malbim*). Alternatively: In one year all your crops will be destroyed by disease and in the next they shall be devoured by locusts (*Radak*).

10. שִׁלַּחְתִּי בָכֶם דֶּבֶר . . . — *I have sent against you pestilence* . . . I have decimated the ranks of your youth whom you sent on horseback to Egypt to procure provisions during the hunger. Some died from pestilence which I sent down upon them; others were murdered by marauding gangs along the way, who

יא הָפַכְתִּי בָכֶם כְּמַהְפֵּכַת אֱלֹהִים אֶת־סְדֹם וְאֶת־
עֲמֹרָה וַתִּהְיוּ כְּאוּד מֻצָּל מִשְּׂרֵפָה וְלֹא־שַׁבְתֶּם
יב עָדַי נְאֻם־יהוה׃ לָכֵן כֹּה אֶעֱשֶׂה־
לְּךָ יִשְׂרָאֵל עֵקֶב כִּי־זֹאת אֶעֱשֶׂה־לָּךְ הִכּוֹן
יג לִקְרַאת־אֱלֹהֶיךָ יִשְׂרָאֵל׃ כִּי הִנֵּה יוֹצֵר הָרִים
וּבֹרֵא רוּחַ וּמַגִּיד לְאָדָם מַה־שֵּׂחוֹ עֹשֵׂה שַׁחַר
עֵיפָה וְדֹרֵךְ עַל־בָּמֳתֵי אָרֶץ יהוה אֱלֹהֵי־צְבָאוֹת

killed them and took their horses captive. The bodies of these youths lay rotting in the sun, raising a stench that nauseated all passers-by, including those among you who followed — in wave after wave — to seek to alleviate your hunger, only to be met with the same fate (*Radak*; *Abarbanel*).

Rashi renders: I sent upon you pestilence in the way of Egypt — i.e., just as I sent upon you in the desert when you were traveling from Egypt (cf. *Kara; Alshich*).

11. הָפַכְתִּי בָכֶם . . . — *I have overturned you* . . . I rained upon you fire from the heavens as I did to the cities of Sodom and Gomorrah (*Ibn Ezra*), and you were charred like a brand plucked from the fire (*Rashi*).

Alternatively: I destroyed entirely portions of your land, just as I destroyed the cities of Sodom and Gomorrah. Those of you who remain are thus likened to a brand extracted from a fire just before it, too, is about to be consumed (*Radak*). I laid waste to the lands occupied by the tribes of Reuben, Gad, and part of Manasseh to the east of the Jordan River (see *Seder Olam* ch. 15) as well as to the area inhabited by the tribe of Naphtali, which was conquered by Assyria before the remainder of the kingdom of Israel (see *II Kings* 15). Those of you who remain are like a brand plucked from the flames, and it would behoove you to repent of your evil ways before you, too, are destroyed (*Abarbanel*; *Malbim*).

12. לָכֵן כֹּה אֶעֱשֶׂה־לְּךָ יִשְׂרָאֵל . . . — *Therefore, so shall I do unto you, Israel* . . . Because you have not repented and returned to Me, I will bring upon you all of the evils which I have described. Having received such tidings from your prophets, you would be well advised to prepare yourselves through repentance and righteous deeds in order to receive the Almighty. Because He is your God, Who involves Himself in your destiny to a degree unique among all the nations, He will accept your repentance and repeal the evil decree, and bring good in its stead (*Rashi*; *Radak*).

Others see this as the issuance of a sarcastic challenge: Now that you have heard what the Almighty has in store for you, prepare yourselves as well as possible to go out and meet Him in battle (*Ibn Ezra; Abarbanel*).

Malbim sees in this verse an allusion to another principle. Because it is the will of the Almighty to bestow only blessing upon His people, any time they transgress His will and force Him to punish them they thereby cause Him great anguish — so to speak — since His will is thwarted. Thus: *Therefore* — because you have acted evilly — *so shall I do unto you, Israel; because [you have made] Me do this to you* — the fact that you have caused Me anguish by forcing Me to bring punishment upon you is in itself sufficient cause for which to exact further retribution.

The Sages derive from this verse a halachic principle, that one is required to prepare himself by donning the proper attire before going to encounter the Almighty in prayer (*Shabbos* 10a). They further extract

[11] *I have overturned you like the Almighty's overturn of*
Sodom and Gomorrah and you were like a brand sal-
vaged from the fire, and you did not return unto Me,
says HASHEM. [12] *Therefore, so shall I do unto you, Israel;*
[and] because I will do this to you, prepare to [go out]
towards your God, O Israel. [13] *For behold, He forms*
mountains and creates winds and relates to a person
what his deeds are; He renders dark the dawn and
treads upon the heights of the earth; HASHEM *the God of*
Hosts is His Name.

that one who must attend to his bodily needs may not pray until he has done so (*Berachos* 23a).

13. יוֹצֵר הָרִים וּבֹרֵא רוּחַ — *He forms mountains and creates winds.* The Almighty is omnipotent and does with His creation as He pleases (*Radak*). He forms mountains which are mighty and visible to all (*Radak*) from pre-existing earth (*Malbim*), and He creates (ex nihilo — *Malbim*) winds which cannot be seen yet are capable of overturning those powerful mountains (*Radak*).

וּמַגִּיד לְאָדָם מַה־שֵּׂחוֹ — *And relates to a person what his deeds are.* Do not think that the Almighty does not observe all that you do; He relates to a person through His prophet (*Radak*) all of his deeds — even those actions done and words spoken instinctively, without full realization (*Malbim*) — so that he should repent and perfect himself (*Kara*).

Rashi interprets: He enumerates to a person all of his deeds at the time of his death.

The Sages interpret שֵׂחוֹ to refer specifically to speech: Even the casual speech between a man and his wife is recounted to him at the time of his death (*Chagigah* 5a).

עֹשֵׂה שַׁחַר עֵיפָה וְדֹרֵךְ עַל־בָּמֳתֵי אָרֶץ — *He renders dark the dawn and treads upon the heights of the earth.* The Almighty converts the dawn of His blessings into the darkness of His harsh judgment when the deeds of mankind so require. And, conversely, a decree which has already been rendered can be revoked and turned to blessing if the people repent of their misdeeds (*Kara*).

Others interpret: He makes the dawn shed light and, if He so desires, turns it to darkness by eclipsing its light (*Radak*). He makes the dawn shed light for the righteous, and He turns the light to darkness to bring punishment upon the wicked (*Targum; Rashi*).

ה׳ אֱלֹהֵי־צְבָאוֹת שְׁמוֹ — HASHEM *the God of Hosts is His Name.* He is the Lord of the Hosts — the Lord of those who dwell in the heavens above and the earth below, and He judges all of them and acts with them in accordance with His will. Therefore, O Israel, it behooves you to prepare yourselves to greet Him with repentance and self-perfection, so that He should bestow upon you His blessing and not His punishment (*Radak*).

Abarbanel interprets this verse as foretelling the invasion of the Land of Israel by Sennacherib, King of Assyria: The Almighty created the mountains of Samaria and those that surround it, and He has created a spirit (רוּחַ) which He infused in Sennacherib, moving him to conquer those mountains. He communicates His speech (שֵׂחוֹ) to you, His people, through His prophets [and has let you know His intention to] cover the dawn with darkness and trample upon the heights of your land. For He is the Lord of all Hosts in the heavens and on earth, and He shall bring upon you the hosts of the king of Assyria.

א שְׁמוֹ: שִׁמְעוּ אֶת־הַדָּבָר הַזֶּה אֲשֶׁר
ב אָנֹכִי נֹשֵׂא עֲלֵיכֶם קִינָה בֵּית יִשְׂרָאֵל: נָפְלָה לֹא־
תוֹסִיף קוּם בְּתוּלַת יִשְׂרָאֵל נִטְּשָׁה עַל־אַדְמָתָהּ
ג אֵין מְקִימָהּ: כִּי כֹה אָמַר אֲדֹנָי יֱהֹוִה
הָעִיר הַיֹּצֵאת אֶלֶף תַּשְׁאִיר מֵאָה וְהַיּוֹצֵאת מֵאָה
ד תַּשְׁאִיר עֲשָׂרָה לְבֵית יִשְׂרָאֵל: כִּי
כֹה אָמַר יְהוָה לְבֵית יִשְׂרָאֵל דִּרְשׁוּנִי וִחְיוּ:
ה וְאַל־תִּדְרְשׁוּ בֵּית־אֵל וְהַגִּלְגָּל לֹא תָבֹאוּ

V

In this chapter, the Almighty Himself laments the destruction of the kingdom of the ten tribes of Israel, which He has decreed upon them due to their wickedness. Since the *Shechinah* did not reside among them in the first place, it was not exiled along with them. The lamentation is thus for the people alone but not for the Almighty's Divine Presence. This stands in contrast to the subsequent destruction of the kingdom of Judah, in which the Divine Presence which had dwelt among them was also exiled. In reaction to that catastrophe, the Almighty declared, "Call to the lamenters and have them hurry to lament you." Since the Almighty was among the victims — so to speak — He was also among the subjects of the lament, and He therefore left it to others to express it (*Abarbanel*, from *Pesikta*).

The Almighty's lamentation over the impending destruction and His description thereof are interspersed with some verses describing the transgressions which are the cause of the destruction, and others exhorting the people to abandon their wickedness and avert catastrophe.

1. שִׁמְעוּ אֶת־הַדָּבָר הַזֶּה אֲשֶׁר אָנֹכִי נֹשֵׂא עֲלֵיכֶם קִינָה בֵּית יִשְׂרָאֵל — *Hear this word that I raise over you [in] lamentation, House of Israel.* Since you refuse to heed My words of warning and repent, hearken [instead] to My words of lamentation over your upcoming destruction (*Radak*).

2. נָפְלָה לֹא־תוֹסִיף קוּם בְּתוּלַת יִשְׂרָאֵל — *The virgin of Israel has fallen and shall no longer rise.* The virgin kingdom of Israel, which has not hitherto been despoiled by any foreign master (*Radak*), shall lose her nationhood now and forever (*Rashi*, cf. *Ibn Ezra*). Never again shall the ten tribes enjoy their own sovereignty. Even after their redemption in the times of the Messiah they will be reunited with the rest of the Jewish people as part of the kingdom of David (*Abarbanel*).

Others interpret this as alluding to the exile of the populace at the hands of the king of Assyria. They will not return to their homeland for many generations to come — unlike the people of Judah, who returned to the Land of Israel seventy years after being exiled to Babylonia (*Radak*).

The Sages suggest a more optimistic interpretation of this phrase: *She has fallen but shall not continue* [to do so]; *arise, virgin of Israel* (*Berachos* 4b). [I.e., the nation has descended to the lowest depths that it will have to endure; the future holds only the improvement of their situation and, ultimately, redemption.]

נִטְּשָׁה עַל־אַדְמָתָהּ אֵין מְקִימָהּ — *She has been abandoned upon her soil, with no one to lift her up.* While still residing upon her own soil she has already been abandoned to her fate. As she becomes

[1] Hear this word that I raise over you [in] lamentation,
House of Israel. [2] The virgin of Israel has fallen
and shall no longer rise, she has been abandoned upon
her soil, with no one to lift her up. [3] For so said HASHEM/
ELOHIM: The city from which goes forth a thousand
shall leave a hundred, and one from which goes forth
a hundred shall leave ten to the House of Israel. [4] For
so said HASHEM to the House of Israel: Seek me and
live. [5] And do not seek Beth-el, and to Gilgal do not go,

continually weakened at the hands of her enemies there is no one to raise her up and restore her to glory, for her kings and princes do not arouse her to repent and to thereby merit being freed from oppression (*Radak*).

This follows the interpretation of the majority of commentators. *Rashi* renders: *she is strewn out upon her soil, there is no one to raise her.*

Others interpret this verse slightly differently: The virgin of Israel has fallen and shall never again be able to raise herself by her own efforts out of the abyss. Only the Almighty Himself is henceforth capable of elevating her to her previous state of glory. Now, however, she has been abandoned upon her soil, and מְקִימָהּ, *He Who must uplift her*, i.e., the Almighty, אֵין, *is not* with her (*Abarbanel*; cf. *Alshich, Malbim*).

3. כִּי כֹה אָמַר ... — *For so said* ... [The devastation which the people shall suffer will leave them decimated beyond repair.] A town from which a thousand men go out to war will be left with but one hundred of them, and a town from which a hundred depart will be reduced to ten. The majority shall be destroyed by the sword and by hunger — and even the tenth who survive will be sent into exile (*Radak*; cf. *Abarbanel*).

The cities themselves are depicted as destroying the bulk of their inhabitants and leaving only a small remnant, because the Holy Land cannot abide the presence of sinners in its midst and will therefore be the cause of their destruction (*Alshich*).[1]

4. כִּי כֹה אָמַר ה׳ לְבֵית יִשְׂרָאֵל דִּרְשׁוּנִי וִחְיוּ — *For so said HASHEM to the House of Israel: Seek me and live.* Although the sentence of destruction has already been issued, if you will only seek me and pursue my service [the decree can yet be abolished and] you will be allowed to continue to dwell upon your land in peace (*Radak; Abarbanel*).

Rashi interprets: Go up to Jerusalem for the Festivals and fulfill your pledges to offer sacrifices there.

5. וְאַל־תִּדְרְשׁוּ בֵּית־אֵל וְהַגִּלְגָּל לֹא תָבֹאוּ — *And do not seek Beth-el, and to Gilgal do not go.* Do not seek the service of the golden calves in Beth-el and do not go to worship at the idolatrous altars of Gilgal (*Abarbanel*; see 4:4). For it will not suffice that you serve Me along with your

1. The Almighty created the world and placed all that is below into the hands of the heavenly forces above. Accordingly, he allocated to every nation and to every land a heavenly prince that guides its destiny. The Land of Israel alone is the portion of Hashem that remains directly under His control in all its aspects. Therefore, one who sins in the Land of Israel has thereby defiled a higher degree of sanctity than exists in other lands and is subject to harsher retribution. For this reason, the Holy Land cannot tolerate the presence of evildoers in its midst and it 'spits them out' if they persist in their wrongdoing. Indeed, the decadence of the Canaanite nations was no greater than that of other heathen nations, but because they pursued their evil ways in the Land of Israel they were destroyed (*Ramban* to *Leviticus* 18:25).

וּבְאֵר שֶׁבַע לֹא תַעֲבֹרוּ כִּי הַגִּלְגָּל גָּלֹה יִגְלֶה
ו וּבֵית־אֵל יִהְיֶה לְאָוֶן: דִּרְשׁוּ אֶת־יהוה וִחְיוּ
פֶּן־יִצְלַח כָּאֵשׁ בֵּית יוֹסֵף וְאָכְלָה וְאֵין־
ז מְכַבֶּה לְבֵית־אֵל: הַהֹפְכִים לְלַעֲנָה מִשְׁפָּט
ח וּצְדָקָה לָאָרֶץ הִנִּיחוּ: עֹשֵׂה כִימָה וּכְסִיל וְהֹפֵךְ
לַבֹּקֶר צַלְמָוֶת וְיוֹם לַיְלָה הֶחְשִׁיךְ הַקּוֹרֵא
לְמֵי־הַיָּם וַיִּשְׁפְּכֵם עַל־פְּנֵי הָאָרֶץ יהוה שְׁמוֹ:

false gods; you must abandon your idolatrous ways entirely (*Alshich*).

וּבְאֵר שֶׁבַע לֹא תַעֲבֹרוּ — *And Beer Sheva do not cross over.* Do not pass through Beer Sheva on your way to the idols of Beth-el and Gilgal. Until that point you are still traveling the roads which lead to Jerusalem as well; once you pass Beer Sheva, only the route to the false gods lies before you (*Rashi*; cf. *Radak*).

Alternatively: Do not seek Beth-el nor go to Gilgal to serve the idols there, and you will not need to pass through the border town of Beer Sheva when you are exiled from the land. I.e., if you repent, the exile can still be avoided (*Abarbanel*).

כִּי הַגִּלְגָּל גָּלֹה יִגְלֶה וּבֵית־אֵל יִהְיֶה לְאָוֶן — *For Gilgal shall be completely exiled and Beth-el shall be vanity.* Gilgal shall fulfill the destiny implied by its name and be exiled — גָּלֹה; Beth-el, too, shall live up to the connotation of its contemptuous nickname of בֵּית אָוֶן (see *Hosea* 4:15) and be rendered futile and empty by the banishment of its inhabitants (*Rashi*).

Alternatively: Because of Gilgal you shall be exiled and due to Beth-el you shall become vanity — i.e., because of the idolatry practiced in these cities, the nation of Israel shall be destroyed (*Abarbanel*).

6. דִּרְשׁוּ אֶת־ה׳ וִחְיוּ ... — *Seek* HASHEM *and live ...* Those of you who have thus far survived the wrath of the Almighty are like a brand plucked from the flames which have engulfed whole sections of your land (4:11). Know, however, that you too will soon be destroyed if you do not abandon your evil ways. For if your present behavior continues, the flame of His anger will burn in the House of Joseph (*Malbim*) and consume all the people of Samaria who worship their gods in Beth-el (*Abarbanel*; cf. *Targum*).

Others render יִצְלַח to mean to split: lest like a roaring fire He will split the House of Joseph (*Ibn Ezra; Radak*).

Malbim interprets this verse as alluding prophetically to the split in the nation which was caused by the opposition of Hosea ben Elah, king of Israel, to the idol in Beth-el. At that time, the nation was divided into two opposing camps, who engaged in battle and consumed each other in the fires of fratricide (cf. comm. to 3:4).

7. הַהֹפְכִים לְלַעֲנָה מִשְׁפָּט וּצְדָקָה לָאָרֶץ הִנִּיחוּ — *Those who turn justice to wormwood, and righteousness they leave upon the ground.* In addition to your involvement in idol-worship, there is yet another cause for the destruction which has been decreed upon you (*Malbim*). Your officers and judges distort justice to meet the needs of the wealthy and powerful, thereby rendering it bitter like wormwood to the downtrodden whom they oppress. Rather than pursuing righteousness, as would be proper, you have chosen instead to engage in corruption, leaving righteousness lying abandoned upon the ground (*Radak*).

Alternatively: You react to the sweetness of the Torah and its ways of justice and righteousness as if they were bitter wormwood in your mouths (*Abarbanel*).

and Beer Sheva do not cross over; for Gilgal shall be
completely exiled and Beth-el shall be vanity. 6 *Seek*
HASHEM and live, lest His [anger] burn like a flame
the House of Joseph and consume in Beth-el with none
to quench it, 7 *those who turn justice to wormwood,*
and righteousness they leave upon the ground. 8 *He*
Who made the Pleiades and Orion and turns black-
ness to morning and day He darkens [like] night;
Who calls to the waters of the sea and pours them
out upon the face of the earth; HASHEM is His Name.

8. The prophet seeks to awaken the people to the magnitude of their wickedness in turning from the ways of Hashem: [Behold what you have done:] You have abandoned the service of the One [Who created the celestial bodies and light and darkness] (*Targum*).

עֹשֵׂה כִימָה וּכְסִיל — *He Who made the Pleiades and Orion.* He created these two clusters of stars, each of which effects the earth in its appropriate time. Pleiades [a cluster of stars within the constellation Taurus] possesses extreme cold, and causes the fruit here on earth to harden. The constellation Orion, on the other hand, contains great heat which softens the fruit (*Radak* from *Berachos* 58b).

וְהֹפֵךְ לַבֹּקֶר צַלְמָוֶת וְיוֹם לַיְלָה הֶחְשִׁיךְ — *And turns blackness to morning and day He darkens [like] night.* He set in motion the rotation of the earth, causing it to alter daily from darkness to light and from light to darkness (*Abarbanel; Metzudos David*). Alternatively: During the summer He turns darkness to light by lengthening the days and shortening the nights. In the wintertime, He brings about the reverse, thereby turning day to night (*Radak*).

Rashi interprets this phrase metaphorically: He brings light to those who dwell in darkness and darkens the lives of some of those upon whom the light of day shines favorably. [I.e., He rescues the righteous from dire straits and brings punishment upon the wicked in the midst of their prosperity].

הַקּוֹרֵא לְמֵי־הַיָּם וַיִּשְׁפְּכֵם עַל־פְּנֵי הָאָרֶץ — *Who calls to the waters of the sea and pours them out upon the face of the earth.* He raises the salty waters of the seas up into the clouds and transforms them into the sweet waters which rain down upon the earth (*Radak*).

Alternatively: Although He decreed that the dry land should appear through the waters, when man's wickedness so requires it He floods the land with the waters of the seas (*Abarbanel*). Particularly, He flooded a third of the world in the times of Enosh when mankind began to pursue idolatry (*Rashi*).

ה׳ שְׁמוֹ — *HASHEM is His name.* He is the Almighty God Who rules in the Heavens above and upon the earth below and deals with all His creatures according to His will (*Radak*).

Therefore, you who rule and judge here on this world, why do you not ponder His might and His ability to continuously change the forces of creation? For He will similarly overturn your positions of authority and prestige and bring upon you great misfortune in their stead if you do not mend your wicked ways (*Ibn Ezra; Abarbanel*; cf. *Rashi*).

Radak interprets the thrust of this verse somewhat differently: Just as the Almighty is constantly involved in making fundamental changes, so are you.

ט־י הַמַּבְלִיג שֹׁד עַל־עָז וְשֹׁד עַל־מִבְצָר יָבוֹא׃ שָׂנְאוּ
יא בַשַּׁעַר מוֹכִיחַ וְדֹבֵר תָּמִים יְתָעֵבוּ׃ לָכֵן יַעַן
בּוֹשַׁסְכֶם עַל־דָּל וּמַשְׂאַת־בַּר תִּקְחוּ מִמֶּנּוּ בָּתֵּי
גָזִית בְּנִיתֶם וְלֹא־תֵשְׁבוּ בָם כַּרְמֵי־חֶמֶד נְטַעְתֶּם
יב וְלֹא תִשְׁתּוּ אֶת־יֵינָם׃ כִּי יָדַעְתִּי רַבִּים פִּשְׁעֵיכֶם
וַעֲצֻמִים חַטֹּאתֵיכֶם צֹרְרֵי צַדִּיק לֹקְחֵי כֹפֶר
יג וְאֶבְיוֹנִים בַּשַּׁעַר הִטּוּ׃ לָכֵן הַמַּשְׂכִּיל בָּעֵת הַהִיא
יד יִדֹּם כִּי עֵת רָעָה הִיא׃ דִּרְשׁוּ־טוֹב וְאַל־רָע לְמַעַן
תִּחְיוּ וִיהִי־כֵן יהוה אֱלֹהֵי־צְבָאוֹת אִתְּכֶם כַּאֲשֶׁר

However, He alters the forces of nature to the benefit of mankind, whereas you overturn His righteous statutes in order to do evil.

9. הַמַּבְלִיג שֹׁד עַל־עָז וְשֹׁד עַל־מִבְצָר יָבוֹא — *Who strengthens the robbed over the powerful, and the robbed shall come upon a fortress.* Just as the Almighty constantly alters the forces of nature, so shall He overturn your stations here on earth (*Alshich*). Thus, He will fortify a weak and lowly nation with the strength to defeat a mighty people like yourselves, and they will come upon your fortresses and conquer them (*Targum; Rashi; Mahari Kara;* cf. *Radak; Abarbanel; Metzudos; Malbim*).

10. שָׂנְאוּ בַשַּׁעַר מוֹכִיחַ וְדֹבֵר תָּמִים יְתָעֵבוּ — *They hate the admonisher by the gate, and he who speaks purely they despise.* The people leave Me no option other than to destroy them, as their behavior allows no hope for improvement (*Malbim;* see fn. to v. 14). For the judges who sit in their courts by the gates of the town (*Radak*) hate all those who admonish them there (*Rashi*) publicly (*Radak*). Those who castigate them sharply for their misdeeds they detest, and even those who reprove them gently, seeking to inspire them to repentance with pure and lofty words, are despised by these evildoers (*Alshich*).

Alternatively: They hate those who rebuke them by the gates for their corruption of justice and their oppression of the downtrodden; and they despise as well those who reprove them concerning matters between man and God (*Malbim*).

11. ...לָכֵן יַעַן בּוֹשַׁסְכֶם עַל־דָּל... — *Therefore, because you have trampled upon the poor man ...* You trampled upon the poor man and oppressed him (*Rashi; Abarbanel;* cf. *Radak*), and the burden of grain which he carried to his home for sustenance you took from him, taking advantage of his inability to defend himself (*Radak*). Therefore, the houses of hewn stone which you constructed by means of robbery and oppression will be seized from you by the invading hordes, and you will not dwell in them for very long. Nor shall the precious vineyards, which you coveted and stole from the poor, provide you with much wine, for you will soon be sent into exile by the enemy (*Radak*).

Rashi interprets מַשְׂאַת־בַּר — *the grain which you make for a heavy burden.* You raise the prices of grain, thereby requiring the poor to buy it on credit with interest. In this manner you impose upon them such a burden of debt that they must sell their properties in order to pay.

12. ...כִּי יָדַעְתִּי — *For I know ...* Do not deceive yourselves into thinking that I do not see your evil ways. I see and note your many misdeeds and your substantial transgressions (*Radak*). You oppress the righteous, and you accept bribery

9 *Who strengthens the robbed over the powerful, and
the robbed shall come upon a fortress.* 10 *They hate the
admonisher by the gate, and he who speaks purely they
despise.* 11 *Therefore, because you have trampled upon
the poor man, and a burden of grain you exact from him,
houses of hewn stone you have built but you shall not
dwell in them; delightful vineyards you have planted
but you shall not drink their wine.* 12 *For I know that your
iniquities are many and your sins are substantial: oppressors of the righteous, takers of ransom, and the [jus-
tice of] the destitute they distort by the gate.* 13 *Therefore
shall the prudent man keep silent at that time, for it is a
time of evil.* 14 *Seek good and not evil so that you may live,
and HASHEM the God of Hosts will thus be with you as*

from those who are guilty of capital crimes as ransom for their souls (*Kara; Metzudos David*). In addition, you rob the poor by rendering corrupt judicial decisions against them in the courts that convene by the gates of the cities (*Abarbanel*).

Others interpret: You oppress the righteous in return for the ransom you accept from their litigants (*Radak; Abarbanel*).

Malbim notes that the term פֶּשַׁע is used for sin performed out of rebellion, whereas חֵטְא is used to refer to one who submits to his desires. Thus, the former tend to be substantial but few, whereas the latter occur more often but are generally of lesser magnitude. In your case, however — declares the prophet — this distinction does not exist. Your oppression of the righteous is constant (רַבִּים פִּשְׁעֵיכֶם), as you do it not merely for the sake of gain but out of hatred for the righteousness they personify. And your indulgence of your desires extends even to sins of great magnitude (עֲצֻמִים חַטֹּאתֵיכֶם). For you accept bribery not only to distort monetary justice but even to take ransom from those who have committed capital crimes, thereby filling the land with depravity (*Malbim*).

13. לָכֵן הַמַּשְׂכִּיל בָּעֵת הַהִיא יִדֹּם כִּי עֵת רָעָה הִיא — *Therefore shall the prudent man keep silent at that time, for it is a time of evil.* Even those who would normally rebuke you for your misdeeds (*Malbim*) are prudently silent in the face of your evil, for fear that they will be killed if they speak up (*Radak*). Thus, there is no longer any basis to hope for your repentance. Therefore, it has been decreed that you be destroyed (*Malbim*).

Alternatively: The prudent man shall keep silent and not turn to the courts to rescue him from his oppressor, for his misfortune will only be compounded by their corruption (*Abarbanel*).

Others interpret this verse as alluding to the time when punishment shall befall the people for their wickedness. At that time, the wise man will remain silent and not question the justice of all this misfortune, for he will understand that the people have brought it upon themselves with their wickedness (*Rashi; Kara*).

14. דִּרְשׁוּ־טוֹב וְאַל־רָע לְמַעַן תִּחְיוּ וִיהִי־כֵן ה׳ אֱלֹהֵי־צְבָאוֹת אִתְּכֶם כַּאֲשֶׁר אֲמַרְתֶּם — *Seek good and not evil so that you may live, and HASHEM the God of Hosts will thus be with you as you have said.* Now that you are aware of the terrible misfortune

טו אֲמַרְתֶּם׃ שִׂנְאוּ־רָע וְאֶהֱבוּ טוֹב וְהַצִּיגוּ בַשַּׁעַר
מִשְׁפָּט אוּלַי יֶחֱנַן יהוה אֱלֹהֵי־צְבָאוֹת שְׁאֵרִית
טז יוֹסֵף׃ לָכֵן כֹּה־אָמַר יהוה אֱלֹהֵי
צְבָאוֹת אֲדֹנָי בְּכָל־רְחֹבוֹת מִסְפֵּד וּבְכָל־חוּצוֹת
יֹאמְרוּ הוֹ־הוֹ וְקָרְאוּ אִכָּר אֶל־אֵבֶל וּמִסְפֵּד
יז אֶל־יוֹדְעֵי נֶהִי׃ וּבְכָל־כְּרָמִים מִסְפֵּד כִּי־אֶעֱבֹר
יח בְּקִרְבְּךָ אָמַר יהוה׃ הוֹי הַמִּתְאַוִּים

which is destined to befall you because of your misdeeds (*Abarbanel*), pursue good rather than evil so that [the decree may be annulled and] you be allowed to live (*Metzudos David*).[1] For if you will do so, the Almighty will [in turn] be with you, and He will assist you (*Rashi*) in achieving all that you have declared — or even considered — to be desirable and beneficial (*Radak*).

Alternatively: *And let the Almighty be with you* — i.e., through cleaving to Him and following His ways — just as you vowed when you accepted the Torah at the foot of Mt. Sinai (*Abarbanel*).

15. שִׂנְאוּ־רָע וְאֶהֱבוּ טוֹב וְהַצִּיגוּ בַשַּׁעַר מִשְׁפָּט — אוּלַי יֶחֱנַן ה׳ אֱלֹהֵי־צְבָאוֹת שְׁאֵרִית יוֹסֵף *Despise evil and love good, and establish justice by the gate; perhaps HASHEM the God of Hosts will grant grace to the remnant of Joseph.* Do not suffice with restraining yourselves from pursuing evil. Now that you have glimpsed its results you must despise it entirely (*Malbim*) [and love only good]. Accordingly, you must [once again] establish justice in the courts which convene by the gates of your cities (*Radak*).

Some view this verse as being adjoined to the previous one. Concerning areas of righteousness between man and God, seek good and not evil — pursue the service of the Lord and abandon that of your false deities. In regard to your dealings with your fellow man, despise injustice and love good and uprightness, and, accordingly, establish justice by your gates (*Abarbanel; Malbim*).

אוּלַי יֶחֱנַן ה׳ אֱלֹהֵי־צְבָאוֹת שְׁאֵרִית יוֹסֵף — *Perhaps HASHEM the God of Hosts will grant grace to the remnant of Joseph.* Although you have sinned greatly, the Almighty remains gracious and merciful. Accordingly, if those of you who still remain from the exiles which have already taken place will only repent, He may yet have mercy upon you and deal with you graciously (*Radak*).

Despite the certainty of God's mercy, His graciousness in this case cannot be guaranteed — only offered as a possibility. This is because, as stated by the Sages (*Yoma* 86a), one who sins in a manner that desecrates God's name cannot achieve full atonement through repentance alone. Rather, he must undergo afflictions and even death before his soul is completely cleansed. Therefore, it is not certain that His grace will extend so far as to accept your repentance and forgive you your misdeeds, since these have caused a great desecration of His Holy Name (*Abarbanel*).[2]

1. Despite His repeated declaration above that there is no hope for their improvement (see comm. to vs. 10, 13), the Almighty nevertheless exhorts the people to repent. Although there are misdeeds and transgressions for which it is very difficult to repent — and thus repentance is not to be realistically expected — if one overcomes all hurdles and persists in his repentance it is accepted by Hashem (see *Rambam, Hil. Teshuvah* 4:6).

2. [This seems contradictory to the prophet's unequivocal declaration in the previous verse: *And HASHEM the God of Hosts will thus be with you as you have said*. Accordingly, *Abarbanel's* commentary here is seemingly based upon his interpretation of that verse, that it is a continuation of God's exhortation to His people and not a description of His response if

5/15-18 *you have said.* [15] *Despise evil and love good, and establish justice by the gate; perhaps* HASHEM *the God of Hosts will grant grace to the remnant of Joseph.* [16] *Therefore, so said* HASHEM *the God of Hosts, the Lord: In all the plazas mourning and in all the streets they shall say, 'Woe! Woe!' and they shall call the farmhand to mourning and those skilled in wailing to lamentation.* [17] *And in all vineyards lamentation, for I shall pass in your midst, said* HASHEM. [18] *Woe to those who desire*

שְׁאֵרִית יוֹסֵף — *The remnant of Joseph.* This refers to the kingdom of Ephraim (*Radak*) [i.e., the kingdom of the ten tribes, which was established by Jeroboam from the tribe of Ephraim]. Alternatively, the entire Jewish nation is called in Joseph's name, because he sustained them [in Egypt] (*Rashi*; cf. *Yalkut* from *Bereishis Rabbah* 71:2).

16. לָכֵן כֹּה־אָמַר ה׳ אֱלֹהֵי צְבָאוֹת ה׳ בְּכָל־רְחֹבוֹת מִסְפֵּד וּבְכָל־חוּצוֹת יֹאמְרוּ הוֹ־הוֹ — *Therefore, so said* HASHEM *the God of Hosts, the Lord: In all the plazas mourning and in all the streets they shall say, 'Woe! Woe!'* If you will not heed My warning and repent (*Radak*), [I will carry out the decree] which has already been issued from before Me (*Abarbanel*). So great will be the evil I bring upon you (*Radak*) that the public squares will all be filled with people gathered in mourning. And in the narrow streets that adjoin the squares, the women and children who live there will respond to the mass mourning with cries of woe (*Malbim*).

וְקָרְאוּ אִכָּר אֶל־אֵבֶל וּמִסְפֵּד אֶל־יוֹדְעֵי נֶהִי — *And they shall call the farmhand to mourning and those skilled in wailing to lamentation.* They will summon the farmhand to participate in the public mourning, since all his toil in the field will be negated by the blight which befalls the vegetation (*Radak*).

Others interpret: *and the farmer shall 'meet' with the mourner, and those who lament with those who know how to wail* (*Targum; Rashi*) — [i.e., the land shall be filled with the cries and wails of those in mourning until they encompass all facets of society].

17. וּבְכָל־כְּרָמִים מִסְפֵּד כִּי־אֶעֱבֹר בְּקִרְבְּךָ אָמַר ה׳ — *And in all vineyards lamentation, for I shall pass in your midst, said* HASHEM. The vineyards shall be filled with lamentation over the fact that they contain no grapes, for I shall pass in your midst to afflict you (*Radak*).

18. Up until this point, the prophecies of Amos have been directed to the northern kingdom of the ten tribes of Israel, rather than to that of Judah. In the following verses, he turns to the latter and addresses his words to them. However, there are various views as to where this change takes place. According to *Abarbanel*, this verse begins the new phase of Amos's prophecy, as will be explained. The Midrash follows this approach in its interpretation of v. 19. *Radak* understands the transition as occurring somewhat later, in verse 21. However, the basic assumption of this change is not certain;

they repent (see commentary there). However, such an assumption may not be necessary. It is possible that the people are guaranteed that Hashem will be with them if they repent, and He will eventually fulfill all their desires. However, they may first have to undergo a measure of affliction in atonement for their desecration of His name. Thus, the achievement of total grace and clemency by virtue of their repentance alone can be held out only as a possibility.]

אֶת־י֣וֹם יְהוָ֑ה לָמָּה־זֶּ֥ה לָכֶ֛ם י֥וֹם יְהוָ֖ה הוּא־חֹ֥שֶׁךְ
יט וְלֹא־אֽוֹר׃ כַּאֲשֶׁ֨ר יָנ֥וּס אִישׁ֙ מִפְּנֵ֣י הָאֲרִ֔י וּפְגָע֖וֹ
הַדֹּ֑ב וּבָ֣א הַבַּ֗יִת וְסָמַ֤ךְ יָדוֹ֙ עַל־הַקִּ֔יר וּנְשָׁכ֖וֹ
כ הַנָּחָֽשׁ׃ הֲלֹא־חֹ֛שֶׁךְ י֥וֹם יְהוָ֖ה וְלֹא־א֑וֹר וְאָפֵ֖ל
כא וְלֹא־נֹ֥גַהּ לֽוֹ׃ שָׂנֵ֥אתִי מָאַ֖סְתִּי חַגֵּיכֶ֑ם וְלֹ֥א אָרִ֖יחַ
כב בְּעַצְּרֹתֵיכֶֽם׃ כִּ֣י אִם־תַּעֲלוּ־לִ֥י עֹל֛וֹת וּמִנְחֹתֵיכֶ֖ם
כג לֹ֣א אֶרְצֶ֑ה וְשֶׁ֥לֶם מְרִיאֵיכֶ֖ם לֹ֥א אַבִּֽיט׃ הָסֵ֣ר
מֵעָלַ֔י הֲמ֖וֹן שִׁרֶ֑יךָ וְזִמְרַ֥ת נְבָלֶ֖יךָ לֹ֥א אֶשְׁמָֽע׃

Rashi (v. 24) apparently contends that the entire chapter continues to deal with the northern kingdom of Israel.

הוי הַמִּתְאַוִּים . . . — *Woe to those who desire* . . . Woe to those who respond [cynically] to the Lord's declaration that His day is coming. They say, 'Let Him hurry; Let Him hasten His deed' (*Isaiah* 5:19) (*Rashi; Ibn Ezra; Radak*) — thereby expressing their disbelief in the impending calamity (see *Radak* ad loc.). [Why do you challenge the Almighty in this manner, as if the day of Hashem was something to be desired? Know that when that day arrives it will be a time of darkness and tragedy, not one of light and cheer.]

Others explain that the Jewish people were aware that there would come a 'day of Hashem,' in which His glory would be revealed in the world (see *Joel* 3:4). Accordingly, they anxiously awaited that day, in which the enemies of the Lord would be destroyed and the Jewish nation would flourish. In reference to this the prophet declares: Woe is to those who desire the day of Hashem. Why do you seek this day of Hashem? — Although it will be a day of salvation for the Jewish people in the end of days, that will occur only when you are righteous and upright, following the ways of the Torah. However, as long as you persist in your present behavior, the day of Hashem's glory will be one of darkness and gloom, with no light of salvation in its wake (*Malbim*).

The Sages offer a parable of a rooster and a bat that were awaiting the dawn. The rooster said to the bat: I await the light because the light is mine, but you — why do you seek the light? (*Sanhedrin* 98b).

Abarbanel interprets this verse as being directed to the neighboring kingdom of Judah. Because of the deep enmity which existed between the two nations, the people of Judah eagerly awaited the day of doom which had been prophesied against the kingdom of Israel. To this the prophet declares: Why do you desire the day of Hashem's retribution from the ten tribes? Do not think that you will benefit from it, for it will be a day of only darkness, and not one which brings light and rejoicing to you.

19. כַּאֲשֶׁר יָנוּס אִישׁ . . . — *Like a man who flees* . . . [When the day of Hashem arrives,] you will be plagued by misfortune after misfortune (*Radak*), so that even as you escape from one you will soon thereafter be struck by the next (*Ibn Ezra*).

The Sages interpret this verse as depicting the four nations who were to exercise sovereignty over the kingdom of Judah. First you will be conquered by the lion, Nebuchadnezzar, king of Babylonia, and sent by him into exile. When the iron chains of his rule are broken, you will encounter the kingdom of Persia and Media — depicted by the bear — who will enjoy sovereignty over you. After they too have passed from the scene, you will have access to the House of God — i.e., the Holy Temple — under the

the day of HASHEM*; Why do you [seek] this day of*
HASHEM*? It is darkness and not light.* 19 *Like a man who*
flees from before the lion and is encountered by the bear,
and he comes to the house and leans his hand upon the
wall and is bitten by the snake. 20 *Is not the day of*
HASHEM *darkness and not light, blackness without a*
glimmer? 21 *I hate and loathe your festivals, and I will not*
be appeased by your assemblies. 22 *For if you offer up to*
Me burnt offerings and your meal offerings, I will not
accept [them], and the peace-offering from your fatlings
I will not regard. 23 *Remove from before Me the multitude*
of your songs, and the music of your lutes I will not hear.

auspices of Greece [and her Hellenistic successors]. Ultimately, however, you will be fatally bitten by the snake, representing Rome, who will destroy the Second Temple and send the Jews into exile (*Midrash Shocher Tov*, cited by *Yalkut*).

Alshich notes that in the phrase *the day of* HASHEM (v. 18), the prophet uses the Name הוי׳ which represents the attribute of mercy. Thus, the prophet declares to the people: Although you anxiously await the arrival of the day in which the Almighty's mercy will be revealed, do not think that this will bring an end to your misfortune despite your wicked ways. Rather, as long as you do not repent, His mercy will manifest itself only by the division of your punishment among four eras — allowing you a chance to recover from each phase and thereby survive. However, your retribution will not be negated entirely [unless you mend your evil ways].

20. הֲלֹא־חֹשֶׁךְ יוֹם ה׳ וְלֹא־אוֹר וְאָפֵל וְלֹא־נֹגַהּ לוֹ — *Is not the day of* HASHEM *darkness and not light, blackness without a glimmer?* Why do you so eagerly await the day of Hashem (*Ibn Ezra*), when its arrival shall bring only the darkness of tragedy (*Radak*), without any light or hope for salvation (*Malbim*)? Indeed, it shall be a time of total blackness, without even a glimmer of light to be seen (*Radak; Malbim*).

21. שָׂנֵאתִי מָאַסְתִּי חַגֵּיכֶם וְלֹא אָרִיחַ בְּעַצְּרֹתֵיכֶם — *I hate and loathe your festivals, and I will not be appeased by your assemblies.* Do not think that your sacrifices in the Temple will protect you from disaster (*Ibn Ezra; Abarbanel*), for I have come to detest the offerings that you bring on your festivals and those which you offer up to me when you call mass assemblies (*Radak*).

Alternatively: *Your festivals* refers to the festivals themselves rather than the sacrifices brought then: I have come to loathe the occasions when you gather together from across the land to celebrate the three festivals of Passover, Shavuos, and Succos in the Holy Temple (*Abarbanel*).

22. כִּי אִם־תַּעֲלוּ . . . — *For if you offer up* . . . Your burnt-offerings — which are intended to effect appeasement for minor transgressions — will not succeed in appeasing Me. And your peace-offerings I will not regard whatsoever (*Malbim*), even if they are brought from the choicest fattened animals (*Abarbanel*; cf. *Isaiah* 1:11ff).

23. הָסֵר מֵעָלַי הֲמוֹן שִׁרֶיךָ וְזִמְרַת נְבָלֶיךָ לֹא אֶשְׁמָע — *Remove from before Me the multitude of your songs, and the music of your lutes I will not hear.* [Do not come to Me] with the many songs that the Levites sing in the Temple to accompany the offering of the sacrifices, along with the

כד וְיִגַּל כַּמַּיִם מִשְׁפָּט וּצְדָקָה כְּנַחַל אֵיתָן׃
כה הַזְּבָחִים וּמִנְחָה הִגַּשְׁתֶּם־לִי בַמִּדְבָּר אַרְבָּעִים
כו שָׁנָה בֵּית יִשְׂרָאֵל׃ וּנְשָׂאתֶם אֵת סִכּוּת
מַלְכְּכֶם וְאֵת כִּיּוּן צַלְמֵיכֶם כּוֹכַב אֱלֹהֵיכֶם
כז אֲשֶׁר עֲשִׂיתֶם לָכֶם׃ וְהִגְלֵיתִי אֶתְכֶם
מֵהָלְאָה לְדַמָּשֶׂק אָמַר יְהוָה אֱלֹהֵי־צְבָאוֹת

music they play upon their lutes (*Radak*). Since you persist in your illicit dealings and your distortions of justice (*Rashi*), your offerings and services will be to no avail. What good to Me are your sacrifices if you rebel against My statutes even as you worship Me (*Radak*)?

This follows the translation of *Ibn Ezra, Radak,* and *Abarbanel*. Others render הֲמוֹן to mean the din of your songs (*Targum; Metzudos*). As long as you continue your evil practices, your sounds in the Temple are not music to Me but merely an irritating cacophony of noise (*Malbim*).

24. וְיִגַּל כַּמַּיִם מִשְׁפָּט וּצְדָקָה כְּנַחַל אֵיתָן — *And let justice be revealed like water and righteousness like a mighty stream.* This you must do in order to appease Me: You must uncover the justice that you have subdued and concealed and allow it to flow in your midst like surging waters, and uncover righteousness as well so that it shall flourish among you like a powerful stream (*Rashi*).

This translation follows the majority of commentators. Others render: *Let justice flow like water and righteousness like a mighty stream* (*Ibn Ezra; Radak*). Justice (מִשְׁפָּט) is a natural phenomenon which is rooted in human nature, since it is necessary for the maintenance of society. Thus it is likened to surging waters, which, if only left unimpeded, will flow on their own initiative. Righteousness between man and God (צְדָקָה), on the other hand, must be derived from the statutes of the Torah and received by the human being, like a stream into which waters flow from outside sources (*Malbim*).

25. הַזְּבָחִים וּמִנְחָה הִגַּשְׁתֶּם־לִי בַמִּדְבָּר אַרְבָּעִים שָׁנָה בֵּית יִשְׂרָאֵל — *Did you offer sacrifices and meal-offerings to Me for forty years in the desert, O House of Israel?* Do you think that it is your sacrifices and meal-offerings that I desire from you? Why, for forty years in the desert you did not offer any sacrifices unto Me, save the *pesach*-offering which you brought the first year (*Rashi*).

While still encamped in Sinai you had ample livestock, wine, and grain, and were thus able to bring the required sacrifices. Once you left there and traveled in the arid desert, however, where there was no grazing land for your beasts and no vineyards from which to procure wine, your offerings in the Tabernacle ceased. Yet I issued no complaints about this situation; I demanded of you only that you practice justice and righteousness (*Ibn Ezra; Abarbanel*).

This follows the simple meaning of the verse. However, the Sages disagree as to its correct interpretation. R' Eliezer states that indeed, although the Jewish people were commanded as to the laws of the *olah* sacrifice at Mt. Sinai, they did not actually bring it until they entered the Land of Israel. R' Akiva, however, contends that they offered it at Sinai and continued to do so throughout their sojourn in the desert. This verse indicates only that the tribe of Levi alone, who did not sin with the golden calf, brought these sacrifices, but not the rest of the nation (*Chagigah* 6b). Elsewhere, a similar dispute is recorded in regard to the

[24] *And let justice be revealed like water and righteous-*
ness like a mighty stream. [25] *Did you offer sacrifices*
and meal-offerings to Me for forty years in the desert, O
House of Israel? [26] *And you shall carry Siccuth your*
king and Chiun your images; Kochav your god which
you made for yourselves. [27] *And I shall exile you to*
beyond Damascus, said HASHEM, *whose Name is the*
God of Hosts.

pesach-offering. The first (unnamed) *Tanna* maintains that they brought only the one *pesach*-offering on the first year in the desert. R' Shimon ben Yochai follows the view of R' Akiva, that the tribe of Levi fulfilled the sacrificial requirements throughout the forty years in the wilderness (*Sifrei* to *Num*. 9:2).

26. The prophet now returns to his earlier theme of the coming darkness of God's punishment which shall soon descend upon the Jewish nation (*Rashi*; cf. *Radak*, below).

וּנְשָׂאתֶם . . . — *And you shall carry . . .* When you go into exile because of your sins, your conquerors will force you to carry along the idols which you worshiped (*Rashi*).

סִכּוּת מַלְכְּכֶם — *Siccuth your king.* This is the name of one of the false gods they worshiped (*Rashi*). Others interpret מַלְכְּכֶם to refer to another deity, which was called thus either because they referred to it as their king or because it is the dominant star of one of the constellations and is thus described as ruling over that cluster (*Radak*). Still others render: *And you shall bear* (וּנְשָׂאתֶם) *[the burden] of your kings* — the punishment you receive will come about because you followed the ways of your idolatrous kings (*Abarbanel*).

כִּיּוּן צַלְמֵיכֶם — *Chiun your images.* This, too, is the name of one of their deities (*Rashi*), specifically the planet Saturn, of which they made images and worshiped them (*Ibn Ezra*; cf. *Radak*).

כּוֹכַב אֱלֹהֵיכֶם — *Kochav your god.* Another false god (*Rashi*) — specifically the constellations in the Heavens which the people worshiped (*Mahari Kara*). Alternatively, it means *the star of your gods* — the star images which you made to represent your false gods (*Ibn Ezra; Radak*).

27. וְהִגְלֵיתִי אֶתְכֶם מֵהָלְאָה לְדַמֶּשֶׂק אָמַר ה׳ אֱלֹהֵי־צְבָאוֹת שְׁמוֹ — *And I shall exile you to beyond Damascus, said* HASHEM, *whose Name is the God of Hosts.* Do not think that I will bring upon you only the hordes of neighboring nations, who at worst will transplant you to nearby lands. Rather, I shall deliver you into the hands of Sennacherib king of Assyria, who will carry you far from your homeland, beyond the borders of nearby Syria (*Rashi*), to the distant lands of Halah and Habor (*Radak*).[1]

Abarbanel interprets this verse as being directed to the kingdom of Judah: When the time comes for your punishment, you will not be sent to the neighboring lands of Damascus and Syria, with whom you are presently at war, but rather to a distant land far beyond Damascus.

1. [According to *Radak's* approach, it is unclear at which point the prophet ceased to address the tribes of Judah and Benjamin and redirected his words to the northern kingdom of the twelve tribes.]

א שְׁמוֹ: הוֹי הַשַּׁאֲנַנִּים בְּצִיּוֹן
וְהַבֹּטְחִים בְּהַר שֹׁמְרוֹן נְקֻבֵי רֵאשִׁית הַגּוֹיִם
ב וּבָאוּ לָהֶם בֵּית יִשְׂרָאֵל: עִבְרוּ כַלְנֵה וּרְאוּ
וּלְכוּ מִשָּׁם חֲמַת רַבָּה וּרְדוּ גַת־פְּלִשְׁתִּים
הֲטוֹבִים מִן־הַמַּמְלָכוֹת הָאֵלֶּה אִם־רַב גְּבוּלָם
ג מִגְּבֻלְכֶם: הַמְנַדִּים לְיוֹם רָע וַתַּגִּישׁוּן שֶׁבֶת חָמָס:
ד הַשֹּׁכְבִים עַל־מִטּוֹת שֵׁן וּסְרֻחִים עַל־עַרְשׂוֹתָם
וְאֹכְלִים כָּרִים מִצֹּאן וַעֲגָלִים מִתּוֹךְ מַרְבֵּק:

VI

1. הוֹי הַשַּׁאֲנַנִּים בְּצִיּוֹן וְהַבֹּטְחִים בְּהַר שֹׁמְרוֹן — *Woe to the serene in Zion and the secure in Mt. Samaria.* Woe to the wealthy people of Zion, the capital of the kingdom of Judah, and to those dwelling in Samaria — the capital of the kingdom of Israel and the last of its cities to be conquered by the Assyrian invaders. [You continue to wallow in your luxuries,] untouched by the destruction of your brothers in the remainder of the kingdom of Israel and untroubled by the possibility of meeting the same fate (*Radak*). [However, you, too, are soon to be defeated and exiled].

נְקֻבֵי רֵאשִׁית הַגּוֹיִם וּבָאוּ לָהֶם בֵּית יִשְׂרָאֵל — *Who were called the foremost of the nations, but the House of Israel came to them.* You were once lauded by all as the most praiseworthy of people in the family of nations, but now you have turned to the other peoples and chosen their ways and statutes (*Rashi*).

Alternatively, this refers specifically to the cities of Zion and Samaria. These were the first areas inhabited by the peoples of the seven Canaanite nations and their fields were considered the choicest in all the land. They were conquered by the Jewish people: not by your own might and prowess — declares the prophet — but by the Hand of the Almighty, Who gave you the bountiful lands in His beneficence. Despite all this, you have abandoned His ways and chosen the decadent life styles of the nations who inhabited this land before you (*Radak*).

2. עִבְרוּ כַלְנֵה . . . — *Cross over to Calneh . . .* Why do you abandon My ways, as if I had mistreated you? Take a look at the great cities of Calneh, Hammath, and Gath — are they superior in quality or greater in size than those which I have given to you? If not, what claim do you have against me (*Rashi; Radak*)?

Calneh is either a city in Babylonia (*Rashi*) or a major city in the land of Sumeria (*Radak* from *Gen.* 10:10). Great Hammath is another name for Antioch (*Rashi*) [the capital of ancient Syria, now located in Southern Turkey]. Gath was the most prominent of the five major cities of Philistia (*Rashi; Radak*).

Malbim interprets these verses differently, noting the fact that the kingdom of Israel was the first in that vicinity to be conquered by the Assyrians, while the kingdom of Judah was the first to be overrun by Babylonia. Each was conquered first despite the presence of other nations in the area, which were smaller and weaker and thus more vulnerable to invasion.

Thus, *Malbim* explains, the prophet challenges the people of Zion and Samaria with this paradox: Residents of Zion, you are totally serene and unaffected by the Assyrian invaders who have not yet attacked your land. Inhabi-

1 Woe to the serene in Zion and the secure in Mt.
Samaria, who were called the foremost of the
nations, but the House of Israel came to them. 2 Cross
over to Calneh and see, and go from there to Great
Hammath and descend to Gath of the Philistines; are
they better than these kingdoms; is their border greater
than your border? 3 Who distance the day of evil and
convene a session of lawlessness. 4 Who lie on ivory
couches, stretched out on their beds, and they eat the
fattened of the sheep and calves from within the stall.

tants of Samaria, although the target of the invaders, you are nevertheless secure behind your strong fortifications and great military might. You [i.e., the Jewish people as a whole] were considered the paramount power in the region, and yet the nation of Israel was the first to be exiled into the neighboring countries. Can you explain this puzzling phenomenon? Know that it is the will of the Almighty, Who is sending you into exile at a time when the great cities of the other nations are still intact. The reason for this is so you should pass through cities in your exile and observe them in their glory, and thus note that they are neither greater nor mightier than your own. By so noting, you will be forced to conclude that your destruction was not a natural event but rather the will of Hashem, Who has punished you for your misdeeds.

3. הַמְנַדִּים לְיוֹם רָע וַתַּגִּשׁוּן שֶׁבֶת חָמָס — *Who distance the day of evil and convene a session of lawlessness.* You proclaim that the prophets I send to foretell the evil that will befall you are discussing events in the distant future. Thus reassured, you continue to sit by the gates of your towns and judge the people corruptly, thereby creating a society filled with dishonesty and lawlessness (*Ibn Ezra; Radak*).

Targum renders: They distance the day of evil, but you bring close robbery in your assemblies. *Malbim,* following along these lines, interprets the verse in accordance with his approach to the previous two (see above): The other nations have done all they can to ward off the day of their destruction, but you have brought close your plunder at the hand of Assyria by virtue of your evil ways, as described in the following verses.

Others translate הַמְנַדִּים to mean motion: You move yourselves towards the day of evil, and thus bring closer the time when you will be exiled from your homes and forced to dwell in the land of Esau, the man of lawlessness (*Rashi; Kara* from *Vayikra Rabbah* 5).

4. ... הַשֹּׁכְבִים — *Who lie ...* You have indulged yourselves in every conceivable luxury without giving any thought to your impending destruction and exile (*Radak*).

הַשֹּׁכְבִים עַל־מִטּוֹת שֵׁן וּסְרֻחִים עַל־עַרְשׂוֹתָם — *Who lie on ivory couches, stretched out on their beds.* This follows *Rashi's* translation. *Radak* renders: with their bedcovers hanging over the sides of their beds as a sign of indulgence. The Sages interpret: They befoul their beds with the semen of others when they indulge in sinful relations with each other's wives (*Shabbos* 62b).

וְאֹכְלִים כָּרִים מִצֹּאן וַעֲגָלִים מִתּוֹךְ מַרְבֵּק — *And they eat the fattened of the sheep and calves from within the stall.* They

ה הַפֹּרְטִים עַל־פִּי הַנָּבֶל כְּדָוִיד חָשְׁבוּ לָהֶם
ו כְּלֵי־שִׁיר: הַשֹּׁתִים בְּמִזְרְקֵי יַיִן וְרֵאשִׁית שְׁמָנִים
ז יִמְשָׁחוּ וְלֹא נֶחְלוּ עַל־שֵׁבֶר יוֹסֵף: לָכֵן עַתָּה
ח יִגְלוּ בְּרֹאשׁ גֹּלִים וְסָר מִרְזַח סְרוּחִים: נִשְׁבַּע
אֲדֹנָי יֱהֹוִה בְּנַפְשׁוֹ נְאֻם־יהוה אֱלֹהֵי צְבָאוֹת
מְתָאֵב אָנֹכִי אֶת־גְּאוֹן יַעֲקֹב וְאַרְמְנֹתָיו שָׂנֵאתִי

pass before the flocks of sheep and the stalls of cattle to seek out only the choicest lambs and calves for their indulgence (*Mahari Kara*).

5. הַפֹּרְטִים עַל־פִּי הַנָּבֶל כְּדָוִיד חָשְׁבוּ לָהֶם כְּלֵי־שִׁיר — *Who sing along to the tune of the lute; they consider themselves like David in regard to musical instruments.* As they indulge in their sumptuous feasts, they entertain themselves with music to enhance their pleasure (*Alshich*). So enamored are they of their prowess that they compare themselves to King David, who was a master of all musical instruments (*Radak*). In reality, however, the comparison is baseless, for he dedicated his music to Hashem, whereas they employ it merely to satisfy their desires (*Rashi; Metzudos David*).

הַפֹּרְטִים עַל־פִּי הַנָּבֶל — *Who sing along to the tune of the lute.*

They alter the notes of their songs in accordance with the music of the lute (*Rashi; Mahari Kara*). Alternatively, this refers to the music itself, which is played in many different notes according to the melody (*Radak*).

Others interpret פֹּרְטִים to be derived from *perutah*, the smallest coin in their monetary system: They give *perutos* to those who entertain them by playing the lute (*Radak; Alshich*).

6. הַשֹּׁתִים בְּמִזְרְקֵי יַיִן — *Who drink wine from basins.* They guzzle wine straight from large receptacles rather than from glasses of an appropriate size (*Radak; Abarbanel; Alshich*).

Alternatively, מִזְרָקִים are vessels with more than one mouth, from which two people drink at one time (*Rashi* from *Shabbos* 62b; see ibid.).

וְלֹא נֶחְלוּ עַל־שֵׁבֶר יוֹסֵף — *And they are not pained by the destruction of Joseph.* The citizens of the kingdom of Joseph[1] pay no heed to the prophecies of their impending doom and the destruction of their nation (*Rashi*).

Alternatively, those who were spared from the exiles that already took place and still remain in the Holy Land have no feelings whatever for the citizens of the kingdom of Joseph who have already been exiled (*Radak*).

According to *Abarbanel*, this criticism is directed at the people of Judah, who were not at all concerned with the plight of their exiled brethren from the kingdom of Joseph.

7. לָכֵן עַתָּה יִגְלוּ בְּרֹאשׁ גֹּלִים — *Therefore, they shall now be exiled at the head of exiles.* Because they continuously require the first quality of all in which they indulge, it is fitting that they be the first to be exiled (*Ibn Ezra*). Therefore, the

1. The northern kingdom of the ten tribes is referred to as the kingdom of Joseph for several reasons: Firstly, the kingdom was established by Jeroboam son of Nabot from the tribe of Ephraim the son of Joseph. In addition, the tribe of Ephraim was the largest and most influential among the ten tribes. Furthermore, when Jacob blessed the sons of Joseph he stated, 'and my name shall be called upon them' (*Gen.* 48:16) — i.e., my descendants will be called in their name. Finally, since Joseph was singled out to replace Reuven for the rights of the firstborn, the kingdom was called in his name (*Radak*).

5 Who sing along to the tune of the lute; they consider
themselves like David in regard to musical instruments.
6 Who drink wine from basins and with the choicest
oils they anoint themselves; and they are not pained
by the destruction of Joseph. 7 Therefore, they shall
now be exiled at the head of exiles and the banquets
of the haughty shall cease. 8 HASHEM/ELOHIM has
sworn by His soul, declares HASHEM the Lord of Hosts:
I loathe the glory of Jacob and his palaces I detest,

ten tribes of Israel will be sent into exile prior to the banishment of the kingdom of Judah (*Mahari Kara; Alshich*; cf. *Radak*).[1]

Malbim interprets: Because of the factors cited above, the people of Israel will be the first to be exiled, prior to all of the other nations conquered by Assyria, and the kingdom of Judah will be the first to be banished by the Babylonians (see comm. to v. 2; cf. *Abarbanel*).

וְסָר מִרְזַח סְרוּחִים — *And the banquets of the haughty shall cease.* [With the coming exile,] the festive banquets of the great and haughty will be ended [once and for all] (*Rashi*; cf. *Targum*).

Others render: *and mourning* (מִרְזַח) *shall approach those who are stretched out* [on their beds] (*Radak*; cf. *Moed Katan* 28b) — [those who lay indolently on their beds and couches in pursuit of pleasure and enjoyment will soon mourn the loss of all they desire] (see also *Radak*; *Ibn Ezra*).

8. The prophet conveys the Almighty's sworn determination to annihilate the Jewish kingdoms — offering a graphic illustration of the extent of the destruction that will occur. He stresses, however, that the two nations will not share similar fates, for the kingdom of Judah will recover — at least partially — and return to their land long before the redemption of the ten tribes.

נִשְׁבַּע ה׳ אֱלֹהִים ... — *HASHEM/ELOHIM has sworn ...* The Almighty proclaims that He has made the following oath by the very essence of His Being: I have come to loathe (מְתָאֵב) the Holy Temple,[2] the glory and splendor of the nation [due to the wicked ways of the

1. [This follows the view of the majority of commentators, that the previous verse refers specifically to the citizens of the kingdom of Israel. Thus they are the subject of the prophecy of doom in this verse as well.] According to *Abarbanel*, the subject of these verses is the kingdom of Judah. He interprets the phrase *the head of exiles* to allude to the fact that the nation of Judah was destined to suffer yet another exile several centuries later at the hands of the Romans (see ibid.). [Since they were to undergo repeated banishments they are called *the head of exiles* — i.e., the leader in experiencing that fate.]

2. [It is somewhat difficult to comprehend such a statement: Why should the Almighty loathe the Holy Temple because of the people's misdeeds? However, several possible explanations come to mind.

First, as hinted above (5:21), the people relied on the sacrifices they offered in the Temple to achieve atonement for their transgressions, and, with the assurance of a clean slate, they continued in their wicked ways. Thus, the Temple had become a tool for their decadence, and is therefore depicted as the subject of Hashem's hatred.

In addition, because the Temple provided the potential for towering heights of spirituality, it greatly magnified the scale of their wickedness in abusing such great potential and defiling such intense holiness. Thus, the presence of the Temple contributed significantly to the extent

ט וְהִסְגַּרְתִּי עִיר וּמְלֹאָהּ: וְהָיָה אִם־יִוָּתְרוּ עֲשָׂרָה
י אֲנָשִׁים בְּבַיִת אֶחָד וָמֵתוּ: וּנְשָׂאוֹ דּוֹדוֹ וּמְסָרְפוֹ
לְהוֹצִיא עֲצָמִים מִן־הַבַּיִת וְאָמַר לַאֲשֶׁר בְּיַרְכְּתֵי
הַבַּיִת הַעוֹד עִמָּךְ וְאָמַר אָפֶס וְאָמַר הָס כִּי לֹא
יא לְהַזְכִּיר בְּשֵׁם יהוה: כִּי־הִנֵּה יהוה מְצַוֶּה
וְהִכָּה הַבַּיִת הַגָּדוֹל רְסִיסִים וְהַבַּיִת הַקָּטֹן בְּקִעִים:
יב הַיְרֻצוּן בַּסֶּלַע סוּסִים אִם־יַחֲרוֹשׁ בַּבְּקָרִים

people], and I shall therefore deliver the city of Jerusalem and its inhabitants (*Rashi*) into the hands of the enemy (*Radak*).

Others translate מְתָאֵב as *desire*: In truth I love the Holy Temple, says the Almighty, but I have come to detest the palaces of Jacob, where the people engage in their decadent behavior. Therefore, I must destroy the city of Jerusalem and all that is in it, even the Temple itself (*Abarbanel; Metzudos David*).

9. וְהָיָה אִם־יִוָּתְרוּ עֲשָׂרָה אֲנָשִׁים בְּבַיִת אֶחָד וָמֵתוּ — *And it shall be that if ten men remain in one house they shall die.* [The devastation shall pervade in all places, and the destruction shall be all-encompassing.] Thus, if ten men — or any other number of people (*Ibn Ezra; Radak*) — shall escape the sword of the enemy and seek refuge together in one house, they too shall be destroyed, for the enemy will burn down the house with them inside once he has captured the city (*Rashi; Metzudos David*). Alternatively: A plague of pestilence shall infiltrate the house and wipe them out completely (*Radak; Abarbanel; Malbim*).

10. וּנְשָׂאוֹ דּוֹדוֹ וּמְסָרְפוֹ לְהוֹצִיא עֲצָמִים מִן־הַבַּיִת — *And his kinsman who saves him from burning shall carry him to take out the bones from the house.* Because no one from the immediate family will survive the destruction, it will be left to an uncle (*Malbim*) — or any other relative sufficiently close and concerned — to extract the bones of the victims before they are consumed by the flames, and to take them [to be buried] (*Targum; Rashi*).

Ibn Ezra cites *R' Yehudah ben Karish* who renders: *His paternal uncle and his maternal uncle shall take out etc.*

Others render מְסָרְפוֹ, *the one who burns him* — as a reference to the embalming of corpses with pungent spices to eradicate their stench (*Mahari Kara; Radak*) and prevent the spread of disease (*Malbim*).

וְאָמַר לַאֲשֶׁר בְּיַרְכְּתֵי הַבַּיִת הַעוֹד עִמָּךְ וְאָמַר אָפֶס — *And he will say to the one who is at the end of the house, 'Are there any more with you?' and he will say, 'None.'* This relative will call out to his companion, who had entered the house to investigate further, and inquire of him whether there is anyone else alive aside from himself. The latter will respond in the negative, for all within the house will be dead (*Rashi*).

וְאָמַר הָס כִּי לֹא לְהַזְכִּיר בְּשֵׁם ה׳ — *And he will say, 'Remove them,' for they were not [wont] to mention the Name of* HASHEM. The relative will direct his accomplice to remove all of the corpses

of Hashem's wrath (cf. *Michtav MeEliyahu*, Vol. 2, s.v. דוד המלך ובנין בית המקדש).

Finally, because of the sins of the people, the בֵּית הַמִּקְדָּשׁ שֶׁל מַעְלָה — the Heavenly source from which the Temple drew its unique level of holiness — had been defiled and rendered bereft of its potency (see *Nefesh HaChaim* 1:4). Accordingly, the Temple which remained standing here on earth was an empty shell, drained of its 'spirit,' and thus stood as a mockery of the very sanctity it represented.]

and I shall deliver the city and its inhabitants. 9 *And*
it shall be that if ten men remain in one house they
shall die. 10 *And his kinsman who saves him from*
burning shall carry him to take out the bones from
the house, and he will say to the one who is at the end
of the house, 'Are there any more with you?' and he
will say, 'None,' and he will say, 'Remove [them],' for
they were not [wont] to mention the Name of HASHEM.
11 *For behold, HASHEM commands and shatters a large*
house into slivers and a small house into chips. 12 *Will*
horses gallop on a rock; will one plow [it] with cattle,

from the house. And he will comment further [in response to the entire situation]: This punishment befell them because they refused to mention the Name of Hashem when they were alive (*Targum; Rashi; Mahari Kara*).

Others translate הָס to mean *be silent* (*Ibn Ezra; Radak; Alshich; Metzudos; Malbim*): Refrain from bewailing this terrible tragedy, for it has come upon us because we consistently refused to mention the Name of Hashem, and mentioned instead the names of our idols (*Radak*).

Alternatively: The relative will command, 'Be silent and do not publicize this awful occurrence, lest it cause the people to despair.' However, it will not occur to anyone to mention the Name of Hashem and acknowledge the truth of His judgment (*Ibn Ezra*).

11. כִּי־הִנֵּה ה׳ מְצַוֶּה ... — *For behold, HASHEM commands ...* The Almighty shall issue the command, and the enemy shall smite (*Metzudos David*) the greater kingdom such a mighty blow that it shall shatter into tiny slivers. The smaller nation shall also be smitten, but less violently, so that its fragments will be larger than those of the former (*Targum; Rashi*). I.e., the kingdom of the ten tribes will be destroyed so completely that it will be many generations before it is restored. The smaller nation of Judah will also be defeated, but its fragments will remain sufficiently large to allow for its renewal within a short period of time (*Mahari Kara; Abarbanel; Metzudos David*).

Others interpret: The great houses of the nation's rulers will be smashed to small fragments (*Ibn Ezra; Alshich*) for they bear responsibility for the misdeeds of the multitudes who follow their lead. The smaller houses of private citizens will be dealt lesser blows, as they are only culpable for their own transgressions (*Alshich*).

Radak interprets the verse more literally to refer to a great earthquake — depicted earlier (3:15) — which will destroy the larger houses along with the smaller ones.

12-14. Why do you persist in your wrongdoing when all logic points to the folly of your ways? All of the sources of your imagined security will be to no avail if you do not abandon your evil ways, and there will be no avoiding your terrible fate.

12. הַיְרֻצוּן בַּסֶּלַע סוּסִים ... — *Will horses gallop on a rock ...* Can horses run up rocky cliffs (*Mahari Kara*) in defiance of the laws of nature? Can a man plow with cattle upon those cliffs? Why then do you think that you can successfully alter the natural order, turning justice and righteousness into poison weed and

ו/יג־יד כִּֽי־הֲפַכְתֶּם לְרֹאשׁ מִשְׁפָּט וּפְרִי צְדָקָה לְלַעֲנָה׃
יג הַשְּׂמֵחִים לְלֹא דָבָר הָאֹמְרִים הֲלוֹא בְחָזְקֵנוּ
יד לָקַחְנוּ לָנוּ קַרְנָיִם׃ כִּי הִנְנִי מֵקִים עֲלֵיכֶם
בֵּית יִשְׂרָאֵל נְאֻם־יהוִה אֱלֹהֵי הַצְּבָאוֹת גּוֹי
וְלָחֲצוּ אֶתְכֶם מִלְּבוֹא חֲמָת עַד־נַחַל
ז/א א הָעֲרָבָה׃ כֹּה הִרְאַנִי אֲדֹנָי יֱהוִה וְהִנֵּה
יוֹצֵר גֹּבַי בִּתְחִלַּת עֲלוֹת הַלָּקֶשׁ וְהִנֵּה־לֶקֶשׁ

wormwood [and still escape retribution] (*Rashi*)? Alternatively: Just as you understand quite clearly that such events would be an upheaval of the natural order, know that you, too, are perverting that natural order with your corruption of justice. For justice and righteousness are the pillars of civilization, and their corruption is thus as destructive as the deadly poison weed. The natural fruits of righteousness are peace and all that is good, but you have [replaced it with behavior that breeds] only wormwood (*Radak*).

Others explain this verse as an allegorical description of the land. Your land has been rendered indefensible, like a sheet of rock upon which horses are unable to gallop to battle. Nor does any produce grow in the fields, just as they would not be able to grow in rocky soil. Why has this occurred? Because, כִּי, you have distorted justice — in the merit of which the Almighty brings victory in war — and transformed it into poison weed. And the righteousness which would bring blessings of prosperity you have turned to wormwood (*Malbim*; cf. *Abarbanel*, *Malbim*).

13. הַשְּׂמֵחִים לְלֹא דָבָר — *Those who rejoice over nothing.* You revel in your greatness and wealth as well as in the tranquility they bring, but your rejoicing is of no consequence and will not be long lasting (*Rashi*; *Radak*).

Alternatively: You rejoice in your refusal to heed the words of the prophet — as if there were no such words (*Mahari Kara*), and you exult in your lack of concern for the impending destruction that such a policy will bring (*Alshich*).

הָאֹמְרִים הֲלוֹא בְחָזְקֵנוּ לָקַחְנוּ לָנוּ קַרְנָיִם — *Who say, 'Is it not with our might that we have taken for ourselves horns?'* When Jeroboam ben Joash defeated the enemies of Israel and restored her boundaries (see *II Kings* 14:25,28), you attributed it to your military might. You boasted of your mighty horns which overpower the enemy as the wild ox gores with his horns, rather than acknowledging that it was God's mercy upon His people that wrought your victory (*Radak*; *Malbim*; *Metzudos David*; cf. *Abarbanel*).

Targum renders: *who say, 'Is it not with our might that we have acquired for ourselves possessions?'* — as a person's wealth raises his status and provides him with 'horns of glory' (*Mahari Kara*; cf. *Rashi*).

14. כִּי הִנְנִי ... — *For behold ...* In retribution for your many transgressions against Me, I shall raise up against you a nation (*Metzudos David*) — the mighty forces of the king of Assyria. And because you insist upon taking credit for your victories rather than acknowledging My beneficence to you, he will — with the removal of My providence from you — oppress you in those very lands which Jeroboam conquered, and subsequently drive you out from them entirely (*Radak*).

Rashi explains that Hamath is in the northwestern corner of Eretz Yisrael, whereas the Wadi Arabah is the brook of

6/13-14 *that you have turned justice into poison wood and the
fruit of righteousness into wormwood? [13] Those who
rejoice over nothing, who say, 'Is it not with our might
that we have taken for ourselves horns?' [14] For behold, O
House of Israel, I will raise up against you a nation,
declares HASHEM the Lord of Hosts, and they will oppress
you, from the approach to Hamath to the Wadi Arabah.*

7/1 [1] *Thus showed me HASHEM/ELOHIM: and behold He was
forming locusts as the later growth was beginning to
sprout, and behold [there appeared] the later growth*

Egypt in the southwestern corner. [Thus, the prophet declares that the forces of Assyria will conquer the whole of the kingdom of Israel.]

VII

As described earlier, the Almighty brought upon the Jewish kingdom a series of calamities in order to motivate them to repent and thereby avoid the final destruction of their nation. In this chapter, Amos describes how the Almighty showed him those catastrophes in advance, and how he beseeched Him to limit their scope in His mercy so as to prevent total destruction (*Abarbanel; Malbim*).

1. כֹּה הִרְאַנִי ה' אֱלֹהִים . . . — *Thus showed me HASHEM/ELOHIM* . . . The Almighty showed me a vision in which He was creating locusts (*Targum; Radak*) at the time of the sprouting of the second crop of the growing season (*Rashi; Radak*) — which appears at the time of the second rainfall (*Ibn Ezra*). Indeed, after the first growth had been mowed while still grass — before its stalks appeared — in order to feed the animals of the king,[1] the shoots of this later growth were beginning to appear (*Rashi; Radak*).

Others translate יוֹצֵר to mean *gather* — I saw Hashem gathering together an army of locusts (*Ibn Ezra; Radak*).

Abarbanel offers an entirely different interpretation to this verse. He maintains that גֹּבַי is rendered collectors — i.e., the agents through which the Almighty will collect His debt from the Jewish people for their wickedness. As described in chapter 4 (vs. 6-9), these agents — who will bring about the loss of the crops — may come in the form of drought, blight, or an invading enemy who decimates the produce of the fields.

Thus the prophet relates: I saw a vision in which the Almighty was conceiving His agents of collection, through which He would exact retribution from the Children of Israel by destroying their crops. This will occur after the crops have already appeared in the fields, thereby maximizing the disappointment and anguish of the people. To further increase the effect of this punishment, He chose a time immediately after the king had cut away the possessions of the people through exorbitant taxes, leaving them eagerly anticipating the new year's yield in order to ward off famine. At that time, Hashem set out to devastate their crops and bring them to utter destitution and despair.

1. *Mahari Kara* explains that the first growth was harvested when the shoots were still soft in order to allow for a second growth of larger and stronger stalks.

ב אַחַר גִּזֵּי הַמֶּלֶךְ׃ וְהָיָה אִם־כִּלָּה לֶאֱכוֹל אֶת־
עֵשֶׂב הָאָרֶץ וָאֹמַר אֲדֹנָי יֱהוִה סְלַח־נָא מִי יָקוּם
ג יַעֲקֹב כִּי קָטֹן הוּא׃ נִחַם יהוה עַל־זֹאת לֹא
ד תִהְיֶה אָמַר יהוה׃ כֹּה הִרְאַנִי אֲדֹנָי
יֱהוִה וְהִנֵּה קֹרֵא לָרִב בָּאֵשׁ אֲדֹנָי יֱהוִה
וַתֹּאכַל אֶת־תְּהוֹם רַבָּה וְאָכְלָה אֶת־הַחֵלֶק׃
ה וָאֹמַר אֲדֹנָי יֱהוִה חֲדַל־נָא מִי יָקוּם יַעֲקֹב כִּי
ו קָטֹן הוּא׃ נִחַם יהוה עַל־זֹאת גַּם־הִיא לֹא
ז תִהְיֶה אָמַר אֲדֹנָי יֱהוִה׃ כֹּה הִרְאַנִי
וְהִנֵּה אֲדֹנָי נִצָּב עַל־חוֹמַת אֲנָךְ וּבְיָדוֹ אֲנָךְ׃

2. וְהָיָה... — *And it came about* ... In my vision, I saw the locusts devouring all of the grass, signifying that a plague of locusts will come and destroy all vegetation, causing a total famine (*Metzudos David*). I therefore turned to the Almighty in prayer and beseeched Him: Please forgive Your people and do not bring upon them so great a calamity. For Your nation is small and will be unable to survive such a disaster (*Radak*). They will not have the means to feed themselves, and the gentile nations who detest them will certainly not render assistance (*Metzudos*). Nor will they be able to strengthen themselves and improve their behavior — and thereby earn the removal of their misfortune, for their spiritual stature at the present time is very low (*Malbim*).

Alternatively: Who will sustain Jacob, as he is small (*Targum; Rashi*)? If I will not plead their case, who among them will arise to beseech You to abolish the decree, for there are very few among them in this generation who are truly righteous (*Kara*).

3. נִחַם ה׳ עַל־זֹאת לֹא תִהְיֶה אָמַר ה׳ — *HASHEM relented concerning this: 'It shall not be,' said HASHEM.* Hashem acceded to my prayers and nullified the decree (*Rashi*).

Abarbanel explains that only the decree of total destruction was abolished, but the majority of the crops were nevertheless devoured. *Malbim*, however, notes the use of the word סְלַח, *forgive*, as opposed to the word חֲדַל, *refrain*, used in the following vision. He explains that in this case there was still sufficient merit among the people to allow for actual forgiveness and total annulment of the decree. The second vision, however, which followed further sinfulness, could only be mitigated in scope, but it could not be negated entirely.

4. כֹּה הִרְאַנִי ה׳ אֱלֹהִים... — *Thus showed me HASHEM/ELOHIM* ... I was shown another vision, in which Hashem called together His heavenly hosts to prepare to do battle with the nation of Israel by afflicting them with fire (*Rashi; Ibn Ezra; Radak*). Alternatively, the fire symbolizes a great heat wave, which will prevent the rain from falling and will destroy all vegetation like a consuming flame (*Ibn Ezra; Radak*; cf. Kara).

וַתֹּאכַל אֶת־תְּהוֹם רַבָּה — *And it consumed the great depths.* The fire consumed the waters lying beneath the surface of the earth (*Radak*). *Alshich* explains that when the Jewish nation sinned in the desert, the Almighty punished them with a raging fire that consumed some of the nation. Then, in response to the prayers of Moses, the fire sunk beneath the ground (*Num.* 11:1,2; *Rashi* ad loc.). Now, once

after the king's reaping. 2 *And it came about when*
He finished devouring the grass of the earth that I
said, 'HASHEM/ELOHIM, pray forgive. How will Jacob
survive, for he is small?' 3 *HASHEM relented concern-*
ing this: 'It shall not be,' said HASHEM. 4 *Thus showed*
me HASHEM/ELOHIM: and behold HASHEM/ELOHIM was
summoning to contend by fire and it consumed the
great depths and devoured the lot. 5 *And I said,*
'HASHEM/ELOHIM, pray refrain; how will Jacob sur-
vive, for he is small?' 6 *HASHEM relented concerning*
this; 'It too shall not be,' said HASHEM/ELOHIM. 7 *Thus*
He showed me: and behold HASHEM was standing
on a plumbed wall with a plumbline in His hand.

again, the Almighty recalled that same fire from the bowels of the earth in order to exact retribution from the kingdom of Israel. It first wrought destruction beneath the earth's surface, drying up the depths of water, and then began to rise to the surface to continue its destructive course. At that point, the prophet beseeched Hashem for mercy and the fires receded once more to the core of the globe.

וְאָכְלָה אֶת־הַחֵלֶק — *And devoured the lot.* It consumed the portion of the field (*Rashi*). According to *Ibn Ezra*, this refers to the entire land surface of the country. *Radak* interprets it to refer specifically to the fields of the king. Since the king set the tone for the moral standard of the nation, he was held to be primarily responsible for its decadence, and was therefore singled out for punishment.

Others understand the fire described in this verse to allude to a plague of pestilence which devoured the nation, as foretold earlier (4:10) (*Abarbanel; Malbim*). First it affected those who went down to Egypt, whose surface lies lower than that of the Land of Israel. It then traveled to the Land of Israel itself, the Jewish nation's portion of the earth's land surface (*Malbim*; cf. *Abarbanel*).

5. וָאֹמַר ה׳ אֱלֹהִים חֲדַל־נָא מִי יָקוּם יַעֲקֹב כִּי קָטֹן הוּא — *And I said, 'HASHEM/ELOHIM, pray refrain; how will Jacob survive, for he is small?'* [Once again, I pleaded with the Almighty to stay His hand.] This time, however, I sought only that He limit the scope of His punishment, for I recognized that total forgiveness was no longer possible (*Malbim*; see comm. to v. 3).

6. נִחַם ה׳ עַל־זֹאת גַּם־הִיא לֹא תִהְיֶה אָמַר ה׳ אֱלֹהִים — *HASHEM relented concerning this; 'It too shall not be,' said HASHEM/ELOHIM.* [Once again, the Almighty relented and spared the Jewish people the retribution they deserved.]

7. The prophet now goes on to describe the Almighty's decree of the invasions to be suffered by the kingdom of Israel, which would be conquered piecemeal by successive waves of Assyrian forces. First, the tribes dwelling east of the Jordan River were conquered and exiled by Pol, king of Assyria; subsequently, the provinces of Zebulun and Naphtali were overrun by Tiglath Pileser [and finally, the entire nation was conquered by Sennacherib] (*Abarbanel*).

כֹּה הִרְאַנִי וְהִנֵּה ה׳ נִצָּב עַל־חוֹמַת אֲנָךְ וּבְיָדוֹ אֲנָךְ — *Thus He showed me: and behold HASHEM was standing on a plumbed wall with a plumbline in His hand.* [A

ח וַיֹּאמֶר יהוה אֵלַי מָה־אַתָּה רֹאֶה עָמוֹס
וָאֹמַר אֲנָךְ וַיֹּאמֶר אֲדֹנָי הִנְנִי שָׂם אֲנָךְ בְּקֶרֶב
עַמִּי יִשְׂרָאֵל לֹא־אוֹסִיף עוֹד עֲבוֹר לוֹ:
ט וְנָשַׁמּוּ בָּמוֹת יִשְׂחָק וּמִקְדְּשֵׁי יִשְׂרָאֵל יֶחֱרָבוּ

plumbline is a line from which a weight is suspended to determine verticality (or depth). A plumbed wall is a wall that has been made to stand perfectly straight by means of a plumbline.] In this third vision, I saw the splendor of the Almighty atop the straight wall of justice (*Rashi; Radak*). He held the weights of strict justice within His hand — in order to maintain control over them and thereby mitigate them with a measure of benevolence (*Radak*).[1] The wall indicates that although the Almighty is the wall of Israel — its fortification and protection — the haven of His mercy shall henceforth be limited by His judgment of our deeds (*Abarbanel*).

The Sages interpret: Behold, the Almighty stood upon a wall of fraud, and in His hand was fraud [i.e., the fraudulent acts which had angered Him], like a debtor who comes with his documents to collect his debts (*Vayikra Rabbah* ch. 33; *Yalkut Shimoni*). All [misdeeds are punished] through an agent, with the exception of fraud, which is dealt with directly by God, as it is stated, *with fraud in His hand*[2] (*Bava Metzia* 59a; *Yalkut Shimoni*).

8. וַיֹּאמֶר ה׳ אֵלַי מָה־אַתָּה רֹאֶה עָמוֹס וָאֹמַר אֲנָךְ — *And HASHEM said to me, 'What do you see, Amos?' And I said, 'A plumbline.'* The Almighty asked me, 'What do you see in this vision, that you do not cry out immediately in supplication on behalf of the Jewish people as you did in the previous two cases' (*Radak*)? And I answered, 'This time I perceive that You intend to judge them cautiously, not simply destroy them as in the earlier visions' (*Radak*).

Others explain that the Almighty questions Amos here in this vision because this prophecy is not self-explanatory as were the others (*Abarbanel; Metzudos David*).

הִנְנִי שָׂם אֲנָךְ בְּקֶרֶב עַמִּי יִשְׂרָאֵל — *'Behold I am placing a plumbline amidst My nation Israel.'* Behold I shall judge My nation with the straight measure of justice (*Rashi*). However, I shall not punish them all at once; rather I will implement My judgment *amidst My nation* — affecting only a portion of the kingdom [at first] (*Abarbanel*).

The Sages comment: *And I said, 'a plumbline'* — this is the great Sanhedrin, which consisted of seventy-one judges — the numerical value of the word אֲנָךְ (*Vayikra Rabbah*, loc. cit.; *Yalkut Shimoni*). I.e., I see that even the highest court in the land has rendered justice fraudulently [and retribution is therefore unavoidable] (*Radak*).

לֹא־אוֹסִיף עוֹד עֲבוֹר לוֹ — *'No longer shall I continue to forbear him.'* I can no longer forbear the iniquities of the people (*Rashi*) without exacting retribution

1. [*Radak* adds this insight in interpretation of the phrase וּבְיָדוֹ אֲנָךְ, *with a plumbline in His hand*. The other commentators, however, seem to understand this verse to be describing a strict measure of justice unmitigated whatsoever by the attribute of mercy.]

2. When the Almighty exacts retribution through an agent [i.e., through one of the heavenly forces through which He works His will], there are times when that agent is impeded by other factors and cannot carry out its mission immediately [thus allowing time to prevent the misfortune from arriving by means of prayer and repentance]. However, when Hashem Himself punishes the wicked, no force in creation can impede or delay Him, and His vengeance is swift and sure (*Rabbeinu Yonasan*, cited by *Shitah Mekubetzes*, ad loc.).

[8] *And HASHEM said to me, 'What do you see, Amos?' And I*
said, 'A plumbline.' And HASHEM said, 'Behold I am plac-
ing a plumbline amidst My nation Israel; no longer shall
I continue to forbear him. [9] *And the altars of Isaac shall*
be laid waste and the sanctuaries of Israel destroyed;

from them (*Radak*). Therefore, do not seek to enjoin Me with your prayers to retract this decree, for it will be to no avail (*Abarbanel*).

The Sages see this phrase as an expression of God's mercy: Said the Almighty: I shall afflict him in this world, but I shall no longer cross over (עֲבוֹר) to him [to punish him] in the world to come (*Vayikra Rabbah* ad loc.; *Yalkut Shimoni*).

Ibn Ezra translates אֲנָךְ to mean lead, and interprets the verse as follows: I have placed a wall of lead between Myself and My nation, and I shall not pass through it (עֲבוֹר) in order to see them [and thereby be aroused to mercy by their plight].

Malbim offers a unique interpretation to these verses: The plumbed wall represents the entirety of creation, which was established with an inherent system of justice to allocate reward and punishment to all of mankind. However, that system has two limits: First, it is a general system dealing with the entirety of creation and, as such, does not respond to each person on an individual basis. [I.e., when all of mankind — or even a large segment — is deserving of a certain manner of treatment, individuals within that segment are included in that treatment — even if they as individuals merit otherwise for better or for worse (see *Gen.* 19:15).] Second, because it relates to an entire system, there are times when appropriate punishment is delayed due to other factors within the system. [E.g., one man's retribution may be withheld because of its effect upon others.]

However, in addition to the plumbed wall, the vision portrayed the Almighty with a plumbline in His hand. This indicated that He was holding the implementation of justice in His own hands in order to exact retribution on a personal level from those individuals who deserve it — unbound to the general system at large and not limited to its constraints.

Thus, in response to the Almighty's query, *'What do you see,'* Amos replies, *'I see a plumbline.'* I.e., in addition to the natural system of justice I observe that You hold a plumbline in your hand. This indicates that You intend to mete out justice to some [individual or] nation in a manner untied to the general system. To this Hashem declares: *Behold I have placed a plumbline amidst My nation Israel.* No longer shall I leave their iniquities to the natural system of justice. Rather, I shall personally see to their punishment, so that it will take effect amidst the nation — not only affecting the nation as a whole but even the individuals in their midst. Furthermore, *I shall no longer continue to forbear him* — I will no longer wait for the general system of justice to respond to their actions. Instead, I shall exact retribution at once, even if from the perspective of creation as a whole the time is not appropriate.

9. וְנָשַׁמּוּ בָּמוֹת יִשְׂחָק — *And the altars of Isaac shall be laid waste.* The altars that the children of Isaac have built to their false gods shall be rendered desolate due to the lack of anyone to worship upon them (*Metzudos David*).

The nation is referred here to as the children of Isaac — rather than of Israel, as throughout Scripture. This is to note the contrast between Isaac himself, who allowed himself to be bound on an altar to be offered to the Almighty, and his descendants, who used altars to rebel against Hashem (*Radak*). Alternatively, it is meant to intimate that they have chosen the standard of the children of Isaac rather than of Israel — i.e., they have followed in the ways of Isaac's other son, Esau (*Alshich*).

Others render יִשְׂחָק to mean mockery: The altars which are but a mockery in the eyes of the Almighty shall be laid waste (*Abarbanel; Malbim*).

וּמִקְדְּשֵׁי יִשְׂרָאֵל יֶחֱרָבוּ — *And the sanctuaries of Israel destroyed.* The cities of Beth-el (*Rashi*), Gilgal, and Dan, which

י וְקַמְתִּי עַל־בֵּית יָרָבְעָם בֶּחָרֶב׃ וַיִּשְׁלַח
אֲמַצְיָה כֹּהֵן בֵּית־אֵל אֶל־יָרָבְעָם מֶלֶךְ־
יִשְׂרָאֵל לֵאמֹר קָשַׁר עָלֶיךָ עָמוֹס בְּקֶרֶב בֵּית
יִשְׂרָאֵל לֹא־תוּכַל הָאָרֶץ לְהָכִיל אֶת־כָּל־
יא דְּבָרָיו׃ כִּי־כֹה אָמַר עָמוֹס בַּחֶרֶב יָמוּת יָרָבְעָם
יב וְיִשְׂרָאֵל גָּלֹה יִגְלֶה מֵעַל אַדְמָתוֹ׃ וַיֹּאמֶר
אֲמַצְיָה אֶל־עָמוֹס חֹזֶה לֵךְ בְּרַח־לְךָ אֶל־
אֶרֶץ יְהוּדָה וֶאֱכָל־שָׁם לֶחֶם וְשָׁם תִּנָּבֵא׃

were the designated sanctuaries of the service of the idols, shall be destroyed (*Radak*). Alternatively: This refers to the sanctuaries which were built in every town for the worship of the false gods (*Abarbanel*).

וְקַמְתִּי עַל־בֵּית יָרָבְעָם בֶּחָרֶב — *And I will ascend upon the House of Jeroboam with the sword*. [I will bring death by the sword to the family of] Jeroboam the son of Joash (*Rashi*). Although Jeroboam himself will die a natural death (*Malbim*), his son Zechariah will be slain by Shallum the son of Joseph, thereby ending the dynasty of his ancestor, Jehu (*Radak*).

Abarbanel interprets the phrase *with the sword* as referring back to this entire prophecy. Whereas the first vision foretold a plague of hunger, and the second one of pestilence, this vision prophesies the suffering of the people at the hand of the enemy's sword.

10. Amos digresses in the midst of his prophecies to relate an event which occurred while he was involved in transmitting the word of Hashem. A priest of idolatry named Amaziah heard the prophecies of Amos in Beth-el and sought to silence him. First, he informed upon him to the king of Israel, accusing him of inciting rebellion and treason. When that failed to produce results, he tried to convince Amos himself to flee to the kingdom of Judah where his prophecies would be appreciated. Amos responds by refuting his arguments and goes on to foretell the climax of the catastrophes about which he has prophesied.

וַיִּשְׁלַח אֲמַצְיָה כֹּהֵן בֵּית־אֵל אֶל־יָרָבְעָם מֶלֶךְ־יִשְׂרָאֵל לֵאמֹר — *And Amaziah the priest of Beth-el sent to Jeroboam king of Israel saying*. Amaziah, who was a priest of the idols in Beth-el (*Rashi*), heard the prophecies uttered there by Amos. He then sent the following message to King Jeroboam, who was not present at the time of Amos's prophesying (*Radak*).

קָשַׁר עָלֶיךָ עָמוֹס בְּקֶרֶב בֵּית יִשְׂרָאֵל — *Amos has conspired against you amidst the House of Israel*. Amos seeks to incite the people against you. He has uttered a prophecy foretelling your death, thus encouraging your enemies to rise up against you and claim that they are thereby fulfilling the will of the Almighty (*Abarbanel*). Furthermore, he has uttered this prophecy publicly, in the midst of the populace, rather than in secret [to avoid inciting a rebellion] (*Radak*).

לֹא־תוּכַל הָאָרֶץ לְהָכִיל אֶת־כָּל־דְּבָרָיו — *The land will not be able to tolerate all his words*. Do not be afraid to strike him down for his effrontery (*Malbim*), for the people of the land will not tolerate such rebellious behavior in their midst and they will support you in your response (*Ibn Ezra; Malbim*).

Alternatively: If you do not act against him, he will succeed in inciting the people to rebel, for they will not be able to tolerate the message he bears without acting upon it (*Abarbanel*).

and I will ascend upon the House of Jeroboam with
the sword.' 10 *And Amaziah the priest of Beth-el sent*
to Jeroboam king of Israel saying: 'Amos has con-
spired against you amidst the House of Israel; the
land will not be able to tolerate all his words. 11 *For so*
said Amos: "By the sword Jeroboam shall die, and
Israel shall be exiled from upon its land."' 12 *And*
Amaziah said to Amos: 'Seer, go, flee to the land of
Judah; and eat bread there and there you shall prophesy.

11. כִּי־כֹה אָמַר עָמוֹס בַּחֶרֶב יָמוּת יָרָבְעָם וְיִשְׂרָאֵל גָּלֹה יִגְלֶה מֵעַל אַדְמָתוֹ — *For so said Amos: By the sword Jeroboam shall die, and Israel shall be exiled from upon its land.* With what has he sought to incite rebellion? He has prophesied that you, the king, shall die — thereby encouraging your enemies, and that the nation shall be exiled — thereby arousing in them a fear which could lead to rebellion (*Abarbanel*).

In truth, however, Amaziah's accusations against Amos were unfounded. He did not prophesy the death of Jeroboam himself, but only that of members of his family (*Rashi*; see v. 9). Furthermore, he did not foretell — at this time — the exile of the entire nation, but only the destruction of a portion of the land at the hands of invading forces (*Abarbanel*; see comm. to v. 9). Nevertheless, Amaziah distorted the truth in order to incite Jeroboam to have Amos executed (*Radak*). This was because he saw in Amos's prophecies a threat to his position as priest, since if Amos successfully aroused the people to repentance they would no longer worship in the sanctuary of the idols (*Abarbanel*; cf. *Mahari Kara*).

Despite Amaziah's efforts, he was unable to arouse the king's wrath. Rather, Jeroboam responded, 'God forbid that that *tzaddik* should speak thus, and if he did, what shall I do to him? The *Shechinah* has so instructed him' (*Pesachim* 87, cited by *Radak, Abarbanel, Malbim*; see comm. to *Hosea* 1:1).

12. וַיֹּאמֶר אֲמַצְיָה אֶל־עָמוֹס — *And Amaziah said to Amos.* Upon seeing that Jeroboam would not be moved to act against Amos, Amaziah attempted to persuade Amos himself to flee the kingdom of Israel in order to avoid retribution against him from the king for his prophecies (*Radak*). According to *Abarbanel*, he presented himself as a friend seeking Amos's welfare and urged him to escape with his life.

וֶאֱכָל־שָׁם לֶחֶם — *And eat bread there.* There they will appreciate your prophecies, and will consequently provide you with sustenance (*Kara; Alshich; Malbim*). Whereas in the kingdom of Israel, it is the false prophets who are fed and supported for their prophecies, there in Judah they honor the prophets of Hashem (*Ibn Ezra; Radak*). Furthermore, they will certainly support you when they hear you foretelling doom to their enemies, the citizens of the northern kingdom (*Radak*).

Abarbanel explains that there was then a famine in the land of Israel, as foretold above by Amos, but in the land of Judah, there was bread to be had.

Rashi interprets this phrase as being stated degradingly: Go to the land of Judah where they will feed you scraps of bread in exchange for your prophecies.

וְשָׁם תִּנָּבֵא — *And there you shall prophesy.* In Judah lies the Temple of the Almighty God in Whose Name you prophesy (*Rashi*), and the atmosphere there is thus more conducive to the

יג וּבֵית־אֵל לֹא־תוֹסִיף עוֹד לְהִנָּבֵא כִּי מִקְדַּשׁ־
יד מֶלֶךְ הוּא וּבֵית מַמְלָכָה הוּא׃ וַיַּעַן עָמוֹס וַיֹּאמֶר
אֶל־אֲמַצְיָה לֹא־נָבִיא אָנֹכִי וְלֹא בֶן־נָבִיא אָנֹכִי
טו כִּי־בוֹקֵר אָנֹכִי וּבוֹלֵס שִׁקְמִים׃ וַיִּקָּחֵנִי יהוה
מֵאַחֲרֵי הַצֹּאן וַיֹּאמֶר אֵלַי יהוה לֵךְ הִנָּבֵא
טז אֶל־עַמִּי יִשְׂרָאֵל׃ וְעַתָּה שְׁמַע דְּבַר־יהוה אַתָּה
אֹמֵר לֹא תִנָּבֵא עַל־יִשְׂרָאֵל וְלֹא תַטִּיף עַל־
יז בֵּית יִשְׂחָק׃ לָכֵן כֹּה־אָמַר יהוה אִשְׁתְּךָ בָּעִיר
תִּזְנֶה וּבָנֶיךָ וּבְנֹתֶיךָ בַּחֶרֶב יִפֹּלוּ וְאַדְמָתְךָ
בַּחֶבֶל תְּחֻלָּק וְאַתָּה עַל־אֲדָמָה טְמֵאָה תָּמוּת

achievement of the level of sanctity required for prophecy (*Alshich*).

Alternatively: There they worship the Almighty in His Temple, and they will therefore allow you to prophesy in His Name without fear of retribution (*Kara; Abarbanel; Malbim*).

13. וּבֵית־אֵל לֹא־תוֹסִיף עוֹד לְהִנָּבֵא כִּי מִקְדַּשׁ־מֶלֶךְ הוּא וּבֵית מַמְלָכָה הוּא — *But continue no longer to prophesy in Beth-el, for it is the sanctuary of the king and the house of royalty.* Prophesy no longer in Beth-el, for the Name of Hashem is not mentioned there, only those of the idols [and you will therefore find no sympathy for your cause] (*Rashi; Mahari Kara*). Furthermore, it is the sanctuary of the king, where he is often to be found, and thus the officers who accompany him may overhear your words and put you to death (*Metzudos David*; cf. *Alshich*). Indeed, Beth-el is *the house of royalty*, where the king dwells for long periods of time as if in his own house [and you are thus even more likely to incur his wrath] (*Radak*).

Two sanctuaries of idolatry were founded by Jeroboam ben Nebat, one in Dan and one in Beth-el. The one in Beth-el was closer to Samaria, the capital city of the kingdom, and was therefore the one patronized by the royal family (*Abarbanel*). In addition, because Beth-el had been designated by Jacob as a House of God (*Gen.* 28:17) it was considered to be a place of singular holiness — comparable to Jerusalem — and was thus deemed an appropriate site for religious worship (*Radak; Abarbanel*).

Others interpret: *he is of a house of royalty* — since Jeroboam comes from a line of kings, his claim to royalty is well established, and one who seeks to undermine his authority will thus be dealt with very harshly (*Alshich*; cf. *Metzudos*).

14. ... וַיַּעַן עָמוֹס — *And Amos replied ...* I am not a prophet from my youth (*Radak*) — learned in the ways of prophecy and the preparations for its achievement (*Abarbanel*; see comm. to 1:1). Nor did I inherit the mantle of this greatness from my father (*Abarbanel*), as he himself was also not a prophet and thus could not have taught me the ways of prophecy (*Radak*).

Others interpret: I am not one of your false prophets who take pay for their prophecies (*Rashi*).

According to *Alshich*, Amos here responds to Amaziah's reference to him as a 'seer,' which is a lesser level of prophecy than indicated by the word 'prophet.' To this Amos replies: You are correct in calling me a seer, for I am not a prophet nor the son of a prophet — and the higher level of prophecy has remained beyond my reach (see comm. to 1:1).

13 *But continue no longer to prophesy in Beth-el, for it*
is the sanctuary of the king and the house of royalty.'
14 *And Amos replied and said to Amaziah: 'I am not*
a prophet nor am I the son of a prophet, for I am a
cattle herder and an inspector of sycamores. 15 *And*
HASHEM took me from behind the sheep, and HASHEM
said to me: "Go prophesy to My nation, Israel." 16 *And*
now hear the word of HASHEM: you say do not
prophesy concerning Israel nor speak about the House
of Isaac. 17 *Therefore, so said HASHEM: Your wife shall*
be promiscuous in the city and your sons and daugh-
ters shall fall by the sword, and your land shall be
divided by lot, and you shall die on unclean soil,

כִּי־בוֹקֵר אָנֹכִי — *For I am a cattle herder.* All my life I have been a cattle herder, and from this I have earned my livelihood. I thus have no need for anyone else's bread to sustain me (*Rashi; Kara; Radak; Alshich; Malbim*).

וּבוֹלֵס שִׁקְמִים — *And an inspector of sycamores.* I inspect sycamores to see which are ready to be pruned, and which are fitting to be cut and made into beams (*Rashi*; cf. *Radak*). Alternatively, this phrase is translated *one who mixes sycamores* — I mix the fruit of the sycamore together with other foods in order to feed my cattle (*Radak*).

15. ... וַיִּקָּחֵנִי ה׳ — *And HASHEM took me* ... I did not leave my work on my own volition. Rather, Hashem took me from behind the sheep which I shepherded, and imbued me with the spirit of prophecy, thus coercing me to go out and relate His words. As such, you cannot demand of me to cease to prophesy, for Almighty God has commanded that I continue (*Radak*).

מֵאַחֲרֵי הַצֹּאן — *From behind the sheep.* I achieved prophecy while herding sheep, rather than cattle. This is because the former require less attention and effort, thus allowing more time for solitude and introspection, which are conducive to spiritual ascension (*Alshich*). In addition, many leaders of Israel were previously tenders of sheep — e.g., Moses and King David — for it is an activity which is similar in nature to leading a nation (*Abarbanel*).

וַיֹּאמֶר אֵלַי ה׳ לֵךְ הִנָּבֵא אֶל־עַמִּי יִשְׂרָאֵל — *And HASHEM said to me: Go prophesy to My nation, Israel.* The Almighty commanded me to relate His prophecies to the nation of the ten tribes of Israel, not that of Judah, and I thus am unable to flee to Judah and prophesy there (*Malbim*). Furthermore, as an agent of the Almighty, I need not fear retribution from a king of flesh and blood, and I thus have no reason to flee (*Alshich*).

16. ... וְעַתָּה שְׁמַע דְּבַר־ה׳ — *And now hear the word of HASHEM* ... Because you have sought to dissuade me from fulfilling the mission of God to prophesy to His people, this is the fate He has in store for you (*Radak*).

17. ... לָכֵן כֹּה־אָמַר ה׳ — *Therefore, so said HASHEM* ... I have come in the Name of Hashem with several goals. I seek to prevent the people from betraying their allegiance to the Almighty by prostituting themselves to other gods, and [I hope to arouse them to repent and to thereby]

א וְיִשְׂרָאֵל גָּלֹה יִגְלֶה מֵעַל אַדְמָתוֹ׃ כֹּה
ב הִרְאַנִי אֲדֹנָי יֱהוִה וְהִנֵּה כְּלוּב קָיִץ׃ וַיֹּאמֶר
מָה־אַתָּה רֹאֶה עָמוֹס וָאֹמַר כְּלוּב קָיִץ וַיֹּאמֶר
יהוה אֵלַי בָּא הַקֵּץ אֶל־עַמִּי יִשְׂרָאֵל לֹא־אוֹסִיף
ג עוֹד עֲבוֹר לוֹ׃ וְהֵילִילוּ שִׁירוֹת הֵיכָל בַּיּוֹם הַהוּא
נְאֻם אֲדֹנָי יֱהוִה רַב הַפֶּגֶר בְּכָל־מָקוֹם הִשְׁלִיךְ
ד הָס׃ שִׁמְעוּ־זֹאת הַשֹּׁאֲפִים אֶבְיוֹן וְלַשְׁבִּית

avoid the enemy's invasion and conquest of their homeland. This would involve the death of many people at his hand, as well as the subsequent exile of the survivors from the land. Because you have sought to impede my efforts, you shall be punished in a manner appropriate to your sin. For encouraging the prostitution of the people to other gods, you shall suffer the prostitution of your own wife here in the city, even before she is sent into exile. For hampering my endeavors to save the nation from their tragic fate, you personally shall experience that same fate. Thus, your children will be felled by the enemy's sword; your land will be divided by lots among the conquerors; and you yourself will be exiled to foreign soil, where you will subsequently die (*Abarbanel*; cf. *Alshich*).

וְיִשְׂרָאֵל גָּלֹה יִגְלֶה מֵעַל אַדְמָתוֹ — *And Israel shall be exiled from upon its land*. That which you falsely claimed to have been included in my previous prophecies shall truly come to pass (see comm. to v. 11); the nation of Israel shall indeed be exiled from its soil (*Abarbanel; Alshich; Malbim; Metzudos David*).

VIII

Having prophesied explicitly that the end of the kingdom of Israel had been decreed by Hashem, Amos goes on to elaborate on that theme. According to some commentators, these three verses are still part of his response to Amaziah (see comm. to v. 3).

1. כֹּה הִרְאַנִי ה׳ אֱלֹהִים וְהִנֵּה כְּלוּב קָיִץ — *Thus showed me HASHEM/ELOHIM: and behold [I saw] a basket of summer fruits.* The Almighty showed me yet another vision, in which I saw a basket of fruits which ripen in the summer (*Targum; Ibn Ezra; Radak; Abarbanel; Metzudos David*). Alternatively: He showed me a basket of late figs, which are of inferior quality (*Rashi*). There are some figs which ripen as early as the month of Tammuz and are superior in quality. Others ripen in Av [and are not quite as good]. Those which do not ripen until Elul are referred to as קָיִץ — or, in the language of the Sages — קְיָצֵי תְּאֵנִים (*Kara*).

Malbim interprets כְּלוּב as a basket which is normally used for carrying birds which have been trapped. In this vision, such a basket was filled with figs (see comm. to v. 3).

2. בָּא הַקֵּץ אֶל־עַמִּי יִשְׂרָאֵל — *The end has come to My nation Israel.* The appearance of the fully ripened fruit (קַיִץ) indicates that its growing period has ended (*Ibn Ezra*) and it is now time for it to be plucked from the tree and consumed. So too has the period [of sovereignty] ended (קֵץ) for My nation Israel, and they shall now be exiled to another land (*Radak*). Unlike the previous vision of the plumbline (7:8), which depicted the conquest of only portions of the land (see comm. ad loc.), this prophecy portrays the final destruction of the nation (*Abarbanel*).

and Israel shall be exiled from upon its land.'

8/1-4 1 *Thus showed me* HASHEM/ELOHIM: *and behold [I*
saw] a basket of summer fruits. 2 *And He said,*
'What do you see, Amos?' And I said, 'A basket of
summer fruits.' And HASHEM *said to me, 'The end has*
come to My nation Israel; I will no longer continue to
forbear him.' 3 *And they will wail the songs of the*
banquet hall on that day, declares HASHEM/ELOHIM; *so*
many corpses — in every place, 'Cast away! Remove!'
4 *Hear this, you who devour the needy, decimating*

לֹא־אוֹסִיף עוֹד עֲבוֹר לוֹ — *I will no longer continue to forbear him.* I can no longer tolerate his transgressions and withhold the punishment which is due him (*Targum; Radak; Metzudos David*, cf. comm. to 7:8).

Alternatively: I can no longer pass that end [which I have designated for him] (*Ibn Ezra*) and push it off to a later date (*Malbim*).

3. רַב הַפֶּגֶר בְּכָל־מָקוֹם הִשְׁלִיךְ הָס — *So many corpses — in every place, 'Cast away! Remove!'* The corpses of the dead will increase and multiply until everywhere that people go they will say, 'Cast away and remove these corpses from here!' (*Targum; Rashi*).

Others translate הָס to mean silence: Everywhere that the many corpses will be cast will be enveloped by silence, for those who see will restrain themselves from crying out in anguish so as not to overwhelm the populace with fear (*Ibn Ezra; Metzudos David*). Alternatively: Wherever people are involved in casting out the corpses one will say to another, 'Be silent! Let us not cry out! Rather we must acknowledge the justice of our plight' (*Radak*; cf. 6:10).

Another rendition of this phrase is: *So many corpses He has cast everywhere. Silence!* The Almighty will send the sword of slaughter throughout the land and He will thereby cast out corpses in every place (*Abarbanel*). Following a similar line of thought, *Malbim* sees this as the interpretation of the bird-trapper's basket in Amos's vision: The corpses will abound until they are everywhere — like the corpses of birds killed by the trapper. Indeed, they will be cast out into the streets — as depicted by the basket which contained no birds, only fruits, because its normal contents had been cast out.

The final word, *silence*, is spoken by Amos to Amaziah: Be silent, Amaziah, and utter no more statements like that which you said to me. For it is a time of evil for the Jewish people, and you yourself will witness the fulfillment of my prophecies (*Abarbanel*).

Alternatively: *Silence!* There is still more to this prophecy, but the Almighty does not yet wish it to be revealed. In accordance with this injunction, Amos himself disclosed no more. Nevertheless, with the word הָס he alluded cryptically to the nature of that additional prophecy. It was left to Isaiah to reveal it explicitly, when he declared (*Isaiah* 7:8): *And in another sixty-five years Ephraim shall be broken from being a nation*. The Sages (*Seder Olam* ch. 28) explain these sixty-five years — the numerical equivalent of the word הָס — as dating from the prophecies of Amos (*Malbim*; cf. *Abarbanel*).

4. Having been interrupted by the interference of Amaziah and his own response, the prophet now returns to his original flow of prophetic castigation of the people for their wickedness (*Abarbanel*; cf. *Mahari Kara; Malbim*).

שִׁמְעוּ־זֹאת . . . — *Hear this . . .* Hear my words, you people of means, who swallow up the needy with your deceit and fraud, and seek to eradicate them entirely

ה °עֲנִיֵּי ק׳ °עֲנוּי־אָרֶץ: לֵאמֹר מָתַי יַעֲבֹר הַחֹדֶשׁ
וְנַשְׁבִּירָה שֶּׁבֶר וְהַשַּׁבָּת וְנִפְתְּחָה־בָּר לְהַקְטִין
אֵיפָה וּלְהַגְדִּיל שֶׁקֶל וּלְעַוֵּת מֹאזְנֵי מִרְמָה:
ו לִקְנוֹת בַּכֶּסֶף דַּלִּים וְאֶבְיוֹן בַּעֲבוּר נַעֲלָיִם
ז וּמַפַּל בַּר נַשְׁבִּיר: נִשְׁבַּע יהוה בִּגְאוֹן יַעֲקֹב
ח אִם־אֶשְׁכַּח לָנֶצַח כָּל־מַעֲשֵׂיהֶם: הַעַל זֹאת
לֹא־תִרְגַּז הָאָרֶץ וְאָבַל כָּל־יוֹשֵׁב בָּהּ

from the land by taking all that they possess (*Radak*).

This follows the approach of the majority of commentators. *Malbim* translates הַשֹּׁאֲפִים to mean *who aspire* — those who aspire to devour the needy (cf. 2:7, comm. ad loc.).

עֲנוּי־אָרֶץ — *The poor of the land.* This word is written ענוי, *the humble*, and read עֲנִיֵּי, *the poor*. Indeed, it is often the impoverished who are humble (*Radak*).

5. לֵאמֹר — *Saying*. Those of you who own stores of grain (*Ibn Ezra*) express your plan to devour the needy, as follows (*Rashi*).

מָתַי יַעֲבֹר הַחֹדֶשׁ וְנַשְׁבִּירָה שֶּׁבֶר — *When will the month pass and we will sell grain.* When will the month in which the grain is harvested pass? During that time, there is ample grain left as *shikchah* for the poor in the fields, in accordance with the laws of *leket*, *shikchah*, and *peah*.[1] Once that period is over, however, they will have to come to us for sustenance (*Radak; Abarbanel; Alshich; Metzudos David*).

Others render: *when will the month be delayed and we will sell grain*: When will a leap year be declared, thereby delaying for a full month the offering of the *Omer* sacrifice[2] on Passover? Such an occurrence extends the time that the previous year's crop must supply the populace. Thus, when it comes, the supply dwindles, thereby raising the price of grain (*Targum; Rashi; Kara*).

וְהַשַּׁבָּת וְנִפְתְּחָה־בָּר — *The Sabbath, and we will open [the stores of] grain.* When will pass the Sabbatical year of *shemittah*, during which the produce of the fields must be left available to all? This allows the poor ample produce, precluding the necessity of their purchasing from the storeowners. Once it is over, however, we will once again open up our stores of grain and sell to the needy to meet their needs (*Abarbanel; Metzudos David*).

Others assume the opposite connotation: When will the *shemittah* year arrive, when supplies will be low and we will thus be able to sell the grain stocked away in our storehouses (*Rashi; Malbim*)?

Radak interprets *the Sabbath* to mean a week: When the year is intercalated with an extra month, and the poor

1. One who harvests his field in the Land of Israel is limited in his intake by several *mitzvos* which require him to help provide for the poor. First of all, he must leave one corner of the field uncut, to be reaped and gathered by the needy. This is *peah*. Stalks which fall in units of one or two when the grain is being reaped or collected are *leket*, and must be left where they drop to be gathered by the poor. In addition, those sheaves — cut or uncut — which he leaves behind him when gathering his crops may not be retrieved, but must rather be left for the poor (see *Rambam, Hil. Matnos Aniyim* ch. 1).

2. The *Omer* is a *minchah*-offering brought on Passover which renders the grain of that year's crop permissible to eat.

the poor of the land. [5] *Saying, 'When will the month*
pass and we will sell grain; the Sabbath, and we will
open [the stores of] grain, to reduce the ephah and
enlarge the shekel and to distort scales of deceit?
[6] *To purchase the poor with silver and the destitute*
for shoes; and the refuse of grain we will sell?'
[7] *HASHEM has sworn by the Glory of Jacob: I will*
not forever forget all their deeds. [8] *Shall not the land*
quake for this, and all its inhabitants be destroyed?

therefore come to seek provisions, we will delay them until the following week. [We will continue in this manner] until the prices rise and we can exact more money in payment.

לְהַקְטִין אֵיפָה וּלְהַגְדִּיל שֶׁקֶל וּלְעַוֵּת מֹאזְנֵי מִרְמָה — *To reduce the ephah and enlarge the shekel and to distort scales of deceit.* We will reduce the *ephah*-measurement by which we sell and demand a large *shekel*-coin in payment (*Radak*). And when exchanging our produce for other goods, we will alter the scales so as to distort the weighing in our favor (*Abarbanel*).

6. . . . לִקְנוֹת בַּכֶּסֶף דַּלִּים — *To purchase the poor with silver . . .* We will pursue this policy until our buyers are so poor that they will be forced to sell us their fields and vineyards — or perhaps even themselves, as slaves (*Radak; Abarbanel*). The truly destitute, who are left with nothing at all, will sell for the nominal price of a mere pair of shoes (*Malbim*).

An alternate translation of בַּעֲבוּר נַעֲלָיִם is *in order to inherit them* (*Targum; Rashi;* cf. 2:6).

In addition, when they come to purchase our produce, we will give them the refuse that is separated from the grain in the sieve. This is normally given only to domesticated fowl. However, they will be forced to accept it for themselves, for the price of actual grain will be well beyond their means (*Rashi; Radak*).

7. נִשְׁבַּע ה׳ בִּגְאוֹן יַעֲקֹב אִם־אֶשְׁכַּח לָנֶצַח כָּל־מַעֲשֵׂיהֶם — *HASHEM has sworn by the Glory of Jacob: I will not forever forget all their deeds.* [In response to this wickedness,] the Almighty has made the following oath by His Holy Name — the Name that has been revealed only to the Children of Jacob (*Ibn Ezra*). Alternatively, He has sworn by His Glory that resides among the Children of Jacob in the Holy Temple (*Radak*).

I shall not forever refrain from exacting retribution from them for their evil deeds. Even if I do not take action immediately, their prosperity shall not last forever. Eventually I shall punish them for all that they have done (*Abarbanel; Malbim*).

The Sages interpret this oath as applying to the following categories of wrongdoers: those who store produce — i.e., they buy up the produce and hoard it in order to cause the prices to rise (*Rashi*), those who lend with interest, those who decrease the *ephah* [that they sell], and those who jack up their prices above the market value (*Bava Basra* 90b).

8. הַעַל זֹאת לֹא־תִרְגַּז הָאָרֶץ וְאָבַל כָּל־יוֹשֵׁב בָּהּ — *Shall not the land quake for this, and all its inhabitants be destroyed?* Does such evil not warrant that the land undergo a great earthquake, thereby destroying all its inhabitants? For who can tolerate such corruption and lawlessness? Just as the earth was destroyed by the Flood because of robbery, and Sodom and Gomorrah were likewise destroyed for the same reason, so shall the land [of Israel] be destroyed for its inhabitants'

ח/ט־יא וְנִשְׁקְעָה ק׳ וְעָלְתָה כָאֹר כֻּלָּהּ וְנִגְרְשָׁה °ונשקה כִּיאוֹר
ט מִצְרָיִם׃ וְהָיָה ׀ בַּיּוֹם הַהוּא נְאֻם אֲדֹנָי
יֱהוִה וְהֵבֵאתִי הַשֶּׁמֶשׁ בַּצָּהֳרָיִם וְהַחֲשַׁכְתִּי
י לָאָרֶץ בְּיוֹם אוֹר׃ וְהָפַכְתִּי חַגֵּיכֶם לְאֵבֶל וְכָל־
שִׁירֵיכֶם לְקִינָה וְהַעֲלֵיתִי עַל־כָּל־מָתְנַיִם שָׂק
וְעַל־כָּל־רֹאשׁ קָרְחָה וְשַׂמְתִּיהָ כְּאֵבֶל יָחִיד
יא וְאַחֲרִיתָהּ כְּיוֹם מָר׃ הִנֵּה ׀ יָמִים בָּאִים

similar behavior (*Radak*). *Malbim* adds: Earth itself cannot tolerate such wrongdoing. Just as the natural order of civilized human interaction has been overturned by this corruption, so will the system of nature respond in kind [with upheaval and disruption] that will destroy its inhabitants.

This follows the translation of the majority of commentators. Others render: *Shall not the land be destroyed for this* (*Targum; Rashi*)?

וְעָלְתָה כָאֹר כֻּלָּהּ — *And [water] shall rise like the river over all of it.* It is fitting that the land be flooded over with water, just as the land of Egypt is flooded periodically by the surging waters of the Nile. Therefore, when it shall be struck by that great earthquake, the fissure will be filled with water which will cover the entire land (*Radak*). Alternatively: The Almighty shall bring down torrents of rain until the entire land is flooded (*Abarbanel*).

This follows the view of most commentators, who interpret the word כָאֹר to mean כִּיְאוֹר, *like the river*, as stated explicitly in a parallel verse below (9:5). *Rashi*, however, explains that this is a different word, which means 'a raincloud.' Thus: *It shall rise up in its entirety like a rain cloud* — i.e., the land shall be enveloped in darkness like a dark rain cloud.

וְנִגְרְשָׁה וְנִשְׁקְעָה כִּיאוֹר מִצְרָיִם — *And it shall move and sink like the river of Egypt.* The earth shall move out of place [due to the earthquake] and sink beneath the water that fills the fissure, just as the land surface of Egypt sinks beneath the overflowing waters of the Nile (*Radak*).

Alternatively: *It shall be cast up and sink like the river of Eygpt.* The Nile overflows once in forty years and waters the land. When it rises, it brings up mud and silt onto its banks; and when its waters subside, the mud and silt remain behind. In a similar manner, the land shall spew out the evildoers in its midst and only then will [the turbulence] subside and [the land] rest (*Rashi*).

Abarbanel understands this verse as describing allegorically the overrunning of the land by the armies of Sennacherib (cf. *Malbim*).

Alshich explains the choice of metaphor in the following manner: The Sages state that when a wicked person treads upon the land, the earth itself trembles. This is because, as described in *Genesis* (1:9), the Almighty decreed that the land surface of the world should miraculously float upon the waters which lie beneath it without sinking under, in order to uphold the world. However, when this miracle is utilized to maintain the existence of the wicked, the earth begins to tremble, as if to say, 'Why should I remain miraculously atop the waters in order to keep such people alive?' Thus, it would be a fitting reaction to the decadence described above if the earth were to tremble violently and sink beneath the waters upon which it sits, thereby destroying all of its inhabitants.

9. וְהָיָה בַּיּוֹם הַהוּא . . . — *And it shall be on that day . . .* When the time will come to punish you for all your misdeeds (*Abarbanel*), I will bring disaster upon you suddenly in the midst of your prosperity and tranquility (*Rashi*). I will cause the sun to set from above by removing from you My Divine Providence, and by

And [water] shall rise like the river over all of it and
it shall move and sink like the river of Egypt. 9 *And*
it shall be on that day, declares HASHEM/ELOHIM, *that*
I will bring down the sun at midday and I shall
darken the land on a day of light. 10 *And I will turn*
your festivals into mourning, and your songs into
lamentation; and I will bring upon all loins sack-
cloth, and baldness upon every head; and I will place
it as if in mourning for an only [son], and its end
like a day of bitterness. 11 *Behold, days are coming,*

obstructing the celestial forces that work in your favor; and I will darken your lives from below by weakening your might and confounding your wicked plans (*Malbim*).

This alludes specifically to the death of Josiah king of Judah[1] at the hands of Pharaoh-Neco of Egypt, which occurred at a time when there were no hostilities between the two nations. Pharaoh-Neco sought to pass through the Land of Israel in order to pursue his campaign against Assyria, whose army was encamped on the Euphrates River. Josiah, however, understood the verse (*Lev.* 26:6) *and a sword will not pass through your land* to refer even to a non-belligerent army passing through in order to wage war against others. Accordingly, he confronted Pharaoh-Neco in battle in order to stop him, and was killed in the process (*Rashi, Kara*, from *Moed Katan* 25b; *Taanis* 22a; cf. *II Kings* 23:29ff, *II Chron.* 35:20-24). [Thus, the sun set with catastrophe at a time when all had been bright, with no conflict or oppression in process.]

10. וְהָפַכְתִּי חַגֵּיכֶם ... — *And I will turn your festivals ...* In order to clearly demonstrate that your idolatry is the cause of your downfall, I will bring your punishment upon you on those very days which you have designated as festivals for your false gods — thereby turning them into days of mourning. The songs which you sing during those days of merriment will thus be turned into dirges of lamentation for all who die at that time. Upon your loins, which you gird to run to your idol worship, I will place sackcloth [as a sign of your mourning], and your heads which you bow in submission to your idols I will smite with baldness (*Alshich*). Like the intense mourning of a father for his only son shall be the mourning that pervades the land (*Rashi; Radak*), for only a minute few shall survive the holocaust that engulfs you (*Alshich*). But unlike the mourning for an individual, which eventually fades and is nearly forgotten, the calamities I bring upon you will end in bitterness (*Alshich*), for you will ultimately be exiled from your land (*Abarbanel*).

Rashi interprets this verse, too, as referring to the death of Josiah: *And I will turn your festivals into mourning* — as stated (*II Chron.* 35:24): *And all Judah and Jerusalem mourned for Josiah. And all your songs into lamentation* — as stated (ibid. v. 25): *And all the singing men and singing women spoke in their lamentation.*

11. You have defiled and abused the sanctity of your souls, until their true nobility is no longer discernible. Nevertheless, there still exists within you a deep

1. [Although these prophecies were directed primarily to the kingdom of Israel, their application apparently extends to that of Judah as well.]

נְאֻם֙ אֲדֹנָ֣י יֱהֹוִ֔ה וְהִשְׁלַחְתִּ֥י רָעָ֖ב בָּאָ֑רֶץ לֹֽא־
רָעָ֨ב לַלֶּ֜חֶם וְֽלֹא־צָמָ֣א לַמַּ֗יִם כִּ֣י אִם־לִשְׁמֹ֔עַ
יב אֵ֖ת דִּבְרֵ֥י יְהוָֽה׃ וְנָעוּ֙ מִיָּ֣ם עַד־יָ֔ם וּמִצָּפ֖וֹן וְעַד־
מִזְרָ֑ח יְשֽׁוֹטְט֛וּ לְבַקֵּ֥שׁ אֶת־דְּבַר־יְהוָ֖ה וְלֹ֥א
יג יִמְצָֽאוּ׃ בַּיּ֣וֹם הַה֗וּא תִּתְעַלַּ֜פְנָה הַבְּתוּלֹ֥ת הַיָּפ֛וֹת
יד וְהַבַּחוּרִ֖ים בַּצָּמָֽא׃ הַנִּשְׁבָּעִים֙ בְּאַשְׁמַ֣ת שֹׁמְר֔וֹן
וְאָמְר֕וּ חֵ֤י אֱלֹהֶ֙יךָ֙ דָּ֔ן וְחֵ֕י דֶּ֖רֶךְ בְּאֵֽר־שָׁ֑בַע

link to the Almighty, which shall yet reverberate within your hearts and relentlessly demand satisfaction. These verses contain tidings of gloom, for they describe the frustration and sorrow of a people seeking to renew their closeness to Hashem to no avail. But on another level they are verses of solace, reaffirming the deep bond with the Creator that is intrinsic to the Jewish identity.

הִנֵּה יָמִים בָּאִים . . . — *Behold, days are coming* . . . Because you have despised and disgraced the words of the prophets (*Radak*), the time is coming when all of the prophets will die (*Ibn Ezra*) and a great hunger and desire will pervade the land. Not a hunger for bread nor a thirst for water, but a deep spiritual yearning for the words of the Almighty as communicated through His prophets. A yearning which will not be fulfilled, as the word of Hashem will no longer be forthcoming (v. 12). This will occur in the times of the Second Temple after the death of the prophet Malachi, as well as afterward in the days of exile, when prophecy will no longer exist among the Jewish nation (*Radak*).

Alshich interprets this verse as bearing a message of hope and comfort. Do not despair of ever again regaining the good graces of the Almighty. For the day shall come when you will abandon all of your decadence and self-indulgence, and you will hunger instead for the words of Hashem and for His presence among you. Eventually, you will thereby be motivated to repent with all your hearts and regain your lofty level of attachment to the Almighty.

12. וְנָעוּ מִיָּם עַד־יָם . . . — *And they shall journey from sea to sea* . . . The people will travel from the Red Sea south of the Land of Israel, to the Mediterranean which lies to the west (*Ibn Ezra*); and from the northern border to that on the east. Across the length and breadth of the Holy Land shall they wander, seeking the word of Hashem. But they will not find it — not there in Israel and certainly not outside the Holy Land (*Radak*).

Alternatively: They shall seek the word of Hashem in the four corners of the earth, but they shall not find it (*Abarbanel*).

Malbim interprets these two verses as depicting two different periods in Jewish history. In the times of the Second Temple, once the last vestiges of direct prophecy are finally gone, the word of the Almighty will still be available by means of *Ruach Hakodesh* — the holy spirit — and *bas kol* — a heavenly oracle. These will be pursued hungrily and avidly, for the people will be filled with the desire to receive the word of Hashem. After the Temple's destruction, however, they will wander across the length and breadth of the Land of Israel, trying to discover the Almighty's word. But it will no longer be available.

The Sages comment concerning these verses: When our Sages entered Kerem B'Yavneh (the great yeshivah and seat of the Sanhedrin in the city of Yavneh) they said, 'The Torah is destined to be forgotten from Israel, as it is stated: *Behold, days are coming* etc. . . . R' Shimon bar Yochai said: God forbid that Torah should be

*declares HASHEM/ELOHIM, that I will send hunger into
the land; not a hunger for bread nor a thirst for water,
but to hear the words of HASHEM.*
12 *And they shall
journey from sea to sea, and from the north unto the
east; they shall wander to seek the word of HASHEM,
but shall not find it.*
13 *On that day, the beautiful virgins
and the young men shall faint with thirst.*
14 *Those
who swear by the guilt of Samaria and say, 'As your
god lives, Dan,' and 'as the way to Beer-sheba exists';*

forgotten from Israel, as it is stated (*Deut.* 31:21): *For it shall not be forgotten from among his seed*. Rather, what is meant by the words *they shall wander to seek the word of HASHEM and they shall not find it*? That they shall not find clear halachah and clear scholarship in one place (*Shabbos* 138b-139a) — i.e., the halachah will not be established with such a clarity of reasoning so as to leave no room for further dispute' (*Rashi* ad loc.).

13. בַּיּוֹם הַהוּא תִּתְעַלַּפְנָה הַבְּתוּלֹת הַיָּפוֹת וְהַבַּחוּרִים בַּצָּמָא — *On that day, the beautiful virgins and the young men shall faint with thirst.* Even the beautiful young men and women, whose tendency it is to be involved in mundane pleasures and desires, will be so obsessed with the pursuit of Godliness that they will faint from the anguish and despair brought on by their failure to find it (*Radak; Abarbanel*).

Targum interprets the beautiful virgins as referring to the Jewish nation — depicted elsewhere as the virgin of Israel (see 5:2). The virgins — i.e., the virgin kingdoms of Judah and Israel — and the young men — i.e., all of the tribes of Israel — will faint from the anguish and despair of fruitlessly seeking the word of Hashem (*Abarbanel*).

Malbim contends that this verse depicts the fainting from physical hunger and thirst which will occur at the time of the destruction and exile of the kingdom of Israel. Whereas the time will come when the primary endeavors and aspirations of the people will involve spiritual pursuits, that is still far off in the future. When the ten tribes go into exile, however, they will suffer from simple physical hunger and thirst — as they are not gripped by the loftier desire to seek the word of Hashem.

14. ... הַנִּשְׁבָּעִים — *Those who swear ...* As today they despise the word of Hashem and opt instead for the service of the idols they have chosen, so shall they yet seek and desire that holy word, only to have it elude them (*Radak*). *Abarbanel* explains this as referring explicitly to the people of Judah, who were included in the prophecy of the previous verses. They too shall yet hunger fruitlessly for the word of Hashem, for they have also followed the example of their brothers in the kingdom of Israel and worshiped the idols which the latter established.

בְּאַשְׁמַת שֹׁמְרוֹן — *The guilt of Samaria.* This refers to the golden calf which stood in Beth-el. It is called 'the guilt of Samaria' because that was the seat of the royalty responsible for the prevalence of idolatry among the people (*Radak*).

וְאָמְרוּ חֵי אֱלֹהֶיךָ דָּן וְחֵי דֶּרֶךְ בְּאֵר־שָׁבַע — *And say, 'As your god lives, Dan,' and 'as the way to Beer-sheba exists.'* When they wished to pronounce an oath they would swear by the idol which stood in Dan or else by the road to Beer-sheba, which was the route to the idols of Dan and Beth-el (*Mahari Kara*; cf. 5:5; comm. ibid.).

Radak explains that Dan and Beer-sheba were on the two ends of the nation's borders. The people would travel

א וְנָפְלוּ וְלֹא־יָקוּמוּ עוֹד: רָאִיתִי אֶת־אֲדֹנָי
נִצָּב עַל־הַמִּזְבֵּחַ וַיֹּאמֶר הַךְ הַכַּפְתּוֹר וְיִרְעֲשׁוּ
הַסִּפִּים וּבְצַעַם בְּרֹאשׁ כֻּלָּם וְאַחֲרִיתָם בַּחֶרֶב
אֶהֱרֹג לֹא־יָנוּס לָהֶם נָס וְלֹא־יִמָּלֵט לָהֶם פָּלִיט:

from one end of the land to the other to worship their idols in order to increase their reward for their devotion.

Targum renders: as the customs of Beer-sheba exist. He thus understands *the way of Beer-sheba* to refer to their way of life (*Radak*).

וְנָפְלוּ וְלֹא־יָקוּמוּ עוֹד — *They shall fall and no longer rise.* Those who act in this manner shall fall, never to rise again (*Radak*).

Alternatively: Once the kingdom of the ten tribes is exiled, they shall no longer return (*Kara*) — i.e., they shall not return with the redemption of the people of Judah in the time of the Second Temple. However, they will return with the final redemption (*Metzudos David*; see 5:2).

IX

Having prophesied at length concerning the downfall of Samaria and the kingdom of Israel, Amos now directs his words to Jerusalem and the kingdom of Judah. If, as suggested above (see comm. to 8:14), the events depicted at the end of the last chapter applied to Judah as well, the following verses are an elaboration of that prophecy (*Abarbanel*; cf. *Malbim* to v. 1).

1. רָאִיתִי אֶת־ה׳ נִצָּב עַל־הַמִּזְבֵּחַ — *I saw* HASHEM *standing upon the altar.* In a vision of prophecy I beheld the Glory of the Almighty standing atop the altar in the Holy Temple (*Ibn Ezra; Radak*). This was one of the ten phases of the Almighty's withdrawal of His Divine Presence from the Holy Temple (*Rashi, Kara* from *Rosh Hashanah* 31a). According to one version, it was the second phase, in which He traveled from the cherubim to the golden altar in the Temple proper (*Targum*). Another view interprets this as the fourth stop — when His presence ceased to fill the Temple courtyard and was confined to the altar situated within it (*Rosh Hashanah* loc. cit.).

The prophecy which follows is prefaced with this vision to indicate the Almighty's displeasure with the *Kohanim*, who performed the service of the altar (*Radak*).

וַיֹּאמֶר — *And He said.* The Almighty commanded one of His angels as follows (*Ibn Ezra; Radak*).

הַךְ הַכַּפְתּוֹר וְיִרְעֲשׁוּ הַסִּפִּים — *Strike the lintel and the sideposts shall quake.* Strike the lintel atop the roof and cause the sideposts supporting it to tremble (*Rashi*). I.e., slay Josiah king of Judah and bring about the destruction of the Temple (*Mahari Kara* from *Targum*).

Alternatively: Slay Josiah and cause the officers of the nation to tremble (*Rashi; Abarbanel* from *Vayikra Rabbah* 23:3). After Josiah was killed, the Judean royalty was weakened and the power of the nation's officers was usurped. Indeed, when they subsequently elevated Yehoachaz to the throne, the king of Egypt removed him from office and imposed a punishment upon the land (see *II Kings* 23), and they were henceforth unable to appoint a king on their own authority (*Metzudos David*).

Targum renders: If the people of the House of Israel do not repent, extinguish the menorah [i.e., the source of light]; King Josiah will be killed, the Temple destroyed, and the courtyard demolished.

they shall fall and no longer rise.

9/1

1 I *saw* HASHEM *standing upon the altar, and He said: 'Strike the lintel and the sideposts shall quake, and shatter [those] at the head of them all, and the last of them I will slay by the sword; no fugitive among them shall flee and no refugee among them shall escape.'*

כַּפְתּוֹר literally means a circular object. It is used to describe the lintel to the Temple because it was customary to sculpt a large ornamental circular shape above the entrance to which the sideposts were adjoined (*Ibn Ezra, Radak*).

וּבְצַעַם בְּרֹאשׁ כֻּלָּם — *And shatter [those] at the head of them all.* Shatter (*Rashi; Ibn Ezra*; cf. *Radak*) the *Kohanim*, who are the leaders of the nation, for they too have rebelled against Me (*Ibn Ezra; Radak*). Alternatively, this phrase is to be understood in the future tense rather than the imperative. *He* — referring either to the Almighty[1] Himself or to the enemy He will send against them — *shall destroy the leaders of the nation first* (*Radak*).

Targum renders: *and the vessels of the Temple will go into captivity* — i.e., before the Jewish people themselves will be exiled, Nebuchadnezzar will confiscate the treasures of the Temple (*Metzudos David*; see *II Kings* 23:14).

The Sages interpret בְּצַעַם to mean *their robbery*: [Their robbery is at the forefront of all of them — i.e., all their transgressions.] Said R' Yehudah in the name of R' Yochanan: From a *se'ah* filled with transgressions, which prosecutes at the head of them all? Robbery (*Vayikra Rabbah* 33:3).

Abarbanel interprets: *Their split was at the head* — the split in the Jewish kingdom which took place in the time of Jeroboam was the ultimate source of all the tragedy that befell them, for when the Jewish nation is divided the Almighty is no longer with them.

וְאַחֲרִיתָם בַּחֶרֶב אֶהֱרֹג — *And the last of them I will slay by the sword.* The remainder of the nation I will slay with the sword of the enemy (*Radak*). Alternatively: this phrase refers to the decimation of their children (*Ibn Ezra; Metzudos David*).

Others explain these two phrases to be describing the order in which the destruction shall take place: I will begin the destruction with Josiah and complete it with Zedekiah, who will be slain along with his officers and children (*Mahari Kara*). Alternatively: The kingdom of Israel, which was conceived from the division of the nation (see above) will be the first to be conquered and exiled. They will be followed by the kingdom of Judah, whose citizens will be slain by the sword of the enemy (*Abarbanel*).

לֹא־יָנוּס לָהֶם נָס וְלֹא־יִמָּלֵט לָהֶם פָּלִיט — *No fugitive among them shall flee and no refugee among them shall escape.* [Not all of the people shall be slain] as there are those upon whom only the decree of exile has been issued. However, none of those who are designated to die will succeed in escaping with their lives (*Radak*).

[Perhaps this phrase can be understood as having a dual connotation: No fugitive from among those who are meant to be exiled shall flee captivity, and none of those who have been sentenced to die will succeed in escaping with their lives.]

Malbim interprets this verse as depicting the sequence of events that led to the destruction of the kingdom of Israel. As described above (see comm. to 3:15), the invasion by Sennacherib was precipitated by the act of Hosea ben Elah who destroyed the

1. Although Hashem refers to Himself in this very verse in the first person, it is consistent with the style of Scripture to use alternating references in this manner (*Radak*).

ב אִם־יַחְתְּרוּ בִשְׁאוֹל מִשָּׁם יָדִי תִקָּחֵם וְאִם־יַעֲלוּ
ג הַשָּׁמַיִם מִשָּׁם אוֹרִידֵם: וְאִם־יֵחָבְאוּ בְּרֹאשׁ
הַכַּרְמֶל מִשָּׁם אֲחַפֵּשׂ וּלְקַחְתִּים וְאִם־יִסָּתְרוּ
מִנֶּגֶד עֵינַי בְּקַרְקַע הַיָּם מִשָּׁם אֲצַוֶּה אֶת־הַנָּחָשׁ
ד וּנְשָׁכָם: וְאִם־יֵלְכוּ בַשְּׁבִי לִפְנֵי אֹיְבֵיהֶם מִשָּׁם
אֲצַוֶּה אֶת־הַחֶרֶב וַהֲרָגָתַם וְשַׂמְתִּי עֵינִי עֲלֵיהֶם
ה לְרָעָה וְלֹא לְטוֹבָה: וַאדֹנָי יֱהֹוִה הַצְּבָאוֹת
הַנּוֹגֵעַ בָּאָרֶץ וַתָּמוֹג וְאָבְלוּ כָּל־יוֹשְׁבֵי בָהּ
וְעָלְתָה כַיְאֹר כֻּלָּהּ וְשָׁקְעָה כִּיאֹר מִצְרָיִם:
ו הַבּוֹנֶה בַשָּׁמַיִם מַעֲלוֹתָו וַאֲגֻדָּתוֹ עַל־אֶרֶץ יְסָדָהּ

altar of idolatry, thereby causing the division of the nation into two warring camps. In the heart of their struggle, those opposed to Hosea related to Sennacherib that the former had sought aid from Egypt against him, thus inciting him to invade and conquer the land. In this prophecy, Amos is shown these events:

Strike the lintel so that the sideposts shall quake — Hosea will command that the altar of idolatry be smitten and shattered, until the corners of the altar are cut off (3:14). *In the beginning they will all be split and in their end I shall slay them by the sword* — the beginning of their downfall will be the split into two warring camps, which will set off a series of events leading to their destruction.

2. . . . אִם־יַחְתְּרוּ — *If they shall dig down* . . . There will be no place for them to hide and escape from Me, not in the depths below nor upon the heights above (*Radak*). If they dig deep pits into the ground in which to conceal themselves they will not thereby evade the enemy's clutches, for when they eventually come up he will discover them and take them captive. And if they try to flee to the hills and mountains which surround Jerusalem, that, too, will be to no avail. For I will send the enemy to bring them down from there (*Abarbanel*).

3. . . . וְאִם־יֵחָבְאוּ — *And if they shall conceal themselves* . . . If they will seek refuge in the caves at Mt. Carmel, I will seek them out and hand them over to the enemy. Even if they conceal themselves on the ocean floor they will not escape their fate, for I will command the serpent who dwells there — i.e., the Leviathan — to bite them (*Radak; Metzudos David*). [Although this is obviously impossible,] the prophet uses this exaggerated scenario as a metaphor (*Metzudos David*) in order to bring fear to the hearts of those who do not appreciate the might of Hashem (*Ibn Ezra*).

Alternatively: If they will try to hide at the tops of the towers of the fortified cities, from there I will appoint searchers who will seek them out. And if they will hide from me on the islands of the sea, I will send a nation as mighty as the serpent to kill them (*Targum; Rashi; Abarbanel*).

4. . . . וְאִם־יֵלְכוּ בַשְּׁבִי — *And if they shall go into captivity* . . . Those who will place themselves in captivity in neighboring lands in order to escape the sword of the conqueror — such as Johanan ben Kareah, who fled to Egypt in defiance of the orders of Jeremiah (see *Jeremiah* 42:15-17) — will nonetheless be felled by the sword (*Radak*).

Alternatively: If they will submit willingly to their conquerors' authority in order to gain their favor and escape destruction, this too shall not succeed, for

2 If they shall dig down into the grave, from there
My hand shall take them; and if they shall ascend
to the heavens, from there I will bring them down.
3 And if they shall conceal themselves on the top of
Carmel, from there I will seek [them out] and take
them, and if they shall hide from My eyes on the floor
of the sea, from there I will command the serpent
and he shall bite them. 4 And if they shall go into
captivity before their enemies, from there I will com-
mand the sword and it shall slay them; and I will
fix My eye upon them for evil and not for good. 5 And
HASHEM is the Lord of Hosts, Who touches the land
and it melts and all its inhabitants are destroyed,
and [water] rises like the river over all of it and it shall
sink like the river of Egypt; 6 Who built in the Heavens
His strata and His group He has founded on earth;

they will be struck down by the sword (*Abarbanel; Metzudos David*; cf. comm. to v. 1, s.v. לא ינוס).

וְשַׂמְתִּי עֵינִי עֲלֵיהֶם לְרָעָה וְלֹא לְטוֹבָה — *And I will fix My eye upon them for evil and not for good.* Do not think that I will merely remove My Divine Providence from them and thereby leave them to their natural fate. Rather, I will involve Myself directly in their affairs [just as I do in times of prosperity]. However, in this instance, I will do so to punish them rather than to assist them (*Malbim*).

5. ... וַה׳ אֱלֹהִים הַצְּבָאוֹת — *And HASHEM is the Lord of Hosts* ... [Now that you have been forewarned of the Almighty's wrath which hangs over you,] know and recognize that when the great earthquake described earlier (8:8) shall befall you, it will not be a natural disaster (*Malbim*) but rather the hand of the Almighty God, Who rules over the hosts of heaven and earth. In His omnipotence, He will touch your land and thereby cause it to melt — as it will first tremble and quake and then sink into the water which shall flood the fissures caused by the quake (*Radak*; cf. comm. to 8:8).

6. ... הַבּוֹנֶה בַשָּׁמַיִם — *Who built in the Heavens* ... [Given the warnings issued above,] how do you not tremble in fear from His vengeance? Do you think you can escape the wrath of Him Who is the Creator of the entire world and Who judges and oversees all that exists (*Radak*)? Know that there is nowhere to hide and escape Him, for all of creation is in His hands, and He will reward those who heed His voice and punish those who sin against Him (*Ibn Ezra*).

הַבּוֹנֶה בַשָּׁמַיִם מַעֲלוֹתָו — *Who built in the Heavens His strata.* He created the elements of air, cold, and fire which lie above the earth, one layer over the other (*Ibn Ezra*). Alternatively: This refers to the nine celestial spheres which lie one above the other (*Radak*; cf. *Abarbanel*).

וַאֲגֻדָּתוֹ עַל־אֶרֶץ יְסָדָהּ — *And His group he has founded on earth.* The society of His living creatures He has placed here on earth (*Rashi; Ibn Ezra*). Alternatively: The four elements of physical existence

הַקֹּרֵא לְמֵי־הַיָּם וַיִּשְׁפְּכֵם עַל־פְּנֵי הָאָרֶץ יהוה
ז שְׁמוֹ: הֲלוֹא כִבְנֵי כֻשִׁיִּים אַתֶּם לִי בְּנֵי
יִשְׂרָאֵל נְאֻם־יהוה הֲלוֹא אֶת־יִשְׂרָאֵל הֶעֱלֵיתִי
מֵאֶרֶץ מִצְרַיִם וּפְלִשְׁתִּיִּים מִכַּפְתּוֹר וַאֲרָם מִקִּיר:
ח הִנֵּה עֵינֵי | אֲדֹנָי יֱהוִֹה בַּמַּמְלָכָה הַחַטָּאָה

— earth, water, fire, and air — He created here on earth (*Radak*).

Others render: *His group is the foundation of earth* — the righteous, who are indeed His group — are the foundation of all creation, for all that exists here on earth, and even in the Heavens above, exists in their behalf (*Rashi*).

The Sages state (*Menachos* 27a): Israel placates [the Almighty] only when they are all in one group, as it is stated: *Who built in the Heavens His strata and His group is the foundation of earth* — only when His people are in one group, righteous and wicked together [are they the proper foundation of the earth. Thus, only then] are their prayers answered (*Rashi* ad loc.).[1]

Elsewhere (*Yalkut Shimoni*), the Sages express a similar thought but base it on an opposite interpretation of this verse: Abaye said: When Israel is united with one counsel below, His great Name is praised above, as it is stated: *And there will be in Yeshurun a king* — when? *When the heads of the nation are gathered together*. And so it says: *And His group on earth is founded* — but not when they are made into separate groups [i.e., when they are divided into separate groups they remain here on earth and do not reach the Heavens]. R' Shimon ben Yochai says: This can be likened to two ships tied together upon which is built a palace. As long as the ships remain together the palace stands; if the ships separate, the palace cannot stand. So too, when Israel fulfills the will of God, His heights reach the Heavens; when they do not, His group is founded here on earth.

הַקֹּרֵא לְמֵי־הַיָּם וַיִּשְׁפְּכֵם עַל־פְּנֵי הָאָרֶץ — *Who calls to the waters of the sea and pours them out upon the face of the earth.* He summons the waters of the earth to rise up into clouds from where He sends them down to water the earth with rain (*Ibn Ezra; Metzudos David*). Alternatively: Just as He created all that exists, He can also destroy it. If the people rebel against Him, He may flood the earth with water, as He did in the time of the great deluge (*Radak*).

Targum renders: Who says to gather camps as numerous as the waters of the sea and scatters them over the face of the earth (cf. *Mahari Kara*).

ה׳ שְׁמוֹ — *HASHEM is His Name.* He is the Almighty God Who is all-powerful, and there is thus no way to escape His will (*Metzudos David*).

Abarbanel interprets: He is the same God when He blesses you with His kindness as when He punishes you in His wrath. The change is due to your aberrant behavior and not to any transformation on His part.

7. הֲלוֹא כִבְנֵי כֻשִׁיִּים אַתֶּם לִי בְּנֵי יִשְׂרָאֵל — *'Are you not like the children of Cushites to Me, O Children of Israel?'* [Although the entire creation indeed belongs to Me,]

1. [Even Moses was told by the Almighty (*Ex.* 32:7): לֶךְ־רֵד כִּי שִׁחֵת עַמְּךָ, *Go descend for your nation has been corrupted* (by the sin of the golden calf) — Go down from your greatness; I bestowed greatness upon you only for their sake (*Rashi* from *Berachos* 32), for the unique relationship which exists between Hashem and the Jewish people includes the entire nation. Therefore, each individual can achieve his full potential only as part of the whole of *Klal Yisrael*, as a single entity in harmony serving Hashem.]

Who calls to the waters of the sea and pours them out
upon the face of the earth; HASHEM is His Name. 7 *'Are*
you not like the children of the Cushites to Me, O
Children of Israel?' declares HASHEM; 'Did I not bring
up Israel from the land of Egypt as well as the Philis-
tines from Caphtor and Aram from Kir?' 8 *Behold the*
eyes of HASHEM/ELOHIM are upon the sinful kingdom,

I chose you alone to be My nation and to serve Me for eternity — like the people of Cush, who have been sold into permanent slavery to their masters (*Mahari Kara; Radak; Abarbanel; Metzudos*).

Rashi interprets: Why should I refrain from punishing you if you do not repent before Me? Are you not from the children of Noah just like all the other nations? Specifically, you are like the Cushites whom you particularly resemble. Just as a Cushite cannot change his skin, so do you not improve your wicked ways (see *Jer.* 13:22).

הֲלוֹא אֶת־יִשְׂרָאֵל הֶעֱלֵיתִי מֵאֶרֶץ מִצְרַיִם וּפְלִשְׁתִּיִּים מִכַּפְתּוֹר וַאֲרָם מִקִּיר — *'Did I not bring up Israel from the land of Egypt as well as the Philistines from Caphtor and Aram from Kir?'* You became My nation when I took you out from slavery in the land of Egypt to serve Me instead (*Mahari Kara; Radak; Abarbanel; Metzudos*), but because you have not kept My treaty you are no more worthy in My eyes than other nations whom I have saved (*Mahari Kara*). Did I not rescue the Philistines from the hands of the Caphtorites who conquered them (see *Deut.* 2:23)? Do I not intend as well to redeem the people of Aram — who are destined to be exiled by Sennacherib to Kir — when the Assyrian Empire declines? Yet I did not take these people to be My nation [and I will treat you no differently if you do not serve Me loyally] (*Rashi*).

Radak interprets this as referring to the final exile of the Philistines during the reign of Zedekiah (see *Jer.* 47) and the exile of Aram to Kir, from which — *Radak* maintains — they were never redeemed. Although neither of these events had yet occurred, the prophet refers to them as if in the past because the prophecies issued by Hashem are as certain as if they had already taken place. Thus, the Almighty demands of the Jewish nation: *Did I not bring up Israel from the land of Egypt? [Did I also bring up] the Philistines from Caphtor and Aram from Kir?* I.e., did I redeem these other nations from their exile as I redeemed you from slavery in Egypt? No, I did not! Rather, once I punished them for persecuting you they were exiled forever, never to return.

Others interpret this verse — as well as those which follow — as words of solace offered by the prophet after having depicted the great catastrophes which will befall the nation (see *Abarbanel*, s.v. הכונה הכוללת). In this vein, *Malbim* interprets: *Are you not like the children of the Cushites to Me?* Just as the Cushites are recognizable everywhere for their dark skin, so too shall you stand out as My chosen nation wherever you are exiled — distinguishable to all as a people apart. *Did I not bring up Israel from the land of Egypt?* Although you were enslaved there for many years, you did not become totally assimilated into Egyptian society, and it was thus possible for Me to redeem you from there as a separate nation. [*Did I bring up*] *the Philistines from Caphtor and Aram from Kir?* When the ancient Philistines were conquered by Caphtor and eventually returned to their land, were they still the same Philistine nation as before, unmixed with the peoples with whom they had lived in the meanwhile? Will Aram go out from Kir a separate nation, unassimilated with its conquerors? No! Only the Jewish nation has retained its own unique identity which separates it from the entire family of nations.

8. הִנֵּה עֵינֵי ה׳ אֱלֹהִים ... — *Behold the eyes of HASHEM/ELOHIM ...* My eyes are fixed upon the kingdom of Ephraim,

וְהִשְׁמַדְתִּי אֹתָהּ מֵעַל פְּנֵי הָאֲדָמָה אֶפֶס כִּי לֹא
ט הַשְׁמֵיד אַשְׁמִיד אֶת־בֵּית יַעֲקֹב נְאֻם־יְהוָה׃ כִּי־
הִנֵּה אָנֹכִי מְצַוֶּה וַהֲנִעוֹתִי בְכָל־הַגּוֹיִם אֶת־בֵּית
יִשְׂרָאֵל כַּאֲשֶׁר יִנּוֹעַ בַּכְּבָרָה וְלֹא־יִפּוֹל צְרוֹר
י אָרֶץ׃ בַּחֶרֶב יָמוּתוּ כֹּל חַטָּאֵי עַמִּי הָאֹמְרִים לֹא־
יא תַגִּישׁ וְתַקְדִּים בַּעֲדֵינוּ הָרָעָה׃ בַּיּוֹם הַהוּא אָקִים
אֶת־סֻכַּת דָּוִיד הַנֹּפֶלֶת וְגָדַרְתִּי אֶת־פִּרְצֵיהֶן
יב וַהֲרִסֹתָיו אָקִים וּבְנִיתִיהָ כִּימֵי עוֹלָם׃ לְמַעַן יִירְשׁוּ
אֶת־שְׁאֵרִית אֱדוֹם וְכָל־הַגּוֹיִם אֲשֶׁר־נִקְרָא שְׁמִי

which has been consistently sinful from the times of Jeroboam ben Nevat until those of Hosea ben Elah (*Ibn Ezra; Radak*; cf. *Rashi*). Therefore, I will obliterate that kingdom from the face of the earth (ibid.) and the ten tribes of which it is comprised shall be exiled (*Mahari Kara*). However, although their sovereignty will be lost, they will not be destroyed as a nation. Rather, the House of Jacob will remain a separate people among the nations of the world (*Malbim*).

Others explain this verse as a continuation of the previous one. Having declared that He chose the Jewish people to be His nation when He brought them up out of Egypt, the Almighty continues to explain: Although I have also brought up the Philistines from Caphtor and Aram from Kir, their redemption is in no way analogous to yours. For they and all other kingdoms who sin before Me will be totally destroyed, never to recover as an independent nation. The House of Jacob, however, although conquered and sent into exile, will not be totally destroyed. It shall rather remain extant until the end of time and will eventually be redeemed and restored to glory (*Abarbanel; Alshich*).

9-10. These next two verses describe afflictions which are to come upon the Jewish nation. According to *Ibn Ezra*, they refer to the exile of the ten tribes. *Mahari Kara* interprets them as discussing the exile of the kingdom of Judah during the reign of Zedekiah. *Abarbanel* offers two other theories: One is that the prophet is depicting the birth pangs of the Messiah — the turbulent times which will precede the final redemption. Alternatively, he is describing the experience of Jewish exile in general [which applies to each such occurrence in its time].

9. כִּי־הִנֵּה אָנֹכִי מְצַוֶּה . . . — *Behold I decree . . .* I will disperse the Jewish people among the gentile nations amidst great tribulation, just as one shakes the grain in the sieve in order to remove its chaff. Nevertheless, just as the holes of the sieve allow only the small grains of chaff to fall out, but the pebbles, which are larger, remain inside despite all the shaking, so too shall the righteous of the Jewish nation and those who repent their misdeeds survive the turbulent experience of exile; only the wicked will be destroyed. Thus, the righteous among them who are living at the time of redemption shall survive the events which precede it, and those already passed on shall be resurrected (*Ibn Ezra; Radak; Metzudos David*; cf. *Abarbanel; Malbim*).

Rashi interprets this verse as depicting the intensity of the Exile. One who sifts with a sieve shakes it with all his might once the finer chaff has been removed [to separate the coarser pieces of refuse — which cannot easily fall through the holes — from the grain itself]. So too shall the Jewish nation undergo a great degree of

and I will destroy it from upon the face of the earth; but
I will not totally destroy the House of Jacob, declares
HASHEM. 9 *Behold I decree that I will scatter the House*
of Israel through all the nations as grain is shaken
around in a sieve and not a pebble falls to the ground.
10 *All the sinners of My nation shall perish by the*
sword; those who say, 'The end shall not approach and
hurry due to us.' 11 *On that day I will raise up the fallen*
booth of David; and I will repair their breaches, and its
ruins I will raise up, and I will build it up as in days
of old. 12 *So that they upon whom My Name is called*
shall inherit the remnant of Edom and all the nations,

tribulation when they are scattered extensively among the nations.

10. בַּחֶרֶב יָמוּתוּ כֹּל חַטָּאֵי עַמִּי הָאֹמְרִים לֹא־תַגִּישׁ וְתַקְדִּים בַּעֲדֵינוּ הָרָעָה — *All the sinners of My nation shall perish by the sword; those who say, 'The end shall not approach and hurry due to us.'* Just as the useless chaff is removed from the grain by the sieve (*Ibn Ezra*), so shall be destroyed all those sinners among the people who contest the prophecies of impending disaster. They declare, 'Come let us do as our hearts desire, for no evil will befall us as a result of our deeds. Even if catastrophe occurs, it will not be because of our actions but by mere chance, as is wont to happen in the natural course of events' (*Radak*).

Malbim explains: The evil which is coming close will not befall us because of our deeds but will be mere coincidence. Indeed, our actions cannot even hurry these events and hasten their arrival, for our deeds have no bearing whatsoever on the course of history.

11. בַּיּוֹם הַהוּא... — *On that day...* After Israel shall undergo all of these trials, there shall finally come the day which is destined for their redemption (*Rashi*). At that time, I will reestablish the kingdom of David over Israel (*Targum; Rashi; Radak*) — called the booth (סֻכָּה) of David because it covers them — סוֹכֶה — with protection (*Radak*). When this occurs, I will also mend the breaches within the Jewish nation and rebuild the ruins among them, and I will restore the kingdom to its former glory (*Radak*).

Abarbanel interprets the latter half of the verse as referring entirely to the kingdom of David: It shall not be like the era of the First Temple after the death of Solomon, in which the Davidic kingdom was dealt a gaping breach by the division of the nation into two separate kingdoms. Nor will it resemble the times of the Second Temple, during which the dynasty lay in ruins, as the Jewish nation had no independent sovereignty whatsoever, save for the eras of the Hasmoneans and the house of Herod, neither of whom were descendants of David. Rather, I will restore the kingdom to its former glory in the times of David and Solomon, who ruled over a united Jewish nation in its entirety (cf. *Malbim*).

Mahari Kara interprets *the booth of David* as referring to the Temple itself. According to *Ibn Ezra*, this verse describes the monarchy of Hezekiah, the descendant of David, who was saved from the hand of Sennacherib by Divine intervention.

12. לְמַעַן יִירְשׁוּ אֶת־שְׁאֵרִית אֱדוֹם וְכָל־הַגּוֹיִם אֲשֶׁר־נִקְרָא שְׁמִי עֲלֵיהֶם נְאֻם־ה׳ עֹשֶׂה זֹּאת — *So that they upon whom My Name is called shall inherit the remnant of Edom*

יג עֲלֵיהֶם נְאֻם־יְהוָה עֹשֶׂה זֹּאת׃ הִנֵּה
יָמִים בָּאִים נְאֻם־יְהוָה וְנִגַּשׁ חוֹרֵשׁ בַּקֹּצֵר וְדֹרֵךְ
עֲנָבִים בְּמֹשֵׁךְ הַזָּרַע וְהִטִּיפוּ הֶהָרִים עָסִיס
יד וְכָל־הַגְּבָעוֹת תִּתְמוֹגַגְנָה׃ וְשַׁבְתִּי אֶת־שְׁבוּת
עַמִּי יִשְׂרָאֵל וּבָנוּ עָרִים נְשַׁמּוֹת וְיָשָׁבוּ וְנָטְעוּ
כְרָמִים וְשָׁתוּ אֶת־יֵינָם וְעָשׂוּ גַנּוֹת וְאָכְלוּ
טו אֶת־פְּרִיהֶם׃ וּנְטַעְתִּים עַל־אַדְמָתָם וְלֹא יִנָּתְשׁוּ
עוֹד מֵעַל אַדְמָתָם אֲשֶׁר נָתַתִּי לָהֶם אָמַר יְהוָה
אֱלֹהֶיךָ׃

and all the nations, declares HASHEM *Who shall do this.* The restoration of the monarchy to its former glory will precipitate (*Radak*) the conquering of the remnant of the land of Edom and all the neighboring lands by the Jewish nation, upon whom My Name is called (*Targum; Ibn Ezra; Mahari Kara; Radak*; cf. *Rashi*). The nation of Edom will be wiped out entirely, as Obadiah declares (v. 18): *there shall be no survivor to the house of Esau*. When that occurs, a portion of their land shall be totally destroyed and left in ruins as a remembrance of their oppression of the Jewish people and the punishment they received. The remaining land shall be settled by the Children of Israel (*Radak*).

Others render: *So that they shall inherit the remnant of Edom and all the nations upon whom My Name is called* (*Abarbanel; Malbim*): Even the conquered nations shall then be called in My Name, for they, too, shall recognize the truth of My existence and accept upon themselves to serve Me faithfully (*Malbim*; cf. *Abarbanel*).

נְאֻם־ה׳ עֹשֶׂה זֹאת — *Declares* HASHEM *Who shall do this.* I.e., I shall carry out the decree which I have issued, for I am the Almighty God in Whose power it lies (*Radak*).

Alshich interprets: Perhaps you are concerned that the Jewish nation may yet exercise their free will incorrectly and lose the merit to be thus redeemed. Know, then, and recognize that I am the Almighty God Who has promised that this shall come to pass, and I guarantee that the Jewish people will ultimately repent all their misdeeds and be redeemed (cf. ibid.).

13-15. The prophet ends his prophecies with a brief description of the peace and prosperity that the Jewish people will enjoy during the Messianic era (*Alshich*).

13. וְנִגַּשׁ חוֹרֵשׁ בַּקֹּצֵר וְדֹרֵךְ עֲנָבִים בְּמֹשֵׁךְ הַזָּרַע — *And the plowman shall meet the reaper and the treader of grapes him who carries the seed.* So abundant and plentiful shall be the produce of your land that before the harvest is finished it will again be time to till the soil. Similarly, before the grapes have been sufficiently trodden to draw out their wine it will be necessary to replant their seeds for the next year's growth. This parallels the promise of the Torah (*Lev.* 26:5): *and your threshing shall overtake the vintage, and the vintage shall overtake the plowing* — and even exceeds the promise of that verse (*Radak*; cf. *Rashi*).

וְהִטִּיפוּ הֶהָרִים עָסִיס וְכָל־הַגְּבָעוֹת תִּתְמוֹגַגְנָה — *And the mountains shall drip wine and all the hills shall melt.* So much blessing will be bestowed upon you, with so little effort on your behalf, that it will seem as if the mountains themselves drip with wine — as well as the juices of all the

declares HASHEM *Who shall do this.* 13 *Behold, days are*
coming, declares HASHEM, *and the plowman shall meet*
the reaper and the treader of grapes him who carries the
seed, and the mountains shall drip wine and all the hills
shall melt. 14 *And I will revoke the captivity of My*
nation Israel, and they shall [re]build desolate cities and
settle [them]; and they shall plant vineyards and drink
their wine; and they shall cultivate gardens and eat
their fruits. 15 *And I will plant them upon their land and*
they will never again be uprooted from their land that I
have given them, said HASHEM *your God.*

other fruits growing upon them. And the hills will be so saturated with milk from the flocks of sheep grazing upon them that they will appear to be melting into liquid (*Radak*).

According to *Radak*, עָסִיס refers to any juice which is squeezed from fruits. *Targum* renders it sweet wine. Others interpret it simply to mean wine (see comm. to *Joel* 1:5).

Targum renders תִּתְמוֹגַגְנָה to mean split: Ground which has been worked breaks up with the fall of rain upon it. [Thus, the prophet is actually depicting the fact that all the land will be tilled.]

The Sages interpret this verse metaphorically to be describing the degree of unity which will prevail among the Jewish people at that time (*Abarbanel*): *The plowman* refers to Judah, as it is stated (*Hosea* 10:11): *I will cause Ephraim to ride; Judah shall plow. The reaper* is Joseph, as it is stated (*Gen.* 37:7): *And behold we were binding sheaves. The treader of grapes* is Judah, as it is stated (Zechariah 9:13): *For I will tread for Me Judah. Him who carries the seed* [lit. who draws the seed] is Joseph, who drew the seed of Jacob to Egypt. *And the mountains shall drip wine* — this refers to the tribes, who shall say, 'The kings [of the gentile nations] are battling one with the other, but it is not our concern' (*Yalkut*).

14. וְשַׁבְתִּי אֶת־שְׁבוּת עַמִּי יִשְׂרָאֵל — *And I will revoke the captivity of My nation Israel.* I will return the children of My nation from captivity (*Targum*; see comm. to *Joel* 4:1). *Metzudos* interprets: I will settle in peace and tranquility the children of My nation who were hitherto in captivity.

וּבָנוּ ... — *And they shall [re]build ...* They will reap the benefits of all their toil; none of it shall be for nought (*Radak*). They shall rebuild the cities that lay desolate during their exile and will never again be banished from them. They will plant vineyards and cultivate gardens whose fruits they themselves shall enjoy, for no alien nation will conquer them and consume the fruits in their stead (*Metzudos David*).

This verse further intimates that the Jewish nation will enjoy universal prosperity at that time. Thus, each person will enjoy the fruits of his own labors, and no one will need to turn to others for sustenance (*Alshich*).

15. וּנְטַעְתִּים עַל־אַדְמָתָם ... — *And I will plant them upon their land . . .* I will plant them in their land, never again to be uprooted, for they shall continue forever to serve Me and fulfill My will [thus meriting My continued protection] (*Radak*).

אָמַר ה׳ אֱלֹהֶיךָ — *Said* HASHEM *your God.* This is the statement of the Almighty to the prophet (*Radak*).

Alshich notes the use of the singular term אֱלֹהֶיךָ, rather than the plural אֱלֹהֵיכֶם

that is generally used when addressing the entire nation. He further questions the seemingly redundant repetition of the theme of this verse, that the Jewish nation will never again be uprooted from their land. He therefore interprets the verse in the following manner: The roots of the Jewish nation lie in the spiritual realms of creation which constitute the World to Come — referred to in many places in Scripture as the land which has been allotted to them (see *Ex.* 12:20, *Kiddushin* 39b; *Isaiah* 60:21, *Sanhedrin* 90a). Because of this lofty level of existence which they enjoy, they were given the Land of Israel, which is the location here on earth most closely linked to those spiritual realms. Thus, when the Jewish people fulfill their potential and sanctify themselves, they thereby reinforce their connection to their lofty roots and are allowed to live in peace in the Holy Land. However, when they stray from the ways of Hashem, their link is severed, and the Land of Israel cannot abide them in its midst.

Thus, the Almighty declares: When that day of redemption shall arrive, I will arouse My nation to achieve great spiritual heights through which they will implant their souls steadfastly in the spiritual realms to which they are linked. Therefore, they will never again be uprooted from their soil here on earth in the Land of Israel. At that time, they will reach such a totality of devotion and unity that I will be referred to as אֱלֹהֶיךָ — in the singular term, for the entire nation will be viewed as one single unit of existence.

Ovadiah

א חֲזוֹן עֹבַדְיָה כֹּה־אָמַר אֲדֹנָי יֱהֹוִה לֶאֱדוֹם
שְׁמוּעָה שָׁמַעְנוּ מֵאֵת יהוה וְצִיר בַּגּוֹיִם
ב שֻׁלָּח קוּמוּ וְנָקוּמָה עָלֶיהָ לַמִּלְחָמָה: הִנֵּה
קָטֹן נְתַתִּיךָ בַּגּוֹיִם בָּזוּי אַתָּה מְאֹד:

I

1. חֲזוֹן עֹבַדְיָה — *The prophecy of Obadiah.* Obadiah was an Edomite proselyte who was the administrator of the estates of Ahab, king of Israel. When Jezebel, Ahab's queen, had all the prophets of Hashem murdered, Obadiah hid one hundred of them in a cave and sustained them throughout the course of the edict (see *I Kings* 18). As a reward, he was granted the gift of prophecy (*Rashi, Radak* from *Sanhedrin* 39b; see *Ibn Ezra*, who disputes this assumption of the Sages and identifies this Obadiah with the one in *Kings*; and *Abarbanel*, who defends it against his arguments).

כֹּה־אָמַר ה׳ אֱלֹהִים לֶאֱדוֹם — *Thus said HASHEM/ELOHIM concerning Edom:*[1] Why did Obadiah direct his prophecies to Edom? Said R' Yitzchak: Said the Almighty: Let Obadiah, who dwelt among two evildoers [Ahab and Jezebel] and did not emulate their deeds, exact retribution from the wicked Esau, who dwelt among the righteous people, Isaac and Rivkah, and did not emulate their deeds. Said Ephraim Mikshaah the disciple of R' Meir: Obadiah was a proselyte from Edom. This is what people say, 'From within itself the forest is destroyed by the hatchet [i.e. the handle of the axe comes from the very forest which it returns to destroy]' (*Sanhedrin* loc. cit).

Ibn Ezra interprets the bulk of the chapter, with the exception of the final verses, to be discussing Biblical Edom. He cites as proof the description of the fact that Edom stood by and watched the destruction of Israel (vs. 11, 12). This applies only to the destruction of the First Temple, since the Romans themselves carried out the destruction of the Second Temple (cf. *Yalkut Shimoni* from *Seder Olam* ch. 20).

Radak contends that the events described herein will take place in the end of days, when the Jewish people are returned forever to their land. Although the inhabitants of the land of Edom are no longer the descendants of that nation, the kingdom of Rome originally consisted of Edomites [and is thus the subject of these prophecies]. Even the misdeeds of Edom described in verses 11 and 12 refer — according to *Radak* — to events which took place during the destruction of the Second *Beis HaMikdash* (see comm. ibid.).

Abarbanel and *Malbim* also understand the destruction of Edom to refer to their final annihilation which will take place in the Messianic era (with the exception of verses 5-7, which they interpret as portraying earlier catastrophes that occurred to them). However, the misdeeds which are described as

1. Edom has two separate identities in the words of the prophets. Firstly, it is the Biblical nation of Edom, which bordered the Land of Israel and was often involved in the persecution of the Jewish nation (cf. *Amos* 1:11, 12). Biblical Edom was conquered and its inhabitants exiled by Nebuchadnezzar, king of Babylonia, around the time of the destruction of the First Temple. In addition, the city (and empire) of Rome is described by the Sages as having been originally settled by the people of Edom, and prophetic reference to Edom is often interpreted as referring to the Roman Empire. 'Rome' is considered to be perpetuated by Christian civilization which the empire made dominant in the world, and its final destruction will not occur until the times of Messiah (see *Abarbanel* to v. 2). There are various opinions as to whether the Edom discussed by Obadiah is Biblical Edom or Rome.

[1] *The prophecy of Obadiah: Thus said* HASHEM/
ELOHIM *concerning Edom: We have heard tidings
from Hashem and an envoy has been sent among
the nations [saying], 'Arise and let us rise up
against her for battle.'* [2] *Behold, I have made you
small among the peoples; you are most despised.*

being the cause of their retribution refer both to those perpetrated by Biblical Edom during the times of the First Temple and those of the Roman Empire.

שְׁמוּעָה שָׁמַעְנוּ מֵאֵת ה׳ — *We have heard tidings from Hashem.* The nations shall say concerning Edom, 'We have heard the call from the Almighty urging us to wage war against Edom' (*Radak*).

Alternatively, the first portion of this verse should be understood in inverted order: *We, the prophets of God, have heard tidings from Hashem, that the Almighty has said as follows concerning Edom* (ibid.). Indeed, nine different prophets prophesied about the downfall of Edom: Balaam, Obadiah, Isaiah, Joel, Amos, Jeremiah, Ezekiel, Malachi, and King David in *Tehillim* (*Abarbanel*).

וְצִיר בַּגּוֹיִם שֻׁלָּח קוּמוּ וְנָקוּמָה עָלֶיהָ לַמִּלְחָמָה — *And an envoy has been sent among the nations [saying], 'Arise, and let us rise up against her for battle.'* It will be as if an envoy had been sent among the nations carrying the message from one to the other: Let us arise and unite to wage war against Edom (*Ibn Ezra; Radak*).

Some interpret this as referring to the war of Gog and Magog, which is destined to take place between the Christian nations and the Arab world (see comm. to *Joel* 3:1). At that time, the united Christian nations will invade the Arab lands, beginning with Egypt, and they will conquer *Eretz Yisrael* as well. This will incite all the Arab nations to gather together in order to attack the invaders and drive them from their lands (*Abarbanel; Malbim*).

The next few verses describe in brief the rise and fall of the forces of Edom. They began as a small inconsequential nation and grew into a mighty world power, but they are destined to fall once again and to be totally eradicated from the face of the earth.

2. הִנֵּה קָטֹן נְתַתִּיךָ בַּגּוֹיִם בָּזוּי אַתָּה מְאֹד — *Behold, I have made you small among the peoples; you are most despised.* In the early years of your kingdom in the land of Edom, you were a small unimportant nation of no stature whatsoever (*Abarbanel; Malbim; Metzudos*). Indeed, even your progenitor Esau, although referred to by his father and mother as their elder son, was small and unimportant in My eyes (*Rashi*).

Radak interprets this as referring to the *future* of Rome: I will make you a lowly people among the nations, all of whom will despise you and will not be at all concerned if you are destroyed.

According to the Sages, this verse demeans the stature of Rome at the height of its glory: *I have made you small among the peoples*; for the Romans did not crown a king the son of a king — as the Caesars were not succeeded by their sons but were rather chosen by the Senate [and thus did not have the total authority of royalty] (*Abarbanel*). *You are most despised*: for they did not have a script or a language [1] (*Avodah Zarah* 10a).

1. Although Latin was the language of Rome, it was not their own original tongue but was rather derived from the languages of other nations (*Rashi* ad loc.) — primarily Greece (*Abarbanel* to v. 9). *Tosafos* question this assumption and explain that their language was not a prominent one to be used by kings.

ג זְדוֹן לִבְּךָ הִשִּׁיאֶךָ שֹׁכְנִי בְחַגְוֵי־סֶלַע מְרוֹם
ד שִׁבְתּוֹ אֹמֵר בְּלִבּוֹ מִי יוֹרִדֵנִי אָרֶץ׃ אִם־תַּגְבִּיהַּ
כַּנֶּשֶׁר וְאִם־בֵּין כּוֹכָבִים שִׂים קִנֶּךָ מִשָּׁם אוֹרִידְךָ
ה נְאֻם־יהוָה׃ אִם־גַּנָּבִים בָּאוּ־לְךָ אִם־שׁוֹדְדֵי
לַיְלָה אֵיךְ נִדְמֵיתָה הֲלוֹא יִגְנְבוּ דַּיָּם אִם־בֹּצְרִים
ו בָּאוּ לָךְ הֲלוֹא יַשְׁאִירוּ עֹלֵלוֹת׃ אֵיךְ נֶחְפְּשׂוּ
ז עֵשָׂו נִבְעוּ מַצְפֻּנָיו׃ עַד־הַגְּבוּל שִׁלְּחוּךָ כֹּל
אַנְשֵׁי בְרִיתֶךָ הִשִּׁיאוּךָ יָכְלוּ לְךָ אַנְשֵׁי שְׁלֹמֶךָ

3. זְדוֹן לִבְּךָ הִשִּׁיאֶךָ שֹׁכְנִי בְחַגְוֵי־סֶלַע מְרוֹם שִׁבְתּוֹ אֹמֵר בְּלִבּוֹ מִי יוֹרִדֵנִי אָרֶץ — *The wickedness of your heart seduced you, [you] who dwells in the clefts of the rock in his lofty abode, who says in his heart, 'Who will bring me down to earth?'* Now that you have developed into a mighty empire, you allow yourself to be seduced by the haughty feelings in your heart. Thus, you view yourself as if you dwelled in the impregnable clefts of the rocks where no one could approach you, and you exult in your heart, saying, 'Who could possibly bring me down to a lower station on earth?' (*Abarbanel; Metzudos Dovid*).

Others interpret: *the wickedness of your heart seduced you* to sin against the Almighty (*Mahari Kara*). Alternatively: to turn with pride against your brother Jacob — even when you still dwelled on Mt. Seir in the land of Edom, you considered yourself perched securely atop your heights, invulnerable to foreign invasion (*Radak*).

שֹׁכְנִי בְחַגְוֵי־סֶלַע מְרוֹם שִׁבְתּוֹ — [*You*] *who dwells in the clefts of the rock of his lofty abode. Targum* renders: You are like an eagle which dwells in the clefts of the rock of his lofty abode.

Rashi interprets: You relied upon the [protective] cloak of [the merit] of your forefathers, Abraham and Isaac, but they will not help you.

4. אִם־תַּגְבִּיהַּ כַּנֶּשֶׁר וְאִם־בֵּין כּוֹכָבִים שִׂים קִנֶּךָ מִשָּׁם אוֹרִידְךָ נְאֻם־ה׳ — *If you will soar like an eagle and if you will place your nest among the stars, from there I will bring you down, declares Hashem.* If you will elevate your dwellings like the eagle, who soars above all other birds (*Radak*), [and even if you will raise yourself all the way to the stars,] I will nevertheless bring you crashing down to earth and hand you over to your enemies (*Metzudos*). Indeed, I shall allow you to attain such lofty heights only in order to increase the intensity of your impact when you come plummeting down (*Malbim*).

The Sages comment: In the future, when the Holy One, Blessed is He, will judge Esau the evildoer, what will Esau do? He will wrap himself in his cloak and come sit with Jacob — as it is stated: *and if you will place your nest among the stars* — and 'stars' refers to none other than Jacob, as it is stated (*Num.* 24:17): *a star has trodden from Jacob*, and it is written (*Gen.* 15:5): *Look please at the heavens and count the stars.* And Jacob shall say: My brother, you shall not be like me, as it is stated (*Hosea* 13:14): *I will be your words of death; I will decree the grave upon you* — the decrees which you decreed upon me to worship idols — if I fulfilled them I was culpable for death at the hands of Heaven, and if I did not serve them you would kill me.

The prophet now goes on to depict the totality of the destruction which Esau will incur, and the means whereby it will be brought about. As noted above (fn. to

3 The wickedness of your heart seduced you, [you]
who dwells in the clefts of the rock of his lofty
abode, who says in his heart, 'Who will bring me
down to earth?' 4 If you will soar like an eagle
and if you will place your nest among the stars,
from there I will bring you down, declares Hashem.
5 If thieves came to you, or plunderers of the
night, how were you cut off; would they not steal
[only] as much as they need? If vintagers came to
you, would they not leave over gleanings? 6 How was
Esau searched [and] his hoards ransacked? 7 All of
your allies escorted you until the border; your con-
federates seduced you [and] prevailed over you;

v. 1), this refers either to the final destruction of Edom which will take place in the Messianic era or to the ravages of war inflicted upon her in the course of history.

5. אִם־גַּנָּבִים בָּאוּ־לְךָ אִם־שׁוֹדְדֵי לַיְלָה אֵיךְ נִדְמֵיתָה הֲלוֹא יִגְנְבוּ דַּיָּם אִם־בֹּצְרִים בָּאוּ לָךְ הֲלוֹא יַשְׁאִירוּ עֹלֵלוֹת — *If thieves came to you, or plunderers of the night, how were you cut off; would they not steal [only] as much as they need? If vintagers came to you, would they not leave over gleanings?* Thus shall wonder those who witness your ultimate total destruction in the end of days: How did you come to be so completely decimated? If thieves came to you at night while you were sleeping, and you did not sense their presence and fend them off, would they not plunder as much as they could carry off and leave the rest alone? Even if marauders came by day they would leave something behind, just as vintagers, who return time after time to harvest the crop, but nevertheless leave over the gleanings (*Radak; Metzudos,* cf. *Ibn Ezra; Alshich*).

Others translate אֵיךְ נִדְמֵיתָה — *How were you silent* until they stole all they desired (*Targum;* cf. *Rashi*)?

Abarbanel interprets this verse and the two that follow as describing calamities which were to befall Edom long before their final destruction in the times of the Messiah. It refers either to the many conquests suffered by Biblical Edom or to the invasions of Rome by the heathen races of Europe (cf. *Malbim*).

6. אֵיךְ נֶחְפְּשׂוּ עֵשָׂו נִבְעוּ מַצְפֻּנָיו — *How was Esau searched [and] his hoards ransacked?* How did it come about that Esau was so thoroughly searched and looted? Not only did the marauders search the house for all visible objects, but they even ransacked all of the places where treasures were concealed (*Mahari Kara*).

This follows the bulk of the commentators. Others render: *And his hoards revealed* (*Targum; Malbim*).

7. עַד־הַגְּבוּל שִׁלְּחוּךָ כֹּל אַנְשֵׁי בְרִיתֶךָ הִשִּׁיאוּךָ יָכְלוּ לְךָ אַנְשֵׁי שְׁלֹמֶךָ — *All of your allies escorted you until the border; your confederates seduced you [and] prevailed over you.* Those who had sworn to assist you escorted you to the border and encouraged you to wage war against your enemies, but they then turned away and left you standing there to face your foes alone (*Rashi; Mahari Kara; Alshich; Malbim; Metzudos*).

Others interpret: Your allies and confederates in whom you placed your faith escorted you to the border when you

ח לַחְמְךָ יָשִׂימוּ מָזוֹר תַּחְתֶּיךָ אֵין תְּבוּנָה בּוֹ׃ הֲלוֹא
בַּיּוֹם הַהוּא נְאֻם־יהוה וְהַאֲבַדְתִּי חֲכָמִים מֵאֱדוֹם
ט וּתְבוּנָה מֵהַר עֵשָׂו׃ וְחַתּוּ גִבּוֹרֶיךָ תֵּימָן לְמַעַן
י יִכָּרֶת־אִישׁ מֵהַר עֵשָׂו מִקָּטֶל׃ מֵחֲמַס אָחִיךָ
יא יַעֲקֹב תְּכַסְּךָ בוּשָׁה וְנִכְרַתָּ לְעוֹלָם׃ בְּיוֹם עֲמָדְךָ
מִנֶּגֶד בְּיוֹם שְׁבוֹת זָרִים חֵילוֹ וְנָכְרִים בָּאוּ שְׁעָרָו
וְעַל־יְרוּשָׁלִַם יַדּוּ גוֹרָל גַּם־אַתָּה כְּאַחַד מֵהֶם׃

were taken into captivity by your enemies, as if to comfort you and share in your grief. However, in reality they assisted your enemies and enabled them to prevail over you (*Radak*; cf. *Ibn Ezra*).

לַחְמְךָ יָשִׂימוּ מָזוֹר תַּחְתֶּיךָ — *[Those who eat] your bread put a wound in your place*. Those who share your bread [in friendship] brought misfortune upon you while you were residing in your own land (*Ibn Ezra; Metzudos Dovid*). Alternatively: *they placed the wound beneath you* (תַּחְתֶּיךָ), i.e., they hid the wound that they meant to place upon you beneath a veneer of friendship (*Radak*).

Rashi interprets: Your brother Jacob made even your food for you a source of injury, for he gave you bread and a pottage of lentils and you thereby came to despise the birthright.

אֵין תְּבוּנָה בּוֹ — *He is bereft of understanding*. Esau was bereft of understanding, for he did not comprehend the intent of his supposed allies and thus did not guard against their treachery (*Radak; Metzudos Dovid*).

Military prowess depends upon two factors: the quality of the strategic and tactical planning and the valor and strength of the actual armies. Accordingly, the prophet foretells in the next two verses how both of these qualities will be withheld from the forces of Edom thereby precipitating their total annihilation (*Abarbanel*).

8. הֲלוֹא בַּיּוֹם הַהוּא נְאֻם־ה׳ וְהַאֲבַדְתִּי חֲכָמִים מֵאֱדוֹם וּתְבוּנָה מֵהַר עֵשָׂו — *Shall I not on that day — declares Hashem — eradicate wise men from Edom and understanding from the mountain of Esau?* On that cataclysmic day, I shall eliminate the wisdom of the sages of Edom so that they will be unable to plan properly for battle. Thus, those who originate from the mountain of Esau will be left without the necessary understanding to achieve military success (*Radak; Metzudos*).

According to *Abarbanel* and *Malbim*, this verse begins anew the description of the destruction of Esau in the end of days. This will be unlike the conquests endured by Edom in other times, in which there were still wise men and mighty warriors among the Edomite people [capable of limiting the extent of their losses]. At that time, however, they will be bereft of wise men or men of valor and their annihilation will thus be total (*Malbim*).

9. וְחַתּוּ גִבּוֹרֶיךָ תֵּימָן — *And your warriors from the southland shall be broken*. Your mightiest warriors, who hail from the southlands of your nation, shall be broken in strength and spirit and rendered totally ineffectual in battle (*Targum; Abarbanel*).

Alternatively: Your mighty warriors will be broken in spirit and they will flee in terror to the south (*Rashi*, as cited by *Abarbanel*; cf. *Rashi* in our editions). Still others interpret תֵּימָן as referring to the son of Elifaz [and the grandson of Esau] by that name, from whom the greatest Edomite warriors were descended (*Ibn Ezra; Radak*; see *Amos* 1:12).

[those who eat] your bread put a wound in your place; he
is bereft of understanding.
8 *'Shall I not on that day' — declares Hashem —*
'eradicate wise men from Edom and understanding from
the mountain of Esau? 9 *And your warriors from the*
southland shall be broken, so that [every] man shall be
cut off from the mountain of Esau due to the slaughter.'
10 *For the oppression of your brother Jacob, disgrace shall*
envelop you and you will be cut off forever. 11 *On the day*
that you stood from afar, on the day that strangers cap-
tured his wealth, and foreigners came to his gates and
cast lots on Jerusalem; you, too, were like one of them.

לְמַעַן יִכָּרֶת־אִישׁ מֵהַר עֵשָׂו מִקָּטֶל — *So that [every] man shall be cut off from the mountain of Esau due to the slaughter.* So great and extensive shall be the slaughter that will prevail among the people of Edom that all whose roots originate in the mountain of Esau and the Edomite nation that dwelled there shall be wiped out (*Ibn Ezra; Radak; Abarbanel; Metzudos*).

Others interpret, 'so that every man *of might and valor* shall be cut off from the mountain of Esau due to the extensive slaughter' (*Targum; Rashi*).

In the next verses, Obadiah explains the reason for the terrible calamities he has prophesied upon Edom. Their fate has been sealed because of their continuous persecution of the Jewish nation, particularly in light of the fact that they are actually brother nations, both descended from the patriarchs Abraham and Isaac.

10. מֵחֲמַס אָחִיךָ יַעֲקֹב תְּכַסְּךָ בוּשָׁה וְנִכְרַתָּ לְעוֹלָם — *For the oppression of your brother Jacob, disgrace shall envelop you and you will be cut off forever.* Because you have oppressed your brother Jacob, you will be covered completely with humiliation and shame, and you shall be cut off forever, never again to rise (*Metzudos*).

According to *Ibn Ezra*, this refers to the oppression inflicted by the Edomites upon the Jewish nation at the time of their exile at the hands of Nebuchadnezzar. *Radak* contends that it refers to the fact that the Roman nation, descended primarily from the Edomite people, destroyed the Second *Beis HaMikdash* and exiled the Jewish people from their land. *Abarbanel* interprets this verse as alluding to both misdeeds. *For the oppression of your brother Jacob* — i.e., for that which you watched in pleasure as he was destroyed by Nebuchadnezzar, and even lent a hand to aid in the destruction — *disgrace shall envelop you* — you will be punished in a manner that will bring upon you disgrace and humiliation. But for that which you yourselves destroyed the Second Temple and sent My nation into exile — *you will be cut off forever* — never again to appear upon the face of the earth (cf. *Malbim*).

11. בְּיוֹם עֲמָדְךָ מִנֶּגֶד בְּיוֹם שְׁבוֹת זָרִים חֵילוֹ וְנָכְרִים בָּאוּ שְׁעָרָו וְעַל־יְרוּשָׁלַםִ יַדּוּ גוֹרָל גַּם־אַתָּה כְּאַחַד מֵהֶם — *On the day that you stood from afar, on the day that strangers captured his wealth, and foreigners came to his gates and cast lots on Jerusalem; you, too, were like one of them.* On the day that Nebuchadnezzer conquered and plundered Jerusalem, you

יב וְאַל־תֵּרֶא בְיוֹם־אָחִיךָ בְּיוֹם נָכְרוֹ וְאַל־תִּשְׂמַח
לִבְנֵי־יְהוּדָה בְּיוֹם אָבְדָם וְאַל־תַּגְדֵּל פִּיךָ בְּיוֹם
יג צָרָה׃ אַל־תָּבוֹא בְשַׁעַר־עַמִּי בְּיוֹם אֵידָם אַל־תֵּרֶא
גַם־אַתָּה בְּרָעָתוֹ בְּיוֹם אֵידוֹ וְאַל־תִּשְׁלַחְנָה
יד בְחֵילוֹ בְּיוֹם אֵידוֹ׃ וְאַל־תַּעֲמֹד עַל־הַפֶּרֶק לְהַכְרִית
אֶת־פְּלִיטָיו וְאַל־תַּסְגֵּר שְׂרִידָיו בְּיוֹם צָרָה׃

stood from afar and offered no assistance to your brother Jacob (*Rashi*). For this, I consider it as if you had actually participated in the destruction (*Rashi; Abarbanel; Metzudos Dovid*).

Alternatively: Not only did you not come to your brother's aid, you even participated in his destruction by murdering anyone who escaped the Babylonian forces, despite the fact that you had no share in their spoils (*Yalkut Shimoni; Mahari Kara; Alshich*).

Radak follows his approach, that all of Obadiah's prophecy refers to the Roman oppression of the Jewish nation. He explains that at the time of the invasion of Jerusalem by Titus, Edom was still inhabited by descendants of Esau, as well as being ruled by Rome, which itself was ruled by the Edomites in the nation. Thus, when the Romans conquered Jerusalem, the Edomites dwelling nearby rejoiced in the downfall of the children of Israel, and whenever possible delivered their refugees into the hands of the Romans. This is considered a grave transgression, if only because they were actually brothers to the Jewish nation. It is particularly heinous in light of the fact that the Jewish nation was enjoined from attacking Edom on their way from Egypt to the Holy Land due to that brotherhood.

In the next three verses, the prophet elaborates upon the details of Edom's oppression of the Jewish nation. He does so in a poetic format, as if he were addressing the Edomites prior to their misdeeds and enjoining them from performing them in the first place.

According to *Ibn Ezra*, all of the events described in these verses occurred during the destruction of the first Temple. *Radak*, as cited above, interprets these words as addressing the Romans and Edomites who took part in the destruction of the second. *Abarbanel* and *Malbim* follow their approach that both eras are included in the prophet's rebuke. [We will follow this view, as developed by *Abarbanel*, in the commentary.]

12. וְאַל־תֵּרֶא בְיוֹם־אָחִיךָ בְּיוֹם נָכְרוֹ וְאַל־תִּשְׂמַח לִבְנֵי־יְהוּדָה בְּיוֹם אָבְדָם וְאַל־תַּגְדֵּל פִּיךָ בְּיוֹם צָרָה — *Gaze not on the day of your brother, the day of his estrangement; and do not rejoice over the children of Judah on the day of their destruction; and do not expand your mouth on the day of misfortune.* How cruel and improper it was for you to gaze upon your brothers in their hour of estrangement and exile from their land, as you stood from the distance and offered no aid. Even if you were unable to help them, you should at least have gone to your homes rather than shaming them by watching what transpired. How much greater then is your guilt for the fact that you actually rejoiced over their plight when they were destroyed and opened your mouths wide in exultation at the time of their misfortune (*Radak; Abarbanel; Metzudos Dovid*).

בְּיוֹם נָכְרוֹ — *The day of his estrangement.* This follows the translation of *Radak* and *Metzudos*. Others render *the day of his destruction* (*Targum; Mahari Kara*). According to *Rashi*, it means *the day of his delivery* — i.e., into the hands of his enemy.

[12] *Gaze not on the day of your brother, the day of his estrangement; and do not rejoice over the children of Judah on the day of their destruction; and do not expand your mouth on the day of misfortune.*
[13] *Enter not the gate of My nation on the day of their calamity; gaze not, you too, upon his evil on the day of his calamity, and do not extend [your hands] to his wealth on the day of his calamity.*
[14] *And do not stand by the crossroads to cut off his fugitives and do not deliver his remnant on the day of misfortune.*

The prophet now castigates the people of Edom for their persecution of the Jewish nation at the time of the destruction of the Second *Beis HaMikdash*. According to *Ibn Ezra*, the subject is still the era of the First Temple, as cited below.

13. אַל־תָּבוֹא בְשַׁעַר־עַמִּי בְּיוֹם אֵידָם אַל־תֵּרֶא גַם־אַתָּה בְּרָעָתוֹ בְּיוֹם אֵידוֹ וְאַל־תִּשְׁלַחְנָה בְחֵילוֹ בְּיוֹם אֵידוֹ — *Enter not the gate of My nation on the day of their calamity; gaze not, you too, upon his evil on the day of his calamity, and do not extend [your hands] to his wealth on the day of his calamity.* You Romans who descend from Edom, what right did you have to enter the gates of My people to conquer their cities and destroy their Temple? And those of you living on Mt. Seir near *Eretz Yisrael* — you had no business gazing upon My nation in their hour of disgrace. Certainly you should not have extended your hands to plunder their wealth when they were rendered defenseless by the conquering invader (*Abarbanel; Metzudos;* cf. *Malbim*).

14. וְאַל־תַּעֲמֹד עַל־הַפֶּרֶק לְהַכְרִית אֶת־פְּלִיטָיו וְאַל־תַּסְגֵּר שְׂרִידָיו בְּיוֹם צָרָה — *And do not stand by the crossroads to cut off his fugitives and do not deliver his remnant on the day of misfortune.* You acted wickedly when you stood by the crossroads where many paths converge, in order to capture any Jewish people fleeing the enemy (*Radak*).

Alternatively, this refers to the generations after the exile, when the Jewish people lived under Roman rule: Your culpability increased significantly when "you stood over" the destruction of My people — i.e., when you extended the destruction through the generations by persecuting and murdering many of the refugees from the exile you inflicted upon them, and by incarcerating others of their remnant in your horrible prisons and dungeons (*Abarbanel; Metzudos*).

Ibn Ezra interprets both of these verses as referring still to the destruction of the First *Beis HaMikdash*: It was wrong of you to stand by idly at the time of their distress without offering any assistance, and you certainly should not have taken advantage of their plight and plundered their possessions. You further increased your guilt when you stood by the crossroads from which many paths extend, and showed the Babylonians the road taken by the Israelite refugees in order to deliver them into their hands.

Having described in some detail the sins of the people of Edom, the prophet returns to his original theme of the punishment that is to befall them, along with all those who pursued similar paths.

טו כִּי־קָרוֹב יוֹם־יהוה עַל־כָּל־הַגּוֹיִם כַּאֲשֶׁר עָשִׂיתָ
טז יֵעָשֶׂה לָּךְ גְּמֻלְךָ יָשׁוּב בְּרֹאשֶׁךָ׃ כִּי כַּאֲשֶׁר
שְׁתִיתֶם עַל־הַר קָדְשִׁי יִשְׁתּוּ כָל־הַגּוֹיִם תָּמִיד
יז וְשָׁתוּ וְלָעוּ וְהָיוּ כְּלוֹא הָיוּ׃ וּבְהַר צִיּוֹן תִּהְיֶה
פְלֵיטָה וְהָיָה קֹדֶשׁ וְיָרְשׁוּ בֵּית יַעֲקֹב אֵת
יח מוֹרָשֵׁיהֶם׃ וְהָיָה בֵית־יַעֲקֹב אֵשׁ וּבֵית יוֹסֵף
לֶהָבָה וּבֵית עֵשָׂו לְקַשׁ וְדָלְקוּ בָהֶם וַאֲכָלוּם

15. כִּי־קָרוֹב יוֹם־ה׳ עַל־כָּל־הַגּוֹיִם כַּאֲשֶׁר עָשִׂיתָ יֵעָשֶׂה לָּךְ גְּמֻלְךָ יָשׁוּב בְּרֹאשֶׁךָ — *For the day of Hashem upon all the nations is close; as you have done [so] shall be done to you; your requital shall be returned upon your head.* It would have been better for you, Edom, had you not pursued your evil ways. For the day of Hashem is coming, in which He will exact retribution from all of the nations who have persecuted the Jewish people. At that time, you will be dealt with in accordance with your deeds: Just as you slaughtered by the sword so shall you be slaughtered and just as you destroyed Jerusalem with fire so shall you be afflicted with fire and brimstone from Heaven (*Abarbanel*). Although that fateful day may yet be a long way off, it is as certain to arrive and impossible to avoid as if it were imminent (*Radak; Abarbanel; Alshich*).

Malbim interprets גְּמֻלְךָ to refer to the intensity of emotion behind the act. Thus: for the evil deeds themselves — *as you have done [so] shall be done to you.* And for the hatred and cruelty which filled your heart and incited your actions — *your requital shall be returned upon your head.*

16. כִּי כַּאֲשֶׁר שְׁתִיתֶם עַל־הַר קָדְשִׁי יִשְׁתּוּ כָל־הַגּוֹיִם תָּמִיד — *For just as you drank on My holy mountain [so] shall all the nations drink ceaselessly.* Just as you celebrated with food and drink over the destruction of My holy mountain, so shall you — and all nations who are evil like you — yet drink from the cup of affliction (*Targum; Rashi; Radak*) continuously and ceaselessly, until all of the wicked among you have been annihilated (*Radak*).

Alternatively, this verse is directed to the Jewish people: Just as you have been forced to drink from the cup of affliction by your conquerors, so shall they yet drink from that very same cup (*Ibn Ezra; Abarbanel; Alshich; Metzudos Dovid;* see *Abarbanel, Malbim*).

וְשָׁתוּ וְלָעוּ — *And they shall drink and be befuddled.* The cup of affliction from which they drink will leave them stunned and bewildered as if they had drunk themselves into a stupor (*Targum; Rashi; Metzudos Dovid*). Others render: *they shall drink and swallow* (*Ibn Ezra; Radak;* cf. *Mahari Kara*).

וְהָיוּ כְּלוֹא הָיוּ — *And be as if they never were.* So great shall be their devastation that their land will be totally unrecognizable, as if it had never been settled (*Radak; Abarbanel*). Alternatively, they will be obliterated from the face of the earth as if they had never existed (*Metzudos Dovid*).

[The prophet now includes Israel in his words, describing their role in the destruction of Edom.] *Ibn Ezra* cites Japeth as explaining this to refer to the future [in the times of the Messiah], which is the view of the majority of the commentators. However, he also cites the view of R' Moshe that it refers to the times of Hezekiah, and that of R' Yehoshua, that the prophet is discussing events which

[15] *For the day of Hashem upon all the nations is close;*
as you have done [so] shall be done to you; your requital
shall be returned upon your head. [16] *For just as you*
drank on My holy mountain [so] shall all the nations drink ceaselessly, and they shall drink and be befuddled and be as if they never were.

[17] *And on Mt. Zion there shall be refuge and it shall be holy, and the house of Jacob shall inherit their bequeathers.* [18] *And the house of Jacob shall be fire and the*
house of Joseph flame and the house of Esau [shall turn] to straw, and they shall ignite them and devour them,

occurred in the time of the Second *Beis HaMikdash*.

17. וּבְהַר צִיּוֹן תִּהְיֶה פְלֵיטָה — *And on Mt. Zion there shall be refuge.* Whereas the nation of Edom shall be eradicated entirely, the children of Israel will find refuge on the Mountain of Zion (*Mahari Kara; cf. Ibn Ezra*). Alternatively, although many of the Jewish people will perish in their exile, a large remnant will survive and will yet return to Mt. Zion (*Radak*).

וְהָיָה קֹדֶשׁ — *And it shall be holy.* The mountain of Zion will be sanctified, and no one uncircumcised or *tamei* — ritually unclean — shall tread upon it (*Abarbanel; Metzudos*). Alternatively, this refers to the Jewish nation that will dwell on Mt. Zion. They will be fully imbued with holiness and will never again include among them one who is uncircumcised or *tamei* (*Radak*).

וְיָרְשׁוּ בֵּית יַעֲקֹב אֵת מוֹרָשֵׁיהֶם — *And the house of Jacob shall inherit their bequeathers.* The children of Jacob shall inherit once again the land which was previously bequeathed to them, and they shall settle as well the lands of Edom, Moab, and Philistia (*Radak; cf. Targum*).

Others translate: *and the house of Jacob shall inherit those who chased them out* — i.e., they will reconquer their lands from those nations who banished them (*Mahari Kara*).

18. וְהָיָה בֵית־יַעֲקֹב אֵשׁ וּבֵית יוֹסֵף לֶהָבָה וּבֵית עֵשָׂו לְקַשׁ — *And the house of Jacob shall be fire and the house of Joseph flame and the house of Esau [shall turn] to straw.* And the house of Jacob shall be powerful like a fire and that of Joseph like a blazing flame. The house of Esau will be weak like straw and will thus be destroyed by the Jewish nation, just as straw is devoured by a roaring flame (*Targum; Radak*).

וּבֵית יוֹסֵף לֶהָבָה — *And the house of Joseph flame.* This may be merely a repetition of the previous phrase, as from the time of the division of the Jewish kingdom the children of Israel are often referred to as the house of Joseph (*Radak*; cf. comm. to *Amos* 5:15). The Sages, however, state (*Bava Basra* 123b) that the descendants of Esau will fall only into the hands of the children of Joseph (*Radak*). Thus, the descendants of Joseph, who will ultimately return from the exile imposed upon them by the Assyrian Empire, will come upon Edom like a raging fire and consume the entire nation (*Abarbanel; cf Malbim*).

וְדָלְקוּ בָהֶם וַאֲכָלוּם — *And they shall ignite them and devour them.* They shall ignite them in flames as easily as a blazing fire ignites a pile of straw. However, they will not be consumed immediately. Rather, they shall be destroyed slowly,

וְלֹא־יִהְיֶה שָׂרִיד לְבֵית עֵשָׂו כִּי יְהוָה דִּבֵּר׃
יט וְיָרְשׁוּ הַנֶּגֶב אֶת־הַר עֵשָׂו וְהַשְּׁפֵלָה אֶת־
פְּלִשְׁתִּים וְיָרְשׁוּ אֶת־שְׂדֵה אֶפְרַיִם וְאֵת שְׂדֵה
כ שֹׁמְרוֹן וּבִנְיָמִן אֶת־הַגִּלְעָד׃ וְגָלֻת הַחֵל־הַזֶּה
לִבְנֵי יִשְׂרָאֵל אֲשֶׁר־כְּנַעֲנִים עַד־צָרְפַת וְגָלֻת
יְרוּשָׁלִַם אֲשֶׁר בִּסְפָרַד יִרְשׁוּ אֵת עָרֵי הַנֶּגֶב׃

through a long torturous process, as something of substance is devoured slowly by fire (*Alshich*).

וְלֹא־יִהְיֶה שָׂרִיד לְבֵית עֵשָׂו כִּי ה׳ דִּבֵּר — *And there shall be no survivor to the house of Esau, for Hashem has spoken.* Even those Edomites who escape the hand of Joseph and flee — as well as those who are elsewhere when this great battle takes place — will nonetheless be eradicated from the face of the earth. For their destruction is the decree of the Almighty God and is thus not limited to the natural means whereby it is carried out (*Alshich*).

And where was this decree pronounced? Where it is stated (*Num.* 24:19): *Out of Jacob shall come a ruler and he shall destroy him that remains in the city (of Edom)* (*Rashi*).

With the destruction of their nemesis Esau, the Jewish people shall settle in peace in the Land of Israel and inhabit, as well, the neighboring lands which once belonged to their oppressors.

19. וְיָרְשׁוּ הַנֶּגֶב אֶת־הַר עֵשָׂו וְהַשְּׁפֵלָה אֶת־פְּלִשְׁתִּים וְיָרְשׁוּ אֶת־שְׂדֵה אֶפְרַיִם וְאֵת שְׂדֵה שֹׁמְרוֹן — *And [those of] the southland shall inherit the Mountain of Esau and [those of] the lowlands the Philistines;* and they shall inherit the field of Ephraim and the field of Samaria. The Jewish people living in the southlands of *Eretz Yisrael* shall inherit the mountain of Esau which is near their borders, while the dwellers in the lowlands shall inherit the neighboring lands of the Philistines along with Mt. Ephraim and Mt. Samaria (*Targum; Rashi; Ibn Ezra; Mahari Kara*).

Others render: *And they shall inherit the southland of the Mountain of Esau, and the lowland of the Philistines, and the fields of Ephraim and Samaria.* The children of Israel will inherit from Esau their low-lying southlands, while Mt. Edom proper will be completely desolate and uninhabitable. They will settle, as well, the lowlands of Philistia, which, together with the lands of Edom, will suffice to provide them with all their needs. Thus, there will be no need to toil upon the mountains and to cultivate them and no need to use the highlands for protection from the enemy. Similarly, they will inherit the fields of Ephraim and Samaria. Whereas they once needed the hills of Ephraim and Samaria for agricultural and defensive purposes, it will now be sufficient to work only the fields upon the plains (*Radak*; cf. *Abarbanel; Metzudos Dovid*).

וּבִנְיָמִן אֶת־הַגִּלְעָד — *And Benjamin [shall inherit] Gilead.* The children of Benjamin shall inherit the land of Gilead on the other side of the Jordan River (*Ibn Ezra; Metzudos Dovid*). The children of Manasseh, whose land will be taken over by the expanding tribe of Benjamin, will themselves expand their territories eastward, enlarging the original eastern borders of *Eretz Yisrael*.

20. וְגָלֻת הַחֵל־הַזֶּה לִבְנֵי יִשְׂרָאֵל אֲשֶׁר־כְּנַעֲנִים עַד־צָרְפַת וְגָלֻת יְרוּשָׁלִַם אֲשֶׁר בִּסְפָרַד יִרְשׁוּ אֵת עָרֵי הַנֶּגֶב — *And this exiled host of the children of Israel who [wandered to] the Canaanites until Zarepheth, and the exile of Jerusalem which is in Sepharad shall inherit the cities of the south.* The exiled nation of the ten tribes

and there shall be no survivor to the house of Esau, for
Hashem has spoken. 19 *And [those of] the southland*
shall inherit the Mountain of Esau and [those of] the
lowlands the Philistines; and they shall inherit the field
of Ephraim and the field of Samaria; and Benjamin
[shall inherit] Gilead. 20 *And this exiled host of the*
children of Israel who [wandered to] the Canaanites
until Zarepheth, and the exile of Jerusalem which
is in Sepharad shall inherit the cities of the south.

of Israel (*the children of Israel*), who wandered to the lands of the Canaanite nations and onward until France — as well as the children of the kingdom of Judah who were exiled to Spain — shall inherit the cities in the southern portion of *Eretz Yisrael* (*Rashi*). Alternatively, the exiles of the northern kingdom of the ten tribes will be those who inherit the lands cited above in the previous verse; those who were expelled from the southern kingdom of Judah (*the exiles of Jerusalem*) will recapture the cities in the province of Judah to the south (*Radak*).

וְגָלֻת הַחֵל־הַזֶּה — *And this exiled host.* Others render: the exiles of this valley (*Rashi*).

אֲשֶׁר־כְּנַעֲנִים עַד־צָרְפַת — *Who [wandered to] the Canaanites until Zarepheth.* This follows the translation of *Rashi*. *Radak* renders: *who are among the Canaanites until Zarepheth.* When the Jewish people first conquered the Holy Land, many of the Canaanites fled before them and migrated to the lands of Germany [as well as to France]. Thus, when the Jews dispersed across Europe after they were exiled by the Romans, many found their way to these lands, which were already inhabited by descendants of the Canaanites (*Ibn Ezra; Radak*).

Abarbanel disputes this theory concerning the Canaanites. He interprets *Targum* as explaining Zarepheth to refer to the city by that name in the land of Sidon, a Canaanite nation. Thus, the beginning of this verse is rendered as follows: *And this exiled host [will inherit] the lands of the Canaanites until Zarepheth* (cf. *Malbim*).

Abarbanel himself interprets this verse in a different manner. Having stated earlier that the children of Israel shall inherit the mountain of Esau, the prophet now goes on to specify which of the Jewish people will be allotted those lands. According to *Abarbanel*, the word הַחֵל is to be rendered 'initial.' אֲשֶׁר־כְּנַעֲנִים is interpreted *who, like the Canaanites* — i.e., who fled their land and were dispersed across Europe, as were the Canaanites who fled from the Jewish invaders. Thus, the verse is understood as follows: *And this initial exile of the children of Israel, who — like the Canaanites — [migrated] until France* — i.e., the exiles from the Roman invasion and destruction of the Second Temple, who traveled through Italy until France — *and the exiles of Jerusalem who are in Spain* — i.e., those who were exiled from Jerusalem by the Babylonians with the destruction of the First *Beis HaMikdash*, and who were already dwelling in Spain at the time of the second exile (see *Abarbanel* to end of *II Kings*) — *shall inherit the cities of the south.* These exiles, who suffered the greatest degree of persecution among all the dispersed of the Jewish nation, shall be granted the choice cities in the southern lands of Edom.

Although there are no longer any Jews in France or Spain [i.e., in the times of *Abarbanel*], this prophecy will be ful-

כא וְעָלוּ מוֹשִׁעִים בְּהַר צִיּוֹן לִשְׁפֹּט אֶת־הַר עֵשָׂו
וְהָיְתָה לַיהוָה הַמְּלוּכָה׃

filled with the descendants of those who once dwelled there. Alternatively, it applies to those families who remained in those countries and practice their Judaism in secret.

21. וְעָלוּ מוֹשִׁעִים בְּהַר צִיּוֹן לִשְׁפֹּט אֶת־הַר עֵשָׂו וְהָיְתָה לַה׳ הַמְּלוּכָה — *And saviors shall ascend Mt. Zion to wreak judgment upon the Mountain of Esau and dominion shall be Hashem's.* Saviors shall ascend to Mount Zion and exact retribution from the descendants of Edom for their oppression of the Jewish people (*Targum; Rashi*). This refers to the Messiah and the seven shepherds and eight princes who will accompany him (*Radak* from *Michah* 5:4).[1]

Ibn Ezra interprets: And saviors — the judges of Israel — shall ascend to Mount Zion to judge the remnant dwelling in the Mountain of Esau. *Abarbanel* disputes this view, as the prophet has already stated (v. 18), *And there shall be no survivor to the house of Esau.* He contends that the saviors cited are the legions of the gentile nations who will gather together and conquer the nation of

1. The Sages state: Who are the seven shepherds? David in the middle, Seth, Chanoch, and Methuselah on his right and Abraham, Jacob, and Moses on his left. And who are the eight princes? Jesse, Saul, Samuel, Amos, Zephaniah, Hezekiah, Elijah, and the Messiah (*Succah* 52b).

1/21

[21] *And saviors shall ascend Mt. Zion to wreak judgment upon the Mountain of Esau and dominion shall be Hashem's.*

Edom, as described above (v. 1). Thus, the prophet describes here how the annihilation foretold above will be carried out.

This relates to the interpretation the Sages (*Bereishis Rabbah*) give to Jacob's statement to Esau (*Gen.* 33:14) that he should go at his own pace *until I will come to my master to Seir*: Where do we find that Jacob traveled to Seir? Rather this refers to that which it is stated: *and saviors shall ascend to the Mountain of Esau*. Thus, Jacob himself has vowed to ascend to Edom to wreak judgment upon them, and it is therefore he, along with the others cited, who will carry out that prophecy when the time arrives (*Alshich*).

וְהָיְתָה לַה׳ הַמְּלוּכָה — *And dominion shall be Hashem's.* At that time, Hashem alone shall exercise dominion [over the entire world] (*Radak*) for all of mankind will recognize Him as king and accept His sovereignty (*Abarbanel*).

Rashi comments: This teaches you that the throne of the Almighty is not complete until He exacts retribution from Amalek.[1]

1. *Rashi* here follows the version he cites in his commentary to *Chumash* (*Ex.* 17:16) that this idea refers specifically to the nation of Amalek, the grandson of Esau. *Yalkut Shimoni,* however, cites a *midrash* from *Bereishis Rabbah* (78:) which applies this comment to the entire nation of Esau.

This volume is part of
THE ARTSCROLL SERIES®
an ongoing project of
translations, commentaries and expositions
on Scripture, Mishnah, Talmud, Halachah,
liturgy, history and the classic Rabbinic writings;
and biographies, and thought.

For a brochure of current publications
visit your local Hebrew bookseller
or contact the publisher:

Mesorah Publications, ltd

4401 Second Avenue
Brooklyn, New York 11232
(718) 921-9000

MW00657585